SOMEONE WOULD HAVE TALKED

DOCUMENTED!
THE ASSASSINATION OF PRESIDENT JOHN F. KENNEDY
AND THE CONSPIRACY TO MISLEAD HISTORY

SOMEONE WOULD HAVE TALKED

DOCUMENTED!

The Assassination of
President John F. Kennedy
and the Conspiracy to Mislead History

LARRY HANCOCK

JFK LANCER PRODUCTIONS & PUBLICATIONS

The goal of JFK Lancer Productions & Publications, Inc. is to make research materials concerning President John F. Kennedy easily available to everyone. Our prime concern is the accuracy of history and the true story of the turbulent 1960s. We are results oriented and actively support the continued investigation of the JFK assassination and related events.

For additional copies of this publication, please contact:

JFK Lancer Productions & Publications, Inc.
100 Stonewood Court
Southlake, TX 76092
Tel. 817-488-8694
Email: catalogorder@jfklancer.com

More information and documents for *Someone Would Have Talked* are available electronically on the World Wide Web at the following address: www.larry-hancock.com

Printed in the United States

ISBN 0-9774657-1-3

Cover design by Ken Jacobs
Book design by Debra Conway
Edited by Jamie Hecht
Final Editing by Debra Conway

TABLE OF CONTENTS

Preface   xi

Introduction   vii

Acknowledgements   xv

Section A: They're Going To Kill Kennedy

Chapter 1   They're Going To Kill Kennedy   1
Chapter 2   …An ex-Marine, An Expert Marksman   19
Chapter 3   They Came From New Orleans   33
Chapter 4   It Begins   49
Chapter 5   Persons of Interest   61
Chapter 6   "As soon as they take care of Kennedy"   83
Chapter 7   Shadow Wars and Shadow Warriors   91
Chapter 8   "Well we took care of that S.O.B. Didn't We?"   123
Chapter 9   John Roselli, "Strategist"   139
Chapter 10   Standing the "Night Watch"   159
Chapter 11   "Cuba, the Guns, New Orleans, Everything"   185
Chapter 12   The "Anti-Castro People"   199
Chapter 13   Plans, Patsies, and Motives   219
Chapter 14   "All Sorts of Rumors"   239

Photo Section

Section B: Afterwards

Chapter 15   "If I Told You"   271
Chapter 16   Wheeling and Dealing with Bobby   313
Chapter 17   "We can't check every shooting scrape"   323
Chapter 18   The Anti-Castro People, Afterwards   335
Chapter 19   End Game   363

Appendices:
A.   Leverage   411
B.   Crossing Paths in the CIA   413
C.   Barnes , Hunt and Friends   421

D.   The Way of JM/WAVE   433

E.   Student Warrior   445

F.   Another Rumor - Same Source?   451

G.   The Word in the Underworld   461

H.   Odio Revisited   471

I.   Echos from Dallas   481

J.   A Small Clique in the CIA   495

Names From the Secret War   505

Endnotes   519

Selected Bibliography   575

Index   587

INTRODUCTION

Someone Would Have Talked deals with people, with observations, confessions and things said to family and close personal friends–things generally not stated for any official record or investigation. It deals with remarks heard by informants and information known but not reported by either individuals or government agencies.

It also deals with "slips," with people that knew things they should not have given the timing and context of their statements. And it deals with people who kept information to themselves to protect their persons, their family, their jobs and positions; people who had heard or seen something they sincerely would rather have never known.

Its subjects are people who actually tried to tell what they knew, what they knew that did not fit the official record. It catalogs their rejection–in some cases it details the actions taken to make sure they were kept off the record at key times. In the process it becomes very clear that government Committees and Hearings are simply not effective mechanisms for dealing with criminal investigations.

People are always the "sticky" part of any investigation, especially one with criminal implications and penalties, not to mention the possibility of "accessory" charges. The questions are: *who to believe, who to trust, who to expect to lie and cover-up?*

It is an arena where context, corroboration and social networks become key. In this arena circumstantial evidence becomes a legitimate tool of inquiry. Science and quantitative analysis demonstrate their limitations. In the end the reader must make the final call based on objective evaluation and mutual judgement.

For that reason and to the extent possible, this manuscript is supported with not only references but extensively with exhibits. Exhibits ranging from contemporary newspaper articles through testimony to investigative reports and memoranda. In many instances the exhibits present contradictions which must be evaluated; in some they show errors, mis-statements or lack of information in the official record.

The intent of this book, its appendices, exhibits and photographs is to allow the reader to have all the relevant information in context and to display it against pertinent timelines. After more than 40 years of concealed records releases and private research, this gives the reader a major advantage over previous investigators and researchers.

It also allows each reader to make their own evaluation of the information, the connections, the analysis and the implications presented here. The reader will make final judgement; hopefully ending up far closer to the actual truth than that presented in the FBI report of 1963 and the Warren Commission Report of 1964–and much closer to real history than found in our textbooks.

The discussion of individuals and officials does not mean that those individuals are in any way connected with the JFK assassination. Many are mentioned to establish the historical context of the events discussed and the social networks relating to individuals being quoted. Likewise, the mention of an individual named as a JFK conspiracy suspect in the work of other authors, in agency source and informant reports or in investigative memoranda does not mean that the author considers that individual to have any knowing involvement in JFK's death.

Every effort has been made to describe the author's assessments as speculation, premise or theory.

FORWARD

The 2006 edition of *Someone Would Have Talked* contains three years of additional research as well as a number of new elements which we hope will assist the reader:

- Where possible, new research has been inserted directly into the relevant text or into end-notes. Chapter level references and endnotes have been consolidated and are all located at the rear of the book.

- New documents and research on some subjects have been so extensive that they could not be incorporated into chapter text without serving as a major diversion for the first time reader. To avoid that, this edition contains a number of new appendices; several of these appendices are also supported by their own document exhibits.

- Exhibits and hundreds of pages of document references for this edition are now provided via an internet WEB site at http://www.larry-hancock.com for online access rather than being distributed via CD. This allows for ongoing updates of support material.

- Many of the names and groups discussed in the book will be very new, readers are encouraged to routinely consult the section "Names from the Secret War"; this section has been updated and expanded in this edition. The book also contains a photo section showing many of the individuals discussed. A greatly expanded set of photo pages, supporting the individual chapters in the book, are provided on the book web site. They are listed (as are the documents and exhibits) by chapter and readers are encouraged to browse the reference material while reading the book.

- This edition contains an index of names and places discussed in the book. Where available, CIA groups and operations are referenced along with their code names. CIA employee crypt names are also provided as well as crypts assigned to various assets and contacts. Crypts are found extensively in the reference documents and hopefully the presentation of crypts in the chapter text and index will assist the reader in reading these documents.

- A number of important books on the JFK assassination were published towards the end of 2005. Where possible, relevant information from these books has been added with special reference in the chapter text. An expanded list of related books and publications is provided in the bibliography, presented at the rear of the book.

PREFACE

Forty plus years after the murder of President Kennedy, the same intuitive and popular belief exists that was common in the first hours after his assassination–that his murder occurred as the result of a conspiracy. The document releases, transcripts and tapes which have become available in the last decade only serve to confirm how many individuals and indeed witnesses privately held this belief, beliefs which were expressed privately but which for the most part did not enter the public record.

One common challenge to the concept of a conspiracy is that either the institutions of law or of government would have ensured that people with knowledge of a probable conspiracy would bring it before the public and make it a matter of historical record. The book you are about to read will demonstrate that, as of 2006, such knowledge has become a matter of record–fragmented in memos, taped conversations, surveillance reports, biographies and anecdotal remarks to friends and family–but certainly not recorded in the official histories.

This book is the product of a quest for that buried history, the real history rather than the "packaged" history of the Warren Commission report-a report built not on a true criminal investigation conducted by the Dallas Police or the Justice Department but rather on just another "report". A report prepared by the FBI in no more than a single week. A report which the Director of the FBI himself tried to qualify with a private memorandum to the new President that he would like to make it conditional on further investigation. A memorandum that was ignored by President Johnson, who at the time was on the telephone daily, assuring prospective members of the Warren Commission that their role was simply to accept and certify the FBI report to the public of the United States.

You will find "buried history" in this book, and in the hundreds of pages of documents which are being made available with it for reference. You will also find a response to the other two common challenges to the concept of a conspiracy. The first being that if there had been a conspiracy "someone would have talked", because after all we know from movies and TV that someone always does. The second being that a conspiracy which could remain secret for forty years would have to be so "good" as to be unbelievable.

The history you will read will demonstrate that indeed people did talk, both before and after November 22. And that neither the conspiracy nor the cover-up were all that good.

Someone Would Have Talked deals with people, with observations, confessions, things said to family and close personal friends as well as slips and remarks heard by people who were not prepared to fully understand what they were hearing. It also deals with witnesses and informants who gave testimony to committee staff who lacked the context and related data to fully evaluate what they were being told. Staff who were not supported by criminal investigative personnel and certainly not by the proactive support of either the FBI or CIA–as the document releases of the 1990's now fully demonstrate.

Someone Would Have Talked also deals with "slips", with people who knew things they should not have given the timing of their remarks. It deals with people who kept information to themselves to protect their persons, their families, their jobs and positions. People who had heard or seen something they would rather not have known.

And finally, it deals with people who actually tried to tell what they knew about a conspiracy, stories that did not fit the official record, the accepted history. It catalogs their rejection–and in some cases the actions that were taken to make sure these people did not make it into the official record at key times. In the process it illustrates how ineffective Committees and Hearings can be in dealing with a criminal investigation.

In short, this book deals with people, not forensics nor trajectories nor medical analysis. Of course people are always the "sticky" part of any investigation, especially one with potential criminal implications and the related penalties and risks, not to mention the possibility of "accessory after the fact" charges. The question is always who to believe, who to trust, who to expect to lie, to commit "CYA" or engage in protective obfuscation.

In this arena, context, corroboration, connections and propinquity become key. Circumstantial evidence comes into play–and for a jury circumstantial evidence is perfectly admissible. As The Evidence Handbook states, all facts which tend to establish a chain of evidence are admissible and "proof of a significant set of circumstances often produces belief beyond a reasonable doubt...even in the absence of direct proof of the ultimate fact."

For that reason this book is supported not only with the normal references and bibliography but also with an extensive library of exhibits and documents. Exhibits range from contemporary newspaper articles through testimony and telephone transcripts to diaries, investigative reports and memoranda. In many instances the exhibits present contradictions which must be evaluated; in some cases they reveal official errors, mis-statements or simply "holes" in the official record.

This history is no longer buried in the archives, it's in front of you. As the jury you have to make the final call based on objective evaluation and judgment. Belief "beyond reasonable doubt" will be your decision. The history here is real, not "canned" in a report or a textbook. The decision for or against conspiracy and cover-up is yours.

ACKNOWLEDGEMENTS

Someone Would Have Talked offers an alternative view of President Kennedy's assassination. In doing so it presents a picture of 1950s and 1960s cold war history that is a good deal different than most readers will have taken away from their United States history classes.

It has taken well over 40 years of dogged work by hundreds of Warren Commission "critics" to develop the historical context for what is in this book. Beyond that it has taken both congressional actions and a host of individual Freedom of Information Act filings to obtain and release the documents and data that form its foundation.

Without those efforts a book such as this would have been impossible. It would also have been impossible without the assistance and active support of a network of researchers who graciously allowed me access to their own work and collections. Who helped guide me through NARA to obtain what I would never have found on my own. Who willingly shared new finds with me–and helped me understand what I was seeing.

For me, the beginning wasn't with any web site, no online searches, no NARA document search tool. They would come in time, but for me the beginning was Anna Marie Kuhns Walko. Anna Marie had been one of the first researchers to build a collection of files by physically immersing herself in the national archives. Anna Marie shared her files, her document collection and even her copy machine with me. True, most homes don't have a full sized copy machine adjacent to the kitchen but hers did and all three of us became friends. Anna Marie's work was my starting point–before there was a NARA online index and before there was a Records Review Board and before there were "RIF's", Anna Marie had been toiling away on her own in the D.C. Archives. And then there was the "Queen" of documents, Mary Ferrell. Mary began collecting and analyzing JFK materials within days of the assassination. Her collection grew not to fill just a room but a small building. A collection seemingly fully stored and indexed in her fantastic memory. My only regret is that I was never able to spend the sort of time in Mary's "archive" that I was with Anna Marie's copy machine.

More recently I was able to turn to Malcolm Blunt, my "guru" of the national archives, always willing to share and help me understand the most recently discovered and most obscure paper trails. Always there with a continuing stream of new documents - one of my favorite dinner companions at the JFK Lancer conferences in Dallas, always with new documents in his jacket pocket.

Aid and assistance came in all forms. Kathy Emberton sent in requests to NARA so large that they gave us estimates in months ...maybe years. Stuart Wexler tackled NARA in person when there just wasn't time to wait. Bob Dorff mailed me a year's worth of Vice Presidential diaries fresh from the Johnson Library. Russ Shearer was there with articles and original materials from 1963 I'd never even thought about and Alan Kent could locate all the "lost" magazine articles from the last 40 years. Bill Bretz had the kindness to send me hundreds of pages on Cuban exile and fellow traveler activities retrieved from the Miami newspaper archives–it was only after reading Bill's collection that I began to develop a real world context for the efforts against Fidel Castro.

Debra Conway was the fastest file "burner" in the west, sending me CD loads of files for the mere asking, and allowing me to become personally entertained by seven years of FBI surveillance reports on Johnny Roselli (all except for the six months missing out of those seven years, but we'll get to that). David Boylan, contributed all his work including FBI and ATF documents on gun running in Dallas so I could finally get the real picture of what happened there in the fall of 1963. Lisa Pease allowed me use of the testimony of Robert McKeown, 100 pages of it. And there was help from many more individuals over the years. They all have my sincere thanks, and the responsibility for all those file cabinets that are really beginning to grate on my wife's nerves.

And then there were the online document resources, JFK Lancer operated by Debra Conway, History Matters operated by Rex Bradford and Gordon Winslow's Cuban Information Archives, the Mary Ferrell Foundation site. Thank you Debra, Rex, Gordon, and Ollie.

And I can't forget all the books, nor fail to mention my good friend Andy Winiarcyk, and his Last Hurrah Bookshop. How else would I find how who owned major shares in every Las Vegas Casino in 1963 except to call Andy and have him pull the right book off the shelf and get it to me in the next day! Andy is at 570-321-1150 in Williamsport, PA if you need a book you should call him.

Government documents, contemporary history sources, reference books–they are the first foundation of this book.

Then there were the pathfinders, the second foundation. The people who went in first and did the hard work, the leg work, in dark places and sometimes with dangerous people. Gaeton Fonzi with the House Select Committee on Assassinations "discovered" David Phillips and picked up the lead on David Morales. Brad Ayers and Bob Dorff did the legwork on David Morales. Anthony Summers and Bill Kelly interviewed John Martino's family. Noel Twyman pursued details with Morales' friends and explored elements of the Interpen personnel and their exile associates. Harold Weisberg went to New Orleans and gave us the real story of Dean Andrews as well as Orest Pena, especially the parts the local FBI didn't want to report. Dick Russell tracked down Richard Case Nagell and spent a decade digging into his story. Vince Palamara's dogged research on Secret Service protection of the President and his recording of what the Agents would and would not say. Lamar Waldron's work on the suppression of Secret Service agent Abraham Bolden's information. Ian Griggs' persistence in interviewing Dallas witnesses no one else put on record. Martha Moyer and Betty Windsor helped me understand Jack Ruby, and Seth Kantor who dug out the real story on Ruby that the Warren Commission had to work so hard to avoid. Richard Mahoney was still locating new sources and new facts over three decades after the assassination. And William Law, who continues to develop new material from witnesses who are only now talking after 40 some years, talking only due to William's perseverance.

There are many more names to list, too many. Certainly I need to thank my wife who at least tolerates my obsessive–compulsive behavior. The people who worked so diligently editing and fact checking this second edition including Jamey Wecht, Sherry Gutierrez and Debra Conway. A special thanks to James Richards who shared his magnificent photo collection and developed all the photo pages you will find in the book and the much more extensive collection on the book's web site. And to Phil Hopley who came to the rescue with illustrations intended to help in tracking at least some of the many names and events, a request from readers of the first edition.

One of the challenges of the first edition was to point out leads which might be developed to further corroborate premises presented in the book. A number of individuals volunteered to work on certain of these areas and developed corroborative material; you will find the material in this second edition. When possible the contributing individuals have been named. Some have chosen to remain anonymous and that request has been honored. My thanks go out to both the named and un-named contributors.

And finally, my thanks to Kathy Emberton and Connie Kritzberg, who shared their time brainstorming "what if" games with me until one day we came up with the ultimate "what if" connection–and went on to actually find the evidence for it a year later.

Thank you one and all!

Larry Hancock, September, 2006

Section A

THEY'RE GOING TO KILL KENNEDY

CHAPTER 1

"THEY'RE GOING TO KILL KENNEDY!"

MIAMI, FLORIDA: NOVEMBER 22, 1963

Hearing a piece of coverage of the President's travels on the radio, John Martino exclaimed to his wife, "Flo, they're going to kill him. They're going to kill him when he gets to Texas."

John Martino knew that President Kennedy was going to be killed in Dallas. He didn't know all the details but he knew the people who were involved–he had helped them during his trips to Dallas that fall. Martino was nervous that day, wanting to distance himself from what was going to happen and knowing that he couldn't.

Perhaps nervous energy prompted him to announce to his family that he would paint the breakfast room. He asked his son, Edward, to stay home from school that Friday. No reason given and no explanation offered. During the morning, Martino asked Edward not to help paint, but instead to watch television and notify him immediately of any special news or bulletins.

That afternoon when Edward ran to his father with the news of an attack on the President, he watched his father turn white as a sheet. As the afternoon passed, Martino began receiving a series of telephone calls from Texas.[1]

For decades Martino's wife, Florence, along with other members of his family kept his prophetic words of November 22 strictly to themselves. The House Select Committee on Assassinations (HSCA) had been given a lead by one of Martino's close friends that Martino had prior knowledge of the assassination. When questioned by the committee Florence denied that her husband had any foreknowledge. However, months before her death, Florence finally revealed the details of the truth to author Anthony Summers, with confirmation from her son. Martino's actual involvement only became popularly known with the publication of Summers' article in *Vanity Fair* magazine in 1994.[2]

As will be discussed further in this chapter, John Martino eventually provided more details about the conspiracy to murder President Kennedy than were indicated by his remarks to his family on November 22. He did so only to two people. One was a close friend and business partner; the other was one of the reporters who covered Martino's return from imprisonment in Cuba. In both cases, he talked about the matter almost in the manner of a confession and only in the last months of his life.

In order to appreciate and evaluate Martino's remarks, it is necessary to fully understand the life of John Martino, his associates, his activities in 1963, and his activities immediately following the assassination.

JOHN MARTINO, HISTORY AND ASSOCIATIONS

John Martino was born in 1911 in Atlantic City, New Jersey. As a youth he was arrested for being involved in gambling. In 1935 he moved to Miami and was arrested for running a lottery. A year later he married Florence Williams in Miami Beach.

In 1943 John and Florence moved back to Long Island, New York, where John was arrested for loansharking, also becoming involved with racing sheets. Clearly, he was making his living as a petty racketeer.

Self-taught, he also learned a great deal about electronics and electrical equipment, specializing in gambling-related electronic paraphernalia. From repairing slot machines and casino vending machines, he moved into security systems, "bugs," and a variety of devices used to tilt the odds even further toward the advantage of the house.

In 1955 the couple and their two sons moved back to Miami when Martino began facing medical problems that required special kidney medication. He continued his electronics work and in 1956 traveled to Havana, Cuba, at the invitation of Allen Roth. Roth was involved in the management and operation of then new Deauville Hotel and Casino that was leased to Roth by Santo Trafficante Jr. and Everisto Garcia. In his HSCA testimony, Roth stated that Martino was involved in various jobs during the casino's construction.

The Castro revolution eventually resulted in the closure of the Deauville, but over the period of 1957-59, Martino became very much involved with the casino and the FBI reported that in 1958-59 he made an extended series of trips back and forth between Havana and Miami.[3]

Deauville Hotel and Casino Alumni

The Deauville Casino itself had some very interesting alumni. They include Irwin Weiner, a silent stockholder in the Deauville and reportedly a financial money agent for Sam Giancana in Chicago.[4] When subpoenaed by the HSCA, Weiner proved a very difficult witness. First he admitted that he had told unidentified individuals about owning an interest in an unnamed Cuban hotel and "losing his shirt to Castro." The HSCA had previously determined from FBI files that, Weiner's gambling holdings in Havana arose as a result of his friendship with Trafficante. For a while Weiner tried to rescind the remark about his business interest, claiming that his several trips to Cuba were mere vacations—until he was finally forced to admit to business dealings in Havana.

Further, Jack Ruby called Weiner on October 26, 1963, and when contacted by the FBI on November 27, 1963, Weiner simply refused to speak. Weiner testified to the HSCA that Ruby had called him about a bond that Ruby needed issued in Dallas. Weiner said he told Ruby he had no ability to issue a bond in Texas and had no connections that could assist Ruby. But the HSCA determined that the bonding for the Dallas Cabana hotel and restaurant was handled by one of Weiner's Chicago bonding associates, Sol Schwartz.

When asked how Jack Ruby would have known of Schwartz, Weiner stated that Ruby's brother, Earl, was a longtime friend of Weiner's and must have directed Ruby to him. However, when asked about Weiner and Ruby, Earl Ruby stated that he had no knowledge that Weiner knew Ruby and mentioned nothing about ever talking to Jack Ruby about Weiner.[5]

Irwin Weiner was far from being the most important Deauville connection to Ruby. Two of John Martino's co-workers at the Deauville were R.D. Matthews, an associate of both Santo Trafficante and the Campisi family in Dallas, and Louis McWillie. Ruby visited McWillie in Cuba in 1959 during the time Ruby was actively engaged in exploring opportunities for supplying Castro with arms and materials.[6]

This was the same period in that Ruby temporarily became an active FBI informant. During this period, Ruby contacted Robert McKeown, one of the major Castro/Prio gun runners who was doing business from Texas at the same time Frank Fiorini, aka Frank Sturgis, was working for Castro buying and smuggling in arms and materials for the movement against Batista. At this stage, that movement constituted an alliance between Batista's deposed predecessor, Carlos Prio, and Fidel, Batista's eventual successor.

Although apparently out of touch for approximately four years, Jack Ruby began making numerous phone calls to Louis McWillie at the Thunderbird Casino in Las Vegas. The calls began in May and continued through August of 1963. Several casino employees and others in Las Vegas reported that Ruby was in Las Vegas circa November 17, only days before the assassination.[7]

The Arrest

On July 29, 1959, John Martino and his son Edward were arrested in Havana, Cuba. A Castro supporter, a house physician at the Deauville named Dr. Estevez, informed the authorities he had heard Martino make unsympathetic remarks about Castro and Castro's Communist leanings. Martino was accused of attempting to arrange the escape of Batista-connected Cubans. He claimed that he was simply carrying news from Miami Cubans to their relatives while on a business trip to set up a new electronics company in Cuba.

The end result was a trial that left Martino imprisoned in Cuba from 1959 to 1962. He received virtually no support from the American Embassy, partially because FBI headquarters had previously advised its legal attaché that Martino was engaged in "criminal or revolutionary activities."[8]

Hugh Kessler, Welfare Officer at the Embassy, reported Martino as being addicted to drugs, demonstrating a total misunderstanding of Martino's kidney ailments and related medical requirements, and apparently caused the Embassy to refuse requests to assist Martino in obtaining medicine while in prison.[9]

While in prison, Martino encountered and became acquainted with numerous Castro opponents. He was eventually imprisoned along with David L. Christ, aka Daniel Carswell, a senior CIA electronics (bugging) specialist whose team had been captured while in Cuba on a mission to obtain Chinese Communist codes. The CIA first considered hiring

Cuban criminals to help Carswell's team escape, but later turned to legal representation. The legal mission was headed by James Donovan, the New York lawyer who had negotiated the exchange of the Soviet spy Rudolf Agbel for Gary Powers, the U-2 pilot. It intervened on behalf of several of the Americans still in prison after the negotiated release of the Bay of Pigs prisoners. This group approach was used in order not to focus attention on Christ/Carswell's team, all of whom were released—along with Martino—in October of 1962.[10]

MARTINO'S CONNECTIONS IN 1963

Upon his return to Florida, Martino publicly announced that his business was gone and he had no income. He quickly became very much involved with anti-Castro activities in Miami and related a variety of prison horror stories to various reporters, including John Cummings of the *Miami Herald*. (Cummings would become one of the two individuals to whom Martino would eventually confide his involvement in the Kennedy assassination.) He became a public spokesman against Castro and associated with other Miami based activists.[11] Martino was also apparently debriefed by US intelligence agencies.

After his release, Martino came to be associated with many of the non-CIA aligned activists in Miami including Felipe Vidal Santiago, Eduardo Perez Gonzalez aka "Eddie Bayo", and Gerry Hemming. He also met and was in communication with activist Frank Fiorini/Sturgis, who since 1960 had been a CIA informant reporting to Bernard Barker and to Jose Joachim Sanjenis Panderaeo, aka "Sam Jenis".

Later we will explore the relationship of Sanjenis with David Morales of the CIA and his role with the covert exile group that has been popularly described as Operation 40. Since 1962, Fiorini had been assigned to associate with, and report on any anti-Castro activities not directly under CIA supervision. He reported on unsanctioned exile operations and rogue activities, and generally acted as a "snitch" for the Agency.

Martino himself referred to his association with Fiorini and Vidal when being interviewed by the FBI. He was careful to deny them as possible sources for his stories about Oswald being prepared *in Cuba* for a role in the JFK assassination. Martino specified that his source was neither of the two men. However, at the time Fiorini was actively promoting the same information in regard to Oswald.[12]

For future reference, it is also important to establish some background for Bernard Barker in the context of Miami anti-Castro activities. Barker was a former Batista secret service policeman who became a CIA employee reporting to E. Howard Hunt. He served as liaison and paymaster to many exile groups. Reportedly, he also played a liaison role with Operation 40.

Operation 40 was the unofficial designation for a Cuban exile intelligence and action team that was to accompany the Bay of Pigs Brigade as it advanced into Cuba. It has been rumored that selected exile activists were to identify and target Castro and Communist cadre, neutralize, and if necessary, eliminate them. It is also rumored they were encouraged to target leftist exile leaders and politicians following Castro's anticipated overthrow.[13, 14]

Barker was also associated with Miquel Suarez of Ameritas, a Miami real estate partnership and cover for exile actions. Ameritas made the hotel reservations for the Watergate burglars, including both Barker and Fiorini/Sturgis who were among those arrested in that affair. Shortly before the Kennedy assassination, Christina Suarez, Miquel's sister, had told nurse Marjorie Heimbecker that President Kennedy would be killed by Castroites.[15]

THE BAYO-PAWLEY MISSION (OPERATION "TILT")

Eduardo Perez Gonzalez, aka Eddie Bayo, fought under Raul Castro against Batista and had demonstrated extreme tenacity and bravery in combat. He turned against Castro's Communist regime and served on the CIA sponsored infiltration ship the Tejana III. Bayo was also reportedly involved in an assassination mission against Raul and Fidel Castro that was organized out of the Guantanamo Naval Base. He later became an organizer of Alpha 66, leading that group's raids against Russian elements in Cuba.

After John Martino's release, sometime during the winter of 1962, Bayo became the major proponent of a very significant story then circulating in the exile community in Miami. The story was that *two Russian officers inside Castro's Cuba wanted to defect*; that the officers were in contact with anti-Castro forces in Cuba, who in turn had advised

Bayo of the situation. Also that the Russian officers had information indicating that, though the Missile Crisis had been resolved months before, several atomic warheads and missiles were still in Cuba.[16] The story had supposedly emerged in a letter from an underground cell in Cuba whose members had been smuggled out through Mexico City and Spain.[17]

Other proponents of the "Russian Officer" story included Howard Davis of Hemming's "Interpen" group, who established a contact with the White House through a New York financier named Theodore Racoosin. Davis introduced Racoosin to Bayo, who claimed that the Russians were with his underground group hiding out in the mountains in Cuba. Racoosin later returned to tell Bayo that his contacts in Washington had been unable to find anything to support this story and encouraged Bayo to take an intelligence agent into Cuba to verify the story. Bayo refused on the grounds that his men no longer trusted the CIA and he would need support to go in alone.

At that point, the Russian officer affair apparently came to a temporary end. But Davis was encouraged by Racoosin to assemble exiles in Miami who were willing to bring their issues with the CIA to the Administration. President Kennedy and his brother Robert were apparently open to the idea that the CIA might not be sharing the full picture of activities against Castro. To this end, Kennedy administration confidant Bill Boggs, the chief Latin American reporter of the *Miami News* and Hal Hendrix, who specialized in Latin American affairs also for the *Miami News* and an important CIA media asset, met with Racoosin, Hemming, Fiorini, local DRE members, and Martino.

During this time Martino had become a very visible anti-Castro personality.[18] Martino was then working with a politically conservative ghostwriter named Nathaniel Weyl, author of *Red Star Over Cuba*, 1961. Weyl was also working with ex-Flying Tiger and millionaire William Pawley on his autobiography.[19]

Martino arranged for two ex-CIA agents on Pawley's payroll to attend the second Davis coordinated meeting along with selected conservative Florida leaders. While the discussions focused on the shortcomings of the CIA, Martino had the chance afterwards to introduce Bayo and to float his Russian officer story once again.

The upshot was that a few days later, William Pawley himself received a call from Senator James Eastland, chairman of the Senate Internal Security Subcommittee. Eastland had been briefed by

John Martino and felt the matter should be pursued.[20] With known intelligence connections and assets in Cuba (where he had owned the Cuban National Airline and other major businesses before the Castro revolution), millionaire William Pawley was on first-name terms with former CIA director Allen Dulles. Pawley had been US Ambassador to Peru and Brazil, and had served as special assistant to the US Secretary of State. He was also an extremely vocal and aggressive opponent of Kennedy administration policies towards Cuba.[21]

So Pawley was asked if he could arrange to get Bayo into Cuba and bring out the pair of Russians to testify for Eastland's committee—an event that would have caused immense political embarrassment to the Kennedy Administration. It was an appealing opportunity for Pawley, who enjoyed extensive contacts with senior levels of the CIA. These included Richard Helms (then Deputy Director for Plans), as well as most of the other Deputy Directors and Hemisphere Chiefs including J.C. King. He'd also had previous access to the highest levels of the Eisenhower administration.[22]

With this sort of intelligence clout, Pawley decided to go directly to Theodore Shackley, the head man at the CIA's giant JM/WAVE station in Miami, and pursue the Bayo matter with him. Shackley decided to cooperate with Pawley and informed his immediate superior. We also know that Pawley himself was in direct communication with Marshall Carter, Deputy Director of Plans, in regard to the mission. It was Carter who gave the high level approval for participation by *Life* magazine including photographic coverage. There is no indication that plans for this incursion into Cuba were passed on to the SGA (Special Group Augmented), the executive operations group headed by Attorney General Robert F. Kennedy, who was in charge of all operations in the secret war against Cuba.

Though Pawley and Shackley privately described Martino as an unsavory low life, they did invite Martino to join the Bayo-Pawley mission into Cuba.[23]

The CIA's involvement with Bayo-Pawley project (crypt TILT) is often minimized, but at least three Agency military personnel were on the mission, including Rip Robertson of the JM/WAVE staff and Mickey Kappes.[24] Robertson was one of only two US CIA operations personnel with Brigade 2506 at the Bay of Pigs.[25] He served as military advisor to TILT, supplying ample high-quality equipment and weapons.[26]

A native Texan, Robertson had played football at Vanderbilt and was a Marine Captain in the Pacific during WWII. He performed military support for the CIA in its activities in the Guatemala coup along with David Morales but temporarily became an Agency outcast to senior officer J.C. King when Robertson took his own initiative to bomb a British ship that he had mistakenly identified as possibly Russian. Robertson remained active in Latin affairs; he joined a gold mining venture in Nicaragua and eventually became a close friend of the Samozas.[27]

However, he was brought back into CIA operations for the Bay of Pigs commanding the supply ship Barbara J and led exile frogmen onto the beach. Robertson later became affiliated with JM/WAVE operations and was the officer who debriefed Martino upon his release from Cuban prison. Florence Martino identified someone she knew only as "Rip" making numerous visits to their house. (Robertson died in 1970, supposedly of the aftereffects of malaria contracted during service in Vietnam.)

The navigator and coastal guide for the mission was one of Robertson's close associates, the legendary Eugenio Rolando Martinez. Having guided over fifty pre-Bay of Pigs penetrations, Martinez had become the chief pilot of Mongoose missions. A decade later, he would be arrested as one of the participants in the Watergate burglary (along with Barker and Fiorini/Sturgis).

Recently available documents also show that David Morales was one of the signers of an order authorizing the deployment of the CIA ship Leda to provide radar surveillance for the Pawley yacht.

The Leda was one of only two operational CIA motherships specially equipped vessels used to carry, service and generally support the smaller craft deployed in maritime espionage and raids. The cover for both motherships was blown when the Leda was captured, severely hampering the ability of the CIA to operate covert, deniable missions out of Florida. Leda's sister ship, the Rex, would be compromised later in the year during a Cuban penetration, resulting in public exposure of both the Rex and the Leda and a major public relations nightmare for the administration. [28, 29]

Another passenger on the expedition was one Richard "Dick" Billings, a *Life* magazine staff writer brought in through the Pawley-Luce connection. Given what we know about the extensive CIA operational involvement in the mission and the participation by several very key operations personnel (including Robertson and Martinez), it seems almost unbelievable that the CIA officers allowed a public photographic record. This was a direct violation of all operational security procedures and of course would have compromised both CIA personnel and assets. Pawley himself discussed the challenge in gaining high level agency approval for such media involvement. However, with CIA documents that became available in 2004, we can confirm the *Life* magazine participation was cleared at a level significantly beyond even that of Shackley and JM/WAVE.

It was actually authorized in personal correspondence between Pawley and Marshall S. Carter, Deputy Director of Central Intelligence, who was later to become the head of the National Security Agency. In a letter on his own personal CIA stationary, Marshall Carter responded to a communication from Pawley that contained a *Life* magazine letter "in connection with the publishing of a story, apparently based on a conversation with Hunt" (George P. Hunt, *Life* managing editor). This letter was a follow up to an earlier personal exchange between the two men in which Pawley had refused to have any part in the "defector operation" if it involved a story by *Life*. From the text of the letter it appears that Pawley was communicating the insistence of the Cubans to coverage of the project by *Life*. In a follow-up letter from Carter to Pawley on June 1, 1963, Carter states that Carter's "people" in both Miami and D.C. had gone along with the idea of a *Life* photographer accompanying the Pawley boat mission. Carter did state that the CIA people are not to be identified to *Life* and if their CIA affiliation is exposed, *Life* must promise not to mention the CIA "in any way, shape or form in the operation."[30]

Clearly, even the possibility of obtaining Russian defectors who would verify that missiles remained in place was seen to have justified the extensive security risks in this mission. Carter describes it as a "golden opportunity" even though he rated the chances as slim. Certainly the Cuban exile mission participants were aware and had absolutely insisted on their activities being photographed for publication.[31] They knew that they would all very likely receive the national visibility that had been given to earlier DRE and Alpha 66 missions by *Life* photo-journalists.

And the photo coverage of the trip was extensive (as can be seen in a set of the photographs included on this book's website) and include Eugenio Martinez, one of the CIA's most experienced and renowned covert mission boat guides. Another TILT alumni, Richard Billings, the journalist on the mission, went on to have several connections with the President's assassination. Afterwards he was sent to Dallas to be a part of the *Life* investigative team. Then he played a lead role in the *Life* probe of the Jim Garrison investigation, establishing a close relationship with the DA, creating an extensive series of notes and spearheading what came to be a *Life* media critique of Garrison's efforts.[32] Finally, Richard Billings was hired by Robert Blakey, of the House Select Committee on Assassinations, as the editorial director for the final report of the HSCA. Billings and Blakey would later co-author a book called *The Plot to Kill the President* on the Kennedy assassination.

The tiny Bayo-Pawley mission, like the Bay of Pigs invasion, was an utter debacle. The landing team disappeared inside Cuba where it was never officially heard from again. CIA assets reported no word of the team, or of the capture or death of Bayo. Nor did any such announcements appear in the Cuban press, where they would have been eagerly received; it would have been extremely inconsistent for the team to have been captured or killed without publicity within Cuba. An "after operations" CIA report concluded that the Russian defector story was false, and had probably been fabricated to garner Agency support in placing an exile team into Cuba.[33] Alternative speculation is that the mission was actually a well-covered covert infiltration of an exile Castro assassination team. This speculation is somewhat justified by a close examination of the size of the team and the weapons with which it was equipped.

After his return from the expedition, John Martino completed his book, *I Was Castro's Prisoner*, and began book promotion and speaking engagements sponsored by various right-wing and anti-Communist organizations. His book tours took him to New Orleans and twice to Dallas. While in Dallas, he commented on the fact that the daughters of Amador Odio, who he said was a fellow prisoner he had met in Cuba, were living in Dallas. Martino's remark appears to have been a slip, as his book relates that he was never on the Isle of Pines where Amador Odio was in prison and certainly makes no mention of Odio. His knowledge and interest in the Odio girls in Dallas will be examined later in following chapters.[34]

AFTER THE KENNEDY ASSASSINATION "THE BIG LIE"

Other than the above, we have little concrete detail on anyone else that John Martino might have been associating with during the fall of 1963. The next time that he went on the public record was immediately after the Kennedy assassination.

In 1963 and 1964, Martino very publicly told a much different story—a story of Lee Oswald as a Castro-sponsored assassin. That same story was repeated so frequently that it eventually began to sound very much like a script, with other individuals touting similar claims. At the time, it was striking enough to bring Martino to the attention of J. Edgar Hoover and the FBI. This was fortunate for us, since it is the FBI inquiry and its related documents that provide us with much of the background we need to put Martino in the proper historical perspective.[35]

At that time, both he and Nathaniel Weyl actively promoted the story that Oswald had been in Cuba beforehand and that he had been in contact with Cuban intelligence and even Castro himself. Their story described Castro's motivation as revenge for continuing attempts on Castro's life by the United States government.[36] To substantiate Castro's motivation, Martino wrote that the Kennedy administration had "planned to eliminate Fidel Castro…through a putsch (coup)….a left wing administration would be set up."

Martino would not have been privy to the level of information on covert US assassination plots against Fidel Castro that he claimed to know. Much later, one of the individuals directly involved in those operations, John Roselli, began telling a story that was very similar to the one Martino was relating in December of 1963. However, Roselli was actually in a position to know about these highly secret Castro assassination attempts. He himself was the gambling syndicate associate recruited by the CIA in 1960 to use criminal resources and personnel to kill Castro.[37]

Roselli was involved in Castro assassination activities before they became part of the official Mongoose program and he continued to be involved in them after the project was assigned to William Harvey, the officer in charge of CIA activities in support of the Mongoose project.[38] During these activities of late 1962 and 1963, Roselli became the personal confidante of Harvey. We also know that Harvey was authorized by

Richard Helms to continue operation of the CIA's Executive Action (assassination) program, ZR/RIFLE, during 1963. [39]

Immediately following the assassination, FBI and CIA informant Richard Cain (an associate of Sam Giancana and participant in the very early Roselli organized attempts against Castro) began aggressively reporting that Lee Oswald had been associated with a FPCC group in Chicago that had held secret meetings in the spring of 1963 planning the assassination of President Kennedy.

Cain speculated that Oswald had been in the Chicago area in April just prior to his purchasing the gun used in the assassination. Because Cain's report was circulated within the FBI and included a reference to Oswald's gun in the memo title, it has wrongly been stated that Cain was involved in locating the source of the Oswald rifle in the first hours after the assassination. [40] Other reports out of the Chicago area attempted to associate Jack Ruby with a Communist Party cell outside Chicago and had him in contact with them during his Army enlistment in WWII.

Following the assassination, John Martino and Frank Fiorini/ Sturgis of Miami, and Carlos Bringuier of New Orleans, all began telling the same story about Oswald visiting Cuba and being a personal tool of Fidel Castro. Strangely enough, on the afternoon of November 22 after Oswald's arrest, J. Edgar Hoover also related that the FBI had monitored Oswald on visits to Cuba.

Hoover, wrote in a 4:01 PM EST memo on November 22: " Oswald ...went to Cuba on several occasions but would not tell us what he went to Cuba for." Hoover repeated this information again an hour later in a memo of 5:15 PM EST. Of course, this is only one of many *apparently* incorrect pieces of information in the Hoover "first day" memos. [41]

But unlike random pieces of information coming from Dallas, it would seem to be something that would have to come from FBI files or prior knowledge and suggests unreported FBI contacts with Lee Oswald. As we will see in a later chapter, there are indications that Oswald did attempt to get to Cuba on multiple occasions and that the FBI was aware of these trips and investigated them.

The Pedro Charles Letters

In another effort to link Oswald with Castro, a letter was delivered to Oswald's Dallas post office box after the assassination. It was signed by Pedro Charles and postmarked Havana, Cuba, November 28, 1963.

The letter describes seeing Oswald in Miami and urges Oswald to close up business, remarking that he would receive a warm welcome in Cuba afterwards. This letter and two other letters mailed to Johnson and to RFK identify Charles as a Castro G2 agent responsible for using Oswald to kill Kennedy. But the FBI found that all three letters were typed on the same typewriter and mailed in envelopes from a single batch. They suggest a reactive and amateurish plan to tie Oswald and the assassination to Castro.[42]

With one exception, virtually all the propaganda moves to tie Oswald and the assassination to Castro were poorly organized and, like Martino's efforts, had no credible sources. This lack of verifiable sources eventually caused Hoover and the FBI to reject Martino's information, although it was investigated intensely. Hoover even expressed a desire to take Martino to the Warren Commission if his Oswald information could be verified. But Martino could produce no identifiable sources and his story was eventually viewed as discredited by the FBI.

The exception referred to above, relates to a series of CIA informant reports that placed a young pro-Castro, Fair Play for Cuba Committee member in Chicago, Tampa, Dallas and crossing the border into Mexico as soon as it was reopened after being closed following the assassination. The young man, like Oswald, had Russian connections, had made a trip to Mexico City earlier in the fall of 1963 in relation to traveling to Cuba, and had gotten into a fist fight that summer over his pro-Castro sympathies. Gilberto Policarpo Lopez, the subject of many mysterious CIA memoranda, held a job on one of the President's November motorcade routes, and was reportedly in Chicago, Tampa and Dallas during the President's scheduled motorcades and was investigated for possible involvement in the assassination.

Gilberto Lopez represented a suggestive lead in regard to Cuban involvement in the assassination and several authors have argued for that view. However, a closer examination of the various CIA reports suggests that many of them are second and third hand. It also appears that some of the first reports originated with David Morales' shadow intelligence assets. Other CIA memoranda suggest there may have been some interest in approaching Lopez (before his trip to Cuba to visit his ailing mother) because he had a brother who was undergoing military training in Russia.

All in all, the saga of Gilberto Lopez more probably reveals the creation of an another Cuban associated suspect than a lead to a Cuban conspiracy. However, clearly it would be an example where someone with access to CIA intelligence assets would have had to manage the positioning of Lopez as a suspect. Lamar Waldron examines these reports and the story of Gilberto Lopez at considerable length in his 2005 book, *Ultimate Sacrifice.*[43]

MARTINO TALKED

John Martino died in 1975. In the last months of his life, he related his participation in the conspiracy to assassinate President Kennedy to two individuals. The first was John Cummings, the former Miami *Newsday* reporter who had covered Martino's return from Cuba and who had stayed in contact with him over the years.

The second was Fred Claasen, Martino's business partner in Latin America where they had teamed up to sell various sorts of military gear in the decade following the Kennedy killing. Martino himself had spent a good deal of time out of the country during the years immediately following the assassination, as had many of the more radical Cuban exiles and many of the JM/WAVE alumni. These individuals generally ended up in either Latin American anti-Communist activities or in Vietnam.

Martino himself spent time in both Guatemala and Honduras, initially representing the Roths (formerly of the Deauville Casino in Havana) with real estate interests, but eventually going on to organize deals for both guns and bulletproof vests with the Guatemalan government (Claasen was his partner in the vest deal).

Martino's statements to his wife and family, and those to Cummings and Claasen, were very consistent. First, he simply stated that there had been a conspiracy and that he was involved in a very peripheral way, serving as a courier and delivering money or facilitating matters. He certainly did not represent himself as a planner or organizer and what observations he had were limited and in line with his own contacts.

Martino's role was actually brought to the attention of the HSCA by a very hesitant and concerned Fred Claasen. At first, Claasen approached the Committee under an alias, but eventually revealed himself for the record.

The Committee took him seriously and verified the general background of his statements and his connection to Martino. However, its only direct source for verification was Martino's wife Florence, who allowed them access to some of Martino's papers. She refused to give the Committee any corroboration to the conspiracy story.[44]

Considering the potential ramifications and her husband's recent death, Florence Martino's silence at the time is easily understood. What is perhaps less easy to follow is the Committee's failure to go beyond the most elemental work on Martino's background.

In addition, it appears that HSCA Cuba specialists, such as Gaeton Fonzi, were not aware of Martino's JM/WAVE connections. Had they been given access to the details we now have on Martino and especially the level of his contacts, including Congressmen, JM/WAVE personnel and established exile military leaders such as Bayo, their investigations might have ended quite differently.[45]

At this point, available information passed from John Martino to Claasen and Cummings, as well as from Martino's own family, gives us the following insights to the conspiracy. These insights involve the Cuban exile participants and the contact with and management of Oswald, which seems to have been the area in which Martino performed his tasks.[46]

1. Cuban exiles played a significant role in the conspiracy, managing Oswald and incriminating him as a Castro-sponsored assassin (the "story line" for the plot). Two of the exiles performed as shooters in Dallas. Given Martino's role, he would know about exile shooters. However, this does not suggest he knew the full plan and all the possible participants.

2. Oswald was approached and manipulated by anti-Castro exiles who represented themselves as pro-Castro operatives. At the time he was contacted, Oswald was being "run" in a counter-intelligence operation by a US government agency, without doubt the FBI, but possibly as part of a joint agency operation.

3. Oswald was part of the plan, but not a shooter ("hit man" was Martino's term) and was supposed to meet an exile contact at the Texas Theater. Oswald's understanding was that he was being taken out of the country. However, the actual plan was to kill him—apparently outside the country, and very possibly in a location and fashion that would tie him to Cuba and Castro. The killing of Officer Tippit was definitely not part of this plan and indeed aborted the contact. One of the shooters was actually waiting in the Texas Theatre to contact Oswald and was released by the police after Oswald's arrest. According to Martino, the

planners had to have Ruby kill Oswald, indicating that Ruby definitely was under the control of the conspirators.

4. The motorcade route was known in advance and the attack was planned in detail before the assassins arrived in Dallas.

SUMMARY

John Martino had pre-knowledge of the plan to kill John Kennedy in Texas. John Martino "talked" in a very believable and credible fashion. At first, he talked only to his immediate family, nervously, hesitantly, and excitedly. Shortly before his death, he talked with two longtime friends—part confession and part simply recollection. He made no grand claims, down played his own role and limited his statements to things he would have personally come in contact with in playing the role he described with the Cuban exiles whose cause he was demonstrably devoted to at the time. His story is consistent with his documented activities and personal associations in 1963. Martino's personal involvement also helps us to estimate the start date and time frame for the plot.

- Martino's method of relating his knowledge of the conspiracy is credible and consistent.

- Martino does not exaggerate his position nor claim knowledge beyond his described role.

- Martino's switch from his post-assassination public crusade to his private confession is significant and consistent with his overall remarks about his role.

- Martino was demonstrably connected to the anti-Castro people he implicates.

- Martino offers a unique insight into Oswald's role, associations, and manipulation—one that can be investigated for corroboration.

- Martino provides insight into tactical details in Dallas that can be investigated for corroboration, including the elements of advance personnel on the ground, a motorcade route known in advance and figuring in the tactical plan, Oswald as a patsy tied to the route, Oswald framed as a Castro connected shooter, and a planned meeting and extraction of Oswald from Dallas.

John Martino provides a unique insight into a conspiracy by anti-Castro elements to kill President Kennedy in revenge for his perceived betrayal of the exile cause and to tie the President's murder to Fidel Castro and Cuba in a manner that would trigger an American invasion of the island. The immediate question is whether or not the historical record has sufficient evidence to support Martino's information. The larger question, that we will examine later, is how this Cuban exile milieu and its conspiratorial efforts fit into the agenda of the individuals who appear to have been driving the action of the Cuban exiles.

According to one source who will be quoted later in this book, "... the street level Cubans felt JFK was a traitor after the Bay of Pigs and wanted to kill him. People above the Cubans... wanted JFK killed for other reasons."

As a starting point, we will examine the record for evidence that Oswald was not the "loner" portrayed by the Warren Commission, that indeed he was associating with and otherwise connected to a variety of individuals, including suspicious Latinos who appeared to be pro-Castro or Castro connected.

CHAPTER 2

"...AN EX-MARINE, AN EXPERT MARKSMAN"

The official Warren Commission perception of Lee Oswald was that he was very much a loner, with no significant connections or associations. Perhaps because they had no radical group with which to associate Oswald's actions, they experienced some difficulty in establishing a viable motive for his alleged murder of President Kennedy. Especially since the people who had heard Oswald comment on President Kennedy related nothing in the nature of any animosity on Oswald's part. In fact, this loner view is strongly challenged by John Martino's information.

Martino describes Oswald as having associations with several U.S. agencies. Agencies that were using him as an intelligence dangle; a function that led Oswald into contact with a variety of Cuban exiles and eventually Cuban and Russian personnel in Mexico City. In fact, Oswald himself approached both anti-Castro and pro-Castro organizations, groups and individuals. Consequently, he was contacted by exiles of both stripes, presenting themselves as having particular interests and agendas. Many of the individuals were monitoring Oswald; some to ascertain who he was in contact with, and others simply trying to figure out what game he was really playing. As a result, undoubtedly by August of 1963, Lee Oswald was known and of interest to a good number of people involved in the secret war between the Kennedy administration and Fidel Castro. And, in the end, some of them would be in a position to use their knowledge of Lee Oswald to portray him as a tool of Fidel Castro and establish him as a patsy in the murder of President Kennedy.

Martino places Lee Oswald in contact with Cuban exiles during the summer of 1963, frequent contact. If Martino is telling the truth it should be possible to find some sign of this in New Orleans and perhaps even in Texas.

DALLAS, LATE SEPTEMBER 1963

One evening in late September, three men appeared at the apartment door of Sylvia Odio, a young Cuban mother whose sister, Anne, was staying with her to help with the children while Sylvia packed for a move to a larger apartment. Mrs. Odio and her two younger sisters were in Dallas, but their father and mother were both imprisoned in Cuba for actions against the Castro regime.

Her father, Amador Odio (a trucking magnate who was one of the richest men in pre-Castro Cuba), had given shelter to Reinol Gonzalez, one of the members of Manolo Ray's anti-Castro underground group which had planned to attack Castro from an apartment near the Presidential Palace.

The apartment had been rented by Antonio Veciana's mother. Gonzalez had been located and captured on Amador Odio's land by Castro security forces. Since October 1961, Amador Odio had been imprisoned in the infamous Isle of Pines facility.[1]

Sylvia Odio's visitors were three men, including two who were described by both Anne and Sylvia as looking more Mexican than anything else, and one American who spoke poor Spanish, apparently understanding even less. The men initially asked for Sylvia's sister Sarita Odio, a University of Dallas college student, but Anne determined they were actually seeking the married sister, Sylvia.

Sylvia Odio had been modestly active in exile activities, including efforts to obtain weapons for JURE, a liberal exile group co-founded by her father and Manolo Ray. Although she was not a public participant in the Dallas JURE organization, Sylvia remained connected to the highest levels of the JURE leadership. Earlier in 1963, while on a trip to Puerto Rico to get her children, she had reported directly to Manolo Ray in regard to her unsuccessful attempts to locate arms suppliers for his group. The moderate politics of the JURE members of the Cuban Revolutionary Council had been one of the major reasons that CRC leaders including Ray, despised by right-wing Cuban groups and their allies in Miami, had been locked up in Florida during the Bay of Pigs invasion.

Ray had also been among the "leftist" exile leaders who would have possibly been on the target list for Operation 40, a covert operations team trained by David Morales and organized in support of the Bay of Pigs. The team's mission reportedly included seizure of strategic facilities and the kidnapping or elimination of targeted Communists, left wing politicians and Castro cadre.[2] Due to the failure of the invasion, most Operation 40 personnel did not land in Cuba. Although the group was officially disbanded after the invasion, we now know that certain individuals were retained as a shadow intelligence group (see Chapter 8 for details and sources). Persons reportedly associated with Operation 40 and with Sanjenis (its leader) continued to appear in anti-Communist and criminal activities for another decade or more.

Sylvia Odio's two Latin visitors introduced themselves as JURE members and friends of her father—they even knew Amador Odio's "war name." Sylvia questioned them as to who had sent them; whether they were sent by Eugenio, or by Ray himself? They told her that they were acting on their own and that they *"had just come from New Orleans."*[3]

The men then asked Sylvia to write a set of proper English letters to be used in soliciting financial support for JURE. Sylvia refused to commit to the letters since she instinctively did not trust the visitors. They left with the American, stating that they would be in touch with her.

One or two days later, Sylvia received a call during which one of the men made the casual comment that the American with them was named "Leon." "He was an ex-Marine, an expert marksman and he would be a tremendous asset to anyone, except you never know how to take him. He could do anything, like getting underground in Cuba, like killing Castro. He says we Cubans don't have any guts, we should have shot President Kennedy after the Bay of Pigs. He says we should do something like that."[4]

The fact that these remarks were not made by Oswald in front of Odio suggests that Oswald was not fully aware of how at least one of the exiles was positioning him. However, this description of Oswald is similar to remarks noted by Dr. Frank Silva of East Louisiana State Hospital. Silva encountered Lee Oswald in the summer of 1963. Dr. Silva was interviewed by Joan Mellen in 2000 and described in her 2005 book, *A Farewell To Justice*.[5] In this interview Dr. Silva describes Oswald as talking to hospital attendants about "what it will take to bring Castro down", bragging about his Marine service, his proficiency with guns, and about his intentions to go to Cuba. Specifically, Oswald remarked, *"I'm involved with getting rid of Fidel Castro.... I'm using my skills as a Marine."* Oswald presented himself at the hospital as looking for work and gave Dr. Malcolm Pierson as a reference. Silva remarked to Mellen that the young man was disrespectful, impolite and generally made a spectacle of himself.

Sylvia Odio never heard from the men again after the visit and phone call, but she was sufficiently worried about them to write a letter to her father in Cuba. She also mentioned it to the doctor who was treating her for stress and fainting spells—the result of her exile and having been abandoned by her husband. The fainting spells had stopped by September. They started again on November 22 when she heard the news of the President's murder.[6]

Both the letter to her father and her remarks to her doctor occurred well before the assassination, and they confirm the incident. The Odio visit is certainly a major example of Lee Oswald being in contact with suspicious individuals—who could be viewed either as Castro agents attempting to infiltrate the exile organizations or exiles trying to figure out Oswald and use him for their own agendas.Sylvia's father responded to her letter with great suspicion about the visit. "Tell me who this is who says he is my friend—be careful. I do not have any friend who might be here through Dallas, so reject this friendship until you give me his name."[7]

Odio's reaction to the visit was one of considerable suspicion, with good reason given subsequent events. If she had become more closely associated with her visitors, or written documents for them, she could have been used to associate JURE with Castro agents—as well as anything more radical involving Oswald himself. Such an association would have eliminated Manolo Ray from any future Cuban politics as easily as Oswald's paper trail to the Fair Play for Cuba organization was destroyed after November 22, 1963.

Sylvia Odio's uncle, Augustin Guitart lived in New Orleans and was very much aware of Lee Oswald. Guitart attended the court hearing on Oswald's Fair Play for Cuba leafleting in New Orleans (which John Martino observed, according to his family). Sylvia's uncle was also associated with Anthony "Tony" Varona. Varona participated in two of the Roselli-CIA assassination attempts against Fidel Castro and had been recommended to Roselli by Santo Trafficante. Varona was reported to have been in New Orleans in November 1963, staying with Augustin Guitart on November 14 and 15. Varona and Martino have been cited in FBI reports and by other authors as having been acquainted with Rolando Masferrer in 1963. It should be noted that one of Masferrer's brothers was living in the same Dallas apartment complex as Sylvia Odio at this time. Just weeks after the assassination, in an article previously referenced, Martino described efforts by Oswald to infiltrate the JURE organization. *There is absolutely no record of any contact between Oswald and JURE—except this visit to Sylvia Odio.* Additionally, Martino evidently gave away his knowledge of this incident before any word of it was made public.[8]

Varona was a long time enemy of Manolo Ray and his JURE organization. Although Varona's CRC organization had been largely dismantled during 1963, he had begun to attach himself to the new leaders favored by the Kennedy Administration, particularly Artime. The politics of Artime's activities and his role in a new Kennedy Cuban initiative (and that of the involvement of other Kennedy "insiders" such as Harry Ruiz Williams) are discussed in some detail in Chapter 12 and in immense depth in Waldren's *Ultimate Sacrifice*. It does seem clear that if this new initiative had succeeded in ousting Castro, leaders such as Artime and Varona would have wanted JURE and Ray out of the picture in any new Cuban government. Considering the size and effectiveness of Ray's group, that might have been difficult. This at least raises the speculation that the Odio incident, in addition to associating Oswald with possible Castro agents, might also have had the objective of associating JURE with Oswald, something that would have had a very damaging effect on JURE if the plot we are following had succeeded. This must at least be considered given Varona's apparent ties to Sylvia Odio's uncle in New Orleans (who had direct knowledge of Oswald) and Varona's link to Pedro Gonzalez in Abilene, Texas (and the note left for Oswald in Gonzalez mailbox). Details on the Abilene incident are reviewed later in Chapter 14.[9]

Would Sylvia Odio's going public with a story about Oswald and suspected Castro agents have received a hearing? Very likely, especially if she included the remarks made during the private follow-up call in regard to Oswald being a very dangerous individual. Very possibly, because although she had been in Dallas only a short time, Sylvia had become close friends with the family of one John Rogers, who owned the prominent company Texas Industries. She was also reported to have dated the son of one of the owners of Neiman-Marcus. Indeed, her doctor described her as being much better connected to the top of the social ladder in Dallas than to the local exile community.

But on November 22, after hearing the news of the assassination, Sylvia fainted at work and ended up in the hospital over the weekend. When she recognized Oswald on television she was further shocked and agreed with her sister Anne not to speak about the incident. Her story was investigated after her younger sister, Sarita, naively made remarks to a friend, who then mentioned the encounter to the FBI when being interviewed about a completely unrelated incident.Sylvia's statements to the Warren Commission were extremely consistent with her later remarks to HSCA investigators. The Warren Commission was very concerned about the implications of her story. The "Odio incident" presented such problems for the official Oswald "lone nut" scenario that FBI Director Hoover charged his personnel specifically to "disprove her allegation." Hoover suggested to his field offices that they work the "mental illness" angle. "In light of Sylvia Odio's mental and nervous condition the Bureau believes that the most productive method of disproving her allegation lies in an investigation to develop further specifics of her mental status."[10]

The FBI pursued this angle with her brother, with other exiles including Ray and Cisneros, and with her uncle in New Orleans. These individuals refused to follow the FBI's lead. So did Odio's doctor, Burton C. Einspruch, who stated "She does not have any problems concerning hallucinations ...she is telling the truth and not exaggerating." Einspruch also verified that Odio had mentioned a visit by three men—two either Cuban or Latin and one Anglo, before the assassination.[11]

Only at the last minute, before their report was to be finalized, did the Warren Commission manage to reckon with the implications of Oswald being seen with possible co-conspirators a short time before the assassination. It discarded the Odio incident based on an FBI report that supposedly identified the three men, including an Oswald look alike. Afterwards, two of the men (William Seymour and Lawrence Howard) denied being in Dallas at the time and provided proof, while the third (Loran Hall) recanted his statement to the FBI and maintained that the Bureau had pushed him into it.[12] (Further detail on this subject is provided in *Appendix H, Odio Revisited*.)

In regard to the FBI solution of the Odio incident as being a visit by Hall, Howard and Seymour, CD 1553D is of special interest. This memo, out of the Miami Florida FBI office on October 2, 1964, specifically states that Hall "recalled no contact with Odio" in his visits to Dallas in 1963. It also describes interviews with Lawrence Howard and William Seymour in September of 1964 in which they each had no knowledge of any contact with Sylvia Odio. In validation of these statements *the FBI showed photos of the three to Sylvia and independently to her sister Annie and both declared that the individuals were not their visitors.* In regard to Seymour, presented by the FBI as the individual misidentified as Lee Oswald, the FBI also determined from his employment records at Beach Welding and Supplies that he was working in Miami at the time of the reported visit.

This Miami report totally undermines the false impressions conveyed by the FBI to the Warren Commission. It also tends to support Hall's contention in his HSCA testimony that he did not change nor recant his story. Instead when contacted by the FBI he had stated that he had no knowledge of Odio—but that he had visited lots of people and he could not deny that she was someone he might have met. It also appears that the FBI only showed him her photo on the second interview when he denied ever having met her.

The same FBI letter also makes mention of Mrs. Odio stating that upon being re-interviewed she did not know anyone locally named Kiki Ferror but that a Masferrer family lived in her apartment complex. The FBI notes that the apartment manager also had no knowledge of any Ferror living in the complex. The FBI seems to have totally missed the fact that the Masferrer family living near Sylvia Odio was one of the brothers of the very high profile Cuban politician and militant anti-Castro exile Rolondo Masferrer. Masferrer and Lawrence Howard appear to have owned the lease on the No Name Key property where Lawrence Howard conducted a good deal of training, including training of Masferrer military personnel, and other Interpen associates.

During the HSCA investigation in the 1970's, the CIA tried to use the Odio incident to point toward a possible Castro conspiracy, proposing three individuals as possible Odio visitors, all of them Castro agents.[13]

When HSCA investigator Gaeton Fonzi first began working with Sylvia Odio, who had totally avoided any publicity, book offers and private researchers, she remarked to him that she had told the truth to the Warren Commission but that they seemed not to want to hear it.

Upon being told that the HSCA would not take her testimony during their open hearings, a very frustrated and cynical Sylvia Odio remarked that she would never tell her story again as she now knew *"that they don't want to know."* [14]

Sylvia Odio's story was a major stumbling block for the official Warren Commission story and the HSCA concluded that it believed Oswald had visited her in the company of others, supporting its eventual conspiracy finding. The Odio incident alone leaves us with solid evidence of Oswald's association with unknown and mysterious individuals. Unfortunately, Sylvia Odio could never put names or faces to her "Mexican looking" visitors who seem to have been completely outside the list of known or publicly visible Cuban exiles. Sylvia Odio was not the only person to receive suspicious visitors in late September, 1963.

"YOU'RE THE MAN THAT RAN ALL THE GUNS TO CASTRO?"

BAY CLIFF TEXAS, BETWEEN DALLAS AND HOUSTON
LATE SEPTEMBER, 1963

Two men drove up to Robert McKeown's house on a Saturday morning as he and his wife were finishing a late breakfast with their friend Sam Neal. Neal had been staying with the McKeowns due to a pending divorce. When she saw the red car drive up, Mrs. McKeown ran upstairs to dress while two visitors got out of the car and proceeded to knock on the door. One man was younger and in shirtsleeves, while the other was Latin, dark skin but not black, just less than six feet, older, late 30's and dressed in a suit and tie.

The younger man opened the conversation, "I'm Lee Oswald; I finally found you. You are McKeown are you not?" He introduced the man with him as "Hernandez." Hernandez had been driving the car. After a bit of conversation the younger man came to the point, "I understand that you can supply any amount of arms ...we are thinking about doing a revolution in El Salvador."

McKeown, a longtime close associate of former Cuban President Carlos Prio Soccares, was still on probation for handling shipments of guns for Prio Soccares and getting them delivered to Fidel Castro in Cuba. Hence, McKeown wanted nothing to do with any new gun deal.

As quickly as possible he got the two out of the house and told Sam Neal, "Sam, ain't that a hell of a mess?"

But the men came back to the door and McKeown stepped out as if leaving the house and Oswald tried again: "Mac, would you do me a favor? It will not involve you in any way. I can give you $10,000 if you can get me four rifles, 300 Savage automatics with a telescopic sight."[15]

McKeown thought about it but decided no way; after all, anybody could walk into any Sears Roebuck in Texas and get the same rifles for only a few hundred dollars. Obviously there had to be a catch and by being circumspect, McKeown avoided the possibility of having Oswald—or anyone—found with weapons that could be traced to a very well known Castro connection.

Decades later, the HSCA interviewed McKeown. The Congressmen seemed to be totally unable to understand or reconcile why anyone would be willing to pay McKeown that sort of money for the guns. But with our current information and John Martino's direction, it seems rather obvious: McKeown had been in the newspapers when Castro visited the United States; in fact, Castro himself actually visited Houston and met with McKeown after his UN appearance in 1961.[16]

McKeown had worked for Prio Socarres and Castro. He had moved weapons from Arkansas and Texas and other locations to Cuba, through Louisiana, Texas and Mexico. He was doing this at the same time that Frank Fiorini/Sturgis was doing the same thing for the same people. McKeown was aware of Fiorini/Sturgis and both of them had been in Prio's house in Florida. Fiorini/Sturgis went to Cuba with Castro and took a job there after the revolution. McKeown was offered a job by Castro but declined. Indeed McKeown's visibility was such that he was widely viewed as an approachable connection to Castro, contacted by numbers of people who wanted to do business in Cuba, to get people out of Cuba, or to reopen casinos in Cuba, particularly the San Souci and the Tropicana.

Perhaps his most interesting visitor then had been named Jack Rubenstein: Jack Ruby.[17, 18] Ruby visited McKeown four times in 1959, offering big money for a letter of introduction to Fidel Castro. But Ruby never came up with the money; so McKeown never facilitated an opening that Ruby would presumably have used to try to release some of his friends who were in jail in Cuba, or to pitch his supplies of jeeps and slot machines.

After the assassination of the President, FBI agents visited McKeown. They didn't explain why, but they had lots of questions about Jack Ruby and his visit. McKeown recalls that they asked him if he was a friend of Oswald. McKeown repeatedly told the HSCA members he did not "know" Ruby—who visited him 4 times at length; nor did he "know" Oswald either, who visited him once for perhaps half an hour.

> "Now wait a minute," McKeown said when I interviewed him in 1976. "I think the question put to me about Oswald through the FBI, I think he put it, *'Are you not a friend of Oswald's,'* or something of that sort, and I said *'I do not even know Oswald.'"* - from Dick Russell's interview in 1976[19]

Surely, McKeown had reason to be cautious as a solid "yes" to the FBI's question about being a "friend of Oswald" could only have meant big trouble for anyone in January of 1964.

The committee members were troubled that McKeown had not aggressively detailed his visit from Oswald with the FBI, and by the fact that the agents' report stated that McKeown didn't know Oswald. But they were not troubled enough to pursue the matter with Sam Neal (whom McKeown said was still alive and in Texas), or with Dan Rather's investigation team who had surfaced McKeown's story, or with McKeown's attorney—Mark Lane. Indeed they proceeded to grill him over and over, stating for the record that he was most likely a liar and was telling a story to get book royalties or television payments (although no book contract was in place and the total TV payments had been $100). Anyone taking the time to read the transcript of his interview will be amazed at McKeown's patience and impressed by his sincerity. This seemed to be lost on the Commission who obviously disregarded the real implication of this Oswald visit.

> **Congressman Fithian:** Mr. Chairman, I am not sure that further questioning would be all that productive. I think the record that we have three, if not four or five, inconsistencies in the witness's testimony and the record will show that the witness is in the process [of], if not fictionalizing this, at least commercializing this, in a book arrangement and I think that this is really what we have learned today, and I have no further questions.

Mr. McKeown: You see I just think that I told the truth. I know I told the truth. Lee Harvey Oswald came to my door. I know that as well as I know my name. I know it was him and any commercial outside of it, I have not made one dime except for my expenses to Texas and the $100 that the British Broadcasting fellow by the name Scott Malone, I guess he just gave it to me.

Mr. McKeown: I just wanted to do this the best I can. I do not want to tell you a lie, for God's sake. I do not want to tell you any lie. What would I gain by telling you a story? I would not gain anything. I would just jeopardize myself. That is all I would do.

Congressman Dodd: I thank you. I should also warn you, advise you, rather, that you will be continuing under subpoena subject to recall by the Committee.

No book ever appeared, of course, no TV show, no movie. The committee put McKeown in the record all right, but they most definitely did not investigate him or his story. The Commissioners missed something more than the purpose of Oswald's visit to McKeown, possibly much more important. They missed the Hernandez connection.

In 1976, Dick Russell interviewed McKeown, no longer living in the little Texas town between Dallas and Houston. Sixty-five years old, he was living with his daughter in a little wooden house in Miami. In a less hostile environment than that of his HSCA interview, McKeown was willing to share one last bit of information. "One thing is, I knew that Cuban with Oswald from before. His name was Hernandez. Knew him from Cuba. Except he didn't know that I knew."[20]

Hernandez from Cuba? A Prio supporter? A Castro supporter before Castro was known to be Communist? Of course if John Martino's information is correct, the Cubans who were manipulating Oswald in the late summer and fall of 1963 were exiles in violent opposition to Castro. They were in the process of representing themselves to Oswald as Castro supporters and working to the best of their abilities to link Oswald himself directly to Fidel Castro.

If McKeown was making it all up, why did McKeown add a Cuban? Why not add Jack Ruby and make it really exciting? Why four rifles with scopes? The trail is cold now. It wasn't in 1976, when the trail led back to New Orleans. And beyond, to Miami.

SUMMARY

John Martino described a conspiracy in which Lee Oswald was manipulated and set up to be a patsy for the murder of President Kennedy; a patsy connected to Cuba and to Castro, in fact a willing tool of Fidel Castro.

The Warren Commission was very troubled by one well-documented incident of Oswald in association with mysterious Latinos. It appears that it never seriously considered the McKeown story that corroborates an attempt to connect Oswald with suspicious Latinos and a known Castro gunrunner.

In the Odio and McKeown incidents we have corroboration for Martino's basic revelation about Oswald and the conspiracy. These incidents also give us dates that help define the timing of the conspiracy.

- Lee Oswald was to be set-up by associating him with remarks about shooting Kennedy and in an effort to obtain sniper-type weapons from a very well known Castro gunrunner.

- In one instance, the potential witness (Odio) was close to the leadership of one of the three exile groups being closely monitored by JM/WAVE in the fall of 1963. This was a group that was very strongly disliked by both ultra anti-Communist CIA officers and activist exiles, including several individuals involved in supporting the new Kennedy backed Artime project.

- Sylvia Odio was known to both John Martino and to exiles involved in Oswald's pro-Cuban protests in New Orleans in the summer of 1963.

- Sylvia Odio's visitors stated they had come directly from New Orleans.

- One of Sylvia Odio's visitors accurately described Lee Oswald, set him up as willing and able to shoot John Kennedy and advocating that Cubans do so. However, this action was done privately, after the visit itself and may indicate separate agendas being in play by the Cuban participants in the visit.

- McKeown's visitors attempted to buy guns from a well-known Castro arms supplier for yet another Latin revolution. When that failed, they tried to obtain four high quality rifles equipped with telescopic sights.

Both incidents corroborate each other and John Martino's description of the attempts to set up Oswald as a patsy. The McKeown incident points us toward people who were working with the Prio network in Cuba smuggling arms to Castro during the revolution against Batista. The Odio incident points us directly back to New Orleans.

And in New Orleans, we will find even more evidence of Oswald being anything but "a loner." He was associating with people that were unknown in New Orleans and thought to be possible Communist or Castro agents.

CHAPTER 3

THEY CAME FROM NEW ORLEANS

If John Martino knew when and where Lee Oswald had first come to the attention of the conspirators, he didn't pass it on to his friends. Then again, given Martino's limited role, it is very likely that he didn't know such details, or indeed, much about the actual genesis of the idea; but he gave us two key leads.

First, we should see evidence of Oswald in association with exiles who could get away with representing themselves as Castro agents; mystery men who no one recognizes and who have no local Cuban connections. Second, we should see some indication of Oswald being used either actively or passively as a low-level intelligence agent. That means we should see Oswald associating with a variety of people who might be of interest to U.S. intelligence. In 1963, that meant both pro and anti-Castro exiles and their supporters. And that's exactly what we see when we examine Lee Oswald's time in New Orleans, immediately before his move to Dallas. In addition, we will see that these individuals included Mexican-looking Latinos with identical descriptions to those given by Sylvia Odio for her visitors who had just driven in from New Orleans.

NEW ORLEANS, SUMMER 1963

Lee Oswald did make contact with a variety of Cuban exiles in New Orleans during the summer of 1963. His apparent attempt to infiltrate at least one exile group (DRE), his leafleting for the Fair Play for Cuba Committee and his radio debate with Carlos Bringuier all established his visibility as an avid Castro supporter. It all helped to publicly associate the FPCC with Oswald and with Communism. Oswald's personal presentation of himself as a Marxist during his radio debate was likely far too fine a distinction for most listeners in New Orleans.

"CUBA EXILE TELLS OF OSWALD BOAST – WOULD AID CASTRO AGAINST US"

This *New York Times* newspaper headline hit the streets only days after the Kennedy assassination; meanwhile in New Orleans, Carlos Bringuier and the DRE were actively promoting the same story of Oswald as a Castro agent that Martino was pitching to both the media and the FBI in Miami. The newspaper story was based on a visit by one of Bringuier's aides to Oswald's apartment. According to Bringuier, the aide Carlos Quiroga attempted to infiltrate Oswald's organization and represented himself as an interested Castro sympathizer. Exactly what the two said to each other is not known, nor is the total extent of Quiroga's possible involvement with Oswald.[1]

We also know that Quiroga was an FBI informant (NO T-5) and that he filed a November 30 report with the Secret Service. In this report, he stated Oswald had told him that if the US should invade Cuba, Oswald would fight for the Castro government (the source of the *New York Times* newspaper headline). Quiroga offered to infiltrate Oswald's organization for the FBI, but they apparently did not respond. Were they getting Oswald's information first hand?[2]

Certainly Oswald was in communication with the FBI in New Orleans, as seen in his request to speak to the FBI after his arrest during his second FPCC leafleting foray outside the New Orleans Trade Mart. In *A Farewell To Justice,* Joan Mellen cites her 2002 interview with Irvin Magri who was present when Larry Howard interviewed former NOPD Lt. Martello in the early 1990's. In that interview, Martello admitted concealing the fact that he was specifically asked to pass a note to FBI agent Warren deBrueys–a name given to him by Oswald. Oswald had handed Martello a note on a piece of paper torn from his notebook and pointed to a number scribbled on top of the paper. "Just call the FBI… tell them you have Lee Oswald in custody. When they arrive, hand them this note." Oswald had then told Martello that he wished to be visited by a particular agent–Warren deBrueys.[3]

Mellen elaborates on Oswald's visibility to the FBI and the problems this generated for them during the Garrison investigation. At that time agent deBrueys was gone, but Regis Kennedy remained in New Orleans and was available to be called for testimony. However, Attorney General Ramsey Clark ordered that Agent Kennedy reveal no information gained in the course of his official duties. Mellen describes local US attorneys being concerned that this might lead to judicial review and advised Agent Kennedy to use his own judgment. So Kennedy invoked privilege regarding knowledge of Jack Ruby's New Orleans contacts, on the question of whether the FBI had investigated Clay Shaw immediately following the assassination, and on whether he was aware of any connections between Lee Oswald and any Cubans. He only admitted that federal agents in New Orleans had known of Oswald.[4]

Oswald's Known Cuban Associates

Carlos Quiroga may have had an easier time presenting himself as a Castro supporter than we might at first imagine. As recently as 1961, Quiroga had been investigated by the CIA for his reported pro-Castro leanings. Only late in 1961 had he become fiercely anti-Castro. Indeed it appears that both he and the local CRC representative, Sergio Acarcha Smith, had been widely suspected within the New Orleans exile community of being secret Castro supporters and perhaps spies.

In 1962 the CIA was apparently considering recruitment of Quiroga as a counter-intelligence agent based on his conversion. The common interpretation of the Oswald-Quiroga connection is that Quiroga was testing Oswald. However, it is also possible that Oswald was being used to test Quiroga and others in the New Orleans exile community.[5] Quiroga was later investigated by D.A. Garrison and proved to be widely connected within the right-wing community, participating in the Houma arms theft with David Ferrie and Gordon Novel.

Garrison forced Quiroga into a polygraph examination. The answers found Quiroga lying on many pertinent subjects and would suggest that he knew others who did go on to recruit Oswald for a conspiracy. But the polygraph was administered under highly stressful conditions and was adamantly and aggressively challenged by Quiroga.

The building that housed Bannister's detective agency just happened to be situated at the address stamped on a number of Oswald's FPC leaflets. In addition, one of Guy Bannister's aides testified that he had been introduced to a "Leon" Oswald by Carlos Quiroga and that he had been asked to leave the room when he came across Quiroga and Oswald in a meeting with Bannister and David Ferrie.[6] In this context it is significant that individuals in New Orleans were introduced to "Leon Oswald" and that Sylvia Odio's visitors from that city referred to the American they were with as "Leon."

UNKNOWN CUBANS

There is solid evidence that Oswald was also associating with other Latinos who were not part of the New Orleans exile community and who were never investigated at all. Given Oswald's highly visible pro-Castro persona, and given Quiroga's success with Oswald, it seems reasonable that when Oswald made new "friends" in New Orleans, they would have been individuals representing themselves as "fellow travelers" to Oswald's stated interests or even representing themselves as Castro agents. And they would not have been individuals from the known or visible anti-Castro community.

If we are to follow the conspiracy leads given us by John Martino, we need to look for contacts and names that would represent either unknown Cubans or exiles who might appear a bit more Mexican than Cuban, perhaps because of Mexican cultural affectations or physical appearance. Dean Andrews, New Orleans lawyer and assistant DA for Jefferson Parish is one source for this connection:

> The Mexicano I associate with Oswald is stocky ...athletic build ...160, 165 pounds, butch haircut... about 26... around Oswald's height.[7]

Dean Andrews was most accurately described as a clever and colorful New Orleans lawyer; his clients were primarily from the city's less refined strata. He handled a good number of morals charges and had a reputation of being able to talk "jive" as well as file briefs with the court. Andrews was far more approachable for many non-establishment individuals than were most of the legal firms in the city. In 1964 he became Assistant District Attorney for Jefferson Parish, Louisiana.

In the summer of 1963, Andrews testified that one of his clients was Lee Oswald. He identified Oswald with no difficulty and was quite certain of his identify. Oswald had been looking for help in overturning his dishonorable discharge from the Marines, and on visits

Oswald was accompanied by the Mexicano Andrews described. The Mexicano spoke only Spanish and made no remarks during the visits. Apparently, he was just along keeping Oswald company.

Dean Andrews is a very important and very convincing witness, a witness who at first told the truth—until he "saw the score" and decided that his life and his family would be best served by backing off from much of what he first related. But one thing that he never recanted was the visit from Oswald and the Mexicano. Paris Flammonde's *The Kennedy Conspiracy* gives an excellent overview of Andrews' eventual moves to protect himself.[8] Harold Weisberg's books *Oswald in New Orleans* and *Whitewash* are also invaluable for developing an understanding of Andrews and of Orest Pena, another key witness in our search.[9]

> A Mexican, about 28 years of age ...5' 8" in height... weighing about 155 pounds and having very hairy arms.

Orest Pena and Everisto Rodriguez gave this description of Oswald's companion. Rodriguez worked as a bartender for Pena at the Habana Bar, where Lee Oswald was seen with the Mexican described above. The Mexican went out of his way to bring attention to himself by calling the owner of the bar an imperialist and capitalist—the bar was located in the same area as Carlos Bringuier's store, a hotbed of anti-Castro and anti-Communist activism. Oswald also drew plenty of attention to himself, this time by violently vomiting up a drink across much of the bar after first ordering a lemonade and then rejecting it. Pena confirmed the observations of his bartender. It was a minor incident but one well remembered by all those in the bar, perhaps a sort of practice run to see how sensitive Oswald was to being "positioned".[10]

Here is Sylvia Odio's description of one of the men who visited her in late September, saying they had driven straight through to Dallas from New Orleans:

> Very Mexican looking... very hairy... lots of hair on the chest... about 170 pounds... stocky.[11]

Telling officials about Oswald associating with an unknown Mexican was not something that put Pena in anyone's good graces. During the height of the Garrison investigation Pena was badly beaten as he began to tell his story again.[12]

Though he had been a numbered, willing FBI informant before the Bureau received his Oswald information, Pena claimed that his FBI testimony was badly handled and misrepresented. Like McKeown and others, Pena found that placing Oswald with associates appeared to lead to problems with his FBI reports. The descriptions given by Andrews, Pena and Odio are too much of a match for coincidence. Moreover, their personal opinions of the FBI agents they talked with also have much in common.

There is one further observation of this strong, Latin individual in Oswald's presence. Miguel Cruz, present during the contacts and eventual fight between Oswald and Bringuier, reported that when Oswald was doing his leafleting, he observed such a person with a camera in front of the Maison Blanche Building. The individual was around 20-30 years old, taller than Oswald, and would have weighed close to 200 pounds. The man was asking people in the area where they were from and taking pictures. He was dressed in a suit and wore dark glasses. This large Latin cameraman caught others attention as well. In early August 1963, a 16 year old teenager named Jim Doyle was visiting New Orleans with his family and noticed a commotion along Canal Street, walked over to investigate, and began filming. His footage shows Lee Oswald, with his back to the camera, is talking with Carlos Bringuier. Doyle noticed the large man and made the observation that he thought it odd that the man was wearing a gray suit in August and that he had an exceptionally expensive camera.[13]

It appears, just as Martino described, that unknown persons were associating with Oswald from July through September 1963 and that their activities as well as their descriptions are remarkably consistent. Martino was of the opinion that Oswald was oblivious to his manipulation by these individuals.

In a later chapter, we will examine that premise and some alternative possibilities. However at this one point one major question jumps out: why Mexicans? These people approaching Oswald were not part of the known exile community, nor New Orleans natives, but they were commonly described as Mexican in appearance. This suggests that perhaps they were Cuban exiles who had come out of Cuba through Mexico, spending enough time there to pick up the clothing, haircuts and general appearance of Mexicans. Perhaps one might even have been of Mexican descent.

Martino's information certainly is corroborated by events in New Orleans. We even know what at least one or two of Oswald's first manipulators looked like; indeed we have a real name for one of them from McKeown. Using the remarks of Richard Case Nagell and Cuban counter intelligence, we can trace at least one of them back to Mexico City and even back to Cuba. Before coming to New Orleans, they had most recently been in Miami. Citing Nagell and/or former Cuban intelligence sources obviously raises questions of credibility, but it is clear by now that "standard sources" are not necessarily the places to look for the truth in the Kennedy assassination. And "credibility" ought not to be strictly associated with official reports and memoranda, since the latter can on occasion be shown to contain either misinformation or be missing important details (according to the sources involved).

RICHARD CASE NAGELL

"I would rather be arrested than commit murder and treason," Richard Case Nagell told FBI agents during transport in El Paso, Texas on September 20, 1963.[14] Nagell was a decorated Korean War Army veteran and at the age of 22 was perhaps the youngest man to receive a field promotion to captain. In 1955 he completed Army Counter Intelligence Corps training and was designated a CIC Officer, given a Top Secret clearance, and assigned to Japan. He served in counterintelligence in Korea and Japan before apparently resigning from the Army. After his separation, he allegedly continued to perform as a contact/informant for both CIA and Military Intelligence; very possibly working for the DIA, the relatively new Defense Intelligence Agency. As with all intelligence informant relationships, this is virtually impossible to verify, but even the CIA was forced to admit that names found in Nagell's notebook were indeed CIA personnel. And recent research suggests that Nagell's mysterious Mexico City CIA contact "Bob" may very well have been Henry Hecksher, a CIA officer described in Appendix B, "Crossing Paths in the CIA."

As background to Nagell's actions and insights, two observations are critical:

"Nagell... was a maverick, he wanted to do things the right way, by the book all the time... didn't ask you to do anything he wouldn't do... he did not know what fear was."— Nagell's company sergeant in Korea, John Margain.

"Nagell... rigid in his thinking... very moralistic in attitude and pattern."— Springfield psychiatric team which found Nagell to be competent to stand trial for bank robbery.

On September 20, Nagell walked into the State National Bank in El Paso approximately half an hour before closing time. He approached a teller window and politely asked for one hundred dollars in American Express traveler's checks. When the clerk placed them on the counter, Nagell silently reached into his jacket, drew a Colt .45, deliberately aimed it towards the ceiling and fired two shots. He then returned the pistol to his belt, turned and walked out the front door. He made no demand for money at any point.

Upon exiting the bank, he stopped briefly at a street corner, then walked to his car and briefly waited there. Eventually, he pulled into the street and was motioned to pass by another motorist. But then Nagell noticed a young policeman, backed his car up on the sidewalk and waited for the officer to approach. When the officer came up to his window, Nagell calmly told him, "I guess you've got me, I surrender" and raised his hands.

The ramifications of this El Paso incident are extensive. Dick Russell explores them in detail in his book, *The Man Who Knew Too Much*. That extensive work considers elements of Nagell's remarkable career that are beyond the scope of this book. Russell explores Nagell's activities in 1963, the legal manipulations he suffered (including the prosecution's frequent recourse to psychiatric examinations to keep him off the stand and off the record), the refusal to provide him with his own possessions confiscated upon his arrest for use in his trial, his long and painful struggle to regain custody of his children, and his efforts to communicate what he knew to Congress and various investigations.

Analysis of the official CIA and Secret Service reports on Nagell show a number of untruths and inaccuracies. In some cases, third party information is presented as fact. Because of this, it is very important to examine all the documents in context in order to evaluate their content. This is also true for Nagell's own statements, especially in later years as he was attempting to locate and obtain custody of his children; he apparently was able to successfully maneuver the CIA into actually assisting him in this by leveraging his information and knowledge about Lee Oswald. Readers who wish to evaluate Nagell in detail should consult *Richard Nagell, Chronology and Documents* by this author, which provides virtually all available sources, documents as well as timelines and analysis.[15]

Most important for our immediate purposes is the fact that Nagell had come to El Paso from New Orleans. When at his suggestion the trunk of his car was examined, authorities found a number of very interesting items. Unfortunately, the majority of these were never formally entered into the record and only a few were returned to Nagell after his conviction for bank robbery was eventually overturned. The items that are identifiable sound strikingly similar to items in the possession of Lee Oswald. They include:

- One miniature Minolta camera and developing kit.

- Fair Play for Cuba leaflets.

- The P.O. box for the Fair Play for Cuba committee in Los Angeles.

- Cuban and Communist literature including "The Case Against Cuba" by Corliss Lamont, one of the documents also being used in New Orleans by Lee Oswald.

- A notebook containing the telephone number of the Cuban embassy, the same number as found in Oswald's notebook.

- In the same notebook, names of individuals from the CIA's Los Angles office. These names were submitted by the FBI to the CIA in October 1963 and eventually verified by the CIA as being names of actual employees.

Additionally, while reviewing the legal files for Nagell, author Dick Russell found a military ID with Nagell's photo and the name and signature of Lee H. Oswald. Neither Russell nor attorney Bernard Fensterwald, Jr. could ascertain where Nagell could have gotten the copy. After seeing the photocopy, Warren Commission historian Mary Ferrell wrote to Fensterwald, "I stress the point that this card does not appear in anything else–not the [Warren Commission] Report, not the [commission] volumes, in no other book..."[16]

After being charged with bank robbery, Nagell wrote his sister Eleanor from prison, telling her he would have to accept his conviction due to his unwillingness to tell the real story behind his actions in the bank. On November 4, Nagell filed a writ of habeas corpus stating, "*I had a motive for doing what I did but my motive was not to hold up the bank. I do not intend to disclose my motive at this time.*"

On December 19, Nagell was interviewed by the Secret Service. No reason was given for the interview, but Nagell stated that he had sent a note to the Secret Service on the afternoon of November 22. An FBI agent involved in investigating and prosecuting Nagell's bank robbery charge accompanied the Secret Service agents. For that reason Nagell refused to make any comment beyond stating that he had met Lee Oswald in Mexico City before the assassination.[17] On January 1, 1964, Nagell provided a statement to the FBI that he had been approached by foreign agents in Mexico City, as well as by an American working for a foreign government. He cites those contacts, his resulting activities, and subsequent coercion as being the factors behind his action in the Bank.

The next day he wrote to the Chief of the Secret Service protesting the FBI's participation in his interview. Agent Fred Morton of the FBI filed a report stating that Nagell had accused him of violating his civil rights and advised from that point on, Nagell would not be interviewed alone.[18]

The interview resulted in a Secret Service summary report that listed some items of Nagell's property. The first two pages of this document are missing from the document currently available at NARA. They apparently contain the full evidence list that, of course, could be extremely supportive of Nagell's statements. This Secret Service report is the first of several that contain inaccurate information. It states that Nagell fought with the arresting officer during an escape attempt, a far different story from that told by the arresting officer in court.

From this point on the investigation of Nagell and his claims becomes very murky. Nagell had stated he had written a warning letter warning letter to J. Edgar Hoover describing an action against the President being planned for the Washington, D.C. area in September. A letter which received no response. When Special Agent Robert Jameson of the Secret Service interviewed Marina Oswald about Nagell on January 20, 1964, she remarked that the FBI had already talked with her about him—but there is no such record in the FBI files.

One instance could have been FBI agent James P. Hosty's questioning of Marina on November 27, assisted by the Russian speaking Secret Service Agent Leon Gopadze, who had been sent to Dallas to interview Marina himself and acted as translator for Hosty and fellow FBI agent Charles T. Brown.[19] At the conclusion of that interview, Gopadze continued with a short list of questions, some of which did not make the record. As author Dick Russell wrote, "The FBI has not yet seen fit to open its full Nagell file to public scrutiny. Nor, judging from oblique references made in the Secret Service's record on Nagell, has the CIA been forthcoming with all of its Nagell pages either."

Agent Gopadze followed with another interview the next day, November 28, accompanied by Paul Gregory, a member of the Dallas Russian community who met Lee and Marina Oswald in 1962. One of recorded questions is whether or not Marina had *"any knowledge of Lee's trips to Mexico or Washington?"*[20] This is revealing because Nagell would later recount that Lee Oswald had been recruited by two anti-Castro exiles representing themselves as Castro agents. Nagell was privy to some of their discussions and the plan that was presented to Oswald at that time involved an action in the Washington D.C. area in September 1963. The FBI question seems to be a solid corroboration for Nagell's letter and story.

Further corroboration comes from the letters Oswald wrote about his planned move to the northeast at the end of August, 1963. Following a letter on August 28 to the Communist Party of the USA asking whether or not he should go "underground," on August 31, he wrote to the managing editor of *The Worker*, the official CPUSA newspaper, and offered his services as a photographer since he was planning a move to "your area".

On September 1, Oswald wrote two more letters, one to the Communist Party USA and one to the Socialist Party USA. Both asked for instructions on how to contact their representatives as he was planning a move to the Baltimore-Washington area. Clearly, this was an impressive and quite deliberate paper trail (although the ideologies of the two parties were very much at odds, and a sincere adherent of either one would be unlikely to approach the other). If Lee Oswald had been associated with some action in Washington, there would have been a clear link between Oswald and Marxist organizations. Combining this with his public demonstrations in support of Castro makes it easy to imagine the headlines after such an incident.

The interesting point is that the FBI questions for Marina—asked before Nagell's first documented meeting with the Secret Service with the FBI in attendance—suggest that either Nagell's letter, or some other information connecting Nagell to Oswald, was indeed in the FBI's possession. Nagell himself did not openly mention the Washington D.C. matter and the Hoover warning letter until 1975, when he wrote to Congressman Edwards, head of a congressional committee investigating S.A. Hosty's post-assassination destruction of a note from Lee Oswald to the FBI.

Nagell had made general reference to FBI inaction, but supposedly had only privately described the Hoover letter to his sister and her husband, who were holding some of his belongings for him. They told Dick Russell that a copy of the letter to Hoover was among those items missing from their home the day after a team of FBI agents visited them in 1964 requesting to examine Nagell's belongings. They requested the letter copy but were refused. *"We're sure the FBI broke into our home that night to find out what he knew."*

The planned Washington incident is further confirmed by a conversation between Lee Oswald and a young woman who was accompanying her mother on a visit to Marina Oswald. Ruth Paine had written to a New Orleans Friends (Quaker) group searching for someone who could assist Marina and the girls mother was serving as a volunteer in that organization, which led to the visit. Oswald began a conversation with the girl and remarked about his planned travel to the D.C. area. When she asked him the purpose of the visit he appeared flustered and made some remark about going there to "get a gun."[21]

On March 20, 1964, Nagell sent a letter to J. Lee Rankin of the Warren Commission:

"I informed the Federal Bureau of Investigation in September 1963 that an attempt might be made to assassinate President Kennedy. Was the Commission advised that the day before Mr. Kennedy visited Dallas, I initiated a request through jail authorities to the FBI asking that they contact the Secret Service in order to inform them of the same information?"

The commission apparently did not respond to this letter and no evidence of Richard Case Nagell is contained in any of its 26 volumes of information. His saga would continue for several years. Nagell objected, but was not allowed to speak in his legal defense, and his court-appointed lawyer pursued an insanity defense that ended up on the court record, tainting Nagell's information about Oswald.

On May 5 Nagell was tried and convicted in the court of Judge Homer Thornberry. The judge, a longtime friend of then President Johnson had ridden in the Dallas motorcade, flown to Washington, D.C. in AF1, and spent the evening and the next few days after the assassination at Johnson's home in the new president's company. Within a relatively short time after his involvement in the Nagell legal actions, Judge Thornberry was nominated for a seat on the United States Supreme Court of Appeals by President Johnson. Judge Thornberry had been a Texas congressman until the fall of 1963, when he resigned his House seat to join the Federal Bench for West Texas—a post granted as part of the Texas patronage allowed to Vice President Johnson by President Kennedy. Before returning to the Nagell trial, consider another Johnson's appointments to the Supreme Court—in addition to Thornberry, LBJ nominated and successfully placed Abe Fortas on the nation's highest judicial body. Fortas had been serving as legal counsel for the notorious Bobby Baker before leaving him to become part of Johnson's inner circle. Abe Fortas was among the first people Johnson telephoned in the days following the assassination, and was assigned responsibility to coordinate all the assassination investigations for the new president. Fortas' term on the Supreme Court bench was relatively brief, as he was forced to resign over a scandal involving payments from a criminal appearing before the Court. (Judge Thorneberry's remarks on the Nagell case are discussed in Chapter 25 of Russell's book; the roles of Johnson and Fortas in the events following the assassination are further addressed in Chapters 15-17 of this work.)

During Nagell's trial he engaged in a heated exchange with his lawyer. "The real reason that I did not leave the country at the time was not because of my love for the United States but was because of my children... who at that time were quite young... if I had been allowed to take my children with me, I would have taken them but the circumstances were such at the time that I was told because I was not leaving the country through legal channels I could not take my children with me." After sentencing, Nagell protested vigorously: *"Why weren't the real issues brought out in court? They will be some time!"*

Nagell's attorney had not been interested in any defense beyond an insanity plea, nor apparently had the court. Indeed the sentence rendered by Thornberry was really rather strange. It specified that the sentence was conditional and that Nagell might be released at any time based on a parole board's decision. This would appear to offer Nagell a "deal" if he decided to shut up. He refused to do so and paid with years in prison and federal medical institutions. As his sergeant said, *"Yeah, old Nagell was a maverick... he wanted to do things the right way, by the book all the time."*

In 1968, after Nagell had begun providing information to D.A. Garrison in the New Orleans investigation—via a Garrison volunteer investigator who was later determined to have a history with the CIA—the Fifth District Circuit Court of Appeal, to which Judge Thornberry had recently been appointed, overturned Nagell's conviction over the legal issue that no "intent to rob" was ever demonstrated. However, the court also claimed that Nagell was very likely not mentally competent at the time.

Based on the previous court history of an insanity defense, this follow-on decision provided the court with an obvious reason to dismiss Nagell's retrial petition that might have resurfaced alternative motives during the Garrison case. Only after all possibility of further legal action had been eliminated were some of Nagell's personal possessions returned to him. These had been taken into custody upon his arrest and continually refused to him for use in his defense. Some were returned to him, but not all.

Nagell was never able to bring legal attention to the actual motivation and circumstances behind his action in the El Paso bank. He was forced against his will to take court-assigned counsel, who focused all efforts on a defense of insanity in spite of the fact that there was absolutely no evidence whatsoever to support the formal charge of robbery, as was eventually verified by the appeals court. As to the validity of his lawyer's strategy, Nagell's lawyer would tell Dick Russell two decades later that he never explored any aspect of the case other than the insanity defense: *"Oh, they found him with some paraphernalia, Freedom for Cuba... similar to some of that stuff that guy Oswald had... but that's the only similarity... now if you could establish that he was in Mexico City."*[22]

Of course, Nagell was most definitely in Mexico City. It's where he met two radical Cuban exiles who were members of Alpha 66 and who were busy conducting actions against Cuban embassy staff in Mexico City, including bombing attacks against embassy facilities. The same two men would later monitor and consider recruiting Vaughn Snipes, an ex-Marine FPCC activist in Los Angeles, for an attack on President Kennedy. One of these same two men reappeared to establish contact with Lee Oswald in New Orleans in the summer of 1963.

SUMMARY

Lee Oswald was associating with a variety of Cubans in the summer and fall of 1963 and his activities made him visible to exile groups and individuals in both New Orleans and Miami. Martino remarked that certain exiles approached Oswald and led him to believe that they were Castro agents and that they were looking for Oswald's cooperation. These individuals were not a part of the visible exile movements and were unknown in New Orleans. They did match the description of Sylvia Odio's visitors from New Orleans.

- Both Orest Pena and Carlos Bringuier reported suspicious newcomers to New Orleans to the FBI. These newcomers were suspected of being Communist spies.

- Orest Pena and others observed Oswald in the company of an unknown Latin who was very prominently making Communist-type remarks.

- Dean Andrews observed Oswald in the company of a Mexican-looking individual matching the description given by Sylvia Odio.

- Nagell independently reported Oswald in association with exiles presenting themselves as pro-Castro agents and was unable to get Oswald to break the contact.

- Nagell reported that one of these individuals had come from Mexico and had been affiliated with the Alpha 66 organization there.

- Nagell reported that while in New Orleans in August, these individuals recruited Lee Oswald for an action against President Kennedy in the D.C. area in September.

- Oswald's correspondence with the Socialist Workers Party as well as the FPCC documented his intent to move to the D. C. area in early fall of 1963.

There is clearly evidence and corroboration for Martino's contention that Oswald was approached by individuals representing themselves as Castro agents and that to at least some extent, Oswald was cooperating with them in late August. As far as John Martino knew, this was the genesis of the conspiracy that led to Dallas. However, based on verifiable information from Richard Nagell, it is very possible that the concept behind the Dallas plot was many months older than that and that Oswald was not the first candidate for the role of unwitting pro-Castro patsy.

CHAPTER **4**

IT BEGINS

John Martino described it as a simple plan, kill Kennedy and blame it on a patsy. A patsy who had a clear history of being a Castro supporter, and who could be framed as a Castro agent. The idea of killing Kennedy didn't spring into existence in New Orleans or Miami in August of 1963. It was first voiced after the Kennedy Administration's resolution of the Missile Crisis with the Soviets. After the exiles realized there would be no American invasion to remove both the missiles and Castro; and after the first rumors of a non-invasion deal began to circulate.

Don Bohning, in his book, *The Castro Obsession*, quotes long-time exile military leader Rafael Quintero as stating "Talk about the word 'Treason' at the Bay of Pigs, this was even bigger for us, the people involved." Bohning writes that for Quintero and many Cuban exiles, "Washington's action in the missile crisis was seen as a far greater betrayal than the Bay of Pigs. The exiles were convinced that this conflict would be the end of Fidel Castro."[1]

Other Cuban exiles were reported to have held the same opinions following the missile crisis compromise. Exiles in Mexico City went much further, they called for revenge, they voiced the "kill Kennedy; blame Castro" strategy. Then they brought their cry for revenge into the US through Miami, shared it there, and began their own initiative to put it into play, long before Dallas.

Mexico City, 1962

Antonio Veciana, co-founder of Alpha 66

"At that time, the only way to get in and out of Cuba was though Mexico; we had four people there in the fall of 1962. Their main job was to inform the movement here in Miami of people who were visiting Cuba, and what the Cuban consulate was up to. They did check on the personnel of the Cubans, to see if we could bring them over to our side."[2]

In 1961 the US-organized Cuban Brigade movement against Castro had come to grief at the Bay of Pigs. The follow-up Kennedy Administration effort, Mongoose, was falling far short of its goals. Among the *exilios* there was a growing distrust of the official US projects organized and coordinated by the huge CIA JM/WAVE station in Miami.

Beginning in early 1962, an aggressively independent exile group began to wage its own war, not only against Castro, but also directly against his Russian allies. Alpha 66's targeting was more efficient than that of the CIA's JM/WAVE operations, and its raids were extremely effective. During 1963, JM/WAVE planned 88 missions, canceled 15, and achieved only 4 successful sabotage missions.[3]

In contrast, between September 1962 and March 1963, independent exile teams conducted major raids on Russian facilities, construction sites and ships, killing and injuring dozens of Russians and damaging or sinking Russian ships. These raids introduced an element of direct military challenge to the Russians and helped to maintain and focus both media and political attention on the Soviet military presence in Cuba.[4] Alpha 66 raids continued in the fall of 1962 during the Cuban Missile Crisis and could easily have triggered a direct conflict between the United States and Russia.

The most successful and visible Alpha 66 leaders were media figures by 1963. They were Eddie (Perez) Bayo, the future point man for the Bayo-Pawley mission in the summer of 1963, and Tony Cuesta. Alpha 66 raids were both military and propaganda victories. Several were covered by photojournalists from *Life* magazine and were featured as cover stores, constantly "tweaking" the Kennedy Administration and raising the issue of the Russian military presence in Cuba.[5] Although Alpha 66 operations were a major irritant for the Kennedy Administration, we now know that the group received ongoing support from some contacts within the CIA, and that US Army intelligence established exceedingly strong connections to certain Alpha 66 members.

By January of 1962, Army counter-intelligence had been established on Alpha 66 members, and contacts were made throughout 1963. In particular, Army CI had made contact with Antonio Veciana in October 1962. He was assigned code number DUP 748 on January 30, 1963.

A sampling of the information Army intelligence obtained from Veciana in October includes:

- There was a working agreement between Alpha 66 and CIA. Veciana stated "CIA persons nice but constantly asking for information and giving no assistance."

- CIA had made numerous attempts to determine the exact plans of Alpha 66, where weapons were obtained, etc., but Alpha 66 information given to the CIA had been false.

- Alpha 66 had to feed 300 people daily.

- Prior to the La Isabela raid, an Alpha 66 member stole approximately $600 worth of explosives from the CIA.

- Alpha 66 had American members.[6]

In Mexico City, as Antonio Veciana explained to Dick Russell, the "secret war" was more a matter of intelligence and counter-intelligence. Mexico City was the place of observing, of recruiting, and of intelligence dangles. It was the place where the CIA, US Army intelligence, the FBI and Alpha 66 watched, infiltrated, and spied upon Castro's diplomatic and intelligence personnel, his Mexican and American supporters and upon each other.

Given the passions and emotions involved, things were not always subdued and covert. Veciana related matters this way as described by Andres Nasario Sargan, another Alpha 66 co-founder:

"There were scattered Alpha delegates there in the early 60's, some Cubans had gotten out through Mexico and decided to stay there instead of facing an entirely different environment. When we had an office there in 1962-1963, there was trouble. The Cuban consulate was on one street and Alpha was close by. This was a very hard time, very trying for our people there."[7]

Of course, the Castro government had a different view of the situation. During a conference between Cuban government officials and researchers in the 1990's, General Fabian Escalante (an official of the Ministry of the Interior with close connections to Che Guevara, State Security and Cuban intelligence) remarked that the anti-Castro faction in Mexico City went as far as murdering several of the consulate staff.[8] Although he made only cursory allusions these Mexico City incidents, Escalante did describe at least two of the people involved.

Escalante stated, "One man was named 'Hernandez'; he had originally been a Castro supporter. After the revolution he began to disagree with Castro's policies." Given the fact that Escalante described "Hernandez" as a manager in the Sans Souci hotel and Casino in Miami, Castro's policy of controlling and eventually closing much of the gambling in Cuba could have been the trigger for Hernandez's changing sides. Of Hernandez's followers, Escalante only named one other, a "Garcia" who had been in Hernandez's group in Cuba and followed him to Mexico City.[9]

We have previously encountered the name "Hernandez" as the name given by Robert McKeown for the Latin who accompanied Lee Oswald when Oswald made the attempt to purchase rifles from McKeown. That Hernandez was a man whom McKeown had known from his trips to Cuba when McKeown was running arms and supplies to Castro's supporters. Of course, Hernandez is a common name, as is Garcia. However, a Garcia, one Herminio Diaz Garcia, is the man identified by Cuba as one of the gunmen in Dallas on November 22, 1963. This information reportedly came from Tony Cuesta after his capture and imprisonment (see Chapter 18, Exhibit 18-2 of this book).

Tony Cuesta

One of Alpha 66's most prominent field leaders, Cuesta was captured in Cuba after the Kennedy assassination on a mission with Diaz Garcia in which Garcia was killed. Herminio Diaz Garcia is reputed to have been a bodyguard for Santo Trafficante in Cuba before Trafficante was expelled by the Castro regime. Diaz Garcia is also rumored to have been one of the contacts within Cuba for the initial

CIA-Roselli assassination attempt against Fidel Castro. Unfortunately, the names, which Roselli did mention to his attorneys and apparently to the HSCA during his confidential testimony, have been redacted from the minutes of that session.   But it is a matter of record that in the first attempt against Castro, Roselli received approval from Santo Trafficante to use his network in Florida and Cuba to locate contacts that could support or accomplish the task.[10]

A following chapter details how the casino network was used to provide arms for the Castro revolution. All we have are names and connections, but those connections make Robert McKeown's encounter with and his recognition of a man named Hernandez not only credible but perhaps very revealing. Names and connections are only a starting point until they are corroborated, as these have been and by a credible source—Richard Nagell.

Richard Case Nagell

Arthur Greenstein recalled his friend Richard Nagell and their acquaintance in Mexico City in the fall of 1962:

> "He came on real bitter. He didn't say too much about being in Military Intelligence but he was bitter that his wife had cost him his security clearance, being married to a Japanese foreigner. *Looking back, that seems like a cover; maybe he had a very excellent security clearance all the time?"*[11]

Richard Case Nagell elected to take an honorable discharge from the Army in October of 1959. The reasons for this are explored in detail in Dick Russell's book, but essentially, Nagell reportedly was appalled by many of the activities of US intelligence, especially its tampering with the laws and rights of individuals in the countries in which it operated overseas. He was also constitutionally incapable of dealing with the continual violation of the regulations and even laws that those duties involved.

The same conflicts occurred in his civilian jobs, working first as an investigator for the State of California and later in its Alcoholic Beverage Control division. Again and again, Nagell would come up against the gap between the law and its practice in real life and each time it would cost him a job.

These ongoing conflicts with the system ended with Nagell's dismissal from his state jobs in California. We may never know if this was simply a personality conflict or whether Nagell was cooperating in a "sheep dipping" effort to create the image of disaffected ex-Army intelligence officer. As Russell convincingly developed, the truth may be a combination of both elements. In any event, on August 17, 1962, Nagell obtained a Mexican tourist card and on the 24th he crossed the border at El Paso for the first time.

In September, Nagell visited the US Embassy in Mexico City and indicated he planned to renounce his US citizenship. But like Lee Oswald in Moscow, he did not actually do so. Instead, according to Nagell, he began acting as a triple agent—that is, he represented himself to a Soviet contact as a pro-Soviet double agent, while secretly retaining his loyalty to the United States.

A document confirming Nagell's visit to the American embassy in Mexico City has recently been provided by researcher Bob Boyles; it is an FBI Memo from the Legat in Mexico City dated October 2, 1962. The "Legat" is the FBI representative stationed in the US Embassy. The cover sheet and distribution for the document are missing; the document itself was recovered from CIA Security files. The memo is 7 pages in length and confirms all of Nagell's remarks to Dick Russell about his initial arrival in Mexico City, his connection to the Hotel Luma, his friend Arthur Greenstein, etc.[12] It also confirms that Nagell specifically threatened to go from Mexico to another country where he would exchange information of value to the United States. In making this statement Nagell had already described himself as a former military intelligence agent with security clearance. Given these remarks we should expect to find Nagell under surveillance in Mexico City or at least a lengthy security file for Nagell in 1962/1963. No evidence of either has yet to be found—suggesting either a massive internal security failure or the possible use of Nagell as a security dangle. The other alternative is that the Nagell files have been sanitized for that period of time.

Nagell was known to the Russians from his Army counter-intelligence work in Tokyo, where he first expressed his dissatisfaction with US policies in a way that became known to the "other side." When they approached him in Mexico, the Soviets had two tasks for Nagell. He was to penetrate a group of Cuban exiles whose Mexico City members had been heard making threats of revenge against John Kennedy for his treachery at the Bay of Pigs. The exiles clearly intended to implicate the Cubans and Russians. The last thing the Soviet Union wanted in the fall of 1963 was to risk being somehow blamed for the assassination of the US President.

Next, Nagell was to return to the US to monitor a former Soviet defector who, along with his Russian wife, might potentially become an embarrassment to the Soviet Union. Nagell knew the defector because he had also been serving as a very minor "dangle" to the Russians and their local Japanese Communist agents in Tokyo. The defector's name was Lee Oswald.

Many authors have examined Oswald's behavior in Japan, but they seem to miss some of the more curious personal aspects. Even Anthony Summers devoted only a single page to Oswald's newfound Japanese romantic interests. But those exploits may have a hidden significance. Early on in his deployment at Atsugi, Oswald started taking two-day trips to Tokyo and apparently became involved in an affair with a very sophisticated and beautiful hostess at one of the most expensive Tokyo nightclubs. Dick Russell explored this in detail and elaborated on Oswald's likely first experience as an informant—an informant on the Communist "honey traps" being set for young American servicemen working at the Atsugi installation. Atsugi was a prime intelligence target, housing a major CIA installation and the only U2 base in Japan.

David Bucknell

A Marine friend of Oswald's, Bucknell related to Mark Lane that Oswald had told him about being approached by an attractive Japanese woman in a particular bar (the Queen Bee). Oswald reported this to an officer who proceeded to involve him in an intelligence operation, giving him money to spend there. During this period he also received treatment for venereal disease, and this was recorded in his medical record as something connected with his *duty*.[13]

On October 21, 1962, Nagell left Mexico City for the US and stopped briefly in Dallas to monitor Lee Oswald. He proceeded to contact and monitor Cuban exiles in New York and by January was in Miami where he again involved himself with various exiles. It appears that he soon began to focus in on a couple of exiles who had made their way there from Mexico City.

By April both Nagell and the two exiles were in Los Angeles, where Alpha 66 had just opened an office and was engaged in a massive recruiting campaign. Apparently, the two Cubans were sent to L.A.

to continue something they had practiced at length in Mexico City, identifying undercover Castro infiltrators.

Nagell's conversations with Dick Russell indicate that while in Mexico, Nagell had convinced exiles from this organization that he was sympathetic to their cause. Nagell's Army intelligence credentials may have helped in this because even Antonio Veciana remarked that Alpha 66 had been offered assistance by both CIA and Army intelligence operatives; however only the Army came through.

Based on newly released documents discussed previously, we know that by 1963 these Army contacts had evolved into a relationship with the merged Alpha 66/SNFE (II Front) organization, and that Veciana had an officially assigned Army "handler" and designated contact number. Alpha 66 viewed the Army and its military professionals much more favorably than were the majority of its CIA contacts.

In Los Angeles, Nagell observed the two exiles monitoring an individual whom they saw as being perfect for a plan they had originally conceived of in Mexico—an idea that had previously leaked to Russian intelligence sources in Mexico City. It involved convincing a Castro supporter that President Kennedy was ultimately responsible for allowing the survival of the rightist Cuban exile cause, that he was supporting ongoing efforts to overthrow the revolution, even efforts to kill Castro— that he must be stopped.

Their recruitment target in Los Angeles was a man named Vaughn Snipes, later to change his name to Marlowe due to his association with Nagell and the implications it had for him after the Kennedy assassination. In a letter of March 22, 1967, to D.A. Jim Garrison, Marlowe recalled the spring of 1963: "Ex-Captain Nagell...was checking me out, slowly, carefully, for a reason unknown to me even today." Marlowe was an ex-Marine who ran a "left-wing bookstore" and was an executive officer of the Los Angeles Fair Play for Cuba Committee. He also had a local reputation (which he had encouraged for his own protection) as a good man with a rifle.

Indeed Nagell suggested to Russell that he may even have identified Marlowe as a prospect for the two exiles using his earlier connections developed with L.A. police and the local "Red Squad." Snipes would eventually go on record as knowing Nagell in Los Angeles. He would provide documentation of this and Nagell also possessed letters from Snipes/Marlowe written to him after Nagell was jailed.

For some reason, Snipes was not actually approached by the exiles, and President Kennedy visited Los Angeles in June of 1963 without incident. It appears that at this stage Nagell was seeing nothing more than an idea being worked out, not a specific plan but just an idea held by a limited number of fanatically anti-Castro Cuban exiles.

Indeed ideas about getting at the Kennedys may have been circulating among more than one set of exiles. In at least one incident, an exile plot against the Kennedy family definitely was reported to the FBI, who sent people to Miami to seriously investigate it. That report came from a man named Garrett Trapnell.

Garrett Trapnell

The black sheep of a distinguished military family, Trapnell was a stalwart Castro supporter who had gone to Cuba on his own initiative. He was also a bank robber, later a plane hijacker and eventually a long term Federal prisoner.[14] He had been in Cuba with Castro's fighters where he was captured by Batista's forces and deported to Miami in 1958. Apparently, Trapnell retained some peripheral contact with some of the Cubans he had known while on the island, and these Cubans supposedly encouraged him to come from Baltimore to Miami for a meeting in early May of 1963.

Garrett Trapnell's conspiracy report, and most especially his follow-on information must be approached with caution. There is little doubt that Trapnell was an opportunist and he apparently enhanced his initial story both after the assassination and during the Church Committee investigation.[15] In August of 1963, while in jail for passing a bad check Trapnell made the claim that he'd been approached that spring by Cubans with a plot to kidnap or otherwise attack Robert Kennedy and possibly other members of the Kennedy family. Though the FBI investigated Trapnell's claims, it did not forward his report to the Secret Service or to the Warren Commission. The FBI did verify that Trapnell traveled from Baltimore to Miami in early May 1963. They interviewed him repeatedly and he continued to stick by his story until one last meeting in February of 1964, when he officially admitted making the entire story up.

His recantation is covered at length in the summary of the FBI report, although Trapnell later stated that he was advised to recant for his own good, and having his own best interests at heart, he agreed.

He recalled the FBI's parting words: "Don't worry, just be crazy and everything will be alright."[16]

In September of 1964, Garrett Trapnell's wife was worried enough about his involvement in a conspiracy and her potential exposure as an accessory to seek a divorce. Trapnell himself was more concerned that she might say the wrong thing during the divorce proceedings. This information concerning Trapnell's wife is found in a CIA report originating in the JM/WAVE station and forwarded to various offices. Based on the tracking sheet attached the report, it appears that CIA WH security and Counter-Intelligence monitored Trapnell for two years during 1964 and 1965 after the FBI had officially written his story off as fakery.[17]

In the final analysis, the Trapnell incident does not seem to be directly relevant to the Dallas conspiracy and the specific individuals we are following. Possibly Trapnell did talk with some exiles in Miami who were proceeding with a similar concept, a concept which would ensure that the United States would have a good reason to take action against Castro.

Trapnell said that he was approached to participate in a plan that would be instigated as if Castro were behind it. Perhaps as a known Castro sympathizer, Trapnell was indeed prospected by counter-intelligence elements of the exile community and fed a line as a test—an incident that he later decided to use to his own advantage. The FBI's failure to inform the Secret Service is troubling, as is the fact that Trapnell never ended up under any sort of ongoing Protective Services monitoring even though he most definitely did report a plot against the President. The Trapnell incident may be only one of several indications that militant exiles were talking more seriously about direct action against President Kennedy.

SUMMARY

John Martino gave us an insight into the recruitment and manipulation of Lee Oswald as a patsy, a visible and active Castro supporter who had been convinced by exiles that they were actually Castro agents operating within the United States. However, Martino may only have seen the final execution of a concept that had been in circulation for over a year. Many individuals may have come in contact with this idea, with its proponents or even with iterations of a plan to implement it during the course of those twelve months. Certainly the idea of an "evolving" conspiracy is much more likely than one that sprang full blown in late September of 1963. It also accounts for the number and variety of incidents that seem to indicate that such an idea was being discussed and was evolving during 1963. As we will see, a standing threat to President Kennedy seems to have been known and hinted at by Santo Trafficante Jr.—not long after it was first discussed by former members of his Cuban gambling network who resided in Mexico City and later entered the US through Miami.

Based on Richard Nagell's additional information, we can picture the genesis of the concept that led to Dallas.

- Nagell operated as a triple agent in Mexico City, establishing contact with Alpha 66-connected exiles who came there from Cuba after turning against Castro.

- These exiles began talking of a plan to kill President Kennedy in revenge for his betrayal of the exiles and his agreement with the Soviets.

- The key element of this plan was the need to implicate Fidel Castro in the assassination.

- Cuban intelligence has identified two casino/Trafficante-connected individuals who moved to Mexico City in 1962, one named Hernandez and the other Garcia.

- The first known statement that Kennedy would be "hit" came from Santo Trafficante Jr. in the fall of 1962.

- According to Nagell, the first "hit" site discussed by the Cuban exiles was the Orange Bowl, where President Kennedy would make a speech to the returned Bay of Pigs Brigade. Nagell did not know that both a dynamite bomb and a sniper were eventually reported at this event.[18]

- Vaughn Snipes/Marlowe confirmed contact with Richard Nagell in early 1963.

- Nagell described Snipes as the FPCC, pro-Castro, and ex-Marine prototype for a patsy.

- Nagell stated that one of the Mexico City individuals contacted Oswald in New Orleans.

- Mexico City to Miami; Miami to L.A.; L.A. to Miami; Miami to New Orleans; finally: Dallas.

Something seminal happened in New Orleans in the summer of 1963. Somehow individuals who had been considering a plan to gain revenge against John Kennedy and simultaneously trigger an US invasion of Cuba became aware of, and established contact with, Lee Oswald.

The next challenge is to pursue the Miami-New Orleans connection, especially in the context of John Martino's associates. Somewhere among those associates may be, in today's terminology, "persons of interest" in the conspiracy.

CHAPTER 5

PERSONS OF INTEREST

John Martino said that he played a low-level role in the Kennedy conspiracy, that of courier. When John's wife, Florence, was interviewed by HSCA investigators, she permitted them to examine a set of records and memorabilia left by her late husband. The airline tickets and speakers' schedules document Martino's trip to New Orleans on September 27, his speech in Dallas on October 1, and a return trip to Dallas on October 27. Martino's speaking schedule gave him an excellent cover for his courier work. His travel also helps us establish a time frame for the preparations. As we will see later in this chapter, at least one close friend of John Martino's was also traveling to Dallas in the fall of 1963. Martino's friend was there on November 22. Whether that explains the calls Martino began receiving from Dallas that afternoon is, of course, speculation.

It appears that until he was incarcerated, Martino may have first played a similar role of courier in trips to Cuba after the Castro revolution. In prison, Martino proved himself to be trustworthy, with a proven record of keeping his mouth shut under extreme pressure. He also showed his commitment and personal courage by going in person on the Bayo–Pawley mission into Cuba, CIA Operation TILT. Unquestionably, John Martino had demonstrated that he had the attitude and character for conspiracy.

Knowing that Martino was part of the conspiracy and was in communication with individuals in Texas on November 22, allows us to explore persons of interest which could have brought both Lee Oswald and John Martino into a conspiracy. Particularly relevant are Martino's known associates and other persons of interest, obviously that includes Lee Oswald.

New Orleans, August 28, 1963

On August 28, Oswald wrote to the Fair Play for Cuba Committee headquarters about a planned move. He followed it with another letter on September 1 mentioning a move to Baltimore.

This move very possibly represents the first moment when Oswald was actively being manipulated by exiles posing as Castro agents. By the end of August, Lee Oswald had been identified as a potential patsy and was in contact with persons planning a move against JFK. At that point Dallas was not yet in the plan. As August ended, the plan was for Washington in September.[1] However, Oswald did not move to Baltimore in September. By the end of the month, it appears that he was passing through Texas on his way to Mexico City and very possibly passing through Houston with a man named Hernandez.

Hernandez is a common Hispanic name. We've already come across one Hernandez in Mexico City—an exile out of Cuba. He was associated with Alpha 66, had connections to the old Havana casino crowd, and was very likely on his way to Miami. In New Orleans, in July of 1963, another Hernandez turned up. This Hernandez was involved with Cuban exiles and a well-known ex-Havana casino owner in a plot to stage a bombing attack on Cuba.

Victor Hernandez arrived in New Orleans in July. He had with him a U-Haul trailer loaded with explosives purchased in Illinois. These explosives were to be used to prepare bombs for an airborne raid on Cuba—a raid sponsored by Mike McClaney of Miami, formerly of Havana.

In June 1963, Carlos Eduardo Hernandez of Miami was approached by Victor Espinoza Hernandez who wanted Carlos to become involved with a planned bombing raid on Shell Oil refineries in Havana. Carlos, aka "Bata" Hernandez, was active in the DRE and served as its military planner. But his only activity in this operation was to drive a truck with explosives to the plane, no planning and no information. He later came to learn that Victor Espinoza was serving as a contact man for Sam Benton, who in turn was fronting for Mike McClaney. Carlos eventually came to believe his recruitment and involvement was simply a show intended to associate McClaney and his gambling associates with a well-known exile activist and possibly with a highly visible exile group like the DRE.[2] McClaney's efforts appear to reflect efforts by a number of crime figures to establish connections with exile groups. Other exiles approached included Sierra of the JCGE in Chicago, Tony Varona of the CRC and Harry Ruiz Williams, a personal associate of RFK and part of his new Cuba coup initiative.

This first raid involving Hernandez was staged out of Florida, but it was compromised and several of the participants including Carlos Hernandez, Victor Hernandez and Sam Benton were taken in for questioning. No charges were filed.

In early July, Carlos Hernandez was again approached by Victor Espinoza Hernandez in regard to another bombing raid, this one to be staged out of New Orleans. Carlos did drive to New Orleans and went to a farm that was owned by Mike McClaney's brother.

Carlos also told the HSCA of a prior meeting in Miami that occurred at a location easily identified as Mike McClaney's residence. In his testimony, Carlos again expressed his opinion that the arrangements for this raid were "childish," with the wrong aircraft to be used and total incompetence in regard to bombs and explosives. This caused the exile pilot to refuse participation. [3,4]

The FBI report on the McClaney farm raid revealed that on July 15, 1963, Victor Hernandez had transported explosives to the farm from Illinois. It was later determined that they were purchased from Richard Lauchli, a Minuteman arms dealer who at the time was active in selling arms in Miami and in the Midwest to the Paulino Sierra Junta. The report also reveals that the FBI was tipped off by an informant in Miami who identified one of the individuals who had traveled to New Orleans and who then provided great detail about locations and the exact materials involved. The FBI in New Orleans received this tip on July 18 and conducted the raid on the McClaney farm on July 31.

The issue of the New Orleans camps has been of considerable interest to researchers since it has been speculated that in his role as a dangle, Oswald was collecting information on such exile activities. At this point, we can concretely account for at least four such camps.

One camp was an actual CIA training facility used prior to the Bay of Pigs. Another never became operational but was to be sponsored by the CRC and was being organized by Gerry Hemming, Frank Sturgis, David Ferrie and Sturgis' associate Larry DeJoseph in 1962. The CRC cancelled these plans due to the Kennedy Administration crackdown on US staged Cuban raids. Photographs are available showing Ferrie and DeJoseph together during a planning trip for this camp.[5]

During the summer of 1963, we have detailed information on two New Orleans camps, one of which was simply a U-Haul parked at the McClaney farm. This U-Haul was the one that Victor Hernandez had brought down from Illinois. The other 1963 camp was one being organized out of Miami, as part of a proposal that Richard Davis had brought to the Christian Democrat/MDC organization. Later investigation of the Christian Democrat/MDC/Richard Davis camp revealed that it never really jelled; partially because it was apparently a scam by Davis, and partially because the FBI raid and arrests at the McClaney property scared away the participants.[6] These events put Victor Hernandez in New Orleans at the same time Lee Oswald was achieving visibility for his FPCC activities and public support of Cuba.

What we know of Victor Hernandez is limited; the Warren Commission did not investigate him. The HSCA did become interested in him; however, by that time he was living in Europe. The HSCA investigation revealed that he trained for the Bay of Pigs in Guatemala in 1960-1961 (infiltration training) with Carlos Hernandez. He was born at Matanzas, Cuba on August 26, 1937, and admitted to the US on May 2, 1960. Victor Hernandez's occupation was listed as self employed, a decorator. On April 11, 1960, he listed as a friend one Michael J. McClaney of Pine Tree Drive, Miami Beach, Florida. The HSCA also found that Victor Dominador Espinosa Hernandez had trained with the CIA in Panama, Guatemala and New Orleans. They confirmed, as related by Carlos Hernandez in executive testimony, that after the assassination, Victor Hernandez had traveled through numerous European countries. Carlos Hernandez stated that he had heard that his friend Victor had problems in France, perhaps something to do with drugs.[7] With this background in hand, the HSCA actually managed to locate Hernandez and persuade him to come to the US to offer testimony. The results of those interviews and a synopsis of what we now know (and the key areas that the HSCA missed) are covered in *Appendix E, Student Warrior.*

In addition to completely failing to question Victor Hernandez about his activities during the second half of 1963 and 1964, the HSCA interview also failed to explore the remarks in Carlos Hernandez's testimony in regard to his travels and activities overseas. The HSCA at least did pursue in detail the relationship between Victor and Rolando Cubela.

Major Rolando Cubela had led a DRE unit into Havana after Batista's ouster but his patron, Carlos Prio, had been cast aside by Castro and by 1961, Cubela began to think about defecting. At that time, he was recruited by the CIA and eventually became a player in a CIA assassination effort targeting Fidel Castro—an effort organized and sponsored by Desmond Fitzgerald in 1963.[8, 9] The fact that Victor Hernandez was a personal friend of both Mike McClaney and Rolondo Cubela indicates that Hernandez had connections and sources of information far beyond the average anti-Castro exile.

Unfortunately, we have nothing beyond the previously discussed New Orleans proximity to connect Victor Hernandez to Lee Oswald. Still, his activities and associations certainly show that he had the opportunity to identify Oswald as a target of opportunity for certain elements in Miami. Other connections between New Orleans and Miami included Carlos Bringuier, one of the few DRE members in New Orleans. Bringuier became one of the most active DRE members promoting Oswald and Ruby as Castro agents after the assassination. Antonio Varona also had established CRC ties to New Orleans. In 1963 Varona reportedly traveled to New Orleans and was there in November, staying with Sylvia Odio's uncle. Odio's Uncle had attended Lee Oswald's court appearance after his leafleting encounter with Bringuier and other exiles.

News of Lee Oswald traveled from Miami to New Orleans. Whether it was via Hernandez, Bringuier, Varona or someone else is uncertain. One incident that lends weight to speculation on Hernandez as the channel, an indication that McClaney-connected Cuban exiles were aware of Lee Oswald and his potential, is suggested by the following incident:

> On November 11, 1963, in Miami, Jorge Soto Martinez was apparently trying to impress Mrs. Lillian Spingler, an employee at the Parrot Jungle gift shop in Miami. Martinez bragged that both he and his friend Lee (who was living in either Mexico or Texas) were sharpshooters. Lee also spoke Russian, and he and Martinez both hated Kennedy; he could "shoot Kennedy between the eyes." Mrs. Spingler had described this conversation to other employees before the assassination and it was reported to the FBI in late December.

Former Dade County Circuit Judge Alfonso Sepe investigated the Spingler story again in 1977 and found it highly credible. He also located one of her former co-workers, Mrs. Aliese Trigg, who recalled hearing of the conversation before the murder of the President.

However, when the FBI had interviewed her (Special Agent James O' Connor) she was given a firm suggestion: *"Just drop it …They told me not to talk about it …Goodbye."*[10]

Mrs. Spingler took O'Connor's advice seriously and became unresponsive to any further investigation.

Employees at the Parrot Jungle recalled the visitor and the incident well enough to recognize the man when he returned to the gift shop some months later, and they provided his license number to the FBI. The FBI located Jorge Soto Martinez and brought him in for questioning. He denied making any of the remarks attributed to him.

The FBI asked Mrs. Spingler to come to the office and confront him in person. She declined because she was afraid of personal harm from Martinez. At that point, Agent O'Connor determined that Mr. Martinez did not know Lee Oswald and was not involved in the assassination, closing the case.

The FBI did not consider that Martinez might have simply been repeating elements of gossip that he had heard from fellow workers or fellow exiles–gossip which might have led to something worthy of investigation. They did, however, record that at the time of his questioning, Martinez was working as a bellhop at the Fontainebleau Hotel and that his job had been obtained through a referral from Mike McClaney.[11] The Bureau probably also knew that he was a recent exile from Cuba, that he had worked for Mike McClaney there, that his entry into the US had been assisted by McClaney, and that he had lived on Mike McClaney's estate on Pine Tree Drive in Miami Beach.

Mike McClaney was a well-established member of the old Havana casino crowd; in fact, he later became the employer of Lewis McWillie, John Martino's former co-worker at the Deauville hotel in Havana. McWillie had been visited in Havana in 1959 and in Las Vegas in November, 1963 by his self-described friend and personal admirer, Jack Ruby of Dallas. These visits were reported to the FBI/Warren Commission but not included in the Warren Commission listing of Ruby's travels.[12]

Undoubtedly, Martinez did not personally know Lee Oswald, nor was he involved in a conspiracy to kill the President; but Martinez apparently heard some things he should not have, and it's likely he picked them up as gossip from other Cuban exiles.

We will see that there was more exile gossip regarding an action against President Kennedy by November of 1963. Like others, Martinez said something he should not have, and then denied it. But as with the others, his associations point us in the same direction: to Cuban exiles and associates of the casino crowd, to individuals and groups most definitely known to Victor Hernandez who was working on anti-Castro projects with Sam Benton and Mike McClaney in 1963 and in New Orleans in July and August of that year.

Chapter One provided an introduction to John Martino and his activities in 1963. It is important to emphasize that Martino was not a mobster or a gangster in the general sense, although he certainly was not an average law abiding professional. He had grown up and worked his entire life within the venues of racing and gambling. His profession was that of technician, an electronics expert in gaming machines, racing totalizer systems, and racing wire among other things. Martino's employers were racetrack and casino operators and his Havana co-workers included pit bosses and casino managers including R.D. Matthews and Lewis McWillie. Martino was definitely part of the old Havana casino crowd and had connections within the Batista political infrastructure as they all did. His arrest on his last trip to Cuba very likely came about because of his contacts with and attempts to assist Batista regime associates.

While he was certainly connected to the Havana casino crowd, Martino was not a CIA employee, contract agent, front company employee or asset. His only official association with CIA personnel was in regard to the Bayo-Pawley mission, CIA crypt TILT; he does appear to have had other, possibly unofficial contacts with David Morales and Rip Robertson. The lobbying for TILT earned Martino a broad exposure throughout the more radical elements of the exile community, particularly among the Alpha 66 personnel who ended up supplying the majority of the manpower used in the mission. It also earned Martino a great deal of respect within the exile community and this, combined with his ongoing media visibility enhanced by his vehemently anti-Communist and anti-Castro book, solidified his standing as one of the strongest independent supporters of "La Causa," the exile struggle against Castro.

Martino was definitely viewed as a heavy hitter within exile and anti-Castro circles with political connections, casino associates and connections to CIA officers and JM/WAVE. He handled himself so well and his intelligence profile was so low that during the FBI's investigation of him in 1964 it was able to report to Hoover that Martino had no known or reliable connections to Cuba; hence his stories about Cuban sponsorship for Lee Oswald had to be simple self-promotion on his part.

In our search for persons of interest in the Kennedy conspiracy, Martino does give us the name of one person who was definitely involved, Lee Oswald. Upon his recruitment in New Orleans, after the abortive plan for some sort of incident in the Washington area, we see the conspirators focusing on setting up Oswald in Texas, first in Dallas, then in Houston.

On his trip to Mexico City we find Oswald visiting the Cuban Embassy there, urgently and aggressively trying to obtain an entry visa for Cuba. Oswald had no money with which to get to Cuba, but it is simple to imagine the effect of a Cuban entry visa found in Oswald's possession on November 22.

While in Mexico City, Oswald was impersonated in a manner that produced a paper trail connecting Oswald not only to the Cuban Embassy, but also to a far more important entity: the KGB chief of sabotage and assassination in the Western Hemisphere. After that we see no more attempts to tie Oswald to Castro. Of course, after Mexico City, with the KGB and Cuban connections established and known to all the US intelligence agencies as well as the directors of the CIA and FBI, anything more could have been viewed by the plotters as overkill.

When he arrived in Dallas, Lee Oswald adopted a low profile politically. No more demonstrations, no leafleting, no rallies, no letter writing campaigns. He also lived by himself in multiple apartments making it difficult to track his activities and associations. There may have been surveillance of Oswald and the FBI might have had records not now available to us. We do have FBI Agent Hosty's slip to a Secret Service agent about Oswald's subversive contacts only two weeks before November 22. We also have the well-documented destruction by Agent Hosty of a note from Oswald, and the FBI alteration to Oswald's notebook to remove an entry showing a contact by SA Hosty after Oswald's return to Dallas.[13, 14] We also have Hosty's remark to his fellow agent Gayton Carver that he contacted Oswald by placing notes under his door. When Carver replied, "You mean the Paines' house?" Hosty responded "No, Oswald's apartment."[15]

All in all, it seems that there is more than sufficient reason to believe John Martino's contentions that Oswald was being monitored by US intelligence; that Oswald was supposed to be opening himself up to contact by possible Castro agents; and that Oswald continued to do just that right up to the time that even he realized that he truly had been made into a patsy. Martino identifies Oswald as a suspect in the events of November 22, one with knowledge that something was going on in relation to the President's visit to Dallas, but he specifically states that Oswald was not a shooter, nor a major participant.

Further indication that Oswald was not an active participant in the assassination comes from a newly available report which documents the fact that Oswald was looking for work at other locations than the TSBD after being hired there—something long maintained by his widow. This information is supported by Oswald's application for employment at the Devilbiss Company. There is no actual date on the employment application. The application was picked up by the FBI only a few days after the assassination but is not specifically mentioned in its report on Oswald's job searches; although there is a dot on the map that Oswald apparently used to help him locate the companies where he interviewed. The report was somehow brought to the attention of Eyewitness News in Dallas and investigated; they determined that Oswald had visited the company about two weeks before the assassination. The location of the company is not in downtown Dallas at all, although it is in the general area of the Trade Mart.

According to Martino, Oswald was to leave his workplace and meet an exile contact at the Texas Theater. He thought he was going to be taken out of the US, in fact, the intent was to kill him in a manner that would imply Castro support for the assassination.[15] Perhaps Oswald had even been told the President's visit would provide a cover to allow him to get out of Dallas, to get him out from under FBI surveillance?

OSWALD IN THE TEXAS SCHOOL BOOK DEPOSITORY (TSBD)

In order to evaluate this view of Oswald's role, it is necessary to examine the statements from a number of witnesses who were either not included in the WC report or whose testimony was manipulated.

Although the Chief of the Dallas Police would admit in his own book on the events of November 22, that "we could not put Oswald in that window with a gun," the Warren Commission largely relied on two witnesses to place Oswald in the so called "sniper's nest."[16]

One witness, Howard Brennan, had failed to identify Oswald as the shooter on November 22. In fact not only did Brennan fail to identify Oswald, but according to the Warren Commission's own report, he was not even officially brought in to view a lineup, possibly for good reason.[17] Though Brennan would later be cited as the primary Warren Commission witness placing Oswald in the window that was a much later development. As of the day following the assassination, the Dallas Police informed reporters that they had no eyewitnesses to Oswald in the alleged sniper's window.

The Unheard Witnesses

Ian Griggs' book, *No Case To Answer* gives perhaps the most comprehensive record of the history of Howard Brennan and the line-up.[18] After a careful review of Griggs' material, this author suggests that part of the long time confusion over the incident may be that Brennan was actually brought—unofficially—to a Dallas Police line up the evening of November 22. Brennan himself stated that Secret Service agent Patterson had taken him downtown that evening to witness a police line up. Apparently when Brennan would not identify Oswald as the man he had seen in the Texas School Book Depository (TSBD) building, he was simply returned home. This left no official record of his attending a DPD line up and left neither the Secret Service nor the DPD with a confirming witness.

The Commission also relied heavily on Charles Givens' statement that he had seen Oswald in the vicinity of the sixth floor as he was leaving to go to lunch at noon. Givens himself had been picked up by the police that day for being missing from the TSBD after the assassination, like Oswald, and for being suspicious due to a prior narcotics record. But Givens' deposition of November 22 made no mention of his seeing Oswald on the sixth floor.[19]

The WC also chose not to credit a variety of witnesses who give a much more detailed picture of Oswald's movements within the TSBD on November 22—that picture definitely did not put Oswald on the sixth floor for an extended period before the shooting, nor did it have him preparing a "sniper's nest" and then waiting there to fire a series of shots.

First, as Oswald's co-workers left the upstairs area, they mentioned that Oswald yelled to them about sending the elevator back up and then at approximately 11:55 AM, his supervisor, Bill Shelley, saw him on the first floor in the vicinity of the pay telephones. Shortly after that, within 5 minutes, Eddie Piper also saw Oswald on the first floor and Oswald made a remark about eating.

During his interrogation, Oswald stated that he ate lunch and saw two of his black co-workers pass by, one named Junior. Junior Jarman and Harold Norman indeed walked by the lunchroom on their way out to the street that noon and recalled seeing someone in the lunchroom. They were not able to, or perhaps felt it wise not to say who the person was.

Oswald was next seen in the second floor lunchroom by Carolyn Arnold. He appeared to be eating lunch and the time was approximately 12:15. Mrs. Arnold, pregnant at the time, had gone for a drink of water before going out to see the motorcade. She was the secretary of the Book Depository's Vice President, and knew Lee Oswald well since he frequently came to her to get change for the soda machine—the same machine where he was observed with bottle in hand after the assassination.

Carolyn Arnold was very definite about the time she saw Oswald in the lunchroom. When interviewed by researcher Anthony Summers in 1978, she was also rather amazed that her earlier FBI statement did not include this information and only included a vague remark about possibly seeing Oswald in the hallway but not being sure about it. Her amazement is similar to other highly reliable witnesses such as Sam Holland and Wayne January when they were later shown their FBI reports and found major errors or omissions in them.[20]

Officer Marion Baker, the first officer to enter the TSBD minutes after the shooting, observed Oswald in the same location that Carolyn Arnold described, the lunchroom. After his encounter with Baker, Oswald was next seen walking slowly and nonchalantly out of the room carrying a soda.

At the same time Carolyn Arnold saw Lee Oswald in the lunchroom, Arnold Rowland observed a man with a rifle standing in a window on the sixth floor of the TSBD. Rowland's observation is important since he was tracking events against the time shown on the clock display on the advertising sign atop the TSBD. Roland recalled the FBI stated: "They told me it didn't have any bearing or some such on the case right then... in fact, they just the same as told me to forget it right then."[21]

A remark hard to believe at first, but after hearing it from enough witnesses it becomes familiar. We hear the same instructions from FBI agents to individuals ranging from President Kennedy's personal aides (when Kenny O'Donnell at first tried to report shots from in front of the motorcade), to a professional photo analyst at the National Photo Interpretation Center (when he remarked on half a dozen or more shots during his initial viewing of the Zapruder film). What Arnold Rowland saw was a man with a rifle in his arms, with a scope, standing a few feet back from a window on the west end of the TSBD sixth floor (not 15 feet to the rear, an impossibility as reported by the FBI), whereas the so-called sniper's nest is the easternmost window, where Rowland also observed a dark-complexioned man who he thought was a Negro.

Approximately 10 minutes later, Carolyn Walthers saw two men together on an upper floor, one with a darker complexion, perhaps a Mexican. Both Arnold and Walthers told their stories to the FBI and the Warren Commission; both were discredited and ignored.

John Powell, an inmate in the Dallas County Jail across the street, was reluctant to speak out at the time and only related what he saw to a friend many years later. Although the friend contacted a newspaper, Powell attempted to avoid publicity even then. Importantly, what he had seen were two men with a gun in a window at the far right (east) of an upper story window (the sniper's nest area). The men were "fooling with the scope" on the gun. One of the men was dark skinned.[22]

Certainly a case can be made that Lee Oswald was not an active participant in the shooting of the President. The one identifiable print on the rifle was a palm print, a print that was not fresh according to Lt. Day of the Dallas crime scene unit. And a print that was in a position that would normally coincide with disassembly of the weapon, not firing it.

THE SECRET TESTING

In confirmation of Martino's information that Oswald was not a shooter, Professor David Wrone in his book *The Zapruder Film: Reframing JFK's Assassination* presents information on a not widely known (and not contained in the Warren Report) series of FBI tests relevant to this point. It is well known that the Dallas Police performed standard paraffin tests on Oswald's right cheek and hands. The casts were sent to the Dallas City-County Criminal Investigative Laboratory and chemical tests were negative for any gunpowder residue on his face and positive for his hands. In the Warren Commission's report the Commission dismisses these tests by asserting, "a positive reaction …is valueless and unreliable." Professor Wrone points out that this remark is disingenuous because the issue was not the unreliability of a positive test, which can be caused by paper, ink and other materials that Oswald might have handled. However the total absence of residue—a negative reaction—is another matter entirely suggesting that Oswald had not fired a rifle on November 22, 1963.[23]

The FBI continued this line of investigation much further, in secret, performing spectrographic tests on the samples and Neutron Activation tests as well. These tests showed that there was nothing in the way of residue which could connect either Oswald's cheek to the rifle or his hands to the pistol in evidence. *Upon receiving word on these findings the FBI ordered agents not to make the results known to anyone in order to* "protect the Bureau."[24]

As the result of a lawsuit initiated by Harold Weisberg, Weisberg discovered an additional issue related to the FBI testing. Weisberg found that the FBI had used a control group of 7 different men who had each fired the Mannlicher-Carcano rifle and then been tested as a reference for the other tests. These control firings had deposited heavy powder residues on all these subject's cheeks, totally unlike the negative test on Oswald.[25] This would seem to be in direct conflict with remarks of the FBI representatives to the commission:

> **CUNNINGHAM:** No, sir; I personally wouldn't expect to find any residues on a person's right cheek after firing a rifle due to the fact that by the very principles and the manufacture and the action, the cartridge itself is sealed into the chamber by the bolt being closed behind it, and upon firing the case, the cartridge case expands into the chamber filling it up and sealing it off from the gases, so none will come back in your face, and so by its very nature, I would not expect to find residue on the right cheek of a shooter.

In conjunction with this legal testimony, there was also reference to an FBI experiment performed after the assassination in which an agent had used C-2766 (Oswald's Carcano rifle) to fire three rounds of M-C ammunition in succession. A paraffin test was then reportedly performed on his hands and cheek with negative test results. While this was offered into evidence, the FBI ensured that there was no access to the information from the actual control firings in conjunction with the NAA testing—which had deposited heavy residues on seven different agents.

The conclusion from all the above is just as John Martino stated, Oswald did not fire a rifle on November 22, 1963.

WHAT OSWALD DID NOT DO

Perhaps even more revealing are the other things that Oswald did not do. Oswald left no notes, wrote no letters, made no confession and gave no statement of cause or motive. Given Oswald's almost obsessive earlier paper trails and high political profile, this is amazing. If Oswald had been an active and willing participant would he not have left a written confession, a note at the scene, a letter mailed to a newspaper or TV station that morning, a note concealed at the Paine's or at his apartment or better yet, with the rifle in the "sniper's nest"? If Oswald had been persuaded by real Cuban agents to actively join in a conspiracy to support Fidel Castro against American assassination attempts against Fidel, surely we would have seen a manifesto? If Oswald had been an intelligence agent fully aware of the attack on Kennedy and actively cooperating with anti-Castro exiles, surely they could have maneuvered him into creating a more immediate, murder-linked paper trail or even a taped message?

If Oswald was fully cooperating with such a plot for any reason, why did he not make himself visible in the window or wave to his co-workers on the street so he could be placed in the location and leave the rifle where he had been seen? Instead, we have a situation where it is extremely difficult to tie him to the crime, suggesting an extremely poor frame and an unwitting patsy. Such a frame works well if the patsy is killed while trying to escape, but it became extremely weak with a live Oswald in custody and a jury trial expected.

For all his "non-participation," we certainly have indications that Oswald was involved in some suspicious activities. A most important point: He wrote a letter to the Soviet Embassy referencing his meeting in Mexico with "Comrade Kostin," reinforcing a connection to the KGB started by the impersonation in Mexico City. However, the nature of the letter itself is perfectly innocent, suggesting Oswald may have had no idea of the potential ramifications just as he himself was not involved in creating the KGB/Cuban connection. The mere fact that he was impersonated again shows a lack of his direct involvement in the actual Kennedy plot. Whatever Oswald knew from his Cuban associates about the ulterior purpose of his own Mexico City trip, it seems certain that he did not know about these impersonations.[26]

Then we have testimony that on the morning of November 22 Oswald made two separate sets of remarks to his co-workers about the events outside the building, with the suggestion that he had no idea that the President was coming, nor that there was a motorcade scheduled to pass the building. Given Oswald's constant reading of the newspapers (even on his lunch breaks, as noted by one of the same co-workers) and his television watching (as noted by the Paines), it seems impossible that Oswald was not aware of the President's visit. This, combined with his interest in politics and a documented positive attitude toward President Kennedy, suggests that some special instructions for the day influenced his decision not to go outside and watch the motorcade but remain secluded inside the building.

Several factors suggest that Oswald was not privy to the entire plan, and that immediately following the assassination he began to suspect that his instructions were putting him at risk. He left the area; he took a taxi that could have taken him directly to the Texas Theatre, yet requested to be dropped off several blocks beyond his apartment house; and he went in the apartment to arm himself before going on to the Texas Theatre.

And what of Martino's final assertion, that one of the exiles was waiting for Oswald in the Texas Theatre and was let go by the police after Oswald was taken into custody? We should have the information on this including the name of that individual since police reports of the time refer to a detailed list of the witnesses in theatre. The fact that individuals were checked for their names and identification has been verified, but we do not have those names because the list in question never made it into the official record.[27]

Did Oswald play some assigned role on November 22? Most likely. Was he a shooter? John Martino says no, and the unheard witnesses seem to validate his assertion.

The framing of Oswald certainly did not include Oswald's cooperation. He would have made an excellent dead patsy but he was a very dangerous live witness. Given that Lee Oswald played only the role Martino described, focusing on Oswald and his activities in Dallas is not going to tell us much about the conspiracy. Unfortunately, the only criminal investigation (a very brief one) ever conducted in regard to the assassination was focused exclusively on Lee Oswald. The police never had any other serious suspects and were ordered by the White House to omit any reference to conspiracy from the charges brought against Oswald, whether or not they had evidence for it.

It is also a fact that the only visible FBI and CIA investigations seem to have involved possible participation by Castro agents. FBI Director Hoover had the Miami FBI office perform an extensive investigation of John Martino's initial information regarding Oswald's alleged involvement with Castro, indicating to his personnel that he would like to be able to take Martino directly to the Warren Commission. Since Martino could not produce a viable informant, the FBI simply closed out his report with no further investigation of Martino's associates. Unfortunately, this means that the trail is very old and very cold. What we do know follows.

MIAMI 1963, MARTINO'S ASSOCIATES

John Martino did have known associates—CIA officers including David Morales and Rip Robertson, Cuban exiles, and Frank Fiorini/Sturgis. When questioned by the FBI, Martino was assertive in stating that the sources for his Oswald story were not Fiorini/Sturgis (who was promoting the same line at that time), nor his friend Felipe Vidal Santiago.[28]

In Chapter One we saw Martino making claims he would later recant, including that Oswald had received calls from Cuba and was in touch with Castro's intelligence agents. "Martino stated the information concerning such an alleged telephone call by Oswald to Cuban intelligence did not originate with his friend Felipe Vidal Santiago, a Cuban exile in anti-Castro activities."[29]

Indeed from this distance in time, Bayo, Vidal, Fiorini/Sturgis, Robertson and Morales appear as the individuals verifiably identifiable as associates of John Martino in the summer of 1963. Of the five,

Robertson was a CIA action officer attached to JM/WAVE and reporting to David Morales. David Morales was known to Martino as a CIA officer and had been assigned to the US Embassy in Havana in 1959. Frank Fiorini/Sturgis was a CIA informant reporting to Bernard Barker and providing information on a wide range of individuals and exile groups. Fiorini/Sturgis had initially offered his services (including the assassination of Fidel Castro) to the CIA while still serving under Castro in Cuba after the ouster of Batista.

Although Richard Helms would deny under oath that Fiorini/Sturgis had ever been associated with the CIA, we now have documents showing Fiorini/Sturgis was an active CIA informant. We also have a copy of a CIA memo recording his initial approach to CIA while on a trip to the United States. CIA (KUBARK) determined that Fiorini/Sturgis should be developed and in a memo advises that, "Base should deal with Fiorini under strict Consular cover."[30] Immediately after the assassination, Fiorini/Sturgis and his associates would become extremely active in gaining media coverage for the "Oswald had been in Cuba and was a Castro agent" story line.

Recently obtained documents reveal that a March 1963 INS notice to Felipe Vidal was the result of information passed by informant Frank Fiorini (Sturgis) to Bernard Barker (crypt AM/CLATTER) and sent on from JM/WAVE to a broad list of CIA offices and government departments. The information from Sturgis describes a variety of exile military operations in preparation. However, the main news was about a strike against Cuba by a 185-foot mother ship and several small boats. This flotilla planned to attack a Cuban ship on the way to the island—as a diversion for two separate landings in Cuba.

The leader of the operation—in March of 1963—was Felipe Vidal. His forces were to include men from both Unidad/UR and MDC. Financing had been obtained from Lobo and Orlando Bosch Avila.[31]

Additional details on Julio Lobo and his New York City associates are contained in *Appendix D, The Way of WAVE*. New documents demonstrate that start-up money for Alpha 66 came from Julio Lobo and Carlos Prio and that at least some of the Bayo mission personnel appear to have had New York connections. The FBI had Bayo and Rene Lamoru under surveillance at an apartment on 351 SW 6th Street (Apartment 2) in March 1963 and was informed by CIA that the Agency had "covert interest" in those individuals as of July, 1963 (the time of the Bayo-Pawley mission).[32]

Vidal, on the other hand, was most definitely not a CIA employee or contract agent in 1963, although he had been one for a time after his defection. Vidal was in a totally different category. So was his friend and associate, Roy Emory Hargraves.[33]

Roy Hargraves was first recorded as one of about 20 Americans described as soldiers-of-fortune who became associated with former Army Major George Tanner (formerly associated with Rolando Masferrer) in April of 1961. Tanner's group was taken over within a couple of months by Gerald Patrick Hemming and the name changed from "Anti-Communist Legionnaires" to "Interpen–Intercontinental Penetration Group." Hargraves and several other Legionnaires were arrested in May of 1961 for fighting with pro-Castro Cuban exiles at Bayfront Park. Approximately two weeks later he was arrested for petty larceny and received a suspended sentence. During 1961, the Hemming group was closely associated with Sanchez Arango's AAA exile group.

The AAA group was an offshoot of the *Authentico* party originally formed to fight Batista, and itself had strong ties to Carlos Prio, to the old Havana casino operators, and to Mike McClaney.[34] AAA was one of the first exile groups to take a hard line in rejecting CIA influence and left the CRC umbrella organization a week after the Bay of Pigs invasion. By November 1961, Hargraves was reported associating with Rolando Masferrer as well as with Hemming's Interpen group. In April, Hargraves was serving as one of the trainers at Hemming's private camp in the Everglades. The first exile trainees were from Arango's AAA.

In August of 1962, an FBI report indicates that Hargraves claimed to have located a ship in Miami conducting commercial trade with Cuba and wanted to blow it up. This incident made Hargraves stand out as one of the most committed, radical and action oriented of the Americans associated with anti-Castro activities.[35]

By November, the FBI reported a scheme between Sam Benton (McClaney's representative to the exiles) and Hargraves to steal pleasure boats in Miami so their owners could collect insurance.[36] That plan would have produced the boats needed for Cuban raids. But it was never pursued; within a month of its formulation, twelve of Hemming's group, including Roy Hargraves, was arrested by the US Customs for illegal arms transport—though the DOJ did not continue the prosecution and dropped charges in February of 1963.

In December 1962, Felipe Vidal Santiago began to express his dissatisfaction with the US and attempted to move his equipment out of the country to Guatemala. At this same time, Hargraves claimed to have participated in a mission into Cuba with the 30 November group.

In February 1963, Roy Hargraves led a group which captured two Cuban fishing boats and took the boats to the Bahamas. Masferrer reportedly provided money for the raid. When Hargraves returned to Miami, the Cubans entered the Bahamas and recaptured the boats.

In March 1963, Felipe Vidal Santiago was given legal notice by the INS. This notice was supposed to restrain Vidal from leaving Dade County. The INS action was part of the overall Kennedy Administration crackdown on unsanctioned exile groups attempting operations from within US territory. Such groups included Alpha 66, 30th November, and the DRE. In April, Vidal was found in a boat off the Florida Keys in violation of his INS restriction.

In June, 1963, Hargraves was arrested for arms violations, but released in only a few days.

By October, Vidal and Hargraves were working closely together. They lacked financing and were supposedly working at developing Cuban missions out of Nicaragua or Guatemala. Vidal traveled to Dallas and stated that he visited General Walker seeking donations. Vidal spent almost two weeks in Dallas from October 31 to November 11. Upon his return, he, too, reportedly stated that Walker had no further interest in Cuban affairs. Vidal was reportedly back in Dallas as of November 21, 1963, still trying to raise money and still in violation of his travel restriction.

From October 1963 into 1964, Vidal and Hargraves continued working together, although they had apparently been unsuccessful in raising money. In April, 1964, Vidal entered Cuba on a penetration mission, where he was captured and eventually executed.

Decades later, Cuban General Fabian Escalante made a point of talking to researchers about the interrogation of Vidal, claiming that Vidal told his interrogators that he had been active in 1963 in informing Cuban exile groups about Kennedy administration attempts to start a dialog with Cuba. This Kennedy initiative was extremely secretive and known only within top circles of the CIA and State Department. Where and how Vidal might have received this information will be explored in a later chapter.[37]

After Vidal's death, Hargraves remained active in anti-Communist activities for several years. In 1968, he was arrested for dynamiting groups in Los Angeles including the Black Panthers. In 1970, he was involved in a complex plan with Cuban exiles to infiltrate Cuba, shell Guantanamo Naval Base, and attack the Presidential enclave in Key Biscayne making both appear to be acts of the Castro government. This plan was intended to provoke warfare with Cuba and a military invasion by the US.

Interest in Vidal and Hargraves, is enhanced by an FBI report released in 1993, titled: "JFK, SUSPECT."[38]   The information that apparently generated the report and an investigation of Hargraves was provided to the FBI by William Blanton Acker. Acker had lived in Miami in 1963 working in a restaurant on Flagler Street. He had met an individual named Art Silva. Silva and his girlfriend moved into a tourist (trailer) court where Silva made the acquaintance of a neighbor named Roy (last name unknown) who was living with a woman in the tourist court.

According to Silva, Roy had several telescopic sight-equipped rifles, grenades, dynamite, etc. in his room. Roy was an ex-Marine and associated with several Cuban exile groups. At a Christmas party in 1963, Roy and Acker almost came to blows as Roy blamed the late President Kennedy personally for the death of one of his close friends who participated in the invasion at the Bay of Pigs. Most importantly, *"Roy had made a trip to Dallas, Texas in late 1963 and was reported by Art to have Secret Service credentials in his possession."*[39]

Acker also stated to the FBI that in the fall of 1963, he talked with Silva about his next-door neighbor Roy and Silva said that Roy could help get Acker into the exile movement. He also said, "Somebody is going to die. Somebody who hasn't hurt anybody. He doesn't know it but he is going to die." Silva would not tell Acker who that was, but stated that, *"Roy is in something big, the biggest thing this country has ever seen."*[40]

In its investigation the FBI determined that Roy Hargraves had an alibi (an unnamed reliable source reported him as being in Miami from November to March) and that there was no way to prove that he was the Roy in question. They discounted Acker as a witness—for having a diseased mind. It seems Acker had spent time in a veteran's hospital after having served in North Africa, Italy, France, Germany and Austria in WWII. The FBI then sealed the report from public view and there is no indication it was brought to the attention of the HSCA.

There is, however, possible corroboration that the individual in question was Roy Hargraves. In June of 1967, Tom Dunkin, a photojournalist for *Life* magazine, wrote a memo to Dick Billings about his experiences with Hemming's Interpen associates in 1963.[41] In that document, Billings describes being in Miami on October 20, 1962, and sitting in a beer drinking session at the Flagler Hotel. Afterwards, he accompanied Roy Hargraves to a nearby Tourist Court where Hargraves was living with his girlfriend Betty whom he later reportedly married.

Since they arrived rather late and rather drunk, it seems Betty had a variety of profane remarks for Hargraves and kept telling him he was wasting his time with a revolution. He replied that he had too much time invested to quit. This story seems to place Roy Hargraves in the same location/trailer court described by Acker and Silva.

Further suggestion that the Roy in Ackers report was Roy Hargraves comes from a 1964 FBI report in which the FBI's own records showed that Roy Hargraves was living in Frank's Cottages, a motel at 4170 S.W. 8th Street in Miami. The report describes Hargraves as a "mercenary, soldier of fortune and adventurer who has been involved with Cuban exiles in Miami Florida for about the past two years." This is an exact match to the descriptions given by Acker.[42]

SUMMARY

There is every reason to believe, as John Martino asserted, that Lee Oswald was recruited and managed by anti-Castro exiles as part of the conspiracy. There is also good reason to believe that Oswald himself was being monitored in contacts with exiles and subversives in some sort of informant role for the FBI. Whether he was a forced informant, a voluntary informant or walking a line in-between will be discussed in later chapters.

- Lee Oswald was identified as a potential patsy in July of 1963. Several possible channels may have served to pass information on Oswald from New Orleans to Miami. One channel may have involved people in communication with Mike McClaney and his associates.

- Lee Oswald was approached and involved in August 1963.

- Oswald maintained contact and cooperated to some extent up to his arrival at a pre-arranged meeting place, the Texas Theatre.

- Oswald was not a shooter and not an active participant in the assassination or in connecting the assassination to himself, to Castro or to Cuba.

Martino did not leave us any names in his final revelations to his friends and no investigation was ever made of his associates or his contacts. Given the lack of any real criminal investigation we are forced to look for additional information among the sorts of leads that can be found only in "slips," things that should not have been said, things that should not have been known, things said by people who got excited, people who got drunk, someone who talked when they shouldn't have.

CHAPTER 6

"AS SOON AS THEY TAKE CARE OF KENNEDY"

The CIA case officers who worked with the Cuban exiles had no complaints about their bravery or their passion. They had absolutely no complaints about their dedication, but almost to a man, they stated that the fundamental weakness in most operations was simply their lack of ability to keep a secret, to not talk about even the most secret plans or projects.

Given this, we should expect to find leads and traces by searching for exile gossip. The gossip is unlikely to reveal the direct participants, but when combined with a detailed examination of group affiliations and the exile social network, it can help us define persons of interest. Fortunately, the record does show instances of such leaks. We have already seen one in Miami; another seemingly well informed remark came from Chicago.

CHICAGO, ILLINOIS, NOVEMBER 21, 1963

Homer Echevarria was an activist in the exile anti-Castro movement. He had been active with a group of Cubans who were bitterly opposed to President Kennedy and he had condemned the United States, advocating a forceful recovery of Cuba by anti-Castro groups. FBI informants had been monitoring him because he was also making approaches to purchase machine guns and other weapons, but the FBI turned over its ongoing investigation of Echevarria to the Secret Service because after November 22, it appeared have become primarily a protective matter. The reason being that on November 21, an FBI informant heard Echevarria say:

> "We now have plenty of money—our new backers are Jews—as soon as they (or "we") take care of Kennedy..."

At that point the conversation was interrupted.[1]

The Secret Service established surveillance on Echevarria and determined that he was personally affiliated with the DRE organization and an associate of Juan Francisco Blanco Fernandez. Fernandez was military director for the DRE and it appears that the arms that Echevarria was soliciting were being financed out of the war chest of Paulino Sierra (whose organization, the Junta or JGCE, will be discussed in detail below and in Chapter 7). Unfortunately, we know little more about Echevarria's connections. The Secret Service did not pursue this assassination lead because the Kennedy murder investigation had been ordered back to the FBI and the FBI "made it clear that it wanted the Secret Service to terminate its investigation."[2] Documents released over the last decade show that the FBI's justification to the Secret Service was that Echevarria's father had been a valuable FBI informant.[3]

Although we know far to little about Echevarria's connections, it appears that we at least know more than the CIA did when they actually began to recruit him in 1964. New documents show that he was first contacted in December 1964; both he and his father were interviewed by the CIA at that time. They both claimed not to have any connections that could be helpful inside Cuba but stated that they might know people inside the United States who "had good contacts". They apparently failed to tell the CIA about Homer's contacts with the DRE, the JCGE, and that he had been investigated by the both the FBI and Secret Service in regard to arms sales–not to mention his remark about "taking care of Kennedy." In turn, during its background and security investigation the CIA failed to turn up any of these associations much less the FBI or Secret Service reports. In February of 1965, he was given a provisional operational approval (a note on his approval form states that there were no JM/WAVE station traces on him). This approval was cancelled in August 1965 due to a lack of interest in operational use. As a side note, it appears that Echevarria had moved out of Chicago and by December 1963 was residing in Alabama.[4]

Chicago was a hotbed of Cuban activity in 1963, the apparent starting point for an explosive new exile movement nominally headed by Paulino Sierra Martinez. The Sierra Junta eventually supported Carlos Prio Soccares as the new President of Cuba once Castro had been forced out of power by the JGCE, Junta of the Government of Cuba in Exile. Sierra established affiliations with the most violent and aggressive of the exile groups sending funds to SNFE-Alpha 66, Commandos L and 30 November.

Sierra's Minister of the Interior was Carlos Rodriquez Quesada, a SNFE (Second National Front of the Escambray) founder associated closely with Alpha 66, Antonio Veciana and Menoyo. Quesada was reputed to be acquainted with Homer Echevarria. Perhaps Echevarria's remark about getting rid of Kennedy came from Quesada? Or Blanco Fernandez, a military officer in the DRE? Blanco was reportedly in Chicago in the fall of 1963, prospecting for weapons – just as other DRE members were in Dallas. Or the gossip about JFK could have come from some other exile doing business in Chicago, with access to the right rumors in Miami, someone like Victor Hernandez. Hernandez was in Miami, Illinois, and New Orleans in the summer and early fall of 1963.

There is no doubt there were a variety of independent exile initiatives in progress during the summer of 1963. It is also clear those involved were not getting either their weapons or their funds from the Kennedy administration. Neither JM/WAVE nor Robert Kennedy's Special Group Augmented was in control of these exiles. As some of these initiatives developed, they became connected to long time players from the Cuban gambling scene.

Paulino Sierra himself was unknown in the Miami exile community. A high level civil servant in the Batista regime, he immigrated to Miami in 1960 but then moved on to Chicago. After taking a law degree he joined the legal counsel for the Union Tank Car Company and founded the exile division of the Cuban Bar Association. Suddenly, in the spring of 1963 Sierra became an activist with independent funding. He also managed to convince Union Tank Car that it could wisely invest in a return to a free Cuba and it allowed him to embark on the formation of his new movement. William Browder, Chief Counsel for Union Tank Car, even managed certain accounts for Sierra in which, he stated, there were "considerable" monies on deposit.[5]

When first seen in Miami, Sierra was in the company of a companion, William Trull, an entertainer from Texas. Later, Trull would say that Sierra approached him and sent him airfare to come to Miami and join him in promoting his plans. It now appears that Trull was recommended through connections between Sierra, his Cuban associates in New York City and Robert Kleberg, of the King Ranch in Texas. Sierra's initial organizing meeting in Miami, May 15, 1963, involved a variety of exile leaders of various political persuasions including Carlos Rodriquez Quesada and Felipe Vidal Santiago.

Trull later stated that Sierra boasted to him that his real money sponsors were "representatives of Las Vegas and Cleveland gambling interests" who had offered him $14M in backing against a 50% share of future gambling concessions in a free Cuba.[6]

It is interesting to note how well this matches the "Jewish" supporters remark by Homer Echevarria and the very special Jewish Mafia contacts of John Roselli. These included Roselli's former Havana connections to the Cleveland "Jewish" Mayfield Road mob, to Moe Dalitz and to Dalitz's Desert Inn casino in Las Vegas. Jack Ruby and some of his associates from the Chicago milieu fit as well.

Sierra's public description of his supporters was much different. He dropped the names of corporate giants such as United Fruit, Standard Oil, Du Pont, and US Steel. He also told of high-ranking army and navy officers who were going to arrange for arms and overseas bases. In June, the Chicago FBI office interviewed Sierra and could find no real evidence of an actual organization or legitimate funding. It concluded some sort of con job was in process and closed his file. However, Sierra was just getting started and the Miami press gave a much more forthright view of the Sierra pitch.

"Gamblers Pop Out Of The Exile Grab Bag"
— *Miami News, May 6, 1963.*

Sierra may not have had a real organization but he traveled around negotiating for bases in Nicaragua and Columbia. Sierra's companions on these high level trips included Carlos Prio Socarres and Tony Varona (Roselli's faithful resource in the anti-Castro assassination schemes). Prio and Varona were making similar contacts with Manual Artime in the same time frame.

Sierra had plenty of money for major arms purchases from Minutemen arms dealers according to an AMOT/AMWORLD memo of August 3, 1963, which quotes Sierra's military affairs representative (Gulberto Rodriguez) as telling a JM/WAVE informant that Sierra had a $650,000 war chest deposit in a Miami bank. For manpower, Carlos Rodriquez Quesada introduced him to certain Interpen associates. These individuals assisted Sierra in moving his arms purchases, including a miniature submarine. He even offered them cash if they would stage raids into Cuba to gain publicity for the movement. Though Sierra's eight month initiative (March–November 1963) would provide considerable money to the more activist exile groups, it, too, quickly evaporated. Sierra's Military Coordinator, Gilberto Rodriquez even complained to Browder about Sierra's style of leadership.[7]

In November, Homer Echevarria heard that someone was planning to remove JFK as an obstacle. He repeated this to an FBI informant. Echevarria made a slip while excited and bragging—a slip such as the one we saw earlier from Jose Soto Martinez at the Parrot Jungle in Miami. It appears that Martinez may have heard gossip within the McClaney circles in Miami.

We do know that Victor Hernandez traveled in those same circles and was working on McClaney projects which took him to both New Orleans and Chicago. We know that a "Hernandez" was involved in the same Chicago area arms purchasing initiative, which included Homer Echevarria. We also know before it was pulled from the investigation of Echevarria, the Secret Service confirmed that Echevarria had been associated with Juan Francisco Blanco Fernandez, Military Director for the DRE. The source of Echevarria's gossip could have been Hernandez or Blanco Fernandez, in either case, with its origin in Miami. Both Sierra and the DRE were looking for weapons in the Chicago area and upper mid-west. The DRE was also shopping for weapons in Dallas. DRE and Alpha 66 members became increasingly active in Dallas by that fall.

Author Eric Tagg reports in *Brush with Destiny*, an excellent manuscript on the life of Buddy Walthers, Dallas County Deputy Sheriff, that Walthers was contacted on the evening of November 22 by his mother-in-law. She lived down the street to the house on Harlandale that had started to receive a lot of mysterious late night visitors in October and November. She had become suspicious of her new neighbors who had moved in only 2-3 months before, and who held frequent meetings lasting long into the nights. Apparently, she felt that these Cubans might be somehow connected to Lee Oswald; in fact she told Walthers that she had seen someone looking very much like Oswald going into the house.[8, 9]

Walthers continued his own investigation of the house and its occupants. He found that one occupant was Manuel Rodriguez Orcarberrio, and that Frank Ellsworth of the ATF was indeed monitoring Orcarberrio's armaments buying efforts at the time of the assassination. Walthers concluded his investigation and on November 26, he submitted a follow-up report:

> "I don't know what action the Secret Service has taken but I learned today that sometime between seven days and two weeks before the President was shot, these Cubans moved from this house. My informant stated that the subject Oswald had been to this house before."

There are no records indicating that the Secret Service ever pursued Walther's report. The CIA did, but was confused (it would seem) by a misspelling of Harlandale in Walthers' original report and dropped its inquiry on the grounds that no such street existed. The FBI managed to locate the address but did no more than simply confirm that the Cubans and Orcarberrio had been there and departed. As we have seen, if the Cubans in such reports were not Castroists, the FBI seems to have had little interest in their activities, even if apparently connected to Oswald.

An examination of an FBI follow-up on Walthers' report is even more revealing. It seems that the FBI had a source within Alpha 66 in Dallas who reported to it that Oswald was not associated with Alpha 66 in any way and had never been in the house on Harlandale. The same report notes that the source later moved to Puerto Rico after the assassination. Since we know that Rodriquez Orcarberrio made such a move, it is possible that the FBI's source clearing the house on Harlandale may have been one of the persons reported as being in contact with Oswald. The FBI report made no mention of the fact that in 1964 the Secret Service listed Orcarberrio as a potential Presidential threat nor does it mention yet another, separate FBI report in which a witness reported Orcarberrio in the company of a man closely resembling Lee Oswald.[10]

In a following chapter there is further explanation as to how and why Echevarria may have heard the gossip he let slip. He was in contact with Cuban exiles known to be hostile to President Kennedy and actively involved in buying arms and preparing for banned Cuban raids. These exiles had gone to Chicago in October and individuals traveling to Chicago at that time were reported by the FBI to the Secret Service as preventive security suspects, i.e., potential threats to the President. It is possible that these individuals were under FBI surveillance and had been since the incident at the McClaney farm outside New Orleans.

In any event, Echevarria did make a slip, one that most likely takes us back to Miami, with people known to have had associations with the old Havana gambling crowd in which Martino had circulated and people who had been in contact with Sierra's group. People such as Felipe Vidal.

When Vidal was captured on a mission into Cuba in 1964, he reportedly told his Cuban captors things having nothing to do with his mission. They say he told them about all his trips to Dallas, about his intense efforts in the fall of 1963 to communicate to the dedicated and activist exiles that John Kennedy was betraying them. Kennedy was negotiating with Fidel Castro and shortly a deal would be cut to leave Castro in power, eject the Russians, and destroy the hopes of the exiles for a return to Cuba. John Kennedy was about to destroy "La Causa" forever. If we can believe the Cuban sources, Vidal had been busy circulating one of the most secret actions of a President. Vidal heard word of contacts, contacts that had been carried out by personal representatives of the President, not even by officers of the State Department. Such a secret would have been guaranteed to brand Kennedy as a traitor in the eyes of many of those to whom it was apparently passed.

SUMMARY

The Echevarria remark from Chicago was troubling to the Secret Service, if not the FBI. It caused a small flurry of interest but was not brought to the Warren Commission's attention at the same level as the Odio incident. There was no coordinated criminal investigation and certainly no centralized investigation. There was no connecting of the names, nothing that associated a remark in Chicago with specific people in Miami or Dallas.

Attempts to identify the source for such gossip takes us in a variety of directions, producing names that seem to lend credibility to the remarks themselves. The money for the related arms search was very likely coming from the Sierra Junta. The Junta's secret financial backers were out of Nevada and included elements of the Jewish branch of American organized crime. These new backers all known to a name which will continue to be of interest in regard to any plot against JFK, John Roselli.

Chicago leads us back to Miami. It branches to New York and Las Vegas. The road to Dallas was not a straight one. There were branches that led to Washington D.C., Chicago, Florida and even Mexico City. There were threats and possibly even preparations for attacks in other cities before Dallas.

One constant does emerge in all the leads, the names, and the gossip—the Cuba factor. In that respect all roads pass by and through the war against the Communist regime in Cuba, the war against Fidel Castro that continued to be waged in 1963. Not a cold war, rather a covert one. A war of shadows—and shadow warriors.

CHAPTER 7

SHADOW WARS AND SHADOW WARRIORS

John Martino's information about some elements of the conspiracy is very specific. For instance he relates that in 1963, the plotters knew Oswald was operating in a counter-intelligence role for an agency, or agencies, of the U.S. Government. He describes Oswald's activities as relatively low level, most likely in what is generally referred to as a dangle; an individual who is circulated among potential intelligence targets strictly to see who responds to or contacts him, and to determine their connections. Martino's impression was that Oswald simply followed orders as an informant and certainly was not a highly skilled intelligence operative.

In the previous chapter, we raised the issue that persons within a certain community of interest had been reported to be in contact with Oswald and that Oswald had been reported visiting a specific exile residence in Dallas only weeks before the assassination.

This chapter will examine information corroborating Oswald's contacts with such individuals, his being under observation by the FBI, and performing the role of intelligence dangle described by John Martino. We will also examine material written by Oswald, writings which give us a much clearer view of his real beliefs and which had to be avoided to sustain the image the Warren Commission needed to establish.

We will also examine elements of the Cuban situation in 1963 and evaluate in much more detail how Oswald's activities fit within certain intelligence and secret war events of the time.

"Hosty mentioned that Oswald had contacted two known subversive agents about two weeks before the Kennedy assassination."[1]

Special Agent James P. Hosty, the FBI agent assigned to Oswald in Dallas, told a Secret Service agent on the afternoon of November 22 that Oswald had been observed meeting with a pair of subversives two weeks before the assassination. S.A. Hosty told Secret Service Agent William Patterson that he felt sure, that in light of events, this sensitive information would be provided to the Chief of the Secret Service. As far as the official record goes, no follow-on information was ever provided to the Secret Service on this subject. Currently (October, 2006), FBI documents are under investigation which may reveal the identity of the two "subversives" and demonstrate a connection between those individuals and John Martino. Information on this and other ongoing research will be communicated on the book web site.

Agent Hosty made similar remarks about monitoring Oswald to Lt. Jack Revill, a Dallas police intelligence officer, immediately following the assassination (the conversation was verified in part by Detective V.J. Brian). Hosty later adamantly denied making the remarks as Revill reported. J. Edgar Hoover went to great lengths to suppress the remarks, to force a DPD retraction, and later to penalize the Dallas Police Department for discussing Hosty's remarks with the press. [2,3]

Agent Hosty has over the years provided many inside details and new documents relating to Lee Oswald and to the Mexico City appearance of Oswald. Unfortunately, Agent Hosty and the FBI can also be shown to have destroyed evidence on two well-documented occasions.

First, a note left for Hosty by Oswald at the Dallas FBI office was purposefully destroyed and not revealed to the Warren Commission. Second, a reference in Lee Oswald's notebook to a contact with Agent Hosty was concealed by the FBI, which totally retyped the contents of the notebook so as to eliminate this one item. The FBI certainly acted as if it had something to conceal in regard to Lee Oswald.[4]

THE REAL OSWALD

The HSCA investigated whether or not the CIA also might have concealed information on an informant relationship with Lee Oswald. One particularly interesting indication is described in a request from Edwin Strakna, George Green, and Leonard Nurk of the HSCA staff to Mr. Scott Breckinridge of the CIA. Breckinridge was the CIA coordinator for HSCA information requests and the letter is a request to CIA for copies of all documents pertaining to an informant report concerning a Minsk Radio Plant.

Dear Mr. Breckinridge:

In connection with its investigations into the circumstances surrounding the death of President Kennedy, the Select Committee on Assassinations has been informed that during the summer of 1962, a CIA contact report concerning the Minsk Radio Plant was routed to the Foreign Documents Division in the Soviet Branch of the Directorate of Intelligence. The source of this contact report is believed to have been a former Marine and defector to the Soviet Union who returned to the United States with his family during the summer of 1962. The source is believed to have stated that he had been employed at the Minsk Radio Plant. The Committee has been further informed that this contact report was filed in a volume of material concerning the Minsk Radio Plant and that this volume is retrievable from the CIA's Industrial Registry Branch, which in 1962, was a component of the Office of Central Reference.[5]

Though the HSCA request is in the record, no response from the CIA has been located.

Actually, we do have a very detailed informant report on the Minsk Radio Plant, more accurately the "Minsk Radio and Television Plant".[6] It includes plant production numbers, personnel breakdowns and staffing by type of job and male-female ratio as well as quite detailed facilities and logistics descriptions.

This Minsk material is contained in a manuscript prepared by Lee Oswald after his return from Russia in 1962. When Lee Oswald returned to the United States, he approached Pauline Bates, a Fort Worth stenographer, asking her to work with him to complete a manuscript. This manuscript contains detailed information about his time in Russia including extensive details about the Minsk Radio Plant where he worked.

Perhaps one of the reasons why Oswald's manuscript did not receive more attention in the Warren Commission investigation is the fact that parts of Oswald's writing are decidedly anti-Communist and not supportive of the official view of Lee Oswald, as illustrated by the following:

> The Communist Party of the United States has betrayed itself! It has turned itself into the traditional lever of a foreign power to overthrow the government of the United States, not in the name of freedom or high ideals, but in servile conformity to the wishes of the Soviet Union ... *The Soviets have committed crimes unsurpassed ...imprisonment of their own peoples [sic]... mass extermination... The Communist movement in the United States of America has turned itself into a "valuable gold coin" of the Kremlin.* It has failed to denounce any actions of the Soviet Government when similar actions of the United States Government bring pious protest. *[I have] many personal reasons to know and therefore hate and mistrust Communism.*[7] (emphasis added)

Clearly, this is not the Lee Oswald of the official image–the devout Russophile who avowed his Communist beliefs in the Cuban Embassy in Mexico City in 1963. Nor would such a paragraph be consistent with the Lee Oswald who maintained written correspondence with the Soviet Embassies and the Communist Party of the USA.

It seems worth mentioning that Daniel Schorr of CBS investigated the Minsk radio debriefing report that was adamantly supported by an ex-CIA agent. Schorr interviewed the unidentified ex-agent as well as CIA Director Colby in regard to the report. The ARRB obtained copies of correspondence pertaining to Schorr's interviews. In an internal memo, Colby described his interview with Schorr and his assessment that he had successfully deflected any linkage of Oswald to the CIA. His summary sentence is perhaps the most revealing part of the memorandum:

> "We must, however, insure that Mr. Schorr does not learn anything which would cause the slightest doubt on the above account before he produces the programs in November."[8]

Colby's efforts were at least partially effective. In Schorr's final coverage of the subject, he reported that the CIA had told him the debriefing report was actually from an unnamed re-defector in 1952. The individual was ex-Navy, very similar to Lee Oswald but someone else and in another city, not Minsk.

In contrast, the ex-CIA agent who had agreed to testify to the HSCA on the Minsk report, stated to Schorr that the report he read most specifically had said "ex-Marine" and "Minsk." Schorr concluded with the remark that the CIA could not find the actual report, that it had referred him to the Navy, and that the Navy had no record of such a report, such a re-defector, or any such incident.[9]

The FBI recovered notes made by Lee Oswald for a speech, these notes were not addressed by the Warren Commission but are found in the 26 volumes of exhibits.[10] Visibility for the notes certainly would not have furthered the role Oswald assumed in 1963, nor would it have bolstered the image the Warren Commission needed to establish for Oswald. In these notes Oswald wrote *"there are possibly few other Americans born in the US who (have) as many personal reasons to know—and therefore mistrust—Communism."* He acknowledged that both countries had shortcomings and advantages but went on to note, "only in ours is the voice of dissent allowed opportunity of expression."

Shadow Wars

For our purposes, it is very important to separate Lee Oswald's role as an intelligence dangle from his role in the Kennedy conspiracy. That conspiracy did not begin with Lee Oswald nor was Oswald the first patsy candidate. Several of the elements and activities which are often felt to be unique to Oswald and the conspiracy may be better viewed simply as part of the ongoing secret war against Castro and his influence—part of a war which was fought not only in Cuba but also in the United States, Mexico and eventually across much of Latin America. Unfortunately, this makes matters even more difficult as we can see individuals and activities cross paths in ways both related and unrelated to the conspiracy.

For example, the CIA and FBI actively conducted a counter-intelligence program against the Fair Play for Cuba Committee. The FPCC had been targeted not only because of its support for Fidel Castro but also because it assisted students and others in moving in and out of Cuba. This was a violation of US law and the administration embargo against Cuba, in place since the failed Bay of Pigs invasion.

There was ongoing surveillance and, whenever possible, prosecution of individuals attempting to enter Cuba. In August of

1962, Vaughn Marlowe/Snipes was in Mexico City with other leftists attempting to make his way into Cuba. Marlowe was an ex-Marine, an avowed socialist and an FPCC activist living in Los Angeles. In August of 1962, Richard Case Nagell, former Army military intelligence officer and recently fired ex-employee of various California state agencies, crossed the border into Mexico. Nagell was on military record as being an opponent of certain US foreign polices and in September he visited the US Embassy in Mexico City. There he expressed his intent to renounce his citizenship based on his political views, much as Lee Oswald had done years before at the US Embassy in Moscow. However, also like Lee Oswald in Russia, he never actually carried out this action, making it possible for him to return to the United States. But this action did make him very visible as a target for Soviet block recruitment as a disaffected ex-US military officer.

Nagell did not meet Vaughn Marlowe during the brief period when they were both in Mexico City. He did become rather close to him in Los Angeles several months later, a fact elaborated on and supported in great detail in statements by Marlowe to various investigators, including D.A. Garrison.

The shadow war against Castro's control of Cuba spawned a number of covert activities. Some of them, including intelligence operations against the Fair Play for Cuba Committee and special operations and projects controlled by Robert Kennedy's Special Group, were in line with Kennedy Administration policy. Other activities, such as independent intelligence operations of the FBI, CIA, and Army Intelligence against the Cuban exiles and each other, reflect the vested interests of each organization. Beyond that, certain projects conducted at the personal discretion of senior CIA officers needed to be protected not only from the opposition but also from non-included colleagues within a given branch or office.

SHADOW WARRIORS

The following chronology outlines a few of the major activities of this secret war as revealed over the past 35 years.[11] Selected headlines are from *Miami Herald* articles.

"Miami Hears Anti-Castro Blows Near"
– 30th Of November (June 16, 1962)

"Raiders Shot Up Hotel In Havana" – DRE, Student Revolutionary
Directorate (August, 1962)

"Anti-Castro Group Plans Next Attack" – Alpha 66 (September, 1962)

September 1962

Immediately before and during the Cuban Missile Crisis, Alpha 66 began targeting attacks on Russian installations and ships in Cuba. These attacks proved to be very successful and showed signs of high quality field intelligence as well as great personal skill and commitment by the participants. The small Alpha 66 complement in Mexico City continued to perform counter intelligence, monitoring the movements of traffic to and from Cuba and identifying potential agents and sympathizers. In addition, it conducted an offensive against individual Cuban embassy personnel. According to Anthony Veciana, the Alpha 66 Russian attacks (which received immense press coverage) were being encouraged and supported by a person named Maurice Bishop. A strong case can be made that Bishop was in fact CIA officer David Atlee Phillips. What remains in doubt is the extent to which his activity with Veciana in regard to these attacks against the Russians reflected a personal initiative on Phillips' part. Information presented in Appendix D, *The Way of WAVE*, suggests that at least certain elements of the Agency were far more aware of Alpha 66 operations than we have previously known. Whether they went further in manipulating the group remains a matter of speculation.

However, as far as Veciana was concerned, he was most certainly not taking orders from or acting under direction of the CIA itself. His mentor and advisor, Bishop has been identified elsewhere as CIA officer Phillips. This identification was strongly denied by the CIA and by Phillips himself. In 1962 and 1963, Phillips (previously with Operation Mongoose as C/WH/4 Propaganda) was stationed in Mexico City and was charged with both intelligence and propaganda operations against Cuba. He had been the CIA lead in joint CIA-FBI activities against the FPCC since 1961 and US citizens visiting Cuba were among the major targets of this operation.[12] Court Wood, a young man who had returned from Cuba to start an FPCC chapter, had become a major target for an early joint FBI-CIA infiltration of the FPCC managed by Phillips himself.

October 1962

In October, the first rumor of a Castro-sponsored effort to murder John Kennedy entered the official record. A CIA informant in Guatemala (solidly anti-Communist by this time and heavily under the influence of the CIA apparatus which had ousted the Arbenz government), reported a detailed conversation by Castro agents which included discussion about Kennedy being eliminated within the coming year.

In addition, a letter intercepted in Miami and destined for an out-of-country anti-Communist radio station appeared to substantiate the Castro plot. The note revealed a purported effort by Castro agents to kill the US President. It resulted in an extensive FBI investigation that was unable to trace the letters to any Castro personnel or agents. Suspicion was expressed that it was actually a propaganda operation aimed against the Castro regime by Cuban exiles.

Given what we now know, it is possible to speculate that such a propaganda effort, using an exile radio station in Latin America, could have been part of the psychological warfare being conducted by the CIA's Cuban propaganda specialist, David Phillips.[13]

At this same time, according to Richard Nagell, the Russians in Mexico City had been hearing rumors that certain anti-Castro exiles were beginning to talk seriously of eliminating Kennedy themselves in retaliation for his perceived treason at the Bay of Pigs and for reaching a "hands off Cuba" accommodation during the missile crisis. Nagell described being approached to collect information on these rumors as well as to investigate the possibility that an individual he was acquainted with in Japan, Oswald, would somehow embarrass the Soviets.

Oswald himself, only two days back in Dallas after his return from the Soviet Union, had obtained a job as a photo technician at Jaggers-Stovall, a film processing company with US Army contracts that was also involved in processing classified U2 aerial photography.

Immediately upon his return to Texas, Oswald began subscriptions to a variety of radically left wing publications including Russian magazines. On September 28 he had subscribed to *The Worker* and a FBI memo from New York City had advised the Dallas bureau of this on October 17.

In October Oswald applied for membership in the Socialist Workers Party and later sent them samples of his photographic work. Despite this, in the same month the FBI closed its active file on Lee Oswald.

In the winter of 1962 John Martino and the Bay of Pigs prisoners were back in the United States after their imprisonment in Cuba. Shortly after their return a story began to circulate about missiles remaining in Cuba and Russian officers who were in anti-Castro hands and willing to talk about the missiles.

"Alpha 66 Runs Arms Into Cuba" (October, 1962)

"Exiles Sign War Pact" – Alpha 66 / SNFE; Second National Front Of The Escambray (November 1962)

"Exile Charges US Betrayal" "Our thesis is to carry the fight to Cuba and we will do that" SNFE (November, 1962)

"Exiles Warn Fidel Raids Are Coming" – Commandos L (November, 1962)

November 1962

Nagell left Mexico for New York City to visit his family and began infiltration of the active exile movement there. The "White Rose" movement in New York was widely known and was reported to have received backing from gambling figures. When jailed in Cuba, Martino had been charged with being a White Rose supporter and agent. One of the more visible and violent of the anti-Castro figures, Rolando Masferrer, had relocated to New York City and was also associated with the White Rose movement.

Recent information suggests that Nagell may have been targeted on Masferrer, one of the most crime-connected of the exiles, by CIA officer Henry Hecksher. In 1963 Hecksher would become a senior political officer for the new Kennedy autonomous group project, designated AM/WORLD. As addressed by Waldron in *Ultimate Sacrifice*, one of the concerns of this initiative was how to exclude crime-connected exiles from any new Cuban provisional government. Hecksher's primary focus in this new project was to establish Manual Artime in a leadership role for the hoped for exile alliance. Background for this observation on Nagell and Hecksher is provided in *Appendix B, Crossing Paths in the CIA*.

Before leaving Mexico City, Nagell described making contacts with two exiles who had come directly to Mexico City from Cuba. He related meeting these same individuals again in both Los Angeles and New Orleans during the course of 1963. It is possible that these individuals were Herminio Diaz Garcia and a former Havana San Souci casino manager named Hernandez—Alpha 66 associates in Mexico City.

December 1962

President Kennedy addressed the exile Brigade in the Orange Bowl and William Harvey was officially removed from his position with Task Force W of Operation Mongoose. Task Force W was renamed the Special Affairs group and Harvey was replaced by Desmond Fitzgerald.

In Dallas, Lee Oswald corresponded with the Hall-Davis Committee, a Communist front in New York. He also subscribed to *The Militant*, purchased speeches by Castro from Pioneer Press, and, through the Soviet Embassy in New York, ordered subscriptions to the Soviet magazines *Ogonek*, *The Agitator*, and *Krokodil*.

Of course, this interest was in direct conflict with Oswald's previously stated rejection of the Soviet system as well as his opposition to Russian communism. The manuscript drafted by Oswald immediately after his return from Russia clearly expressed his total rejection of the communist society in Russia and as referenced earlier had even stronger words for the Communist Party of the USA as a Russian political tool.

In accordance with its Russian mail monitoring policies, the Post Office, assisting an FBI program, monitored Oswald's mail and opened it. Oswald filed Post Office form 2153X instructing the Post Office to always deliver his foreign mailings and protested "this intimidation."[14] Oswald continued in his job at Jaggers for well over six months while continuing to demonstrate his Communist and Socialist leanings through his letter writing and subscriptions.

January 1963

Nagell moved from New York City to Miami and began monitoring selected exiles including Rolando Masferrer, Manuel Artime and Orlando Bosch. In Cuba, James Donovan continued discussions with Cuban officials, which had begun as part of the negotiations that ultimately led to the release of all the Bay of Pigs prisoners and several other American citizens. Donovan was debriefed after each visit and he described Castro as cordial and intimate.

Upon his departure from Cuba in January, Castro's personal physician and aide-de-camp, Rene Vallejo, broached the subject of re-establishing diplomatic relations with the US Vallejo extended Castro's invitation to return to Cuba for further talks on relations.

March 18, 1963

Alpha 66 attacked a Russian freighter at Isabela de Sagua and, shortly afterwards, Commandos L (accompanied by a *Life* photographer) attacked the freighter Baku.

March 30, 1963

The Kennedy administration launched a major crackdown on exile raids into Cuba originating from the United States and its territories. This crackdown was announced by both the Justice and State Departments but was opposed by CIA Director McCone. Alpha 66 continued to increase its raids into Cuba and its attacks on Russian facilities.

Sylvia Odio arrived in Dallas to join her younger sister, Sarita.

Agent Hosty of the FBI reopened Oswald's file. The reason given was Oswald's subscription to *The Militant*. Much later, Hosty would state concerns over Oswald's employment. However, nothing in Hosty's reports of this period mentions Oswald's job or any related security issues or concerns. Of course when the FBI had originally learned of a subscription to this same magazine they had *closed* his file. Supposedly Hosty did not actually make a move to interview Oswald at this time, and in the interim Oswald lost his job and left Dallas with no contact information. However, the day after the Oswald FBI file was re-opened Oswald rented his first post office box in Dallas and supposedly placed an order for a rifle in the name of Hidell. This post office box and the rifle order would become immensely important after the assassination. But it could have proved troublesome if Oswald had ever gone to trial, because three different postal records are missing. The signature record of individuals allowed to receive mail in both this box and the box which Oswald was still using in November are gone, contrary to postal regulations.

Peter Dale Scott provides a compelling explanation for the apparently self-defeating purchase of the rifle through the mail:

> To order guns by interstate mail is of course an irrational way for a potential assassin to purchase his murder weapons: it lays a paper trail linking the weapon to the purchaser, or at least his

post-office box. Conversely, if one is investigating firms known to sell weapons illegally through the mails, a paper trail is precisely what is needed.

In Texas anyone in 1963 could go to a gun shop and purchase a weapon untraceably over the counter. Only in interstate purchases did the law require identification, and Oswald was interested only in making interstate purchases.

Scott quotes the Warren Report's (WR 723) statement that Oswald had purchased his pistol from Seaport Traders located in Los Angeles and his rifle (actually a mere carbine) from Klein's Sporting Goods located in Chicago. But, says Scott:

> The Warren Report did not mention that in 1963 Seaport Traders and Klein's Sporting Goods were being investigated by the ATF unit of the US Treasury's Internal Revenue Service, as well as by Senator Dodd's Juvenile Delinquency Subcommittee of the Senate Judiciary Committee... As Senator Dodd announced, the existing situation had been studied, by actually tracing firearms through the mail, from firms under investigation. "A.J. Hidell's" purchase of a pistol from Seaport Traders on January 27, 1963, without even a minimum proof of identification, was only two days before the Dodd subcommittee hearings on the matter opened on January 29. Sometime later, a corresponding purchase in Texas from Seaport Traders was duly noted in the committee's sample statistics.[15]

The rifle purchase is further complicated by the disappearance of the postal receipt. The FBI would come up with order forms for Oswald's purported weapons, but the confirmation of his being the only one who could actually have received them, which should have been readily available, was not. Furthermore, the paperwork in evidence can be viewed as highly suspect.[16]

Within days after the opening of his new FBI file, the opening of the post office box, and the rifle order, Oswald was dismissed from Jaggers. On March 31, the FBI began a new mail intercept program targeted at the Fair Play for Cuba Committee.

In March, Cuban minister Raul Roa Garcia sent a letter to U.N. Secretary General U Thant hinting that Cuba was interested in friendly relations with the United States.

By the spring of 1963, the administration Cuban non-invasion pledge had been obviated by the failure of the Russians to convince Castro to accept the UN inspectors who were to verify that all missiles had been removed. At that point the Kennedy Administration's secret war strategy turned to sanctioned exile leaders and autonomous exile groups operating strictly outside the United States territory. This policy involved an even more active FBI and Customs crack down on any groups or individuals operating from US or even British possessions. This dual policy of a new and totally deniable off-shore initiative plus shutting down exiles operating inside the US placed a further premium on obtaining intelligence on the unsanctioned exile outsiders, in regard to arms purchases, military operations and even political contacts.

An example of this effort was CIA case officer Bernard Barker's use of the highly visible anti-Castro activist, Frank Fiorini/Sturgis. In, 1963, Fiorini was assigned to circulate as widely as possible among groups inside and beyond the US, and specifically to report any planned exile raids or missions.[17] However, as we noted earlier in mentioning Army intelligence contacts with Alpha 66 and Antonio Veciana, the more serious and organized exile groups such as Alpha 66, SNAFE and Commandos L were very much aware of the CIA's priorities and by mid-1962 were working hard at keeping their CIA contacts in the dark as they ratcheted up their own attacks.

In the face of the often expressed Kennedy administration annoyance with the exile raiders and the officially announced crack downs on their activities, recently obtained documents reveal that the Alpha 66 and Commandos L raids on Russian targets in Cuba–with their high profile *Life* magazine media coverage–were known to JM/WAVE in advance and that no efforts were made to block them. A long time CIA asset, Alberto Fernandez, routinely reported on the movements and plans of independent raider groups including Alpha 66 and Commandos L.

It is quite surprising to find the following statement within a CIA memo.[18] "Both the L-66 raid on the Soviet vessel Baku and the Manuel Quiza raid, which aborted on Cayo Blanco were reported pretty accurately in advance by AMDENMIM/1 (Fernandez) and AMDENIM/13". These and other JM/WAVE documents suggest that from September of 1962 through much of 1963, officers at JM/WAVE and CIA headquarters were very much aware of exile military operations that the Kennedy Administration was concerned about stopping.

April 1963

In April, an organizational cross-agency meeting was held on the subject of the newly formed AM/TRUNK project, an effort to produce an internal revolution against Castro in Cuba. David Morales attended the organizational meeting. The AM/TRUNK project was heavily opposed by many CIA officers because the Cuban principals put forward as leads in the project, Manolo Ray (Rey) and Huber Matos were considered by many to be virtual Communists. Ray had formed the JURE organization and JM/WAVE suspected JURE of trying to infiltrate its own operations. Both Theodore Shackley and Morales were adamantly opposed to AM/TRUNK.[19]

In April, Lee Oswald wrote his first letter to the Fair Play for Cuba Committee, (specifically, on this occasion he wrote to its headquarters and director, V.T. Lee), in which he remarked on his having demonstrated in support of Cuba in Dallas. Later in the month, Oswald left for New Orleans.

In the same month, Alpha 66 opened a new chapter in Los Angeles and Nagell stated that this was his next encounter with the two men he first met in Mexico City. He did not state why they were in Los Angeles, but given their Alpha 66 association and earlier work in Mexico City it seems likely that they were playing a role in the new chapter, possibly monitoring for Castro agents and infiltrators.

After extensive political networking, the Bayo Russian officer story had been accepted and William Pawley had won the support of CIA JM/WAVE chief Ted Shackley for a penetration into Cuba to recover the purported Russian officers.

William Harvey returned to Miami for over a week on what was reported as a ZR/RIFLE operations trip. Harvey apparently met John Roselli as well as an unknown individual who had flown in from Chicago. Neither Harvey nor Roselli was officially assigned to any sponsored action at this point and Task Force W itself had been replaced. Documents clearly show the authorized expenses for the trip to have been charged against the ZR/RIFLE project (which recent document releases show us was authorized and funded for the full year of 1963). This trip and the relating expense report seem to confirm that the original Roselli initiative had moved to become part of Harvey's ZR/RIFLE project and that the project was still operational in 1963.

In April, Paulino Sierra of Chicago launched a major new initiative to organize all the more aggressive exile groups under a common Junta.

The Junta was to have Carlos Prio Soccares as the designated President of the new Cuban government-in-exile and among its officers were Carlos Quesada, leader of the 30th of November group and Gilberto Rodriguez. Sierra made a formal appearance in Miami in May to begin organizing in that city. This timing is remarkably close to the itinerary of the mystery visitor from Chicago who attended the Harvey–Roselli meeting in Miami.

The origins and funding of the new Junta were unclear, perhaps deliberately so. At one point, Sierra stated that he received a call from an anonymous caller he assumed to be Harry Ruiz-Williams, one of Robert Kennedy's personal friends among the exiles. Sierra apparently tried to involve RFK, or at least create the impression that RFK was behind his initiative and that he had contacts with RFK's staff.[20]

The RFK connection seems questionable on three significant points. First, there is no evidence of any series of contacts between RFK, his staff, and any of Sierra's Junta members. Robert Kennedy was very open in his personal and social attachments to a number of the exiles whom he was actively supporting in 1963. Second, the person Sierra's Junta picked to be the new head of a revolutionary government was Carlos Prio Soccares, clearly not an individual popular with either John or Robert Kennedy. Prio was a figure of the Batista era and had gambling syndicate connections that were not a good fit with the Kennedys' political agenda, which was focused around Ray. Third, and perhaps most importantly, the FBI questioned a man named Richard Cain who had been involved with Giancana and Roselli in one of the very first assassination attempts against Castro when they investigated Sierra's operation. Cain specifically stated that John Roselli was a key figure behind the Sierra initiative.[21]

Cain's statement seems to be very consistent with the details that we do have on Sierra and the fact that virtually all of the money raised by Sierra was distributed to extremely reactionary exile groups. These were groups whose leaders were most definitely not those individuals with whom RFK was closely involved in 1963, and their activities had a lengthy history of embarrassing the Kennedy Administration (specifically groups such as 30th of November led by Carlos Rodriquez Quesada in 1963, Commandos L and SNFE-Alpha 66).

In regard to the origins and funding of the Sierra Junta, at least two new documents seem to confirm its close ties and possible manipulation by certain gambling figures. A CIA document generated by the LA Division of the LAD/JFK task force provides some interesting background.[22] It relates that Sierra was first approached by William Trull in February 1963, the same month Sierra and Cesar Blanco had a meeting with Burton B. Mold and John Lechner, gamblers who said they represented substantial investments in Cuba and wanted to unite all exile groups with a view towards overthrowing Castro.

When pressed by Blanco for further references, they gave the name of Jack Lansky, whose name Blanco recognized as the brother of Meyer Lansky, the US gambler and syndicate man. Blanco also remembered that the Lansky brothers had contacts with Santo Trafficante, a known narcotics operator.

An attached background sheet notes that Trafficante reportedly gave financial aid for arms and ammunition to Aldo Vera Serafin.... for independent commando raids against Cuba. This is referenced to an "Eyes Only" 7 Feb 63 cover sheet in the AM/TRUNK operations file. Serifin was the first Chief of the Cuban National police and headed the American Patriotic Action Movement; he supported Sierra and his Junta during the time frame he was taking money from both Trafficante and Sierra. He was shot to death in San Juan, Puerto Rico on October 25, 1976.

In addition, an interview with Santiago Alverez Rodriquez on May 23, 1963, relates his remarks about a meeting with Sierra in April. In this meeting, Sierra asked him to meet an American coming from Chicago with $30,000 in donations for select exiles. The American was giving the money on condition that the group he represented would receive certain concessions in Cuba in the future. He was said not to represent the US government but to have good contacts with the government. The nature of the concessions was not specified; Alvarez felt the man obviously had spent some time in Havana in the past, was a white male about 45, 5'10", 180 pounds, well dressed, businessman type and had indicated he was from Chicago. Alvarez stated he felt the man to be completely unreliable. [23]

The extent to which the continuing 1963 Alpha 66 activities proved an intense public relations pain for the Kennedy administration is covered by Anthony Summers in the second issue of his book *The Kennedy Conspiracy [Not in Your Lifetime].*[24] He provides a detailed overview of the activities of Virginia Prewett, a Washington journalist who specialized in Latin American affairs and wrote extensively for the North American Newspaper Alliance (founded by Prewett's friend

Ernest Cuneo, a member of the Committee to Free Cuba and OSS veteran). Prewett's articles often referred to Castro as the "Betrayer" and the exiles as "Patriots", a term which surfaces in other interesting places relating to the Kennedy assassination. A number of Prewett's articles in support of the Alpha 66 raids and bitterly condemning the Administration for an "all time low in foreign policy" were read into the Congressional Record.[25]

In contrast to all the new exile anti-Castro initiatives, Lisa Howard, an ABC journalist, obtained the first extended interview with Fidel Castro since 1959. Howard got the interview through a personal introduction by James Donovan. He was the New York lawyer who acted as the principal in negotiations with Castro for the survivors of the Bay of Pigs prisoners and two dozen assorted US civilians including John Martino and David Lemar Christ's undercover CIA bugging team, which had been captured on a mission to obtain Chinese codes. The Howard-Castro interview aired on May 10. During the interview, Castro commented that an improved relationship with the US was certainly possible if Washington wished it.[26]

Howard briefed the CIA in detail on the interview, telling them of even more pointed remarks by Castro about improving relations. These included possible moves on the issues of the Soviet presence in Cuba, the expropriation of American properties, and Cuban support for revolutionary activities in the rest of Latin America. CIA Director McCone adamantly opposed Howard's approach to Cuba, arguing that it would compromise CIA operations against Castro.

May 1963

In the late April–early May time frame, Nagell observed two people he knew from Mexico City monitoring an individual in Los Angeles. The individual was viewed as a potential recruit in a planned attack on President Kennedy during a scheduled visit by JFK to Los Angeles in June for the premier of the movie *PT 109*. Nagell also implied that he might have used his former contacts in the LAPD to find a potential candidate for their recruiting, a Castro sympathizer who could be turned into a patsy implicating Castro. The candidate targeted was Marlowe/Snipes, the ex-Marine FPC activist who had a reputation for being good with a rifle. Marlowe confirmed an association with Nagell, though he was never actually contacted by the exiles. In New Orleans, Lee Oswald continued his FPCC correspondence.

June 1963

President Kennedy visited L.A. with no incident.

In New Orleans, Lee Oswald requested and obtained a passport in one day.

By June, Paulino Sierra had obtained considerable amounts of funding and by July he was passing money to all the major activist groups and individuals including Commandos L, SNFE-Alpha 66, Bosch's MIRR and Aldo Vera Serafin's group.

CIA supported operation TILT launched into Cuba with John Martino and Eddie Perez (Bayo); CIA personnel including Rip Robertson and Eugenio Martinez were among those involved as was a CIA "mother ship", used for radar screening. Heavily armed Alpha 66 personnel served as the exile element of the force.

Carlos Eduardo Hernandez was approached by Victor Espinoza Hernandez who wanted Carlos to be involved with a planned bombing raid on Shell Oil refineries in Havana. Carlos (aka "Bata") was active in the DRE and served as its military planner, however his only activity in this operation was to drive a truck with explosives to the plane - no planning, no information. He later came to know that Victor Espinoza was serving as a contact man for Sam Benton who in turn was fronting for Mike McClaney–casino operator and long time organized crime contributor to anti-Castro activities. Carlos eventually came to believe his involvement was simply a show effort to associate McClaney and an underworld initiative with himself and a known exile group.[27]

On June 19, President Kennedy approved a new NSC-approved sabotage program involving a series of missions into Cuba.

On the "peace front," by June 5, the CIA had accumulated a half dozen intelligence reports "suggesting Cuban interests in a rapprochement with the United States."[28]

July 1963

In early July, Carlos Hernandez was again approached by Victor Espinoza Hernandez in regard to another bombing raid; this one to be staged out of New Orleans. Carlos did drive to New Orleans and went to a farm that was owned by Mike McClaney's brother.

Carlos also described to the HSCA a prior meeting in Miami that occurred at a location easily identified as Mike McClaney's residence. In his testimony, Carlos again details that the arrangements for this raid were "childish" with the wrong aircraft to be used and total incompetence in regard to bombs and explosives causing the exile pilot to refuse to participate.[29]

The FBI report on the McClaney farm raid reveals that on July 15, Victor Hernandez had transported explosives to the farm from Illinois; where they were purchased from Richard Lauchli, a Minuteman arms dealer who was active in selling arms in Miami and also to the Sierra movement at the time. The report also reveals that the FBI was tipped off by an informant in Miami who identified one of the individuals who had traveled to New Orleans, who in turn provided great detail about locations and the exact materials involved. The FBI in New Orleans received this tip on July 18 and conducted the raid on the McClaney farm on July 31.

Lee Oswald lost his New Orleans job on July 19, but the same day he remarked to his friend Adrian Alba that he had found his pot of gold, and seemed extremely happy.

During the latter half of July, exiles associated with the independent Christian Democrat exile group initiative begin arriving outside New Orleans. But their plans were interrupted by the FBI raid on the McClaney house on July 31 that drew far too much attention toward Cuban exiles in the area. The exiles were returned to Florida as quickly as possible by bus.

Fidel Castro's détente-oriented interview with ABC's Lisa Howard occurred in July; in October, it eventuated in a talk between Kennedy and French journalist Jean Daniel. Daniel carried a message from Kennedy to Castro in mid-November. These feelers went through none of the normal State Department channels, though both State and CIA knew them; and both organizations reacted negatively to the possibility. This same information apparently began spreading among select activist exiles in the fall.

August 1963

Orest Pena and Dean Andrews observed Oswald associating with Mexicanos. Pena and others observed two suspicious men whom Carlos Bringuier would later describe as being associated with Mexican Communists.

On August 4, Lee Oswald wrote to the FPCC headquarters in New York City informing it of his street altercation during leafleting: "Through the efforts of some exile *gusanos*, a street demonstration was attacked and we were officially cautioned by police. This incident robbed me of what support I had, leaving me alone." The problem with his communication to the FPCC is that the letter was written five days before the street conflict occurred![30]

Lee Oswald was arrested on August 9 for an encounter with Carlos Bringuier while conducting a very public leafleting incident. Following his arrest and while still in custody, Oswald requested a Saturday meeting with a specifically named FBI agent. Immediately after his release, Oswald sent news clips to both the FPCC and the Communist Party of the United States. He also went on radio for an interview and a debate that became a major propaganda tool used by numerous anti-Communist and anti-Castro groups.

Richard Nagell related that in July, Oswald was approached and recruited by one of the two men Nagell had first met in Mexico City. These men represented themselves as Castro supporters. They recruited Oswald for an incident to occur in September in Washington DC. It appears that Oswald accepted their proposal as he began writing a series of letters at the end of August regarding a planned move to the D.C. area. These letters created a further paper trail linking Oswald to the Socialist and Communist organizations.

It seems Nagell was then ordered to either convince Oswald that he was being used or to eliminate him. He attempted this and provided proof that the two men were actually anti-Castro agents. Nagell could not understand why Oswald refused to break his contacts with them, but neither could he bring himself to take any action against Oswald. When he became aware that he was being followed and was obviously under suspicion, Nagell left New Orleans and headed towards Mexico.

By the end of summer 1963 another new Kennedy administration secret war project was moving into operation. This project reflected a major change in strategy. The new direction was to involve a combination of totally autonomous Cuban exile groups with leaders selected and operations personally coordinated by Robert Kennedy. Key exile leaders included Harry Ruiz Williams and Manuel Artime. The strategy was to give these leaders a great deal of autonomy while providing financial and operational support, under the agreement that military operations would be staged from bases totally outside the United States or its territories. Some operational and public relations support was to come from within the CIA. However, this support was to be compartmentalized even within the CIA itself, independent of JM/WAVE and independent of CIA station personnel outside the US in locations including Mexico City and other Latin American countries. Within the CIA the project was designated AM/WORLD. It had its own separate operations staff within a separate area in Miami (designated as LORK) and in Mexico City the only officer designated to organize safe houses and related activities for AM/WORLD was David Phillips. (RIF 104-10098-10093; COS Mexico City to Chief Western Hemisphere, subject: AM/WORLD safe house). AM/WORLD activities, especially the recruiting and operational activities of Artime, were intended to be totally deniable in terms of United States sponsorship or funding.

The AM/WORLD head and Artime case officer was Henry Hecksher; designated as H/H on AM/WORLD documents and serving as a special assistant to Desmond Fitzgerald. The ranking exile under Artime was "Chi Chi" Quintero who worked with CIA paramilitary officer Carl Jenkins. The AM/WORLD group was actually very small and consisted of Hecksher's secretary Mrs. Bobbie Hernandez, her husband Raul Hernandez, and Richard B. (Dick) Beal. Beal was a career logistics employee assigned to AM/WORLD along with his secretary Mrs. Gwen Thornton. Other individuals with AM/WORLD knowledge were Seymour Bolten, Al Rodrigez and Raford (Ray) Herbert (super grade assistants to Fitzgerald and individuals with extensive personal connections to the old Cuban sugar business network which had relocated to New York City; reference Appendix D). M.K. Holbick was security officer for the project.

The AM/WORLD project, the AM/TRUNK project and planning organized outside the CIA, involved Califano and Vance (Department of Defense), Cottrell (State Department) and Haig and Krulak (Army) in the new strategy being organized by Robert Kennedy in 1963. Reportedly a wild card in this planning was a covert and very private Kennedy agreement with Juan Almeida, the third most powerful official in Cuba in 1963, after Fidel and Raul Castro. Almeida's military clout placed him in a position to eliminate the Castro brothers. This secret Kennedy effort is described in detail in Waldron's *Ultimate Sacrifice*, 2006 edition. Elements of the general coup contingency planning are also discussed in *Inside* by Joseph A. Califano Jr.[31] Names from the AM/WORLD project also appear later in *Appendix J, Echoes of Dallas*). The author is indebted to the research of Malcolm Blunt for much of this new information on the AM/WORLD project and personnel.

October 1962 to October 1963: Twelve Months of Shadow War

In these twelve months there emerged an idea, an idea for an act against President Kennedy, an act involving a person with the right image; a person who could be positioned as a patsy to implicate Fidel Castro in an attack on President Kennedy. The first candidate was Vaughn Marlowe/Snipes, an FPCC activist who had been in Cuba. The final selection was Lee Oswald, ex-Marine, defector, FPCC activist.

During these twelve months Lee Oswald demonstrated a massive disconnect in his personal writings and public image. Shortly after Oswald returned from Russia to Fort Worth, he began preparation of an anti-Communist manuscript concerning his observations of the Soviet Union. He hinted to the stenographer that he had gone to the Soviet Union as an agent but during later work on the manuscript he became increasingly fidgety and worried.

However, shortly after expressing his aversion to both the Russian system and to its tool, the Communist Party of the United States, Oswald subscribed to *The Worker*, the newspaper of the Communist Party in the USA as well as to a variety of other similar journals including the Russian periodical *Krokodil*.

During the summer of 1963, Oswald visibly campaigned in favor of Fidel Castro, an avowed Communist while repeatedly stating that he himself was definitely not a Communist. During this same period, Oswald would continue his extensive letter writing to organizations including the Communist Party of the United States and individuals at *The Worker*. And in at least one newly reported incident, he made public remarks about going to Cuba and getting rid of Castro.

By fall of 1963, Oswald would be in the Cuban Embassy in Mexico City attempting to get a visa for travel to Cuba and using as reference his own FPCC and radical credentials including CPUSA membership.[32] Oswald's appearance in Mexico City also demonstrated a variety of totally inconsistent actions, presented and evaluated at length in works by John Newman[33]. Further in depth analysis of Oswald in Mexico City is available in Peter Dale Scott's *Deep Politics II* and *Deep Politics III*.

For our understanding of Oswald's true role, it is important to examine the "Oswald in Mexico City" events along with some of his other September-October activities. To evaluate them against John Martino's statements:

> (a) that Oswald was being used as an informant by an agency of the US government, and (b) that in this role, Oswald was successfully

manipulated and used as a patsy by the anti-Castro Cuban exiles who were involved in the murder of John Kennedy.

When viewed from this perspective, Oswald's activities during this period make considerably more sense. They also explain Nagell's inability to sway Oswald from his contacts with the anti-Castro elements as well as the FBI's cover-up of its own contacts with Lee Oswald in October and November of 1963.

New document releases reveal additional context for the use of Lee Oswald as a penetration agent. The FBI can now be shown to have been using credible civilians having the *appearance and other attributes for the role of a pro-Castro revolutionary,* to penetrate pro-Castro organizations, in particular the FPCC, since 1960. In December of 1962 they began cooperation with the CIA in a project designated by the CIA as AM/SANTA. This project used FBI informants to develop intelligence on Cuba and the Castro regime. We know little about the overall project but in July 1963, one such asset used his FPCC connections to obtain a visa from the Cuban government and to travel illegally to and from Cuba (apparently via Mexico City on Cubana airlines). The asset was briefed by the CIA on intelligence targets prior to his trip and debriefed afterwards. Shortly before going he had been asked to join the CPUSA. One of the individuals mentioned in the context of this briefing, CIA officer Anita Potocki, also shows up on an HSCA document apparently relating to Lee Oswald's NSA file. [34]

September 1, 1963

In the last week of August, Antonio Veciana of Alpha 66 traveled from Miami, where he was officially confined to Dade County to prevent his participation in the Alpha 66 Cuban raids, to Dallas, Texas, in order to meet with his long time advisor Maurice Bishop. As he located Bishop in the lobby of the Southland Building, he observed Bishop talking with a young man. Veciana identified this young man to HSCA investigator Gaeton Fonzi as Lee Oswald.[35] In a more recent interview, Veciana told Thom Hartmann that the purpose of his trip was to get rid of Castro and that he heard remarks from Oswald on the same subject.

This reported meeting follows Oswald's loss of his New Orleans job and his remark to his friend Alba that he has found his pot of gold. It also follows a frenetic burst of intense Oswald's Fair Play for Cuba Committee activism that included much newspaper and television coverage and finally a radio interview that made public Oswald's Russian stay and connections. This series of events constituted a major propaganda action against the FPCC and provided volumes of materials that were used by a variety of private anti-Communist groups–the most effective of which have clear connections to the CIA's propaganda specialist, David Atlee Phillips.

There are numerous reasons to suspect the Maurice Bishop reported with Lee Oswald in Dallas was David Phillips (reasons for this belief are further expanded on in Chapter 10). This identification was aggressively denied by Phillips himself and only hinted at by Veciana. However, Fonzi's work for the HSCA has been supplemented by additional revelations and confirmations. Ron Cross, a CIA officer at JM/WAVE, confirmed to Fonzi and the HSCA that he knew a David Phillips who worked through JM/WAVE to assist the exile groups with propaganda efforts. Cross knew Phillips to use the alias Bishop. Phillips and E. Howard Hunt (CIA officer and Watergate burglar) had worked together on both the Guatemala and Bay of Pigs operations. Hunt himself had used the alias Knight and was known to his Cuban charges simply as Eduardo.[36]

Jim Hougan authored the book *Secret Agenda: Watergate, Deep Throat, and the CIA*.[37] Hougan had gotten to know former CIA agent Frank Terpil while working on a PBS documentary. Terpil kept talking about David Phillips, whose politics he disliked. He told Hougan that he first met Phillips while living in Florida with the daughter of Hal Hendrix, a man whose role as a media channel for the CIA is well established (in September of 1963 Hendrix wrote a piece for Scripps-Howard about the ouster of the Dominican Republic's Juan Bosch—the only problem with the piece was that the actual event did not occur until a day later). When he would come around with Hendrix, Phillips would use the name Bishop.

Hal Hendrix was also the source given to Seth Kantor by his Washington D.C. editor on the afternoon of November 22, 1963, when Kantor was seeking information on Lee Oswald. Kantor was provided a detailed background on Oswald's defection and his FPCC activities including the New Orleans leafleting.

The best overall summary of the Phillips–Bishop controversy as well as Phillips' contradictory and inaccurate HSCA testimony is found in the 1989 edition of Anthony Summers' *Conspiracy* (pp. 504-519). David Atlee Phillips went to great lengths to deny the Bishop connection, some of them rather incredible, such as claiming to never have heard the name of Veciana—unbelievable for the CIA head of Cuban Operations. But Phillips admitted to being in Texas at the time specified for the Oswald meeting reported by Veciana; he claimed he was then visiting his family in Fort Worth.

In the larger context, a connection between David Phillips and Lee Oswald seems extremely reasonable and logical. David Phillips had been in charge of propaganda operations ranging from the CIA's success in Guatemala to their failure at the Bay of Pigs. His specialty was media, print, radio, psychological operations, and "the big lie".

Stationed in Washington D.C. during 1960, he had coordinated propaganda operations against Fidel Castro in preparation for the planned invasion. He also appears to have had a definite connection to New Orleans.

It is rarely observed that there were supporting operations for the Bay of Pigs staged out of New Orleans, including a very mysterious operation relating to the mission of Nino Diaz. This operation placed a boatload of exile troops dressed in Cuban uniforms in the vicinity of the US base at Guantanamo during the Bay of Pigs action.[38] We will likely never know the full story of this incident, but we do have a memo about a training site at Belle Chase on a Naval Ammunition Depot. The depot had been inactive for five years, and had supposedly been completely sterilized by base and Navy personnel on April 21, 1961. The training camp was entirely Agency controlled with training conducted solely by Agency personnel. A report on this base was prepared during the Garrison investigation. It described the sanitizing of the base on April 21 and is signed "David Phillips, WH/COG."[39]

A Chain of Command Chart for the Bay of Pigs operation also lists the Nino Diaz Group and shows Diaz as Chief of Training at the Belle Chase camp. Indeed this camp was even noted by the Miami press along with the major Guatemala training facilities.[40] Phillips' memo refers to the training of some 300 Cubans over a six week-period. One group was trained as an assault battalion and was sent to Guatemala on March 22 to join the April invasion. Additional documents located by William Davy seem to associate three names with Agency related anti-Castro activities in the New Orleans area: Sergio Arcacha Smith, Gordon Novel, and David Ferrie.[41]

These names are very enlightening because they connect to the removal of a large quantity of explosives and related materials that were apparently removed under CIA auspices from a storage facility of the Schlumberger Corp. These materials may have been destined for very secret use in a deniable mission staged out of New Orleans in support of the Bay of Pigs invasion, the Nino Diaz mission.

Schlumberger Well Services Company had storage bunkers at the former Houma blimp base there; ostensibly those contained supplies for use in Schlumberger's commercial activities. Jim Garrison investigated the removal of material from a bunker on this facility by Gordon Novel, David Ferrie and anti-Castro Cubans. Novel had obtained a truck for Arcacha Smith and was given a key that allowed the group enter the bunker and load a supply of grenades, bazooka shells and small arms ammunition. The materials were in InterArmco boxes, possibly surplus that had not gone to the CIA Guatemala camps. Reportedly these supplies found their way onto the Santa Ana in support of the Nino Diaz mission associated with the Bay of Pigs landing. For more details, see *Let Justice Be Done* by William Davy.[42]

The robbery of this material by Novel, Acarcha Smith and Ferrie was apparently staged in order to allow Schlumberger to claim insurance on the contents. Acarcha's attorney stated that in the end, the CIA apparently reimbursed the insurance company.

When Gordon Novel was sought for questioning by D.A. Garrison, he first fled New Orleans through Ohio and Chicago to McLean, Virginia, the area immediately adjacent to CIA headquarters.[43]

In this way Novel managed to avoid extradition and testimony to the Garrison investigation. What little we know directly from Mr. Novel comes from his legal counteractions against Garrison and as importantly, his suit against *Playboy Magazine* that had published an extensive interview with Garrison. Novel's depositions in the *Playboy* case and other sources have been evaluated in excellent research articles by Lisa Pease; these are invaluable for a full understanding of Novel and the New Orleans affairs.[44] For our purposes, the most important revelation by Novel was that he was able to claim CIA privilege – not only due to his participation in the Houma affair and various front operations pertaining to the Bay of Pigs, but also because he had attended a certain meeting in New Orleans in late 1960. This meeting was in conjunction with the activities of Sergio Arcacha Smith and involved a media project to organize a telethon that would have raised money for the exile cause; but most importantly, it was to show what

Castro's Cuba had become and create a dramatic view of his treatment of his opposition.

The initial meeting for this project was attended by Arcacha Smith, Guy Bannister, and a certain Mr. Phillips. Novel stated that Mr. Phillips from Washington exhibited a very commanding presence and was definitely "running the show." The project itself did not come to fruition, but Novel continued to see Mr. Phillips in the area a few more times.[45]

The fact that the Propaganda Chief for the Cuba project would be in New Orleans organizing a major propaganda event only a few months before the invasion seems quite consistent. That David Atlee Phillips would be aware of Guy Bannister and Arcacha Smith, who were acting as civilian supporters of the CIA in the Houma raid, is also reasonable.

September 1, 1963, in Dallas

Lee Oswald was seen with Maurice Bishop, the same Lee Oswald who had just been the main player in an immensely successful anti-FPCC propaganda operation in New Orleans, using FPCC leaflets stamped with the address of the same building that housed Guy Bannister's offices. Phillips' first operation against the FPCC in 1961 involved the insertion of one agent and one dangle into a new chapter that was being organized by Court Wood, a young man who had recently returned from Cuba. The Wood operation was not nearly as successful as Phillips' recent New Orleans effort in the summer of 1963. This month Phillips received a promotion to GS15 with a new title, Chief of Cuban Operations.

High-level US government contacts with Cuban officials were carried out using back channels outside any government departments or agencies.

September 18, 1963

William Attwood, an advisor to the US Mission to the U.N., wrote a two-page memorandum to Under Secretary of State Averell Harriman and U.N. Ambassador Adlai Stevenson. This memorandum on Cuba laid out an argument for being given permission to establish discrete, indirect contact with Cuban authorities and was the result of Lisa Howard's personal approach and presentations to Attwood.

September 20, 1963

Stevenson obtained approval from President Kennedy to authorize direct contact between Attwood and Carlos Lechuga, the Cuban ambassador to the United Nations. This contact was made during a private party at Lisa Howard's Park Avenue apartment. During the party, Lechuga hinted that Castro was indeed in a mood to talk. Lechuga's memory of the conversation is that Attwood suggested going to Havana but made it clear that he did not yet have specific instructions or approvals.

September 24, 1963

Attwood met with Robert Kennedy in Washington and reported on the contact. RFK felt the trip to Cuba would be risky, as it was *bound to leak and might result in some kind of Congressional investigation.* He did think the matter would be worth pursuing. But the initiative was pursued throughout the fall with further discussions between Attwood and Lechuga at the U.N. Lisa Howard continued to serve as an intermediary and significant progress was being made. By November, the President had given his personal approval to proceed.

September 16, 1963

The CIA actively initiated a new project with the cryptonym AM/LASH, related to the AM/TRUNK internal Cuban coup project. AM/LASH involved Rolando Cubela, a high Castro government official who supposedly was being used for his contacts with potential Castro opponents within his government. However, at the direction of Richard Helms, Desmond Fitzgerald expanded his role to include a potential assassination action against Castro.

In fact, the entire Cubela contact had been vigorously opposed by Fitzgerald's security officer, Harold Swenson, due to suspicions that Cubela might be a double agent. Cubela had refused the standard CIA polygraph test.[46]

Also in September, a CIA memorandum was sent to the FBI informing them that the CIA was considering action against the FPCC in foreign countries and that they were thinking of *"placing deceptive information which might embarrass the FPCC."*[47] The following day Lee Oswald was in line in New Orleans and obtained a tourist pass for Mexico.

In June 1964, an ultra-secret FBI source ("SOLO," the Communist Party double agent Jack Childs) claimed to have been told by Fidel

Castro himself that Oswald (touting his FPCC activities on his visit to the Cuban Embassy) had lost his temper in the Embassy, shouting, *"I'm going to kill Kennedy for this"* apparently in reference to the restrictions on Cuban travel.[48]

Peter Dale Scott evaluates this incident in chapter VIII of *Deep Politics II*, reaching the conclusion that this and other questionable reports were all post-assassination—entered into the record in order to rationalize the strange actions of US intelligence in Mexico City immediately after November 22. An alternative scenario is that Oswald's US intelligence handlers were raising the ante with a most aggressive Cuban operation, designed to see if the Cubans would pursue Oswald's remarks and perhaps begin a relationship with him. There may well be evidence of further Cuban contact with Oswald that has yet to surface, especially in Mexican intelligence files.

During his Mexico City visit, Oswald was apparently impersonated in two calls to the Russian embassy. These calls associated Oswald with a Russian named Kostikov who was known at the highest levels of the FBI and CIA to be the senior Soviet agent in charge of sabotage and assassination in the Americas. *The wording used in the calls also made it look like Oswald had some special relationship to the Cubans.* We now know all of this to be absolutely false.

This apparent Oswald–Kostikov association was the subject of extensive and anxious cable traffic between the Mexico City station and CIA headquarters in the twenty-four hours following the assassination. It suggests a good deal of confusion among different CIA groups and perhaps indicates that a security operation involving Oswald was in play and unknown outside the CIA's CI/SIG (counter-intelligence) group.[49]

Regarding this incident and its implications, Rex Bradford has written:

> This episode is important because it helps explain why men like Earl Warren might engage in a cover-up. It also narrows the field of potential conspirators considerably. In 1963 these intelligence activities were kept under extremely tight wraps. So who knew that the Embassy (Cuban) phone lines were tapped? Who knew that Kostikov was involved in assassinations and that this fact was known to the US (both the CIA and FBI)? Who knew that this phony Red connection would scare the government into a cover-up?[50]

We also know that these events were fully reported to the local Mexico City FBI staff and other US agencies before the assassination, on October 16. By October 18, Agent Hosty in Dallas had been informed of events in Mexico City concerning Lee Oswald–with the exception of the Kostikov contact and the impersonation. At the end of August, Lee Oswald was a mediocre patsy candidate for the conspirators, better than Marlowe perhaps, with more media visibility. By mid-October, Lee Oswald was a world-class patsy and because some of the most critical incidents in Mexico City were impersonations, Oswald had no idea of his elevated status.

During the next 30 days, the name Oswald would be associated with both the Cuban embassy and the Russian embassy in Mexico City. The Cubans would receive a request for a tourist visa, which they refused. According to Phillips, in a comment to the *Washington Post* that he immediately contradicted in his HSCA testimony, Oswald asked the Cubans for money in exchange for information.

Lee Oswald went to Mexico City. There is every indication his role was an extension of his performance in New Orleans, a dangle to the Cubans and Russians. This could have been viewed by Phillips as a good use of Oswald's new Cuban activist credentials and a test of the Cuban embassy. Oswald being issued a Cuban visa or given a free trip to Cuba would have been excellent CIA media ammunition against the Cuban mission in Mexico City—public relations leverage to help push the Mexican Government into stricter control of civilian traffic through the key access point to Cuba. Beyond that there is the potential of an even more ambitious project designed to get Oswald into Cuba and possibly close to Fidel himself.

What may have been promoted as a brilliant counter intelligence operation against the Cubans may have become a huge problem for the CIA on November 22.

Summary

- Lee Oswald was used as an intelligence dangle and informant by multiple intelligence agencies.

- His initial experience was in Japan and came as the result of bar girls reporting contacts, attempting to solicit young servicemen for minor information.

- At a minimum, his Russian experience resulted in reporting on the Minsk factory where he worked as well as on general observation of Soviet military elements.

- Upon his return to the United States, he was monitored in a broad variety of activities, some of which may simply have been standard security tests (his work at Jaggers) and his correspondence with various Socialist and Communist outlets, as well as with Soviet embassies and the Fair Play for Cuba Committee. It may also have included the ability of known political defectors and suspicious individuals to order guns via mail order, a test of the Post Office monitoring and informant system then in operation.

- At some point, Oswald was included in the FPCC penetration and propaganda efforts being conducted by both the FBI and CIA. From that point on, he served as a dangle to both pro- and anti-Castro elements.

- This role brought Oswald into contact with the assassination conspiracy and ensured that he maintained the contacts that led to his use as a patsy in Dallas.

- Oswald's own activities in Mexico City can best be interpreted as an extension of his FPCC propaganda role with possible enhancement as a test of whether or not he could establish himself in an anti-American role with the Cuban embassy.

A broad look at the secret war against Cuba suggests that the threat against President Kennedy was initially triggered by his compromise during the Cuban Missile Crisis and that an action against him became urgent in reaction to the Kennedy Administration's back-channel initiative towards a political reconciliation with Fidel Castro. These communications were known only to a select few at the highest levels of the CIA and State Departments, including the senior members of the JM/WAVE station, Theodore Shackley and David Morales.[51] And apparently known to John Martino as well, based on his article describing such a compromise.

This leads us to a much closer examination of David Sanchez Morales—a man known well enough to John Martino to be mentioned in Martino's own book.

CHAPTER 8

"WELL, WE TOOK CARE OF THAT S.O.B., DIDN'T WE?"

We began our study of persons of interest by looking at people who were associated with John Martino in 1963, individuals with whom he was involved in anti-Castro activities. That study showed us that Martino was indeed associated with some very interesting individuals including Eddie Bayo of Alpha 66, the legendary Eugenio Rolando Martinez (boat commander with Rip Robertson at JM/WAVE and later Watergate fame), Felipe Vidal Santiago, and CIA informant Frank Sturgis (also a Watergate burglar).

Based on remarks in his book about his imprisonment in Cuba, Martino was also familiar with a very senior CIA officer, David Sanchez Morales–a man whom we now know as truly synonymous with black, covert operations. Martino knew Morales well enough to write about his position in the US embassy in Havana, his filling a CIA slot, and even about Morales' personal protests to Washington that Fidel Castro was a Communist; protests that were ignored, according to Morales, until Castro's commitment to Communism became overt.

An inquiry into David Morales teaches us a great deal about the CIA. It also instills a healthy respect for the ability of the CIA to separate itself from its employees.

In Wilcox, Arizona, 60 miles east of Tucson, the modest burial marker reads:

David S. Morales
SFC US Army
World War II Korea
1925 – 1978

Morales did indeed join the US Army and did die in 1978, but in 1963 David Morales was Chief Operations Officer at JM/WAVE, the CIA's largest operational facility, reporting directly to Ted Shackley who was running the front line battle in the United States government's secret war against Castro. Ten years later, Morales was back home in Phoenix visiting with old friends. While celebrating at El Molino, a local restaurant, he had his picture taken by a photographer from the *Arizona Times* and gave the reporter, Kevin Scofield, a bit of background on himself. The photograph appeared in the paper and the caption stated that Morales' current job as of 1973 was: Consultant to the Deputy Director for Operations Counter Insurgency and Special Activities in Washington D.C. The article did not point out that this was a position reporting to the Joint Chiefs, but it did quote Morales as saying he had 28 years of government service and had been American Consul to Cuba at the time of the Castro revolution.

In 1975 Morales officially retired and in 1978, shortly after being added to the HSCA interview list, Morales died of an apparent heart attack. His obituary described Morales as being a lifelong foreign service employee working much of the time as a consular official.[1]

Morales' lifelong friend, Ruben Carbajal, told researchers of visiting Morales in Washington at the Pentagon where Morales' personal parking space was one of those reserved for General Staff Officers. Clearly, David Morales was not a Sergeant First Class in the Army and his service ranged far beyond Korea (indeed, there is no evidence he ever served in WWII or in Korea), beginning in Germany and thence to Latin America, Cuba, Miami, Laos and Vietnam. Details of Morales actual service are provided in Appendix B, *Crossing Paths in the CIA*.

What we knew of Morales prior to 2003 had come solely from private investigations following on a name surfaced by Gaeton Fonzi of the HSCA. It was largely the result of private detective work by Bradley Ayers, who served with Morales at JM/WAVE. Ayers' findings have been confirmed by follow-up interviews with Morales' friends by other researchers, including Noel Twyman, who wrote extensively on Morales in *Bloody Treason*.[2] What little third party information we had came from remarks about Morales in books written by two individuals now familiar to us, Phillips and Martino.

Fonzi and the HSCA made absolutely no headway with the CIA while investigating David Morales, also known as El Indio, when they were anonymously given his name. Jim Garrison had also been directed towards El Indio, also known as the "Big Indian" in a letter from Miami. The reference remained totally mysterious until private researchers discovered that Morales had been the Operations Chief at the biggest station ever run by the CIA, the JM/WAVE station in Miami.

MARTINO AND MORALES

We can confirm that Morales was well known to John Martino. Martino went to great lengths in his book to describe all the American Embassy officials in Cuba who let him down and failed to do their jobs. He gave no indication of having had any contact there with Morales and indeed, given Morales' official position with the Embassy, that makes perfect sense. But Martino took the time to identify Morales in his book. More than that, he intimated that Morales had filled a CIA vacancy and related the lengths that Morales went to in order to inform Washington about Castro's Communist leanings. He lamented Morales' personal frustration about being ignored by Washington. Of course, as an average citizen, Martino should not have known such details about Morales. But Martino seems to have known far more about Morales than the CIA would reveal to House Select Committee investigators.

Morales is discussed in Chapter 4 of Marino's book, *I Was Castro's Prisoner*, where Martino gives a very detailed analysis of the behavior of the US Embassy staff in Havana during the period that Castro came to power, up to the point where he declared himself a Communist. He describes Ambassador Smith as giving unwarranted and undue encouragement to the revolutionaries and makes other negative remarks about the Embassy CIA staff. Martino also names Earl Williamson as CIA and describes his activities, stating that Williamson was "quietly withdrawn from Havana and replaced by Morales". He then describes Morales' opposition to Castro and his unsuccessful attempts to move Washington to act against Castro. This sort of detail, published when Morales was acting as Operations Chief at JM/WAVE and the secret war was at its height, is certainly not sanctioned by CIA policies. It seems clear that Martino's book was neither CIA propaganda or vetted by CIA.[3]

Martino may also have remained connected to Morales long after 1963. It appears that Morales may have used the import-export business on occasion as a cover. Certainly after his retirement Morales became involved with a broad variety of import-export activities in Mexico and apparently throughout Latin America.

Martino was also very much involved in import-export in Latin America, in Honduras, Guatemala and Mexico. Martino was investigated by the FBI in regard to his activities in Guatemala. It seems that somehow Martino had become very close to the brother of the Guatemalan President. The FBI was interested in a possible connection between this brother and Martino in regard to Guatemalan drug smuggling. After his death, Martino's name also surfaced in conjunction with an FBI investigation of "Sud Import Export" in Mexico City. Sud apparently had Miami offices at 2323 Alton Road, Miami.[4]

In regard to the Martino-Morales association, it is worth noting that at the time Martino first began doing business in Latin America by dealing in military supplies, Morales seems to have been helping establish counter insurgency elements of the "Condor network" in the same area. Later, after Morales had retired and gone into the commodity business, Martino's business transactions also moved into commodity type import and export.

Martino's book provides the indication that he knew Morales, and that Morales was CIA staff even when stationed in an embassy staff position in Havana. Either David Morales was connected early on to the Havana casino crowd and revealed himself as a CIA officer there, or John Martino became acquainted with him early in 1963 in Miami. Given that the military advisor for the Bayo mission, Rip Robertson, reported directly to David Morales and that Robertson had initially questioned Martino on his return to the US, it seems likely that Morales and Martino were well known to each other during much of 1963.

Interestingly enough, Morales also received a very positive mention in another book, a work of fiction written by Phillips, former CIA Deputy Director for the Western Hemisphere. In Phillips' book *The Carlos Contract*, he described a character who is the best "back alley" operator he had ever known.[5] The character's nickname was "El Indio" and of course "El Indio" was also the nickname for Morales, with whom Phillips had worked in Guatemala, in Cuba, and at JM/WAVE. It is easy to believe that Morales, the operations officer for JM/WAVE and later advisor to the Joint Chiefs on counter insurgency and special operations, deserved Phillips' special description and praise.

EARLY DAYS

David Morales grew up in Phoenix, where his best friend was Ruben Carbajal. After his mother's divorce and remarriage, Morales was virtually adopted by the Carbajal family. In fact, much of what we know about Morales comes from interviews with Carbajal, who remained a staunch friend up to the time of Morales' death. All the details provided by Carbajal have been corroborated by the information in Morales' recently available personnel files and from newly available JM/WAVE related documents. Carbajal undoubtedly knew Morales very well and Morales told Carbajal a great deal about himself and his career.

In 1944 upon graduation from high school, Carbajal, Morales and another friend all went to volunteer for the Navy. Ruben was accepted and ended up in the Seebees while David failed the physical and spent the next two years attending classes at Arizona State, USC, and UCLA. He earned money from a part time job picking grapes for his brother-in-law who had an orchard outside Los Angeles.

By the time Ruben returned from the service, Morales had succeeded in joining the Army and was headed off for paratroop training. At the end of 1946, he was stationed in Munich, Germany. Although he had nothing official to confirm it, Carbajal said that within six months, Morales had been recruited into intelligence. Morales' career cover resume document states that from 1946–1953, he was on active duty with the 82nd Airborne of the US Army in Germany.[6, 7] In addition, his CIA screening background review indicates that Morales had been serving for some time in Army CIC (Counter Intelligence) and had received initial security screening for that position.[8]

We know that CIA dramatically grew its covert operations staff in the period from 1949 (302 covert operations personnel) to 1952 (2,800 personnel). Much of this growth was driven by field operations in Albania, as well as a request from SAC to establish networks within Russia to extract downed flyers and support missions in the event of hostilities.

Morales could very well have supported either mission. His records simply state that while stationed in Germany, he served as a trainer and administrative advisor, attaining the rank of Corporal.

At that time Germany was proving to be the unofficial nursery for the Agency, with many of its future "old guard" serving there in the opening stages of the Cold War. They included Ted Shackley, later to be Morales' boss both at JM/WAVE and later in Laos as well as Henry Hecksher, who would serve in Guatemala, Laos, and Japan, in a senior position with AM/WORLD and eventually as Chief of Station in Chile. German operations also kick-started the career of William Harvey, the first head of CIA counter intelligence and later head of its ZR/RIFLE Executive Action program, as well as those of James Angleton, Harvey's successor at CI (CIA Counter Intelligence) and Richard Helms, Deputy Director of Plans in 1963 and later CIA Director.[9]

In 1953 the State Department's Biographic Register placed Morales at the University of Maryland and later that year listed him as a lumber company purchasing agent. This background apparently prepared him to become a "political" officer with the State Department in Caracas in 1955. By 1958, he was stationed at the American Embassy in Havana, serving there until 1960. Morales' file document lists his positions in both Venezuela and Cuba as Attaché and Second Secretary of the Embassy, a Consular officer position in the US Foreign Service. He lists his duties as diplomatic liaison, preparation of political and economics analyses, and issuance of visas. But beneath this veneer, it was during this period that Morales became part of the very select CIA team that engineered the overthrow of the democratically elected Arbenz government in Guatemala in 1954. Phillips writes in his autobiography that he and El Indio were selected to fly back to Washington for a debriefing and honors ceremony with President Eisenhower; also present for this meeting were J.C. King and Allan Dulles.[10] It is clear that Morales was on a very special fast track, and that he would assume roles and responsibilities far beyond his cover duties.[11]

SUCCESS IN GUATEMALA

It appears that Henry Hecksher was called in as the lead field officer inside Guatemala. He took Phillips in country for intelligence work and may well have been the officer who brought Morales into the project from the Berlin station, referred to inside the CIA as Berlin Operating Base or "BOB". Hecksher is referred to as "Peter" in Phillips' book, *The Night Watch*,[12] according to Joseph Trento in *The Secret History of the CIA*.[13] It is also merits mention that Hecksher was a CIA base chief in Japan in the late 50s while Oswald and Nagell were both stationed outside Tokyo; Hecksher's Japan duty is referenced in his obituary and also cited by Trento in his book. Hecksher was also working out of Miami and traveling to Mexico City during the period in 1962-63 when Nagell reportedly encountered an old CIA acquaintance in Mexico City who was not part of that station's staff and whom Nagell had first met in Japan. Nagell refused to give a name to this individual who seemed to vanish from the scene by the fall of 1963 (when Hecksher assumed his AM/WORLD duties); Nagell would only refer to him by the name "Bob".

Although it is impossible to detail any specific activities of Morales in PB/SUCCESS, we do have further insights into some of the activities developed by the CIA as part of this project. According to a CIA History Staff Analysis made public in June of 1995, the PB/FORTUNE project of 1952 and its follow on, PB/SUCCESS beginning in 1954, included the development of target lists for political assassinations and plans to train Guatemalan exiles as assassins. CIA Plans officers compiled hit lists of individuals to be eliminated after the coup and pledged arms to Trujillo in return for his assistance in execution of targeted individuals. The CIA report states that in the end these plans were abandoned and no officials or communists were killed. Whether this is correct can be argued, but it certainly seems possible that exposure to such activities and thinking was part of Morales' experience in Guatemala.

After his service in Guatemala, Morales moved into an Embassy staff position in Caracas and from there to Havana in 1958. Upon leaving Cuba (following a Cuban arrest order for Morales/Zamka based on raids which had discovered his name on a list of those holding Batista secret police cards), Morales was assigned to the Cuba project, first in Washington and then at the JM/WAVE station in Miami. His cover history document states that in the period of 1960-1965, he advised the US Air Force and the military and police of unnamed foreign governments in investigative, small unit and counter-guerrilla activities, as well as setting up schools and training cadres. That certainly fits his role at JM/WAVE, and he does state that he worked out of Florida and Washington, D.C. in this period.[14]

THREE ROUNDS WITH FIDEL

Morales' real profession is made crystal clear by his assignments at JM/WAVE in Miami, where before the Bay of Pigs he set up the counter intelligence operations for the Cuban Revolutionary Council and prepared CI intelligence personnel to go into Cuba before and with the Brigade, during the invasion. Afterwards, Morales became JM/WAVE Operations Chief reporting directly to Ted Shackley and responsible for JM/WAVE training, infiltration and exfiltration operations relating to Cuba. Morales' subordinate JM/WAVE operations leaders included Rip Robertson (who had also served with Morales in Guatemala) and Grayston Lynch.[15] Both had been with the exiles at the Bay of Pigs where both went on shore, leading advance teams of UDT frogmen.

Morales often remarked to Carjabal that he was over the beach at the Bay of Pigs watching as the Cubans slaughtered his friends and the exiles he had helped train. Based on Carjabal's remarks and Morales' description of his own duties during that period, it appears that Morales did indeed have a connection to preparations for the Bay of Pigs. It also seems consistent that the two American officers advising the Bay of Pigs landing teams would end up working for him at JM/WAVE in Miami in the follow-on rounds with Castro.[16]

Recently, documents have become available which give us a much more detailed insight into Morales' activities before and during the Bay of Pigs. These documents corroborate Morales' remarks as related by his friend Carjabal and validate Carjabal as a reliable source on Morales. The documents include a CIA Memo for the Record prepared by R.D. Shea on June 2, 1962, which summarizes his "Interview with Dave Morales, GS-14, Chief of CI section, Miami Base". The interview was conducted in May of that year, as part of a debriefing process on the failed Bay of Pigs project. Attached are documents pertaining to the JMARC Counter Intelligence Plan and the follow-on JMATE covert action plan developed in August of 1961.

Morales' role in support of the FRENTE (the exile political group organized by the CIA to become the new leadership of Cuba) and the failed invasion involved selecting, training and operating three different groups of Cuban exiles. This work was not only to support the invasion, but also to create and deploy what was to be intelligence service of the new government to be installed by the invasion force. The principal group consisted of 39 highly educated Cubans who were trained as Case Officers, the core of the new intelligence service. They were known as "AMOTs". After being trained they were employed by Morales in penetration of local anti-Castro and pro-Castro organizations in Miami. They also prepared biographical files on all prominent FRENTE members, monitored all radio transmissions out of Cuba and screened all persons recruited for the invasion brigade. They began their screening work in November, 1960 after 300 persons had already been transferred to the camp.

In addition, four of the AMOTs were sent into Cuba in advance to report on CI targets, chiefly the secret service and police. Morales stressed that the AMOTs had received trade craft training far in excess of that given the average CIA staff employee.

It seems reasonable to speculate that one of the tasks of Morales' group was to prepare a list of Cuban political and security leaders including Castro and Communist cadre. A similar black list had been created for the Guatemala operation, although the CIA claimed it was never used to actually target individuals for elimination. A similar list may well have been provided to select "Operation 40" personnel who were to work along side but independently of the Brigade itself.

A second group prepared by Morales involved 100 Cubans who were trained as future CI officials and Civil Government Officials. Of the 100 trained, 61 were sent to the camp in Guatemala for training with the Brigade and accompanied the Brigade on the invasion. Of the 61, two were killed, nine captured and the rest escaped because their steamer, the Lake Charles, was not able to land its troops. These men had been given the job of penetrating inland as fast as possible with the troops, identifying and seizing documents and records; they were then to set up the temporary civilian government of Cuba.

In general, the members of these teams returned to Miami and resumed private lives. However, the documents make it clear that some of these individuals were recruited back into infiltration and intelligence operations into Cuba. The individuals were known to and controlled by David Morales. The CIA report also specifies that the FRENTE leaders had attempted to incorporate many of these individuals into new activities but that this had been anticipated and that security files were removed and secured by the AMOTS, who were organized as a *shadow intelligence organization* reporting to Morales.

New documents also reveal that there was a separate paramilitary effort involving select exiles who were trained and infiltrated into Cuba in advance of the invasion—for military intelligence purposes as well as more radical activities, apparently including one or more projects to assassinate Fidel Castro prior to the invasion. These highly select small teams and individual agents appear to have been managed by Carl Jenkins, long time CIA paramilitary trainer and infiltration specialist. Jenkins had come into the Cuba project from small team training and operations in Asia, including Indonesia, Singapore, Malaysia and the Philippines. Following the failure at the Bay of Pigs he would go on to serve as Special Warfare Advisor to I Corps Commander in DaNang and work with the Army Special Forces there. He returned in the fall of 1963 to work on the AM/WORLD project as military advisor and case officer for Quintero. Further background on Jenkins is presented in Appendix I, *Echoes of Dallas*.

Bradley Ayers, an Army officer assigned to JM/WAVE to conduct paramilitary training, writes of his contacts with Dave and describes him as impressive, hard nosed, intimidating and bad tempered with no toleration for anyone questioning his practices.[17]

In David Corn's biography of Ted Shackley, *Blond Ghost*,[18] Shackley is said to have fired his previous operations chief and brought in David Morales from Mexico City. However, that appears to be questionable since we know Morales was already working on the Cuba project and at JM/WAVE as early as May of 1960.[19]

A recently discovered memo from Mexico City Station Chief Win Scott to William Harvey shows that Morales was reassigned to Task Force W in November of 1961 at Harvey's request.[20] It also suggests that Morales may have had some special projects and assignments in Mexico City that we know nothing about.

In November of 1961 Harvey was instructed to apply his ZR/RIFLE Executive Action program in support of Operation Mongoose, the secret war on Castro. Harvey had been placed in charge of the CIA portion (Task Force W) of Operation Mongoose in the summer of 1961; but the assassination program that he had set up in Staff D of the CIA organization was not officially part of the action against Castro until November. Even then it was extremely covert, so covert that the officer in charge of the Bay of Pigs would lie to the CIA's own Inspector General about being aware of a Castro assassination program.[21]

In November 1961, Shackley was in Washington D.C. and at Camp David wrestling with decisions pertaining to the Berlin Crisis and was not called to serve at JM/WAVE until early 1962. This suggests that

Morales performed some special support work for Harvey as well as went on to head training and operations for Shackley.[21] Morales was already in place when Shackley arrived, and before Harvey promoted Shackley to replace the JM/WAVE Chief of Station who had become involved in a public drinking incident. William Harvey had been in charge of Task Force W for several months before calling on Morales for Task Force W assignment. Given the exact timing of the start date for ZR/RIFLE under Harvey's Task Force W (targeting Castro) and Morales' assignment, it seems possible that Morales was used to provide tactical and logistical support for the Castro assassination project involving Roselli.

DAVE'S FRIENDS

Later in his career, Morales was able to assist his friend Carbajal, who was working in Mexico doing commodities import-export deals with Mexican politicians. Morales was a big help to Carbajal as he always had inside information about the Mexican economy and whom to see or where to look for exactly what Carbajal needed. Later, in the 1970s, Morales would become a silent partner with Carbajal and Harvard Law graduate Robert Walton in commodities trading throughout Latin America.

On visits to Washington, Morales introduced his friend and partner to some of his Agency associates, including Ted Shackley, Tom Clines and Ed Wilson (the movers and shakers, along with Oliver North, Felix Rodriquez and Quintero of Iran-Contra and similar extra-legal military activities of the time). Reuben also received an introduction to Manuel Artime. Morales had received high praise for his training of Artime and Quintero in the winter of 1963; the training was on running operations as well as on UDT (Under Water Demolitions) and maritime operations. A memo praising Morales (crypt "Zamka") and the training was written by Henry Hecksher. The training was part of the AM/WORLD project (memo on Ambiddy 1 singing highest praises of Reuteman/Zamka training).[23] There is no doubt that Morales was a back alley expert as described by Phillips. He was also a field operations and counter-intelligence specialist who developed associations at the highest level of the Agency. Without a doubt, Morales' foreign service assignments were a cover for his real duties with the CIA.

Additional information has been obtained which further develops the link between Morales and Roselli. When questioned about Morales's friends, Ruben Carbajal mentioned that Morales was acquainted with the Fischetti brothers.[24] The Fischetti brothers were members of the Chicago Outfit who obtained positions of some significance by being cousins of Al Capone. Of the brothers, Joe Fischetti, aka Joe Fish, was perhaps the best known because he managed talent bookings for the various mob-connected hotels and casinos. Joe Fish was especially close to Frank Sinatra and members of his so called "Rat Pack"; he took Sinatra to Havana to meet and mingle with all the senior Mafia figures in 1947 when Luciano sneaked back from Italy to try and maintain his hold with the organization. In the 60s Joe Fish spent much of his time in Miami.

Morales' friend Carbajal confirmed that David Morales (Didi to him) was close to Roselli, and that Morales visited Las Vegas, staying at the Riviera and sometimes meeting Roselli there.[25]

We also know that Morales continued to be involved in some activities going on in Mexico City. According to Bradley Ayers, he was often "off station" from JM/WAVE and reportedly in Mexico City for extended periods of time in 1963.[26] The details of what Morales may have been doing via his Mexican connection are a total mystery, however we have one document that reveals that Phillips and Morales were continuing to work together. The document deals with a maritime exfiltration of an unnamed but key "Headquarters asset" out of Cuba. Apparently the exfiltration was being handled by Morales while Phillips was the contact person in Mexico City for information being brought out relating to the project. Information was coming via Mexico City by pouch to arrive on November 22. An agency asset apparently related to this project was also coming via Mexico City, his crypt was given as "Sloman." Sloman is now known to have been a very deep cover, very long-term covert agency asset by the name of Tony Sforza, also a long time personal friend of David Morales.[27]

Additional documents lead to the speculation that this highly important exfiltration maybe have been related to getting Fidel Castro's sister out of Cuba; Sloman is referenced in regard to that action, although it seems to have slipped to a considerably later date than late November or early December 1963.

After JM/WAVE

Both Morales and Shackley were Harvey's assets. Morales would later work for Shackley in Laos but from 1961 to 1963, he appears to have been playing a dual role at JM/WAVE. Indeed it is very likely that Morales played a dual role throughout the Secret War combining a normal military operations job with support of political assassinations activities against Communist targets. He would apparently continue the same sort of dual role when called to Laos by Shackley. There Morales was given charge of the CIA base at Pakse in 1966. Pakse was home of the "Hardnose" Ho Chi Minh Trail disruption project as well as the Palace Dog black program for putting US troops into Laos under cover of military duties for the Air Attaché. Shining Brass and Prairie Fire intelligence and assassination missions were also staged out of Pakse and it was rumored to be a key transit point for drug shipments out of Laos.

During later service in both Latin America and in Laos, Morales was working under an AID (International Development Agency) cover. Carbajal told researchers that during this period when he needed to call Morales, he was given a telephone number for AID. Morales' resume document relates working with AID as a Public Safety Advisor training the Peruvian National Police and as a counter-insurgency advisor. He describes serving with AID in Laos as a Community Development Officer and going from there to Vietnam, where he worked for the Department of Defense as a training advisor to the government of The Republic of (South) Vietnam.[28]

Following his service in Southeast Asia, Morales was assigned back to Latin America and served as a counter insurgency advisor to the governments of Argentina, Panama, Paraguay and Uruguay. This was in the period of 1971-1975. In this instance, Morales arrived in Latin America before Shackley, who was placed in charge of the Western Hemisphere Division in 1972. According to Carbajal, Morales arrived in time to support the massive CIA project of covert operations against the democratically elected Chilean government of Salvador Allende, and personally assassinated a leading Chilean general. A key general, Rene Schneider, was indeed murdered in that time frame.

At that point, the Chief of Station in Chile was Henry Hecksher. Hecksher was extremely active in trying to prevent Allende from coming into or staying in power, and one of his major obstacles and targets was General Schneider. The same Schneider who was mysteriously murdered after Morales arrived in Chile.[29] During this assignment, Morales' resume describes him as working as a consultant for the Joint Chiefs, the same title he gave to the reporter in Phoenix. We know that it was during this period that under US advice, the military leaders of several right-wing governments in this area formed the Condor coalition. This coalition involved Paraguay, Uruguay, Chile, Brazil and Argentina. It targeted left-wing political dissidents and began the era of the notorious death squads who executed thousands of supposed leftists. Given that the project used training and techniques taken from manuals originally developed and used in Vietnam, and that it was coordinated by officers working for the Joint Chiefs, it seems reasonable to speculate that Morales may have played a support role during the emergence of the so-called Condor network.

In his own resume, Morales states:

> From 1971-1975, I served as a counterinsurgency advisor for Latin American matters to the Joint Chiefs of Staff in Washington, D.C. During this period I traveled extensively throughout Latin American countries, primarily Argentina, Panama, Paraguay and Uruguay. In all these assignments I worked directly with senior officials of the government of the country to which I was assigned. In all cases my responsibility was one of insuring that US Government policies were understood and, insofar as possible, coordinated, supported and carried out.

MORALES AND JFK

Everyone who came into contact with Morales described him as an extreme patriot. Carbajal called Morales the biggest patriot he had ever known. "He didn't want anybody to even talk against the United States. I never saw a man so dedicated to his country."[30]

It's also clear that like many of the men directly involved with the Bay of Pigs, Morales felt that President Kennedy was a coward and very likely a traitor to his country. Morales expressed his tremendous anger about seeing his Cuban exile friends butchered in remarks to both Carbajal and his lawyer and business partner, Robert Walton. Morales felt especially strongly about President Kennedy. At one point while in

Walton's office, Morales noticed a small Kennedy ceramic decal and immediately offered to break it into pieces for Walton.[31]

On one special evening after approximately eight hours of extremely heavy drinking, Morales went a good deal further than that. It was in the spring of 1973, five years before his death. Morales entered into a heated exchange with Walton while Carbajal and Walton's wife listened; the subject was John Kennedy.

At some point, Walton began to talk about himself, his background, his interest in politics and doing volunteer work for Kennedy's campaign. At that point, Morales flew off the bed of the hotel room in which they were drinking and started screaming curses against Kennedy and talking about how Kennedy had been responsible for him having to watch all the men he had recruited and trained get wiped out.

Several minutes later after he had worn himself out, Morales sat back on his bed and after a minute of silence simply said to himself, "Well, we took care of that SOB, didn't we?" Not bragging, not bluster, just talking to himself.[32]

SUMMARY

When a man of Morales' rank, position, experience, and reputation makes a first person remark about "taking care of" the President of the United States, it deserves to be taken seriously, especially as Morales can be shown to have had an established association with Martino, a man who related his own personal participation in a conspiracy to murder the President.

- Morales was a CIA legend in covert operations.

- Morales was personally involved in some of the most successful (as viewed at the time) covert operations in CIA history: Guatemala, Laos, Chile, and the anti-Communist military coalition in Latin America in the 1970s.

- Morales was renowned for his bad temper, secrecy and personal projects.

- Morales bragged to his best friend about his many personal executions of leading Communists and their supporters.

- In his JM/WAVE position, Morales was aware of the moves towards a reconciliation with Castro which were being discussed at several levels within the Kennedy Administration in 1963, including within the Special Group meetings which Morales sometimes attended (he is on the attendance list for at least one meeting in which the subject was discussed in the summer of 1963).

- Morales stated that John Kennedy was a traitor to his country.

- Morales was a strongly patriotic anti-Communist and displayed a seemingly fanatic hatred of President Kennedy.

- Morales remarked about having helped "take care of Kennedy."

It seems reasonable to speculate that Morales had the qualities and respect which would have made it possible for him to instigate select exiles into action against President Kennedy. However, Morales was not the only individual working out of JM/WAVE with a recent history and motivation to incite action against the 35th President of the United States. In fact, the CIA had recruited another individual from the gambling syndicate who supposedly had exactly the right connections for just that sort of thing.

CHAPTER 9

JOHN ROSELLI, "STRATEGIST"

John Roselli enters our search for persons of interest from a different direction than most of the individuals previously discussed. To this point, we have examined Martino's personal associations as well as individuals with apparent prior knowledge of a plot against President Kennedy. The search has focused on people who can be shown to have known Martino, or those in the circles in which he traveled in 1963. While we have no documented evidence of any direct association between Roselli and Martino, we do have ample indication that Roselli was part of two separate networks in which the conspiracy developed and finally jelled.

Roselli was extremely well established within the casino crowd whose members were associated in both Las Vegas and Havana. Roselli was so well connected that he was selected by the CIA to tap those networks for resources in a project to assassinate Castro; those resources, particularly elements of the Trafficante network in Cuba, were used in this effort over a period of three years.

As a result of that project, Roselli became a very covert part of the JM/WAVE station operations. He also became a close friend of William Harvey who was an organizer of the CIA Executive Action program, so close that Harvey would eventually violate all standard CIA procedures to continue his personal relationship with Roselli. As part of this project, Roselli also became known to Morales.

It seems unlikely that Roselli himself would have been the sole driving force behind the Kennedy conspiracy, although he had extensive private reasons to wish John Kennedy gone. Not the least of which was Robert Kennedy's personal crusade against the syndicate and Roselli's exposure to deportation because of his being an illegal alien; RFK had Carlos Marcello forcibly taken out of the country for the same status. However, Roselli did have resources and assets available to influence and support a conspiracy. We will examine those at length in following chapters, but first, before we can speculate on Roselli's possible role, we need to become familiar with John Roselli.

JOHN ROSELLI, "STRATEGIST"

That was the title on his business card, a good indication of how Mr. Roselli felt about himself. For an accurate vision of how he was viewed by others, the best source is his biography, *All American Mafioso: The Johnny Rosselli Story* by Charles Rappleye and Ed Becker. It details his career in organized crime and is essential to an appreciation of Roselli's capabilities and connections. A few excerpts from this work will give a sense of his character and profession.

Jimmy Fratianno described Roselli as the brains behind the operations of the L.A. mafia family: "See, Jack Dragna respected Johnny. *He was in on everything. Johnny, you know, he gave the orders because he was smarter than all them guys*."[1] In L.A., Dragna and Roselli had locked up the racetrack gambling racket before Roselli moved into the film industry. When the mob moved into Las Vegas, Meyer Lansky led the way launching the Thunderbird. Moe Dalitz, the entrepreneurial leader of Cleveland's Mayfield Road mob, opened the Desert Inn in 1950. Both men were viewed as members of the so-called Jewish Mafia. Roselli moved from the film industry into Las Vegas affairs not long after Lansky and Dalitz. A recently released FBI document confirms Roselli's connection to the Cleveland group in the period 1961-1962.[2]

Roselli moved into Las Vegas affairs in a major way, serving as a deal-maker and facilitator. However, before and early on during his Vegas success, he also took his services to Guatemala, reportedly becoming involved with the Standard Fruit efforts to take business from United Fruit. Roselli significantly aided Standard Fruit by helping tie key army officers into the newly emerging gambling interests there and in arranging for rebel attacks on United Fruit properties at key intervals. Standard Fruit was known to have good relations with the Marcello network in New Orleans. Although obviously not from Guatemala, Marcello held Guatemala citizenship; Robert Kennedy earned Marcello's hatred by having him picked up and literally dumped into Guatemala in 1961. How Roselli himself became involved in Guatemala is unclear, but when he made his first major deal in

Las Vegas it involved investments not only from his old friend Sam Giancana in Chicago, but also from Marcello and Lansky.

As Rappleye and Becker describe it, "Roselli's work in Las Vegas was nebulous but crucial. He maintained open channels to all the out of town factions and served as a conduit to political fixers. Roselli also provided muscle." As Fratianno more simply put it, "Johnny was more or less the engineer."[3] Sam Giancana, head of the Chicago syndicate, had sponsored Roselli in his move to Las Vegas because Chicago was far behind in the flow of money from Las Vegas. Roselli's unique combination of tact, personality and muscle quickly rectified this and he became particularly renowned for his success with the Tropicana.[4] Given that the only money engine for organized crime comparable to Las Vegas were the casinos in Havana, Roselli seemed destined to become a key operator in Batista's Havana. He was employed for a time in the management of the Sans Souci Casino. As noted earlier, the Sans Souci was reputedly the former workplace of the Hernandez who left Cuba for Mexico City along with Diaz Garcia—a Trafficante employee. Both have been proposed as suspects in the assassination.

Refugio Cruz, a former casino manager at the Hotel Nacional described Roselli's visits in 1957 and 1958, "It was as if royalty was visiting." In Havana, Roselli was observed in the company of Moe Dalitz from Cleveland and at dinner with Meyer Lansky.[5] It was during Roselli's time in Havana that Morales was serving in his CIA cover position at the American embassy in that city.[6] Unfortunately for Roselli, it was Castro who diverted him from the good life in Havana. At first the casino owners were supporters and major arms suppliers to Castro and his financial backer Carlos Prio Soccares, partly for profit and partly to obtain protective leverage in the event that Batista's obviously foundering regime was overthrown.

When Castro forcefully ousted the American gangsters, first by control and then by closing many of the casinos, it was the casino crowd that took the leading role in opposing him. Before the US government took a position against Castro, before the CIA began its Secret War, and before the Cuba Project or Operation Mongoose, the casino figures were already supporting anti-Castro rebels and had put the first contract out on Castro himself.

"GAMBLER FACES QUIZ IN CASTRO DEATH PLOT"[7]
— Headline from the Miami Herald, April 24, 1959.

David Rosen, convicted gambler and associate of Meyer Lansky, was sought for questioning in regard to a plot to assassinate Cuban Premier Fidel Castro. Reportedly, eight men had been hired to kill Castro during his visit to the United States. Rosen, a mob man with strong Las Vegas connections, had been identified through information given to New York police by the Cuban intelligence service. In addition to the Rosen contract, one of Giancana's men, Richard Cain, a specialist in electronics and wire taps had been at work in Havana collecting information to use in plots against Castro.[8]

Richard Cain is a name to remember, a possible participant in the Roselli attempts against Castro and also an informant for the FBI. Cain had picked up prior experience inside Cuba by installing wiretaps for Prio Soccares.[9]

"...certain gambling interests ...might be willing to assist"

In the fall of 1960, when the CIA itself first undertook to eliminate Castro, it turned to organized crime and specifically Roselli to execute a formal contract on the Cuban leader. Numerous books examine the CIA assassination effort in great detail and the Church Committee of the US Senate conducted a formal investigation of it.

Thirty years of disclosure have given us considerable insight into this project. The following are excerpts from a State Department document — *Foreign Relations of the United States, 1961-1963, Volume X, Department of State 337 Memo, May 14, 1962*. This was a briefing for the Attorney General on the sensitive CIA operation initiated in August 1960. It gives a good sense of the overall nature of the "sensitive" (sensitive = assassination) project:

[A]pproached by Mr. Richard Bissell, DDP, to explore the possibility of mounting a sensitive operation against Fidel Castro. It was thought that certain gambling interests which had formerly been active in Cuba might be willing to assist and might have intelligence assets in Cuba and communications between Miami, Florida and Cuba. Mr. Maheu was approached and asked to establish contact with a member or members of the gambling syndicate... Mr. Roselli showed interest... indicated he had some contacts in Miami that he might use... *met with a courier going back and forth to Cuba... never became part of the project current at the time for the invasion of Cuba... no memoranda... no written documents... orally approved by said Senior Officials of the Agency.*

In the early 60s, the CIA contract on Castro, the use of the gambling syndicate by the CIA and the existence of an official Executive Action program (ZR/RIFLE) sponsored by the US Government for use against foreign leaders were among the most secret subjects imaginable.[10] Further commentary on the possible use of assassination abroad during this period is contained in *Appendix C, Barnes and Company.*

We can judge the depth of the secrecy from a staff memo; Aaron to Miller, Schwartz, Smothers and Bader, March 27, 1975. In this memo, advisor and speechwriter to President Kennedy, Dick Goodwin remarked that it was "pretty foolish" for Robert McNamara to even mention "Executive Action" as a side comment to Goodwin at a Cuban Task Force meeting with others present. For our purposes of understanding the Roselli–Morales connection that had developed by 1963, it is important to have a clear view of the origin and evolution of the Castro assassination project under Task Force W as headed by William Harvey. A basic timeline of its origins is shown below:

September 1960

Roselli was approached by a third party CIA contact. A first formal meeting followed with CIA officers in which Roselli rejected money for the job but said that he would cooperate for patriotic reasons. Although the CIA representatives proposed a classic mob-type hit with gunmen, Roselli persuaded them to use covert tactics and poison.

March 1961

The first poison attempt was organized in Cuba, very likely using Richard Cain out of Chicago as the designated go-between to Trafficante contacts in Cuba.[11] Cain's participation is further suggested by his posing as a *Life* Magazine/newspaper correspondent in an attempt to enter Cuba during this timeframe.[12] Jack Mobley, a Chicago columnist and Bob Ajamian of *Life* both had knowledge of Cain's attempt to enter Cuba. The first attempt failed. The contacts and Cuban assets for these initial attempts were identified and referred by Santo Trafficante and were part of the pre-Castro Trafficante casino operations in Havana.

April 1961

A second poison attempt was rushed into action immediately prior to the Bay of Pigs invasion using one of Prio Soccaras' men, Antonio de Varona (aka. Tony Varona) another longtime Trafficante contact. This attempt was a rush effort to ensure that Castro would be dead at the time of the Bay of Pigs invasion on April 17; the attempt failed as did the invasion. The failure was partially due to Varona being confined by E. Howard Hunt due to fears that the exile leadership would leak information or otherwise compromise the invasion. Varona's participation in the Roselli assassination project was apparently unknown to CIA political officers such as Hunt.

May, 1961

Sheffield Edwards of the CIA finally responded to a standing request from FBI Director Hoover to explain why the FBI's pending wiretap prosecution of Arthur Balletti was being described by Bob Maheu as relative to Anti-Castro activities. Hoover's request dated back to an incident in October of 1960 when Maheu, as a favor to Sam Giancana, had used CIA funds to bring Balletti in from Miami to place a bug in Dan Rowan's hotel room. Giancana had been fiercely jealous of Rowan's engagement to Giancana's girlfriend Phyllis McGuire.

Edwards had vaguely confirmed that the CIA was working with Maheu and certain of his associates and was opposed to prosecution of the wiretap case. Hoover demanded a much fuller explanation and on May 3, Edwards was forced to state that Giancana had been recruited to work with the CIA's covert activities against the Castro government. Hoover wasted no time in bringing this to the attention of Robert Kennedy, who wrote in the margin of the memo to his aide, Courtney Evans, "I hope this will be followed up vigorously," after being assured the alliance had been discontinued by CIA's Edwards.[13]

June 1961

The State Department document previously referenced lists a third assassination attempt having been made in June. It also confirms the March and April attempts but gives no details or references to participants, other than relating that the individual used for the first attempt was replaced by an alternate for use in the second and third.

Summer 1961

The Kennedy administration formed the Special Group Augmented (SGA) with the goal of fermenting a revolution against Castro. The SGA initiated the Mongoose project. Mongoose was a dual track activity. The first track involved military staff to train exiles in paramilitary operations and support intelligence gathering and sabotage operations against Castro. The second track involved CIA resources in propaganda, intelligence collection, communications intercepts, human intelligence and covert operations. General Lansdale was in overall charge of Mongoose while William Harvey headed Task Force W, the CIA track. The JM/WAVE station in Miami served as operational headquarters for Mongoose.

November 1961

Harvey was ordered to activate a ZR/RIFLE assassination project against Fidel Castro. Covert JM/WAVE operational support for such activities would have been obtained from either Morales, or later in 1962 from Shackley.

April 1962

Harvey formally took charge of Roselli and initiated a second round of Castro assassination attempts. His first order to Roselli was to cease any involvement of Giancana or Trafficante with the Castro assassination plots. In April, Harvey and Ted Shackley, the new head of the JM/WAVE facility, personally dropped off a U-Haul trailer full of explosives and technical devices to Tony Varona. In exchange, Varona was to organize contacts for another poisoning attempt. The fact that Shackley and Harvey personally conducted this operation shows the level of secrecy involved and the separation from normal JM/WAVE operations. This was an example of CIA bartering supplies in exchange for services from Cuban exile groups, bypassing the normal supply chain and accounting for the JM/WAVE facility.

May 1962

Following a lunch with Robert Kennedy, Director Hoover formally requested that the CIA make a formal response in regard to the FBI's intent to prosecute the Balletti case. Edwards responded with a memo that such prosecution would result in a most damaging embarrassment to the US government.

Additionally, on May 7, RFK met with Richard Helms who briefed him on the early Castro assassination plots and described their termination. RFK ordered that he be told if there were further organized crime contacts. Apparently RFK was not told that William Harvey was in the process of reviving the Castro assassination project with John Roselli.

January 1963

Desmond Fitzgerald took over Task Force W, replacing Shackley. Harvey was fired for independent activities during the Cuban Missile Crisis and for his personal conflicts with Robert Kennedy whom Harvey had come to detest and vocally complain about in the strongest, often obscene terms.

February 1963

According to official statements, Harvey formally closed out the ZR/RIFLE project against Castro and terminated official relationships with Roselli. Harvey had been reassigned to be Chief of Station in Rome, apparently due to the intercession of his associate and supporter, James Angleton. Research mentioned previously reveals that the project actually continued on throughout 1963 and that Roselli and Harvey continued to meet.

There remains a good deal of controversy about just how personally active Roselli was in secret war operations and about the possibility that other assassination options than poison were pursued, especially beyond 1962. Hinckle and Turner make reference to Roselli going on missions to Cuba and to his having control over exile rifle teams used in assassination missions. Bradley Ayers describes visiting a virtually autonomous exile training group, under loose JM/WAVE supervision, but from time to time being used by Colonel Roselli for raids and clandestine mission. This was a camp where snipers trained for assassination missions against Castro. Roselli himself apparently told Jack Anderson that he had obtained scoped rifles from Mafia sources but that the CIA had insisted on substituting Belgian FAL assault rifles which were in use by the Cuban Army and hence deniable in terms of US sponsorship. None of this information fits well with the known Roselli FBI surveillance records or with Roselli's testimony. On the other hand, this is reportedly an area that was going to be explored when Roselli was called back for another round of testimony just prior to his murder. The only real lead we have is the FAL rifles with which the CIA supposedly equipped Roselli's people.

We know of two specific instances of FAL weapons in use by Cuban exiles in 1963. The first is on the TILT mission, documented in the *Life* photographic record; Eddie Bayo and others are shown using FAL's. As related in *Deadly Secrets*, Pawley had told Hinckle and Turner that the CIA had given him weapons for TILT and that Rip Robertson gave the Cubans a crash course on board ship. This does seem to verify Roselli's remark about deniable weapons. A second set of photos also shows FAL weapons in use by Alpha 66 exiles. They were photographed at an Alpha 66/Menoyo connected training camp in Florida in August 1963. Reportedly the photographer taking these photos was invited in by the exiles and then ordered away suddenly when Rip Robertson showed up at the camp. Photographs from the camp show practice with scope equipped weapons (not FAL's), clearly the exiles were preparing for sniper type actions. We can only speculate as to whether or not these individuals were in any way linked to Roselli or a specific Castro assassination mission.[14]

By late spring 1963 RFK would become concerned enough about blow-back from ongoing actions against Castro to order the formation of a multi-Agency group to monitor and plan for any signs of Castro-sponsored retaliation against senior US officials or the President. The first public visibility of that planning was contained in an article in the *Boston Globe* in May of 1976.

"BEFORE DALLAS, RFK FORMED COVERT UNIT TO PROBE POSSIBLE CASTRO DEATH PLOTS"
- Boston Globe headline, May 28, 1976[15]

Although apparently not investigated or disclosed in the published records of the HSCA, the story revealed a cover-up of information at the highest levels. Specifically, it stated that RFK had formed an inter-departmental committee charged with monitoring potential attempts on the lives of US government officials. The CIA official mentioned in conjunction with the article was William Harvey. Apparently, the Senate Intelligence committee became aware of the existence of this unit based on witnesses referring to the RFK committee.

Further work by Lamar Waldron reveals that the article's author, Tad Szulc, had written the May 28 piece as well as a slightly different version published in the *New Republic* on June 5, 1976. Szulc had been influential in the concept behind the AM/TRUNK project and in 1963 had championed Ray to the Kennedys in contrast to their choice of Artime who became the primary focus on AM/WORLD. Waldron provides details of Szulc's information of *Ultimate Sacrifice*, including contingency planning conducted in the event that Castro decided to retaliate against the new Kennedy initiatives.[16] Unfortunately, it appears that this planning had not directly involved either the Secret Service or the FBI. Equally unfortunately, Robert Kennedy and the personnel of the working groups involved chose not to inform the Warren Commission of these concerns or of the contingency planning.

April 1963

William Harvey was in Miami for an official trip, which he documented with an expense voucher. The voucher is coded to ZR/RIFLE operations.[17] For a full week, from April 14 to 21, Harvey met with two unofficial Americans. He expensed calls to Los Angeles (the telephone number involved has been traced to the Friar's Club, a known Roselli hang out) and to Las Vegas as well as to a number that was likely at JM/WAVE. He chartered a private boat, despite having access to a virtual fleet available from JM/WAVE, and he paid for someone's first class ticket to and from Chicago. One of Harvey's meeting participants gave a home address on Wilshire Blvd. in Los Angeles and all the expenses were charged to ZR/RIFLE operations. One of the meal receipts lists Harvey's guest as "Mr. John A. Walston" while Roselli commonly used aliases including "John A. Ralston" and "John Ralston."[18]

Available FBI surveillance records on John Roselli lend corroboration to the speculation that Harvey was meeting with him in Florida. Roselli had been placed under both physical and telephone surveillance in 1960 and this surveillance continued for several years, well beyond 1964. One particular report, for April of 1963, describes the fact that agents had observed Roselli's car parked near the Friar's Club on April 12. Roselli was seen leaving the club on the 12th. The next observation records his car being parked in a stall near his apartment on April 23. But the next day a strange car was parked in his stall and the report notes that no information was obtained during the period from April 17 through April 24 when Roselli was in Los Angeles. On April 18, the report also advises that the Las Vegas office had not been able to locate

Roselli in any of his normal haunts there nor in his favorite hotels on the strip. Roselli had managed to elude his surveillance during the exact window in which the Harvey meeting occurred in Miami.[19]

It seems very likely that Harvey, Roselli and at least one other person were still doing something related to ZR/RIFLE in April of 1963. It would be even more interesting to know exactly who approved Harvey's travel and expenses for the meeting at a time when he was officially separated from all Cuban activities and assigned to a CIA position in Rome.

Roselli was under intense FBI surveillance related to the Justice Department crackdown on organized crime. Like most other things, this did not daunt Roselli and he constantly used effective techniques to avoid his monitors. As far as can be documented, Roselli only departed from his standard L.A./Vegas routine twice in 1963: The first incident is described above. The second is detailed by Mahoney in *Sons and Brothers*.

The week before the Kennedy assassination, Roselli made advance airline reservations in his own name. He made hotel reservations in his own name in Arizona, and he and a male friend accompanied by two women—went on a vacation. However, once at the Arizona resort he immediately left, and on his way to Las Vegas the FBI lost him, until after November 22.[20]

His run appears to have taken him into the Las Vegas area in roughly the same time frame that Ruby was sighted there. This is especially interesting because during the investigation of Roselli's eventual murder, FBI investigators supposedly came across Miami office surveillance reports showing Roselli meeting with Jack Ruby twice in Florida in the fall of 1963. These records were described to a reporter writing on Ruby but have never been provided as copies. (This incident will be discussed in more detail in a later chapter.) The meetings occurred during a period in which Ruby was out of Dallas traveling to New Orleans with no record of his day-to-day activities.

Despite the extensive FBI surveillance of Roselli, virtually nothing has currently been located on the period from August to November of 1963. The reports seem to simply be missing, the only missing interval out of a several year period. In addition, there are absolutely no reports from the Miami office, this despite well-documented travel by Roselli to Miami as part of the Castro project—a project the FBI was fully aware of due to Giancana's wire tap incident.

The FBI continued to monitor Roselli during 1964 and 1965. Roselli in turn connected with his old friend Maheu and brought in Joe Shimon to perform counter bugging and surveillance against the taps on both he and Giancana.[21] In spite of this, the Justice Department significantly neutralized Giancana in Chicago mob circles by 1965. Chicago PD intelligence reports show that he had been losing influence with his fellow crime lords for several years and they had become fed up with the attention he was drawing from the Justice Department. After his brief jail sentence, Giancana left the US in 1966 for Mexico. He no longer had a significant organization in Chicago.[22]

In 1966 the FBI broke Roselli's assumed identity and presented him with the fact that he was an undocumented illegal alien subject to deportation. It also let him know that, based on their bugging of Giancana, it was fully aware of Roselli's association with the CIA. As usual, Roselli did not panic. He simply moved back to Los Angeles, leveraged his movie industry and local gambling contacts and went into an apparent early retirement.

...A POLITICAL H-BOMB!

Roselli also reacted to the FBI's attempt to spook him with its knowledge of his illegal alien status and CIA involvement by meeting with a powerful Washington D.C. attorney, Edward Morgan. Morgan had excellent connections with the FBI and the Republican Party and Roselli used him to plant a very interesting story. It seemed that Roselli had some special knowledge of the Kennedy assassination that he now needed to share.

According to Roselli:

> The last of the sniper teams dispatched by Robert Kennedy in 1963 to assassinate Fidel Castro were [sic] captured in Havana. Under torture they broke and confessed to being sponsored by the CIA and the US government. At that point, Castro remarked that, if that was the way President Kennedy wanted it, Cuba could engage in the same tactics.

Of course, just how and from whom Roselli could have acquired such a first hand quotation is difficult to understand. The alleged result, according to Roselli's story, was that Castro infiltrated teams of snipers into the US to kill President Kennedy and Roselli himself knew two such snipers who were still living in New Jersey in 1966.

Roselli elaborated on the story as time went on, telling Jack Anderson that the team members, all of them Trafficante Mob men, were brainwashed and sent back to murder the President. Edward Morgan's first call on the story was to Jack Anderson, a close personal friend; within a month, Anderson had taken it to his boss, Drew Pearson—a good friend of Earl Warren. Pearson met with Morgan at Morgan's home and within a week he had introduced Morgan to Warren.

Warren wanted nothing to do with any more conspiracy issues and Pearson suggested that Warren hand it off to the Secret Service. They, too, would have none of it and passed it off to the FBI which determined that no investigation needed to be conducted. With Morgan's failure to leverage his inside contacts, the story was brought to public attention in an Anderson column on March 3, 1966, with the headline, "President Johnson is sitting on a political H-Bomb." Anderson, and for that matter Morgan, had not a single piece of evidence or source other than Roselli.[23] However, the column was enough to start inquiries into CIA assassination activities, moving US intelligence agencies into a defensive position at the same time the Garrison investigation of the Kennedy assassination was moving ahead in New Orleans.[24]

Roselli's intent in taking his story to Morgan is unclear since Roselli was not in any serious legal trouble at the time. Indeed it became clear later that his CIA role was no particular help in addressing his legal problems. John Roselli had immediately taken steps to notify the CIA when the FBI let him know that it was fully aware of his and the CIA's Castro assassination activities. In Roselli's biography, *All American Mafioso*, Rappleye and Becker speculate that Roselli might even have started this exposure effort at the request of his CIA contacts, generating a public smoke screen to refocus attention on Castro as the force behind JFK's assassination during the Garrison investigation rather than on the CIA itself.

Roselli's friend Maheu had been very upset about the fact that, "They were putting words in Johnny's mouth, and I was very, very peeved at Ed Morgan about that. He never checked that out with me or anyone."[25] Given that Maheu was Roselli's official conduit to the CIA, it would appear that if Rappleye and Becker are right, Roselli's move may have been undertaken specifically in support of his old friends from JM/WAVE in Miami. Speculation that this might have been another ploy to divert attention from activities in New Orleans or from CIA contract employees seems very much on target given new documents released in 2001.

Previously, we had only anecdotal stories that the Garrison investigation had been discussed in senior staff meetings of the CIA. Now we have memoranda that describe the first two of a series of CIA Garrison Group Meetings in September of 1967. These meetings were attended by the most senior Agency staff including: Executive Director, Inspector General, General Counsel, DD/P, DD/S, Roca of Counter Intelligence staff, and Director of Security. This first meeting was convened to establish a Garrison Group which would be assigned to evaluate and proactively deal with exposure from the Garrison inquiry. The group was given an introduction that included the following:

- General Counsel discussed his dealings with Justice and the desire of Clay Shaw's lawyers to make contact with the Agency.

- Roca [of Counter Intelligence] stated that he *felt that Garrison would indeed obtain a conviction of Clay Shaw for conspiring to assassinate President Kennedy.*

- The first meeting examined actions that the CIA could take before, during and after the Shaw trial. The second meeting recorded that the Justice Department had obtained from Shaw's lawyers a list of individuals they believed might be implicated in the trial.

- Executive Director asked how complete our [CIA] records are of contacts with Cubans. DD/P explained that they are adequate with individuals but not when they were with Cuban groups. The Executive Director remarked on the impressive number of contacts we [the CIA] seem to have who might now be implicated by Garrison. He said we should think of our course of action should be [sic] in the event our position on executive privilege becomes unstuck.

In that particular meeting, two records show that special attention was being paid to *the part of Garrison's story which was based on alleged CIA involvement in a plot to kill Castro.*[26]

But the CIA was not alone in reacting to Jack Anderson's column and the Garrison investigation. We now know that President Johnson used Anderson's information to prod Attorney General Ramsey Clark into certain actions in defense of the Warren Commission's findings—just as he had used the Mexico City material to force Warren onto the cover-up commission that will forever bear his name. In typical Johnson fashion, he called Clark and suggested it would be in the best interest of the Department of Justice to ensure that something had not indeed been missed in the original Kennedy investigation; not that the Justice Department had been involved. Clark seems to have initiated a number of actions based on this including convening the Clark Medical Evidence panel which certified the validity of all the Kennedy autopsy materials. This questionable effort is examined in Chapter 15. Recently released Garrison era documents also demonstrate that the Justice Department itself was directly involved with the Shaw legal defense team. The release of the Clark panel medical evidence at the time of the Garrison trial was a major blow to Garrison's contention of conspiracy. More will be presented on Garrison's investigation in Chapter 18 of this book.

In 1978, *LBJ and the JFK Conspiracy*, a very interesting paperback by Hugh McDonald and Robin Moore, was published and presented as highly factual and related a conspiracy to kill JFK that had originated at the highest levels of the Politburo and which had been supported by a pact between the Soviets and then Vice President Lyndon Johnson.[27] This book has remained something of a curiosity until newly released CIA documents that show an extensive history of the CIA's own investigation of McDonald's book. The CIA investigation included memoranda indicating that McDonald's only known CIA source was a low level analyst who had been released after only a short term of service. These records make it clear that McDonald had no high level connection to the Agency, as his book implies. His only association was by way of a photo identification tool which he had developed and in which the CIA had an interest. The documents relating to McDonald are all searchable and available though the National Archives JFK collection.

It appears that some organized effort may have been underway to create diversions and possibly apply pressure to certain individuals in the event that the Garrison investigation led to something serious. This speculation appears to be supported by an FBI report relating that in 1967 Irving Davidson telephoned the Bureau and related being contacted by the representative of an Eastern Group which was putting up a ton of money to learn the truth about the assassination of President

Kennedy. Davidson related that he had been contacted to help develop information on George DeMohrenschildt, but that he had refused and was determined to report the project to the FBI as an effort to spread disinformation about President Johnson. The FBI dismissed the incident while commenting that its files indicated that Jack Anderson's office mate (Davidson) was an unsavory individual. This is curious in that recent file releases show Davidson to have been a frequent and ongoing FBI informant as well as a self-confessed arms dealer; further investigation of his report might have pointed to the dis-information group.[28]

Interestingly, McDonald's book had not been published in 1967 or 1968. It only went into print a decade later during the House Select Committee investigation. Davidson's earlier report and remarks resurfaced before the HSCA, who interviewed him with no notable results.

At the time of the Garrison investigation, even after Ed Morgan's behind-the-scenes efforts with Earl Warren and Jack Anderson's columns, John Roselli was still not publicly identified with the assassination attempts or the CIA. That would come later.

A CHARACTER REFERENCE GOES BAD

Roselli continued to circulate between L.A. and Las Vegas. Unfortunately for him, one of his local gambling connections eventually led to his prosecution and eventual conviction as an accessory in an illegal gambling scam at the Friar's Club. A good deal of what became public knowledge about ZR/RIFLE and specifically Roselli's CIA involvement came from his lawyer's decision (without Roselli's approval) to introduce Roselli's cooperation with the CIA as a character reference at his sentencing. Unfortunately for the lawyer and for Roselli, the judge did not feel that participation in a government-sponsored assassination program against the leader of a foreign country called for leniency.

Roselli's next stop was McNeal Island prison where the weather and local conditions had a very serious effect on his health. Fortunately for him, his good friend Fred Black, a man with very powerful political connections—a business associate of Bobby Baker, among many others—managed to pull strings to get Roselli transferred to a much nicer, white collar facility until his parole in 1973.[29]

When enough information had eventually leaked about the Secret War against Castro and the US official Executive Action programs, the US Senate convened the Church Committee to investigate what appeared to be an out-of-control intelligence community. Due to the information released during his trial, Roselli was on the witness list, as were Giancana and Trafficante. Trafficante immediately left for Costa Rica and avoided giving testimony. Giancana was murdered only days before his scheduled testimony—in a fashion clearly indicating a warning to others not to talk: multiple gun shots in a circle around his mouth. At the time of Giancana's murder, Roselli was already in Washington D.C. waiting for his first round of testimony and staying with his good friend Fred Black.[30]

Roselli appeared to be undeterred by Giancana's murder. He did not attempt to avoid testimony and gave considerable, if incomplete, detail about the assassination program. While he talked at length about the initial meetings and the first poison attempts before the Bay of Pigs, he avoided any mention of the second phase of his activities at JM/WAVE or any events of 1962 or 1963. According to comments from his lawyers, what he did say had the Committee enthralled, and nervous enough not to go any further. However, when the committee finally decided near the end of its term that it had come across elements that might connect with the JFK assassination, Roselli was called a third time. At that point, he stopped talking.[31] That decision did not prevent someone from playing it safe and silencing him; he was brutally murdered before his next scheduled appearance–after Fred Black had called him and warned him that his old friend Santo Trafficante held a contract on Roselli's life and that *the Cubans were after him*.[32]

Later, the HSCA managed to obtain the records of an FBI wire tap on Santo Trafficante. The tape was made after Sam Giancana's murder. On the tape, Trafficante was heard to say "now only two people know who killed Kennedy and they aren't talking."[33]

Apparently, someone became concerned that one of the two might begin to talk after all.

SUMMARY

There is no doubt that Roselli was one of the brightest and best-connected individuals among the casino crowd and to crime figures including Giancana, Lansky, Trafficante and Marcello. His connections and ability led him to be used by the CIA for the executive action project targeting Fidel Castro. Roselli had access to syndicate assets in Miami, Cuba, Chicago, the Midwest, Los Angeles, and as we will see in future chapters, Dallas, Texas. Roselli was the man who could help make things happen–make a call here, an introduction there, get a name, find out who could be used, blackmailed or coerced into getting the desired results. Roselli was a strategist, an influence peddler, a self declared patriot, an asset.

- Roselli not only worked on the Castro assassination project but also was a close personal friend of William Harvey.

- Roselli was established at the highest levels of the JM/WAVE operational structure that supported the Castro assassination project.

- Roselli was reported to be close to David Morales both operationally and personally.

- Roselli had worked in Havana, was well acquainted with Santo Trafficante, and may have personally known some of the individuals on our exile suspect list including Diaz Garcia.

- Roselli was very supportive of the exile crusade against Castro and may have been a key influence in connecting the Nevada Group and obtaining financing from the Jewish Mafia to support the independent Sierra initiative in 1963.

- Roselli reportedly met with Jack Ruby in the fall of 1963 and as we will see in a later chapter, he very likely initiated the process that brought Melvin Belli in to defend Jack Ruby (in what was to become one of the very few significant failures in Belli's career –a defense still puzzling to experienced trial lawyers).

- Roselli used his influential Washington D.C. connections and his media contacts to help plant the infamous disinformation line that Castro orchestrated the killing of President Kennedy in retaliation for Kennedy/CIA assassination attempts.

Roselli served as yet another advocate of the "Castro did it" propaganda line—a reiteration of the same story that Martino originally proclaimed. And in the end, like Martino, Roselli also talked to someone.

When Roselli did talk, he talked about his personal involvement in the Kennedy assassination, confiding it to his attorney under full attorney/client protection. Roselli was a strategist even when it came to confession. He related his personal involvement in the Kennedy assassination to his long-time friend and attorney, Tom Warden. Warden in turn confided Roselli's involvement to his former law partner, William Hundley—who had once been head of the Justice Department's Organized Crime Division.[34] Unfortunately, we have no details from Roselli, nothing like what we have from Martino. In later chapters we will develop Roselli's possible role in the Kennedy assassination conspiracy and perhaps as importantly, in the cover-up of that conspiracy.

But that comes later. First there is one other figure from the secret war that deserves our attention. A man who was an avowed advocate that there was no conspiracy involved with JFK's death (other than perhaps some suspicion of Cuban involvement with Oswald), someone who seemingly underwent a very revealing reversal shortly before his own death.

CHAPTER 10:

STANDING THE "NIGHT WATCH"

As with John Roselli, we are led to explore David Phillips' possible connection to the Kennedy conspiracy not by any direct connections to John Martino, but rather by Phillips' own activities and associations. These activities suggest Phillips may well have been involved with both counter-intelligence and propaganda projects that, in 1963 had begun to involve Lee Oswald. Such an association would explain many of the conflicts in Oswald's behavior as well as resolve much of the mystery of his travel to Mexico. But first, we must start with the basics, with David Phillips and his career in the CIA.

THE MAN WHO STOOD THE NIGHT WATCH

David Phillips wrote his own biography titled *The Night Watch*.[1] In it, CIA Director Colby provided the introduction, stating that the book contained "the truth behind the sensational headlines of twenty-five years in Latin American history." In reality, the title of the book may tell us a good deal more about Phillips' view of himself, than the book tells us about Latin American history. Without a doubt, Phillips did view himself as standing a lonely night watch against Communism and against Fidel Castro. How alone, and all that he may have done on that watch, are matters for speculation. The challenge is determining the truth about a man who loved covert affairs and who was an actor by training, profession and preference both before and during his career in the CIA–an actor who went on to become one of the most senior intelligence officers in the Agency–leaving the service as a GS18.

Phillips was without doubt a CIA general. An officer with credentials and rank comparable to David Morales, Phillips' operations counterpart in assignments beginning in Guatemala and continuing through Havana, JM/WAVE and eventually much of Latin America. While Morales, in Phillips own words, made a career for himself in the "back alley" (e.g. Special Affairs), Phillips himself established his reputation in propaganda operations with the "big lie."

Some of what we need to know, Phillips tells us in his own book about himself, *The Night Watch*. Much of the rest is conjecture based on remarks by the people who worked with Phillips, his propaganda/media network, his political network, and his "assets"—individuals with confidentiality, legal (and in some cases, even stronger) motivations not to put too much on the official record.

RECRUITED

Phillips was an actor and a budding playwright when he moved to South America, where he felt he could support himself with writing. However, the CIA approached him for contract work because of his ownership of *The South Pacific Mail*, South America's oldest English language newspaper. His potential media cover and CIA access to his printing press appear to have figured in his recruitment.[2]

His first intelligence role, as it is for many contract employees, was as a dangle for Communist sympathizers, local Communists and eventually even KGB agents. Phillips began his contract work for the CIA representing himself as an American Communist and went on to become a master of the dangle and of recruitment.[3] On a trip back from Chile to the US on special assignment, he also had his first experience with being given an order to commit perjury. He was forced by Agency order to plead guilty on a charge of intent to commit fraud. The charge had resulted from an incident in which he presented a check in his real name, and had to verify his identify. Unfortunately for him, the identification papers in his billfold consisted only of "mint-fresh phonies printed by the CIA in a false name."[4]

Throughout his book, Phillips highlights examples of his supposed moral quandary, questioning ethical issues in his CIA assignments. But he never mentions a single example of refusing to comply with questionable orders or rejecting the assignments involved.

As with his constant presentation of himself as a political agnostic and Kennedy supporter, this ethical self-positioning is called into question by many of his actions and associations. Phillips' first trip back to the US saw his initial encounter with Tracy Barnes, a very senior (GS16) officer in the Directorate of Plans (Phillips translates this as overseas covert operations e.g. clandestine projects). Barnes recruited Phillips to head propaganda operations in the CIA's effort to unseat the elected government of Guatemala—an action that has since led to the loss of several hundred thousand Guatemalan lives—thus preventing the emergence of a leftist state in Latin America. By the time of his deep cover arrival in Guatemala, Phillips noted that *leading two lives, being two persons was becoming increasingly familiar for me.* By the 1960's, we see ample evidence of Phillips' impressive ability to handle two identities and even two jobs.

SUCCESS IN GUATEMALA

In Guatemala, Phillips' radio propaganda proved to be one of the major enablers of the CIA's success in forcing out and replacing the elected president of a country. He created the "big lie" of an opposition radio station broadcasting from the capital when in reality it was safely outside the country. He used 180 degree spin (stating an untruth as officially denied) in a fashion so as to make the listeners assume a denial meant an event was true. For example, a fake official announcement that the city water supply had not been poisoned and was totally safe was intended to make listeners conclude that the rebels had indeed contaminated the water. Phillips demonstrated such a mastery of this technique that he was among a very select group presented to President Eisenhower after the success of PB/SUCCESS.[5] His success also gained him the ongoing support of well placed Agency advocates such as Tracy Barnes and later Desmond Fitzgerald. As the CIA's first major political success, both Guatemala and David Phillips became legends within the Agency.

Among the group flying back from Guatemala to a hero's welcome was another operative who would go on to become one of Phillips' most frequent CIA co-workers, proceeding afterwards to assignment in Havana, Cuba. Both men would be there during the Castro revolution, both would make contacts with anti-Castro Cubans in Havana and both would leave Cuba to take their next assignments in support of the Cuban project which would end in disaster at the Bay of Pigs.

David Sanchez Morales, the ultra-secret "shadow warrior" whose tombstone shows him to have been only a NCO in the Army, is identified only three times in print. Once by David Phillips in his biography, where he mentions him only as "El Indio", and again in Phillips' fictional work, *The Carlos Contract*. The third identification was by our primary person of interest, John Martino. In the chapter on Morales, we noted Martino's friend in the Latin American import-export business was described as a retired CIA officer. A DEA report circa 1973 stated that Martino had visited Guatemala where he had some politically influential friends. Given Martino's lack of personal experience in Latin America, this suggests that he may well have received an introduction from one or more of his CIA friends who had been so successful earlier in Guatemala.

OUR MAN IN HAVANA

David Phillips' description of his activities while under deep cover in Havana contains little detail. However, he does mention a special assignment where he made contact with an anti-Castro group plotting against the new Castro regime. In this contact, Phillips suggests he *used both a false identity and a disguise.* Antonio Veciana, knew the man who approached him in Havana and worked with him in anti-Castro projects over a period of almost two decades only under the name of Maurice Bishop.

New information may reveal more about the special assignment mentioned in Phillip's book as well as how he could have come to focus on Veciana as a contact. In early 1960, Veciana had approached the CIA (contact crypt Olien) with a proposal for a plot to *"wipe out"* Prime Minister Castro and his top aides. The memo disclosing this information also relates that Veciana worked for Julian Lobo's bank. We now know that Lobo, his New York connections and his contact to Alberto Fernandez and Unidad were all key CIA contacts for intelligence into the early counter-revolutionary activities against Castro; we also know that Lobo was among those providing start up funds for Veciana's Alpha 66 group. This information suggests that Phillips may have been targeted on Veciana due to Veciana's own offer to the CIA to eliminate Castro. [6] Veciana's relationship to Phillips apparently became so close that Veciana refused to identify Phillips for the HSCA, later admitting to both Gaeton Fonzi and Anthony Summers that he would never have done so without talking with Phillips first and receiving his permission.

Phillips also became good friends with Paul Bethel. During his time in Cuba, Bethel was a US AID employee (See Chapter H, "Volski document" www.larry-hancock.com.) handling public relations. He and Phillips both participated in amateur theatricals in Cuba. Later, Bethel apparently became a key part of the media and political network that would represent one of David Phillips' major achievements in anti-Castro propaganda. Bethel's own politics were right-wing and "Red Menace" oriented. Paul Bethel had worked on a trial basis for JMWAVE from October – December, 1961 as a writer and analyst on Cuban press and press plans. He was released when JMWAVE determined that his contributions did not justify his $1,000 per month salary (after leaving USAID upon his return to Miami, Bethel was employed on a trial basis by JMWAVE from Oct-Dec of 1961).

Bethel was only one of Phillips associates who seem to have held aggressively conservative political agendas—friends with whom the supposedly apolitical Phillips established strong bonds. Phillips' friends included Claire Booth Luce of the Luce magazine empire and Gordon McLendon, founder of national radio and movie chains. Claire Booth Luce, once ambassador to Italy, was not known for her restrained remarks, once remarking that Vietnamese Buddhist monks who died in flames had "made a good deal for themselves" by assuring their own sainthood.

Claudio Accogli, in his book *Kennedy e il centro-sinistra,*[7] points out that Claire Boothe Luce, US ambassador to Italy during 1953-1956, was known to have been heavily involved in covert anti-Communist political maneuvers in Italy, as were local CIA personnel. With no-holds barred political activism and heavy spending (including the support of the SIFAR/Italian Army Secret Service, the same Service which would later identify Oswald's Carcano carbine as "unique in the world with that serial number"), Luce and the CIA managed to block the probable takeover of the center-left governments, an alliance between Christian Democrats (DC) and the Socialist Democratic party (PSI).

Mrs. Luce's views are also illustrated by her remark that President Kennedy had "put Bobby in control of the US secret police–the FBI."[8] Strangely enough, Drew Pearson once described Luce as a fighting, intelligent liberal. As we have seen, Pearson and Anderson also went to great lengths to propagate Roselli's "Castro blowback" disinformation story and to use their media clout to present Roselli as a patriot for his Mongoose program activities.

In *The Night Watch*, Phillips narrated numerous occasions on which he had decided to leave the CIA in his early years. But each time it seems he was offered a project, a position, or a promotion that kept him in place. This happened again after his departure from Havana when he and all officers who have recently served in Havana were recruited for the new Cuba project. Offered the propaganda shop, Phillips felt he could not refuse and within hours found himself among a select few in a Cuba project kick-off meeting with Allen Dulles, the head of the CIA.

THE CUBA PROJECT

Phillips' book suggests that his Cuba Task Force activities were largely built around establishing yet another virtual radio station. However, in this instance we have enough third party information to appreciate that he significantly understated his actual roles in his own biography. Phillips' major task actually involved leveraging the anti-Castro exile groups, their activities and their information from Cuba into a media campaign targeted both towards Cuba and to the exiles within the United States who were needed as recruits for the invasion force that the Cuba project eventually required. Phillips established strong connections within the Cuban Revolutionary Council and personally dictated press releases to go out over its officers' names (using Lem Jones Associates, a New York City public relations firm). In fact when E. Howard Hunt resigned his position, due to his aversion for the leftist politics of certain CRC leaders, Hunt went to work for David Phillips.[9]

Three examples help to demonstrate the range of Phillips' Cuban Project activities while assigned to WH/4/Propaganda in Washington. These examples are very consistent with what we know to have been CIA tasks as designated by the Special Group Augmented assigned to oversee and coordinate the Cuban Project at the Executive level. The tasks assigned to CIA in this planning included:

Political Task #5: *Assure optimum value from CRC (Cuban Revolutionary Council) and refugee groups in the United States.*
Intelligence Task #16: *Collection of psychological information from Cuba and third countries.*

Psychological Task #9: *Ready the "Voice of Cuba" and develop propaganda based in "local events simulating a location in Cuba but actually located offshore."*[10]

Each of the following examples illustrates how Phillips was personally and operationally involved in these activities in Washington, D.C., in Miami, and elsewhere. The first example is indicated by a simple reference in a summary report on Bernard Barker's activities. It notes that Phillips needed to be informed concerning problems relating to Miami safe-houses and their administration. Additional administrative help was being assigned. Without this simple note, we would not know that Phillips was involved with details down to the level of operating the Cuban exile safe-houses in Miami.[11]

The second example further shows the scope of Phillips' interests and activities. During 1961 the Fair Play for Cuba Committee (FPCC) was viewed by the CIA and FBI as a major vehicle for Communist advocacy, not only in the United States but also in Latin America. The FPCC was also suspected of being an infiltration channel due to its sponsorship and advocacy of student travel to and from Cuba. In what appears to have been equal parts counter intelligence and propaganda, the CIA initiated a program to dangle a student into the FPCC, encouraging the student to use the cover of being interested in starting a new FPCC chapter. This action occurred within the three months before the Bay of Pigs. It involved Western Hemisphere and CIA Security Office use of an Agency employee who knew Court Wood, a student recently returned from Cuba. Conveniently, this employee worked for WH/4 and the WH man supervising the operation was Phillips.[12] In fact, it appears that at this early stage, Phillips was in charge of both counter-intelligence and propaganda efforts targeting the FPCC, successfully manipulating a young man who was in the process of organizing an FPCC chapter and tracking activities to illegally travel to and from Cuba.

Of course, this sort of action might have been considered illegal under the charter of the CIA (as a domestic covert operation targeting US citizens), but it continued from February though July of 1961. Phillips was removed from the project only when the FBI found out about the operation and claimed it as part of its own new (legal) project targeted against the FPCC.[13] FPCC chapters in Newark, Chicago and Miami were infiltrated by the FBI, which routinely conducted break-ins and mail monitoring at FPCC offices.

Some of Lee Oswald's FPCC correspondence seems to have come into FBI hands in that manner and had to be disguised by referring to confidential informants rather than breaking and entering. It appears that FBI procedure sometimes required reporting information obtained through bag jobs, wire taps or mail intercepts as originating with unnamed informants.

During and after the Bay of Pigs, Phillips was running a counter-intelligence operation against the FPCC, not just worrying about radio propaganda and leaflet drops as *The Night Watch* implies. And he was not just working in D.C. and Miami.

Phillips and New Orleans

But even before that, Phillips had apparently been active in both Miami and New Orleans using the Cuban Revolutionary Council activities as a tool to generate propaganda against Castro. In New Orleans, the Council operated under the leadership of Sergio Arcacha Smith. Smith was heavily involved in fundraising and the recruiting of young Cubans for the upcoming invasion. The New Orleans area also contained a very important exile training camp in 1961. The Belle Chasse Camp provided military training, including explosives and demolitions. It also served as the staging point for the Nino Diaz mission into Cuba in support of the Bay of Pigs invasion.

The CIA exile training in the New Orleans area is confirmed by a recently declassified CIA memo titled "Garrison Investigation: Belle Chasse Training Camp."[14] The camp is described as opening on February 12, 1961, at the Belle Chasse Naval Ammunition Depot that had been inactive for five years at the time. The memo states that approximately 300 Cubans were trained there over a six-week period. The only known list of trainees was available at headquarters but had not been located. Training consisted of weapons firing, demolition, guerilla warfare, communications, UDT (Underwater Demolitions Training for frogmen), etc. One group was trained as a strike force assault battalion and was sent to Guatemala on March 22, 1961, to join the Bay of Pigs invasion force. The author of the memo adds that "the training camp was entirely Agency controlled and the training was conducted by Agency personnel."

Although Phillips apparently could not find the trainee list, we now have a good idea as to the identity of one individual trained and expelled from the Belle Chasse camp. It's a name known to us already– Victor Hernandez. The CIA Inspector General's report describes contacts between Victor Espinoza Hernandez and the INS, FBI and CIA. These contacts concerned his friend Rolando Cubela (AM/LASH). However, on page 105 we find the following remarks about Victor Hernandez: "... a former MP trainee who was terminated as a malcontent on 20 March 1961..." On page 131, in a section about the training of Cubans for small team insertion, the report describes their being trained in various camps in Guatemala and Panama until they ended up in New Orleans:

> The morale of the remaining trainees was low and their anger was high. This caused a great many problems in New Orleans. Some of these men had been held in five different camps over a ten-month period. On March 30, about three weeks before the invasion, the remainder of the group of about 20 who were transferred to Miami and turned loose, were described as a collection of spoiled individuals distinguished by bad conduct.

This information about the CIA training camp outside New Orleans provides further corroboration for Orest Pena as a source. Pena had described knowing exiles that had been brought into the area by the CIA for training prior to the Bay of Pigs. The author of the training camp memo was Phillips.[15]

As discussed in future chapters and in Appendix E, *Student Warrior*, details from Victor Hernandez's own HSCA testimony suggests that these CIA reports were very probably a cover for individuals assigned to invasion support missions relating to Operation 40. Hernandez speaks of being removed to a safe house in New Orleans and then being sent on to Cuba but not having the chance to land. New documents provided by researcher Malcolm Blunt confirm that Sanjenis, the individual in charge of Operation 40, was actually the number one exile in the AMOT organization trained and prepared by David Morales.[16] The CRC was actively recruiting in New Orleans while the brigade was being formed. The local CRC head was Sergio Arcacha Smith; Guy Bannister had helped Smith find space in the building that contained Bannister's own offices, and he had been conducting background checks for Smith's student CRC recruits.[17] Another individual involved with Smith and Bannister was Gordon Novel, previously mentioned in discussion of the Houma incident.

Novel described his first meeting with Phillips in a sworn deposition during the Garrison investigation. The meeting was in late 1960; Ed Butler had recently introduced Novel to Guy Bannister and some of his associates. Butler was in the process of organizing an anti-Communist propaganda and media effort to be known as INCA, the Information Council of the Americas. Butler was both a CIA informant and asset; it is very likely that both he and INCA were to become a significant part of the media/propaganda network being developed by David Phillips. Arcacha Smith had invited Gordon Novel to a meeting in Guy Bannister's office. The attendees as sworn by Novel included "Mr. Bannister, Mr. Arcacha Smith and Mr. Phillips." Phillips was "running the show," he "was from Washington," and he was interested in organizing a telethon. "The idea was to raise money and to show what Castro's Cuba was like at the time, especially the Isle of Pines. Mr. Phillips seemed to be reading from a typewritten sheet covering topics." The telethon idea didn't come to fruition; there may not have been enough time given the approaching invasion, but Novel did see Phillips once or twice later in New Orleans as Phillips was coming out of the Federal Building."[18]

In summary, it seems that in addition to radio broadcasts, Phillips' Cuban Project assignment led him into activities involving domestic-counter intelligence dangles against the FPCC and into the exile community of New Orleans. It involved him with some individuals whose names would become familiar during the Garrison investigation and Shaw trial.

Connections such as these go a long way toward explaining the extreme concern of the CIA over the Garrison investigation and the Clay Shaw trial. They help explain the Agency's and the Justice Department's active but covert activities against the investigation and perhaps they also explain the following remarks from the minutes of the CIA Garrison Investigation Team meeting number two:

> Executive Director asked how complete our records are of contacts with the Cubans. DD/P explained they are adequate where contacts were with individuals but not when they were with Cuban groups. The Executive Director remarked on the

impressive number of contacts we seem to have who might now be implicated by Garrison.

The CIA man with the Cuban groups is often thought of as E. Howard Hunt, although Hunt ended up working for Phillips in Miami. The CIA had a good paper trail on agency exile penetration/intelligence assets like Barker and Fiorini/Sturgis who operated out of JM/WAVE. However, group contacts were often for propaganda purposes and sometimes they seem to reveal the fine hand of David Phillips–despite Phillips' reputation inside the CIA for "keeping his fingerprints" off his operations.[19] It's possible to get a feeling for how obscure CIA-Exile connections were from the following examples:

> FBI Memorandum – Subject: Anti-Fidel Castro Activities; Internal Security – Cuba 12/22/61.

> On 12/21/61, Central Intelligence Agency (CIA) Headquarters advised it was financing Sergio Rojas, former Cuban Ambassador to Great Britain who was engaged in this type of Anti-Castro propaganda (leaflet drops over Cuba) and that Rojas could have engineered the 12/17/61 leaflet dropping without CIA's cognizance since CIA does not oversee his detailed activities. CIA had previously advised in October 1961, that it was financing Rojas and that Rojas and his associates were responsible for the leaflet dropping over Camaguey in October 1961. CIA noted, however, that it was not involved in this particular operation and did not know it was to take place.

Carlos Hernandez, in HSCA executive testimony, described his relations with Americans who contacted him in his position with the DRE. He remarked that the DRE was getting CIA money for propaganda but not for military purposes. He characterized many of his contacts with the following remark: "We were dealing with people that we didn't know what agency they belonged to and we never learned their real names."

A HSCA summary document on E. Howard Hunt's personnel file states that Phillips was the man in contact with the DRE. Interestingly enough, the HSCA showed Carlos Hernandez a photo of Phillips (whom he apparently did not recognize, at least for the record) and inquired as to whether he had ever had any contact with Morales, aka

El Indio. The HSCA had reason to be interested in undocumented exile group contacts of both Phillips and Morales.

We know that Phillips had staff members at JM/WAVE who did project work for him and may have served as "cut-outs" or surrogates in much of the propaganda work and intelligence collection from the groups.[20] One of his assistants in Miami, Ron Gupton, told Fonzi that *Phillips was actually in charge of two sets of operations*. Phillips' operation in Miami was at least partially run by Gupton who kept Phillips fully informed. Gupton described keeping in touch by telephone and cable but remarked that Phillips visited Miami "quite often."[21]

MEDIA REACH

David Phillips relates one of his propaganda efforts in support of the Bay of Pigs invasion. He was tasked with having the world conclude that the planes bombing Cuban airstrips were actually defectors from the Cuban Air Force who used the planes to attack their own installations. Phillips calls it an incredible charade. He remarked that when specially prepared and marked B-26's were flown into Miami (carefully peppered with machine gun bullets to make it look as if they had been under fire in the bombing raids), one Miami newsman noted that one of the planes had its machine guns covered with tape. The CIA planes based in Nicaragua had their barrels covered to keep out dust. But the first stories out of Florida still generally accepted the deception that Castro pilots had blasted their own air force in a blow against Castro before defecting! This seems to be another characteristic Phillips' understatement. He omits the fact that reporters had also noticed that the planes' bomb racks were corroded and that the Plexiglas noses were clear rather than opaque as were those on Castro's planes.

In reality, Phillips had an ace in the hole with the Miami media community, a hole card that he definitely did not describe. The extent of his influence and disinformation stands out in an April 15, 1961 *Miami News* article by Hal Hendrix, which authoritatively stated:

> "It has been clearly established now that there will be no mass invasion against Cuba by the anti-Castro forces gathered at bases in Central America and this country. The News has stated this for several months."[22]

It certainly appears that Phillips had developed his own network of media contacts that were well positioned to ensure the CIA version of Cuban events got maximum media coverage. The core of his captive media network appears to have been Hal Hendrix. Fortunately for Hendrix, his pre-invasion pitfall was eclipsed by the fact that his "coverage of the Bay of Pigs invasion seemed to be deeper and more detailed than [that of] any other journalist."[23] Hendrix went on to garner a Pulitzer for his very well informed reporting of the Cuban Missile Crisis and by 1963 was covering Latin America for the Scripps-Howard News Service. We now know that Hendrix's inside information originated with the CIA.

In the case of the missile crisis, it had come direct from the head of JM/WAVE, Ted Shackley. Hendrix's CIA connections were well known to the insiders, in fact William Pawley introduced the managing editor of the *Miami Herald* to Shackley after pointing him out in a restaurant and identifying Shackley as the man who had fed information to Hendrix.[24] Interestingly, Antonio Veciana had also remarked that his advisor Mr. Bishop had referred him to Bethel as a good media outlet in Miami.

A good example of this inside connection appears to have occurred in September of 1963. Hendrix wrote a detailed story on the coup against Juan Bosch in the Dominican Republic, which would be Phillips' new station in 1964. But Hendrix's story was filed *the day before* the coup, suggesting his sources were actually within the CIA and not on the street. Seth Kantor (a Scripps-Howard writer) noted that Hendrix's intelligence connections were so obvious that he was referred to as "the spook" within the Scripps-Howard D.C. office. Hendrix appears to have had a general relationship as a resource for the Agency and a personal connection to Phillips as well. According to CIA agent Frank Terpil, who was living with Hendrix's daughter in Miami, he frequently met Hendrix in company with Phillips in the latter's "Maurice Bishop" persona.[25]

Hendrix further exposed his agency relationship in 1970. While on assignment in Chile, he sent a memo to an ITT executive with highly confidential information regarding Salvador Allende. Phillips was in charge of the CIA anti-Allende project at the time. When questioned under oath as to how he had obtained such information, Hendrix told a Senate committee his source was as a Chilean friend. Three years later, a CIA cable was discovered which proved that Hendrix's actual source was a CIA officer. The memo also indicated that the CIA knew Hendrix was going to lie to the Senate committee.

Hendrix was supportive of CIA agendas for well over a decade, from Miami to South America, but he and David Phillips were often at odds with the Kennedy Administration and the President. Hendrix's own agenda can be seen in a November 1963 story containing quotations that he attributed to unnamed Cuban escapees. The story described the success of spontaneous Cuban sabotage efforts "which increase Castro's inability to cope with Communist Cuba's steady economic disintegration." He continued, "considerably more could be done to make life increasingly miserable for Castro if infiltration and raiding parties were not harassed by both British and United States authorities." This was written at a time when the Administration, the Special Group, and supposedly JM/WAVE were doing everything in their power to shut down independent exile actions, and receiving extensive media criticism for this policy from all the elements of the Luce-Phillips media network.[26]

Seth Kantor's interest in Hal Hendrix began on November 22, 1963. Kantor called his home office at Scripps-Howard after the arrest of Lee Oswald and was told that his best source of information on Oswald would be Hal Hendrix in Miami. When Kantor contacted Hendrix he found that the latter had a wealth of information on Oswald's time in Russia, his connection with the Fair Play For Cuba Committee and all the details of Oswald's activities in New Orleans including the radio debate. Although New Orleans was not on Hendrix's Latin America beat, it seems that for some reason his sources had kept him fully briefed on Lee Oswald. *In fact, Hendrix had immediately contacted Scripps-Howard after the assassination and made them aware that he had Oswald's background for anyone who might need it.*

Hendrix was only one cog in the CIA media network that was developed in the early 60s. The anti-Communist media that Phillips could reach stretched from Hendrix and Scripps-Howard to influential editorialists such as Virginia Prewett in Washington, D.C. and, via Claire Booth Luce and her husband, the entire Luce owned *Time-Life* network. An outline of the network can be seen in the more well known members of the Citizens' Committee to Free Cuba founded and led by Paul Bethel, Phillips' old friend from Havana. The Citizens' Committee to Free Cuba included William Pawley (of the Bayo-Pawley mission), Claire Booth Luce (of the *Life* sponsored and front-page featured

Alpha 66 raids against Russian targets in Cuba), Hal Hendrix, Virginia Prewett and Ernest Cuneo of the North American Newspaper Alliance. Cuneo, an OSS veteran had also served as an unregistered agent for the Chinese Nationalist government and was well-connected to Drew Pearson. The politics of all these individuals was aggressively anti-Castro and anti-Communist. They are probably best summarized in a book which Bethel wrote in 1969 entitled *The Losers*, a book which identified John Kennedy, Robert Kennedy and Martin Luther King, as well as certain State Department and CIA personnel as facilitating the Communist agenda.[27]

Given Bethel's friendship with Phillips it seems reasonable to speculate that Bethel and the Committee to Free Cuba more accurately reflect Phillips' personal politics than do his liberal declarations in *The Night Watch*. Phillips' brother, James, claimed David was actually "extremely critical of JFK and of his policies."[28]

And according to *The Night Watch*, the day of the Bay of Pigs invasion was the "worst day" of Phillips' life. He went home, got drunk and spent hours alternating between being sick and sobbing. For once, Phillips did not understate an event—the failure at the Bay of Pigs obviously affected him as strongly as it did David Morales, who would curse John Kennedy the rest of his life while talking about his good friends dying on the beach.

After the Bay of Pigs, Phillips became head of Cuban operations in Mexico City.

INTELLIGENCE WARS IN MEXICO CITY

In *The Night Watch*, Phillips clearly described his role and duties in Mexico City. "Each intelligence service in Mexico City plays the cat-and-mouse game of trying to infiltrate the other's organization." This ranged from what Phillips describes as very aggressive monitoring of telephone calls, bugging of facilities, photography of visitors and staff at the Cuban embassy to monitoring the Soviets. In addition, Phillips describes spending considerable time on anti-Castro propaganda and also becoming very familiar with Secret Service procedures during the visit of President Kennedy to Mexico City.[29]

Phillip's activities in 1962 and 1963 can be best understood in terms of the role of the Mexico City CIA mission. The following is excerpted from a synopsis of activities at the Mexico City station:

> The Mexico City station devoted a major part of its time to running or supporting operations against Cuba; 47 percent of its cable traffic concerned Cuban operations....WH Division assigned top priority to recruiting agents in place in Cuba, and Mexico City station not only ran its own operations but supported the tentative plans of other stations. The variety and volume of technical operations created a heavy workload managing safe-houses, listening posts, and vehicles. For photography alone the station had six base houses commanding the entrances to target embassies, two mobile photo-surveillance trucks and three agents trained in photo-surveillance on foot (this could certainly support SA Hosty's information from Mexico City about photo surveillance of Oswald outside the Cuban and Soviet embassies). It was such projects that provided information on the visits of Lee Harvey Oswald, President Kennedy's assassin, to the Cuban and Soviet Embassies....[30]

Phillips also describes having his job changed in 1963 at the personal behest of Desmond Fitzgerald, the new CIA Chief of Cuban Operations. Phillips states that one of his major tasks was monitoring the Cuban Embassy in Mexico City; beyond that, his remarks are relatively general and discuss relatively minor incidents. He does mention the appearance of Lee Oswald in Mexico City but dismisses Oswald as only one more blip on the station's radar screen. He reports in his book that CIA staff monitored Oswald's contact with the Soviet Embassy but that it took days for Washington to be queried about the incident because it was so minor.

One of the long standing issues in regard to Oswald's visits to the Cuban and Soviet embassies has been the total absence of surveillance photographs of Lee Oswald obtained from either location. A variety of innocent explanations have been offered for this including one that equipment covering the Cuban embassy was not in operation in September and October.[31] However, a recently released FBI memo seems to suggest something much more suspicious behind the lack of photos. Early in 1964 the FBI was continuing to explore reports that Oswald had been seen inside and outside the Cuban embassy, in contact with suspicious Cubans or others and very possibly receiving payment or orders for some act against President Kennedy. The FBI went to the CIA in an effort to verify if one informant, Pedro Gutierrez Valencia, had indeed been in the Cuban embassy as he asserted. The FBI received a response from the CIA, from David Phillips.

In this response Phillips asserted that CIA could not substantiate Valencia as visiting the embassy—not because they did not have photos for the period in question *but rather because their coverage and files were so complete they could assure that he had not been there!*

Phillips cites Allen White, A/IC as giving the opinion that if he had indeed been there the CIA equipment would definitely have photographed him as the equipment was in full operation during daylight hours of September 30 through October, 4, 1963. CIA made available to the FBI photos from September 27 (a confirmed date for one Oswald visit to the Cuban embassy; a telephonic intercept also places him making a call from the Cuban embassy on September 28) and October 9 of individuals which contained a vague resemblance to Valencia. They also provided an additional 20 photographs of possible Americans photographed by the CIA at the Cuban Embassy during the period of September and October, 1963.

According to Phillips and White, as of February 1964 they had been able to consult the complete set of photo files from September and October of 1963 and were unable to identify Valencia as "visiting the Cuban embassy of September or October 1963". No qualifications or mention of equipment problems or routinely shredded photos is mentioned—leading to one rather obvious question: If the files and coverage were good enough to exclude Valencia as a visitor, why were there no photos available capturing Oswald's multiple entrances and exits during the period of September 27 through October 4? The exact surveillance period in which the photo files were cited by the CIA as disproving any visit by Valencia![32] We now know that the Oswald visit constituted a major incident in the Mexico City station and that both the FBI and CIA intensely investigated Oswald contacts with both the Cuban and Soviet embassies. They also investigated his apparent relationship to the head of KGB sabotage and assassination for North America. In regard to Oswald's visit Phillips' book simply appears to be untrue. The fact that Phillips own autobiography cannot be trusted is one more reason to question his denial of activities under the name Bishop.

THE PHILLIPS/BISHOP SAGA

The following synopsis is taken from research and analysis in Gaeton Fonzi's *The Last Investigation* and Anthony Summers' *Conspiracy*; it is cross referenced to remarks in Phillips' own book.

Havana, 1958 – 1960

Phillips was under deep cover in Havana as the owner of a public relations agency, a private businessman. In *The Night Watch*, he describes his activities in recruiting intelligence sources (p. 80) and establishing contact with a group planning a coup against Castro (p. 81). He discusses cultivating conspirators using a false identity and in disguise (p. 82), and one instance *escaping detection because a group he had contacted was arrested, but none of them knew his real name* (p. 83). Phillips mentions that his favorite luncheon place in Havana was the Floridita Restaurant (p. 65). Antonio Veciana also described his first meeting with Bishop who took him to lunch at a fine restaurant called the Floridita.

Havana, 1960 – 1961 (Veciana quotes are from Fonzi, pp. 125-131)

A man identifying himself as Bishop, describing himself as a businessman, approached Antonio Veciana, then employed with a major Havana bank. Over a period of some months, Maurice Bishop made it known to Veciana that he was interested in him as an individual who might be willing to organize others in a movement against Fidel Castro and communism in Cuba.

"He was not in a position to let me know for who he was working for [sic] or for which agency he was doing this."

"Bishop told me several times that psychological warfare could help more than hundreds of soldiers, thousands of soldiers."

"The main purpose was to train me to be an organizer, so I was supposed to initiate a course of action and other people would be the ones to carry it out."

"Bishop always wanted to be informed what was going on within the various groups."

Bishop was supposedly not directly associated with the US Embassy although he knew individuals there well enough to give introductions to Veciana. Veciana's meetings with Bishop ceased several months before the Bay of Pigs, but Bishop did return and met with Veciana again in Cuba before Veciana left the country after a failed Castro assassination attempt.

Miami 1961 – 1963

Shortly after his arrival in Miami, Veciana was re-contacted by Bishop and they began planning anti-Castro strategies. The Bishop-Veciana relationship would last over a period of 13 years. The next major fruit of their planning was the formation of Alpha 66 with Veciana its chief officer and spokesman. As far as the public and media knew, Alpha 66 was "all Cuban" and Veciana was totally in charge. He only slipped up once, remarking in a press conference (quoted in the September 24 *New York Times*) that planning was being done by people "I don't even know."[33]

According to Veciana, by the fall of 1962, his mentor was taking Alpha 66 and its media exploits in a totally new direction. The goal of their raids (now focused largely on Russians and Russian installations) was very focused: *The purpose was to politically embarrass Kennedy and to force him to move against Castro. As Bishop remarked, they had to put Kennedy's back to the wall, forcing him to act against Castro.*[34]

By 1963, Bishop's meetings with Veciana had become infrequent, perhaps monthly at the most, and he was concerned with their overall strategy and press impact. Bishop would initiate the contacts and fly in for meetings. Many of the meetings were in Miami with a few in Puerto Rico. Occasionally the two would use a third party to relay communications. This person, a woman, recalls both Bishop and a lady with the name Prewett. Veciana recalls the lady as "Virginia," someone in the press. As always, Bishop was interested in what other groups would do and occasionally would share anecdotes about other anti-Castro operations. One that Veciana volunteered to Fonzi was a leaflet drop propaganda project called *Cellula Fantasma*. Bishop mentioned that one of the men involved was much more than a soldier. Apparently Bishop knew that at that time Frank Fiorini/Sturgis was one of the principal contract information sources that the CIA had operating within the exile group community.

In the spring of 1960, Phillips began work on propaganda for the new Cuban Project. His activities from 1960 through 1961 frequently took him to the Miami JM/WAVE station and he also engaged in counter intelligence work against the FPCC. He met routinely with exile groups including the CRC (*The Night Watch* makes no mention of Alpha 66). JM/WAVE personnel have said that Phillips continued to maintain contact with and use Cubans that he had originally met in Havana, and continued this into his next assignment after the Bay of Pigs in Mexico City.

Virginia Prewett appears to have been one of Phillips' significant media contacts and certainly one of the most consistent sources of media coverage for Alpha 66 activities.

The other major source was *Life* magazine, part of the Luce Media family managed by Claire Booth Luce's husband Henry Robinson "Harry" Luce (a member of the Citizens Committee to Free Cuba, along with Phillips' friends Hal Hendrix and Paul Bethel). Articles by Prewitt and editorials by *Time-Life* provided the strongest challenge to the Kennedy position on Cuba and were quite consistent with the type of embarrass and back-to-the wall agendas Veciana attributed to Maurice Bishop.

The Veciana–Bishop relationship continued into the 1970's, but the scope and range of Veciana's activities expanded significantly over that period. In 1968, Veciana managed to get a job with USAID and moved to South America. He was an officer of the International Development Bank in Bolivia.[35]

Veciana was amazed that he was able to get such a job while being legally restricted to Miami by the INS due to charges involving his violation of the US neutrality laws. Fonzi found that his government job application was not even signed. Veciana assumed it was the good connections of Bishop that got him the position.[36] In South America, Veciana engaged in numerous anti-Communist as well as anti-Castro projects, including assassination attempts against Castro in Chile and Venezuela.[37] But these attempts failed, and in 1973 Veciana and Bishop went their separate ways after Bishop arranged a major cash payment to Veciana for his cause.

In 1968 Phillips was appointed Chief of Cuban Operations for the Western Hemisphere, expanding his role to cover all of South America. During this assignment, the Church Committee's report would reveal that the United States sought to foment a military coup in Chile and adopted a policy, both overt and covert, of opposition to Allende. The Church Committee also noted that "the CIA did not consult its congressional oversight committees as required by law on most of the Chilean covert action projects." The track II military coup project was led by Phillips.[38]

The HSCA found Veciana to be an extremely credible and reliable witness. Its report states that he was felt to have been untruthful on only one point, his failure to formally identify Maurice Bishop as Phillips. The identification of Bishop is of great importance to us for several reasons. Perhaps the most significant being where Bishop was observed by Veciana meeting a young man in Dallas in the fall of 1963. Veciana described this young man as being identical in appearance to Lee Oswald.[39]

David Atlee Phillips as Maurice Bishop

Phillips' movements, job, activities and resources are an exact match for the individual described as "Bishop" by Antonio Veciana. This is circumstantially convincing by itself, given the fact that it occurs over a period of some thirteen years. Aside from propinquity, there is the issue of resemblance. Veciana described Bishop in detail early on in Fonzi's investigation. He also worked with a police artist to develop a sketch of "Bishop." During the course of his investigation, Fonzi showed the sketch to Senator Richard Schweiker at the Church Committee who found it familiar.

A short time later, Schweiker independently identified "Bishop" as senior CIA officer Phillips. The Senator suggested that Fonzi obtain photographs of Phillips and show them to Veciana. During the next two years, Veciana would view the photographs, meet Phillips in person and testify to the HSCA on his identification of Bishop. The following is a synopsis of his comments from the first photograph viewing to final testimony:

"It is close but it is not him—but I would like to talk to him."

"Maybe if I saw him I could tell better—well you know maybe it would help if I could talk to him."

"No, he's not him—but he knows."

"It was strange that he (Phillips) did not know my name; I was very well known."[40]

"There is a physical similarity, [but he is not Bishop]," under oath to the HSCA and immediately afterwards to Fonzi as he spotted Phillips in the room: "There's David Phillips."

When asked by Fonzi one last time if Veciana would tell him the truth if Phillips were actually Bishop, Veciana stated, "Well you know, I would like to talk to him first."[41] Later, in an interview with researcher Henry Hurt, Veciana confirmed that given his long-term relationship with Bishop, he would never confirm his true identity for the record. However, during the course of his investigation, Fonzi also showed the Bishop sketch to Phillips' brother in Forth Worth, Texas. His brother's comment was: "Why that is amazing! He certainly does look like David." The office secretary when shown the sketch stated: "That's David." When Phillips' niece Beth was shown the sketch she said: "Why that's Uncle David! That is Uncle David."[42]

In addition to propinquity, the Veciana-Prewett-Bishop connection, and the amazing physical resemblance between Phillips and Bishop, researchers Fonzi and Summers also located two CIA personnel who described Phillips as using the cover name "Bishop." Ron Cross of the JM/WAVE staff accurately described Phillips as using the name "Bishop" while E. Howard Hunt used the name "Knight." He also recalled Phillips' staff assistant (Ron Gupton) in JM/WAVE using the name "Bishop" in reference to Phillips. Gupton's response to this was an extremely careful, "Well maybe I did... but I don't remember."[43]

In an interview with author Jim Hougan, CIA officer Frank Terpil recalled meeting Hendrix and Phillips frequently while Terpil was living in Miami with Hendrix's daughter. Terpil also maintained that Phillips' early retirement and formation of a legally aggressive intelligence officer defense group was an assignment and that the retirement was "phony."[44]

Reviewing David Atlee Phillips as Maurice Bishop:

- At the time, Phillips was chiefly responsible for exile group contacts and propaganda.

- At a time when Alpha 66 was putting Kennedy's "back against the wall" by striking directly at Russians in Cuba, constantly elevating the political necessity for Kennedy to do something about the Russian menace directly offshore.

- At the same time when Phillips was waging an intelligence war against the Cubans in Mexico.

- The same time Bishop was seen with someone identical to Oswald and only weeks prior to Oswald's trip to Mexico City and the Cuban embassy.

If Phillips was Bishop, were his actions in line with a covert CIA project to manipulate the most aggressive group of Cuban exiles? Or might there have been a more personal political agenda in play? Might the same agenda have been in play when *Miami News* Latin American editor Hal Hendrix exposed most of the secret Kennedy autonomous group off-shore plans in an article on July 15, 1963, entitled "Backstage with Bobby." Clearly in that instance, Hendrix was not being supplied with or writing for his official CIA sponsors as before the Bay of Pigs invasion (when he was denying any preparations for action against Cuba). Was the Hendrix article one more attempt to put Kennedy's "back against the wall"?[45]

Summary

There are three indications that Phillips was at least aware of a conspiracy:

- The first indication is in conversations that Phillips had with Kevin Walsh, a former HSCA staffer who went on to work as a private detective in Washington, D.C. In a dialog not long before his death, Phillips remarked: *My private opinion is that JFK was done in by a* conspiracy, likely including American intelligence officers. – David Atlee Phillips, July 1986[46]

- The second comes from an email exchange between researcher Gary Buell and Phillips' nephew, Shawn Phillips. As Shawn described in the email, Shawn's father, James Phillips, became aware that his brother, David, had in some way been seriously involved in the JFK assassination. James and David argued about this vigorously and it resulted in a silent hiatus between them that lasted for almost six years. As David was dying of lung cancer, he called his brother. Even at this point there was apparently no reconciliation between the two men. James asked David pointedly, "Were you in Dallas that day?" David answered, "Yes," and James hung up the phone on him.[47]

- Finally, we have Phillips dialog in the outline of an unpublished fictional manuscript he wrote during the time frame of the HSCA investigation. Phillips novel features a character who seems to be modeled on Phillips himself and who served with CIA in Mexico City. Most interestingly, Phillips has this character state the following:

> "I was one of the two case officers who handled Lee Harvey Oswald. We gave him the mission of killing Fidel Castro in Cuba...I don't know why he killed Kennedy. But I do know he used precisely the plan we had devised against Castro. Thus the CIA did not anticipate the President's assassination, but it was responsible for it. I share the guilt."[48]

Phillips held a seminal position in anti-Castro affairs before and during the time in which the Kennedy conspiracy was formed. He had access to strategic plans and information in regard to Cuban affairs by way of his contacts in Washington D.C. and at JM/WAVE in Miami. He worked in tandem with David Morales at JM/WAVE and in Mexico City and undoubtedly his real politics and feelings were much closer to those of Morales rather than to the liberal picture he paints of himself, as a JFK proponent, in his biography.

That David Atlee Phillips was Maurice Bishop seems almost certain.

- At times Phillips seems to have pursued his own personal anti-Communist and anti-Kennedy Administration agenda.

- Through Veciana, Phillips supported assassination plots against Fidel Castro.

- Veciana was specifically told Veciana his goal was to provoke US intervention in Cuba by "putting Kennedy's back to the wall."

- Phillips had an established history of organizing anti-FPCC dangles and propaganda operations.

- Phillips was involved in a new anti-FPCC initiative in 1963, including a project to extend the effort outside the United States.

- CIA documents reveal that the reason the FBI had Oswald's letters to the FPCC in their hands at the time of the assassination was because a mid-level CIA officer had asked for their help in stealing correspondence and mailing lists from the FPCC. This was in support of a project targeted outside the US.

- Bishop was seen in Dallas, Texas with Lee Oswald immediately prior to Oswald's trip to Mexico City–a trip in which he made contact with both the Cuban and Russian embassies in an attempt to travel through Cuba to Russia. Veciana related to Lamar Waldron that his reason for the meeting was to discuss the elimination of Fidel Castro and that Oswald was there with the same goal. That corroborates Oswald's remarks in front of Dr. Frank Silva.

We do know a good deal about Phillips. What we may never know is the exact nature of his relationship with Lee Oswald or the extent to which Phillips' associates may have participated in the Kennedy assassination conspiracy.

CHAPTER **11**

"CUBA, THE GUNS, NEW ORLEANS, EVERYTHING"

We began our exploration of the Kennedy conspiracy with John Martino, his pre-knowledge, his private remarks and his associates. One name mentioned by Martino remains to be addressed. Martino didn't say much about this man, only that he had been called on after the planned conspiracy had fallen apart due to Oswald being taken into custody—before he could be either murdered or started on his way out of the country as planned.

That remark leads us to a man almost as well known as Lee Oswald, Jack Rubinstein—Ruby. Ruby has been the subject of numerous books, much news coverage and considerable attention from both the FBI and the Warren Commission; rather bafflingly ineffectual attention—until you recall the FBI Director also refused to admit that organized crime existed. The Warren Commission itself had to go so far as to force out its only two real field investigators in order to avoid dealing with their suspicions about Ruby, and to break its promise to the investigators to bring them back for the Ruby interview in Dallas.[1]

In the next three chapters, we will investigate Jack Ruby and his world one more time. We will review evidence that Ruby was a familiar figure to members of the old Havana Casino Crowd that served as a common social and financial network for several of the individuals involved in the Kennedy conspiracy. We will examine ignored evidence Ruby may even have crossed paths with Oswald in his role as a dangle to both pro- and anti-Castro elements. We will evaluate evidence that Jack Ruby was selected for a very different role than anyone might have imagined—evidence that reveals how extraordinarily risky ordering him to eliminate Lee Oswald truly was and demonstrates the failure of the conspiracy as initially conceived. However, before we can address all that, we have to examine the Jack Ruby that the FBI Warren Commission worked so hard to avoid.

EGYPTIAN LOUNGE, DALLAS, TEXAS, APRIL 1957

G.D. Gandy, CID Detective with the Dallas Police Department submitted a routine observation report on the association of certain known and suspected Dallas criminals. Gandy's report describes James "Black Jimmy" Campisi and others sitting in an office at the café. A pair of newcomers, Lewis Joe Martin—aka, Louis McWillie, and Ruby joined them.[2]

There's nothing remarkable about the report; we don't even know if it was part of any specific criminal surveillance or just routine tracking of associations between small time Dallas crime figures. We do know that as of 1957 Ruby was considered to be one of the known members of the Dallas crime scene, one of many things the Warren Commission had to keep quiet in 1964. Perhaps more importantly, the Warren Commission also had to dismiss his role as an FBI informant in 1959, his longstanding interest in Cuba, and his association with gambling syndicate interests in that country.

McWillie and Jack Ruby were friends in Dallas, where McWillie moved in 1942. McWillie was known as a gambler in Dallas with a reputation for paying off the police. In 1946 he killed a man who tried to hold him up. His Social Security records show no earnings in the period from 1952 to 1958, but Elaine Mynier, a friend of both Ruby and McWillie, reported she often saw McWillie and Ruby at the airport going off on their frequent trips. In fact, Jack Ruby later remarked that McWillie was his idol. The reason for that remark appears to be after McWillie left Dallas for Havana in 1958 where he became extremely well-connected and successful in the Havana casino network, gaining connections and "class"—the things that were Jack Ruby's lifelong goals.

During 1958 McWillie went to work as a pit boss at Meyer Lansky's Tropicana resort in Havana. He was forced to move to other locations during the Castro gambling crackdown but ended up being one of the very last gamblers to leave Cuba. He remained there until January 1,

1961, two full months longer than R.D. Matthews, another associate of Jack Ruby's who had moved to the Havana casino scene.

In 1958 Ruby wrote a letter to the State Department's Office of Munitions Controls, *requesting permission to negotiate the purchase of firearms and ammunition from an Italian firm.* The name Jack Rubenstein was also listed in a 1959 Army Intelligence report on US arms dealers. Although clerks located these documents in 1963 and reported on them, the documents themselves have seemingly disappeared.[3] Ruby's apparent interest in becoming an arms dealer was very much in line with other events of 1958.

October 14, 1958

When 317 weapons were stolen from the Ohio National Guard Armory at Canton, Ohio, the burglary was investigated by the Cleveland office of the FBI. As part of this inquiry, the FBI determined that the weapons would eventually come into the possession of an individual who would sell them to Cubans associated with Jose Aleman. The arms purchase would be facilitated though Joe Merola. Both men were then located in Miami, Florida, where Merola had connections to Cuban casino people and Prio era politicians. The FBI reported Merola's arms shopping network ranged up the East Coast into Canada, and that Merola was working in anticipation of major gambling concessions from a new government in Cuba.[4] Later Merola would become a key contact for Mitch Werbell, an individual discussed in some detail in *Appendix J, A Small Clique in the CIA.*

November 4, 1958

A plancload of guns piloted by Stuart Sutor of Hialeah, Florida was seized in Morgantown, West Virginia. These guns were identified as the stolen National Guard weapons, and the principals were involved in a plan to sell stolen Canadian securities and deliver a major cache of arms to Fidel Castro. These individuals were Norman Rothman and Joe Merola, both of Miami. Merola was associated with both Jose Aleman and Carlos Prio Soccares. Aleman was also an acquaintance of Santo Trafficante.

This incident allows us to list Norman Rothman, Joe Merola and Jose Aleman along with Robert McKeown and Frank Fiorini/Sturgis as major participants in the Prio-sponsored supply effort to obtain weapons for Castro. Rothman, Merola and McKeown were caught and served time for gun running. Frank Fiorini/Sturgis was more successful, and spent most of his time in Cuba. He went on to become Castro's appointee to oversee the Cuban casinos in the spring of 1959 after Castro's overthrow of Batista. By 1960, both Rothman and Fiorini/ Sturgis would be involved with separate projects aimed at bombing Cuba and murdering Castro.[5]

In 1978 Norman Rothman gave a deposition to the HSCA where he elaborated on a supposed Castro assassination contract that was offered him by Robert Kennedy as a quid pro quo for avoiding imprisonment in his gun running conviction.[6] Rothman described a meeting with Kennedy aides, however, his positioning of the meeting being at RFK's personal request is doubtful given RFK's concerns about using mob assets in secret war projects. It seems more likely that Rothman was trying to involve himself in Cuban projects to gain leverage if Castro was ousted. However, Rothman's statements do suggest that he was privy to at least general knowledge and gossip concerning the participation of other gambling syndicate members in government sponsored Castro assassination efforts.[7]

In 1958 running weapons and supplies to Castro was very much in vogue. In 1959 it would become important again as part of an effort to establish terms with Castro during his takeover of the Cuban casinos. Lewis McWillie worked for Norman Rothman, the man who shared with Fiorini/Sturgis and McKeown the longest record of attempts at getting weapons into Cuba. McWillie worked for him at both the Tropicana and Sans Souci casinos in Havana and was in Cuba when Rothman's most ambitious plan to get large amounts of weapons to Castro failed. McWillie and the gamblers were in for much tougher times in 1959.[8]

Ruby stated that in 1959 McWillie called him and invited him to Havana for a vacation, sending him prepaid airline tickets. Ruby described his August visit as his only trip to Havana, a ten day stay. A "vacation" in Havana during 1959? The year in which Castro began taking control over the Cuban casinos closing down some, allowing others to be operated only under tight controls, expelling some of the gambling fraternity and arresting others including Santo Trafficante? Indeed, Trafficante had been taken to Triscornia prison before Ruby's trip, and was released at the end of August.

Martino, who had been making a series of trips back and forth between Miami and Havana, had just been arrested in July and was in prison in August. Not the best of times for someone with casino associations to make his first carefree visit to Cuba. There is good reason to look for something else behind Ruby's trip. Perhaps it was not as simple as McWillie throwing some tickets in the mail to Dallas. Elaine Mynier worked at a car rental agency at the Dallas airport, where she had often seen Ruby and McWillie travel together before McWillie moved to Havana. She told the FBI that in May of 1959, she visited McWillie in Havana and carried a short "coded" message from Ruby to McWillie. Her story was found very credible by the HSCA which concluded that Ruby was most likely "serving as a courier to the gambling interests." *We came to believe that Ruby's trips to Cuba were in fact organized crime activities.* The HSCA also concluded that while in Havana, Ruby had met with crime figures detained by the Cuban government.[9] Lewis McWillie himself had visited Santo Trafficante, jailed in Triscornia, and testified, without prompting, that *Jack Ruby could have been out there one time with me.*

Interestingly enough, Ruby's travel records show that he entered Cuba from New Orleans on August 8, left Cuba on September 11, re-entered Cuba from Miami on September 12 and then left for New Orleans on the 13: two trips to Cuba, not one. However, Dallas police records, bank records and FBI records show Ruby in Dallas on August 10, 21, 31 and September 4, all right in the middle of his supposed Cuban vacation. Was Ruby going in and out of Cuba illegally as well as legally? The HSCA concluded that if all the known records were reviewed, Ruby would have had to have made at least three trips to Cuba, not one as he claimed. How he accomplished these extra trips is an open question.[10]

During the same time in August when Ruby was traveling to and from Havana, US Customs surveilled another individual traveling to Miami whom they suspected of being involved in gun smuggling. Following a brief investigation that included a telephone tap, they determined that Eastern Airlines Captain and New Orleans resident David Ferrie appeared only to be "planning an outing for his scouts." Given events of later years, it seems Customs gave up too easily. In any event, based upon Ruby's actual movements and travel, his message to McWillie, and some previous activities in 1959, it appears that Ruby was interested in Cuba for something more than a simple vacation.

Months before his trip(s), Ruby had already been very much interested in Cuba for a number of reasons. Earlier in 1959 he had contacted and made four separate visits to Robert McKeown, the highly visible Houston arms runner for Prio and Castro before the ouster of Batista. Ruby himself described reading about an individual in the Houston area and thinking about "making a buck" by acquiring jeeps or other equipment which might be shipped into Castro's Cuba. Of course Ruby said that nothing came of his momentary interest. When the FBI questioned McKeown about his possible contact with Jack Ruby he told a different story.

In January, immediately after Castro's seizure of power, McKeown began to get frantic phone messages from a man in Dallas who was trying to reach him. When they did connect, the man identified himself as Rubinstein. Rubinstein asked McKeown if he would take money to use his influence in Cuba to get three people released from prison inside Cuba. Rubinstein said that the money would be coming from Las Vegas.

Ruby's contacts with McKeown started in January of 1959, immediately after Castro's takeover. In April of that year that McKeown received newspaper coverage due to Castro's travel to Houston after McKeown refused a position in the Castro government. Ruby referred to this coverage *after* rather than before the Rubinstein calls and visits. So who did pass McKeown's name to Ruby? Perhaps somebody from Havana: someone who had actually worked with Prio and McKeown in the earlier gun running.

In any event, three weeks after the telephone call, Ruby visited McKeown and offered him a large sum of money to write a letter of introduction to Castro. The reason given was that Rubinstein held an option on a large number of jeeps in Shreveport, Louisiana, and wanted to sell them in Cuba. Ruby did not come up with the cash and no introduction was made, although McKeown told the FBI, *Well, I found out later through friends of mine that he did go to Cuba and he did use my name.*[11]

In April, Ruby rented a safe deposit box for the first time and visited it on several occasions during the summer of 1959. He also met with the FBI for the first time as a criminal informant (PCI) and would go on to meet with the FBI a total of 9 times in 1959.[12]

The casino crowd was clearly in trouble in Cuba in 1959. They had only been nominal supporters of Castro, playing both sides of the street with Batista as well. Their efforts to supply Castro with large quantities of weapons had not been notably successful. Lansky had been forced out of Cuba and his chief aide and successor, Santo Trafficante, needed to reach some accommodation with the Castro government that had placed him in prison.

Apparently, Trafficante did indeed reach an agreement with someone in Cuba, as he was allowed to attend his daughter's wedding in Havana and return to his Cuban "prison" to defend himself in October and November. Eventually, he simply left Cuba as the Castro government seemingly lost interest in him.[13]

In recent research conferences, Cuban government representatives have stated that Trafficante was only arrested because the Cuban government thought the US held a narcotics warrant on him. When that was determined to be untrue, he was allowed to leave. It is very possible that is the politically correct version of his departure. It is unlikely that we would be told about any accommodation between Santo Trafficante and Fidel Castro or about the alternative, Trafficante bribing Cuban officials.

There is little doubt that Ruby had some connection to potential deals in Cuba in 1959, and little doubt that he was connected in Havana by his former associate, Lewis McWillie. That he played any grander role than courier and go-between remains unlikely, but even that was enough to make his name known within the ranks of the Havana casino crowd. Ruby was certainly no kingpin of organized crime, but at the end of 1959, he was a known figure to key elements of the casino crowd and to the deep crime underworld in Dallas, a network operated under the syndicate jurisdiction of Carlos Marcello. It would be some time before Ruby would begin calling McWillie again though, not until the spring of 1963.

If 1959 had been a year of opportunity for Ruby, 1963 started off quite differently. Due to a tax mistake by his attorney, Ruby owed a substantial amount of money in back taxes to the IRS—$39,000 to be exact, plus another $2,000 in other taxes, and he was having serious difficulty coming up with it. The club business was supposedly bad that year with lots of competition; amateurs were stripping at his competitors' establishments while he paid union scale. The official story of Ruby has him spending most of the year trying to cope with this situation as things got continually worse, with not even enough cash to negotiate the beginnings of a payout schedule with the IRS. His attorney, Graham Koch, was trying to negotiate a payment of 8 cents on the dollar for the taxes and on November 15, Ruby's business account officially held a grand total of only $246. However, on November 22,

1963, his banker, Bill Cox at the Merchants State Bank, observed Ruby with what he estimated to be over $7,000 in large bills. Upon Ruby's arrest for shooting Lee Oswald, he was found to have over $2,000 in his wallet, including nine 100 dollar bills, plus enough in his car to bring the total over $3,000 thereby confirming Cox's observation of Ruby having lots of cash in large bills. Investigation failed to turn up any signs of loan applications or any source for this influx of cash.

Further indication that Ruby had come into some money is reflected in an interview conducted by Ian Griggs in 2005. Andrew (Andy) Armstrong was Ruby's assistant and Griggs was the first researcher to interview him in decades. In a monograph on the interview, Griggs relates that Armstrong, when he "knew [Ruby] wasn't coming back" took money Ruby had kept in the air-conditioning room at the club to Ruby in jail. On Ruby's instruction he handed the cash over to Ruby's partner, Ralph Paul. Armstrong was not aware of the exact amount but the impression was that it was a substantial four-digit sum.[14]

On November 19, Ruby had told Koch that he had made a connection that would turn up the needed cash for the IRS, and in an unprecedented move for the secretive Jack Ruby, he gave Koch power of attorney.

Actually 1963 was a good year for sales—if you were selling arms to Cuban exiles. Individual groups like Alpha 66, SNFE and Commandos L were in the market and a new round of financing showed up via Paulino Sierra. The casino crowd was investing again, and Mike McClaney was spending money on attempted air raids against Cuba. Even the autonomous exile groups supported by the administration had to obtain arms and materials that were totally deniable. Tony Varona was traveling to Central America with Prio Soccares in search of new bases. Both communicated with Artime who was busy setting up offshore and recruiting exiles who were in training with the US Army.[15]

Groups other than Artime's didn't have a CIA support infrastructure to help them locate and purchase weapons and equipment. They were getting them on their own, buying them from right-wing sources such as Richard Lauchli of the Minutemen and from those who could steal or bribe weapons out of National Guard armories, in the tradition of 1958 and Norman Rothman, Fiorini/Sturgis, and Robert McKeown. Arms were coming from thefts and purchases in the Midwest, Illinois, Ohio, and Michigan, moving through Chicago (described in detail in the FBI surveillance reports and investigation of Homer Echevarria), and going to New Orleans and Miami. The Echevarria investigation showed that individuals scouting for arms in the Midwest included Paulino Sierra, Hernandez (FNU/Full Name Unknown) and Juan Francisco Blanco of the DRE.

It took most of 1963 to establish these connections and the gun-running networks. The process started much earlier in the year, in the spring, just before Ruby began making an extended series of calls to McWillie who had moved to Las Vegas. Did Ruby try to get back into the gun running business in 1963? There are at least three separate incidents that suggest arms traffic was beginning to pick up in Ruby's circles early in the spring of 1963. There also indications that Ruby again began to associate with people who were interested in Cuba, guns and the secret war—their own secret war, not the one run by the CIA or the Kennedy Administration.

Additionally, gun-running may not have made him much money, but it may have escalated Ruby's visibility and led him to re-establish his connection to McWillie. It may explain how Ruby came to the attention of the conspiracy and to the attention of Roselli in 1963.

"A Friend of Jack Ruby's Who was Interested in Running Guns"

In 1967 District Attorney Jim Garrison received two unsolicited and anonymous notes. One note identified an inmate in the Atlanta Penitentiary who had talked about knowing Clay Shaw under the aliases of both Bertrand and Lambert. It also made mention of a Cuban associated with him named Sanchez Diaz. The other described a man serving time on a Federal offense who claimed to have known Oswald. After an inquiry, Garrison sent an investigator to Atlanta and conducted an interview with Edward Girnus, who related a variety of incidents he said occurred during 1963. At the time of the interview, Girnus was serving a sentence for Dyer Act violations, the interstate transport of stolen vehicles.[16]

In January of 1963, Girnus was released from Leavenworth Penitentiary and moved to Pasadena, Texas, just outside Houston, and began using the name Edward Stark. Sometime in March or April, he moved to Dallas and was charged with embezzlement by a gunsmith who owned two gun shops. While in Dallas, Girnus frequented a series of strip clubs and associated with the girls who worked there. During this period, Girnus met a friend of Ruby's who was associated with right-wing groups, had access to money, and was interested in buying guns. Girnus also met another potential customer, this one from New Orleans. Apparently, this man's interest persuaded Girnus to move to a location close to New Orleans where he began buying guns from military men and reselling them. *He thought the guns were ending up ultimately in Central America.* [17]

During May or June, Girnus met several people including Clay Shaw, and their discussions led to the availability of guns and an introduction to Lee Oswald. His discussions centered on Central and South America (where Girnus had traveled), how to get there, and the living conditions there. At this point in the interview, Girnus declared he did not want to provide any further details as he stood to be exposed regarding crimes for which he could be prosecuted. He did agree to have someone send a photo and a flight plan he said would be self-explanatory. When the formal interview ended, the investigator stopped taking notes and Girnus revealed something important: he had driven Oswald to Catulla, Texas, in September of 1963 where Oswald met a friend from Mexico. From there, Oswald and the Mexican man crossed the border at Laredo. There appears to be no further verification of Girnus' story and the one mention of a rap sheet refers to a Dallas embezzlement charge in 1962, not 1963.[18] Unfortunately, Garrison's files have turned up nothing further on this lead other than a copy of a handwritten flight plan dated April 1963, from Hammond, Louisiana to Garland, Texas. The pilot is listed as Ferrie and the passengers as Hidell, Lambert, and Diaz.

There are typed notes on the flight plan: "Here is the flight plan. Check light colored station wagon bought in Houston in Feb. or Mar. (Wagon was 1959 model) of 1963. Check this wagon at Walkers and at Garland Texas airport and on railroad parking lot behind book depository." This note should be evaluated in conjunction with the testimony of Sam Holland as to the station wagon and footprints observed behind the fence in Dealey Plaza, where numerous observers on the overpass noted smoke at the time of the shooting on November 22.[19]

David Ferrie associated with someone named Diaz in New Orleans, with Clay Shaw and Lee Oswald (Hidell). By itself, it is just another "teaser." But there is another report from the Garrison investigation by a young man named Jules Ricco Kimble. He could not have known about the Girnus interview, yet he described a flight that he himself took with David Ferrie, a man named Clay Shaw, and another man who was *either Mexican or Cuban, a heavy set man, dark, balding in the front and in his 30's,* who spoke only broken English. For what it's worth, that's a perfect description for Herminio Diaz Garcia.

The Kimble flight was in a Cessna. The Girnus flight plan also lists the aircraft used as a Cessna and we have photos of David Ferrie with a Cessna in company with an associate of Frank Sturgis' on a 1962 planning trip for a CRC training camp in the New Orleans area.[20]

In his November 26, 1963 interview, David Ferrie "emphatically denied that he had been in Texas for about the last eight to ten years" before his recent road trip to Houston and Galveston. David Ferrie must have been very frightened to lie to the Secret Service. Unfortunately, the Secret Service was not aware that it was a lie. Garrison's files contain a partial record of Ferrie's phone calls while working for Gill Wray. The record shows numerous calls from Ferrie in Texas back to Wray's office in New Orleans in 1962 and 1963. On May 26 and 27, 1963, he called from Dallas and from Dallas and Bay City on June 21, 1963.[21]

Some interesting names from New Orleans and a flight to Texas in April of 1963 with absolutely no validation, but then another flight from New Orleans was reported with the same pilot, same type of plane and a familiar passenger. The same type of plane which David Ferrie used in survey flights for a proposed CRC training camp in 1962. Was David Ferrie shuttling people and possibly weapons with persons of interest in the spring of 1963? Interestingly enough, there is corroboration for just that. It is in a report from the HSCA investigation and a memo from Jack Moriarty to Cliff Fenton (April 27, 1977 re: Robert Allen Price).

HOUSTON, TEXAS, APRIL 11, 1963

Robert (Bob) Price's wife, Delores, was the day manager for the Escapade Lounge on Old Spanish Trail in Houston. The day staff included six girls and a bartender. Bob stopped by on Tuesday afternoon to see his wife and found ten or eleven people in the place.

Four men walked into the lounge just before 1 p.m. that afternoon and as they did, one of the girls yelled "Jack Ruby." She had known

Ruby when she worked at the club next to his in Dallas. Bob had seen Ruby in Dallas himself but did not know him personally. Introductions were made—the report does not say whether the young man with Ruby was introduced as Oswald at the time or not. A third man was older, 28 to 30 with the same build, a crew cut and a few inches taller than Oswald. The fourth man was much older, 41 to 42, balding and with darker hair. He was described as a "high flying inspector pilot."

Bob spent a good while talking with the group as they were just "killing time" until their plane was ready to leave. That evening they were going to "fly to Cuba." One of the bar girls danced with the pilot and afterwards she and Bob walked out front and took a look at the vehicle the group was using. It was a big car, light color, wood trim station wagon with a luggage rack on top.

Bob left before 5 p.m., leaving everyone still there. In the HSCA report, he added that both he and Ruby discovered they had a mutual acquaintance, Candy Barr. At the time of his report, Price had divorced and was running the "525 Club" in Houston.[22]

These are two very independent reports, but both of them put Hidell/Oswald in Texas in April of 1963—one putting him in the company of Jack Ruby.

Back in 1959 Ruby's appearances in Dallas and Cuba during his purported ten day vacation suggest he had some way of getting in and out of Cuba other than on official transport. Perhaps this was no big deal to Ruby, but both reports independently happen to hit one of only two short windows in 1963 in which Ruby is totally unaccounted for: the second week in April, when his long distance call count is abnormally low, with one call on April 10 and only 4 calls April 21–27.

The Girnus report notes discuss a station wagon purchased in Houston and the Price report describes a station wagon in Houston. Was Ruby again trying to make some money off Cuba in 1963?

In May, Ruby had started an extensive series of calls to Lewis McWillie, lasting only from May through June. June is the other month in 1963 when Ruby went "missing" off to New Orleans but with a three day time lag before anybody there saw or heard of him.

At one point after the shooting of Oswald, during his time in jail, Ruby came apart, worried that the prosecution would find out about *"Cuba, the guns, New Orleans and everything."* But whatever was going on in May and April didn't net the cash Jack needed. By June, he had more immediate interests according to Lt. Robert May, Jr. of the Dallas

Vice Squad. Lt. May submitted a confidential report to Chief Curry that described a series of syndicate meetings that had occurred in the week of June 13, 1963. A number of organized crime family members from the Giancana and Genovese families appeared in Dallas and held meetings at three different locations. One of the establishments selected was the Carousel Club, with hosting by Jack Ruby. Nothing out of the ordinary, the subject of the meetings was organization of prostitution and book making in Dallas. May's report was not provided to the Warren Commission that infamously concluded that Ruby had no organized crime associations at all.

The source for the Dallas syndicate meetings in June of 1963 is in Seth Kantor's book *Who Was Jack Ruby?*. Kantor cites the primary source as being the Texas Attorney General's assassination files: "Files of Evidence Connected with the Investigation of the Assassination of President John F Kennedy, Texas Attorney General's Office".[23] It should be noted that although Lt. May had spent several years assigned to Vice, after Lt. Gannaway was promoted to Captain and placed in charge of the Vice unit he had Yates transferred to Auto Theft. Researcher Steve Thomas developed this information confirming May's previous assignment to Vice, where May was mentioned in the Warren Commission volumes as being assigned.

Confusingly, the Commission appears to have been given none of the DPD Vice Squad or CID crime reports on Ruby. They were not initially told that Ruby had been used by the FBI as a PCI (criminal informant; someone with the right connections to give insider tips on the crime scene in Dallas). The FBI even used testimony by people such as Dave Yaras to verify that Ruby had no criminal associations. This is the same Dave Yaras who had been arrested in Miami in 1959 for robbery and money switching schemes against Cuban exiles.[24]

SUMMARY

Jack Ruby had a long history of association with gamblers, syndicate connected criminals, and members of the Havana casino crowd. Beyond that, Ruby had most likely played the role of courier and go-between in efforts related to getting Santo Trafficante out of his Cuban captivity.

It is clear Ruby approached Robert McKeown for a reference that would be paid for with money from Las Vegas, and that would be used to help get Ruby's associates out of Cuba. Within months, Ruby himself was in Havana at the invitation of Lewis McWillie, who in turn was visiting Santo Trafficante.

McWillie virtually admitted taking Ruby on at least one of these visits and within a short period, Trafficante was attending his daughter's wedding in Havana and not long afterwards leaving Cuba for good. Whether Ruby had any direct connection to Trafficante's release is questionable; that he was involved in the efforts seems likely.

- Jack Ruby was a low-level gangster with roots in Chicago, known in Havana and Las Vegas.

- Ruby played the roles of FBI informant and police informant.

- Ruby served as a go-between to Robert McKeown and as a courier into Cuba.

- The same people who sent Ruby to McKeown in 1959 may have acquainted Ruby with Lee Oswald in 1963.

- Ruby consistently demonstrated that he would do virtually anything for money and for attention from the people he idolized in the casino community.

- Ruby began looking towards guns and Cuba as a way to raise money in 1963, making himself visible again to the network he had first worked for in 1959.

Things would get even more interesting for Jack Ruby later in 1963, and he wouldn't have to leave Dallas to find the action. People began showing up in Dallas, and some of them wanted little things, like guns. Some of them wanted something more.

CHAPTER **12**

THE ANTI-CASTRO PEOPLE

John Martino tells us that the Kennedy assassination conspiracy was carried out by the anti-Castro people. However, determining exactly which people Martino was describing is a considerable challenge. We have the exiles involved in the ongoing operations of the JM/WAVE station, the new autonomous activities of AM/WORLD, not to mention other projects such as AM/TRUNK and AM/LASH. Then we have the truly independent groups including Alpha 66, the DRE, nominally under CIA control but with a history of acting on their own, and the new Sierra Junta. The task is even more challenging in that the anti-Castro activities and allegiances of 1963 were far different from 1962 and in some instances, worlds apart from 1960-61.

We began the search for Martino's special anti-Castro people with a study of his own known associates and moved on to the business and social networks in which these people moved. Networks that may well have served as an infrastructure in which conspirators could have met and or moved without drawing any particular attention, even from most of their associates. These networks included the Havana, Miami and Las Vegas casino crowd as well as Prio/Castro revolutionary gun running connections.

Our next step is to revisit these individuals and networks for a closer look at who was doing what, to whom and with whom during the three to four month period leading up to the assassination. In doing so, it will be especially important to identify the individuals who were circulating in the areas where we find leaks, gossip or apparent pre-knowledge of a move against JFK–Chicago, Miami and of course Dallas. Individuals traveling to all three locations will be of special interest.

We need to know who was on the inside with the Kennedy Administration and the CIA, who was on the outside, and who was playing both sides. In particular, we need to know who among this cast of characters might have become familiar with Lee Oswald in New Orleans and who had begun to show any interest in Dallas, Texas.

THE INSIDERS

As 1963 progressed, the Kennedy administration was continuing its projects to either eliminate the Castro regime in Cuba (Track one) or to get the Russians off the island through some sort of agreement with Castro (Track two). The President was reviewing a new Special Group list of Cuban penetration and sabotage missions. These missions would be executed by JM/WAVE's heavily armed speedboats, supported by specially equipped motherships. The Rex, the Leda, and four more motherships were prepared to support dozens of V-120 Swift raider boats.

President Kennedy authorized thirteen new sabotage missions proposed by the Special Group on October 24 and gave final approval for the AM/TRUNK project, a prospecting effort for Cuban military officers who might be willing to support a coup against Castro. Robert Kennedy was involved not only with these CIA focused projects but also with the new autonomous group efforts. Artime–AM/WORLD alone was receiving support to the tune of a quarter million dollars a month. There was also extensive State Department and armed forces contingency planning for a coup inside Cuba, a coup that could have been generated by one of the aforementioned efforts or through private contacts by John and Robert Kennedy.

This independent CIA team, separated from JM/WAVE and with its own designation—AM/WORLD and its own facility—LORK was moving the Kennedy Administration sponsored exiles offshore to start a major new and fully deniable effort against Castro. This effort was scheduled to mount major seaborne attacks into Cuba before the end of 1963, to organize a provisional government that could assume control after a coup against Castro and ultimately lead to a new regime. Within the exile community, word of this new initiative was stimulating competition from both Alpha 66 and DRE, each of which intended to mount its own offshore campaigns.

CIA documents reveal that the DRE push was far too little and too late. They got no serious consideration and had little money of their own to back such a project. Besides, their independent military actions in 1962 had gained the DRE a reputation of being impossible to control.

Artime had money of plenty. In chapter twelve of *Ultimate Sacrifice*, Waldron describes one check issued on November 19, for $167,784 and a sum of $450,000 used by Artime to purchase modern military equipment. As part of the new autonomous operations, extra efforts were supposed to be made to ensure that he, his recruits and their operations were not to be seen as tied to the United States government. Artime named sponsors ranging from private businessmen to Latin American and even European governments; in the end this proved to be as fruitless as the deniability efforts for the 1961 Brigade landing in Cuba.

Artime's approach to recruiting also had to be circumspect; he did, however, have access to the Cuban personnel who had been taken into the US Army and Air Force for training. The following comments are from a memo generated by the 112th Army Intelligence group and reflect the operational constraints of deniability as reflected in Artime's recruiting:

> During the month of June 1963, Manuel Artime, a leading political figure among the Cuban refugees in Miami, Florida, came to Fort Benning, Georgia, for the purpose of recruiting people to go to a revolutionary camp in Nicaragua. Artime informed this group that the US Government was not going to do anything for Cuba and that he had obtained aid and instructors from Europe.

> Help should start to be received by Artime after November 1963.

> Muina is working for, or with, Artime. Muina has indicated that Cuba will not gain its liberty with the assistance of the United States, but needs to look for help from another country. Muina believes that the United States has decided to apply the principle of co-existence towards Cuba.

> There is a group of officers with the Cuban Officers Training Program at Lackland Air Force Base who contemplate submitting their resignations if the United States has not done anything for the freedom of Cuba by December 1963. Many officers have indicated their desire to resign in order to join Manuel Artime

who is supposedly organizing a training camp in Nicaragua. Artime has some contacts that have been undermining the present training program by spreading dissention among their fellow officers.

These men have developed a recruiting campaign to supply Artime with qualified leaders for the Nicaraguan camp... It is rumored that a Latin American country is going to buy planes from England and make them available to Artime... The Samoza regime in Nicaragua has also promised assistance to Artime in the forthcoming operations against Communist Cuba.

In early August, Fernandez-Martinez offered Source $500 if Source would accept a position in Nicaragua with Artime.

During the inquiry, the USARMA, Managua, called attention to intelligence reports he had furnished reporting Nicaraguan press comment on the visit of exiled Cuban refugee leaders Dr. Manual Artime Buessa, Dr. Carlos Prio Soccares, Dr. Manual de Varona... during July and August 1963.

At 1030 hours 19 November, Major Bryce, G-2 Section, Ft. Holabird telephoned... a call from Washington, D.C. on the night of the 18th requesting Jose Raul Varona Gonzalez to come to Washington D.C. the following day. The call was from Lt. Erneido Oliva who was second in command at the Bay of Pigs, and according to Varona, now commander of Brigade 2506. Oliva wanted Varona to come to Washington to meet with Mr. Robert Kennedy, the Attorney General.

Varona was reportedly the G2 for Brigade 2506.

Varona made no mention of seeing Mr. Kennedy.

Mr. Kennedy did confer on 17 November with Manuel Artime Buessa, Roberto San Roman, aka Roberto Peres San Roman, Jose San Roman and Enrique Jose Ruiz William Alfret. They were also scheduled to meet with Mr. Robert Kennedy on either the 21st or 22nd of November, 1963. There is no indication that Ft. Holabird student Varona was present.

This office has no information whether Mr. Kennedy is aware of Artime's alleged recruiting activity."[1]

While such communications demonstrate that Artime was capable of keeping his Kennedy Administration and AM/WORLD associations from parties within the US government, there was less success in keeping his offshore preparations secret. In the Miami press, these preparations were little more secret than the preparations for the Bay of Pigs.

Nicaragua Denies Cuban Exile Force,
The Miami Herald, Tuesday, October 22, 1963

Luis Samoza, eldest of the two heirs who boss this country, is supporting a Cuban liberation group whose members include Carlos Prio Soccares, ex-President of Cuba and Manual Artime, political leader of the 1961 invasion.

An August CIA memorandum from Desmond Fitzgerald to McGeorge Bundy outlined the fact that Samoza claimed to be receiving personal encouragement from the highest levels of the Kennedy Administration and was developing his own Samoza Plan. Fitzgerald even discussed the last resort of dropping hints to Castro that he should not be taken in by the Samoza plan nor be provoked into any retaliatory acts that would provoke an invasion.[2]

By the fall, Artime's fleet was established near Monkey Point, Nicaragua and Samoza himself announced that in November, "strong blows" would begin against Castro. On November 5, the first group of CIA-trained Artime commandos sailed from Norfolk on board the Joanne. At another camp in Costa Rica, Pepe San Roman, Robert Kennedy's unofficial military advisor, had 300 men under arms.[3]

At the same time, Justice, FBI, INS, ATF and the Border Patrol were seriously following their orders to crack down on any attacks against Cuba originating from the US, except, of course, those on the JM/WAVE approved list, each of which had to get Presidential approval. This was a schizophrenic situation at the least: inflammatory, in the end futile and very likely fatal for President Kennedy.

THE OUTSIDERS

With total administration support being thrown to Artime, Williams and San Roman, the independent exile groups were on their own in 1963. The disparate movements of Alpha 66, SNFE and DRE were now separate groups fighting separate wars.[4] The FRENTE had given way to the CRC and by the summer of 1963, it too had largely dissolved amid bitter recriminations and extremely harsh words towards John Kennedy. The CIA maintained contact with as many of the groups as it could. We have records that show that the CIA's main goal was to give minimal support and money, enough to allow the CIA to monitor their activities and at the most, leverage their successes for public relations purposes within Cuba.

The personnel file of Bernard Barker, one of the chief JM/WAVE agents working first with E. Howard Hunt prior to the Bay of Pigs and later under William Harvey as part of the Task Force W CIA staff, gives us a good insight into the change in official directions and relationships with the Cuban exiles during the periods before and after the Bay of Pigs.[5] Barker's assignments circa 1960 ranged from coordination with Tony Varona, who objected to Barker's attitude of treating all the exile leaders equally, through Bay of Pigs propaganda activities in support of E. Howard Hunt and "Mr. Phillips," to helping Treasury officials break up two narcotics rings operating between Cuba and Florida.

After the Bay of Pigs in 1961 Barker faced the virtually impossible task of defending the effort, while beginning to investigate the independents who quickly began to go their own ways–Bosch, Veciana/ Alpha 66. One of his reports mentions that almost immediately after that 1961 disaster, there emerged *"an alignment of gangster groups with the Revolutionary Council [the CRC led by Tony Varona]."* Later, with the "disintegration of the CRC in April of 1963," Barker reported that the new Junta being touted by Paulino Sierra deserved attention, as its freedom from "ties to US apron strings would be particularly appealing."[6]

But in 1963 Barker was being ordered not to associate with certain exiles so as not to create the impression that their groups had re-established an association with the CIA. So he switched his major asset, Frank Fiorini/Sturgis, to primarily collecting information on the independent groups' activities. In April, a Barker report commented on the value of using a trusted cut-out, evidently Fiorini/Sturgis, to procure information without the targets being aware that the information was being passed to the CIA. That applied not only to Cuban exiles but to right-wing militants interested in the anti-Castro effort, such as Clare Chenault Jr.[7] That summer, Barker reported, Tony Varona was working on an accommodation to join forces with Manuel Artime in Nicaragua, and planning to visit there for meetings and negotiations with Samoza.

The implications of Artime's association with both Varona and Prio Soccares were serious. This gave an early appearance that the chosen leader for AM/WORLD was talking with Varona and Prio, although Artime went out of his way to assure both Samoza and the CIA that these old Cuban politicians would never control him. Artime also had a known propensity for loose talk—records reveal his detailed conversations about Kennedy funding and support of Rolondo Cubela, AM/LASH, a possible Castro double agent. It seems likely that Prio and Varona learned many of the details of the new autonomous group/coup initiative. They would have unhappily realized they were dependent upon Artime's good graces should he succeed in ousting Castro. And Varona, deeply enough embedded in the Trafficante network to have been the main "go to guy" for Roselli in three years of Castro assassination plots, can hardly have been expected to keep Artime's news from Roselli or Trafficante.

Without a doubt, Prio and Varona were playing with both the "insiders" and the "outsiders" in exile and CIA affairs, selectively passing on what information they chose, to the ears of whomever they chose. It is extremely likely that both the Kennedy's track one (military/coup) and track two (negotiation) initiatives were known to people who had major issues with John and Robert Kennedy.

The "outsider" independent exile groups were on the move in 1963. They were under intense surveillance in Florida, in the US protectorate offshore islands, even in the British island chains. Alpha 66 had largely moved operations to Puerto Rico. It still needed guns and explosives. If the US would not help Alpha 66, then it was forced to turn to middlemen, primarily the same arms dealers who supplied the American paramilitary organizations such as the Minutemen and the John Birch Society.[8] We find these groups looking for guns in the Midwest, Dallas and in California. We've already taken a brief look at one of their locations in Dallas. The gun deals and the gossip and the subversives in Dallas deserve a much more in-depth look—which will show them to have crossed paths with a man who was just trying to make some money: Jack Ruby.

DALLAS AND THE "HOUSE ON HARLENDALE"

In 1963, an Alpha 66 leader named Manuel Rodriguez Orcarberrio moved to Dallas, Texas. By September, he was in a house in nearby Oakdale. Although the FBI and CIA later performed their standard "weak" investigation of this location (the CIA supposedly could not even locate the address due to a transcription error on a DPD memo), Orcarberrio's neighbor just happened to be the mother-in-law of DPD Detective Buddy Walthers. Walthers filed reports and investigated these mysterious Cubans after the assassination. The Cubans apparently stood out on the block because of their active comings and often late night goings, their meetings on weekends, and the variety of the individuals involved.[9]

We know only a few things about Manual Rodriguez Orcarberrio. We know that he was in Castro's revolutionary army, that he eventually rejected Castro and communism and defected via the Brazilian embassy in Havana. He arrived in the US in 1960 and worked a dish-washing job in Miami before moving to Dallas. We also know from FBI and Secret Service PRS reports that he was violently opposed to President Kennedy, a stance he would deny after the assassination. We know that shortly before the assassination, in Sulpher, Oklahoma, he was reported as being in the company of someone who closely resembled Lee Oswald. The FBI confirmed that Orcarberrio was a leader in Alpha 66, the same action group whose members included Antonio Veciana, Tony Cuesta and Eddie Bayo/Perez—the same group that provided personnel for the Bayo-Pawley mission in which John Martino was involved. [10]

Researchers have described Manual Orcarberrio as being very active in arms purchases. While that seems likely, it still requires corroboration. The ATF agent normally cited as a source for this, Frank Ellsworth, told the HSCA that the name might have come up, but that the individual was not a focus of his investigation. He did not originate the name in his testimony.[11]

GUNS, GOSSIP, JOHN THOMAS MASEN, AND JACK?

John Thomas Masen, one of the more interesting gun dealers in Dallas, was rumored to be connected to the Minutemen as a weapons source for right-wing buyers of many sorts. He was suspected of reworking semi-automatic weapons for full automatic firing, and of trafficking in controlled explosives. Because of these reports, ATF agent Frank Ellsworth began an investigation of Masen in which Ellsworth and another ATF agent eventually placed a purchase with Masen for a number of automatic weapons supposedly for a very right-wing buyer in New Mexico.

> I'd tracked this fellow undercover through another man for several months before I actually met him. I think this began sometime in the summer of 1963. When I finally made contact with him, I led him to believe I was a crook. He claimed to have done some arms smuggling in and out of Mexico, but not when I was dealing with him.[12]

Ellsworth was not aware that Masen was already the object of another undercover inquiry, one in which military intelligence and the FBI were pursuing an offer from Masen to disclose information about an upcoming Cuban exile attack on Cuba. That investigation had begun on October 24, 1963, when George Nonte, an Army ordinance officer at Fort Hood Texas, had reported an offer from Masen to sell such information. Nonte was very well known as an arms enthusiast and expert and had been engaged in starting up a business with Masen. Nonte had previously exchanged ammunition with Masen, who in turn had re-barreled weapons for him.

With his retirement coming up in a little over a year, Nonte was talking with Masen, Leroy Barker (a Dallas chemist), and James Melton (another Dallas gun shop owner) about chemical compounds to be developed for commercial sale by a company then in development by Nonte, Masen and Barker called Black Hawk Chemicals.[13]

During the October 24 call to Nonte, Masen floated the question of whether or not there would be a buyer for information on an upcoming attack on Cuba. Nonte appears to have immediately notified 112th Army Military Intelligence of this and the 112th reported it to the FBI.[14] From that point on, Nonte was requested to stay in touch with and cultivate Masen in order to get additional details and names on the source for the information. Nonte did so over a period of several weeks, eventually meeting Cuban exiles who were attempting to put together a weapons purchase with Masen.[15]

Masen's initial exile contact was Joaquin Martinez de Pinnillos from Miami. While in Dallas and talking to Masen, Mr. Martinez apparently began talking about the new exile plans to take the war to Castro from off-shore, first in boat raids in November, and then with a major invasion. Masen, described by Ellsworth as very much an opportunist, apparently decided to shop this information to Nonte. Although the FBI had a great deal of difficulty in tracking down the identities of all the exiles associated with this arms purchasing effort, we now know that Martinez, George Perrel, and Sam (last name unknown) were all DRE members. Martinez had been in Dallas accompanying DRE officer Manual Salvat.

After Martinez left Dallas, he handed over his shopping list to George Perrel and Sam. Perrel, aka Fermin Goicoecha Sanchez, was a student at the University of Dallas; the same University attended by Sarita Odio. Nonte talked with Sam and eventually met with Perrel, who was interested in buying M1 rifles. Nonte referred him to two commercial firearms dealers, Globe firearms in New York and Interarmco in Virginia. But this was not exactly in Masen's interest, as he was looking to get Nonte to help source the weapons from an underground supplier; an order from Cuban exiles to Globe or InterArmco would not have netted Masen a commission. Besides, such a purchase might have drawn too much attention as the weapons were legal for sale but not for export outside the US.

On November 7, Nonte reported a letter from Masen asking for 75MM and 20MM guns and 50 caliber machine guns. He replied by telling Masen where the first two types could be purchased, giving no response on the machine guns since they were prohibited weapons.

This MI/FBI investigation and Nonte's role was unknown to ATF agent Ellsworth and his sting operation against Masen. Ellsworth came across Nonte as a Masen contact and possible weapons source. And in November, Ellsworth reported visiting Fort Hood and making an inquiry about arms thefts and Nonte. The information given Ellsworth is questionable, as he was told nothing about Nonte's voluntary role as an informant on Masen that had been going on for some time at that point. In fact in his HSCA testimony, Ellsworth gives no indication he was ever aware that Nonte was cooperating in an intelligence collection operation against Masen while Ellsworth was running his own sting.

FBI memoranda, after the apparent date of Ellsworth's San Antonio visit, show Nonte was then reporting that Masen wanted to come down to Fort Hood and was pressuring Nonte to locate spare parts to build a quantity of M-2 rifles. He reported that Martinez and the exiles were apparently not Masen's only buyers, and he apparently had taken another order he couldn't fill. Of course Nonte did not know about the Ellsworth sting or the fact that Masen had a planted (sting) order from the ATF.[16]

Captain Nonte reportedly retired from the Army in 1964 with a final promotion to major. His reporting of the Masen incident and work in the FBI inquiry received favorable comment in a variety of FBI reports.

While these newly released reports show that Nonte and Fort Hood proved to be of no use to Masen in his quest for arms, we also know that Masen did come up with a set of weapons to sell to Ellsworth and the ATF. He managed to find someone who could steal them from a small National Guard repair facility, but his sources ran into a little delivery problem.

THE TERRELL THEFT

Sometime during the evening of November 13, 1963, the Ordinance Maintenance Shop of the National Guard Armory at Terrell, Texas, was robbed of the following nine weapons:

Four .30 caliber rifles
Two .30 caliber automatic rifles
Two .30 caliber light machine guns
One .45 caliber submachine gun

A summary of the robbery investigation concluded that the robbery was essentially a crude break-in to a building with poor construction and no alarm system.

"The thieves had gained entrance to the building through the front door after having first tried a window... placed a steel bar under the door and moved it up and down until they were able to remove the hinge pins. The thieves then entered the office through an open screen door and with an axe and other tools found in the shop, they broke a night latch- type lock which secured a metal-covered door in the strong room."[17]

The Military Police investigation report on the incident makes it clear that the facility robbed was that of the Texas National Guard Headquarters Company and describes the arrest of the thieves, "Whittier" and "Miller," in Dallas. Two of the Terrell automatic rifles, the two machine guns, and the submachine gun were recovered. The other four rifles were not.[18]

As of November 27, Whittier was in Parkland Hospital for injuries sustained in a car accident during the arrest in Dallas; Miller, who had suffered extensive facial lacerations, was in the Dallas County Jail.[19] The guns were in Dallas, because although Masen had arranged for them to be delivered to Agent Ellsworth, the lack of inter-agency coordination had blown the ATF sting. So the intermediary who was to transfer the guns to Ellsworth was never apprehended, and one of the two cars involved in the transfer got away, while the Thunderbird with Whittier and Miller inside did not. John Masen was off the hook until in frustration, Ellsworth had him arrested for possession of dynamite on November 20. Masen was out on bail the next day, but would be back in on the 22nd.

Later investigations would turn up the fact that Whittier happened to be the service man who personally attended to Ruby's car. In fact, it seems at least possible that Ruby himself may have played a minor role in the Terrell weapons theft. It is even possible that one of Ruby's friends within the DPD arranged for the tip that helped blow the ATF sting and allow the man transporting the guns to Whittier and Miller to escape. Corroboration for this speculation goes far beyond the service station connection. It goes to the remarks reportedly heard in the Dallas jail by John Elrod on November 22.

THE ELROD ENCOUNTER

On August 11, 1964, a very troubled John Elrod walked into the Shelby County Jail in Tennessee and told the officers a story that had been on his mind since November 22, 1963. On that day, Elrod had been picked up as a suspicious vagrant shortly after the murder of the president and was placed in the Dallas County Jail. While in a cell with another prisoner, he observed a man with an extremely lacerated face being brought down the hall beside their cell. Elrod's cellmate remarked that he knew the man and that he had been part of a crime that involved guns and a car accident in a Thunderbird. The cellmate also told Elrod about a meeting. This meeting had included him, the man with the cut face, and a fellow named Jack Ruby.[20] Due to the diligent research of a number of individuals including Carol Hewett and David Boylan, we now have the documents showing that John Masen initially had been arrested on November 21 and then re-arrested on November 22.[21]

The initial charge against Ellsworth had been the Federal offense of trafficking in controlled materials: explosives. His release on bail left him open to follow-on local Texas charges that placed him back in the same Dallas Police jail holding area on November 22. ATF agent Ellsworth had described Masen as a virtual look-alike for Lee Oswald, and it seems possible that it was Masen who spoke to Elrod in the cell rather than the normally close-mouthed Oswald. Perhaps Masen simply vented his frustration, and in doing so, revealed that Jack Ruby was involved with the Terrell armory theft. Of course, hearing the name Jack Ruby on November 22 would have been no big deal, but after Oswald's murder by Ruby, the incident could well have made a lasting impression on Elrod.

There is also other circumstantial evidence that Jack Ruby himself may have been very concerned about the Terrell-related arrests. He can be shown to have met and been in telephone contact with Masen's lawyer, to have visited a bondsman (with no outstanding charges open against Ruby himself), and to have met with District Attorney Alexander immediately after the arrest of Whittier and Miller. Ruby's explanations for these contacts are questionable at best.[22]

Additionally, among the material found in Ruby's possession were three un-cashed American Express traveler's checks (others could well have been cashed) that had been endorsed by Samuel Baker, an Army soldier assigned to the Terrell installation. The story was that Ruby had done the service man a favor. Supposedly Baker had just gotten paid, had converted all his pay into travelers checks and had gone directly to Dallas to Ruby's club. So there he was, in the club with no cash and nothing else but travelers checks and Ruby was kind enough to personally go to the trouble to give the fellow cash for the travelers checks—not a standard service performed at clubs. The coincidence of

Ruby doing this for a soldier from Terrell at the exact same time as the theft and gun transaction also brings the explanation into question.

When we add Elrod's story, with the details of the car, the crime and the facial injuries, to the fact that both Elrod and Masen can now be shown to have been in the same jail on November 22, it seems more than likely that Elrod's story of talking to someone he later took to be Oswald is credible. But, he was mistaken and it was not Oswald. The cops and Ellsworth had every reason to think there was a connection between Masen and Miller, so it's no wonder they ran Miller by the cell to see if Masen might say something or acknowledge him.[23] No major surprise in finding Ruby trying to make some side money from guns. And, if the official JFK investigations of Jack Ruby missed his involvement in an armory theft, it is very possible that they missed a few other things Ruby was doing in the weeks before the assassination.

NEWCOMERS IN DALLAS

There were anti-Castro people in Dallas in the fall of 1963; Cuban exiles were shopping for weapons, Alpha 66 was recruiting and raising money. There were those mysterious late night meetings and comings and goings at the house on Harlandale, itself apparently abandoned a few days before the assassination (not long after Oswald had been observed with two "subversives"). Relevant dates, activities and questions include:

November 26, 1963
"I don't know what action the Secret Service has taken but I learned today that sometime between seven days before and the day the President was shot, these Cubans moved from this house. My informant stated that the subject Oswald had been to this house before."
– Buddy Walthers.

November, 1963
Someone resembling Lee Oswald was seen at the House on Harlandale. Someone resembling Oswald was reported in company with Orcarberrio in southern Oklahoma. A note containing an urgent message with Oswald's name on it was left in Abilene at the home of a

Cuban exile who had moved there from Miami, and who was known to be associated with Tony Varona.

Who else might have stayed at the House on Harlandale during this period? Who might have used their Alpha 66 connections to provide cover for contacts and scouting in Dallas? Did the House on Harlandale provide an overnight stopover for the two "Mexicanos" and Oswald during their travel from New Orleans to visit Sylvia Odio, before Hernandez and Oswald went on to try and purchase guns from McKeown in Houston?

Since there was never any serious investigation of these possibilities, it is difficult to do more than clearly demonstrate that associates and fellow travelers of John Martino had connections to Dallas. There is also little difficulty in seeing how exile shooters could move into Dallas with a support infrastructure in place for them. An exile network complete with safe-houses was in place in Dallas and perhaps the guns and ammunition were available too. After all, we know now that John Thomas Masen was one of only two dealers in Dallas to stock Mannlicher Carcano 6.5 mm ammunition and that he was in the habit of reloading the Full Metal Jacket military rounds with softer, fragmenting loads for "deer hunting." Which means that Masen would have had available both types of ammunition that appear to have been used in Dealey Plaza on November 22, 1963.[24]

CHICAGO, "OUR NEW BACKERS," AND MR. HERNANDEZ

Before Dallas, the first place the "outsiders" had turned for arms was the midwest, possibly because right-wing suppliers such as Richard Lauchli were more established there, and had been working with certain elements of the Cuban community all the way back to the Prio-Castro gun running period. The Rothman contract to supply guns to Prio had relied on a robbery from a National Guard armory in Ohio and Frank Fiorini/Sturgis had gone in the same direction to obtain many of the materials he procured for Prio and Castro.

On July 7, 1961, Donald Browder gave a sworn statement to the American Surety Company in which he stated that he had obtained the stolen securities [which] he was arrested with from the 26th of July Movement, Fidel Castro's revolutionary group, in exchange for arms during the summer and fall of 1958. Browder was the purchasing agent for the Rothman gun-running operation to Castro's forces. This memo from well known investigative journalist Scott Malone, dated December 19, 1977 confirms:

> Donald Edward Browder, the ex-Canadian pilot... Browder was in prison for a conviction of receiving, transporting and possessing stolen Canadian securities. The securities were stolen from the Brockville Savings and Trust Company and two other Canadian financial institutions... Both the gun running and the stolen Canadian securities were activities controlled by Norman Rothman. Rothman admits knowing Browder.[25]

Cubans driving station wagons and small trucks were purchasing automatic weapons... Frank Sturgis has admitted to being involved with the operation... Efren Pichardo, associate of Browder, has also admitted to being involved in this operation at the same time with Sturgis. Pichardo was working for Browder at the time. Pichardo also confirmed that many of the weapons were hidden in the marshes of Islamorada Florida, where Ruby has been identified by independent witnesses as "babysitting" a large arms cache.

In October of 1963, a new generation of exile arms buyers returned to Chicago. We first visited some of these memos many chapters ago because they reveal a dramatic slip made to an informant by one of the resident Chicago exiles. Homer Echevarria remarked that the Cubans had new backers, plenty of money, and were ready to move as soon as President Kennedy was eliminated.

Some additional excerpts from these Chicago memos may be even more informative:

> Hernandez had come to Willow Run, Michigan airport... the Cubans wanted to purchase .45 caliber pistols, sub-machine guns, Browning automatic weapons, C-3 explosive, recoilless rifles and ammunition... they indicated that they had the necessary funds and were impatient to consummate the purchase.

> It is not known if delivery was ever made. However, the report indicates that Sierra and Hernandez departed Willow Run by plane for Chicago.

Regarding the name Sierra mentioned above, it is noted that the customs file reflects that the Sierra at Willow Run, Michigan, was constantly referred to as "Doctor" by the other Cubans. A confidential source at Chicago has advised that there is one Paulino Sierra, an attorney, who has been very active in the Cuban movements in Chicago. It now appears possible that this "Paulino Sierra," the Doctor Sierra and the "Mannie" who met Mosley (Mosley was part of the Homer Echevarria contact) may be one and the same person.

A separate Treasury Department Protective Research memo dated January 10, 1963, refers to an investigation of other individuals who may have been in Chicago. The memo regards two individuals who were residing in Miami and were being investigated as to their recent appearance in Chicago. The report's subject is given as "Lee Harvey Oswald; Assassination of President Kennedy."

Unfortunately, no explanation is given for this memo other than that it is a followup in Miami to a Chicago inquiry and that the investigation has been requested by S.A. Edward Tucker on two individuals who had recently been in the Chicago area. The individuals are Francisco Blanco and Homer Echevarria. The investigation determined that:

> The confidential source made personal contact with Juan Francisco Blanco Fernandez and through discrete conversation with him, learned that he had been in Chicago approximately two weeks ago. Fernandez is currently head of the military phase of the Student Revolutionary Directorate at Miami Florida... his mission to Chicago may have been for the purpose of securing military equipment from Thomas Mosley (the Echevarria connection in Chicago).[26]

> In Chicago, we see an individual who was told that his backers, Sierra's "new backers," were Jews and that they had plenty of money. Things were to move as soon as someone got rid of President Kennedy. Hernandez is a name that we have also traced from Cuba to Mexico City, to Miami, to New Orleans and to Houston—always associated with Alpha 66, always dealing guns, and in November, Hernandez was in Chicago flying in a private plane with Sierra.

SCHAUMBERG, ILLINOIS: OUTSIDE CHICAGO

Three days before the assassination of President Kennedy, a man named Hernandez rented a small plane. He and the plane were never seen again. The owners reported theft and particulars about Hernandez to the FBI, which made no move to investigate the incident. A local reporter followed the story and could not determine why the FBI was avoiding the case. It would be interesting to know if that airplane and Hernandez were in Texas three days later.[27]

SUMMARY

This chapter has spent considerable time examining what various anti-Castro people were doing in 1963, who were outsiders and who were insiders relative to the Kennedy Administration and its sanctioned exile activities, what each group was doing, and who had connections between the inside and the outside. This examination is a search for the anti-Castro people that Martino described and a search to find which of them were indeed connected to Dallas in the fall of 1963.

- It is clear that the "insiders" being backed in their off-shore operations were not the people we find in Chicago and Dallas searching for weapons, not the people turning to the casino crowd, the Nevada group or to the Jewish Mafia for money.

- The "insiders" were busy trying to recruit exile troops (and having to distance themselves from the administration and the CIA to do so) and establishing their bases in Nicaragua and elsewhere offshore.

- It is also clear that Manuel Artime made his own position clear to Prio and Varona regarding the new Kennedy backed project which would result in his replacing Fidel Castro. He would be in, and they would have to come to him for any return to power in Cuba. This of course would not have been Robert or Jack Kennedy's view of a new provisional Cuban government but rather Artime's likely version of future events.

- David Atlee Phillips and David Morales both had to be aware of the Kennedy Administration's back-channel approach to Castro. They were also both aware of the alternative offshore Artime project, involving liberal elements each would have personally opposed.

- The "outsiders" had been forced to turn to their own fundraising and to a mix of conservative ex-Batista supporters as well as the casino crowd.

- The "outsiders" were shopping for guns and money and raising funds in Chicago and Dallas by the fall of 1963.

- It was the "outsiders" who carried the gossip about plans to murder President Kennedy.

- It was the "outsiders" who were connected to Martino's associates in 1963.

It is in this anti-Castro segment, the individuals that had no confidence in the Kennedys, who felt them to be an actual obstacle in recovering Cuba and who feared that they might very well be betrayed once again by John and Robert Kennedy where we would find Martino's exiles.

Next we move to consider how a plan for action against the President came into being in the fall of 1963, and how it would jell into a specific plot for Dallas.

CHAPTER **13**

PLANS, PATSIES AND MOTIVES

John Martino's information gives us a direct view to certain elements of the conspiracy as well as its overall goal. This allows us a very different perspective of events than that of the official history, the history produced by the FBI report from Hoover to Johnson and the Warren Report, which simply validated the FBI's view. Martino's view allows us to make a great deal more sense of incidents in September, October and November of 1963. It also turns out to be much more internally consistent, without the loose ends we see all over the official story. An in-depth look at events also leads to the conclusion that there may have been two patsies planned for Dallas, not just one.

PATSY #1: LEE OSWALD

The Dallas script did *not* position Lee Oswald as a lone nut acting entirely on his own initiative. The plot was intended to present the assassination as a conspiracy, one that would lead directly to Fidel Castro and a Castro intelligence organization operating within the United States. The plotters spent considerable effort associating Lee Oswald with purported Castro agents and positioning him as being paid by Castro to participate in the killing of President Kennedy.

This script did *not* present Oswald as a devout Castro activist and revolutionary—as might have been anticipated from the New Orleans FPCC activities of Oswald–but rather as a nut or an unstable gun for hire. That was the characterization presented to Sylvia Odio. Oswald was presented as someone *dangerous, emotional, and unpredictable*. This was also the impression left with Dr. Silva after his personal encounter with Lee Oswald.

The stories floated immediately after November 22 present Oswald as having made secret trips to Cuba from Mexico, from Texas, from Louisiana, and from Miami. He supposedly had gone to Cuba, met with Castro agents or with Castro himself, and been paid to kill Kennedy—all very much a mirror image of the CIA/Roselli project targeting Castro using a paid killer to target Castro. The Oswald impersonations in Dallas continued the same theme. Oswald went out to buy a car and, while taking a test drive, bragged about having been to Russia (leaving no doubt he would be remembered) and that he was coming into enough money to buy a new car shortly. Not the talk of a political activist or Marxist revolutionary, but more the talk of someone better described as a loose canon.[1]

In Mexico City after the assassination, the CIA accepted and promoted what is now known as the Alvarado story, a totally implausible tale of Oswald being seen in the Cuban embassy taking money from a red-headed, black Cuban, to whom he boasted that while the Cubans lacked the guts to kill Castro, he would do it. There were other reports from Mexico City of Oswald being seen around the Cuban embassy with Latinos taking money. The only detail about Lee Oswald in Mexico City that David Phillips repeats in his biography is this story about Oswald coming back to the United States with a large sum of money that was received from a Castro agent in Mexico City. Of course, Phillips does not comment on how thoroughly the Alvarado story was disproved, or on the fact that he personally endorsed and promoted it himself.

This particular story was the stuff of brute-force propaganda. In real life, assassination contracts to kill presidents of other countries are not made and discussed in public view within the sponsoring country's own embassy. Intelligence services do not recruit agents and then bring them to their own embassies ,even to the basements. Neither do KGB agents normally meet military defectors and court them for assassination missions by having them walk in the embassy's front door. The first CIA liaison assigned to the assassination investigation wrote a memo expressing professional skepticism over these sorts of reports and Richard Helms replaced him within days, assigning James Jesus Angleton to all coordination of information with the Warren Commission.

However, the Alvarado story generated a gut reaction from avid Cold Warriors like Ambassador Thomas Mann in Mexico City, and the tale was promoted by David Phillips and James Angleton, experienced covert operations professionals who undoubtedly knew better. They also should have known that Gilberto Alvarado, the originator of the story, was not a Communist as he was first described by the CIA, but rather an operative of the right-wing Nicaraguan intelligence service.

Jack Ruby was also strongly promoted in post-assassination stories as having been involved with both Oswald and Castro. An example of this can be found in the private remarks between Martino and his friend and co-author Nathaniel Weyl, which were related by an undisclosed (i.e., name redacted) CIA informant during a dinner at Weyl's home in December, 1963. The informant was female and a house guest of the Weyls' from December 1963 to January 1964.[2]

Mr. and Mrs. Martino visited the Weyls one evening when a CIA informant [the initial CIA report has the informant's name redacted, but later releases show it as Prisbeck] was present. The informant's report contains the following information:

- John Martino and Nathaniel Weyl are co-authors of the book *I Was Castro's Prisoner*. John Martino is the individual who carries the stories to Nathaniel Weyl and both John and Nathaniel are deeply entrenched with the Cuban anti-Castro forces. Martino claims to have a friend in Miami who keeps him well informed on Cuban matters.

- The Cuban friends of the unnamed individual in Miami know that Oswald contacted the Cuban intelligence service by telephone from a private home in Miami. They also know the man who furnished the information on Oswald to the FBI.

- From the reports given by the Cubans to this unknown individual, it seems very definite that Ruby went to Havana to make a shady deal with a creature [sic] by the name of Praskin, who works with the Cuban Communists and who is also tied up with call girls in Cuba.

- A friend of Nathaniel Weyl, who ran for the presidency of Cuba in 1958, shortly will testify before the Senate Internal Sub-Committee… Sourwine of the Committee contacted Nathaniel to get in touch with the individual.

PATSY #2: JACK RUBY

Jack Ruby was a problem for the Warren Commission. There was the issue of his motive for shooting Oswald. Ruby was presented as emotionally obsessed with the Kennedy family, -but not enough so to have walked a block to view the motorcade. His Jackie sympathy motive was discredited when Ruby himself told Melvin Belli that it had been invented by his first attorney. Then there was Ruby's status as a police snitch and FBI informant; his gambling syndicate connections, his prior history of interest in making money from Cuba, and his earlier visit there at a time when gamblers were being either kicked off the island or locked up. However, if one very important FBI report out of Dallas had received as much attention as the Odio incident, we would have seen the Warren Commission's official story of Lee Oswald as a lone nut challenged by Oswald's self-described connection to the Carousel Club.

If Ralph Yates had reported his story on November 22, it is very possible that Jack Ruby would have been in questioning or under surveillance immediately and we would have had a very different picture of both Lee Oswald and Jack Ruby.[3] Ralph Leon Yates, of 13564 Brookgreen Drive, Dallas, Texas, voluntarily appeared at the Dallas FBI office accompanied by his uncle, Mr. J.O. Smith, and furnished the following information:

> Yates stated that he is employed as a refrigeration serviceman for the Texas Butcher Supply Company... in connection with this employment he was driving a pick-up truck on the R.L. Thornton Expressway at approximately 10:30 AM on either November 20 or 21, 1963. He noticed a man hitchhiking at approximately the Beckley Street entrance to the R.L. Thornton Expressway and he stopped and picked up this man.

> When the man walked up to get into the pick-up truck, he was carrying a package wrapped in brown wrapping paper about 4 feet to 4 and a half feet long. The man said the package contained curtain rods and he would carry it with him in the cab [of the truck].

The man had asked him if he knew a certain party whose name Yates cannot recall now and Yates indicated he did not. The man then asked if he had ever been to the Carousel Club. Yates then brought up the subject of the forthcoming presidential visit.

The man asked Yates if he thought a man could assassinate the President, asked if it could be done from the top of a building or of a window high up... the man pulled out a picture which showed a man with a rifle and asked Yates if he thought the President could be killed with a gun like that one... the man asked Yates if he thought the President would change his route... Yates replied that he doubted it.

The man indicated that he was going on Houston Street ... Yates went off the Expressway, turned off Commerce on Houston and let the man off at the corner of Elm and Houston. He saw the man cross Elm Street... he recalled him saying something about the Triple Underpass but cannot recall exactly what was said. Yates stated that he had mentioned this incident to another employee, one Dempsey Jones, prior to the time the President was assassinated.

Yates stated that the man was identical with Lee Harvey Oswald... Yates is married, has five children and he would appreciate not receiving any type of publicity from the fact he was furnishing this information.[4]

Additional FBI inquiry did indeed verify that Yates had spoken to fellow employee Dempsey Jones about this incident. Jones provided a deposition confirming the conversation with Yates. Yates was also given a polygraph by the FBI that further verified the incident.

A review of Dempsey Jones' actual FBI interview on November 27, 1963 shows:

- Jones confirmed that Yates did talk to him on the same day that Yates gave the young man a ride.

- Yates related he dropped this boy off at Houston and Elm.

- Yates stated the boy had a package and that the boy had talked about the possibility of someone shooting the President from a building.

- Jones also stated that following the assassination, Yates said the boy had told him that the package contained window shades, and that Yates was going to call someone and report the incident.

- Yates clearly did describe the incident with the hitch-hiker *before* the President's visit.[5]

Lee Harvey Oswald, or someone looking very much like him, with a long paper package went to Elm and Houston and talked about the assassination of the President with a rifle from the top of a tall building and focused attention on Jack Ruby's Carousel Club.

Compare the Yates incident with the official story of the Buell Wesley Frazier package observation, the package which was demonstrably too short to carry even a broken down rifle as described by Frazier and his sister. The story was elicited from Frazier in a late night interrogation after he was taken into custody by police, along with his own rifle and taken back to Dallas for some very serious interrogation.

The Warren Commission used two specific observations to place Lee Oswald in the sniper's nest of the School Book Depository with a rifle. The first was Howard Brennan. But Brennan did not officially identify Oswald in any of three Dallas Police line-ups conducted on November 22. Indeed, as we have seen in Chapter 5, there is no record of Brennan's officially participating in any of the line-ups. Chief Curry told reporters on the following day that the police had no witness to Oswald doing the shooting.

Buell Wesley Frazier was the second individual making the official case. Frazier described Oswald carrying an object in a package to as they left for work the morning of November 22, but both Frazier and his sister repeatedly gave descriptions that would not confirm a package long enough to contain even a broken down rifle; the package was carried in Oswald's cupped hand and fitted under his armpit. The genesis of Frazier's information is also not nearly as clear or straightforward as the Yates report to the FBI, at least when examined in light of Frazier's treatment by the Dallas Police.

Frazier's affidavit of November 22, 1963, (dated but with no time specified, it was apparently given that afternoon at the same time as the other employees') is very detailed, running to two pages and covering all the details about giving Oswald a ride, Oswald's carrying a package, the curtain rods, etc. However, after returning home on Friday evening to Irving, Frazier was arrested by Dallas police; his residence was searched, and the police confiscated a rifle, ammunition, and a clip, all owned by Frazier. He and his sister were taken to Dallas, and questioned again, and affidavits were taken from both at that time. The Warren Commission apparently placed the evening affidavits in evidence while the DPD retained the afternoon Frazier affidavit in their records.

At that point, around 9 p.m., Frazier was released and driven back to Irving. But halfway home, the police car received a call and Frazier was returned to Dallas where he was asked by Captain Fritz to submit to a polygraph examination. According to the official record, between 11:20 and 12:10 Frazier did so, passing the exam with flying colors. And yet a few years later, Frazier and the various police participants would give investigative reporter George O'Toole widely varying recollections of what actually occurred during Frazier's late night recall and polygraph test. R.D. Lewis denied any recollection of being called from home to give a polygraph related to the President's assassination. Detective Stovall denied being present during the test and Lt. Gerald Hill claimed Captain Fritz did not believe in polygraph exams at all, so the examination didn't even take place. Fritz himself declined any interviews about the assassination.

O'Toole further points out that the three individuals involved with Frazier—Stovall, Guy Rose and Patrolman Adamcik, who reported to Hill—are the three officers who obtained the most seriously incriminating evidence in their search of the Paine residence.

Detective Hill's statements are also challenged by other officers' rejections of his remarks about Fritz's aversion to the polygraph, and by other statements of his which relate to his personally taking Oswald's wallet from him in the squad car after his arrest at the Texas Theatre. Hill went on record as observing multiple names among the ID in this billfold and radioing in both the names Hidell and Oswald—but nothing of this nature can be found in transcripts of his transmissions on the official police radio log.

We are left with a variety of issues pertaining to the arrest, interrogation, and polygraph examination of Buell Wesley Frazier. O'Toole's use of a voice stress recorder further determined that almost all the statements about Frazier's polygraph exam produced extremely hard stress among all participants, including Frazier.[6]

The Yates' report of Oswald carrying a rifle to the TSBD and deliberately associating himself with both a presidential assassination and Jack Ruby's Carousel Club seems fully as credible as the Frazier information. Indeed both could well be true. And although Yates' story has completely escaped official discussion, it becomes even more important when examined in light of the hard evidence given to the Dallas Police that connected Ruby to Oswald and a conspiracy.

A few weeks after the assassination, Deputy Ben Cash took possession of a box of materials from a very scared woman. In it was a great quantity of material including receipts for motels, telephone call records, notebooks, newspaper articles, voluminous correspondence, and notes on business stationery with a "Paramount Pictures Corp." letterhead. Apparently, the woman—who Cash could only recall by her first name—Mary, had access to Paramount stationary and the young Latin man who had left the box of material had borrowed or used sheets while dating her roommate.

Much of the material discussed the assassination and seemed to be written in the first person by one or more participants, possibly including Lee Oswald. The material clearly discussed both Lee Oswald and Jack Ruby as participants in the conspiracy. One motel receipt from New Orleans showed both their names. The telephone charges included calls to Mexico City. There were references to landing strips in Mexico, references to agents in the border towns of McAllen and Laredo, and two Mexican gunmen.

In addition, the material included notes for a plan to assassinate President Kennedy during a trip to Wisconsin. JFK did visit Wisconsin on a Conservation Tour in the fall of 1963, a repetition of an earlier tour in 1962. The signature of Lee Oswald was found in the registry of a Wisconsin restaurant, dated September 16, just days before Kennedy's visit. This incident was dismissed by the FBI and received virtually no attention outside the state of Wisconsin.

Also among the materials was a press card for the *Daily Worker* issued to Jack Ruby in Chicago. The box and its contents were taken to the Dallas County Courthouse and either seen or examined by several Dallas lawmen before being turned over to District Attorney Henry Wade, who was prosecuting the Oswald murder case against Jack Ruby.

The list of officers handling and reading this material included Deputy Constables Ben Cash, Billy Preston, and Mike Callahan, Constable Forest Keene, and officers Callahan and Stockard. Constable Robbie Love had turned over the papers directly to District Attorney

Henry Wade. Wade acknowledged to Dallas reporter Earl Goltz that this story and the box of materials was familiar to him and that he had been given such a box by Love. *"It might well have happened,"* Wade remarked, *"but I knew whatever they had didn't amount to nothing."*[7]

Neither the contents of this box nor any reports on it survive within the Dallas Police records. Ben Cash speculated that the material was saved by a Latin man as protection against being fingered as a patsy, and that he left it with his girlfriend for insurance, finally abandoning it during an unplanned flight after the assassination; when, as Martino tells us, the whole plan fell apart upon Oswald's capture.

If a report given to District Attorney Garrison is correct, there was even more solid evidence linking Lee Oswald to Jack Ruby: telephone call records. Call records were reported to the Dallas Police by Pete Raymond Acker, a Southwestern Bell Telephone manager. According to Acker's father-in-law and brother, the records remained with the police and Acker was told to shut up and go home. Acker reportedly went on to become Vice President and General Manager of Southwestern Bell in St. Louis. Apparently there was never any official inquiry into this report. But it, and several related incidents tending to corroborate the report are mentioned in a memorandum from Matt Herron to Jim Garrison.[8]

Jack Ruby made numerous remarks and efforts to communicate that he felt he was being viewed as part of the conspiracy, as much of a patsy as Lee Oswald. This was puzzling to most people, since there was no general discussion of his being involved in the conspiracy itself. Ruby's early remarks are quite revealing:

> "Don't you think I make a good actor?" – A question to Sheriff Will Fritz.

> "I have been used for a purpose."

> "To start out, don't believe the Warren Report. That was put out to make me look innocent."

Consider Ruby's remarks to Earl Warren during the Commission's eventual interview of Ruby. It was conducted several months into 1964, and without the two prime Ruby field investigators, Hubert and Griffith; they had been removed from Dallas due to their aggressive investigation and reports on Ruby's criminal connections and possible complicity. Ruby told Warren:

"You can get more out of me."

"Unless you take me to Washington you can't get a fair shake out of me... I want to tell the truth... my life is in danger here... not with my guilty plea... my whole family is in jeopardy... would you rather delete what I said and pretend nothing is going on?"

Ruby's remark regarding his family is often attributed to his accelerating stress and purported mental breakdown, paranoia, and delusions. But it might mean something much more pragmatic and understandable, given the combination of the reported FBI surveillance report of Roselli/Ruby meetings and the fact that Ruby's first visitors in jail were Joe Campisi and his wife. Campisi was reputedly the number two man in the Dallas crime organization under Joseph Civello.

Campisi did not provide much detail about their discussions although he did remark that Jack Ruby expressed his concern for Mrs. Kennedy and the children. This is interesting given the fact that Ruby himself later told his attorneys that Tom Howard, his first counsel, actually gave him the alibi about concern for Jackie. Campisi need not have said anything to Jack Ruby nor have known anything other than that Ruby was under arrest; his visit simply endorsed the syndicate "code": if he kept his mouth shut, he and his family would be supported, if he broke the rules, he knew the consequences. Indeed, Ruby's remarks about his family being at risk can also be taken at face value, indicating normal syndicate practice. Robert Blakey, head of the HSCA, gave a very reasonable interpretation for many of Ruby's remarks while in custody.

"Ruby was trying to tell the truth about the conspiracy he knew existed, but he feared for his life and consequently spoke indirectly, as seasoned criminals often do when they are being interrogated."[9]

Indeed Ruby's descent into paranoia, including his remarks in regard to persecution and mass execution of Jews, could also be interpreted as a back-up insanity ploy, left unused by his attorneys. Yet there is another possible explanation for his behavior, given his visits by Dr. Louis Joylon "Jolly" West. Dr. West's career included pioneering LSD research; once destroying an elephant with a massive overdose for the CIA. West often served as a court-appointed psychiatrist and he served this role in the Ruby case after Ruby's conviction and sentencing. However, he does not appear to have had any legal association with Ruby's defense during the trial at the time of his first visits with Ruby.

These visits and visitors log are described by Eric Tagg in his book on Buddy Walthers referenced earlier.[10] As Tagg notes, two names stand out on the log, two men not associated with either the defense or the prosecution at that point in the Ruby trial. Dr. West of Oklahoma, his first visit, April 29, 1964 lasted about half an hour, with no further visit until 1965 and Robert Stublefield who only visited once, the day following Dr. West, April 30, 1964. Tagg notes that both men had been associated with LSD research and the horrendous CIA mind and behavior alteration project MK/ULTRA under Richard Helms.

No Big Deal for Jack

John Martino did not describe the involvement of Jack Ruby; he merely remarked that they had to have Ruby kill Oswald, something not part of the initial plan. It is very possible that Jack Ruby was recruited by Roselli to perform relatively small tasks involving local intelligence collection, confirming the motorcade route, or possibly even simply maintaining contact with and monitoring Oswald's residences and employment. Ruby himself asked the Warren Commission if they did not think there was anything odd about Oswald getting his job at the Texas School Book Depository.

Although the official investigation asserted that it could prove no connection between Ruby and Oswald, researchers including John Armstrong have collected observations including telephone call evidence that suggests Ruby frequently called the public phone at Oswald's boarding house. All of this suggests that any involvement of Ruby with Oswald was not something that Ruby felt it necessary to conceal. Ruby himself likely had no idea of the scope of events on November 22, the patsy role developed for Lee Oswald, or the plan and materials developed to implicate Ruby himself. This conclusion is supported by an FBI report dated 1975 that fits well with Ruby's observed movements on the morning of November 22:

Dallas, Texas, April 6, 1977

On March 2, 1977, Robert J. Potrykus, Chief Intelligence Division, Internal Revenue Service, Dallas, Texas, hand delivered a letter to Ted L. Gunderson, Special Agent in Charge of the Dallas FBI Office. The letter is on IRS stationery and states:

> Recently, Arlen Fuhlendorf, a Group Manager in the Dallas Intelligence Division, received information from a confidential informant that might be helpful in the investigation of the Kennedy assassination.
>
> The informant stated that on the morning of the assassination, Ruby contacted him and asked him if he would "like to watch the fireworks." He was with Jack Ruby and standing at the corner of the Postal Annex at the time of the shooting. Immediately after the shooting, Ruby left and headed toward the area of the *Dallas Morning News* Building.
>
> If you desire, Group Manager Alan Fuhlendorf can be available to discuss this matter with your agency.

There are no records indicating a response by the FBI.[11]

Given Jack Ruby's Cuban interests, his connections to Lewis McWillie and R.D. Matthews, his possible involvement in the spring of 1963 with "Hidell" and a trip to Cuba, it is very likely that Ruby had been recruited with the promise of some minor role in a glamorous syndicate-CIA Castro project. This was a familiar pitch for John Roselli and one that could not have failed to attract Ruby, especially if it put several thousand dollars into his hands. The money would have been very useful in implicating Ruby as a paid agent not of Roselli of course, but of Fidel Castro. Such a story would only have become needed if anyone had pursued the report of Ruby's banker's supposedly having seen him with a very large amount of cash on November 22.

Numerous witnesses related that Ruby was hard hit by the news of President Kennedy's being shot and killed:

"An uncomprehending look"
– Billy Rhea, first and perhaps the most descriptive witness.

"Ashen white" – Richard Sanders

"In a daze" – Rabbi Silverman

It got worse upon the public announcement of Oswald's arrest with Ruby actually breaking down and throwing up. However, by that evening, he was posing as a reporter in the Oswald press conference and as Seth Kantor details, continuing to stalk Oswald until the time of his murder. The appearance of Ruby at the late night press conference wearing glasses with a notepad and pencil listening intently at the interview and later correcting the name given for Oswald's Cuban affiliation, discredits Ruby's plea that he had no special interest in Oswald until overcome by sheer impulse during a visit to the telegraph office on Sunday morning as Oswald was being transferred.[12] No one called Jack Ruby out of the blue on the afternoon of November 22 and ordered him to kill Lee Oswald. The order was given and he had no choice at all about complying.

Motive, Means, and Names

Jack Ruby and Lee Oswald were both patsies. Both manipulated by the anti-Castro people, who bring us back to Martino's conspiracy and to the core of the matter: motive, means, and names.

The motive is clear. Several of the key figures involved had a personal and visceral hatred for John Kennedy that sprang from their experience at the Bay of Pigs disaster. They had become convinced that Kennedy was a liar, very possibly a Communist, and without doubt a traitor in the fight against communism. They had been told about the non-invasion agreement with the Russians and later, in the spring of 1963, had been told for the first time that Kennedy was exploring an accommodation with Castro, one that would remove the Soviets from Cuba but leave Castro in power.

These individuals were given specifics of meetings and contacts, with names they recognized and details they could confirm. The information came from individuals within the CIA who unquestionably had access to such information. All of the men involved have been described by their friends and associates as fierce patriots. Undoubtedly, they considered their act as patriotism, an act committed in the interests of their country, whether it was Cuba or the United States. Martino calls them the anti-Castro people, not Cubans or exiles specifically although Cubans were present. Richard Case Nagell knew the Cubans who contacted Oswald in New Orleans, but he described the plot as a domestic inspired conspiracy, domestically formulated and domestically sponsored. Nagell describes the individuals he knew to be participants as *four or five madmen out to further their just cause.*

We have also seen that senior CIA officer David Atlee Phillips devoutly and aggressively denounced any explanation of the Kennedy assassination other than that of the Warren Commission. Only shortly before his death did he remark that he believed it was indeed a conspiracy, one organized by American intelligence officers.

Gerald Patrick Hemming remarked to author Dick Russell that the exiles were *used and incited* to anti-Kennedy fervor by being let in on the knowledge that Kennedy was pursuing an accommodation with Castro, told that their dream of retaking Cuba was dead unless something drastic was done. In the end, "they took the bait."[13]

Is there any corroboration that CIA officers in Miami did hate John Kennedy so intensely; that they had access to the top secret accommodation discussions; that they covertly incited exile groups in Miami? There is no single answer, no simple confession other than Morales' drunken remarks, and second hand gossip but again, we find many traces.

As to passion and hate, we know first hand from Morales' best friend about his feelings on John Kennedy, which were personal and violent. Two of the officers working for Morales were veterans of the Bay of Pigs. One, Rip Robertson, debriefed and worked with Martino and with Roselli and his sniper team. Robertson is deceased and we have no commentary from him, however, his co-worker and friend, Grayston Lynch, published a book in 1998 entitled *Decision for Disaster – Betrayal at the Bay of Pigs*. Lynch obviously knows what he is writing about and serious students of history should compare his observations to the CIA Inspector General's report to find the truth. His remarks are invaluable and he fully communicates what was, for the exiles and their supporters, the tragedy of the situation and the opportunity that was lost. But he also makes no bones about his view of President Kennedy and the New Frontiersmen. There is no reason to even suggest that Lynch himself has done more than relate his own observations and the feelings of his associates. However, his words paint a clear picture of the prevailing attitude toward John Kennedy among some of the veterans of JM/WAVE.

> When it came to the "decision for disaster," the cancellation of the Monday-morning strike, the Kennedy apologists waffled, sideslipped [sic] and performed miracles of acrobatic sophistry in a futile attempt to downplay and explain the president's decision to sign the death warrant of the 2506 Brigade.[14]

> The failure in 1961 was just a failure. But not a total failure, for it did accomplish for the New Frontier a solution to one of its problems. It got rid of the 2506 Brigade. Their "dumping" into Cuba was flawless![15]

Was there reason to believe that John Kennedy was prepared to abandon the Cuban exiles again? First the Bay of Pigs, then the Cuban Missile Crisis, the broken promise to the Brigade in the Orange Bowl, and the exile group crackdown starting in 1963. There seems little reason for them to question Kennedy's purported treachery if they were told by those they trusted, told by CIA officers in the know and who they knew to be devoutly anti-Communist, devoted to the anti-Castro cause rather than to Langley, the Special Group or to Kennedy Administration policies.

Rolando Otero was well-connected within the Miami exile community and fanatically opposed to Fidel Castro. He would continue the struggle against Castro for decades. Very much like Antonio Veciana, Otero was also no friend of the official CIA. Veciana told Fonzi that he suspected a conspiracy in the Kennedy killing and that Bishop would know who was involved. Otero also provided Fonzi with information suggesting that CIA personnel were involved in the conspiracy. In his HSCA testimony, Otero related that key individuals within the Miami exile community were told Kennedy had betrayed them, that something big was going to happen and that they should not abandon the cause.[16] Corroboration for Otero's story comes from a very unexpected and independent source.

During a research conference in Bermuda, Fabian Escalante, the former Chief of Cuba's G-2 intelligence agency, related the following: "By mid-1963, we had infiltrated a special group of exiles working with the CIA. A CIA official came to a safe-house in Miami and said to a group of Cuban exiles, 'You must eliminate Kennedy.'" Escalante also related that when they had interrogated Felipe Vidal Santiago, he had made a special point of telling him that he had spent a great deal of effort and time in 1963 informing groups of exiles in the United States about the Kennedy Administration's efforts to have a dialogue with Cuba. "Vidal told us he was very surprised ... it was almost like a bomb, an intentional message against Kennedy."[17]

There is no doubt that top CIA officers were very much aware that there had been multiple approaches offered by Fidel Castro himself. Intelligence officials had debriefed James Donovan, for example, after each of his trips to Cuba negotiating the release of US civilians including an ultra secret team of CIA wire-tappers, with Martino included as a diversion. Donovan had received the first contact from Castro's physician, Rene Vallejo, in April. The CIA had debriefed Lisa Howard after her interview with Castro and learned of Castro's remarks about a rapprochement. The CIA had then expressed their opposition to such a dialogue at the highest levels of the Agency. Richard Helms himself reported to the President that "Fidel Castro is looking for a way to reach a rapprochement with the United States." McCone sent a memo to Bundy recommending that "no active steps be taken on the rapprochement at this time." It was certainly clear to the President and to Bundy that CIA was not supportive of any talks with Castro and in June, the Special Group, whose meetings were periodically attended by both Shackley and Morales, added an "accommodation option" to its planning.

The CIA was also very likely suspicious that Kennedy had begun to exclude it from the decision-making process regarding further Castro contacts. It certainly was not part of the Howard, Attwood, Lechuga connection that developed in New York City in September and October of 1963. In fact, it is very possible that the CIA was monitoring Lisa Howard directly, perhaps even bugging her apartment or her phone line. If so, the CIA officers involved with Cuba knew its opposition to a Castro dialogue was fast coming to naught and if Howard was under surveillance, it would most likely have been from the office of CI/SIG, intelligence, or security. In that case, James Angleton knew about the burgeoning possibility of a Kennedy-Castro rapprochement. And if Angleton knew, then it is very likely that Morales and Phillips could have known far more than they were supposed to about the President's plans.

Of course all of this is raw speculation. Or is it? On September 20, Stevenson obtained the go-ahead from President Kennedy to authorize Attwood's direct contact with Carlos Lechuga, the Cuban ambassador to the United Nations. Lisa Howard approached Lechuga in the United Nations delegates' lounge and invited him to a party at her apartment where he and Attwood conferred in an exchange of views. Lechuga hinted Castro was in a mood to talk. Later, Howard offered her home as a communications center for Attwood to converse directly with Rene Vallejo and a series of telephone exchanges took place in October with Vallejo conveying a message through Howard to Attwood:

> Castro would very much like to talk to a US official anytime and appreciated the importance of discretion to all concerned. Castro would be willing to pick up the official and fly him to a private airport near Veradero where Castro would talk to him alone. The plane would fly him back immediately after the talk.

> If this could not be done, then Castro did not rule out sending an emissary to the United Nations. Howard suggested that Vallejo come to New York himself. Kennedy preferred a meeting between Vallejo and Attwood at the United Nations.[18]

We do know, thanks to research by the HSCA and independently by researcher Vince Palamara, that on November 2, President Kennedy canceled a trip to Chicago at the very last minute. As detailed in earlier chapters, this is the first indication that a group of Cubans were known to represent a potential danger to the President of the United States. Certainly they were not Castro Cubans, indeed, given the Castro-Kennedy dialogue it is very possible that much of what we see of purported Castro threats against John Kennedy and the US may have been positioned or "spun" by David Phillips' media contacts.

In particular, this includes a reported interview with Castro at the Brazilian embassy in Havana. The interview made the AP wire and generated considerable US press, especially in New Orleans where the focus was on Castro personally threatening the President and United States officials. Supposedly, Castro had somewhat uncharacteristically agreed to a spontaneous interview by Daniel Harker following the embassy function. As part of his article, Harker quoted Castro with the following remark: "United States leaders should think that if they assist in terror plans to eliminate Cuban leaders, they themselves will not be safe."[19]

The Cubans themselves took great exception to the report and the slant given by Harker to Castro's comments, saying it was a distortion used to foster right-wing propaganda against Castro. What Castro actually said, according to Fabian Escalante, was this: "American leaders should be careful because [the anti-Castro operations] were something nobody could control."[20] The Cuban position was and remains that Castro was not threatening President Kennedy but rather warning him of the dangers of being involved with the exiles.[21]

After the assassination, Daniel James filed a report with the FBI that a source of his in Cuba had advised him that Castro had publicly remarked at a function at the Brazilian Embassy that, "if the United States causes him difficulty, he has the facilities to "knock off" United States leaders." James was well known for his anti-Red articles and like Virginia Prewitt, worked for NANA, which was managed at the time by Ernest Cuneo. Cuneo and Prewitt were board members of the Committee to Free Cuba while James was the Executive Secretary of the Committee.

James' tip from his personal source appears to be simply one more propaganda effect surfacing the original Harker story directing investigators towards Cuba and Fidel. The FBI report and tip were given additional emphasis when CIA headquarters directed it to the Warren Commission.[22]

Whether incidents such as Harker's story and the James' FBI report simply represent an ongoing propaganda campaign or reflect something more sinister remains a matter of conjecture. Clearly, certain media elements were creating a climate of confrontation at the exact time Kennedy and Castro were pursuing their own personal dialogue aimed at curtailing confrontation.

On November 8, President Kennedy made a very low profile trip to New York City. Immediately following this trip, Protective Research Service agent Glen Bennett was temporarily assigned to the White House Detail of the Secret Service. Bennett was the first PRS agent to have a field assignment to the Presidential Detail and would accompany it to New York City, Miami and Dallas where he would be in the presidential security car. He was present on all three major trips and all the major stops on the tours. When interviewed by Vince Palamara, Bennett denied his presence on the trip to Miami, but Palamara found shift and survey reports locating him in the Presidential Security Car just as in Dallas.[23] In the 2005 edition of his work, Palamara reveals that another PRS agent, Howard K Norton the first "Security Technician" hired by the Secret Service and formerly with OSI, was covertly on the Texas trip, in Austin.

Bennett was on the second Kennedy trip to New York on November 14, the only trip on record that shows the Secret Service conducting a "technical survey," in essence, a search for bugs at the Presidential Suite at the Carlyle Hotel. In November of 1963, the President of the United States had apparently become concerned that he might be under technical/electronic surveillance of some sort.

This leads to the speculation that by November of 1963, the President may have been concerned about surveillance of his and his personal envoys' back-channel dialogues with Cuban representatives and visitors to the United Nations. The Secret Service may have been worried about an elevated threat to the President based on incidents in Chicago and Florida, further indication of the danger associated with the President's Cuban initiatives.

SUMMARY

- The scenario for killing John Kennedy involved using patsies who could be connected to Cuba and to Fidel Castro or his agents.

- The patsies had to have a history of Cuban interest, contacts and connections.

- The patsies had to be credible as men who could be approached by Castro agents.

- There had to be witnesses to suspicious Cuban contacts.

- There needed to be some evidence of anticipated or actual payments to the patsies.

- The patsies had to be unaware that any casual contact, any phone calls, could suggest collusion and conspiracy and be encouraged to engage in such contacts.

- There had to be hard evidence and documents connecting the two patsies.

By the beginning of November all of the elements were in place, the witnesses were there, Odio, McKeown, Yates, Alvarado, the car salesmen, the telephone records, the box of receipts and correspondence—all evidence for conspiracy. The motive for the plan was a combination of revenge, warped patriotism and opportunity for the organizers—a matter of necessity for the participants. Eliminate Kennedy or lose Cuba to Castro for good. Do it now, or stay in exile. This is our last chance. Strong talk, with all sorts of rumors.

CHAPTER **14**

"ALL SORTS OF RUMORS"

It is probably safe to say that the majority of conspiracy research has focused on the investigations conducted after the assassination. Much of it has been an effort to re-examine both evidence and witnesses. The problem is, if there was official interference with the investigation of a conspiracy, if there was "management" of both evidence and information suggestive of conspiracy, then the material presented in and with the official reports may be of limited value. Given that caution, we will take a different approach. We will look further for evidence before the fact, pre-assassination indications that the plot and activities described by John Martino actually existed. Our leads will continue to come from gossip, rumors and leaks–both from the conspiracy and from individuals who had cause to believe President Kennedy was at risk.

Martin "Marty" Underwood was a professional advance man for the Democratic National Committee. By his own description, he became an honorary Secret Service agent and served both Kennedy and Johnson, becoming Johnson's liaison to the Secret Service.

Underwood served as the advance man for Houston on the Texas trip in November, 1963. In 1992 he consented to a personal interview with researcher Vince Palamara. His remark to Palamara was that, "everyone who had anything to do with Dallas in any way, Kenny O'Donnell, the Secret Service, they're practically all dead now. I just think people should know the truth." The truth according to Marty Underwood is that in the days immediately before Dallas, *"We were getting all sorts of rumors that the President was going to be assassinated in Dallas; there were no ifs, ands or buts about it."* Underwood went so far as to relate these reports to the President and Kennedy replied, "Marty, you worry about me too much...the Secret Service told me that they have taken care of everything. There's nothing to worry about."[1]

Unfortunately, we don't have a list of the rumors and sources from Marty Underwood, just the knowledge that there were rumors and leads indicating that a threat existed. After more than four decades of private inquiry, we do at least have a few insights into the types of incidents that fed the rumors.

On at least three planned Presidential trips to Chicago, Illinois and Tampa and Miami, Florida, special precautions had been taken in reaction to reports of possible threats against the President. These threats and their Cuban connections were not presented to the Warren Commission. When the HSCA did attempt to investigate the Chicago incident, their investigators were totally "stonewalled" by memory loss among the Chicago office Secret Service personnel.

As recently as 1995, after being given personal instruction and orders from the Assassinations Records Review Board (under Federal statute) not to destroy any further records, the Secret Service destroyed boxes of documents relating to Presidential travel in the fall of 1963. In addition, the final report of the ARRB suggests that at some unspecified date(s) the Secret Service had also destroyed their records related to potential threats in Dallas and its FPCC file.[2]

A closer look at the last two months before Dallas reveals the following:

October 1, 1963

John Martino traveled to Dallas to deliver a series of speeches relating to his new book against the Castro regime. During this trip, he mentioned knowing that Sylvia Odio and her sisters, the daughters of his friend Amador Odio, were in Dallas. This occurred in the same time frame in which Sylvia Odio had been visited by two suspicious Latinos and Leon Oswald.

In Mexico City on October 1, someone speaking very bad Russian but very good Spanish impersonated Lee Oswald in a call to the Russian embassy. The impersonation created a taped record of an apparent connection between Oswald and the Cubans.

October 3, 1963

Jack Ruby made a call to R.D. Matthews' ex-wife. The content of this conversation remains unknown, but it appears very likely that Ruby had a serious reason for renewing his association with the ex-Dallas mobster and Havana casino alumnus. Matthews had been a co-worker of Martino and Ruby's friend McWillie.

October, first two weeks, exact dates unknown

Roselli was reportedly observed meeting with Ruby on two separate occasions in Florida. This was during the period of time Ruby was out of Dallas, supposedly on a business trip to New Orleans. This observation was contained in the FBI files on Roselli's surveillance and noted by an FBI agent during the investigation of Roselli's murder thirteen years later. The FBI agent confidentially contacted a Washington D.C. investigative reporter, Scott Malone. Malone retained a tape of the telephone call that he played for Rappleye and Becker when they were working on Roselli's biography. Malone reported his findings in an article titled "The Secret Life of Jack Ruby."[3]

This apparent Ruby-Roselli connection is corroborated by Roselli's reported remark to his friend Jack Anderson, to the effect that Ruby was "their boy" in Dallas. It is also corroborated by one of Roselli's associates from the Castro project, Robert Maheu, who stated that Ruby had worked for the mob and probably had ties to Roselli (while maintaining that Oswald acted alone).[4] The implications of such a Roselli-Ruby meeting are key to understanding the events in Dallas.

October 16, 1963

Lee Oswald began work at the Texas School Book Depository.

Mid-October, 1963

An Air Force Security Service monitoring unit monitored a call in which the individuals involved discussed a plot against President Kennedy. This incident was investigated by the HSCA and the documents pertaining to it are still classified. What is known about the Kirknewton intercept is presented in Appendix F, *Another Rumor.*

November 1, 1963

In Miami, Jorge Soto Martinez engaged in a conversation at the Parrot Jungle store bragging that his friend Lee, who was living in either Mexico or Texas was an American Marxist. Lee, who spoke Russian, was a crack marksman. The conversation was reported to the FBI after the assassination and Jorge Martinez denied making any of the reported remarks although several Parrot Jungle employees corroborated the incident.

Mrs. Lillian Spingler, employee, made a detailed statement on the encounter to Jorge Martinez and who was questioned by the FBI in late

December. After a quick investigation, FBI Agent James O'Conner told Mrs. Spingler to, *"Just drop it and not to mention it."*[5]

October 30-November 1

On November 1 in Chicago, Illinois, the Secret Service was investigating potential threats against President Kennedy during a scheduled motorcade and appearance at Soldiers Field for an Army-Air Force football game. The HSCA investigated this incident at length and met with total memory loss among the personnel in the Chicago SS office; even a typist whose initials showed on related reports for the trip could not recall ever having seen the documents though her initials indicated that she had typed them.

"Isn't that the one that was cancelled at the last minute?"[6]

Agent Griffiths at first disclaimed any knowledge, until his memory was refreshed; he then confirmed the trip. We know that the trip was scheduled and cancelled at the absolute last minute on the morning of November 2, though personnel associated with security for the trip and the Presidential motorcade were deployed and waiting. Secret Service Agent Robert Kollar recalled arriving in Chicago a week in advance to conduct preparations for the visit. He also told the HSCA that he received notification of the trip cancellation only on the morning of the day itself and was given no explanation at all. The loss of memory in the Chicago Secret Service office even extended to other agencies.

"I remember that case. Some people were picked up. And I'm telling you it wasn't ours. That whole Soldier Field matter was a Secret Service affair... you'll get no more out of me. I've said as much as I'm going to say on that subject. Get the rest from the Secret Service." – FBI agent Thomas B. Coll.[7]

After much investigation, we can now see that there appear to have been two threats associated with the Chicago trip. The first involved one Thomas Vallee, who had been reported by an associate as making remarks against the President. Vallee was investigated and arrested early on the morning of November 2. He was in police custody at the time the trip was cancelled.

The second and apparently much more serious and confidential threat has been described in detail by no one except Secret Service

Agent Abraham Bolden. Bolden was the first black agent to serve on the White House Detail. As of November, he was reassigned to the Chicago office. After the assassination, Bolden made certain unflattering remarks about drinking and lack of professionalism by some members of the White House Detail on which he had served. He also remarked on the cancelled Chicago visit. On May 18, 1964, Bolden was arrested and charged with a criminal offense in conjunction with his office's investigation of a counterfeiting case.

As events would later suggest, Bolden's remarks seem to have led to his being framed for a crime in order to shut him up and remove him from potential public visibility.   The judge in his trial made some extremely remarkable statements to the jury and legal counsel and refused to consider the fact that the primary witness against Bolden recanted his story and admitted to lying. On January 20, the government's witness against Bolden admitted under oath that he had committed perjury.

Page 6825 of the official transcript of the Joseph Spagnoli trial shows the following dialogue:

Spagnoli: I lied in the Bolden trial.

Court: Are you telling this court under oath that you lied in the Bolden trial?

Spagnoli: Yes, Sir.

Court: You committed perjury then?

Spagnoli: Yes.

The judge in Bolden's case was Judge Perry; he was also the judge in the Spagnoli trial. Judge Perry refused to accept this new information that indicated that Spagnoli had perjured himself and implicated Bolden at the behest of government prosecutor, Richard Sikes. A yellow sheet of paper in Sikes' handwriting was submitted into evidence to verify Spagnoli's allegation and testimony. Prosecutor Sikes stated that "The only thing that I promised Spagnoli was that any co-operation that he gave would be brought to the attention of the judge."

Judge Perry denied a retrial for Bolden on the grounds that he did not believe Spagnoli and that Spagnoli's confession was some sort of a plan by which he could free Bolden thus freeing himself. Abraham Bolden was sentenced to six years in federal prison and his appeal rejected.[8]

Just what was so threatening about the cancelled Kennedy Chicago trip that demanded the false imprisonment of a Secret Service agent; the "scrubbing" of the memories of the entire Chicago Secret Service office staff; and the destruction of four boxes of documents about the trip in direct violation of a Federal order *as recently as 1995*? Bolden himself had no idea. He was very forthright about his being moved off the White House detail because of his complaints to Harvey Henderson and James Rowley about the heavy drinking among the Detail Agents. However, corroboration of Bolden's observations is suggested by the behavior of the full Dallas Secret Service detail and in particular, the motorcade security car unit who partied in a Ft. Worth bar until approximately 3 a.m. on the morning on November 22. This incident was reported, officially investigated, and extensively documented, with no reprimands or disciplinary actions, even in light of the utter failure of the unit to protect the President later that day.

After his complaints about detail drinking, racial slurs against blacks, and blacks being given separate housing during trips to the South, Bolden had been transferred to Chicago.

Bolden's observations on the Chicago JFK incident were simple and unexaggerated. He stated that on the night of October 30, a long teletype was received in the Chicago Secret Service office from the FBI. Prior to the teletype there had been a telephone call from the FBI. It was unusual for the Secret Service to receive alerts from the FBI (another point of Bolden's that seems corroborated by events of the Florida and Texas trips). The FBI communications concerned a potential danger to the President; four persons of interest were identified and surveillance was conducted on the "North Side" of Chicago. The surveillance was blown by mistakes of Agent Jay Lloyd Stocks; only two of the suspects were apprehended and brought in for questioning. Bolden knew this only because of his monitoring of SS channels in his vehicle and through office gossip, especially some rather pointed jibes offered to Agent Stocks.

With only 13 agents in the office, this sort of gossip was common and everyone generally knew a good deal about active cases and investigations in progress. All Bolden observed was that the suspects brought in were apparently questioned late in the evening of November

1 and eventually turned over to the Chicago Police. The other two suspects remained at large. Bolden saw only one suspect and described him as "swarthy and stocky," 5 foot 9 or 10 inches, dark hair and a crew cut. One of the two men was named Gonzalez.

At this point there was a call from Washington D.C. and a sensitive Central Office case number assigned to the file on the incident. This meant that the file would be held separate from the normal office files. After the suspects were handed over to the police, the agent's notes, photos and memos were taken to O'Hare airport and put on a commercial flight to Washington. Bolden stated that he had made a few notes in his personal notebook at the time but that notebook was seized during his arrest and not returned. This leaves us with an indication that people who were seen as a potential threat to the president had traveled to the Chicago area at the time of a planned visit by the president. Given that of the two known threats from Chicago, Vallee was in custody, it appears the fact that two of these individuals were still at large may have led to the cancellation of the President's trip at the very last moment.[9]

November 4, 1963

Following his visit by FBI agent Hosty to Marina Oswald and collection of information on Oswald, Hosty sent an airtel to New Orleans and HQ advising them to make Dallas the office of origin since Oswald was now resident there.[10]

November 8, 1963

"Oswald had contacted two known subversives about two weeks before the assassination." – Special Agent William Patterson, Secret Service.

Agent Patterson engaged in conversation with Agent Hosty after the murder. Hosty informed him that Oswald had contacted two known subversives about two weeks before and a classified security report was generated on the incident. Hosty expressed his belief that the report would be turned over to the Director of the Secret Service, and Patterson recorded the conversation in a memo that he submitted to his superiors. Patterson expressed concern that he was never questioned by his superiors about this incident nor interviewed by the Warren Commission. He also expressed surprise that when he interviewed Marina Oswald on November 23 or 24, the FBI had not interviewed her nor did they request a copy of his interview that was the first official record of her remarks.

This Treasury Department memo highlights the issue of the FBI's actual relationship with Oswald, a relationship that the FBI was so eager to obscure that it verifiably went so far as to destroy and alter evidence. For example, during the time of the initial FBI and WC inquiries, Agent Hosty was ordered to destroy a note brought to the FBI office in Dallas by Lee Oswald on November 12. Hosty did so and made no mention of the note in any of his official reports or statements. In addition, at a higher level, the FBI had Lee Oswald's personal notebook retyped and the pages renumbered to remove a note regarding a contact between Hosty and Oswald. When fully revealed, Oswald's notebook contained FBI Agent Hosty's business number, home phone number, and license plate number. This fact has initially been concealed by the FBI when it removed the Hosty reference and renumbered the diary pages; in a more dramatic incident and acting on orders from his superior, Hosty had actually destroyed a note left by Oswald at the Dallas FBI office. We can only speculate on other pieces of evidence that may have been altered or possibly "gone missing." Such speculation would include the box of Ruby/Oswald materials turned over to Dallas officers after the assassination as well as seven metal file boxes reportedly containing letters, maps, records and index cards with names of pro-Castro sympathizers.[11]

A recently released memorandum from the FBI Director of Security to Director Hoover is one more indication that the Dallas FBI office had been repeatedly informed of Oswald's suspicious activities in Mexico and the USSR before the assassination. This memorandum appears to be a report on the FBI mail intercept of Oswald's letter to the Soviet embassy in which he mentions "Comrade Kostin" (the intercept program was so secret, the source is identified even in the Secret FBI memo as an "informant").[12] The interesting part is that the memo is distributed to Mexico City, to New Orleans and with 2 copies to Dallas. The last paragraph verifies that: *"Information being furnished Dallas for whatever action deemed necessary since that Office is origin and status of (Oswald) investigation is unknown to WFO"* (FBI security office). This document is among the FBI series provided as exhibits for Chapter 15.

In addition to his remarks to Agent Patterson, Agent Hosty also spoke to DPD Officer Jack Revill on November 22, stating that Oswald was a known Communist and had been under observation.

When Revill protested that the information had not been shared with the Dallas Police intelligence unit, he was reminded of the FBI policy forbidding sharing of information pertaining to espionage.[13]

Other indications that Oswald was under some sort of surveillance surfaced immediately after the assassination. However, none of these seems to have been explored in depth by any of the official investigations. These include:

- William Kline, chief of the US Customs Bureau investigative services in Laredo, Texas, stated on November 25 that Oswald's movements were watched at the request of "a federal agency at Washington."

- Eugene Pugh, US agent in charge of the Customs office on the American side of the bridge at Laredo, admitted to the *New York Herald Tribune* that "US Immigration had a folder on Oswald's trip." In addition, Pugh stated that the checks on Oswald during his transit to and from Mexico were "not the usual procedure."[14]

All of this is consistent with what one would expect for a highly visible FPCC activist and Castro supporter being monitored while traveling to and from Mexico. Indeed, from recently released documents and tapes on the afternoon of November 22, we have a statement from Hoover to President Johnson confirming that the FBI monitored Oswald on multiple trips to and from Cuba but had been unable to fully explain his activities and intentions.

An Associated Press dispatch of November 30 from Dallas said that "someone telegraphed small amounts of money to Lee Oswald for several months before the assassination." Whether or not this story was correct is difficult to determine, because shortly after this the FBI instructed Western Union in Dallas that any inquiries about the frequent teletype messages for Lee Oswald would receive no further comment; "any details or comment would have to come from Washington headquarters of the Federal Bureau of Investigation." Based on what we now know to be a matter of record, we can definitely be sure that whatever the truth about the FBI contacts with Oswald, it was not the blanket statement reported in a story published by the *New York Times*. *That FBI statement firmly declared that Oswald was not under surveillance by the FBI as months of checking had indicated that Oswald was "neither a spy nor a saboteur."* Recent document releases showing extensive FBI investigation of Oswald in Mexico City in the two months before the assassination show such a statement to be absolutely false.

November 9, 1963

The FBI conducted surveillance on Joseph Milteer and obtained a tape recording of Milteer describing plans to kill the President by placing a sniper in a tall building during a motorcade; the plan included the use of a patsy to throw off investigators. The informant who was in contact with Milteer stated that "the impression I got from" Milteer was that *this conspiracy originated in New Orleans and probably some in Miami.*" Milteer, a member of the National States Rights Party, had attended an ultra-right wing political meeting (Congress of Freedom) in New Orleans in April, 1963 and was personally connected to some of the right wing speakers that were involved in the fall speaking tour in which John Martino participated. Milteer's information was provided to the Secret Service but is totally un-acknowledged in the official trip memo provided to Chief Rowley. Later investigations have also encountered omissions in the record for Miami similar to those of the aborted trip to Chicago.

November 12, 1963

Oswald entered the FBI office in Dallas and left a sealed note for Special Agent Hosty.

Jack Ruby was meeting for two days with Al Gruber of Los Angeles. The two men had not seen each other since 1947. Gruber would later offer no real reason for the visit, claiming that he drove over to see Jack because he was in Arkansas and it was close! At the time, among other activities, Gruber reportedly ran a card game in Los Angeles.[15] The afternoon of November 22, Jack Ruby made only two long distance calls, one to his sister in Chicago and one to Al Gruber in Los Angeles.

November 15, 1963

A telex from the FBI's San Antonio office related a threat against the President on his upcoming trip to Dallas. The message contains the warning that "....*a militant group of the National States Rights party plans to assassinate the President and other high level officials.*" [16] It is important to note that this is one of two leaks from National States Rights Party members. The Milteer leak previously mentioned may well have had to do with a threat to the President during his extremely long motorcade in Tampa on November 18th. It appears that gossip about a fairly specific threat to the President was circulating among not only Cuban exiles and underworld figures but also certain elements of the ultra-right. John Martino was moving within these same ultra-right circles in 1963 and 1964; he was in great demand for speeches and articles relating to the Communist menace in Cuba, something in which he sincerely believed.

November 16, 1963
"Oswald interviewed by FBI" – *Dallas Morning News* headline, James Ewell, November 24, 1963.

The sources for this newspaper report, anonymous at the time but revealed in the 1990s, were Chief Jesse Curry and his police intelligence unit. Curry refused to blame the FBI for not sharing its surveillance of Oswald and was quoted as saying, "the FBI has no obligation to help the Dallas Police" and confirmed that neither the DPD nor the Secret Service was informed.

Jack Ruby was reported in Las Vegas on November 16. Two separate informants reported this, one to Las Vegas Sheriff Ralph Lamb and the other directly to the FBI. One informant had access to the hotel's front office and verified Ruby's stay with room and telephone records which disappeared from the hotel files. Both sources placed Ruby at the Tropicana, a hotel in which John Roselli had originally been very much involved, as verified by the FBI.[17]

November 17, 1963
RFK began a series of key meetings in preparation for support of a hoped for coup against Fidel Castro. These meetings involved RFK, Artime, two of Artime's leaders and Enrique Ruiz Williams. The meetings are referred to in Army intelligence documents previously discussed and referenced in the Califano papers. The document references further meetings on either November 22 or 23 as well as a meeting between RFK and a Cuban troop leader from Fort Benning, scheduled for November 18 in Washington D.C.[18]

November 17, 1963
At approximately 1:45 a.m. on November 17, a telex was reportedly received in the New Orleans office of the FBI. The teletype was

addressed to all SAC's from the Director. The Bureau security clerk on duty later testified to the HSCA about it.[19]

> Threat to assassinate President Kennedy in Dallas, Texas, November twenty-two... information has been received by the Bureau that a militant revolutionary group may attempt to assassinate President Kennedy on his proposed trip to Dallas. All receiving offices should immediately contact all CI's, PCIS, Local Race and Hate group informants and determine if any basis for the threat. Bureau should be kept advised of all developments by teletype. Other offices have been advised and ack pls."[20]

Walter worked strictly from memory making a reconstruction of the actual message, including the Cuban note. No copy of the teletype exists and the Bureau most adamantly denied it ever existed. Walter testified to the document and also described being on duty the Saturday morning Lee Oswald had demanded a meeting with an FBI agent after his leafleting arrest. Walter had supported the agent, John Quigley, by checking for a file on Oswald. Walter found multiple cards on Oswald and all the related files fell into the "security type, informant type files– 105 and 134 classifications."

Walter's statements were totally rejected by the FBI and discredited by the HSCA, primarily over technical details in the text he provided from memory to them. Walter could only relate that what he had provided was a roughly typed version based on handwritten notes taken at the time and his memory.

By focusing on the technical details of his typed reconstruction, the HSCA interviewers essentially pretended that Walter was trying to deceive them with a forgery. This allowed them to ignore Walter's troublesome claim that the original teletype had once existed:

> "The point is if I wanted to make a teletype look like a teletype, I had the knowledge and the ability to do just that. I made teletypes myself that were approved by supervisors and sent to other field offices. If I had wanted to use correct terminology because I thought that at a later date I was going to use this particular document to make myself look good or for publicity, I certainly would have done a better job."

Walter did not report the teletype at the time of the assassination and continued as an FBI employee for a brief period. When he eventually did talk about the teletype, he related that Bureau personnel were pressed to sign affidavits—not to the effect that the teletype did not exist but that they would not "disclose" information, with the appropriate reminders of penalties for security breaches. Walter concluded with a simple statement: "I had gotten the feeling from everybody I talked to that we know this is true, but we are not going to talk about it.'"

Researcher Mary LaFontaine contacted a former agent McCurley who had been Walter's best man at his wedding. Their conversation shows the extent to which Walter's fellow employees distanced themselves from him:

LaFontaine: Did you know Walter well?

McCurley: Well, I knew him while we both worked at the FBI at that time you know.

LaFontaine: Did you believe this was false testimony that he made?

McCurley: I couldn't say yes or no.

LaFontaine: Did he ever discuss it with you at the time of the assassination?

McCurley: I really don't know, you know.

LaFontaine: Did you ever know him to fabricate stories?

McCurley: No, not really.

LaFontaine: Did the FBI ever talk to you about it?

McCurley: (after a long pause) I can't recall. I might have signed a statement.[21]

An FBI cover document apparently related to this incident specifically states that the originator has been "told not to place the letters in the office files on express instructions of the Deputy Associate Director, James Adams." Unfortunately, the HSCA neglected to use its legal powers to corroborate Walter's information, just as it had evaded the opportunities presented by McKeown, Bolden, and others.

The HSCA could find no motive for any supposed fabrication. Walter had left the FBI in early 1964 in good standing to start a successful career in banking and had never made any attempt to gain publicity or profit from his experience with the telex.[22]

November 17, 1963

In Abilene, Texas, Pedro Gonzalez, a local exile activist and friend of Tony Varona in Miami, received a note. It was left for Gonzalez and seen by a good friend and exile supporter, Harold Reynolds. "Call me immediately – Urgent" with two Dallas telephone numbers and the name Lee Oswald.[23]

An explanation as to how the note may have gotten to Abilene emerged in the completely independent report of W.M. Hannie, who drove from Juarez, Mexico, to Ft. Worth, Texas, a few days before the assassination. He was asked for a ride by a young man and during the trip, the young man talked about having recently been in Mexico City working at the "Book Company," having two small children and Jack Ruby's "honky-tonk" in Dallas. Hannie's girlfriend, Dorothy Marcum, confirmed his story including the fact that the young man left them at every stop to use the telephone. Abilene is a bit over half-way on the trip from Juarez to Fort Worth/Dallas.

Of course according to the official record, Lee Oswald should have been working in the TSBD at this point. However, during October and November there were several concrete reports of someone representing himself as Lee Oswald at a time when Oswald should have been at work. These incidents were all highly incriminating and each should have helped connect the real Oswald to a premeditated, planned and "paid" murder of the President:

1. October 4: Oswald applied for a job as a photographer in the Adolphus Hotel in Downtown Dallas. The Adolphus was across the street from the Carousel Club.[24]

2. October 31: Oswald applied for a job at the multi-story Statler Hilton Hotel in Downtown Dallas.

3. November 1: A rifle associated with Oswald was left at Dial Ryder's gun shop to have a scope installed on his rifle–although the final Oswald weapon in evidence had a scope when purchased.

4. Approximately November 7: Oswald applied for a job at the Allright Parking garage located at 1208 Commerce Street.[25] Jack Ruby parked his car at the Allright on a monthly basis according to a statement from Eugene Dibbles to Detective W.S. Biggio.[26]

5. November 9: Oswald test drove a new car from the Downtown Lincoln-Mercury dealership, gave his name and stated he would soon have enough money to buy the car.

6. November 16: Oswald applied for a job at the Southland Hotel parking garage and asked if the building had a good view of downtown Dallas.

If Oswald had not been taken into custody but rather had been killed escaping as in the plan described by Martino, each of these incidents would have been very useful in establishing his planning and preparations. Certainly they do not represent the last minute, emotional decision to kill President Kennedy that was presented in the Warren Report. This planning and preparation would have been confirmed by a story of Oswald being seen taking money for the assassination from a black Cuban in the Cuban embassy in Mexico City—a story that was given to the CIA immediately after the assassination.

Abilene, Reynolds, and the Oswald Note

Reynolds attempted to report the incident twice after the assassination but stated that agents were uninterested, as no pro-Castro Cubans were involved. Reynolds' story surfaced in the HSCA investigation of original reports. His comments were extensive, including a description of how his friend, Gonzalez, forcefully collected any and all photos of himself and any other exiles before leaving town immediately after the assassination. He also described meetings at Gonzalez's residence that were attended by individuals driving cars with Florida and Louisiana license plates. Two Anglos also attended a meeting with Gonzalez a couple of months before the assassination—a young man resembling Oswald and "a little dried up Anglo from New Orleans, about 5'8" appearing to be in his 50's and with a weathered complexion." This same description could easily be applied to John Martino.

Gonzalez's friend, Tony Varona, had several interesting connections including being a long-time and high-level associate of Carlos Prio Soccares, an associate of Santo Trafficante, and a participant in Roselli's attempts to murder Castro for the CIA. He was also reportedly an associate of John Martino's in 1963 and had apparently become privy to information from Artime about the new autonomous group project.

November 17, 1963

Jack Ruby called Al Gruber, his recent visitor in Dallas. Following this call, Ruby reportedly traveled to Las Vegas. The nature of this trip is uncertain and it was not inserted in the "official" Ruby timeline developed by the Warren Commission, despite several independent witnesses and observations of Ruby in Las Vegas on that date.

John Roselli, who had been under frequent FBI surveillance in the latter part of 1963, conducted a rather elaborate travel ruse that allowed him to shake FBI surveillance and travel to Las Vegas circa November 18.[27]

November 18, 1963

President Kennedy visited Tampa and Miami, Florida. On December 11, 1963, John Marshall, Special Agent in Charge of the Miami trip, sent a summary trip memorandum to James Rowley, Chief of the US Secret Service. Ostensibly this memo detailed all the threats, incidents, warnings and preventive measures taken in regard to the President's trip. However, as with the Chicago trip, we only have hints of certain threats and incidents that did not make it into this report. However, uncovered documents indicate at least two other serious threats to the President on his Florida trip.

- An interview with Robert Jamison states that "the threat of November 18 was posed by a mobile, unidentified rifleman with a high-powered rifle and a scope."[28]

- An interview with Lubert F. deFreese states that, "there was an active threat against the President which the Secret Service was aware of in November 1963 in the period immediately prior to JFK's trip to Miami made by a group of people."[29]

Additional research by Lamar Waldron has detailed a threat in Tampa, the first Florida city visited by the President, and one in which he did participate in an unusually long motorcade which passed the tallest building in the city, the Floridan Hotel. Waldron's interviews, discussed in chapters ten and twenty-four of *Ultimate Sacrifice* show confirmation of the Tampa threat by Chief of Police Mullins and cite another high Florida law-enforcement official as saying that "JFK had been briefed that he was in danger." Waldron also notes that the Secret Service destruction of Presidential travel records (after being officially instructed by the ARRB that no such records were to be touched until reviewed) occurred only weeks after he had informed the ARRB of the threat in Tampa.

Although it is impossible to develop further details of these threats at this point, it is also a fact that car travel between a hotel and a heliport that had originally been planned for Miami was not executed. The President's party was picked up directly by helicopter at the hotel.

November 19, 1963

At Red Bird airfield in South Dallas, Woburn Incorporated had been in the process of selling off a small fleet of DC3 transports that it had purchased to fulfill a contract that ended in 1963. The last of the aircraft was sold in November and the new owner had arrived at Red Bird to collect his aircraft on November 18. As part of the deal, Woburn had agreed to completely check the aircraft and perform any required repairs. They had contracted with Wayne January to meet the new owner and the pilot that came with him. The pilot spoke English with no accent but told January that he had been born in Cuba and eventually revealed that his boss was an Air Force Colonel. The Cuban pilot was extremely proficient with the DC3 and later told January that he had flown that type of aircraft in Cuba as an officer in the Cuban Air Force.

During the next few days, the two men became friendly with each other and the man made remarks which January kept to himself over more than two decades, finally contacting and communicating with a JFK researcher/author only in 1992. Matthew Smith gives the details of the Red Bird incident in Chapter Seven of his book *Vendetta*. [30] By Thursday, November 21, January and the Cuban had become close enough to talk somewhat freely. During their lunch break and after a period silence, the Cuban looked at January and said: *"They are going to kill your President."* January could tell the man was not joking. He had shown no sign of being less than serious before this in any conversation. When January asked him why he was saying this, the Cuban talked about being involved in the Bay of Pigs and about being told how his friends had died because Robert Kennedy had talked John Kennedy out of sending the air support they had been promised for the invasion. He talked about the pain and the embarrassment of those involved. *"They are not only going to kill the President, they are going to kill Robert Kennedy and any other Kennedy who gets in that position."* January knew the man was serious, but it was too much for him to believe and he said so. The Cuban closed the conversation with, *"You will see."*

The DC3, its new owner, and the Cuban pilot departed Dallas the afternoon of November 22. January saw the Cuban again briefly right after the initial report of shots being fired at the motorcade. The Cuban, appearing rather sad, simply said, *"It's all going to happen like I told you."*

During JFK Lancer's 2003 *November In Dallas* conference, Matthew Smith revealed January's name in conjunction with this incident (after his death and with permission of his widow). The aircraft had been sold to the Houston Air Center and the actual FAA registration number of the aircraft was N-17888. During 2004, an individual working with the author managed to obtain the FAA file on this aircraft and the paperwork confirms the basic elements of Wayne January's remarks including the modification of the aircraft for fitting of special radar equipment. The aircraft in question was actually a C-53 (the troop transport version of the DC-3); manufactured in 1944 and eventually sold by the US Liquidator of War Assets to Mid-Continent Airlines in 1949. The aircraft eventually came to Red Bird airfield in Dallas in January of 1963 and was held by two different companies there; Wayne January was involved with both companies. The paperwork also confirms that January did sell the aircraft to Houston Air Center Inc. but it did not actually register the aircraft until 1965, shortly before it was sold outside the United States to Aerovias del Sur of Mexico City.

Names of individuals associated with the purchase and sale of the Aircraft at Houston Air Center include President E. Mitchell Smith Jr. and Vice President Clarence Wrigley. January had told Smith that standard practice was not to actually complete the paper transfer until the plane was resold, thus deferring sales taxes. This practice has been confirmed to the author by a historian at the Houston airport. An interesting side note is the fact that in 1963, the aircraft had indeed been re-classed with the FAA as an R&D, experimental aircraft. In conjunction with its modifications all the seats were removed from the aircraft.

We do know that Artime was acquiring transport aircraft in the second half of 1963. A memo copied to "AM/WORLD Aircraft" discusses chartering a C-47 transport through Sociedad Resposibilidad Limited. The memo is from Raul Hernandez in regard to a conversation with Artime.[31] It is also interesting that the C-53 was resold by Houston Air Center after approximately 18 months, at the point in time in which the Artime off-shore exile initiative had finally been shut down by President Johnson. It may also be relevant to point out that a CIA proprietary airline (Southern Air Transport; crypt ZR/CLIFF) had flown out of Houston. Reportedly, while flying a Douglass 553 transport for Southern Air Transport, David Ferrie kept his plane at the ZR/CLIFF facilities in Houston.[32]

November 19, 1963

Jack Ruby told his tax attorney that he had finally managed to come up with the money to address his substantial back tax problems. On November 22, Ruby would be seen with $7,000 in cash at his bank and was arrested with $3,000 in cash in his possession. As of November 19 the supposedly cash strapped Ruby had begun talking to a realtor about a new location for his club, had inquired with someone in the travel business about a Caribbean cruise and told a friend that he planned on moving into a new apartment on Turtle Creek, at almost double his then current apartment rental rate[33].

SUMMARY

President Kennedy was at risk during the last few weeks of his life. One of his advance men tells us that, and says Kennedy himself knew it, but thought the Secret Service had the threats in hand.

- The FBI and Secret Service were warned of potential threats in Chicago, Florida and Texas; to what extent specific Secret Service personnel knew of these threats and warnings is uncertain.

- Evidence of all such threats was suppressed following the assassination.

- Evidence pertaining to fall Presidential trips was destroyed within the last decade in express violation of warning and penalties communicated to the Secret Service by the ARRB.

- The FBI had information concerning Lee Oswald that Director Hoover shared neither with the President nor the Warren Commission following the assassination, nor was it included in the FBI's own report.

- There is a clear pattern of "Oswald activity" in Dallas that created witnesses that could have been used to portray Oswald as scouting the motorcade route and perhaps selecting alternative attack positions.

- This record would have demonstrated planning on Oswald's part and negated any thought that his action was one of impulse rather than conspiracy.

- The timing and nature of these incidents suggest that Oswald was impersonated. Some of the incidents also suggest that links to Ruby were being established.

The conspirators worked diligently to create the image and establish the witnesses required in to implicate Cuba and Castro in the assassination. They were defeated by a combination of events and official damage control. However, with so many loose ends and so many people aware of threats, how did all this escape the Warren Commission's attention?

That question leads us to examine the second conspiracy in the assassination of President Kennedy—*a conspiracy to cover-up a conspiracy.*

NAMES FROM THE WAR AGAINST CASTRO

John Martino

Eugenio Martinez

Eddie Bayo

Sylvia Odio

David Morales

Rip Robertson

David Atlee Phillips

Antonio Veciana

William Harvey

John Roselli

Tony Varona

Richard Cain

Desmond Fitzgerald

Allen Dulles

Richard Helms

Ted Shackley

Manual Artime

Rafael Quintero

Manual Ray

Carlos Prio Socarras

Roy Hargraves

Felipe Vidal Santiago

Bernardo De Torres

Loran Hall

Frank Sturgis

Bernard Barker

E. Howard Hunt

Virgilio Gonzalez

Sergio Arcacha Smith

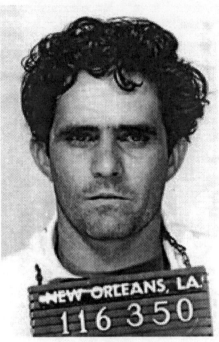

Emilio Santana

David Ferrie

Orest Pena

Tony Cuesta

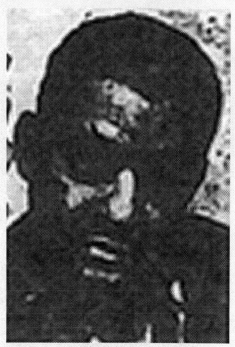

Herminio Diaz Garcia

Eladio Del Valle

Santo Trafficante

Lee Harvey Oswald

Loran Hall

William Seymour

Lawrence Howard

SECTION B

AFTERWARDS

CHAPTER 15:

"IF I TOLD YOU"

There is no indication or evidence that John Martino profited from the murder of John Kennedy. From 1964 through 1966, he continued with his anti-Communist speaking engagements and articles. Later, he became involved in selling military equipment such as bulletproof vests, in Latin America, spending much of his time outside the country for several years. During the months following the assassination, Martino personally crusaded in the media and with right-wing politicians to promote the late Lee Oswald as an agent of Fidel Castro and a Cuba-based conspiracy. Martino also filed a number of incriminating reports with the FBI and encouraged them to investigate Oswald-Castro connections, including the reported presence of Oswald in Cuba immediately prior to the assassination.[1]

Whatever Martino and his fellow conspirators expected (or may have been promised) would follow the murder of the President, it did not happen—no hostilities, no invasion of Cuba—not even any significant escalation in political or military support for operations against Cuba. The existing Special Group sabotage projects against Castro continued haltingly for a year or more. No major coup occurred; Johnson instructed Robert Kennedy and others involved with the Kennedy initiative to turn it off and so inform the military Cuban military officers. The Artime effort and AM/WORLD gradually faded away. Eventually all the attention and resources shifted to Vietnam. Fidel Castro attempted to resume his diplomatic outreach to the United Stages and President Johnson simply ignored him.

FAILURE IN DALLAS

Martino himself tells us very specifically where the plan went wrong. Lee Oswald did not make it to his contact at the Texas Theatre. There was no opportunity to get him out of Dallas and eliminate him in a manner which would directly implicate Castro. The obvious speculation from this is that Oswald had not actively participated in framing himself, certainly not to the extent of leaving an unmistakable trail to Castro. Nor was Oswald prepared to confess himself as a Castro supporter acting for the "revolution" or in response to American assassination attempts against Fidel.

The most radical aspect of this view of the assassination is the implication that *immediately following the assassination, there were actually competing efforts in play.*

Some of the individuals involved were desperately working to carry on their "script" in the face of Oswald's capture. They also had an urgent need to quickly eliminate Oswald to prevent him from directing attention to them—given his realization that he had been set up as a patsy. At the same time, individuals within the FBI and CIA were working to cover up their own use of Oswald as an intelligence tool. And, at the highest level of government, a move was underway to constrain any serious investigation of conspiracy and portray Lee Oswald strictly as a "lone nut".

The question is whether or not a detailed examination of events in the hours and weeks following November 22 supports this view of events. If it does, we would expect to see that the efforts of all parties would be reactive, spur of the moment, reflecting no advance planning and, at times, in direct conflict with each other.

A PUSH FOR CUBAN CONSPIRACY

We have already reviewed some of the many efforts that presented Oswald and even Jack Ruby as being sponsored by the Cubans or generically by Communists. These efforts to establish a direct Oswald-Castro tie can be seen in Miami, Mexico City and New Orleans. They appear weak, with no credible sources, no paper or photographic evidence, no known Castro agents identified—nothing that would be expected in a professional and prepared operation. We don't even find any credible Cuban G2 agents named as Oswald contacts or associates, though there were plenty of credible names available in both the JM/ WAVE and FBI Security files.

Examples of these reactive efforts include a series of incriminating letters from one "Pedro Charles", a self described agent of the Cuban Security Department, which referred to a meeting with Oswald in Miami and Charles' telling the "Chief" about Oswald's marksmanship. The letters were written as if they were pre-assassination encouragement to Oswald, yet were mailed and postmarked after the assassination. Other letters typed on the same typewriter were mailed to Robert Kennedy and President Johnson. The whole incident was such a transparent deception that the FBI was forced to dismiss it out of hand. However, Director Hoover himself was very interested in the letters from Cuba and in December of 1963 he promoted them as one reason not to rule out conspiracy, even as the formal FBI report was being submitted to President Johnson.[2]

In Mexico City, Ambassador Mann, CIA Station Chief Win Scott, and Cuban Operations Chief David Phillips championed a totally bizarre story from an informant initially misidentified as a Communist in reports to Washington. The Mexico City CIA officer sending the memoranda (either Phillips himself or someone under his supervision) described Gilberto Alvarado as "a well known Nicaraguan Communist underground member." This was an absolute untruth. Alvarado was an agent/informant for the Nicaraguan security services. This was quickly and correctly verified by a cable from Managua. Phillips and the Mexico City CIA station had endorsed Alvarado as a source with remarks such as:

Alvarado was, "on a penetration mission for the Nicaraguan secret service."

"Impressed...the wealth of detail Alvarado gives is striking."

"Alvarado is telling truth in general outline but mixed up on dates."[3]

Actually, Alvarado's "wealth of detail" was not merely impressive but also extremely hard to fathom, including such elements as seeing Lee Oswald meeting and talking with: "A tall, thin, Negro with reddish hair," and a "blonde-haired girl with a Canadian passport" named Maria Luisa ("with the address, Calle Jurez 407"). The girl embraced

Oswald during the contact. More importantly, Alvarado also related observing and hearing a Cuban pass money to the Cuban Negro who said to Oswald, *"I want to kill the man,"* with Oswald replying, *"You're not man enough. I can do it."* The Negro then gave Oswald $6,500 in large bills. It is also interesting that Phillips seemingly accepted that Alvarado was able to see and hear all of this happening in a public area of the Cuban Embassy, and even observe the *exact* amount of money paid![4]

Alvarado's detailed story could not be realistically supported for more than about 48 hours despite its active proponents in Mexico City. Like the stories out of Miami, it was implausible, totally lacking in supporting evidence, and in the end it conflicted with the official story of Oswald's movements and activities. Its weaknesses are another example of a "reactive" effort, rather than a professionally pre-planned, credible story with convincing sources.[5] Although this incident proved rather embarrassing to the Agency, it does not seem to have done much damage to Phillips' career. Phillips even mentions it in *The Night Watch*, including the incorrect identification of Alvarado as a Communist and as the source for the rumors that Oswald came back from Mexico City with a large amount of cash. Martino, Fiorini/Sturgis, Weyl and Bethel each promulgated stories about Oswald being in Miami, calling contacts in Cuba, and associating with Castro agents. These stories all contain references to unnamed and unverifiable sources or to individuals not on any intelligence index—sources who just happened to be away from Miami on raids or on penetration missions into Cuba.

The Committee to Free Cuba and Paul Bethel (Phillips' friend) disseminated the story of a confession from one Pasqual Gangora. He confessed that he had been sent into the US on a Castro hit team. However, it turned out that Pasqual had been a mental patient for some time before the assassination. Officials of the Committee to Free Cuba also put out stories that Oswald had visited Cuba before the assassination and that *"Ruby was a Communistic Jew"* who had met with Solomon Pratkins in Havana.[6] It appears that the same story had been hurriedly distributed to the entire anti-Castro "network." There was no documentation, nor any credible sources, to go along with this information. The story elements clashed with the official government investigation on several points—including Oswald's presence in Miami (a common element in almost all the "network" stories), Oswald's trips to Cuba, contact with Cuban agents, and Ruby's participation with

Oswald, as well as Oswald's own Communist leanings and Castro connection. Whether or not some of these elements might actually be true is open to debate. However, since they were contradicted by the positions taken by the FBI and CIA, the "Castro did it" propaganda faced an uphill battle. Within a matter of days, the story coming from the US government and the Johnson administration quickly overwhelmed the "Castro was behind Oswald and Ruby" efforts.

DANGEROUS TO THE COUNTRY

One thing is crystal clear. Based on the records releases of the 1990's, fear was a factor in many of the activities that followed the assassination. President Johnson used fear in the creation of the Warren Commission; he personally gave Earl Warren the responsibility to validate the FBI report, which presented Oswald as the lone assassin. That FBI report, itself generated after no more than a few days of investigation, was leaked to the media even before the report itself was completely finalized.

Johnson himself, with the assistance of his personal political aide Clifford Carter, had contacted and ordered the Dallas Police and the Dallas District Attorney not to file conspiracy charges against Lee Oswald. In addition, Johnson officially took the murder investigation and major pieces of evidence away from Dallas and apparently ordered them into the possession of the FBI prior to midnight on the evening of the murder. The details of this order are difficult to verify because the record of Johnson's telephone calls now contains no reference to a Friday night call from Johnson to Hoover. Such a call was described by William Manchester[7] but does not now appear in Johnson's call log. However, there is no doubt about the fact that key medical and ballistics evidence left Dallas for Washington on November 22.

While any official suggestion of conspiracy was being aggressively neutralized at the Presidential level, the FBI and the CIA were revisiting events in Mexico City, which presented the possibility that Lee Oswald might well have been acting as a tool of the Cuban government of the Soviet KGB. A key element in this scenario was a telephone call in which an individual naming himself as Oswald contacted a known KGB officer and made statements suggesting that he was in close contact with Cuban officials.

We now have tapes of Johnson's telephone conversations that demonstrate that he used events in Mexico City to force individuals such as Earl Warren and Senator Russell into taking part in the Warren Commission—assuring them that they only had to sign off on the FBI report.[8] And warning them that failure to cooperate could put the nation in a dire situation, *risking atomic war and millions of deaths.* In the end he would override people ranging from Ambassador Mann and CIA station chief Scott in Mexico City to J. Edgar Hoover, who wanted his FBI report to include some statement about the possibility of Cuban influence on Oswald. Johnson would have his way but his actions would leave a legacy of doubt at even the highest levels. One insight into the seriousness of the situation can be seen in a remark made by J. Edgar Hoover to the son of wealthy Texas oilman, Billy Byars.

Billy Byars, Sr., a Humble Oil millionaire, was close to Hoover. They used adjacent bungalows at Murchison's California hotel every year during Hoover's vacation. On the afternoon of November 22, Hoover's phone record shows that Billy Byars, Sr. was the only person Hoover called outside the government. Byars' son Billy Jr. spoke with Director Hoover the following year at the Del Charro resort. He related that Hoover, Murchison and Byars frequently dined together.

Billy Byars, Jr. thought that Hoover seemed to be in a strange frame of mind, getting along better with Johnson than Kennedy of course, but with a difference from earlier years. At one point, the young college student got to ask Hoover about the assassination and whether or not he thought Oswald had killed the President. The reply was nothing like what he anticipated, as Hoover's remark was, *"If I told you what I really know, it would be very dangerous to the country. Our whole political system could be disrupted."* J. Edgar Hoover, 1964. That was all he said, and it was obvious that he would say no more.[9]

Was Director Hoover posturing for the son of an old friend? Or was he getting something off his chest? Some see this as a confession of conspiracy; the alternative interpretation would be that Hoover suspected that his arch-enemies, the Communists, had gotten away with killing a US President.

OSWALD - HOT IN MEXICO CITY

September 27, 1963

Lee Oswald reportedly arrived in Mexico City and according to the CIA he made multiple visits to the Cuban Embassy/Consulate, plus three separate telephone calls to the Soviet Consulate. On September 28, he and a woman, purportedly Sylvia Duran, made a call to the Soviet Consulate from the Cuban consulate. The CIA was unable to provide any photos of Oswald entering or leaving the Consulate during the period of September 27 through October 1 while he was in Mexico City, despite the known existence of photo surveillance equipment at both the Cuban and Soviet facilities.

A newly available document relates correspondence from David Phillips, CIA, Mexico City.[10] Phillips conducted a photographic records search in an attempt to corroborate a claim by Pedro Gutierrez Valencia that he had seen an American resembling Oswald at the Cuban embassy in the company of a Cuban on October 1, 1963. *Phillips advised that CIA was unable to identify Gutierrez visiting the Cuban embassy during either September or October.* Phillips stated that *photographic surveillance was in full operation during all daylight hours in this period* and that the photo file would have allowed Gutierrez to be identified if he had indeed entered the Cuban embassy.

Phillips also refers to a comprehensive photo file for the Cuban embassy available for reference in March 1964. This raises the question of why this comprehensive file would not have contained photographs of Lee Harvey Oswald entering or leaving the Cuban consulate embassy during the same period. A period in which Phillips describes full photo surveillance to be in effect, with no down time in September or October which might have missed Gutierrez.

October 8, 1963

CIA Mexico City station had reported Oswald's contacts with the Cuban and Soviet embassies to CIA Headquarters on October 8, including Oswald's apparent contact with Soviet Vice Counsel Kostikov. In response to the Mexico City request for information, CIA HQ responded that Lee Oswald was known to them as an ex-Marine Soviet defector. However, the last activity in his file was his return to the US in May of 1962 and they had no more recent information on him. This misleading response was approved by a variety of individuals—the same people who had also signed off as having read a number of reports on Oswald's leafleting and pro-Castro, FPCC activities in New Orleans only two months before.

This misrepresentation involved Ann Egerter of Angleton's Counter Intelligence staff, Jane Roman, liaison to CI (Counter Intelligence), and Thomas Karamissines, Assistant Deputy Director for Plans (one of the top four executive positions in the Agency). All these individuals, without doubt, signed off on a very incomplete reply concerning Oswald when the true facts would have triggered a much higher level of response in Mexico City.

When interviewed and shown the relevant documents with her signature in the 1990's by Dr. John Newman, Jane Roman admitted that she was *"signing off on something she knows not to be true."* This interview was taped by *Washington Post* reporter Jeff Morley.[11]

The CIA translators in Mexico City were Mr. and Mrs. Tarasoff, identified as Mr. and Mrs. T in Newman's *Oswald and the CIA*. Their full names are given in Peter Dale Scott's *Deep Politics II* [12] where Scott also notes that "Mr. Tarasoff added the important and possibly relevant detail that the name Lee Oswald was known to the CIA station before the October 1 telephone call from someone who identified himself as Lee Oswald." In Tarasoff's words *"they were very hot about the whole thing"* before that call was transcribed.

Also, the author had the opportunity to discuss the Mexico City incidents in further detail with former FBI Agent James Hosty. Hosty repeated a conversation he had with a friend of his who had been working in Mexico City at the time, agent Michael DeGuire. DeGuire had informed Hosty, after the assassination, that Oswald was under surveillance in Mexico City outside of his visits to the embassies and that he had been separately photographed near a fountain at one time during the surveillance.[13]

October 10, 1963

CIA Mexico City sent a memo to various State Dept, FBI and Navy organizations in regard to Oswald's embassy visits; Oswald's apparent contacts with Soviet official Kostikov were not mentioned. However, departments of the INS and FBI in Mexico City were later notified with full information, and an intensive investigation of sources and contacts for information on Oswald was conducted by FBI personnel in Mexico. This information was passed up the chain to Director Hoover. But it apparently was not communicated to the local US FBI offices or to individuals responsible for monitoring Oswald.

October 18, 1963

The FBI legate in Mexico City sent a cablegram directly to J. Edgar Hoover informing him that the CIA had just provided them with information (not to be disseminated) that Lee Oswald had contacted Soviet Vice Counsel Valery Kostikov at the Soviet embassy in Mexico City on September 28 and again on October 1. CIA advised that this Oswald was probably identical with "Lee Henry Oswald" who had been in the Marine Corps and defected to Russia in 1959.[14]

The importance of this telegram could not be understood without recently released records which reveal that in 1962 the FBI had "turned" one of Kostikov's agents in New York City. This agent had identified Kostikov as head of covert operations for North America, and had been providing information on him for months. "Tumbleweed" was an FBI counter-intelligence source known only at the very highest levels of the FBI and CIA; the development of this asset represented a major coup for the FBI.[15]

Certainly Director Hoover was well aware of the significance of any Kostikov contact, especially a contact with a former Soviet defector living in the United States, with a Russian wife. In addition, we now know that these Oswald contacts apparently involved one personal visit by Oswald to the Soviet embassy and follow on telephone calls, apparently from the Cuban embassy, which were tape recorded— possibly by both the FBI and CIA.

More importantly, information from Sylvia Duran and employees of the Russian embassy suggests that the three calls were actually made from the Cuban Consulate on a day in which the Cuban Consulate was closed.[16]

The advisory CIA cablegram makes no reference to probable impersonation or to the fact that the caller actually spoke in Spanish. If the CIA was aware of the impersonation at the time, they chose not to inform the Director of the FBI whose agency was running the Kostikov counter-intelligence project. Immediately after the assassination, Hoover's own personnel in Dallas identified and reported the impersonation by comparing a tape of one telephone call to Oswald's voice.

In Chapter Eighteen of *Oswald and the CIA*, John Newman gives an excellent analysis of the new documents and interviews that demonstrate this impersonation, and both he and Peter Dale Scott concur that a female also appears to have impersonated Sylvia Duran, a Cuban Consulate employee.

October 22, 1963

A Registered Mail Airtel was sent from the SAIC of the Dallas FBI to Director Hoover, and copied to FBI Mexico City, New Orleans, and Little Rock. SAIC Dallas referenced an unavailable Airtel on the same subject from October 2, 1963. He informed Hoover that S.A. Hosty in Dallas has been advised by INS verbally that they are in receipt of a "Secret" communication from their office in Mexico City indicating that Lee Oswald has been in the Soviet Embassy in Mexico City. He also advised that a confidential postal informant in Ft. Worth had related that Lee's brother, Robert, has moved to Little Rock, Arkansas.[17]

It appears that the Dallas FBI had not been informed by Hoover's office of the Kostikov contact. However, it also seems that the FBI may have been routinely monitoring Oswald's entire family. This document, along with Patterson's report on Hosty's remark about Oswald meeting with subversives and the Oswald letter mentioning a November contact with Hosty all cast further doubt on the claim that the Dallas office was not actively interested in Lee Oswald in the weeks before the assassination. There is the definite possibility that other individuals than Jim Hosty might have been involved in monitoring Oswald.

FBI Headquarters did respond to Dallas, simply confirming the facts. They did not escalate the matter nor did they give any advice on Kostikov's importance—*but Kostikov was considered one of the most dangerous Soviet agents in the Western Hemisphere and was on daily surveillance up to and including November 22.*[18] Both the Director of the FBI and the top CI people at CIA HQ were personally aware that an ex-Marine Russian defector had contacted the head of Soviet assassination and sabotage. However, the official record indicates that Oswald was neither contacted nor placed under special surveillance by either agency. One year earlier, Oswald had been investigated by the FBI for doing no more than subscribing to a variety of Russian and socialist publications, yet in the 60 days before his murder (including after his arrest) Oswald was never interrogated by the FBI about his contact with the Soviets.

OSWALD – ON EVERYONE'S RADAR

Because various FBI and CIA documents have been released over the years (and many still await discovery), the sequence of Agency communications has been very nebulous. To assist in a more objective analysis, documents available to the author are included as exhibits. The following provides an overview of these documents although many of them are discussed separately in this chapter. The overview makes one thing strikingly clear. The Director of the FBI had a considerable amount of information about Lee Oswald in his files and available to him on November 22. None of that information is discussed on the tapes of his conversations with President Johnson on November 22 and 23. And Hoover had been in full possession of inflammatory information on Lee Oswald for weeks without apparently ordering any special investigation or surveillance of Oswald.

DOCUMENT OVERVIEW AND TIMELINE

Oct 2
Source: SAIC New Orleans
To: SAIC Dallas referenced in Oct 22 DAS SAIC
Content/Action: Message to Director

Oct 8
Source: CIA Mexico City
CIA HQ
Content/Action: Oswald contact with Kostikov[19]

Oct 18
Source: INS Dallas verbal
To: SA Hosty
Content/Action: Oswald visits to Soviet embassy[20]

Oct 18
Source: Legate Mexico City
To: Director
Content/Action: Oswald Soviet embassy contacts; Kostikov identified;
Request for background info.

Nov 19
Source: SAIC, WFO
To: Director
Content/Action: Oswald letter to Soviet embassy in Washington, D.C. (mail monitoring). Info on intentions to travel to Cuba. Reference to Kostin/Kostikov and comment that status of Oswald investigation unknown to WFO since Dallas is office of origin.

Oct 22
Source: SAIC Dallas
To: Director
Content/Action: Oswald Soviet embassy contacts Mex City reported to Hosty by INS in Dallas.

To: New Orleans FBI
Content/Action: No Kostikov mention.

To: Little Rock
Content/Action: Postal Inspector Office informant reports Robert Oswald moved Ft. Worth to Dallas.

Nov 23
Source: FBI/Sullivan
To: Brennan, Belmont, Rosen
Content/Action: CIA memo confirming memo of Nov. 23 confirming Kostikov contact (Tumbleweed source), Dept 13 association of Kostikov–sabotage and assassinations; Sullivan also repeats "Kostin" intercept info.[21]

Nov 27
Source: FBI/Sullivan
To: Brennan, Belmont, Rosen
Content/Action: Reviews verification memo from CIA about Kostikov contacts, Tumbleweed, lack of photos of visit.[22] Concludes by backing off on absolute connection of Kostikov to KGB.

Nov 27
Source: FBI/Belmont
To: Sullivan

Content/Action: Lists investigative measures to be urgently taken in Mexico to verify possible connection of Cubans, Soviets or other individuals to the Kennedy assassination.[23]

Dec 11
Source: C/WH3 (Scelso)
To: DD/P (Helms)
Content/Action: Memo on plans for "handling" of Oswald Investigation. Concern that FBI report will disclose that FBI had "advance information on the reason for Oswald's visit to the Soviet embassy."[24]

Dec 24 (circa)
Source: C/WH3 (Scelso)
To: Chief CI
Content/Action: Memo on Dec 24 meeting with Chief CI/SI Helms on policy errors and inaccuracies in draft of Oswald (GP/FLOOR) report.[25]

May 13, 1964
Source: Angleton (CIA)
To: Belmont (FBI)
Content/Action: Memo outlining anticipated questions from Warren Commission and advice on answers to be given by CIA.[26]

72 HOURS - FROM CRIMINAL INVESTIGATION TO A REPORT ON LEE OSWALD, LONE NUT

November 22, 1963

Important conversations on the potential Soviet-Cuban sponsorship of Lee Oswald could have been part of now missing Air Force One radio channel traffic. Thanks to the work of the ARRB and senior staff member Doug Horne, we know now that the official transcript entered into the record contains only a third of the actual message traffic that should be expected. The transcript, which does remain in the Johnson Library, shows indications of heavy editing.[27]

Though we have abundant records of Director Hoover's memos and calls on November 22 and 23, none of them makes any reference to an Oswald contact with the KGB. They treat Oswald as a virtual nobody, but we now know the Director of the FBI was very much aware of the contact between the supposed Presidential assassin and the chief of KGB sabotage and assassination for the Western Hemisphere. Oswald's central FBI file contained the Cuban and Soviet consulate contacts, memoranda on the following investigation in Mexico and reports on Oswald's return to Texas as well as information on Oswald's New Orleans political activism. Either the official record of Hoover's communications has been significantly altered, or Hoover had some reason not to disclose this knowledge in communications with the President, the Secret Service or with any member of the National Security Council.

November 23, 1963

At 2:47 AM, a plane and courier arrived in Dallas carrying materials on Lee Oswald from Mexico City. At 10:00 AM the following morning, President Johnson's first recorded call of the day shows his initial question to Director Hoover to be about Oswald in Mexico City. There are no earlier records confirming how and when Johnson was first informed about Oswald and Mexico City. Hoover described the situation as confusing but stated that his men in Dallas had a tape and photos and neither the voice on the tape nor the photos match Oswald. According to Hoover, there seemed to have been a *"second person" down there impersonating Oswald* (obviously this would have been grounds to raise the possibility of Oswald being used as some sort of patsy, just has he had claimed to the media after his arrest).

It may be that we were never intended to know that Hoover had even raised the issue of impersonation in Mexico City. This is suggested by "14 Minute Gap" identified by researcher Rex Bradford.[28] There is indication that an attempt was made to remove the content of the Hoover–Johnson dialogue from the historical record. Although a transcript of this conversation does exist, Bradford's research shows that the actual tape containing this morning call seems to have had only this single 14 minute call erased; the transcript remains, but not the actual voices on the tape.

Shortly after this exchange between Hoover and President Johnson, Shanklin of the FBI in Dallas, talked with Belmont in D.C. who then wrote a memo to Tolson, Hoover's second in command. This memo confirmed that Dallas FBI agents familiar with Oswald had listened to the tape of the conversation (apparently the September 28 telephone call) supposedly from the Cuban to the Soviet embassy. The FBI also had in its possession a mail intercept which contained a letter from Lee Oswald in Dallas to the Soviet Embassy in NYC in which a meeting with "comrade Kostin" was mentioned.

Of course we now know that Hoover had known about that mail intercept for almost two months as had the Dallas office. Although the FBI referred to tapes being listened to and comparisons to Oswald's voice, by around noon on Saturday two different messages from the CIA in Mexico City related that they would be unable to provide tapes to their own headquarters. One stated that they were "unable to compare voices as first tape erased" (that would seem to be the September 28 tape) and a second message stated that as of noon, "regret, complete recheck shows tapes already erased."

This CIA communication itself conflicts with a separate document (Anne Goodpasture) from Mexico City, which spoke of comparing voices. [29] The position that Oswald's conversations were of no importance and would have been routinely erased also conflicts with an interview with the CIA station translator. He stated that the staff in the office had been "very hot about the whole thing" pertaining to Oswald, even before he had transcribed the October 1 tape. [30] Goodpasture also later admitted to the HSCA that tapes were compared. This suggests that the CIA Mexico City staff were aware of the impersonation, but may not have shared it with the FBI, nor have wanted to confirm it afterwards for the official record.

4:45 PM Saturday, November 23, 1963

A communication from Helms of CIA to the Mexico City CIA staff gives an idea of how seriously the whole Kostikov issue was being treated in Washington. In addition to telling them their information was being processed around the clock, Helms instructed them to: *"Feel free to abandon cables and talk plain English,"* so that there can be no mistakes!" Richard Helms DD/P CIA. [31]

6:00 PM Saturday, November 23, 1963

A CIA cable from Mexico City stated "regret complete recheck shows tapes from this period already erased." This claim appears not to have registered because as of Sunday afternoon, CIA Counter Intelligence was still asking for all tapes and transcripts. [32]

November 25, 1963

FBI Headquarters communicates to FBI Mexico City. "If tapes available please forward to Lab including tapes sent to Dallas if they have been returned." FBI Mexico responds: "I think you are confused; we never sent tapes to Dallas."[33] This seems to be in direct contradiction to Hoover's personal remarks to Johnson at 10:00 AM on Saturday morning, the 23 although it may only reflect the confusion over whether the tapes actually sent on Friday night were from the CIA rather than the FBI. More recently information has been developed that both agencies may have had copies of telephone taps.

What Should Have Been Said

On November 22, the FBI and CIA knew at the highest levels that the man charged with the assassination of the President had been in contact with a Russian suspected of being the KGB chief of assassinations for the United States. The Director of the FBI had been privy to this information for almost two months; Kostikov himself was being monitored as a primary contact of the FBI's Tumbleweed intelligence source. We are asked to accept that Hoover and FBI counter-intelligence had taken no apparent action to pursue an investigation in Dallas when Lee Oswald returned to the United States. And that Hoover communicated none of the Kostikov background or implications to Johnson, Bundy or anyone else on November 22 or the following weekend?

A survey of other communications may shed some light on this apparent lack of concern—beyond President Johnson's lobbying individuals to join the Warren Commission and quickly certify a FBI report on Oswald as the sole assassin.

A CIA/CIC memo on December 11, recording a call from Helms to Angleton, addressed the CIA concern that the draft FBI report might disclose the CIA telephone taps. It contains the statement: *"This would compromise our telephone tap operations in Mexico; because the Soviets would see that the FBI had advance information on the reason for Oswald's visit to the Soviet Embassy."*[34]

This suggests that the CIA and FBI had bugs in the Cuban embassy. It also suggests that CIA and FBI were actively monitoring Oswald's activities in real time or that Oswald's activities were part of an agency counter-intelligence operation.

Although the single memo cannot reconcile nor adjudicate between those two options, we are led to a rather basic mystery. As soon as Oswald was arrested and booked on Friday, Helms and Hoover would seem to have had reason to suspect Russian and Cuban involvement in a conspiracy to assassinate President Kennedy. However, there is no evidence that such a contingency was actually registered with the President, his National Security Advisor or the National Security Council. Even when FBI Director Hoover mentioned the explosive issue of impersonation (in calls to the Soviets, which could be interpreted to imply some special relationship between Oswald and the Cubans) to President Johnson, the tape of the conversation contains no relevant reply or remark from the president? Either the historical record has been scrubbed or people the highest levels of these agencies had reason not to act on the potentially explosive issues of the Kostikov contacts and the Oswald impersonations. Certainly they took no advantage of the opportunity to grill Oswald on his Cuban and Soviet contacts!

As of 2005, a search of all Johnson and Bundy communications revealed no evidence of any communication between CIA or FBI and the White House on the subject of Oswald and Kostikov or any further discussion of Oswald being impersonated in Mexico City. There are numerous communications in regard to Oswald's visit to Mexico, but as with the exception of Hoover one remark to Johnson, the Kostikov contacts and implications seem to have been withheld from the White House. This is in dramatic contrast to the Gilberto Alvarado incident, where Alvarado's information about Oswald receiving payment from the Cubans for the assassination was communicated in frequent, detailed messages to the White House and McGeorge Bundy.

THE OFFICIAL INVESTIGATION

With Kostikov and the impersonation of Lee Oswald in mind, it is enlightening to highlight additional details of the days immediately following the assassination.

Friday, November 22, 1963
1:48 PM, Hoover received a call from SAIC Shanklin in Dallas stating that they had heard over the radio that JFK had been shot and

"one witness said a Negro man leaned out a window and made two shots."

2:21 PM, Shanklin called Hoover and stated that agents had learned JFK was dead and that Dallas police had informed them that one man had been picked up and that a Secret Service agent had been killed.

During a media interview that afternoon, DPD Chief Jesse Curry stated, "we have heard that Oswald was picked up by a Negro in a car." This broadcast statement confirms the report of Officer Roger Craig, who saw a man looking like Oswald running down to Elm Street and being picked up by a station wagon with a dark skinned driver.[35]

Craig's movement and observation as well as the presence of a station wagon at the correct location and time are well validated in photographs (Murray series), as well as by the FBI statements given by two drivers in traffic behind the station wagon.[36] Later on the 22nd, Curry replied to the press stating, "Well, there's no one but him" when asked about any indication of conspiracy.

4:19 PM, Hoover memo related that he had told RFK that the killer has "Communist leanings" and is a "very mean-minded individual." Hoover also related and confirmed again in a 5:15 PM memo that the subject Oswald "went to Cuba on several occasions but would not tell us what he went to Cuba for." It is true that Hoover did pass on what appears to be some early misinformation about real time events in Dallas but it is hard to interpret the Cuba reference as a mistake since it would have had to have come from Oswald's files. Hoover does not mention Oswald's activities in Mexico City or New Orleans or any suspicious contacts or connections.

8:06 PM, FBI Director Airtel to all offices: "*All offices immediately contact all informants, security, racial and criminal, as well as other sources for information bearing on assassination of President Kennedy ...utmost priority.*" On Friday evening, Dallas Assistant D.A. William Alexander prepared a set of formal charges for Lee Oswald. These papers charged Oswald with murdering the President "as part of an International Communist Conspiracy."[37] Alexander later remarked that his charges were driven strictly by Oswald's obvious Communist and Castro associations. Given the emotions of the country on Friday evening, the media impact of such a charge would have been tremendous. We now know from Soviet document releases that the Soviets were immensely concerned about a US response based on Oswald's politics and previous defection.

On Friday night the White House placed telephone calls to Dallas D.A. Henry Wade, to Texas State Attorney General Carr and Police Chief Curry requesting that they avoid any official statements, charges, or discussion relating to conspiracy.[38] Johnson's aide Cliff Carter was making the calls and if the individual in question raised objections, President Johnson was used as the authority for the message. The FBI also moved quickly to bring pressure on Chief Curry to retract statements about being told by Hosty that Oswald was known to be a Communist and potentially dangerous and Curry did so.

By midnight that Friday night, several major pieces of evidence had already been removed from Dallas; these had either not been examined or only partially examined by the Dallas Police. These key elements of evidence included the presidential vehicle, clothing of both President Kennedy and Governor Connally, the rifle purportedly owned by Lee Oswald, bullets (not all the hulls, which were transported separately), documents relating to the purchase of the Oswald rifle and handgun and the paper sack purportedly used to carry the dis-assembled rifle into the Texas. School Book Depository.

Some of these items were referenced by Hoover in a call to Johnson's aide Walter Jenkins on the morning of November 24. The transcript of that call also notes that the FBI felt that the crime "involves the Criminal Code on a conspiracy charge under Section 241" and that because of this Hoover wanted the Dallas Police to "shut up" and stop giving information to the press. In particular, Captain Fritz of the Homicide squad had to be gotten under control. This call was made 45 minutes after Oswald's death and mentions that Hoover had an agent at Parkland to take a deathbed confession from Oswald if one were made. It is impossible to tell if his remark about Section 241 refers to the President's murder or to Oswald. However, given the timing it appears Hoover was referring to the investigation of the President's murder and Section 241 "specifically involves two or more persons who conspire to injure, oppress, threaten or intimidate"; it carries a maximum sentence of ten years.[39]

Dallas Police fingerprinting of the Carcano rifle was interrupted and never completed, leaving Lt. Day unable to state that the weapon contained prints from Lee Oswald or even that the rifle had been fired that day. Issues and challenges, including serious apparent gaps regarding their chains of possession, have been raised with all the pieces of evidence that were taken out of Dallas that Friday afternoon and evening.

The bulk of the remaining material collected by the Dallas Police was handed over to the FBI and taken out of Dallas early the following week. In a number of instances, items described by Dallas officers either disappeared or changed description—including a Minox camera that changed into a light meter. These items were photographed in Dallas before release to the FBI; a total of 451 items were photographed and only 251 items were returned. The story of this evidence handling is well covered by researcher John Armstrong and is based largely on statements from DPD Chief Curry and testimony by FBI Agent James Cardigan.[40]

The FBI itself noted the fact that the Commission might inquire into the missing and altered evidence. FBI Section Chief Bill Branigan noticed that certain items referenced in a report by Agent Gemberling were marked "deleted" and was concerned that the Warren Commission might believe something was being held back. His memo to the Dallas office contains the following request: *"The Bureau does not desire that the Commission ask any questions about this, and Dallas should either furnish amended pages and re-number the exhibits so that all the exhibits are accounted for, or else should explain why some of the exhibits are missing."*

Dallas responded with a renumbered exhibit log in much the same way they eliminated the evidence of contact between Hosty and Oswald by re-typing and re-numbering the transcript of Lee Oswald's address book.

Saturday, November 23, 1963

The combination of William Manchester's research and Johnson's diary gives us valuable information about Johnson's knowledge and interests on Saturday morning. After a visit to the West Wing and the President's office around 8:30 AM, Johnson went to McGeorge Bundy's office around 9 AM and according to both Manchester and the diary, preceded to the White House situation room for a "short" briefing by CIA Director McCone.

The reality of the briefing was even "shorter" than that, according to McCone aide Russell Jack Smith. In his book, *The Unknown CIA*, Smith relates that he accompanied McCone to the White House to brief Johnson. They found the new President in the basement secretarial area outside Bundy's office. Johnson stood among the typing and ringing telephones to talk briefly with McCone and Smith and "had no interest whatever in being briefed. After some inconsequential chatting, he turned back into Bundy's office".[41] This narrative only underscores Johnson's apparent lack of any real concern about any national security implications of the assassination.

At 10 AM, Johnson was back in his own office to receive a call from Hoover. Johnson's first question to Hoover was *"Have you established any more about the visit to the Soviet embassy in Mexico in September?"* But up to this point, the record contains no evidence that anyone had talked to Johnson about Oswald's even being in Mexico City.[42]

During the 10 AM call, Hoover described FBI personnel comparing the taped recordings of the Oswald calls, explained the issues and pointed out that this indicated another party was involved: "J. Edgar Hoover: No, that's one angle that is very confusing. We have up here the tape and this photograph of the man who was at this Soviet Embassy, using Oswald's name. That picture and the tape do not correspond to this man's voice, nor to his appearance. In other words, it appears that there is a second person who was at the Soviet Embassy down there." This is the first and last record we have of this subject being discussed with Johnson and we have no way of knowing its resolution, if there was one.

Recently released tapes show Johnson using Mexico City and the threat of a nuclear war to force Earl Warren into heading a government commission to certify the report that the FBI would file. Johnson's use of the nuclear war issue was enough to force Warren to violate his basic beliefs and moved him to tears. Johnson also used the issue to force Senator Russell onto the Commission with Warren.[43] Researchers reviewing these tapes in detail have found Johnson offering different justifications / objectives for the Warren Commission:

- Save 38 Million Americans from death in a nuclear exchange.

- Make sure that Americans did not end up believing that Khrushchev or Castro killed Kennedy.

- Certify an FBI report on the assassination.

- Discourage Congress or Texas from conducting their own independent investigations.[44]

Based on the official record, Johnson's now documented efforts ordering a quick FBI report, one demonstrating Oswald acted alone, was based on a single conversation between Hoover and Johnson in which only impersonation is mentioned. An impersonation never officially resolved nor even discussed again.

11:57 AM, Director FBI to all offices:

> *"Lee Harvey Oswald has been developed as the principal suspect in the assassination of President Kennedy... in view of developments all offices should resume normal contacts with informants."*

In less than one full working day, the FBI had moved from a proactive investigation into one of receiving reports; it was no longer developing leads other than to Lee Oswald.

This directive was issued a little less than 2 hours after Hoover discussed the impersonation of Lee Oswald with President Johnson.[45] And in contrast to any such confidential issues, on November 23, the US media began a series of editorials in major establishment newspapers that effectively quashed any major media discussion of conspiracy. "Americans can take comfort in the fact that the murderers of their President have, in nearly every case, been crazed individuals." *New York Herald Tribune*.

The *Tribune* cited the same book, *The Assassins*, by Robert Donovan, that Allen Dulles would take to the first meeting of the Warren Commission. Donovan would later write the introduction for the *Popular Library* edition of the Warren Commission Report.

Sunday, November 24, 1963

Alan Belmont of the FBI prepared a memo for Deputy Director Clyde Tolson. This memo was the first conclusive statement that Oswald was the lone killer and suggests that the investigation was essentially complete. However, rather than an investigation, Belmont was describing a process by which the FBI would generate a memorandum for the Attorney General and "set forth the items of evidence which make it clear that Oswald is the man who killed the President."

Although two more weeks would pass before the final FBI report was actually submitted, essentially the investigation did not take two weeks but rather had been completed in two days; the rest of the time would be allotted to writing the "difficult report" as Belmont describes it. The following day, Belmont described the FBI memorandum as "settling the dust" just as John J. McCloy of the Warren Commission will later refer to their role as to "lay the dust."

A week later, Belmont would decline to send an FBI representative to the first session of the Warren Commission stating that, "there is nothing we can contribute at this time." The Warren Commission might just be beginning their investigation, but the FBI was busy wrapping up its own report.

Monday, November 25, 1963

According to an internal CIA memo, Gilberto Alvarado "called the American embassy on November 25 and succeeded in speaking to a high official with whom he made an appointment for that same day at 5:30." Two embassy security officers (CIA) met with Alvarado who related an explosive story of having observed Lee Oswald being recruited for a murder by a negro Cuban within the Cuban embassy in Mexico City. Alvarado's story was accepted and enthusiastically promoted by David Phillips of the CIA and Ambassador Mann who was convinced of a Cuban plot; Mann would later become highly agitated at the lack of aggressive investigation of a Cuban-Soviet conspiracy. However, under further questioning, Alvarado gave a date for the embassy incident when Oswald was clearly still in New Orleans.

When confronted with this, Alvarado retracted his claims on November 30. Alvarado's story was relatively quickly disposed of, but for at least three days it appeared to offer strong proof for Oswald as a paid Castro assassin. Given the endorsements from Mann and the Mexico City CIA staff, this incident seemed extremely explosive the week following the assassination. A major effort by Hoover, Johnson and Robert Kennedy was required to suppress the Mexico City demands for a major investigation of Cuban and Soviet involvement in the assassination. If any rumor of this incident had leaked into the press, the dramatic details given by Alvarado could have quickly pushed the United States into a dangerous confrontation.[46]

It is of note that the efforts to suppress the Mexico City, Johnson leveraged both cabinet level officers and agency heads. Reportedly Robert Kennedy was involved as well. This is described in an interview with former Ambassador Mann by the HSCA (RIF 180-10113-10404) in which Mann stated that "the investigations by the CIA and FBI after the assassination did cause him concern." He specifically stated that:

"instructions were received from Washington to stop investigative efforts to confirm or refute rumors of Cuban involvement in the assassination ...Mann said his instructions came from Dean Rusk and he believed that Scott, CIA Station Chief, and Anderson, FBI Legat, had received similar instructions from their respective directors."

"Mann stated that in his opinion, if he had to make a guess, there was a 99 percent chance that the investigation was stopped because it would have resulted in the discovery of a covert US government action ...he also stated that RFK was heavily involved in counterintelligence activity in 1964."

The Director of the FBI seems not have been totally convinced by the pressure to erase all concern over conspiracy. On December 12, he wrote his own note to Tolson about the FBI memorandum that had come to be a full blown report. Hoover stated that Rankin of the Warren Commission had wished to receive something from the FBI that definitively stated that there was no evidence of conspiracy. Hoover had rejected that and appealed to President Johnson who had supported him. In the end Hoover simply took exception to the FBI's own report which contained no possibility of conspiracy. He not only took exception to that position but also wanted to further investigate the Castro angle and the letters that had arrived from Cuba (the Pedro Charles letters discussed earlier). Hoover still made no mention of the Mexico City impersonation or of the Kostikov connection in his remarks. Hoover later assigned his Miami office to an intensive scrutiny of the Castro-Oswald connection reported by John Martino and was apparently disappointed that the office could not corroborate Martino's information so that it could be taken to the Warren Commission.

The WH/Cuban and CI (counter-intelligence) divisions of the CIA also seem to have been greatly interested in pursuing leads to conspiracy if they pointed to Cuba and Castro. Over the next year, first in Mexico City and then elsewhere, various CIA reports would identify possible Castro agents who might have associated with Oswald or in some element of a conspiracy. They generated reports on Miguel Casas Saez (described as a Cuban "gangster" and an agent of Castro G2), and Policarpo Lopez, an FPCC member coming from Tampa, who crossed the border into Mexico on November 22 (he had been trying to leave the U.S for a year but the Mexico City station expressed its suspicions and quoted a source as saying he was involved in the assassination). The CIA reported rumors of conspirators escaping through Mexico City, of pieces of Oswald's luggage being located in transit Mexico City and a variety of other suspicious rumors.

Further evidence of interest in conspiracy leads pointing to Castro shows up in a newly received document which describes that, as of November 26, the NSA was "undertaking a project to determine whether recent radio traffic between Cuba and the US …might indicate a connection between the Cuban Government and Oswald's assassination of President Kennedy." The search was against 3 months of radio traffic and was "considered very urgent at NSA." The FBI encouraged NSA in this project, providing some Oswald associated names and promising more; they described their own investigation of that time as being still underway and very extensive.[47] The NSA eventually summarized their study with a statement that:

> "….on the Cuban target we produced many products on (redacted) as well as from military command and control to (several redactions) communications. There were no reflections in any of these products of any activity that might have been related to the assassination."

The CIA obtained the same negative result from its queries to covert sources inside the Cuban intelligence and foreign services.

NOW YOU SEE IT, NOW YOU SEE DON'T

Only now, after more than 40 years, can we really sketch a full picture of what many refer to as a "cover-up" relating to President Kennedy's assassination. Actually "cover-up" may not even be the best term to describe what actually occurred. What did happen was twofold. First, beginning the evening of the assassination, President Johnson and certain of his staff began an effort to quash discussion of and further investigation of conspiracy. As Admiral Burkley would tell the medical staff as Bethesda, the killer was in custody and it was only a matter of recovering the evidence. As Cliff Carter would tell various law enforcement officers in Texas, discussion of conspiracy was simply too explosive and was not to be done—if they objected to that the President would be eager to discuss it with them personally.

Second, the evidence being collected was managed in a fashion so as to present only those elements that would support the image of Lee Oswald as a "lone nut". It's now clear that some individuals were not all that happy about dropping the investigation of Oswald being associated with persons unknown. Almost immediately several parties began to express reservations about dropping the pursuit of conspiracy (a Communist conspiracy at least). Those objecting included Director Hoover, CIA and State Department staff in Mexico City and certain elements of the counter-intelligence and Cuban divisions of the CIA. Examining both sets of actions shows activities that seem to have been unplanned, conducted piecemeal and often in a very reactive fashion. That they succeeded was largely due to the implication of KGB involvement, the threat of nuclear war, the awesome power of cold war security oaths, and pure presidential pressure (exercised by one of America's very best practitioners of the art of political manipulation). These elements were also substantially abetted by the power of almost universal major media support for the official positioning of Oswald as a "lone nut".

The presentation of Oswald as a "lone nut" marksman was a challenge for the FBI report. It had to cope with the lack of witnesses to his firing shots at the President, not to mention any particular shooting skill or any sign of practice since his Marine qualification of several years earlier. It also had no witnesses to his even being on the sixth floor at the time of the shooting. The FBI's problems extended to the repeated refusal of Oswald to acknowledge any role in the shooting and its inability to develop any obvious motive. On Saturday the 24th, Director Hoover called President Johnson and remarked twice that there was not enough evidence to convict Oswald: "*At the present time it is not very, very strong,*" and "*The case as it stands now isn't strong enough to be able to get a conviction.*" That was approximately twelve hours after Dallas Police had filed formal charges against Lee Oswald for two murders.

At the time the local charges were filed on Oswald, Dallas Police had no identifiable prints on the purported murder weapon; that is verified in statements by Lt. Carl Day, of the Crime Scene unit. Day performed the tests and took the prints; he obtained no proof of the rifle being recently fired. The DPD also faced a negative paraffin test on

Oswald's cheek (suggesting he had not fired a rifle), no line-up with an eyewitness identification of Oswald as the shooter, no witness or photograph placing Oswald above the first floor lunchroom anywhere near the time of the shooting (and two witnesses who would have testified that he was not there fifteen minutes before or three minutes after), no witness showing him bringing anything into the building that day, no confession, no notes or letters to the media, no political declarations and above all, no motive.

Chief Curry, in his own book on the assassination, reviewed the "vast amount" of evidence that was eventually developed but also commented on the fundamental difficulty of "placing Oswald in that window with a rifle."[48] There is an expanding body of research (and documents) that suggest that the evidence confirming Oswald as a shooter was indeed "developed" by the FBI and that contrary evidence was kept from the Warren Commission. The same pattern of evidence management can also be seen in the minimal investigation of Oswald's association with other suspect individuals, reports that should have at least produced a proactive investigation of some sort of conspiracy.

Contrast this initial lack of evidence against Oswald with a Cuban exile plan to assassinate Castro in Chile in October 1971. That plan was coordinated by Antonio Veciana with the assistance of Maurice Bishop (David Atlee Phillips). Details involved concealing a gun in a camera, but most importantly, to quote Veciana:

> "It was very similar to the assassination of Kennedy—because the person Bishop assigned to kill Castro was going to get planted with papers to make it appear he was a Moscow Castro agent who turned traitor and he himself would be killed."

This frame involved using forged papers with appropriate signatures. In a similar attempt, not only forged papers were planted but the plotters managed to obtain photographs of the patsy meeting with a Communist agent. This was done by having someone who appeared similar to the patsy stop the target on the street and ask for a light. Then a hidden photographer took a variety of set shots showing the two individuals conversing.[49]

The framing of Oswald in the Texas School Book Depository was minimal; a much better effort had evidently been planned and set to unfold during the period of Oswald's "escape" out of the country. This minimal evidence is not up to the standards of even rogue professionals, much less the resources of the Central Intelligence Agency, with its capability for generating everything from false radio intercepts to faked photographs or tapes of Oswald meeting with known Castro agents. Any professional CIA plan could certainly have found an Oswald impersonator with a physical resemblance to Oswald for use in Mexico City, and one capable of better language skills than "broken" Russian.[50]

Masking the myriad purported links between Oswald and the pro-Castro community, the "lone gunman" was a creation of official damage control, not an element of the conspiracy. Martino provided no indication that this was an element of the plot. The issues of multiple shooters, more than three shots, more than three bullet strikes and acoustics evidence for at least one shot from the front have been major reasons why the "lone-nut" story has worked with establishment media but not the American public; according to 40 years of opinion polls. The bottom line seems to be that the tactical people in Dealey Plaza were not concerned with any such thing.

The plotters were presenting Oswald as a paid Castro agent associating with Castro operatives. They had one sacrificial patsy but no shortage of shooters; beyond any other consideration they had to ensure that John Kennedy died. Their original concept seems to have included multiple officials as targets, perhaps explaining the shots to Governor Connally. There was no reason for them to limit the number of shots or shooters.

On the other hand, the amount of effort required to adjust the official record to eliminate evidence of multiple shooters has been immense and is best documented in books such as *Six Seconds* by Josiah Thompson, *Murder in Dealey Plaza* edited by James Fetzer and *Cover Up* by Stewart Galanor.[51] We now know that even President Johnson and Warren Commission member Senator Richard B. Russell adamantly disagreed with Arlen Specter's artificial construct of the "magic bullet" and Russell wished to say so officially. We also know that Gerald Ford had to personally alter the location of the purported neck entry wound in the final Warren Commission report in order to preserve even a minimal credibility for the "Single Bullet Theory."

Examples of evidence and witness "management" are numerous. One particular incident is especially indicative of the way such things were done. Two of John Kennedy's closest personal friends were in the motorcade behind him and both of them would later tell Speaker of the House Tip O'Neill that they heard shots from the front of the motorcade, not from the rear in the Texas School Book Depository. However, Kenny O'Donnell specifically stated in his WC testimony that the shots "came from the right rear." When challenged by O'Neill he responded:

> "I told the FBI what I heard, but they said it couldn't have happened that way, and I must be imagining things. So I testified the way they wanted me to. I just didn't want to stir up any more pain and trouble for the family."[52]

In addition to "management" there was brute force manipulation. Over and over again, we hear witnesses describe their interaction with FBI agents similar to Kenny O'Donnell's, "They said it could not have happened that way." We see the same caution made to individuals ranging from a witness who saw a man on the sixth floor in the SW window (at the same time Oswald is seen in the lunchroom), to a presidential aide and even the first photo analyst to evaluate the Zapruder film (who was selecting frames to "storyboard" the shooting). One witness sees men who don't match Oswald's description. Another clearly hears shooting from the front of the President's car. Another sees ample evidence of multiple shooters and more than three shots. The photo analyst, Homer McMahon, gave his professional opinion that the president had been shot from at least three separate directions. The agent carrying the film informed him his opinion was not important and told Homer very simply, "you can't fight city hall."[53]

Another answer given to many witnesses amounted to *I'm sorry, that can't be, because it does not match what we know to be true.* If the cover-up had been pre-planned, if it had been orchestrated at the highest levels within the "CIA/White House/Joint Chiefs," there should not have been the glaring problems we now see in regard to the autopsy. Why would both sets of the original autopsy notes have disappeared? Why would the initial autopsy report have been burned and rewritten? Why would the wounds in the final report not match the locations on the autopsy work sheet? It seems apparent, as with the DPD investigation, the autopsy began authentically and was hijacked in the middle of the night and over the following weekend.

Why the apparent discord over wounds described by the doctors at Parkland and Bethesda? Though their testimonies do conflict on certain points, they agree that there was a massive wound in the rear of the skull that cannot have been caused by a bullet's entry. Unfortunately for the Bethesda doctors, they had to attempt to reconcile their work with the official story of one shooter at the rear while the Dallas personnel did not. [54,55]

Doctor Gary Aguilar sums up the medical evidence situation extremely well: "A huge chasm exists between the credible accounts of myriad, solid witnesses and the hard evidence, between the examining physicians at two different locations and the autopsy photos and X-Rays."[56] The personnel involved in the autopsy and records preparation were not pre-selected, vetted, nor given a script. Records were not prepared and confidentially inserted into the process by "vetted" technicians. Instead, autopsy notes disappeared, the report was rewritten, photos and X-Rays disappeared. Over the following week, the official evidence was organized to support the official story. At first no one could anticipate that the case might not go to trial. If nothing else, the legal "best evidence" had to be prepared to stand and the doctors ordered to defend it. Aguilar's summary lists the points that remain unclear after the ARRB clarification of the original record:

> More negatives were submitted by the autopsy photographers than can now be accounted for, doctors and photographers under military command signed false affidavits and swore untruthfully, witnesses who developed the photographs rejected the supposed authentic images as well as the film on which the images were printed, both of the autopsy photographers and all three of the pathologists have sworn that specific autopsy photographs are missing, why attempts to match the current batch of autopsy photographs to the camera that took them failed.[57]

Dr. Mantik's points tend to corroborate those of Dr. Aguilar; for example: the trail of metallic debris (which reflects a type of ammunition other than that supposedly used by Oswald) was intentionally relocated by the autopsy doctors to support the official shooting scenario; critical photographs were removed from the autopsy record (primarily to cover-up the large exit wound), a second brain was substituted for the real brain which had far too much damage to support the official story, and the autopsy doctors told the truth whenever possible except when they could not risk exposing the official scenario (in which case, they obfuscated).

Doctor Mantik has identified a short list of individuals who must have been ordered to cooperate and lists others who would have warranted Grand Jury investigation for coordinating and managing the cover-up. All the individuals so indicated worked out of the White House and retained their positions in the new administration. Three of the individuals so cited privately expressed their belief in a conspiracy.[58]

Admiral George Burkley, President Kennedy's personal physician, almost gave away the cover-up. Doctor Aguilar notes that during an oral history for the JFK Library, Admiral Burkley was asked if he agreed with the Warren Commission in regard to the number of bullets that entered the President's body. Burkley answered, *"I would not care to be quoted on that."* Ten years later, Burkley's attorney, William Illig, contacted HSCA Counsel Richard Sprague about providing information to the Committee.

"Although he, Burkley, had signed the death certificate of President Kennedy in Dallas, he had never been interviewed and he has information in the Kennedy assassination indicating that others besides Oswald might have participated."

The HSCA did contact Burkley a year later and on a completely different subject. There is no indication that Sprague or the Committee took any action at all to respond to Burkley's eyewitness information on indications of conspiracy. Yet it was Admiral Burkley himself who now appears to have been the individual actually directing, controlling and attempting to limit the Kennedy autopsy. Burkley's involvement began on Air Force One where he informed Jackie Kennedy that for security purposes, her husband's autopsy needed to be performed at a military hospital. At Bethesda, according to Boswell, Burkley briefed the doctors with the information that *"the police had captured the guy who did this and all we need is a bullet."* Boswell relates Burkley's directions for a simple bullet search and the opposition of the autopsy staff to that instruction based on their legal responsibilities. Boswell also relates that someone even instructed him not to examine the clothing as part of the autopsy as it was only of academic interest. He refused to state who this was, other than it was a superior officer, but based on his other remarks it seems likely that he was referring to Burkley.[59]

Morgue assistant Paul O'Connor has been considerably more outspoken, describing Admiral Burkley as "a maniac." "I'd never seen anybody like that in this life, scared the hell out of me. He was yelling and cussin' and carrying on all night. He kept saying 'don't do this because the Kennedy family won't want this done', and 'don't do this and don't do that.' " It is clear that with Admiral's rank, being the personal physician for the former president, and being at a Naval Hospital, Burkley was able to take an active role in control of the autopsy and later of much of the medical evidence (contrary to the official record). Almost all the autopsy participants commented on Burkley's control, generally assuming that it was originating with the Kennedy family members who were in the hospital. That assumption is purely speculative and is addressed in detail by researcher James Folliard in his excellent and detailed work on Burkley's behavior and communications during the autopsy.

Folliard points out that as Boswell described, Burkley began by trying to limit the autopsy and was challenged by the staff until he was finally overridden by Admiral Galloway, Commanding Officer of the Bethesda Medical Center. Burkley stated that Mrs. Kennedy had granted permission for only a limited autopsy. However, the autopsy release in evidence that has Jackie Kennedy's name typed in and Robert Kennedy's signature as witness, lists no such limitation at all (contradicting both Admiral Burkley and Dr. Finck). Neither the documents nor witness testimony conclusively confirm direct Kennedy family intervention in the autopsy process. Apparently some individuals assumed pressure to rush the procedure was coming from the family and there is evidence of regular communication between the family and the autopsy area. However, the observed calls were between Secret Service agents Clint Hill and Roy Kellerman attempting to find out how long the autopsy would take. There was also communication between the family and Burkley in regard to burial preparations.

In any event, the legal document and the orders from Admiral Galloway both required the doctors to perform a full postmortem, which they did. Contrary to statements of certain of the doctors, there are at least two witnesses who describe a full and complete autopsy including Burkley's consent to a study of the adrenals. These witnesses are lab assistant James Jenkins (who describes sectioning of the heart and examination of the organs, adrenals, and testes) and Doctor Robert Karnei (who has described in detail the failure to locate the adrenals). Karnei's information was given to Harrison Livingston and confirmed by Karnei to Dr. Lundberg of the *Journal of the American*

Medical Association. Given the new evidence collected by the ARRB, as well as extensive interviews by Livingston and others, it seems wise to put more faith in observations by Doctor Karnei than those of Humes, Boswell, or Finck. For instance, Finck told his boss that the doctors were specifically restricted by the limitations stated on the autopsy certificate (the document shows none), while Humes gave a detailed listing of those present at the autopsy with no mention at all of Admiral Burkley who was playing a major role in the process.[60]

In addition to all this, we also now have a record of a most unusual conversation between Lyndon Johnson and Attorney General Ramsey Clark in 1967, at a time when Clark had been instructed by Johnson (for unstated reasons) to obtain legal certification of all the autopsy photographs and other materials. We now know that many of the affidavits from this process are questionable and some were given under duress. However, the dialogue makes it very clear that there was concern about the materials not supporting the doctors' earlier reports and testimony. At one point, Clark shows a great deal of relief in being able to report to Johnson that, "It's very clear to them (the doctors) that there's nothing in the autopsy photos that contradicts anything they said." Why this should even be a concern four years after the fact raises some serious questions—as does the fact that Clark identifies a photo described by Dr. Humes in his testimony which is no longer among the official inventory.

Since that raises questions about possession and opens the door to speculation on other photos that might be missing, it was clearly of concern to Johnson and Clark. The dialogue also began to explore the fact that Burkley himself seems to have kept possession of much of the primary material, at least the issue was raised by Clark, until LBJ abruptly terminated the conversation and hung up. This dialogue is especially interesting in that there seems to be a real concern in regard to Dr. Burkley, there is the suggestion that Johnson feels that he could not control him—even though Burkley continued on Johnson's own staff as *his* personal physician.[61] At that point, it is impossible to determine from whom Dr. Burkley was taking his instructions or what his goal was in trying to limit and control the autopsy. It is clear that he did play such a role, and increasingly clear that the official historical record of the autopsy and its related evidence is a *construct* developed over time.

In summary, the view from 2006 shows us a series of highly reactive and iterative actions, very possibly managed out of the White House with the full authority of President Johnson. The same authority which could remove a charge of conspiracy in Dallas provided the perfectly legal power to enforce military orders and back them up with secrecy oaths. What happened has become relatively clear; why it happened is another question entirely. Johnson himself made his official motive quite clear, citing it over and over again to various individuals. Chief Justice Warren's motivation is equally clear—to save 40 million American lives. Even the possibility of a Soviet–Cuban conspiracy in the Kennedy assassination was not worth that. President Johnson says so on tape.

But Johnson himself shows no indication of seriously fearing Soviet involvement. In the hours following the assassination he ordered absolutely no actions pertaining to military preparedness or national security. Nor did he direct any special intelligence activities against either the Soviets or Cubans. This lack of action on Johnson's part is confirmed by a White House memorandum written on December 4, 1963, by Bromley Smith in regard to "Changes in Defense Readiness Conditions as a Result of the Assassination of President Kennedy." This memo summarizes the authority granted to the Joint Chiefs and documents their "Defcon" actions following the assassination. According to the memo, the Joint Chiefs, acting on their own initiative, increased the defense readiness condition from Defcon 5 (the lowest peace time condition) to Defcon 4 at 2:50 EST on November 22 and returned to Defcon 5 at 12:30 on Sunday November 24. The Commander in Chief Pacific (CINPAC) on his own initiative had directed his forces to Defcon 3 at 3:13 PM on November 22, something he was fully authorized to do. This memo provides solid proof that the US military did not move overall to a major elevation of defense readiness, suggesting any fear of foreign involvement or that the assassination was a precursor to an attack.

Beyond that there is no evidence that the Joint Chiefs or the Secretary of Defense took any other than very limited precautions. When the Chiefs were informed of the assassination, they remained in a meeting together, not even dispersing to their respective operational or command centers. Given that the assassination occurred at the height of the cold war (only a year after the Cuban missile crisis), and that certain defense scenarios anticipated elimination of US leaders as part of any Soviet attack, this apparent lack of a stronger reaction seems rather amazing.

What We Do See

We seem to see FBI Director Hoover leaving his office at the regular time on the Friday of the assassination and simply going home. Not to the airport to meet the new president and confer privately, nor to the National Command Center–apparently behaving just as he would at the end of a normal workday.

William Manchester gives a relatively detailed description of a phone call from Johnson to Hoover that evening. Johnson is in the White House after his return from Dallas and Hoover is at home, he had not stayed at the Capital to make himself available to the new President nor direct the investigation personally from FBI headquarters. It is apparently this call that Hoover uses to authorize his commandeering of the investigation and key evidence from the Dallas Police.[62] Yet this call, very specifically timed at 7:25 PM, does not appear in the Johnson diaries available from the Johnson Presidential Library. No such call is logged, even though the others immediately before it are registered to the minute as Manchester reports them–there is no tape and no transcript. If Manchester had a source for this detail, it appears to have vanished.

In Dallas, the paperwork charging Lee Oswald in an international Communist conspiracy was torn up and redone after a call to DA Wade. According to Wade, "Cliff Carter, President Johnson's aide, called me three times from the White House that Friday night. He said that President Johnson felt any word of a conspiracy—some plot by foreign nations to kill President Kennedy would shake our nation to its foundation. President Johnson was worried about some conspiracy on the part of the Russians...

Washington's word to me was that it would hurt foreign relations if I alleged conspiracy—whether I could prove it or not. I would just charge Oswald with plain murder and go for the death penalty."

"Johnson had Cliff Carter call me three or four times that weekend" to stop the charges that Oswald was part of an international Communist conspiracy.[63]

Of course the problem is that at that point in time Johnson had no reason to fear any such conspiracy since he had not been informed of Oswald's full FBI file or the incidents in Mexico City. So exactly why did Johnson aggressively preempt the Dallas charges? Indeed, why was he even thinking about the legal charges in Dallas?

Johnson himself followed the time of the reported Hoover call with dinner, meeting a Congressional delegation, and then telephoning a variety of political leaders before departing from the White House to his home.

One of Johnson's party, Jack Valenti, provided a much more detailed picture of the rest of the evening than did William Manchester. According to Valenti, Johnson invited him to stay until his family arrived in Washington; Valenti lived with Johnson for the next eleven days. Further, Valenti, Bill Moyers, Cliff Carter and others (we know Judge Thornberry was in the party) went with Johnson to his bedroom at 11 PM and sat with him while Johnson changed into pajamas, got into bed and talked while watching television. For four to five hours, Johnson talked about nothing but programs, politics, the Kennedy legislative initiatives and bills until the very early hours of the morning.[64]

We do know that President Johnson eventually did have a relatively confidential meeting with CIA Director McCone. However that did not occur until November 26. Details from that meeting could be extremely informative. In its final report (part 8) the ARRB noted that certain of McCone's records were missing or destroyed. One of them is simply listed as "Date of Meeting November 24, participants DCI (McCone) and Bundy. Subjects covered: Message Concerning President Kennedy's assassination." Perhaps there was something very significant in that message, perhaps not.

However, Dr. John Newman has found a more personal commentary on the events in Mexico City that is far more suggestive. Newman located a memo from a subordinate to Hoover, written only a few weeks after the events in question. The memo discusses plans for working with the CIA to keep abreast of their domestic operations in the United States. Hoover had scrawled on the memo the following:

"O.K., but I hope you are not being taken in. I can't forget the CIA withholding the French espionage activities in the USA nor the false story re. Oswald's trip to Mexico, only to mention two cases of their double dealing!"[65]

Was the lack of national security response to events in Mexico City due to the fact that Lee Oswald was either part of or being manipulated in an intelligence operation against both the Cubans and Soviets?

The alternative is that the new president didn't receive any special communications while on Air Force One, no covert briefings that evening or over the weekend. That the apparent Mexico City impersonation of Oswald was not explained to him. That his actions were not really being driven by the motives that he stated to Warren and Russell.

Is it possible that the conspiracy planners had even more going for them than the knowledge that Lee Oswald as a patsy was a major "poison pill" both to the FBI and CIA?[66] Is it possible that Lyndon Johnson had good reason to feel it to be in his own best interest if Oswald was only viewed as a "lone nut". Was there some other reason he would act to ensure that nobody was even to discuss the possibility that a conspiracy was involved in the assassination, much less actively investigate such a possibility?

Dr. David Mantik has presented a short list of those individuals apparently acting under Johnson's direction. These individuals worked for the White House and retained their positions under the new President. They include Secret Service Chief, James Rowley and Admiral (Dr.) George Buckley. Although it is not now possible to know the exact details of their activities, we can at least list specific actions ordered by Lyndon Johnson himself:

1. Used Presidential pressure via his personal aide to ensure that Oswald was not charged with conspiracy; this effort actually resulted in the initial draft charges prepared by Assistant D.A. William Alexander being rewritten. Alexander would later describe the initial draft as a "joke" on his part.

2. Personally ordered the immediate and complete reconstruction of the Presidential limousine which constituted the actual "crime scene" in the assassination.

3. Personally issued orders to place Bethesda personnel under a gag order in regard to the autopsy; Captain John Stover, Commanding Officer of the National Naval Medical School, reportedly received this instruction from Admiral Buckley on orders from the White House.

4. Appears to have been personally involved in the control of the autopsy

photographs. In a conversation with Attorney General Ramsey Clark, Johnson expressed his displeasure with Dr. James Humes' referring to a photograph that did not officially exist.[67]

5. Personally contacted the Parkland Hospital staff during the treatment of Lee Oswald and instructed the medical staff to assist in obtaining a deathbed confession that would be taken by his representative in the emergency room. "Dr. Crenshaw, I want a deathbed confession from the accused assassin. There's a man in the operating room who will take the statement. I will expect full cooperation in the matter." Dr. Crenshaw did speak to the President's representative who had a pistol clearly visible in his back pocket.[68]

6. During the Garrison/Shaw trial, President Johnson granted Presidential Immunity to FBI agent Regis Kennedy in order to prevent his being questioned about his connections to and knowledge of Lee Oswald.

All of which leaves us with a very uncomfortable question. Is there any possible way in which the Vice-President of the United States could somehow have become influenced by a conspiracy, specifically the conspiracy that we have pictured from John Martino's information and associates?

THE BOBBY BAKER SCANDAL

The possibility for just such a scenario may be found in the scandal that Lyndon Johnson himself stated might make him the first United States President to end his term in prison:

> "John, that son of a bitch (Bobby Baker) is going to ruin me. If that cocksucker talks, I'm gonna land in jail... I practically raised that motherfucker and now he's going to make me the first President of the United States to spend the last days of his life behind bars!" "Tell Nat that I want him to get in touch with Bobby Baker as soon as possible—tomorrow if he can. Tell Nat to tell Bobby that I will give him a million dollars if he takes the rap. Bobby must not talk."[69]

This conversation took place in February of 1964, and referred to a series of investigations, including a Senate investigation of Bobby

Baker, Fred Black and Edward Levinson.   By February, the new president had effectively neutered the investigations; the scandal was receiving nothing like the extreme media visibility that it had been getting in September and October of 1963. And during the course of the investigations, the wife of the government accountant (Lorin Drennan) investigating Baker's finances had been found dead in their home—found by her children in her bathroom, with the unlocked front door open. As related by Joachim Joestin in The Dark Side of Lyndon Baines Johnson, her autopsy was totally inconclusive, finding a death from either homicide or accident—and no significant criminal investigation was conducted.[70]

Lyndon Johnson was indeed very close to Baker. In August of 1958, Democratic Senator Alan Bible of Nevada paid a joint tribute to both Johnson and Baker on the floor of Congress. Bible described Baker as "a man who gets things done with the minimum amount of time and a maximum of efficiency," referring to Baker as "Lyndon, Jr."[71]

Baker was also a neighbor of LBJ's and Johnson was the next-door neighbor to Fred Black (in Spring Valley near Washington D.C.). Baker had moved in to join them in April of 1963 with Black (a lobbyist for North American Aviation) in the middle, Baker on one side and Johnson on the other.

Baker and Black owned 57% of "Serve U Corp." Their ownership was hidden by having the stock in the name of Baker's business associate and law "partner," Ernest Tucker. Baker and Black had paid $1 a share for their stock while their Las Vegas partners Levinson and Sigelbaum had paid $16.52 plus provision of a $150,000 loan.

Among the accusations initially raised in the Baker scandal was the possibility that Bobby Baker had used Johnson's political influence to gain contracts (with North American Aviation, Northrop and Space Technologies) for his "Serve U Corporation" which included as investors Baker, Black, Levinson and Sigelbaum. Johnson felt that these investigations and his connection to Baker had placed him at risk and that he was largely at the mercy of Baker.

Indeed LBJ had a very solid reason for his fear of going to jail. A study of Johnson's Vice-Presidential diaries now shows us that the Juries and Committees investigating the Baker influence peddling scandal never became aware of a fact which seems to provide full confirmation of Baker's influence peddling. On August 21, 1963, in the Executive Office Building, Johnson met with Baker, Black and N. A.

Storm of North American Aviation. The meeting lasted only 15 minutes. It involved the three principal players cited in the Baker lawsuit and investigations and North American Aviation was one of the military contractors whose vending machine business had been recently taken over by Baker, Black and Levinson's vending machine company.[72]

Baker had been associating with Las Vegas gambling interests long before 1961 he was introduced to casino operator Ed Levinson by Black.[73] This introduction occurred the day before the Kennedy inauguration. Black told investigators that Baker must have known Levinson for some years prior to this introduction.[74] It seems likely that Baker's initial introductions to Vegas connections may have been made by Nevada Lt. Gov. Clifford Jones, who had served on the Democratic National Committee before being forced to resign over scandals in Las Vegas.

Jones had investments in the Golden Nugget and Thunderbird casinos (the Thunderbird was a Lansky operation) and was well known in Las Vegas as a source of major political influence and gaming commission influence; Jones was frequently referred to as "Big Juice" among the casino crowd. Baker of course, had been well connected with the Democratic National Committee for a number of years. Levinson himself owned the Vegas Fremont in partnership with Clifford Jones and Levinson had formerly operated a casino in Havana before the Castro revolution.[75]

In September of 1963, Lyndon Johnson was facing the probable destruction of his career over a series of highly visible investigations of Baker—the man who filed a financial statement in September of 1963 showing a net worth of over $2 million dollars on a salary of $20,000 per year—Bobby Baker, who between January of 1962 and November of 1963, deposited over $1.5 million in his bank account including cash deposits over $106,000, a new $125,000 house and the purchase of a townhouse for his secretary—Bobby Baker who literally "kept fistfuls of cash in his Senate office."[76]

Baker's business associate and partner, Black, was also the long time, close personal friend and confidant of John Roselli. Black had the kind of political connections that had gotten Roselli the change in prison venue that saved his life.

Black had telephoned Roselli days before his murder with the message that Trafficante had a contract on him and the Cubans were coming to kill him. Lyndon Johnson had no known connection to John

Roselli. But if Johnson did indeed play the pivotal role in the Kennedy conspiracy cover-up that he appears to have—if he did so for his own reasons, those reasons may have developed from an introduction to Roselli. Could an introduction have been made by someone as close as Johnson's own next-door neighbor, Fred Black?[77]

Black met with Vice-President Johnson in the Executive Office Building as recently as August 1963, in the company of Baker and a North American Aviation executive. Black who would only have to tell the truth about this meeting in Johnson's office to potentially destroy the Vice President's political career.

SUMMARY

Among the difficulties in understanding the Kennedy conspiracy, perhaps the most challenging is reconciling the many elements that appear to be contradictory. This has been made even more difficult for those who have viewed the "cover-up" as an extension of the conspiracy. That difficulty disappears if we first view the conspiracy to frame Oswald as a Castro (or both Cuban and Soviet associated) conspirator, a plan that came totally unraveled when Oswald was taken into custody. And second, we see that the so-called "cover-up" was an independent, largely unplanned and highly reactive effort to ensure that a Lee Oswald would the fall all by himself—as a lone nut.

We may have a much descriptive term than "cover-up", see how much sense it makes when you picture it as "damage control."

- The plot was to show the US President being killed by a Castro sponsored conspiracy.

- The plotters were unable to execute their full plan due to Oswald's capture.

- Due to Oswald's role as an intelligence dangle and his contact with Kostikov, the initial appearance was still that Oswald might have been acting as a Communist dupe.

- Both the FBI and CIA were aware of the Kostikov implications; when, how, and if they shared this information with the new President is unclear.

- Lyndon Johnson personally led the official cover-up to eliminate any public suggestion of conspiracy while leveraging confidential information and the threat of war to make the cover-up work.

- The "lone nut" was a creation of the official cover-up, not of the Kennedy plot.

- The plotters' follow-on efforts to maintain conspiracy were overwhelmed by Johnson.

Johnson's motivation in the cover-up remains uncertain, partially because the historical record has been sanitized to remove any items that would reveal a discussion of conspiracy. However, there is a scenario that would involve a personal motivation on Johnson's part.

CHAPTER 16

WHEELING AND DEALING WITH BOBBY

Establishing Lee Oswald as a "lone nut" was a highly successful tactic for preempting an open ended criminal investigation of Oswald as part of or influenced by a conspiracy. It was also a vital part of establishing a "you can't fight city hall" attitude among law enforcement and military personnel—who were forced to consider their careers and security oaths against any contrary leads or evidence.

Creating gaps and holes at select points in the records also proved to be highly effective. In most cases it was not necessary to introduce anything false but rather to manage what went into the official reports, what was presented to the Warren Commission and what would go into the national archives. However, in regard to President Johnson's actions, these gaps also leave room for concern as to his own personal motives.

Many aspects of Lyndon Johnson's behavior appear either inconsistent or suspicious. Suspicion fueled by a rather dramatic change in the Vice President's behavior and activities during the two months prior to the assassination.

Johnson was under immense pressure as a result of the Bobby Baker scandal. The scandal involved Las Vegas gamblers with connections to John Roselli. Baker was deeply involved with Fred Black, one of Roselli's closest friends. Black was an obvious witness for both Congressional and other official investigations of the scandal. The scandal also gave Black a tremendous leverage over the Vice President. Black held the potential to massively damage Lyndon Johnson's political career simply by telling the truth under oath. We have seen how concerned Johnson was about Baker talking, and Baker was extremely close to Johnson. How much more concerned would Johnson be about someone with no ties to him, someone such as Fred Black? Black "had the goods" on Johnson with his inside information on Baker's peddling of Johnson's influence—and Black had political and media connections that would have made the most of such a story.

WHEELING AND DEALING WITH BOBBY AND FRIENDS IN 1963

In 1963, Bobby Baker's activities had put both the President and Vice-President's political careers at risk. Baker makes no bones about the fact that it was he who introduced John Kennedy to Ellen Rometsch.[1] And the Rometsch scandal, because of its foreign intelligence implications, threatened President Kennedy with political disaster. It is unlikely that JFK somehow overlooked the fact that it was "Johnson's boy" who had put him in a position to be blackmailed by Hoover in the fall of 1963. This incident ended with the Attorney General essentially begging the FBI Director (technically his employee) not to aid the Senate investigation into sex angle of its Baker inquiry, especially into the subject of Baker's introduction of Rometsch to the President.[2]

Hoover possessed two significant pieces of information, either of which could have been politically explosive if leaked during the 1964 election. The first was documented contact between known Mob Hollywood party girl Judith Campbell Exner and John Kennedy. Exner had been introduced to Kennedy in 1960 by Frank Sinatra, during a Kennedy visit to Las Vegas. She carried on an 18 month affair with the President. During this time, the FBI became aware of her close association with both John Roselli and Sam Giancana. The FBI interviewed Campbell in November of 1961, and she was observed in Roselli's company in Beverly Hills in January of 1962. In fact, Roselli allowed Campbell to use his Crescent Heights apartment when he was out of town, knowing full well he was under FBI surveillance and wire tapping. FBI taps and presidential call logs show 70 calls between President Kennedy and Campbell over a year and a half. This activity ended only after Hoover had written to Robert Kennedy in February of 1961 and informed him that Campbell was seeing the President and was a friend of Mafia figures, specifying Roselli and Giancana.

In March, after an unusual private lunch with Hoover, President Kennedy ceased contact with Campbell. Campbell apparently attempted to reestablish contact with JFK, apparently again calling from Roselli's FBI bugged apartment. In *Sons and Brothers*, Mahoney documents a November 4, 1963 memo to Hoover informing him that Campbell was back in telephonic contact with JFK's secretary.[3] Perhaps this was a last ditch effort aimed at baiting JFK into sexual blackmail. If so, it didn't work; that path to JFK was at a dead end.

The Campbell information, combined with the new 1963 Rometsch incident, put Hoover in a commanding position with the Kennedys in regard to both his job and the 1964 election.[4] President Kennedy was the first to suffer media exposure from Baker's personal introductions, while Vice-President Johnson, who was much more strongly associated with the Baker scandal in the public mind, was the second. Johnson was linked to both influence peddling and kickbacks as the result of a lawsuit against Bobby Baker, a lawsuit that would escalate into Congressional and Justice Department inquiries.

THE BOYS FROM VEGAS

Reading through his detailed description of his legal problems, one is struck by Baker's apparent unawareness of the political risk surrounding his business and investment partners. He seems to have been unconcerned that the gamblers from Las Vegas, were connected to the highest levels of syndicate gambling and organized crime on the one side, and to government (especially Johnson) on the other. Baker did acknowledge his work for the Las Vegas casino people and his efforts to help them obtain casino concessions in both the Dominican Republic and Puerto Rico. He claimed that nothing had come of it.[5]

Nothing may have come of it but something of importance must have come up in the conversation. Baker acknowledged that while working for Eddie Levinson, Benjamin B. Sigelbaum, and Clifford Jones (former Lt. Gov. of the State of Nevada, former part owner of the Thunderbird Casino, and long time Nevada delegate to Democratic national conventions) all of them had been repeatedly taped during negotiations with the finance officer of the Dominican Republic.[6] The US had apparently bugged the embassy of the Dominican Republic and had access to Baker and his partners' conversations with the finance officer. The content of these tapes was judged significant enough to place in evidence against Baker until Lyndon Johnson arranged for Secretary of State Dean Rusk to write the judge and request that these *tapes be suppressed in the interest of national security.*[7]

Baker did not detail why these interviews would have been particularly important to Johnson nor did he seem to question why the FBI had routinely bugged the offices and apartments of his business partners including both Levinson and Black. Whatever the details were, they frightened Johnson, who told Speaker McCormick that Baker could not only ruin him but could send him to prison, suggesting at least that some of Baker's illegal activities may have directly involved Johnson's participation or endorsement.

In 1963 Baker accompanied Johnson on a trip to the Dominican Republic. Shortly thereafter, Baker made another trip, this time taking along Levinson and another of their business associates. Whether or not Baker was directly leveraging Johnson's name is a matter of speculation as the individuals they met with were never questioned. We do know of one business deal in the Dominican Republic that netted Baker an ongoing revenue stream. In this instance, Baker seems to have leveraged his and possibly LBJ's extensive influence within the Department of Agriculture. The net result was that in two separate instances, a Murchison-owned slaughterhouse in Haiti, with a history of poor sanitary practices and failed inspections, managed to pass a new Department of Agriculture inspection. This allowed it to sell its product on the Haitian market, netting Bobby Baker a half cent per pound finder's fee.

After the Haitians became dissatisfied with the product, Murchison lobbyist Irwin Davidson facilitated a deal to allow the meat to be sold into the United States through a Chicago company. This required a new and even more demanding USDA inspection–which the company passed with no difficulty. Interestingly enough, Baker's half cent a pound payment finder's fee was continued with the new customer although he had no obvious association with the Chicago deal.[8]

In his autobiography *Wheeling and Dealing*, Baker went to great lengths to relate his business activities and even his financing to Senator Kerr of Oklahoma, merely mentioning that additional investment came from a hotel-casino man named Eddie Levinson and a Miami investor and gambler, Benjamin B. Sigelbaum. He briefly mentions that Fred Black had helped him with introductions to Levinson and Sigelbaum.[9]

Baker describes Black as a super lobbyist for North American Aviation, among other clients. We are already familiar with Black as a close friend and long time associate of John Roselli. Black's importance to both Baker and Johnson may be further indicated by an April 21,

1964, telephone call from President Johnson to Cyrus Vance, in which Johnson indicated to Vance that he was especially sensitive to charges of corruption. He instructed Vance to ensure that the press should find no grounds for charges of bribery in his administration. The call had been prompted by newspaper coverage of the trial of Black for taking $150,000 on behalf of the Howard Foundry Company to intervene with the Air Force in a $2.7 million claim against that firm.[10]

The Chicago-based Howard Foundry was one of Black's two employers of record, paying him $2,500 per month while North American paid him $14,000 a month. Black's associations with Roselli alone might have been enough to inspire the FBI to investigate Black. Baker's other two partners were also involved in business contacts of great interest to the FBI. Sigelbaum and Levinson were the major investors in the Fremont hotel, but in Sigelbaum's case, he was acting as a front man for his close personal friend and Florida neighbor, Meyer Lansky. Anyone who had breakfast every morning with Lansky, as Sigelbaum did, was certainly of great interest to the FBI, which maintained routine surveillance on Lansky.[11]

It remains unclear whether the FBI monitored Baker's meeting with Sigelbaum just before his February 1963, trip to the Dominican Republic with Johnson. In any event, such an association would have been of great interest to the Republicans on the Senate committee investigating Baker. Edward Levinson was a major investor in the Fremont and in the Horseshoe Club along with Benny Binion, formerly of Dallas. Binion's Horseshoe Club employed R.D. Matthews, also formerly of Dallas and an acquaintance of Jack Ruby, Ruby had called Matthews' former wife in the early fall of 1963. Binion had also been known to be a good friend of Lansky but had personally stayed out of gambling activities in Cuba. Perhaps of even greater interest to the FBI, Levinson was involved in business dealings with Moe Dalitz, a major investor in the Desert Inn and the Stardust.[12] The Desert Inn was Roselli's favorite spot in Las Vegas, followed by the Stardust and Horseshoe clubs. The Stardust had been heavily funded by Teamster loans and was known to be a prime source of skim payments to Sam Giancana of Chicago. John and Baker were guests of honor for the opening of the Stardust.[13]

Moe Dalitz had started in business by establishing a string of laundries in the midwest where Jack Ruby's brother, Earl, operated his Cobo Cleaners. Dalitz helped the cleaning industry in the Midwest become a bailiwick of the mob and as early as 1949 he began a close association with James Hoffa. His satisfactory union contract terms allowed Dalitz the financial success to become a major gambling figure both in Havana and in Las Vegas' Desert Inn.[14] His Teamster connections also allowed for multi-million dollar pension fund loans that funded the Las Vegas Sunrise Hospital, involving Dalitz with new friends that he had made at the Desert Inn Country Club, and financing for the Three-O-One Corporation of which Dalitz was a director. After an impressively complex series of transactions, the effects of this funding ended up in his possession of the Fremont Hotel, the deal being concluded with the signature of the Fremont's President, Edward Levinson.

Dalitz was also a partner with Lansky in the Molaska Corporation along with their Cleveland partner, Black Jack McGinty. Levinson and Dalitz's association can be traced all the way back to their being members of the same Midwestern gambling fraternity.[15]

By 1962 Dalitz had become head of the new Las Vegas Resort Hotel Association, a very successful political action effort by the casino owners which allowed Dalitz's candidates to sweep to victory–firmly entrenching Dalitz as the kingmaker in Las Vegas.[16]

Baker's business partners were connected to the very highest levels of the syndicate, to both Dalitz and Lansky. Given Roselli's perennial tie to the Desert Inn, the rumored FBI surveillance of a Roselli-Ruby meeting in Florida in the fall of 1963, and Levinson's business association with the Desert Inn's major investor, Moe Dalitz, it is certainly noteworthy that Melvin Belli's law partner (Seymour Ellison) has related the following.[17] Following Oswald's murder on the afternoon of November 24, Ellison, who had previously done work for Dalitz, a major investor in Desert Inn, received a telephone call. He knew the caller had previously been associated with the casino owners who had been ousted from Cuba.

Sy, one of our guys just bumped off that son-of-a-bitch that gunned down the President. The caller from Las Vegas wanted Belli, who was in Riverside defending an associate of Mickey Cohen, to take on the defense of Jack Ruby. However, Belli was to act as if the job and the money were coming from Jack's brother, Earl Ruby. Ellison called Belli who took an initial $25,000 retainer for Ruby's defense from the Las Vegas caller.[18]

It seems very likely that the FBI was bugging and monitoring Baker's business partners not only because of their connection to Baker and potentially to Johnson, since Hoover always liked to keep his options open, but also because Baker's business partners were linked to two of the biggest names in the syndicate world—Lansky and Dalitz.

Baker may or may not have known the implications. Hoover certainly would have, and certainly the associates of the gambling figures would have been aware of the potential impact of any associations with Baker or LBJ. However, what Black certainly did know and what he very likely told John Roselli was that Black, Baker, and a senior executive from North American Aviation had visited with the Vice-President in his office in the Executive Office Building. Not a long visit, only 15 minutes or so, but *long enough to leave an entry in the official visitors log; long enough to produce concrete evidence that Johnson and the Vice President's office were part of Baker's influence peddling*. This visit was recorded in the Vice President's daily log for August 21, 1963, while Baker's firm was consolidating its control over the lucrative vending machine business for North American and is provided in Appendix A.

There is no doubt that Johnson's association with Baker and his business partners could have exposed LBJ to blackmail. The only questions are whether or not this was communicated to Johnson himself, and whether the approach may have been directly from Roselli. However, as with the Oswald damage control, actions and timing can provide further insight. Johnson's reaction to the Baker scandal becomes visible in the Vice-President's official diary for the months of October and November of 1963. These diaries were maintained by Johnson's secretaries and are immensely detailed, recording virtually all of the Vice-President's activities, often including the time he went to bed and his recreational activities. They are available through the Johnson Library.

The legal proceedings and Congressional investigations of Baker began in September of 1963, and by October the pressure was such that Baker was forced to resign his position with the Democratic National Committee. Baker's legal counsel in October was Abe Fortas, a longtime associate of Johnson, but not Johnson's business or professional counsel. Fortas had not been directly involved with any Johnson legal action since Johnson's infamous Texas Congressional victory and ballot challenge more than a decade before. We have no idea if Fortas was recommended by Johnson to Baker, but the telephone record of calls between Johnson and Fortas suggests that may have been the case. Analysis of Johnson's call records for the six months before this period reveals that Fortas and Johnson had spoken only four times in that period. Three of the calls were from Fortas to Johnson and Johnson only called Fortas once for two minutes. But with the advent of the Baker scandal, there is a dramatic escalation in the level of contact:

Times are maximum times between calls. The actual call times may have been anything less than the maximum shown here; all diary entries are available from the Johnson Library.

October 1
Fortas to Johnson   20 minutes

October 3
Fortas to Johnson   10 minutes

October 7
Fortas to Johnson   20 minutes
(Baker resigns as of this date)

October 8
Johnson to Fortas   20 minutes

October 9
Johnson to Fortas   10 minutes

As of **October 11**, Johnson traveled frequently. He was not routinely in D.C. doing business from this date until the assassination.

October 14, Johnson to Fortas from NYC   5 minutes
Johnson returns to visit Fortas at his home for 1.5 hours that evening then returns to NYC and goes from there to Texas late that night.

October 18
JFK calls Johnson at the ranch at 7:45AM and talks for almost 1 hour. Topic is listed as the Baker-Korth problem.
Johnson calls Fortas at 8:35am   1 hour
Johnson calls JFK back at 9:45   10 minutes
Johnson calls Fortas back at 10:15   15 minutes

October 21
Johnson is back in D.C. Fortas spends the evening at the Johnson residence.

October 27
Upon his return from Boston, Johnson spends 2 hours at Fortas' home. Johnson is driven by Mrs. Johnson in a car borrowed from Sammy Wright. This was quite atypical for Johnson, in many respects including his being driven by Mrs. Johnson in a borrowed car. Certainly it emphasizes his concern for keeping a low profile in his contacts with Fortas and in distancing himself from Baker investigation.

October 29

Johnson to Fortas	45 minutes
Johnson to Fortas	1 hour, then departs for Texas

No further calls are recorded to or from Abe Fortas between October 29 and November 22. During this period Johnson is either at the ranch boating, camping, attending ball games in Texas or traveling to Los Angeles, Belgium and Dallas.

*On **November 1**, the Senate voted $50,000 to fund an expanded investigation of the Baker scandal and a major Congressional hearing was scheduled for the morning of November 22.* Despite this, Johnson's interest and concern over the Baker scandal seems to have vanished, at least as measured against his earlier routine and lengthy contacts with Fortas. Did something happen at the end of October to allay Johnson's concerns? A study of the legal and investigative proceedings shows an ongoing escalation of charges and press coverage. Clearly President Kennedy had made his concerns and feelings strongly known as well.

We are left with a dramatic change in behavior and no obvious explanation for Johnson's apparent loss of interest in neither the scandal, nor his cessation of contact with Fortas at the end of October.

SUMMARY

As of October 1963, Baker's activities and associates had placed Johnson in an extremely exposed position both politically and possibly even legally. The specific individuals who were involved with Baker in this scandal can be demonstrated to be quite closely associated with one of the likely (and reportedly self-admitted) Kennedy assassination conspirators John Roselli.

- Baker obtained introductions and financing from Black and Levinson.

- Baker was involved in negotiations for casino rights in the Caribbean with Levinson.

- Baker, Black, and Sigelbaum were partners and co-defendants in a political influence pedaling scandal which had extended to include Vice-President Johnson.

- Johnson was clearly under great pressure over this scandal, including pressure directly from President Kennedy.

- Black was a close personal friend of Roselli.

- Fred Black was positioned to destroy Lyndon Johnson with his personal testimony.

- Fred Black was a neighbor of, and personally known to, Johnson.

- At the end of October, some unknown factor seems to have abated Johnson's concern in regard to the Baker scandal.

Johnson's motivation for managing the Oswald damage control following the assassination is a matter of personal opinion. However, thanks to transcripts and records that have become available only in the last few years, we at least have a clear view of exactly how Johnson orchestrated the damage control, how the assassination of the President was tied to a single "lone nut". Details of that feat are discussed in the following chapter.

CHAPTER 17

"WE CAN'T CHECK EVERY SHOOTING SCRAPE IN THE COUNTRY"

The damage control following Oswald's capture and his extremely risky elimination by second patsy Ruby, given Ruby's history with crime figures and Cuba, was a three step program.

The first step was to ensure that there were no conspiracy charges filed in Texas and to close down any proactive effort by the FBI to turn up suspects beyond Oswald. The second was to ensure that none of the primary evidence entering the record would unambiguously demonstrate that the President had been fired at by multiple shooters. That effort involved consolidating and controlling the crime scene evidence and ensuring that the final autopsy report would support the lone gunman scenario, exclusively implicating the only individual in custody.

The third step involved the actual management of the official investigations, engineering a process through which a potential criminal investigation became nothing more than a series of reports demonstrating the guilt of a lone nut. The chronology of that process, as it can now be reconstructed, was as follows:

FROM INVESTIGATION TO REPORT

November 22

The Johnson diary records a brief visit with McGeorge Bundy, Special Assistant for National Security Affairs, in the Executive Office Building for no more than 5 minutes, at 6:45PM. This was the first recorded meeting after Johnson's return to the capital. The existing official diary shows no contact between Johnson and Hoover, who apparently had gone home at the end of the workday. However,

| 323 |

William Manchester gives details and a specific time for an evening call from Johnson to Hoover.[1] With Hoover's support, several items of key evidence were removed from Dallas and DPD possession before midnight. Also, several calls from Johnson's aide Cliff Carter were made to Texas; these calls preempted any charges or discussion of conspiracy in the assassination.[2] In spite of that, Dallas Police continued to detain and question possible suspects.

November 23

Johnson had a brief meeting with McGeorge Bundy and CIA Director McCone. This was scheduled as a briefing in the situation room according to Johnson's daily diary. However, a CIA staff member present with McCone has related that the meeting was purely conversational, that no topics of any substance were discussed and that the brief dialog was held in a hallway.[3]

10:03AM, Johnson received a call from Hoover. The very first item of conversation was Johnson asking Hoover about Mexico City. Hoover related the evidence for the impersonation of Oswald in Mexico City telephone calls and the implication of involvement by other parties. There was no discussion by Hoover of Oswald's contact with Soviet Consulate staff member Valery Kostikov, identified by both the CIA and FBI as associated with KGB Department 13/Sabotage and Assassination.

Immediately following this call, Johnson met with Robert McNamara for just two minutes, during which photographs were taken. This was followed by a call from Bundy that lasted for three minutes and a brief (four minutes maximum) meeting with McCone. Calls from Bundy on this and following days were focused on the Kennedy funeral and the attendance and meeting with foreign heads of state who would be attending.

After a meeting with all Cabinet members, Johnson visited briefly with Abe Fortas for no more than 4 minutes.

9:00PM, Johnson called Supreme Court Associate Justice Arthur Goldberg and told Goldberg he was thinking about "what I ought to do to try and bring all these elements together and unite the country to maintain and preserve our system in the world, because if it starts falling to pieces–and some of the extremists are going to be proceeding on the wrong assumption."[4]

This is the second known incident of Johnson raising a vision of calamity in conjunction with expressing caution about not acting on suspicions. The calls to Texas 24 hours before, on the evening of the assassination, were the first.

9:10PM, Johnson called Richard Maguire, Treasurer of the Democratic National Committee and chief fund raiser for the upcoming Presidential campaign.

9:40PM Johnson ended his day with a call to Bundy; Bundy and McCone were the first items on Johnson's schedule for the next day.

November 24

10:09AM, Johnson was in a meeting with McCone and Bundy for up to one hour. If minutes of this meeting still exist they have not been made available and need to be located; Lamar Waldron identifies the meeting subject as "CIA Operational Plans against Cuba."[5] During the afternoon there was a visit by several guests from Texas including Texas Attorney General Waggoner Carr. Photographs were taken of the group but the diary contains no evidence that Carr and Johnson had an actual meeting or even spoke privately at this point. Politicians and governors from all the states had come to Washington for the Kennedy funeral and Johnson met and took photographs with many of them.

5:10PM, Johnson received a brief call from Bundy in regard to the dignitaries who would be attending the Kennedy funeral.

8:55PM, Johnson called Hoover, apparently at home, and talked for a maximum of five minutes. This call concerned a report to be prepared by the FBI demonstrating that Oswald was the lone assassin of President Kennedy. There was also discussion of the negative effects of any other investigations.

This call to Hoover apparently occurred in the midst of a private Johnson meeting on the strategy for the investigation and the political and public relations issues surrounding possible congressional investigations or a possible local investigation in Texas. Johnson referred to such a strategy session in conversations the next day.

Johnson told Hoover that he and his lawyer had worked for three or four hours on this subject and the lawyer left at midnight.

The next day, Johnson told Joe Alsop of the *Washington Post*[6] that he had *"spent most of my day on this"* and had Waggoner Carr fly in; implying that Carr was part of a strategy session. Carr himself, in his autobiography, stated that he went to Washington D.C. because he and three other prominent Texans had been appointed by Connally to represent Texas at Kennedy's funeral.[7]

Carr and Johnson were personally and politically close. Carr had joined Johnson in San Antonio during the Kennedy Texas trip and had ridden in AF2 with Johnson to Houston and then on to Fort Worth.

The diary records that the dinner guests at the Johnson home for the evening of the strategy session included both Abe Fortas and Homer Thornberry, long time Johnson friend, former Texas Congressman and recently appointed Federal Judge. Carr was not in attendance.

November 25

At 10:20AM, Johnson called Hoover: "Apparently some lawyer in Justice is lobbying with The Post because that's where this suggestion came from for this presidential commission which we think would be very bad and put it right in the White House. We can't be checking up on every shooting scrape in the country." Johnson told Hoover they are going to do two things and he wants Hoover to know it. The first is that "they" (although he repeats this as Hoover's proposal from the day before) will have the FBI report on Oswald given to the Attorney General and then the FBI will provide the report directly to the public.

Second, *the Texas Attorney General is "young and able and prudent;" he will cooperate with Hoover and run a Texas "Court of Inquiry."* This is provided for by Texas state law and Carr will have the inquiry associated with "the most outstanding jurists in the country. The Attorney General of the state holds Courts of Inquiry every time a law is violated and the FBI makes these investigations." Johnson instructed Hoover to tell his press people that this is what will happen and that Carr will make the announcement "this morning" to have a state inquiry and Hoover should offer him his full cooperation.

Later, Carr would relate to Manchester that Johnson called him on Monday the 25th to suggest that Texas conduct its own investigation and that Johnson urged him to announce this as Carr's own idea.[8] Carr told a different story in his autobiography, stating that before going to the cathedral for the Kennedy services, he spoke to an unnamed White House staff member and explained the process for a Texas Court of Inquiry. The staff member then talked to Johnson, who instructed him to ask Carr to publicly announce the Texas Court of Inquiry. Johnson clearly wanted everybody to think all these iterations about investigations were somebody else's doing and not picture him as deeply involved with all stages of how things were being positioned.

There is no record of a call from Johnson to Carr on the 24th or the 25th. Either Johnson called Carr privately for some reason or met with Carr privately at some point earlier than related by Carr to Manchester. Carr did indeed announce the Court of Inquiry in a four paragraph statement that morning at the Statler-Hilton in Washington D.C.

It seems likely that Johnson may have called Carr from his home at some point the evening before, perhaps after talking to Hoover while the strategy session with Fortas and Thornberry was in progress.

At 10:40AM, Johnson called Alsop. Johnson described the announcement that Carr would shortly be making: "He has ordered— or will order during the day, probably right after the funeral—a state Court of Inquiry headed by the Attorney General. He will have associated with him one or two of the outstanding civil liberties jurists in the country: perhaps Jaworski, who represented the Attorney General in the Fifth Circuit Negro case, or the head of the Trial Lawyers of America, or Dean Storey."

At that point, *Alsop realized the names involved were all Texas attorneys* and asked about participation from outside. *Johnson told him the FBI would do the investigation but it would be done under Texas law, with Texans.* Johnson also mentioned names like Garwood, the son in law of a former Supreme Court Justice, and cited precedent in the commission set up to investigate the attack on Pearl Harbor. Johnson further shrilly remarked about having spent most of the preceding day on this subject and the legal strategy, and having had Carr fly in from Dallas. He also added that the FBI had been working on preparing its report since 12:30 the previous day. In this call with Alsop, Johnson took strong exception to any independent commission, an idea he attributed to Katzenbach, saying "the lawyers" hit the ceiling over such an idea.

JA: And, I now see exactly how right you are and how wrong I was about this idea of a blue ribbon commission...

LBJ: Now, you see, Katzenbach suggested that and that provoked it ... the lawyers and the council just hit the ceiling ... said, my God almighty...[9]

Finally, Johnson made it very clear to Alsop that what he wanted him to do was to lobby behind the scenes with the press to support

Johnson. There is no evidence that Johnson discussed this plan with anyone in the Justice Department or with any other lawyers besides Fortas and Thornberry prior to telling Texas Attorney General Carr how it was to be handled.

On November 25, Katzenbach sent his infamous memorandum to Bill Moyers:

1. The public must be satisfied that Oswald was the assassin; that he did not have confederates who are still at large; and that the evidence was such that he would have been convicted at trial.

2. Speculation about Oswald's motivation ought to be cut off, and we should have some basis for rebutting thought that this was a communist conspiracy or as the Iron Curtain press is saying, a right-wing conspiracy to blame it on the communists. Unfortunately, the facts on Oswald seem about too pat-- too obvious: Marxist, Cuba, Russian wife, etc.. The Dallas police have put out statements on the communist conspiracy theory, and it was they who were in charge when he was shot and thus silenced.

3. The matter has been handled thus far with neither dignity nor conviction. Facts have been mixed with rumor and speculation. We can scarcely let the world see us totally in the image of the Dallas police when our President is murdered.

By the time Katzenbach's memo was received, Johnson's own strategy for dealing with these issues had already been developed and he was putting it into play, lobbying his media contacts in support of it.[10]

November 25

The CIA in Mexico City received and endorsed a report by Gilberto Alvarado that had Oswald receiving money for the assassination of President Kennedy from an individual within the Cuban Embassy in Mexico City. There is no record that this was communicated to President Johnson until a memo from Bundy the following day.

November 26

On November 26, the day after Carr announced the Texas Court of Inquiry, he was contacted by Fortas. Fortas told Carr that Johnson had assigned Fortas to be the sole liaison between the Court of Inquiry and both the FBI and the Justice Department.

Carr then wrote a memorandum to himself documenting Fortas' communication noting the fact that Fortas was acting at the direction of the President. Fortas had no official connection to either the FBI or the Department of Justice.[11]

1:30 to 3:00PM. Johnson had an extended lunch with Senator Russell.

4:48PM. Johnson met with Bundy for four minutes.

4:52PM. Johnson called Henry Luce and talked for 10 minutes.

6:05-6:50PM. Johnson met with Fortas, Thornberry, Jenkins and Mike Fieldman.

7:25PM. Johnson visited Bundy's office as his last meeting of the day.

According to Michael Beschloss, McCone sent a memo on the 26th, via Bundy, about the Alvarado incident.[12] The wording in the memo— *time prevented me from mentioning this morning developments in Mexico City*—suggests that McCone did not communicate the incident the day that it surfaced in Mexico City. The document is dated November 28, so it is very unclear when the President was informed of the possible witness to Oswald being paid by the Cubans, just as it is unclear if he was ever informed of the Kostikov-KGB-Oswald connection. It is also hard to understand why such an inflammatory report, which we know had been initially endorsed by the Mexico City CIA Station as highly credible would have had such a low priority that it was not to be communicated except via memo. And that one to two days after it was filed in Mexico City!

November 27

At 11:05AM. Johnson began his day with a 5-10 minute meeting with McGeorge Bundy.

4:01PM. Johnson called Alsop for a three minute conversation. He was thanking Alsop for an article praising Johnson as a "man of action" in contrast to his predecessor and as "having all the qualities that are most wanted in a President." Alsop closed by telling Johnson he was impressed with his speech because he had always assumed "acting" rather than speaking was Johnson's strength.

November 28

On November 28, Thanksgiving Day, Johnson delivered a TV address to the nation, spoke with Fortas for two minutes following the speech and then for a few minutes after that with Bundy. He departed the Oval office with no further contacts.

November 29

9:25AM. Lyndon Johnson called Thornberry from his car for approximately five minutes.

11:14AM. Johnson held a cabinet meeting including McNamara, Rusk, McCone and Bundy. The meeting was held in the Oval Office and lasted for a maximum of 30 minutes. Johnson had spoken briefly with Bundy beforehand. Johnson left the cabinet meeting to have a 15 minute telephone conversation with Abe Fortas at 11:15AM.

This call with Fortas went into considerable detail in regard to the formation of a Presidential Commission on the assassination, its structure and a dialogue on names for selection. The names were proposed by either Fortas or Johnson, and Johnson closed by stating that it seemed he would have to call each of them personally although he would have preferred to simply issue an order appointing them. During the course of the day, Johnson conducted numerous calls and meetings with proposed commission members; this activity included meeting with and persuading Earl Warren. He consistently used the threat of nuclear warfare and loss of 40 million people as a means of forcing cooperation. He also made vague references to events in Mexico City as being a concern that must be negated by the commissions' findings. It seems clear that Johnson had deployed the Warren Commission as a device for approving the FBI report in place of his first preference for an *"all-Texas" Court of Inquiry.*

5:41PM. Hoover called Johnson; they spoke for four minutes. Johnson asked Hoover if he was aware of the "proposed" group that "they're" trying to put together to study "your report." Hoover, unaware of Johnson's maneuvering, simply declared that it would be bad to have a "rash" of investigations. Johnson then asked Hoover's opinions of candidates for the Commission.

Johnson himself did not inquire about the progress of the FBI's Oswald investigation. However, *Hoover told him that they expected to wrap it up either that day or by Monday at the latest.* Hoover also related that the investigation had been made more difficult by the report of Alvarado, whom Hoover did not name and they would have to demonstrate its falsity. The two then discussed the rumors of a relationship between Ruby and Oswald. Johnson showed no particular concern over the Alvarado story and gave no indication that he had even heard of it, although according to Michael Beschloss, McCone did write a memo on the subject to Bundy for Johnson's attention on the 26th.[13] The memorandum now in record contains a date of November 28 rather than 26.

8:20PM. Johnson received a call from Bundy followed by another call from Bundy five minutes later.

November 30

10:35AM. Bundy met with Johnson for some period of time prior to conducting a briefing in the Cabinet Room until 12:10. Afterwards, Bundy was in the Oval Office with his mother and photographs were taken with the President, possibly suggesting that Bundy's time with Johnson was not devoted to a high level national security matter.

3:14PM. Johnson received a 2 minute call from McCone, who gave a final opinion that there was nothing to the Alvarado story. Johnson was very nonchalant and is recorded as chuckling during the call.

3:35PM. Fortas and Clark Clifford met in the Oval Office with Johnson for an hour and a half.

December 6

Carr approached the FBI via Katzenbach for a meeting with Hoover. When asked the purpose, Carr, who was virtually begging for the appointment, stated that there was no real reason other than he wanted to be able to say that he had consulted with Hoover before he dissolved the Texas Court of Inquiry. Hoover agreed to see him if Carr did come to Washington, but in the end the two men met only to have a photograph taken.

Nonetheless, on the day of this photo session with Hoover, Carr announced the indefinite postponement of the Texas inquiry and justified it by remarking that he had consulted with Hoover, Katzenbach and Warren, the implication that there were actually serious consultations in regard to the Texas inquiry seems a bit of an exaggeration.[14]

SUMMARY

The conclusion emerging from this chronology is that President Johnson was the driving force in determining and controlling exactly how the murder of President Kennedy was investigated. He instructed Director Hoover to collect the evidence, to take the criminal investigation from the Dallas police and to simply write a report presenting the evidence for Lee Oswald as the lone assassin.

At no point was the Justice Department consulted on strategy or process. The FBI was to prepare the report at its own initiative, not to work as the investigative arm of the Justice department in a criminal case role. The point has been raised that the murder of a President was not legally a Federal crime. However, there is no sign that Johnson ever inquired into that legal issue or that he was even aware of it. Certainly he never mentioned it even as a justification for a Texas inquiry.

With advice from Fortas and possibly Judge Thornberry, Johnson constructed a scenario in which a Texas Court of Inquiry would validate the FBI report. Johnson promoted this concept with the media and maneuvered Carr into announcing the strategy. Carr went so far as to write his own internal memo saying that he had been instructed to coordinate his activities with the President through Abe Fortas, who had no legal standing in the matter.

When the country as a whole began to respond negatively to Johnson's first proposal of a Texas Court of Inquiry, Johnson, in consultation with Abe Fortas, shifted to a presidential commission as the certifying body for the FBI report. Johnson and Fortas identified the potential commission members with Johnson personally doing the recruiting. Members were told it was their duty to assist in avoiding any suspicions that might lead to a nuclear war and that they would only have to validate an FBI report that was already virtually complete.

Following the failure of the conspiracy plan due to Oswald's capture, the plotters responded in two ways. They had no choice but to order Jack Ruby to stalk Oswald and kill him. Then they moved on a variety of fronts to present new evidence that Oswald had been acting under direct influence of Cuba and most likely Castro. Some of this information implicated Ruby as being under Cuban influence as well.

With Oswald in custody, the FBI and CIA also responded; responded with damage control efforts to isolate themselves from any association or more than minimal knowledge of Oswald. Better for them to look incompetent or stupid, than have been involved with an apparent Presidential assassin.

The new President responded as well, with damage control that preempted any charges or discussion of conspiracy, ensuring that the FBI presented Oswald as a "lone nut" and arranging for the Warren Commission to officially sanction that image.

CHAPTER 18

"THE ANTI-CASTRO PEOPLE" — AFTERWARDS

John Martino pointed us towards the anti-Castro people, and we've explored what many of them were doing and saying prior the President Kennedy's assassination. But what did they do afterwards, in the days, weeks and even years following? Perhaps there's something to be learned there as well.

Anti-Castro "Power Players" in 1963

William Pawley

A personal friend of President Eisenhower, Pawley was one of four members of the Doolittle Committee that in 1954 produced a report exhorting the US to abandon its normal principles and turn to subversion and sabotage against the Communists. Pawley had tried to take command of a secret war against Castro, but Dulles and the CIA had prevailed.[1]

Luce/*Time-Life* media network

Life had provided funds and media support the Bayo-Pawley mission. In 1963, *Life* was sending its staff to encourage and provide limited financing and report on the activities of Alpha 66. Both *Life* and *Post* magazines were running frequent articles on Castro's Cuba and the plight of the exiles being restrained by President Kennedy from acting against him.[2]

Theodore Shackley

William Pawley was able to run his 1963 mission into Cuba with CIA support because Theodore Shackley listened to him and endorsed the mission to his superiors. This mission was known to Shackley's boss Desmond Fitzgerald and to the Deputy Director of the CIA, Marshall Carter. However, there is no record of it being authorized or reported to the Special Group or the President who individually authorized operations on the approved Special Group mission list. The Bayo–Pawley mission (CIA designation TILT) was conducted as a covert operation intended to extract Russian officers. These officers apparently would have been made available to a Senate subcommittee, with full details of the mission including photography to be published in *Life* magazine.

The risks involved in this mission were significant. It involved the personal participation of Pawley, *Life* photography of a CIA supported Cuban incursion, and the use of exile personnel not cleared by CIA security. The media and political impact had it succeeded would have been immense including Senate hearings on the failure of the Kennedy Administration to remove missiles from Cuba and major fodder for the ongoing Luce magazine anti-administration propaganda campaign. It seems inconceivable that Robert Kennedy and the Special Group would have supported a personal mission into Cuba by someone with the stature and political clout of William. Former US ambassadors are poor choices for covert military missions, especially at a time when the administration in Washington had assumed a public policy of opposing any actions against Cuba from US territory.

Desmond Fitzgerald

Acting as the successor to **William Harvey,** Desmond Fitzgerald was in overall charge of Cuban operations in 1963.[3] He had promoted and enhanced David Phillips' role both in Mexico City and in conjunction with JM/WAVE. William Harvey had been in charge of Task Force W as part of Operation Mongoose under Edward Lansdale. Lansdale had earlier reported to Fitzgerald in South East Asia. Fitzgerald was well-known for allowing great personal initiative among his subordinates, believing that individuals could and had to make a difference. He had declared his mission in Asia very simply, *"We are here to destroy communism."*[4] While in Southeast Asia, Fitzgerald actually set up a fake Communist Party in China as a "sting" against the Red Chinese.

However, in his role in Special Affairs Staff, he focused on using the CIA's resources and personally paid little attention to the Cuban exiles, writing his daughter in June of 1963, "I have dealt with a fairly rich assortment of exiles in the past but none can compare with the

Cuban group for genuine stupidity and militant childishness."[5] It's clear that other than limited meetings with high level exile leaders such as Artime, Willams and Ray, he left everyday operating contacts with Cuban exiles to his subordinates: Shackley, Morales, Hecksher, Jenkins, Phillips and others.

ANTI-CASTRO PEOPLE, 1963 AND AFTERWARDS

Eduardo Perez (Eddie Bayo) led the mission into Cuba in the summer of 1963 and officially disappeared from view. He was never reported killed or captured by the Castro regime. It would have been a major Cuban propaganda coup to capture a senior Alpha 66 leader, as indeed it was when Castro forces captured Tony Cuesta on the same raid in which Herminio Diaz Garcia was killed. Cuesta's capture was well publicized. The Cubans have since told researchers that while under interrogation, Cuesta named Diaz Garcia as one of the participants in the Kennedy assassination.

Sandalio Herminio Diaz Garcia was a dark skinned Cuban who reportedly had been a Trafficante bodyguard in Cuba. Diaz Garcia may have served as a contact inside Cuba for at least one of the initial Roselli-organized Castro assassination attempts. He had been in Mexico City with Alpha 66 and eventually moved to Miami (Gerry Hemming described Diaz Garcia living with him in 1963).[6]

Diaz Garcia has been offered as a candidate for the "dark" Latin in a Rambler station wagon, who was reported by Officer Roger Craig picking up an individual resembling Lee Oswald on Elm Street shortly after the President's murder.

Recently obtained NARA documents have revealed further background information about Garcia. One document, a State Department report to McGeorge Bundy, described an attempt to assassinate Castro in December 1963. Castro escaped but a man next to him was killed. The memo relates continuing rumors of a plot to assassinate Castro connected to Diaz Garcia, a member of the Cuban Restaurant Workers Union.[7]

Another document from the FBI associates Garcia with Commandos L, the 30th of November Group, and with Prio Socarras. It describes Garcia as a long time counter-revolutionary, states that he is fearless and also was connected in arms sales to Norman Rothman.[8]

In 1966, **John Roselli** told William Morgan a story about the Cuban capture and torture of the last assassination team sent into Cuba to get Castro in 1963. In the first version, the team's capture led to Castro's sending his own rifle teams into the US to get Kennedy one of the circa-1964 stories, as we saw earlier. Roselli even claimed to know the names of some of these individuals; although it is unclear as to how he would have obtained such information, the one name he provided was that of an individual who had been placed in a mental institution in 1964.

Roselli then modified the story to tell columnist Jack Anderson that the team sent to the United States had some of the same individuals on it that had gone in for the CIA, including some who had formerly worked for Trafficante.[9]

In 1977, **Pawley** came under the scrutiny of HSCA investigators. During this period Pawley contracted a nervous ailment (shingles). One week after being placed on the HSCA interview list by Gaeton Fonzi, Pawley committed suicide with a gunshot to his chest.[10] Noel Twyman's interviews with Gerry Hemming produced the following remarks on Pawley's death:

> "He'd become convinced that his participation had gone awry and that he'd become a traitor to his country.[11]"

> "Pawley, he put up some money... It is too bad these guys didn't use the money for what they got the money for. They went and killed Kennedy with it.[12]"

> "This is a guy who deals with the DCI [Director, Central Intelligence Agency], okay? A former ambassador and the ultimate thing occurred. The thing you fear the most. Your people went out and did some shit. The people you financed went out and did some shit they weren't supposed to do.[13]"

Interestingly, in later years, FBI agent Hosty would comment to one researcher that Hosty suspected the visitors to Sylvia Odio were "Pawley's people," engaged in some sort of action against JURE. The thinking behind this statement and indeed Hosty's knowledge about Pawley and his people may be worth further inquiry.

Rip Robertson continued as an operations officer for Cuban exile teams operated by the CIA. As President Johnson demonstrated little interest in the Kennedy Administration's former projects against

Cuba (especially the autonomous group initiative organized by Robert Kennedy), the CIA began to transition these personnel to other wars across Latin America and in Vietnam. In November of 1964, Robertson and a small operational group of his exiles were used in a CIA rescue mission for American citizens in the Congo as part of the joint Belgian-American "Operation Dragon." Cuban exile pilots flew B-26's in air support of the Belgian paratroop assault on Stanleyville. Robertson introduced himself to the Belgians as "Carlos."[14]

Ted Shackley continued to run JM/WAVE as President Johnson gradually began to disassociate the United States from direct Cuban conflict, ordering the Kennedy Special Group sabotage raids ended in April of 1964. But Shackley and Fitzgerald continued to operate a CIA Castro assassination project with **Rolando Cubela** as part of the AM/LASH project. In March and June of 1964, Shackley authorized the delivered of weapons to Cubela, who had been pushing to involve the CIA in new assassination schemes since the fall of 1963. When he was questioned by the Church Committee as to authorization of these activities, the same investigation that showed Desmond Fitzgerald representing himself falsely as Robert Kennedy's personal agent in meeting with Cubela, Shackley insisted he did not recall authorizing the shipments. When shown the cables clearly documenting his own actions and with his signature, Shackley (who was famous with his subordinates for wanting to personally authorize any and all expenditures) insisted that he did not remember ever having seen the cables before.[15] In regard to the JFK assassination, individual JM/WAVE agents recognized the possibility of a connection to the organization's activities, or at least its contacts. However, Shackley believed that since the CIA did not have the primary responsibility for probing Oswald and the assassination, his station only had to collect information in a "passive way" from existing sources. The HSCA committee noted the failure of Shackley's station to debrief its sources and contacts for information and leads pertaining to the assassination.[16]

Shackley's tour at JM/WAVE won him the strong personal support of CIA insiders such as David Morales and high profile agency senior officers such as Desmond Fitzgerald. Shackley received the Intelligence Medal for his Miami Tour. Fitzgerald recommended that Shackley be assigned to the Agency's next major field operation–supervision of the 20,000 man Pathetic Lao CIA army in Laos.

Much has been written of Shackley and the CIA in Laos, including the extent to which heroin traffic became associated with the CIA operational infrastructure. While Shackley's role in this is a matter of debate, the roles of other individuals connected to the CIA and US military are more obvious and can be reviewed in *The Crimes of Patriots* by Jonathan Kwitny.[17]

An old CIA associate in the secret war against Castro, **Santos Trafficante** most definitely did become involved in the drug traffic out of Laos and Vietnam. Trafficante first sent Frank Forci to represent him in Laos in 1965 and finally went to Vietnam himself in 1968.[18]

Desmond Fitzgerald continued his Special Affairs operations through 1964; refusing to abandon the potential of Cubela until Cubela was arrested by Castro, his relatively modest punishment aroused further suspicion that he had been providing information back to Fidel. Like Shackley, Fitzgerald's mission against Cuba was a rather dismal failure. However, Fitzgerald was also awarded with a promotion to Deputy Director of Plans in 1965, the Chief of Covert Operations.

Fitzgerald also proved that he was perfectly capable of keeping crucial information away from assassination investigators. On November 23, when CIA counter-intelligence was desperately searching for information on Oswald's contact with Kostikov in Mexico City, they determined that Kostikov had also met with a Cuban diplomat, Rolando Cubela. CI issued a trace to see if anyone in the agency had been in contact with Cubela or had information about him. Fitzgerald had personally met Cubela in France on October 29. He had agreed to Cubela's goal of assassinating Castro and begun operations to provide Cubela with assassination materials within Cuba. Fitzgerald did not respond to the CI trace. However, Fitzgerald could maintain that technically speaking Special Affairs was compartmented from the rest of the Agency and was not legally required to share information, even within the Agency.

Only Richard Helms knew about the Cubela meeting. Fitzgerald did tell Director McCone's assistant that he had met Cubela in October and an agent had met with him again on November 22. There is no indication that this information was provided to the Kostikov inquiry. Whether or not it was provided to President Johnson in his November 24 intelligence brief is unknown. What is known is that on November 23, Fitzgerald (known as a "stoic" even among his peers) was observed "shaking his head and wringing his hands" while at work. On November

24 while at home watching TV with his wife, he observed the murder of Lee Oswald. For the first and last time in his wife's memory, Fitzgerald began to cry and exclaimed; *now we'll never know*"[19]

Phillips' wife also described her husband's behavior on hearing of President Kennedy's murder. **David Phillips** described himself as a JFK proponent in *The Night Watch*. After the Bay of Pigs failure he had broken down and alternately cried and thrown up for hours. On November 22, *David Phillips came home from work and made no remark at all about the assassination.* Details of the assignments and careers of Shackley, Morales and Phillips are provided Appendix B, *Crossing Paths in the CIA.*[20]

At the beginning of the Church Committee intelligence investigations Phillips took early retirement from the highest level of the CIA; the only officers above him were presidential appointees. In retirement, he organized and led an association of former intelligence officers devoted to countering what he and the others considered irresponsible press and slander against the CIA. The association also assumed an aggressive legal posture against reporters and writers who it felt made untrue or slanderous statements pertaining to its members.[21]

In addition to his involvement in the Bayo-Pawley mission, John Martino was personally involved with **Felipe Vidal Santiago,** Frank Fiorini/Sturgis, and others within the Miami exile community including individuals who had been part of the "casino" scene in Havana.

Vidal mentioned several visits to General Walker during 1963. Walker himself had limited personal funds and relied on his connections to right-wing organizations and in particular, to **H.L. Hunt** who was largely responsible for funding Walker's campaign for governor in Texas. There is no documented account of Vidal meeting with Hunt or Hunt's representatives. However, Hunt's behavior after the assassination suggests that he may have been concerned about somehow being implicated, at least by his associations or remarks.

Gerry Hemming places Hunt, Murchison and Gordon McLendon, a close friend of David Phillips and supporter of Phillips' intelligence agent organization at a Petroleum Club meeting in Dallas where Texans introduced the subject of eliminating John Kennedy along with Fidel Castro. Hemming also stated that Vidal dealt with the Hunts but that they maintained an arms length relationship and did not want to know any details of Vidal's activities.[22]

Felipe Vidal Santiago bears a resemblance to a Latin individual photographed on Elm Street on November 22, 1963. This individual was one of the closest persons to the President at the time of the fatal shot(s). He had been waving his arm up and down, had attracted the attention of several Secret Service agents including the driver of the President's car and in contrast to the others in his area, he remained standing as the others threw themselves to the ground. This individual showed no emotion nor reaction to the shooting, he left the area afterwards, walking west down the street towards the underpass rather than following the crowds up towards the knoll, the fence and the parking lot. He never came forward, was never located and his identity remains a mystery.

Roy Hargraves had been affiliated both with Gerry Hemming's group and with activist exile groups such as 30th November. In the period of September 1963 to March 1964, Hargraves was primarily associated with Felipe Vidal Santiago. Hargraves was reported to the FBI as having traveled to Dallas in late fall and of being in possession of Secret Service credentials.

Hargraves continued his anti-Communist activities for several years. In 1968, he was involved in the bombing of Black Panther groups in Los Angeles. In 1970, Hargraves, along with Ivan Vidal, Felipe's relative, and Gerry Hemming, were involved in a complex plot to simulate attacks on US installations that would implicate Cuba and provoke a military reaction. Also in 1970, Hargraves attempted to introduce Manuel Aguilar to Army Intelligence as a potential asset in anti-Cuban activities. There is also reason to speculate that both Hargraves and Vidal were in contact with an individual representing himself as working with Army Intelligence during 1963.[23, 24]

WHO KNEW—SOMETHING?

H.L. Hunt left Dallas on November 22 traveling to Washington D.C. and staying there for several days. Although he remarked to his aides that he was going "to help Lyndon," there is no official record of any contact between him and the new President in this period. Hunt was particularly well connected to the Dallas FBI office, employing several former agents as top aides. According to Hunt, local FBI officials suggested that he should leave Dallas for his own safety.[25]

Hunt's two chief aides in 1963 were Paul Rothermel and John Curington. The two later crossed paths with Hunt's sons and were ejected from the Hunt companies in a messy exchange which included surveillance and bugging of the employee's telephone lines. The two have reluctantly described two incidents that are extremely suggestive. The first is that before he left Dallas, Hunt instructed Curington to assess the security in place around Oswald at Dallas police headquarters on the evening of his arrest. Curington ended up on the same elevator as Oswald and Fritz. Fritz, knowing Curington well, introduced Oswald to Curington as the "blankety-blank" who shot the President.

The second revelation is that Hunt's interest continued to the time of the Garrison investigation. Hunt sent Paul Rothermel to monitor Garrison and if possible to direct his attention towards a leftist Cuban conspiracy—not a Castro conspiracy per se but leftist exiles (reminiscent of the attempted Odio-JURE frame). Rothermel also related to author Dick Russell that Al Hill (H.L. Hunt's son-in-law) told him once that it was "imperative that Garrison not get the idea that anybody of our family and friends had anything to do with the Kennedy assassination." Like Pawley, H.L. Hunt may have had reason to suspect that people he had contacted and perhaps even paid money to had *done some shit.*[26, 27]

Antonio de Varona and other senior members of the CRC were highly frustrated with Kennedy policy. When the Kennedy Administration discontinued support for the CRC in 1963, its head, Miro Cardona accused Kennedy of "breaking promises and agreements" and stated that he had become a "victim of a master play by the Russians." In 1964, Dr. Varona moved from Miami to New York City where he first worked as a car salesman and the following year became a language teacher for Berlitz. Varona left his high profile, activist exile activities behind him for almost two decades. In 1980, he returned to his former role as a media champion and unifier of splinter organizations. He died in 1992.

Tony Varona had been referred to John Roselli for the attempts against Castro. Varona was a man with well-established gambling and smuggling contacts in Cuba. Howard Hunt's sequestering of Varona along with other CRC leaders may have defeated one of several attempts that were planned to ensure that the Brigade entered Cuba with Castro dead and a leadership crisis at hand. Roselli kept going back to Varona who was his key connection to the Miami exiles, especially those with prior connections to the casino crowd and Cuban crime, people like

Trafficante's former bodyguard in Cuba, **Herminio Diaz Garcia**.[28] In his CRC leadership role, Verona would have to have been associated with Phillips for media and propaganda purposes. Interestingly enough, Varona officially admitted to only knowing E. Howard Hunt, Frank Bender and Bernard Barker. After his "rebellion" against the Agency in 1963, Varona reportedly fell back on the gambling network for his funding.[29]

It seems reasonable to speculate that both Varona and Trafficante may have heard rumors or gossip in regard to the Kennedy conspiracy. Certainly each had channels to the two individuals whose remarks suggest that they had inside information relating to the assassination— John Roselli and David Morales. While US propaganda frequently attempted to put Castro behind the growing influx of drugs, whenever any Cubans were arrested they turned out to be connected to the anti-Castro smuggling and to either the Trafficante or Marcello drug networks rather than to Castro's military or political cadre. Of course successful smugglers make a fine intelligence conduit, one reason that the CIA turned to the gamblers and ended up using Trafficante's network and couriers.[30] It's often pointed out that Cuban officials arrested Santo Trafficante on charges of drug smuggling. In 1956 the FBI investigated a report that Trafficante and Norman Rothman were engaged in cocaine smuggling to the United States, and the traffic only escalated after Trafficante's return to the US.[31]

In late 1962, **Jose Aleman** reported a conversation with Trafficante to two local FBI agents, George Davis and Paul Scranton. Aleman had heard Trafficante remark, in September 1962, that President Kennedy was going to be "hit" before the Presidential election in 1964. It is unclear what report, if any, these agents filed on this incident. The HSCA inquired into Aleman's story and interviewed Aleman at length. He "did not believe that S.T. was personally involved in whatever plan he seemed to know about." Aleman confirmed that there had also been talk of the problems that Hoffa was having, but that Trafficante did not link the two. Aleman reaffirmed to HSCA investigators that he "made no attempt to even infer [sic] that the Hoffa reference was in any way connected to the statement that Kennedy was 'going to be hit.'"[32] Trafficante denied any such remarks when questioned by the HSCA.

This incident coincides in time with the first reported remarks by Trafficante connected Alpha 66 members in Mexico City. These discussions were about killing John Kennedy in retaliation for his treachery at the Bay of Pigs and for his agreement with the Russians not to invade Cuba. After the assassination, Trafficante did not become an object of inquiry. It was not until the Roselli revelations and the Church Committee intelligence inquiry that Trafficante came under scrutiny and as soon as he was listed for testimony, he left the United States for Costa Rica.[33]

While Roselli testified, Trafficante remained out of reach. Meanwhile, during that investigation and after Giancana's murder (with a revolver traced back to Miami), Trafficante was captured on an FBI wire tap stating *"now only two people know who killed Kennedy and they aren't talking."*[34] The two people could well have been Roselli and Morales; both were alive at that point. However, based on warnings to Roselli by Fred Black that Trafficante held a contract on him and that the Cubans were coming for him, it may well be that Trafficante took the initiative to reduce the head count of those who knew.

According to his lawyers, Roselli had "snowed" the Church Committee. But he did reveal to his lawyers the names of three of Trafficante's people who had been involved in the Cuban missions. Any serious investigation of the Kennedy assassination would have come back to Roselli. Once before in a legal venue, Roselli's lawyers had tried to aid his case by revealing old history—not a good precedent for someone who knew as much about organized crime as Roselli. Though Roselli stonewalled the Committee on his third visit, three weeks later he was murdered.[35]

When eventually called before the HSCA, Trafficante stated that he was not aware of any CIA assassination plots to kill Castro and denied any involvement in their operations. Clearly he had something serious to hide if he was willing to commit provable perjury before the HSCA.[36]

Having been jailed and tortured by the Batista regime, **Manuel Rodriguez Orcarberrio** sided with Castro's forces in Cuba until he balked at Castro's communism and defected via the Brazilian embassy in Havana. He traveled to Miami and worked as a dishwasher while associating with activist exile organizations such as Alpha 66, MRP and SNFE (which he described only as a fundraising organization).

In September of 1963, Orcarberrio moved into the house at 3126 Harlandale that became a meeting place for members of Alpha 66 as well as local DRE activists.

An FBI report filed after the assassination placed Orcarberrio and other local Cubans in Sulphur, Oklahoma shortly before November 22 in company with someone very closely resembling Lee Oswald.[37] Questioned about reported threats and violent statements against President Kennedy, Orcarberrio denied all the reports and claimed to have been very much pro-Kennedy. That remark seems about as credible as his description of SNFE/Alpha 66 as being purely a fund raising organization. A Dallas FBI informant had reported him as being "violently anti-Kennedy" and the Secret Service opened a PRS surveillance file on him in 1964 (3/18/64), thus classifying him as a potential threat to the President.[38] Orcarberrio eventually moved to Puerto Rico (the offshore base of Alpha 66). He stated that he had moved because he had been persecuted in the United States for being anti-Communist.

Carlos Rodriguez Quesada was known to be associated with both the DRE and the MRP as well as 30th of November. With the dissolution of the CRC in 1963, Quesada formed the SNFE organization. Later in the year, he affiliated this group with the Sierra Junta and became the latter's Minister of Internal Affairs.[39] Quesada was active in arms procurement and frequented Chicago, associating with Homer Echevarria. He was also associated with many of Gerry Hemming's Interpen members, paying them to help transport weapons and supplies to Florida. Quesada offered money to Interpen group members to conduct raids into Cuba.[40] After Kennedy's assassination, sometime the following year, Quesada was reportedly murdered. The circumstances of his death or disappearance are as uncertain as those of Eddie Bayo.

Victor Dominador Espinosa Hernandez was living in Miami in 1963 and operating in association with old Havana gambling network members such as Mike McClaney, Sam Benton and possibly Norman Rothman. He was arrested for transporting explosives to New Orleans and was involved in Sierra/Quesada arms trafficking in the Chicago area. It appears possible that he was the Hernandez reported in several Illinois and Michigan appearances and was connected to the network which was providing funds to Homer Echevarria. Victor Hernandez had trained in 1960 for the Bay of Pigs but officially got into "trouble" and was discharged in the New Orleans area before the actual invasion. According to Hernandez he was actually moved into a paramilitary group that was to support the invasion; he and this group continued missions into Cuba after the Bay of Pigs disaster. He was also a long time friend of Rolondo Cubela of the CIA (Helms and Desmond Fitzgerald) AM/LASH assassination project begun in 1963, remaining in touch with Cubela in Cuba through 1963 and into 1964. This AM/LASH project used many of the same crime connections that Roselli had leveraged in earlier Castro assassination projects.[41]

After the assassination, apparently before the end of 1964, Victor Hernandez left the United States for Spain and according to his associate, Carlos Eduardo Hernandez, may have gone to France and been involved in something related to drugs. The CIA Inspector General's report on Operation Mongoose revealed that in 1964 and 1965, Cubela (AM/LASH) continued the meetings with CIA representatives in Madrid, Spain, which he had begun in October and November 1963. During this period, he also met with Manual Artime. In addition, the IG report notes that Rafel Garcia-Bongo, a lawyer for Trafficante in Cuba, was in Spain in March of 1965.[42] Bongo claimed to be in contact with dissident Cuban military leaders including AM/LASH. He had formerly represented the Capri Hotel and Casino in Havana and may have been the Trafficante contact who facilitated the gangster's release for his daughter's wedding. Certainly the Trafficante-Bongo-Cubela-Hernandez-McClaney associations are of interest.

Bernardo De Torres was known to have associated with several of Hemming's Interpen members and he was well acquainted with Frank Fiorini/Sturgis. In the years after the assassination De Torres first went to work as a Latin American arms salesman for Mitch Werbell (Werbell is discussed in some detail in Appendix J) and eventually ended up with strong operational contacts in Mexico City. These contacts extended all the way up to Miguel Nazar Haro in Mexican police intelligence. Haro was later revealed as a key individual in drug trafficking into the US and has been associated with both Sam Giancana and Richard Cain. An FBI report on De Torres from the 1970s refers to his "high level contacts" with the CIA, but this is otherwise unexplained. De Torres was not investigated in connection with the JFK investigation until the time of the HSCA, when he came to the attention of Gaeton Fonzi due to the revelations of Rolando Otero. Otero was one of the sources quoted earlier describing an individual representing himself as CIA who was spreading information about President Kennedy within the Cuban community in Miami:

"But prior to that they had a rumor in the Cuban community, like Kennedy was a Communist. Another Cuban would come to you who was working for one of those intelligence groups, and he would tell you Kennedy is a Communist, he's against us, he's messing up the whole cause."[43]

Otero believed there was a non-Castro conspiracy behind the assassination and he gave Fonzi some solid leads on possible participants. These are presented in detail in Fonzi's book *The Last Investigation*, including the orders from Fonzi's supervisor that quashed his effort to obtain solid incriminating evidence by running surveillance on suspects. One of those suspects was an individual still actively operating in the anti-Communist, anti-Castro affairs of the 1970s, one Bernardo De Torres aka "Carlos." De Torres was even reputed by Otero to have had photographs taken in Dallas on November 22. He was a Bay of Pigs veteran who had been held prisoner until December of 1962 (released at virtually the same time as John Martino). De Torres went on to become the military coordinator for Brigade 2506 after the assassination. De Torres became involved in the Garrison New Orleans investigation and apparently diverted Garrison to a certain extent. He also aggressively re-introduced Castro suspicions with his insistent media promotion of a story pertaining to Secret Service fears of a Castro hit team in Miami during Kennedy's visit there shortly before the Texas trip.[44] Between February 18 and February 22, the Garrison investigation received considerable unwanted publicity, much of it based upon inquiries within the Miami Cuban community as well as the involvement of Bernardo De Torres. De Torres was quite visible in his comments and declarations, eventually leading the whole matter off in a direction pointing at a threat against John Kennedy from Castro agents.

By February 19, De Torres had made a variety of statements to New Orleans and Miami newspapers ranging from a conservative observation that the Warren Commission report was incomplete to a statement that, "The Warren Report and the FBI Report will crumble when this investigation is released."

De Torres said that he had been working with Garrison for several months and related the fact that during JFK's Miami trip, he and ten others were recruited by the Secret Service to help spot potential Cuban assassins. De Torres observed that the Secret Service definitely expected a Cuban attack on JFK during his Miami visit. All of this ultimately led to Garrison's first New Orleans press conference with an unprepared Garrison and much follow-on press coverage being focused on a totally irrelevant photo of Lee Oswald in his street leafleting. Garrison made no reference to this photo or to a Cuban involved with Oswald. But the Miami paper printed a photo taken from the WDSI TV Oswald leafleting footage and stated that the stocky man in the plaid shirt matched a head-only blow-up of a man whose photo had been circulated by Garrison's investigators. The article identified this individual as **Manual Garcia Gonzalez**.[45]

The Oswald leafleting photo is clearly *not* a match for Gonzales. Yet someone led Garrison's investigators on a wild goose chase by first claiming to recognize the fellow (who does not seem to have any Latin features) with Oswald and then giving them the Gonzalez identification. Indeed, apart from the press statements we have nothing that really shows that the fellow in the plaid shirt was Garrison's target or that he was the man shown to De Torres. The end result of this high profile press exposure clearly undermined Garrison's chances of turning up any leads within the exile communities in either New Orleans or Miami.[46]

It certainly appears that De Torres' role in the Garrison investigation is suspicious, and it supports Otero's remarks to HSCA investigators that De Torres had "penetrated" Garrison's investigation. It also shows that De Torres had an agenda of his own in addition to getting intelligence about Garrison's investigation and investigators. That agenda involved once again shifting attention to Fidel Castro and a Cuban hit team rather than the activities of the Cuban exiles. Gaeton Fonzi was not allowed to pursue his investigation of De Torres in order to confirm De Torres involvement in the Kennedy conspiracy.

Garrison's own characterization of De Torres is also clear. De Torres approached Garrison offering assistance and even giving the name of the State Attorney General as a reference. Later Garrison told the HSCA that he felt De Torres was "one of his early sources of misinformation" and whatever he provided "never went anywhere."[47]

"Mannie Garcia Gonzalez" and **"Ricardo Davis"** were names initially floated by Dean Andrews to Garrison as Cuban guerilla fighters. Later, Andrews would recant and claim the names were made up. However, as with most of his recanting, it is very likely this was for self protection because a "Manual Garcia Gonzalez" had indeed been arrested in September of 1966 for carrying a concealed weapon in a bar.

Gonzalez was described as "stocky, powerfully built, Latin, five feet seven and around 150 pounds."

Ricardo Davis was also a real person whom Garrison questioned about his involvement in anti-Castro activity. It appears that Garrison may have brought Gonzalez up on narcotics charges to keep him available as he used other charges, including burglary, against many other suspects, including Novel, Thornley, and others.[48]

THE RISKS OF KNOWING OSWALD—AND JACK RUBY AGAIN

The first 48 hours after the murder in Dealey Plaza may also be used to evaluate elements of the Martino—described conspiracy, particularly those pertaining to the real roles of Jack Ruby and Lee Oswald.

> *"Don't you think I would make a good actor?"*
> – Jack Ruby to Will Fritz on Sunday afternoon.

By 3:00 PM Dallas time on November 22, being associated with Oswald in any fashion was not a good thing. It would get Buell Wesley Frazier arrested, interrogated and polygraphed late that night. Others had far more reason to want to distance themselves from Oswald. As of that Friday afternoon, none of Oswald's associates could necessarily expect that officialdom would soon be doing everything in its power to turn Lee Oswald into a "loner," or that institutional cover-ups would emerge to disconnect them from him. There was no reason at all to think that Oswald would turn into just a "nut," much less a "lone nut."

The Warren Commission went to some lengths to record Jack Ruby's activities prior to his shooting of Oswald. In doing so, it gave great credence to the statements of Ruby himself, his relatives, his employees, and his roommate, George Senator. It gave much less credence to independent parties who knew Jack Ruby but were not related or connected to him. Just as it chose to believe known criminals who were adamant that Ruby had no gang connections, the Commission chose to accept the facts provided by exactly those individuals who were the most likely to slant their information to protect Jack Ruby or to protect themselves.

An alternative view of Ruby's movements and moods, based on observations by news personnel, police officers, and police informants tells us much more about Ruby's connection to the conspiracy and his connection to Oswald.

12:25 PM: Ruby and an IRS informant observed the Presidential motorcade pass the corner of Main and Houston. Immediately afterwards, Ruby left hurriedly in the direction of the Dallas Morning News offices. Ruby had invited the informant down to "watch the fireworks." As many of his acquaintances have remarked, Jack Ruby was not a man that anyone would involve "deeply" in a conspiracy. Ruby was far too likely to talk. This incident with the informant suggests that Ruby was told very little and likely had been asked to do relatively little.

Of course, Ruby's invitation was a mistake. Apparently he couldn't resist showing off to someone. *Several of Ruby's friends and associates readily told everyone that Jack could never have kept a secret. The thing is, he didn't. He revealed his knowledge that something special was going to happen that day and afterwards, he repeatedly alluded to a conspiracy.*

12:40 PM: Ruby was back in the *Dallas Morning News* sales offices where he had been earlier in the morning. He was "subdued, numb and pale," not hysterical, shouting, weeping or crying, not even talking. He left the DMN offices around 1:10 PM.[49]

1:30 PM: Ruby was seen by Seth Kantor at Parkland Hospital. Ruby was clearly trying to find out if anyone had actually been wounded, shot or killed. Kantor had worked as a Dallas reporter on the *Times Herald* and was familiar with Ruby. When Ruby approached Kantor at Parkland, he called him by his first name. To Kantor, Ruby appeared "miserable, grim, and pale." After shaking hands, his first question was whether Kantor had any word on the President's condition.[50] Ruby was also reported at Parkland by Wilma Tice, who heard someone call him "Jack." She did not know Ruby but identified his photo and correctly described the clothing he was wearing on Friday.[51] Later, Ruby would deny ever being at Parkland and meeting or talking with Kantor. As we will see, this is part of a pattern of Ruby denying a number of his own activities over that weekend. In that period, he went to great efforts to position himself directly with the press in locations where he would have the best possible access to news about the assassination, in particular news about what Lee Oswald might be saying.

Kantor asks a simple question in his book on Ruby: *"What would make Jack Ruby seek out a news reporter at the hospital on Friday and then deny, after Sunday, having been there?"* Kantor's own rhetorical answer was that, *"Ruby was not involved in a plot to kill anyone on Friday, but by Sunday he was."* Based on the information we have from John Martino, Kantor's observation is absolutely accurate. And Ruby didn't just deny being at Parkland; he denied being in and around police headquarters starting Friday afternoon and extending through Saturday. He denied posing as a news reporter himself numerous times, giving an account of his activities that was egregiously inaccurate. In reality, he became so well-known to one news crew that they gave him a name, "the creep." The same crew immediately recognized "the creep" as Jack Ruby on Sunday morning after he stepped out of the crowd to shoot Lee Oswald.[52]

Ruby left Parkland to go to the Carousel Club where he went about closing his clubs for the weekend. He left there to buy food and went to his sister Eva Grant. When he arrived, according to his sister, "he didn't say nothing, he went into the bathroom and threw up." The man who officially had not been interested enough in the President's visit to go one block down the street to see him in person (and Jack Ruby was famous for seeing and wanting to be seen where anything important was happening) had progressed from being subdued and pale to being physically ill.

Earlier in the afternoon, Ruby had taken the time to place a three minute call to Alex Gruber in Los Angeles, California. Gruber had visited him a few weeks earlier making that the first time they'd seen each other in the previous ten years. Apart from his sister in Chicago, Alex Gruber was the only person Ruby would call long distance that afternoon. Gruber would subsequently tell the FBI he really didn't know why Ruby had called, but Ruby talked about possibly opening up a new business (a car wash) and the fact that he was going to send Gruber one of his pet dogs (the same dogs Ruby referred to as his children). Possibly they talked about something more important than that—*something that would cause his sister to describe Jack as "a broken man" when he arrived at her apartment later in the day.*[53]

Earlier in the afternoon, Ruby had appeared at the Merchants State Bank and talked to Bill Cox. According to Cox, Ruby was in tears, and had approximately $7,000 in large bills in his possession.[54]

According to Curtis Laverne "Larry" Crafard, there had been phone calls coming into the club for Ruby all afternoon. Unlike Jack's regular callers, this man would never leave his name or a message—just kept calling again and again. When Crafard mentioned the calls to

Ruby, Jack told him to mind his own business. Crafard hitchhiked out of Dallas Saturday morning.[55]

7:00 PM: John Rutledge, a veteran Dallas police reporter, saw Jack Ruby step from a public elevator onto the third floor of the Dallas Police Station. Ruby was hunched over, writing on a piece of paper and showing it to one of two out-of-town correspondents as they walked towards Room 317 where Lee Oswald was being interviewed. No longer subdued, pale or physically ill, Jack Ruby was on a mission. Detective Mike Eberhardt, who knew Ruby (as did the guard who passed him into the detective bureau offices), asked him what he was doing and Ruby told him he was acting as a translator for the foreign press![56]

Detective Roy Standifer, also well acquainted with Ruby, exchanged greetings with him in the third floor hallway around 7:30 PM.[57] Following this, Ruby was seen by Victor Robertson Jr., City Hall reporter for WFAA radio and TV. This time Ruby was in the corridor attempting to enter Room 317 while Oswald was in the room. But the door guard turned Ruby away. Robertson described Ruby as "happy, jovial, joking, and laughing."[58]

John Rutledge later observed Ruby mixing with the third floor crowd for some time, pointing out police officials and spelling their names for the out-of-town reporters.

Later Ruby vigorously denied being at the police station at this time because, in his own words, "it looked like I was trying to find out who this Oswald was." Probably not "who" but more likely "what" this Oswald might be saying. If Ruby did already have his orders, the sooner he got to Oswald the better.

The Warren Commission accepted Ruby's word and concluded that the detectives who spoke with Ruby and the reporters who recognized and observed him all must have been mistaken as to the time. Not 7:00 PM but more like midnight, because that was when Ruby admitted he was at the police station. By then, Oswald had been formally charged with the murder of Officer Tippet and was shortly to be charged with the President's murder. Chief Curry had given in to press demands for a conference. Somehow Jack Ruby knew of this and came back just in time to find a place on top of a table at the rear of the room. With glasses, note pad and pen, Ruby's newsman pose was good. Ruby even made himself visible to D.A. Wade and Lee Oswald by yelling out a correction to Wade's misstatement of Oswald's Free Cuba Committee affiliation. In a room full of real reporters, Jack Ruby was the man who knew the correct full name of Oswald's Fair Play for Cuba Committee. It seems that the press conference cheered him up considerably. He had seen the man who killed the President and heard no mention of conspiracy or associates. He had made himself visible to the key investigators and Lee Oswald himself with absolutely no response. For the next several hours, the people who encountered Ruby did not see a morose, distraught, or broken man. Nor did they see a man talking about the dead President with the fate of his wife and children at the top of his thoughts. Instead they saw an animated Ruby, constantly shaking hands, passing out cards and invitations to his clubs, and helping reporters get D.A. Wade's attention. Ike Pappas, a newsman for WNEW radio, encountered Ruby after the press conference and described him as "exhilarated." He gave Pappas a Carousel Club card and invited him to visit.[59]

It seems very clear that Jack Ruby was dedicated to being among the first to know what was going on with Lee Oswald. He seemed extremely happy, possibly because Oswald had not been charged with conspiracy, that the police were not actively pursuing any associates and that Lee Oswald was apparently keeping his mouth shut. Contrary to his own later defense, it is also clear that Jackie Kennedy and her children were not on Jack's mind. Since Ruby eventually disclosed to two of his defense lawyers that Tom Howard, his first counsel, had given him that story, which is no real surprise. The only other person to seriously present that story was Ruby's roommate, George Senator. Tom Howard had met with Senator at length on Sunday night after his meetings with Ruby.[60]

November 23, Saturday morning just before noon, Ruby was back at City Hall and back with the reporters. Frederic Rheinstein, NBC news producer, was annoyed when a man poked his head into their mobile unit to take a look at the monitors—in particular, watching the monitor that was on closed circuit showing activities on the third floor where Oswald was questioned—the monitor which might give a sign that Lee Oswald was about to be transferred to another building. Rheinstein did not know the man's name but he became so familiar to him and his crew (even taking one of their box lunches) that they began calling him "the creep." Ruby told the crew that he knew Wade personally and could get information for them or an interview with Wade. They observed Ruby on the sidewalk outside police headquarters from late morning throughout the afternoon.

They watched "the creep" appear on their third floor monitor as he waked into a third floor office being used by D.A. Wade—an office barred to the reporters and media. They didn't really take note of his name until Sunday morning when he murdered Lee Oswald and then they all recognized him.[61]

Clearly Ruby was monitoring the news, monitoring police gossip within the building (passing freely into controlled areas) and very likely stalking Lee Oswald in anticipation of a transfer. *Fritz and Curry made plans for an afternoon transfer and Ruby knew it.* At 3:00 PM, Sergeant D.V. Harkness noticed him among the loiterers near the vehicle entrance of the country jail (the transfer point) when he asked a small group of people to move out of the area.[62]

Ruby then approached Wes Wise in the KRLD mobile news and told him that Curry and Fritz were examining the assassination scene at the TSBD (they were). Ruby then called disc jockey Ken Dowe at KLIF and told him, "*I understand they are moving Oswald over to the county jail.* Would you like me to cover it because I AM a pretty good friend of Henry Wade's and I believe I can get some news stories?" The planned transfer didn't come off Saturday afternoon due to traffic in the area; but of course, Ruby would be back Sunday morning and given the preceding, it would be hard to imagine that it would be by sheer coincidence.

SOME VERY STUPID THINGS

"I told them, write what you want, that I AM nuts, I don't care...
... you can tell when the steam is on, they are on you like the plague."
– Dean Andrews

Andrews was very straight forward about his reason for recanting various information he initially provided to the Garrison investigation, also explaining his statement to the FBI that the whole thing was a "figment of his imagination."

John Martino related that Oswald was a low level FBI informant, suggesting he was being dangled to generate contacts from leftists, Communists, Castro supporters and possibly even Castro agents.

Martino himself admitted that he had watched Oswald passing out leaflets in New Orleans. Oswald had been dangled in front of anybody and everybody associated with Cuba, Cuban exiles, smuggling, arms deals—pro-Castro, anti-Castro, actively left wing, actively right wing. Anybody who would talk to him—or talk around him.

On the Friday and Saturday following President Kennedy's assassination, several different individuals who had been associated with Lee Oswald in New Orleans panicked, did stupid things and brought themselves to the attention of the authorities. (stupid things that individuals who had actually prepared for the murder of a President would not have done). But stupid things that people who could be shown to have been involved with Oswald in the summer of 1963 might easily do after hearing that Oswald had been with killing the President. Especially if the individuals in question had also engaged in conversations about President Kennedy being a traitor, a traitor who should be eliminated before he sold out the country again. Remarks similar to those that had also been made by H. L. Hunt and his fellow oilmen in Dallas, during talks with various anti-Castro people.

Clay Shaw and David Ferrie did do some very stupid things and both men were investigated shortly after the President's murder—Ferrie by DA Garrison and Shaw/Bertrand by the FBI.[63] This quick FBI investigation of Shaw suggests that FBI security may well have been in possession of informant reports from Oswald describing threatening remarks and perhaps even discussions of killing the President. Reports not shared with the Secret Service prior to the assassination. Joan Mellen does an excellent job of reviewing the indications that FBI agents Quigley, de Brueys and Kennedy of the New Orleans officer were well aware that Oswald was being used as an informant. This is substantiated by the fact that NOPD Lt. Martello was given de Brueys name by Lee Oswald and specifically asked to contact him to visit Oswald after his arrest. Instead agent Quigley visited Oswald and conducted an hour and a half interview (later to say he had burned his notes) because de Brueys had a social commitment that Saturday.[64]

Oswald's New Orleans informant role and the fact that FBI Security had a long established connection to CIA Counter Intelligence (Angleton and Roca) may explain many of the actions of both the FBI and CIA in response to DA Garrison's assassination investigation.

CIA Garrison Group Meeting 1, November 20, 1967

James Angleton had been the CIA coordinator for the Warren Commission and a memo dated February 20, 1964, quotes Birch O'Neal of his department as stating, "the CI staff, i.e. Mr. Roca has the job of determining which pieces of information should be made available to the Commission."[65] At the Garrison's Group's first meeting on November 20, Raymond Roca (James Angleton's number one deputy) gave the group the opinion of CIA Counter Intelligence that *"Garrison would indeed obtain a conviction of Shaw for conspiracy to assassinate President Kennedy."*

Garrison Group Meeting 2, November 26, 1967

The group was given a list of individuals likely to be implicated in the trial; the list had been passed to them from persons at the DOJ who were in communication with Shaw's lawyers. Justice advised that no CIA contact should be made with the Shaw legal defense team; the best policy would be to maintain the safety of executive privilege. The Executive Director of the CIA remarked on "the impressive number of contacts we seem to have who might now be implicated by Garrison."[66]

Later, CIA CI (Angleton's counter-intelligence unit) would compile a list of the trial jurors with background on all of them and supply it to the security division in case of need.[67] Angleton would also work with the FBI to research background on specific Garrison witnesses.[68]

Clay Shaw himself had been an informant on international activities relating to his business and activities in conjunction with the International Trade Mart in New Orleans and with his trade contacts. Shaw also reported on international events such as a trade fair in Basel, Switzerland, and on intelligence collected during his international travels. Shaw was, at a minimum, an informant for CIA domestic contacts and given his covert clearance and the content of some of his reports, apparently much more than a passive informant. Shaw was also a supporter of anti-Communist and anti-Castro efforts. A CIA document reports that he, along with his International Trade Mart associate Mario Bermudez, traveled together to Cuba in 1959 on gun running activities.[69]

Bannister's associate Don Campbell revealed that Shaw was involved with a gun running operation to Alpha 66 exiles in Miami.[70] Campbell had worked at infiltrating left-wing college groups for

Bannister, whose personal involvement with the anti-Castro effort and with Cuban exiles is well known. Much of his work involved counter-intelligence activities, doing checks on potential exile group recruits. His specialty was infiltration. Virtually all of Bannister's agents describe this, including Tommy Baumler who later became a New Orleans attorney.

Baumler reported on left-wing college groups for Bannister and connected Bannister to Shaw in New Orleans intelligence activities. As to Bannister's connection with Lee Oswald, at least five of his employees have related seeing Oswald in Bannister's offices, seeing Oswald's materials in his office space, and/or reporting on Oswald to Bannister and being told not to worry about him. George Higgenbotham described telling Bannister about the three young men he had seen passing out pro-Castro leaflets and quotes Bannister as responding, *"Cool it. One of them is one of mine."* Individuals providing this information included Higgenbotham, Dan Campbell, Bill Nitschke, Alan Campbell and Delphine Roberts.[71] In addition, Tommy Baumler, another former associate of Bannister, was interviewed in 1981 (a safe time after the Garrison trial) and admitted that Bannister and Shaw were associated and that *"Oswald worked for Bannister."*[72]

Confirmation is also available in the Shaw defense files that were turned over to the ARRB. A Wackenhut memo (April 7, 1967) records an interview with Gordon Novel's lawyer, Steve Plotkin. Plotkin revealed to the Wackenhut personnel that another Bannister employee, Vernon Gerdes, had seen Oswald and David Ferrie together with Bannister.

However, perhaps the final corroboration of this and of Oswald's role in New Orleans is Guy Bannister's behavior on the afternoon of November 22.

Bannister spent the afternoon of November 22 with one of his sometime investigators and hanger-on, Jack Martin. They began the afternoon in a very good mood. It seemed Bannister was particularly happy about the death of President Kennedy. Kennedy represented just about everything in the political spectrum that Bannister, a radical right-winger and avowed racist, detested. As they followed the news broadcasts, Bannister began drinking heavily, becoming more unhappy and meaner as the afternoon went on. The news had included the capture and arrest of Lee Oswald.[73]

Bannister's decline in spirits continued after their return to his office, especially after Martin made some remarks about visitors to

Bannister's office during the preceding summer. When Bannister pulled his gun, Martin asked him if he was going to kill him "like you all did Kennedy." This apparently hit home to Bannister's worries; he proceeded to pistol whip Martin in the head, only stopping when his secretary intervened—Martin felt he might have been killed had she not been there.[74]

After hospital treatment, Martin filed a police report. He seemed to take Bannister very seriously because when he talked with officials the next day, he did not associate Guy Bannister with Lee Oswald and a JFK conspiracy but rather pointed the finger at David Ferrie.

Bannister verified his connection to Oswald with his abrupt mood swing and his violence against Jack Martin. Clay Shaw (Clay Bertrand) showed his potential exposure in a much calmer manner—he ran and he called for legal help—help for Lee Oswald.

Shaw was known to a variety of people as Clay Bertrand. That was made abundantly clear in the Garrison investigation; in fact, his use of the alias (most likely for social reasons) had become so commonplace that he was rather casual with it. Garrison obtained a sworn affidavit from an airlines VIP room hostess, Jessie Parker, identifying a photo of Clay Shaw as the man who had signed her guest book as Clay Bertrand the previous December. Bertrand had been in the company of four gentlemen from Caracas, Venezuela. Shaw's defense obtained a counter-statement from a Mr. Alfred Moran who stated that he knew Shaw and had been in the VIP room without seeing him.

Moran's story changed, but recently released CIA reports reveal that he had told his close friend, Hunter Leake of the New Orleans CIA office, that the man in the VIP lounge was definitely Clay Shaw and that he believed Garrison had "an iron clad case" against Shaw. It seems that Moran had become an official DD/P (Deputy Directory for Plans) CIA asset in December 1962. He had submitted some 15 CIA contact reports between 1962 and 1967. The CIA memo also remarks that information from Moran could be critical and that the Agency has connections to get it to Shaw's lawyers without any official tie to the CIA.[75]

Shaw was accustomed to using the Bertrand alias; he may have assumed that it was widely known. While being booked, the processing officer, Aloysius Habighorst, asked Shaw if he had routinely used any aliases. Shaw answered, "Clay Bertrand." The trial judge refused to allow this information to be presented in the trial as he maintained it was protected by Miranda rights. This decision is arguable from a legal perspective, but from a research perspective it is meaningless. Clay Shaw did use, and was known by, the alias Clay Bertrand.[76] As final corroboration, we now have an FBI memorandum dated March 2, 1967, that states: "On February 24, 1967, we received information from two sources that Clay Shaw reportedly is identical with an individual by the name of Clay Bertrand."[77]

Shaw/Bertrand was another individual who panicked in New Orleans, revealing his connection to Oswald. Shaw did a very unwise thing. He called lawyer Dean Andrews, who often handled minor legal matters for some of Shaw's young friends, to ask him to represent Lee Oswald in Dallas.

Andrews had done some work for Lee Oswald, both contesting his dishonorable discharge from the Marines and the two had discussed citizenship proceedings for Oswald's Russian-born wife, Marina. Andrews recalled asking Oswald why he was leafleting for Castro and being told by Oswald that *it was just a job and he was paid to do it.* Andrews received a call from Clay Bertrand on November 23. Andrews was in the hospital, but Bertrand wanted him to go down to Dallas and defend Oswald. Andrews told Bertrand he most probably could not do it, but he did check with Sam Zelden, president of the New Orleans Bar Association and a close friend of Andrews on the following day, Sunday. At that time, Zelden told Andrews that Oswald had been shot and Andrews let it drop.

Andrews' story is verified by two of his employees, Eva Springer and R.M. Davis. Davis specifically recalled hearing Andrews' talk about a call from "Bertrand." Andrews mentioned it again on Sunday and gave the impression that Bertrand was well-known to him. Davis also recalled Andrews' working on a Marine Corps undesirable discharge that summer. Eva Springer also recalled the discharge project and specifically recalls Andrews calling her at home Saturday evening on the 23rd and telling her that he was going to Dallas to defend Lee Oswald at the request of Mr. Bertrand. She even fixed the time of the call as 4:00 PM.

As has been mentioned earlier, along with his own explanation, Andrews later legally recanted his entire story of Oswald and Bertrand, explaining that doing so was a simple matter of protecting himself and his family. The official story given to explain his detailed description of the Bertrand call is that he was under sedation at the time and must have made it all up. However, the FBI checked his hospital records and they clearly show that on the day in question, Dean Andrews received no medication at all until 8:00 PM. Unfortunately, while S.A. Richard Bucaro wrote the memo on the medication, S.A. Kennedy reversed this fact in his summary report, explaining that Andrews was indeed mistaken due to the effects of his medication.[78]

SUMMARY

The anti-Castro people put it together. They manipulated Lee Oswald into a position of appearing to be a paid Castro assassin. They were forced to use Ruby to kill Oswald when the plan went bad in Dallas and they could not get Oswald out of Dallas to conclude the Castro frame. There were loose ends all over the place.

• People associated with a live Oswald could easily have been charged with being accessories to a conspiracy – Jack Ruby, Guy Bannister, and Clay Shaw all lost their nerve, acted stupidly, and belied the official view of Oswald as a loner.

• People like H.L. Hunt and William Pawley had talked about the need to get rid of John Kennedy and about his being a traitor. Pawley had acted aggressively to demonstrate that Kennedy was incompetent and dangerous. They had paid money to individuals they later suspected were involved in Dealey Plaza.

• Hunt left Dallas immediately on November 22 and later had his private investigators monitor the Garrison investigation.

• William Pawley committed "suicide" shortly after being summoned by the HSCA.

• CIA people, Shackley and Fitzgerald, attached to JM/WAVE had reasons to worry that their people were associated with individuals who had been involved with the conspiracy - or at least were aware of it. It was best that they make no inquiries.

• In addition, Shackley and Fitzgerald demonstrated that they would withhold information as required, to protect the CIA.

- Tony Varona left Miami and abandoned the anti-Castro effort for two decades.

- Santo Trafficante left the country during the Church Committee hearings and committed perjury when testifying to the HSCA.

- Felipe Vidal Santiago was captured and executed on a penetration into Cuba in early 1964. He had been warned that it was virtually a suicide mission.

- Tony Cuesta was captured along with Herminio Diaz Garcia on a mission into Cuba.

- Diaz Garcia was killed on a penetration mission into Cuba. Cuesta reportedly identified him as a Kennedy conspiracy participant.

- Victor Hernandez spent a good deal of time overseas, eventually leaving the US entirely.

- Manuel Rodriguez Orcarberrio left the US complaining of being harassed for his anti-Communism.

- Roy Hargraves continued his right-wing activism going on to bomb leftist groups and the Black Panthers in Los Angeles. He also participated in a project to provoke military action against Cuba.

- David Morales, John Martino, John Roselli, and Jack Ruby talked of their involvement—privately to friends, or in Roselli's case, to his lawyer who had to respect attorney-client privilege.

The events following the assassination are very consistent with John Martino's remarks on the conspiracy.

CHAPTER 19

END GAME

There can be no certain conclusion to a work of this sort. Perhaps there could have been—if there had been a true *criminal investigation* in 1963 and 1964—an open-ended investigation using all the tools and legal tactics available. If the agencies and individuals had not felt national security and "CYA" were more important than exploring what might have happened, without regard for consequences. If the new President had demanded such an investigation. Even during the 1970's it might have been possible, especially with use of immunity, witness protection, plea bargaining and perhaps an amnesty program. If the HSCA had been run by experienced prosecuting attorneys and fielded a staff of hard core criminal investigators. If the CIA and other agencies had been forced into proactive support rather than marginal compliance.

40 Plus Years Too Long for Certainty

But not too late to draw a picture, to propose a scenario that matches what we have learned throughout those years. The end game is twofold—setting out a series of premises and then testing them. Premises and supporting points will be presented. Then the reader must weigh the material and reach their own conclusion. The premises address motive, means, opportunity, and method. Whenever possible, each premise is accompanied with a description of additional research to either support or refute it.

Motives

During the last six months of 1963, a small number of action-oriented Cuban exiles and fellow travelers were maneuvered into a conspiracy targeting President Kennedy. The individuals involved were persuaded that unless Kennedy was eliminated he would negotiate a compromise with Fidel Castro which would leave Castro and the Communists permanently in power in Cuba. These exiles were used.

Their decision to actually move against JFK was very likely a mix of motives involving revenge and preservation of their cause. The individuals inciting them to action had a more complex agenda. It was a deadly mix, given final impetus by the secret 1963 Cuban initiatives of John and Robert Kennedy. A mix possibly catalyzed by the success of the Kennedy war against organized crime, in particular its effectiveness against those underworld figures who were closest to John Roselli.

Supporting Observations

The Kennedy backed Castro outreach was kept under the utmost security; contacts were made through private individuals in New York City. In spite of the secrecy, knowledge of a pending "accommodation" was used to incite key individuals within the Miami exile community. Rolondo Otero related to HSCA investigator Gaeton Fonzi that in mid-1963 word was being circulated that Kennedy was betraying them again.

Before the details of the Kennedy-Castro outreach became generally known in the late 1990's, former Cuban Intelligence officer Fabian Escalante related to JFK researchers that, under interrogation, Felipe Vidal Santiago had made a point of telling them that he had spent a great deal of time in 1963 relaying the message about the Kennedy administration efforts to conduct a dialog with Castro. He quoted Vidal as describing the news as "almost like a bomb, in intentional message against Kennedy."[1]

Although this outreach was being conducted through trusted private channels, an agenda item for an "accommodation option" was part of a June Special Group meeting; a meeting attended by David Morales, which made it an open secret.[2] As of June, JM/WAVE and CIA headquarters had also begun accumulating reports suggesting Cuban interest in a rapprochement with the United States.[3] There is also an indication that JFK was actually worried about his own rooms being "bugged" during an early November trip to New York[4]; this was at the time JFK was in the process of giving his personal approval to proceed with Castro contacts.

David Morales, demonstratively hated Kennedy, felt Kennedy was a traitor, and remarked in front of his life-long friend and his lawyer: "We took care of that SOB". David Phillips', an associate of David Morales, admired El Indo as the best "back alley operator" he had ever known. Phillips' brother eventually became aware that David Phillips had been in some way "seriously involved" in the JFK affair and withdrew from him under that belief. Not long before his death Phillips recanted his own anti-conspiracy stance with a remark that he personally felt was that JFK was done in by a conspiracy, "likely involving American intelligence officers."

Certain American intelligence officers, particular in the Plans/ Operations/Paramilitary function of the Agency, would have had good reason to fear their anti-Communist efforts were being compromised by the President's new directions. JFK had already moved to transfer CIA "operations" to the American military in Vietnam. He was focusing covert military operations on Army Special Forces rather than CIA paramilitary. His 1963 Cuban initiatives were being built around inter-departmental (Army and State) efforts, placing the CIA operations staff (such as JM/WAVE) in a supporting rather than controlling role. All of these moves were a direct blow to CIA operational autonomy and would not have gone unnoticed by individuals in roles such as that of David Morales at JM/WAVE or Lucian Conein in Vietnam.

John Roselli, a participant with CIA officers in a three year series of Castro assassination attempts, was operationally involved with David Morales in 1963. Morales was also acquainted with a number of Roselli's "casino" friends and was a frequent visitor in Roselli's Vegas haunts. Roselli later introduced the information story that JFK had been killed by an exile team that had been targeted on Castro—a team captured and turned back on JFK. However, Roselli also disclosed privately to his own lawyer that he had been personally involved in the conspiracy that killed JFK.

Roselli would have brought his own motives to a conspiracy against the President. Roselli himself was the subject of ongoing FBI investigation and Justice Department attention; the FBI would soon discover his illegal alien status and certainly he would have been exposed to deportation—just as RFK had already moved to permanently deport Carlos Marcello. Roselli's friends and business partners within organized crime were also undergoing intense Kennedy administration pressure. Giancana was under lockstep surveillance that was literally ruining his health. Marcello was in court fighting deportation. Trafficante had been made the focus of Congressional hearings, and ongoing IRS investigations; his wife subpoenaed. Both Marcello and Trafficante's drug networks had also suffered major busts in a newly aggressive Kennedy anti-narcotics campaign.

With Roselli's participation, it is highly probable that he would have consulted with these same three individuals, as he had in the anti-Castro assassination projects. Their resources had been used for those efforts (particularly those of Trafficante, including Antonio Varona). Their networks would also have been of value in the move against JFK and of course Roselli would claim a major "marker" for assisting in an action so clearly in their common interest. Indications of their knowledge of a move against Kennedy can be seen in FBI wire taps (many years after the fact) in which Marcello claimed credit for the murder and in Giancana's apparent knowledge that one of the individuals involved was a "Bay of Pigs action officer." Trafficante's knowledge is indicated not only by his personal remarks but also by the nature and timing of the deaths of Sam Giancana and John Roselli.

A tertiary motive may also have come into play among certain exiles who may have knowingly or unknowingly abetted the conspiracy. Their possible connections will be itemized under personnel and operations, but certainly the right wing exiles would have found no joy in a Cuba free of Castro but under the government of individuals such as Artime, Ray and Menoyo. The RFK autonomous group projects initiated in 1963, in particular the coup projects and AM/WORLD (built around Artime) were very likely compromised by Artime's travels and conversations with Prio Soccares and Varona. The three traveled together to Nicaragua in July and August and given Artime's nature, and a variety of JM/WAVE documents, it is clear that Artime was making it clear that he was the chosen leader to form a new Cuban government. Playing a subservient role to Artime would have been galling to both men. That, plus Varona's close association with both Roselli and Trafficante, suggests the significance of Varona associated individuals who may have played peripheral roles in the lead up to Dallas cannot be overlooked. In addition to Trafficante's knowledge, we also have record of at least two incidents in which Carlos Marcello appears in FBI reports, speaking of "getting Kennedy in Dallas" and "having the son of bitch killed". Both incidents occurred after Marcello had been convicted and sent to prison; the former while he was ill and drifting in and out of consciousness–apparently mistaking his prison guards for his former body guards. (This information is referenced in Waldron's *fx*, page 818 and related end notes.)

Suggestions for testing and research

1. It is critically important to recover and examine the complete FBI surveillance records on Roselli, especially those from the Miami office and those for July–December of 1963, (both of which need to be located and analyzed in detail). This task should also include the full ELINT and wire-tap records on Roselli.

2. As with Martino and Morales, no official government assassination investigation ever assessed information on Trafficante and Varona associates such as Diaz Garcia. Complete INS, CIA and FBI records would be vital sources. JM/WAVE exile tracking reports and counter-intelligence files might also help establish Diaz Garcia's associates.

3. Careful study should be given to the intelligence/security operation created by David Morales. The AMMOT, AMFAST and AMCHEER reports should be collected and evaluated to determine individuals who might have been used to distribute information into the exile community and to track any reports of a Kennedy compromise with Castro.

4. JM/WAVE and other intelligence reports pertaining to Varona should be studied for associations, travels and changes in activities during 1963; further research on his 1964 abandonment of political activities and his move to New York City would be of interest.

OPPORTUNITY

Activists in the exile community had been talking about President Kennedy's "treason" since the Bay of Pigs. As Quintaro has described, this attitude became even more pronounced after Kennedy's failure to act against Castro during the Missile Crisis. "Outside" exile groups not being backed by the Kennedy Administration in 1963 certainly viewed JFK as an obstacle. Remarks from October in Chicago express the fact that even with new backers and plenty of money, success in Cuba would still require the removal of JFK. Recently obtained documents disclose that even well respected individuals close to Manual Artime felt that JFK was a significant obstacle to a successful ousting of Fidel and return to Cuba.[5] These activists were well aware that any action they might take against Kennedy could dramatically undermine their own cause. When the President spoke to the Brigade at the Orange Bowl he was threatened by both a sniper and a dynamite bomb placed on his motorcade route but no actual attack occurred.

Two things were required to precipitate an actual attack. The first was concrete evidence that JFK was going betray the exile cause. This became available in June of 1963 when high level CIA officers became aware that a compromise option was on the table, that Castro himself was offering some sort of outreach and that initial contacts had already been made. The prospect of an agreement, which might doom the exile cause, had an explosive impact.

However, the only way individual militant Cuban exiles could act against JFK would be to place the apparent blame on Fidel Castro. No matter how hot their passion or how much support was offered, that was the only method that would allow them to actively target Kennedy without themselves dooming their cause. The use of a Castro-connected patsy was critical. Without a credible and maneuverable patsy, any attack on Kennedy would have been self-defeating. That patsy became visible to them in New Orleans in July of 1963. He became irresistible when they were informed that he was more than simply a naïve revolutionary sympathizer, but was in reality a low-level intelligence dangle who they could play at will.

Supporting remarks and observations

Martino made the patsy element crystal clear; he indicated that was one of the major roles of the exiles in the conspiracy, managing and manipulating Lee Oswald. It was the exiles who contacted him, represented themselves as Castro agents, and continued contact with him up to the time of the assassination. The exiles were aware that Oswald was playing a role himself and that they had to maneuver him by continuing to represent themselves as Castroites.

Martino observed that Oswald was fed elements of a plan to act against Kennedy in some fashion; but Martino DID NOT describe, and could not have known, to whom Oswald reported this information. There is the clear suggestion that some intelligence agency was attempting to monitor these purported Castro agents. Whether or not the agency knew their true affiliations is yet another question.

Oswald's request to talk to a specific FBI agent on Saturday following his arrest for leafleting in New Orleans is telling—from a man whose public and private stance was that he was constantly being observed, harassed, and losing jobs due to FBI actions against him.

There is a clear pattern of Oswald's contact the FBI in New Orleans and Dallas as well as FBI obfuscation of their relationship. This extends to the prevention of testimony by New Orleans agents, destruction of the note from Oswald to Hosty, alteration of Oswald's notebook by the FBI and withholding (and later denial) of Oswald being monitored with subversives in Dallas (a matter described by Hosty to SA Patterson as relating to "espionage".) It also includes the apparent failure of the New Orleans FBI office (which determined that Oswald was using Hidell as an alias in his FPCC activities) to conduct any follow-up action against him—either for using an alias or performing as an officer of an organization classified by the Bureau as subversive.[6] This act alone, under FBI rules, would have required maintaining Oswald on the security watch/pick-up list.

Additional information on a 1963 joint FBI/CIA effort against the FPCC suggests that Oswald was monitored by the CIA and very probably used in efforts against the Cuban embassy in Mexico City.

Further evidence of Oswald's changing role as a "dangle" can be seen in his approaches to both pro and anti-Castro exiles and his remarks in front of Doctor Silva about killing Castro—which followed shortly after his pro-Castro leafleting and radio appearance as a supporter of the Cuban revolution. Oswald's draft manuscript and speech notes made after his return from Russia record his animosity towards the Soviet system and the global Communist party. However, shortly afterwards, Oswald began subscriptions to a number of Russian and political publications which put his mail under surveillance and was used to explain his initial contact by local FBI agents.

The pattern of Oswald's payments towards the debt incurred from the US when he was extended money for return travel to the United States from Russia is suggestive. In 1962 he made payments in the range of a few dollars towards the debt. In the fall of 1963 with one child and another coming, with travel to Mexico and with a very low paying job, he made repayments of much higher amounts. And why would any such debt have concerned the Lee Oswald portrayed by the Warren Commission?

Remarks by William Cline, chief of US Customs Bureau investigative services in Laredo, Texas, that Oswald's movements across the border had been watched at the request of a Federal agency in Washington.

Remarks by Eugene Pugh, US agent in charge of the Customs office at the border in Laredo, that Immigration had a folder on Oswald's trip to Mexico and that the checks on him during his exit and entry were "not the usual procedure."

Oswald's contacts with unidentified Latinos/Mexicanos have been extensively detailed in this work. Perhaps the most revealing point is that the people who saw Oswald with these individuals were broadly acquainted with the exile communities in their locations. That is true of Oscar Pena (an FBI informant in New Orleans), Dean Andrews (well enough informed to give Garrison identifications on two little known locals who were providing supplies to short lived camps outside New Orleans). The individuals associating with Oswald were not recognized by any of these people; they were outsiders–obviously individuals not from the local communities or visible in local exile affairs. Oswald was not just contacting targets of opportunity, he was himself being targeted.

Richard Nagell gives a description of two individuals matching exactly this profile. They worked first in Mexico City, came to the US only in 1963, and performed counter-intelligence activities for Alpha 66 in Mexico, Los Angeles, and New Orleans. These individuals had a twofold mission: a functional mission of counter- intelligence, and their own agenda of finding a Castro-connected patsy who could be moved into a position to cover a rightist exile assassination of JFK. Nagell's description and profiling of two such individuals independently of Martino's remarks about Oswald being manipulated and managed seems to offer strong corroboration for that view.

Consider the timeline of events

July: Dean Andrews observed Oswald with unknown "Mexicano" associate in New Orleans.
August 7: Habana bar incident with Oswald and unknown Latin in New Orleans.

August: Leafleting incident; observed by John Martino on a trip to New Orleans.

August 23: Nagell reports Oswald as meeting with two Cubans representing themselves as agents and recruiting Oswald for an incident targeted to the DC area.

August 31 and September 1: Oswald writes letters to SWP and FPCC about a move to the Baltimore area.

September 13: JFK Texas trip announced for fall.

September 27: Sylvia Odio is visited by Oswald and individuals purportedly traveling from New Orleans.

September 29: Robert McKeown is visited by Oswald and Hernandez.

October 1: Martino's first Dallas visit.

October 5: Dallas papers announce JFK visit.

October 16: Lee Oswald starts work at TSBD.

October 31: Lee Oswald impersonator applies for job at Statler Hilton. The motorcade route had not yet been set; it might only have included Main Street, without passing directly in front of the TSBD.

November 1: Oswald impersonator leaves rifle at gun store to have scope mounted.

Preparations to use Lee Oswald as a patsy in Dallas began in October after his relocation from New Orleans. Oswald had become the key element in the Dallas operation against JFK.

Suggestions for testing and research

* If Eugene Pugh and William Cline of the Customs Service are still living, it would be important to document and explore their reported

remarks about special monitoring and observation of Lee Oswald during his travels to Mexico.

- A detailed follow-up needs to be conducted into the house on Harlandale, including a search for other neighbors or individuals having contact with contemporaneous Alpha 66 members in Dallas. The same needs to be done for the Cubans reportedly in contact with Oswald in Abilene, Texas. Individuals in contact with those Cubans should also be interviewed and local newspapers in Abilene researched for photographs of anyone in that group.

- An investigation needs to be conducted in both Mexico City and Cuba to definitely identify anti-Castro exiles operating in Mexico City circa '61-'62. All background information on Herminio Diaz Garcia needs to be obtained from Cuba.

Personnel

The individuals knowingly involved in the actual conspiracy included both exiles and a small number of their most committed American supporters. Neither the exiles nor the Americans belonged to a single group although some of them likely held membership in Alpha 66, SNFE and other militarily active organizations such as AAA and Commandos L. Some of them had CIA training, military training and had worked for the Agency for periods of time.

It is likely that some of the participants were part of the Morales trained and organized intelligence service that was developed to support the 1962 action against Cuba and which had a political assassination (black list) component. Elements of this group were retained as Morales' intelligence and surveillance force in Miami after the failure at the Bay of Pigs. Some of them had been involved in Agency sanctioned (and possibly unsanctioned) projects to assassinate Castro. This group was unofficially known as Operation 40.

The conspiracy participants were individually recruited and acted as individuals rather than as members of an established group. However, some of those involved had a history with members of the former Havana "casino crowd" and connections to Trafficante organization in Cuba and later in Florida. During 1963, many of the "outsiders" in the anti-Castro community had been forced to return to contacts on the periphery of the Trafficante and Marcello crime networks for ongoing financial support. The influence of their gambling connections had grown during 1963 as the individuals involved had rejected CIA and US government association and funding (as well as its implicit control). This connection explains many the leaks and gossip that we have explored in this work, gossip as specific as a pre-assassination reference in Miami to Oswald being a Russian defector and marksman and a very accurate statement from Chicago, that Kennedy would be removed before a new action against Cuba.

Some of the tactical participants in the Dallas conspiracy may have already been associated through their mutual contacts with the JGCE (the Sierra Junta). The Junta reached out to the entire exile community although it eventually involved and funded only the most militant and militarily aggressive groups and individuals. Virtually all these individuals were openly opposed to the Kennedy Administration and equally distrustful of the CIA and its known contact personnel.

The Sierra Junta presented itself as a "third force" supported by anti-Communist business interests and political figures. We now have documents showing that Sierra met with and apparently was given encouragement by both Bob Kleberg of the King Ranch (original sponsor of the Tejana III) and of various Cuban business connections in New York City. However, there is every reason to suspect that gambling interests (the "Nevada Group" along with members of the Jewish Mafia which overlapped with the Moe Dalitz organization) were very much involved behind the scenes in the Junta's organization. They eventually assumed a primary role in funding Sierra's activities as his other financial backers began failed to expand their initial support.

The Junta initiative brought many of the most radical and independent exile militants in to contact with each other. It also appears to have brought them into deeper contact with elements of the old Havana gambling syndicate, including individuals such as John Roselli who was identified by Richard Cain as a Junta organizer.

In looking for persons who might have been unknowingly involved in peripheral roles in support of the plan, one starting point would be individuals with an established connection to John Roselli, the Trafficante organization and the "casino crowd". Special attention would be given to those individuals who were reportedly associated with Dr. Varona, including Sylvia Odio's uncle Augustin Guitart in New Orleans and Pedro Valeriano Gonzalez in Abilene, Texas.[7]

Supporting observations

John Martino displayed foreknowledge of the attack in Dallas and later admitted being personally, if peripherally involved in the conspiracy. Martino was involved with David Morales and other CIA para-military officers in 1963; he described the attack on the President as being carried out by "anti-Castro people".

As the organizer of the Cuba project Cuban intelligence/security apparatus and with oversight of all JM/WAVE operations, Morales had access to the paramilitary personnel prepared for 1961 and those still operational in 1963. Morales also may have been aware of individuals prepared for Castro assassination attempts prior to and after the failed 1962 Brigade effort.

AM/WORLD documents confirm that paramilitary CIA officers and exiles involved in Castro assassination projects prior to the Bay of Pigs were again actively involved in the Artime initiative in 1963. Their trainees remained operational just as many of the Operation 40 personnel remained active in Miami.

Roselli and Morales remained involved operationally in 1963, despite official cessation of Mongoose. The ZR/RIFLE project remained operational in 1963 and meetings under that project were attended in Florida by William Harvey and John Roselli. Roselli retained control over an exile group under Morales' operational control, supervised by Rip Robertson and reported in ongoing training for sniper attacks against Fidel Castro.

There are indications that Casino interests, specifically Johnny Roselli and his Vegas connections, were involved in funding and influencing Paulino Sierra.

Cesar Blanco, one of Sierra's Junta leaders, stated that in March of 1963, he and Sierra were approached by Burt Mold and John Lechner with offers of financial support. They told Sierra that they represented interests who previously had substantial investments in Cuba including "hotels and other operations connected with them." When asked for names of references, they mentioned Jake Lansky. Blanco assumed the two were representing the gambling syndicate. Blanco was told that the "Nevada group" being represented would assist the Cuban exiles since the US government could do nothing against Castro.

A March CIA report noted that Sierra had mentioned an offer of $10 million in backing for guarantees of Cuban gambling concessions after Castro was thrown out. This was independently confirmed by Sierra's associate, William Trull (a Texas entertainer apparently recommended by Kleberg of the King Ranch following a meeting between Kleberg and Sierra in early Spring), who stated that Sierra had related an offer of $14 million in exchange for a 50% interest in Cuban gambling concessions if Sierra could organize the successful ouster of Castro. Burt Mold later was employed in a Las Vegas casino.

Richard Cain's statement to the FBI was that Roselli was very involved with the Sierra Junta. Roselli had a long time relationship to Jake Lansky in Los Angeles and was known to be exceptionally well connected to the "Jewish Mafia" through the casinos such as the Desert Inn and the Stardust. Skim from these casinos went to both Moe Dalitz of Cleveland and Sam Giancana of Chicago.

In April of 1963, just as the Sierra initiative was moving to make its first Miami exile community contacts, William Harvey and John Roselli appear to have met in Miami with someone previously involved in the earlier Castro assassination effort.

Sierra's first serious recruiting meeting in Miami was attended by Felipe Vidal Santiago, a close personal friend of John Martino. The meeting was also attended by Carlos Rodriquez Quesada, formerly associated with 30th November and SNFE, who became Sierra's "Minister of the Interior."

After the signing of a formal pact with SNFE/Alpha 66, Manuel Pino, a senior Junta counsel member resigned his position over inclusion of such "left-wing" organizations.

Though HSCA summary document on the JGCE (Junta) [8]recounts pledges of support to several groups, actual funds were given only to Aldo Vera Serifin, Tony Cuesta of Commando's L, and members of Sierra's own council staff including Carlos Quesada.

Suggestions for testing and research

- John Cummings, a former reporter to whom Martino supposedly provided details on the conspiracy, remarked to Mary LaFontaine that Martino did mention names that Cummings has never revealed.

LaFontaine reports Cummings as saying that one name mentioned was not known to him at the time but later became quite well known. We do know from FBI reports that Martino was well acquainted with Frank Sturgis whose name became a household word after Watergate. However, he was also well acquainted with Eugenio Martinez of the Bayo raid, of long-standing CIA service, and of Watergate. It is critical that any undisclosed names which Cummings knows be made part of the historical record.

• Mexico City has largely been ignored in terms of identifying and understanding the anti-Castro exiles operating there. CIA and FBI Mexico City station exile and counter intelligence files would be critical sources and Mexico City newspaper files and reporters of the period could offer identification of the more militant exiles who engaged in attacks on Cuban-Castro personnel and supporters in Mexico. If Diaz Garcia and "Hernandez" could be located in Mexico City, it would be key to trace their entry into the US and identify their sponsor.

• The associates and activities of the Junta were intensely investigated by both the FBI and the HSCA; however, no financial details were obtained from Union Tank Car, nor was Paulino Sierra questioned in detail about his associates and activities. Unless Sierra could be located and was willing to supply details, it is unlikely that further information could be obtained at this late date. The alternative would be to attempt to track the money that was supposedly given to SNFE/Alpha 66 or to obtain from Alpha 66 historical information about its activities and contacts with the Junta.

• The good news is that due to the extensive HSCA work and reporting, there is no question at all that a good many of the primary figures of interest in regard to Dallas can be shown to have been known to each other in the second half of 1963, and also known to the syndicate figures who were financing Sierra. These syndicate figures can also be directly connected to Las Vegas, to John Roselli, and specifically to people associated with the Desert Inn and Stardust (David's friend Reuben independently reported that the Stardust was Morales' hotel of choice when visiting his friend Roselli in Vegas.)

HIJACKING THE SYSTEM

The "shadow war" against Castro had been going on for more than three years by 1963; virtually all the military operations, psychological operations, and counter-intelligence activities in this war had been carried out not only in secrecy but with "deniability." In pursuit of this, it had become standard procedure for participants at all levels to conduct their activities in a very compartmentalized fashion—not only in regard to actual missions but also in regard to weapons stores, funding and communications. Many of those involved in anti-Castro and anti-Communist operations had not only had advanced infantry training but special and covert operations training for undercover Cuban penetration missions.

During the early years, the CIA had implemented a rigorous policy of deniability not only with cover stories, press control and front companies, but in its payments and arms transfers to exile organizations. We have previously reviewed examples where even the CIA could not verify for the FBI or other agencies whether a particular mission or project had been carried out at Agency behest or simply by groups or individuals who were receiving Agency funds and support. As the Kennedy Administration ceased its sponsorship of anti-Castro actions launched from American soil and limited its support to very specific groups and individuals, this situation escalated to the point where a good number of intelligence resources were dedicated to determining what the independent exiles were doing or planning, and just who was funding them. It has also been shown that by 1963, the most independent and militant exiles and anti-Castro activists had totally lost faith in the US government and would only take money and direction from individuals who could be seen to be independent of or hostile towards the Kennedy Administration.

This was an environment in which individuals and resources could essentially be "hijacked" by their contacts within pre-existing networks and reporting structures. The Dallas conspiracy took advantage of this situation to use people and networks under the pretext of anti-Castro operations and projects which turned them first into unknowing assets and then into accessories who had to remain silent in order to protect themselves. The list of individuals with the track records and reputations to carry out such actions is a short one; it required the individuals to have demonstrated an opposition to Kennedy Administration policies, and to have proven their ability to provide support for the anti-Communist struggle independent of administration directives. We have seen that Helms, Fitzgerald, Shackley, Phillips and Morales all demonstrated the ability to conduct covert and deniable operations at their own initiative and discretion. This included activities such as the continuation of the Roselli project, the Cubela assassination project, the ZR/RIFLE effort, and the Bayo-Pawley mission.

Supporting remarks, observations and incidents

Carlos Hernandez told the HSCA that the exiles often worked with individuals who simply represented themselves as supporters of their cause, not knowing if they were acting for the US government or other special interests.

Antonio Veciana related that his primary contact in anti-Castro projects for over a decade never acknowledged that he was working for the US government but simply that he represented sympathetic business interests.

The existence and use of the Operation 40 group (led by Joaquin Sanjenis and Felix Gutierrez). This political action team was established for use in support of the Bay of Pigs invasion and was apparently "hijacked" for bombing, assassination and political intimidation activities in Florida for years afterwards. Operation 40 maintained an existence and agenda of its own and was apparently used by CIA officers for their own purposes for years, even after JM/WAVE had been disbanded.[9]

In such instances, CIA officers acted entirely on their own, conducting field operations themselves (including weapons transfers and "trades"). Any CIA personnel or related individuals used in support would have had to assume the operations were fully legal and sanctioned.

This demonstrated ability to conduct totally compartmentalized Special Affairs is illustrated in Fitzgerald's decision not to report AM/LASH contacts with Kostikov during the intense internal inquiry conducted during the weekend following the murder of the President. The level of autonomy afforded to senior officers is also reflected in Shackley's decision not to collect or solicit any intelligence on the Kennedy assassination through his JM/WAVE contacts and resources.

Shackley told the Church Committee that he had no recollection of authorizing weapons shipments to AM/LASH. When the Church Committee showed Shackley copies of cables authorizing shipments with his signature, he denied ever having seen the cables before.

This pattern of CIA compartmentalization and deniability suggests that it would have been perfectly feasible for an extremely small number of senior officers to "pull the strings" which would lead to the assassination of the President. To identify the right individuals and give them the precise information required to push them to action, to give them access to information, intelligence, introductions would take two men, perhaps three. Of course a small number of others would have to know the real goal, the shooters and their "cut-outs." Not even the men who would impersonate and set up the patsy or the men who would support the field action in Dallas would have to know the end game. It could easily have been just another counter-intelligence operation or psychological operation targeted against Castro. They might have suspected. Later they and the others would know for sure, but by then they would all have become accessories to murder.

OPERATING IN DALLAS

The conspiracy had extraordinarily skilled and experienced organizers–not amateurs, but professionals at the peak of their careers. It had access to paramilitary personnel trained to infiltrate Cuba in the face of extraordinarily effective and aggressive security. These individuals were well trained and totally committed, veterans of advanced infantry training, special operations training ranging from ambush to explosives and demolitions, veterans with combat experience, men trained to penetrate occupied territory and conduct sabotage. *What it did not have were two things–time, and a Dallas intelligence network.*

Local intelligence is often the difference between success and failure and these same people had been defeated in Cuba by their own lack of current and accurate field intelligence. The need for these in Dallas was even greater because this was not just a paramilitary operation. They had to set up a patsy whom they could manipulate but who was not a proactive participant; Lee Oswald was not going to do anything to directly incriminate himself in a Presidential assassination. They had to impersonate him in the right places, make him look like a paid shooter, plant at least minimal evidence at the scene, and manage to extract him to some point where they could kill him in a manner that would leave no doubt that Castro was behind the assassination. All of which meant not just putting a shooter team into Dallas a few days in advance but putting agents in Dallas for several weeks to conduct the setup. It also meant staying in touch with Oswald whom they knew to be an informant and under observation. This meant that anyone in contact with Oswald had better have a viable cover (one that would seem in character if observed by the FBI, ATF, or Military Intelligence), and be prepared to communicate through one or more (possibly unknowing) cut-outs.

The Sierra initiative as well as independent groups such as Alpha 66 were under surveillance by almost every US Government agency as well as by JM/WAVE. Exiles and their associates had already been arrested for various federal offenses. Many were under travel interdiction and surveillance and some had reportedly been picked up in Chicago in conjunction with a warning from the FBI prior to a planned Presidential visit.

These circumstances demanded a new set of contacts for Oswald in Texas, a new courier for the field team and an intelligence connection in Dallas. A connection was needed with contacts at the DPD who could get advance information on the motorcade and the security plans without seeming suspicious when asking questions of his or her police acquaintances. Those were the requirements for operating in Dallas when the plan jelled in early October.

The requirements were filled by taking advantage of an existing exile meeting places, use of a Varona connected remote cut-out in Abilene, Jack Ruby's local reputation and police connections, and multiple trips to Dallas by individuals who could be used as couriers.

Supporting observations and remarks

Manual Orcarberrio was reported in the company of someone closely resembling Lee Oswald by two different witnesses on two different occasions, once on Harlandale and once in Oklahoma. The Harlandale observation was in the same time frame that Agent Hosty told a Secret Service agent that Oswald had been seen in the company of "subversives."

The house on Harlandale was a frequent gathering place and residence for a wide variety of exiles, many of whom only appeared late at night. Orcarberrio was reportedly involved in organizing and fundraising for a Dallas chapter of Alpha 66, and was rumored to have been involved in arms purchases. Actual proof of these organizing efforts and arms purchases has yet to be presented. The house was reportedly abandoned several days before November 22.

Pedro Gonzalez was observed to have received a message from Lee Oswald, and the message can be connected to the transport of an individual calling himself Lee Oswald from Juarez, Mexico, through Abilene to Dallas. This individual went to great lengths to mention accurate details about the Oswald family and about Jack Ruby's club.

Pedro Gonzalez had been witnessed to have visitors from both New Orleans and Florida; he was also reported to be a personal friend of Tony Varona. Varona had been a primary resource of John Roselli in at least two separate Castro assassination attempts; he had also established a new connection with Artime in the fall of 1963. Gonzalez fled Abilene immediately following the assassination making great efforts to collect all photographs and other material that might have been used to track him and his associates.

The timing of activities of the named individuals:

September 13: Kennedy trip to Texas announced.

September 25: Odio visited in Dallas by two Latinos and Oswald.

September 27: Martino on speaking tour to New Orleans and Dallas.

September 29 (approx): McKeown visited in Houston by one Latin and Oswald.

October 1: Martino in Dallas.

October 5: Kennedy visit to Dallas announced.

October 1-15: Ruby travels to New Orleans with unaccounted days in his visit (no known contacts); during this period he was reportedly observed by the FBI meeting with John Roselli in Florida.

October 3: Ruby calls R.D. Matthews' wife in Shreveport, La. Matthews had worked at the Deauville Casino in Havana along with Lewis McWillie and was visited there by Ruby and Martino. Matthews had been associated with Ruby in Dallas before his move to Havana and had been reported (and denied) having been approached as a contractor for a pre-Bay of Pigs Castro assassination project.[10]

October 16: Oswald begins work at the TSBD.

October 31: Oswald is impersonated in job inquiry at Statler Hilton. At this point the exact motorcade route remained uncertain beyond Main Street. Vidal is in Dallas from October 31–November 11.

November 4: Oswald's name left on tag for mounting scope on rifle at Irving Sports Shop. On November 24 this tag would be reported by anonymous calls to two separate Dallas papers.

November 8–12: Period in which Oswald's "subversive" contacts are reported by Hosty. Period in which Oswald was reportedly seen at Harlandale house. Vidal reportedly leaves Dallas on November 11. Oswald leaves note for Agent Hosty at FBI office on November 12.

November 9: A man using the name Lee Oswald test drives a car, speaks of the fact that he will be coming into money in two or three weeks, and makes a remark about going "back to Russia."

November 11: Jack Ruby gets prescription for nerve pills; refills immediately.

Mid–November: Al Gruber of L.A. visits Ruby after no contact in previous 10 years. Gruber will later have no reason or explanation for the visit.

November 17: Oswald "call me" note left in Abilene. Ruby calls Gruber in L.A. Ruby will call Gruber again immediately after Oswald's arrest on the afternoon of November 22. Ruby reportedly follows this call with a trip to Las Vegas.

Roselli is in Phoenix on November 17; calls Las Vegas at 3 AM. that night and flies to Vegas on the 18th—losing his FBI tail.

November 19: Ruby informs his tax attorney he now has money to settle his IRS debts.

November 20/21: Ralph Yates gives a ride to a young man who was a look-a-like for Oswald; the man does not give his name but is carrying a four foot long package. He discusses the possibility of someone shooting at the President from a building and asks Yates if he has ever been to the Carousel Club. Yates drops him off at the corner of Elm and Houston at the TSBD.

November 20: Wayne January, operator of a charter air service at Red Bird airfield is visited by a young man and woman interested in chartering a plane to Mexico. The pair acts very suspiciously and their male companion, who closely resembles Oswald, never leaves their car. January had been frequenting the Carousel Club in 1963 and had received a number of suspicious inquiries for charters he felt might involve smuggling; he attributed these inquiries to his visibility at the Carousel Club. The FBI questions January at length about any relationship he might have had with Ruby.[11]

November 21: Vidal back in Dallas.

November 22: Ruby calls Al Gruber following Oswald's capture.

November 24: Ruby murders Oswald; Ruby's eventual chief defense Attorney (Melvin Belli) is reported to have been solicited by a call from the Desert Inn in Las Vegas. S.A. Hosty is ordered to destroy note left by Oswald. The FBI will later retype Oswald's entire address book to remove reference to Hosty.

Suggestions for testing and research

- Inquiries should be made in Abilene to locate any photos, articles or interviews with Pedro Gonzalez, who should be traced. All individuals exposed to him should be interviewed with appropriate photo references to try and identify his visitors.

- All Roselli FBI surveillance reports for the second half of 1963 must be obtained and a detailed travel time-line developed; in particular the report of Ruby's meeting with Roselli must be followed up and the agent identified and interviewed and his deposition taken. Any surviving documents or tapes must be obtained.

- Al Gruber's criminal files should be obtained and his associates documented–especially those within the L.A. gambling community that could connect to John Roselli.

- The FBI reports of Ruby's Las Vegas trip of November 17 should be re-examined, witnesses interviewed, and determination made as to why this travel was left out of the material reported to the Warren Commission.

- The Belli legal case files should be obtained and examined to verify the true source of his employment in the Ruby case as well as all related payments.

MODUS OPERANDI

The methods and tactics used in Dallas were well known to those involved. They included standard paramilitary tactics for a well-structured ambush including:

1. Diversion of security personnel both before and during the attack.

2. Concealed shooters.

3. Slowing and blocking of the target vehicle.

4. A back-up.

In addition, the plot included the ploy of planting evidence to implicate a patsy of the opposite political persuasion. Ample instances of these methods at work are visible wherever David Phillips and David Morales operated in Latin America. *Antonio Veciana gave an example of a Castro assassination attempt in Chile which involved multiple shooters with concealed weapons, an attempt to slow Castro's car with a stalled vehicle, and a car bomb as back-up.* A second back-up included a plane attack on Castro's aircraft. This particular project also included manipulated photographs and fake documents planted on the assassin to make him appear to be a Moscow Castro agent who had turned traitor. The patsy was supposed to be killed after the attack. *Veciana described the project as "very similar to the assassination of Kennedy."*

Neither the Secret Service nor the Dallas Police were prepared to deal with experienced paramilitary teams. Their preparations were built around dealing with known "nuts" and troublemakers or with organized political groups or agitators. An examination of the trip planning meetings shows that the DPD was focused on crowd control and traffic control; its only proactive intelligence work was targeted against protests and demonstrations by the right-wing groups that had harassed Ambassador Stevenson on a recent visit.

The following elements suggest professional planning and manipulation; they deserve investigation at a level far beyond what local FBI and DPD devoted to them:

- During the weeks prior to the President's visit, the ambulance company scheduled to handle ambulance coverage for the motorcade received ten to twelve bogus calls for ambulance runs to the corner of Elm and Houston. Upon arrival there was never anyone there and this became suspicious to them after the assassination. It is easy to imagine the tactical advantage of putting an ambulance into the intersection at the time of, or slightly before, the President's arrival. Given the fact that the motorcade was close to ten minutes behind schedule on November 22, it is significant that an emergency call to the same location on November 22 placed an ambulance in the intersection beside the TSBD approximately ten minutes before the President.[12]

- Driver Aubrey Rike says the significance of the calls was not apparent to any one crew because they were spaced over separate shifts over time. However, after the assassination the FBI visited the company asking for the call logs and offering the explanation that there might have been something suspicious about them, this word got out to the drivers. Rike relates that although the November 22 call described a man with a seizure, no signs of that were apparent on the pick-up although the man did have a red spot on his forehead suggesting he had fallen on the pavement or sidewalk. The man was conscious and apparently coherent but refused to talk to the drivers at the scene.

- The evening before the assassination, the majority of the Secret Service detail stayed out at a club until the early morning hours – 2 to 3 AM and later. Although only a few members admitted to drinking alcohol, at a minimum, their effectiveness was reduced by the late hours and lack of sleep. This incident occurred at "The Cellar" in Fort Worth and a number of the girls serving at the Cellar also worked for Jack Ruby. The owner of the club, Pat Kirkwood, was named as a friend of Jack Ruby and an associate of Jack Ruby and R.D. Matthews. Although the drinking incident was investigated by the Secret Service, no disciplinary action was taken and the details (and people) involved in the genesis of the incident are cloudy at best.[13] A Cellar employee, Jimmy Hill, related to author Jim Marrs that they had received a call from the White House asking them not to say anything about the Secret Service visit as their image had already suffered enough. Hill's comments suggest that more of the agents were actually drinking than is reflected in the internal Secret Service report on the incident.

- At approximately 10:40 on the morning of November 22, a green and white pick-up truck became stalled on Elm Street in the vicinity of the railroad overpass. The truck blocked one lane of traffic and occupied the attention of at least three policemen assigned to security duty on the overpasses during the next hour and a half. One left the area with the driver while the other officers kept a watch on the vehicle and remaining occupant. The driver returned with another pick-up and the first vehicle was pushed off—where it was pushed to remains unspecified. Much has been made of the fact that a motorist reported a man removing a gun case from the vehicle, but nothing has been made of the fact that this vehicle had diverted the officers closest to the fence, parking lot and knoll. No concrete identification was made of the vehicle's owner, and the police officers were not questioned about the incident in detail. The vehicle was not searched at the time. Clearly the officers had no concern for any danger from weapons such as radio triggered "car bombs."

- At approximately 12:10, an ambulance arrived at the intersection of Elm and Houston to pick up an individual reportedly suffering a seizure. Ambulance personnel determined it was not a seizure but transported the man, who was dressed in camouflage clothing, to Parkland Hospital. The individual recovered at Parkland, received no treatment and managed to leave the holding area at a time when it was blanketed by Secret Service personnel and when the ambulance drivers were essentially being held under guard in the same area. The man was located afterwards but simply stated he had not felt well, had recovered at the hospital and walked out unnoticed. No further investigation was conducted.

- At 12:15, while the pick-up truck was being pushed away, the attention of the officers at the corner of Elm and Houston and on the overpass was diverted by the collapse of a man standing in front of the TSBD.

- The first gunshot at the motorcade sounded from the rear. It caused several Secret Service personnel to turn around and look behind them, not up and behind but behind at street level (as though the shot had come from a lower floor of the Dal-Tex building, whose fire escape window appears open in the Altgens photograph).

- At that time, to the front of the motorcade and at street level, a man began pumping an open umbrella up and down. This drew the attention of several Secret Service personnel including William Greer, the driver of the President's car. The "Umbrella Man" did not come forward after the assassination even though he was one of the closest witnesses to the shooting. During the HSCA investigation, a man admitted to being this individual. However, his statements as to his actions and movements are extremely inconsistent with the photographic record. The man, Steven Witt, also claimed not to have noticed the Latin individual standing next to him although photographs show them apparently talking. Witt's remark that he recalls a "Negro man" sitting down next to him and repeating, "They done shot them folks" is also extremely unconvincing. More interesting, however, is the unknown object that can clearly be seen under the Latin's jacket.

- At the time the fatal shots were being fired, a rifle barrel was being pushed out the "sniper's nest" window on the sixth floor of the TSBD. This rifle barrel was far enough out the window to attract the attention of witnesses on the street below and of people in vehicles coming down Houston Street. Witnesses comment that the rifle was "slowly" pulled back into the building. The position of this rifle is dramatically at odds with the seated firing position illustrated in the Warren Commission report. It suggests that the rifle was a visual cue intended to draw attention rather than one being used in the attack.

- Approximately three minutes after the final shots, a train passed over the Elm Street overpass; one of the policemen stationed there stated to the Warren Commission that the train blocked his view of the motorcade and shooting. Given that the motorcade was a few minutes behind schedule, the train did indeed almost pass over the motorcade, a major security violation and again a ready-made vehicle for a remote, radio controlled bomb that could have collapsed the bridge onto the President. A review of the Secret Service motorcade planning, which included railroad representatives, clearly shows that arrangements were made and orders given to stop all train movement across any overpass on the route for a considerable period both before and after the planned passage time. No investigation of the train security incident was made.

- One of the first officers to enter the parking lot behind the fence on the knoll, DPD Officer Joe Marshall Smith, challenged a man in civilian clothes (and with dirty hands) who produced Secret Service identification. Smith allowed him to continue out of the area. After extensive research for over three decades, it is clear that no official Secret Service personnel or other agents were behind the fence at that point. Another early arriving officer, W.W. Mabra, was discouraged from conducting a search in the rail yard behind the parking lot. A uniformed DPD officer approached him and Officer Orville Smith and told them he had been stationed in the rail yard, "I was stationed in the rail yards and had this entire area in view. Nobody came this way." When they hesitated, he expanded, "Fellas, I've been here for an hour, there hasn't been a thing in here, not even a stray dog." Based on this, Officer Mabra and Orville Smith stopped their inspection of the cars. Based on DPD records, we now know that there was no officer officially assigned to the rail yard directly behind the parking area.

- We also have the testimony of Lee Bowers describing several automobiles driving in the area and at least two men behind the fence at the time of the shooting. J.C. Price described a man fleeing into the railroad yard from behind the fence. The uniformed officer who dissuaded Mabra was either badly mistaken or something much more sinister. Officer Mabra was interviewed in 1992 and was adamant that the officer was DPD and after his initial conversation with the researcher, refused to talk further about the incident.[14]

- At 12:45, the police broadcast a description of a suspect. The description was for "an unknown white male, approximately 30, slender build, height five feet ten inches, weight one hundred and sixty five, reported to be armed with what is believed to be a .30 caliber rifle." This is a highly unusual description in that it makes no mention of clothing but is specific on the type of rifle; it sounds like it has been read from a file rather than given by a witness. The Police Captain who received the description gave instructions for the witness to be taken in for questioning, but the witness simply "disappeared."

At the time and taken individually, most of these incidents were treated matter-of-factly or at best closed out with minimal investigation. Some of them were not even recognized as suspicious until years later when reference reports and information such as duty rosters and summary reports from the Secret Service and Dallas Police were available for review. Some of them may indeed be benign or coincidental. But it's clear they were not investigated in detail nor viewed as possible "fingerprints" of an organized covert operation. Whether any law enforcement agency was prepared to detect the "fingerprints" of a covert "special affairs" type operation in 1963 is questionable. However, from this distance in time we have no excuse for not looking for them.

Suggestions for testing and research

1. Clearly too much time has passed to resolve suspicions about how the Secret Service party at The Cellar could have been manipulated or stage managed. However the manager of that evening should be contacted to verify the report that several of Jack Ruby's girls were "working" The Cellar that night.

2. Advertisements might draw out the individuals involved with the stalled pick-up truck, but it is unlikely that the surviving DPD officers on the overpasses would take kindly to questions about whether and how it diverted their attention. Photo examination reveals that cars and vans were parked along the access route to the Stemmons freeway and would have been directly beside the route of the President's vehicle; such a vehicle would have been in the ideal position to serve as a "last resort" car bomb.

3. It is possible that a thorough background check on the seizure victim or on Witt might turn up something revealing. Another extended photo analysis should be done to evaluate how far Witt's remarks actually vary from the Umbrella Man's actions.

4. A professional photo analysis of the Latin Man as compared to persons of interest, including Felipe Vidal Santiago should be conducted.

5. Officers Mabra and Smith should be re-contacted about their encounter in the railroad yard and shown the official DPD logs indicating they were misled.

6. Researcher Ulric Shannon should be contacted in regard to his interviews with Mabra and any further research he has done on the subject.

7. Finally, advertisements and good field work might clarify the issue of the railroad train and its passage.

S.N.A.F.U.

In the author's opinion, Lee Oswald was not a knowing participant in the actual attack on the President nor did he have prior knowledge of others' intent to kill the President in Dallas. Oswald was, however, engaged in ongoing contact with *subversives* who were representing themselves as Castro supporters and who had led Oswald to think that they would assist him in leaving the United States and get him to Cuba. Oswald's unannounced Thursday evening visit to Marina and his children, as well as his actions on November 22, suggest that he was told, with short notice, that November 22 was the day that he would be taken out of Texas. It is even possible that it was suggested to him that the President's visit would serve as a diversion for any ongoing FBI surveillance of him or his contacts.

Whether or not he was asked to do anything that would have later been seen as incriminating remains an open question. Clearly he was not asked to do anything before hand that would have made him suspicious that he was being used as a patsy. As soon as he became aware of the actual shooting of the

President it is very likely he began to develop that suspicion. In short, November 22, 1963 was not a normal day at work for Lee Oswald.

He was planning to leave Dallas, very likely planning to simply leave work during the lunch hour, walk out a door and disappear. However he had to have been told something that would keep him inside during the passing of the motorcade, something that would keep him from compromising the frame by being visible during the shooting. It may have been as simple as giving him a time to make or receive a telephone call. However, his chance encounter with Carolyn Arnold only minutes before the arrival of the motorcade was a significant glitch in the plan and could have been a disaster if Oswald had gone on trial and she had been called as a witness for the defense. It may well be that Oswald was to exit though a rear door and simply take a taxi to the Texas Theatre, that would have isolated him from the crowd and he might have known nothing or little about the attack on the President. After all, it took some time for individuals other than the immediate witnesses on Elm Street to know that the President had been hit and likely killed, many in the Plaza area only knew that something had happened...at first they hoped it had only been fireworks or some sort of protest.

However, Officer Baker's weapon drawn confrontation of Oswald in the break room would have ensured that Oswald didn't leave out the rear. It would have been only too obvious if he tried to sneak out the back he might have been shot first and questions asked later. At that point Oswald's only course of action was to walk slowly and casually out the front door and make some inquiries. But even at then exactly what had happened remained unclear to him. What is clear was is that Oswald's suspicions were aroused enough so to have a taxi drop him off away from his apartment so that he could scan the area as he returned, enough to get him to pick up a pistol and be armed on his way to the Texas Theatre.

- The Lee Oswald who left his apartment armed, suspicious and possibly scared was not part of the plan.

- An armed Oswald and a dead police officer were not part of the plan.

- And a live Oswald in police custody as a cop killer was definitely not part of the plan.

For Lee Oswald to be found dead apparently while escaping towards Cuba (with additional incriminating evidence planted on him) would have ensured that authorities acted against a Cuban-Communist conspiracy. Oswald in jail represented an immediate opportunity for the DPD to declare an immediate victory—which they did. It also left the conspiracy, and the plotters, in grave jeopardy.

Supporting observations and remarks

The evidence relating to Oswald as a shooter in the TSBD is much more indicative of a frame than of anything else—when contrasted to what should have been found if he were a real shooter:

- There is no witness to Oswald taking a rifle to the TSBD. Frazier and his sister, the only two witnesses to observe him with a package that day, were adamant that the package he carried was far too short to have contained even a broken down rifle. Dougherty, the only witness to observe Oswald enter the building, testified that Oswald carried nothing into the School Book Depository. The package entered into evidence was not photographed at the crime scene nor was it found to contain any evidence (oil stains, for example) of ever having contained a rifle. The rifle shows no scratches or other marks which might be expected if a several parts were thrown into a bag and carried by hand; the rifle also shows no scratches associated with re-assembly indicating that it would have been done with a screwdriver, not a coin as the Warren Commission speculated.

- If Oswald had been actively involved in an effort to frame himself, we should see the same sort of remarks made to Frazier such as those that were made to Yates when he dropped a passenger with a long package at the corner beside the TSBD—remarks about the President's visit, or threats against the President or his being at risk—and a package long enough to leave no doubts about its holding a rifle.

- No prints or other evidence tied Oswald to the firing of the rifle found on the sixth floor. There were no prints on the barrel, trigger guard, rifle clip or hulls. There was only an "old" palm print found under the stock, placed when the rifle was disassembled, but not present on November 22 according to Lt. Day of the DPD. A cooperating Oswald certainly should have been able to leave fresh fingerprints on the fully assembled rifle, even if it required an effort on his part.

- No witness identified Oswald in the TSBD window at the time of firing; only a rifle barrel was seen sticking out the window. The witness later offered by the Warren Commission did not identify Oswald on November 22, in fact, there is no record of his officially participating in a line-up, much less identifying Oswald. DPD officers made it clear that they had no witness to Oswald in the window (D.A. Wade told WFAA "people cannot positively identify him there e.g. in the window"), and Chief of Police Curry stated in his book on the assassination that they never could put Oswald in that window with a gun.

- A description of the shooter was given to the Dallas Police and announced on police radio. The source of the description is unknown; the source described by a DPD Captain never gave a deposition and apparently left after being ordered to go to the police station. This source described the shooter with a different type of rifle and gave no description of the shooter's clothing although he gave a comprehensive physical description of height, age and weight.

- A cooperating Oswald could easily have waved to his co-workers from the upstairs window immediately before the arrival of the motorcade; he could have done so and even announced he was coming downstairs. A cooperating Oswald would have made his presence on the sixth floor known and either stayed there or certainly not advertised himself as not being up there continuously—furiously engaged in building a sniper's nest and assembling his rifle. But in reality Oswald took great pains to make sure his co-workers knew he had not remained on the upper floors at the lunch break. First he called them to send him an elevator. Then he went downstairs and was seen by four different people including Shelley at 11:55, Piper at 12:00 noon, and Arnold at 12:15. Only minutes after the shooting, he was seen in exactly the same place as described by Arnold at 12:15.

- An Oswald with instructions to be prepared to sneak out the back door while everyone was outside watching the motorcade would do exactly what Oswald seems to have done: stay inside, downstairs with easy access to the stairs and back door. However, when Oswald was confronted first by Officer Baker and then by Roy Truly, he became aware that there were people coming up the stairs. Baker had pulled a gun on him; running out the back door could get him shot. Going slowly and calmly out the front door was his safest way out and that is exactly what he did, being observed by Mrs. Reid with his coke in his hand and moving very slowly–as he always did.

• Roger Craig related hearing a loud whistle and watching a man who looked like Oswald come down the grassy knoll to Elm Street and get into a station wagon that had pulled over to the curb and which then rapidly went west on Elm into the Oak Cliff area. Craig's statement was not pursued by the DPD; certainly it was out of favor once the official story had been formalized. Only decades later did researchers determine that a series of photographs existed which proves every movement described by Roger Craig. They show a station wagon on Elm and show a man resembling Oswald coming down the knoll. In addition, researchers found statement records from three different individuals including two motorists who had watched the station wagon slow down, pull to the curb and take a passenger. This incident seems amazingly daring. It would have absolutely ensured that Oswald was portrayed as part of a conspiracy, especially since a clear copy of a photo taken that day shows Craig looking at a man coming down the knoll who resembles Oswald in company with another man as he comes away from the School Book Depository.[15]

• Oswald's instructions to leave quietly and covertly might work well to move him on to his point of extraction. However, it would have done little to support the conspiracy that was in operation. Perhaps that explains what occurred in front of the School Book Depository on Elm Street and the statement by DPD Chief Curry to WFAA news that, "We have heard he was picked up by a Negro in a car." Curry's statement is a matter of historical record, but Chief Decker would later deny having paid any attention to the information given to him by his award winning officer, Roger Craig.

• Another incident may relate an escape plan that had to be aborted after Oswald's arrest. At approximately 2:30 PM, a tower operator at Red Bird airport had his attention drawn to a green and white Piper Comanche aircraft. This aircraft had baggage stacked by it and three men in business suits were observed. Although the tower operator could not or would not later state exactly what drew his attention, he felt that the aircraft and people were suspicious (this is reminiscent of Lee Bowers' statements about the men behind the fence at the time of the shooting and his inability or reticence to state exactly what drew his attention to them). At that point, the tower operator tried calling the FBI and encountered a busy line. The plane shortly departed and his suspicion was enhanced because the plane's pilot had stated a southbound departure yet reversed his flight to come around and fly to the north. The tower operator was concerned enough to look up the registration on the plane and found that it was owned by a firm in Ohio. He continued trying to call the FBI but could not get through. About 40 minutes later, the plane returned to Red Bird, landed, and taxied to the TexAir terminal where two men got out. In his statement, not given until 1967 during the Garrison investigation, he related that this led him to believe that the plane had simply flown to Love Field to drop off a passenger for a commercial flight. He could not verify this but simply stopped his calls to the FBI. This incident points up two things of interest. First, this particular plane apparently had stayed in place at the airport until almost immediately after the news media began to broadcast that Oswald was in custody. Second, no investigation at all was made of private or commercial air traffic out of Dallas either before or after Oswald was arrested.

- Shortly after the public announcement of Oswald's arrest, we find Jack Ruby going through another mood swing and on the phone for a call to Gruber in Los Angeles. Ruby's behavior from the time of the assassination through his shooting of Lee Oswald is discussed in detail in Chapter 16. There are ample indications of Ruby having a new role forced upon him, of his relief and exuberance when Oswald does not react to him in the late night press conference and when he learns Oswald is dead. There is also ample evidence that Ruby was to be used to establish Oswald as part of a conspiracy. This evidence was contained in the box of material turned in as evidence by Deputy Ben Cash and seen by at least six other officers as well as by District Attorney Wade. The evidence was not used in the Ruby trial and apparently just disappeared.

Suggestions for testing and research

There may be little that can be done with many of these elements. The observations by witnesses such as Carolyn Arnold and others who saw Oswald in the wrong place at wrong time for the official story, or saw other men on the sixth floor before or after the shooting, are quite clear. They simply were not placed in the official record.

- Roger Craig's story was discredited before the photos were studied and other witness reports were located; there is no doubt that what he reported occurred. However, technical photo analysis of the individuals coming down the knoll might indeed lead to the identification of the Oswald figure or of his apparent companion.

- Perhaps one of the most important opportunities for research is to pursue the box of Ruby–Oswald evidence. Earl Goltz developed this story, is still alive and approachable; likewise many of the named officers including Ben Cash, Billy Preston, Mike Callahan, Forest Keene, and Stockard.

VESTED INTERESTS

The people who implemented the Dallas conspiracy very much wanted the world to see a Castro-sponsored conspiracy; the instigators wanted John Kennedy dead and any blame associated with that to fall on Communists. Even the quickest scan of Oswald's public history and activities prior to November 22 would make the average person suspect that he might have been influenced to act, if not directly assisted. The earliest news coverage out of Dallas suggested conspiracy; reports of a burst of shots, witnesses describing shots from multiple locations and Oswald seen being picked up leaving the scene in a car driven by someone else. Conspiracy charges were prepared in Dallas but then rewritten. Kennedy died, but at one level the conspiracy failed—not for any one reason or any major failure on the conspirators' part. It failed because of bad luck, vested interests, lack of due process, and basic human nature. However, the failure was aided and abetted by two types of special agendas: "institutional" and "executive."

The law enforcement men on the scene in Dallas had every reason to quickly locate and arrest the participants in the President's murder. There is every indication that they moved quickly and aggressively. Based on their remarks to the press in the first few hours, there is also little doubt that they were open to multiple suspects and to a conspiracy. Indeed some of these remarks began to prove very uncomfortable for the executive damage control that began the evening of November 22.

The DPD and Chief Curry would suffer from their openness for years afterwards.

However, once the DPD had a suspect in custody who had also evidently killed a police officer, they also had every reason to declare a quick victory. Law enforcement organizations find and charge criminals. They build cases against them; they do not defend them and they have little motivation to explore whether or not their suspect has been framed. The legal system (supposedly) provides that protection. In most cases, when a credible suspect is framed in a crime it either takes a strong legal defense, a family champion, or a third party to expose the frame and conspiracy.

Lee Oswald had no legal counsel, no legal defense, no family champion, and no friendly organizational sponsor. The liberal organizations that might have defended him were very busy distancing themselves from him. From November 24 on, the reaction of the Dallas Police became one of, "we got our man." Any objections to that could be viewed as a personal challenge to individual or Department integrity. After the murder of Lee Oswald, there was an added DPD institutional (and in some cases personal) incentive not to deal with Jack Ruby's activities as a police "groupie," nor was there an incentive to address the use of Ruby as an unofficial informant to DPD personnel, an official informant to the FBI, and a figure with documented connections to organized crime.

After the murder of Lee Oswald, the case was closed in Dallas. However, the case for a Castro–Communist sponsored conspiracy was still very much alive and was promoted to both the CIA and FBI and was made visible to President Johnson. The case for conspiracy was also still being promoted by Ambassador Mann in Mexico City and taken to the media by a host of anti-Communist "Patriot" groups and politicians.

Field offices of both the FBI and CIA received numerous reports and indications of conspiracy; that is a matter of record. There is little indication that either agency proactively performed any search for conspiracy on their own. On the contrary, high level CIA officers elected not to solicit information and in some cases chose not to respond to requests even within their own agency. FBI personnel acted to cover up their associations and contacts with Lee Oswald and the Director elected not to pursue concrete evidence of a conspiracy involving Oswald in

Mexico City. Unfortunately, the past 40-plus years of experience have shown these practices to be endemic within both agencies.

The FBI has a well-earned reputation within law enforcement for monopolizing access to information, especially vis-à-vis local law enforcement. It also has a reputation for protecting its image.

The CIA has repeatedly demonstrated that it feels duty-bound to conceal and, if necessary, to lie to protect its "sources and methods." It considers these vital to the security of the country and CIA professionals feel honor-bound to protect their "networks." CIA officers have told Congress that they would consider it their duty to withhold sensitive information and senior officers have been accused of, and in some cases, cited for both perjury and contempt by Congress.

In addition, documents of the CIA and DOJ now prove that the Justice Department under Ramsey Clark and the CIA both actively involved themselves in undermining the Garrison investigation. The Justice Department went so far as to actively support Clay Shaw's defense, and the CIA proactively took legal measures to ensure that CIA personnel would be blocked from offering testimony. The FBI went so far as to obtain presidential immunity from testimony for key personnel in New Orleans.

This sort of response by Federal agencies seems to have become institutionalized and has continued for decades—extending to virtually any investigations that the agencies feel could damage their operational capabilities, place their personnel at risk, or even simply cause them adverse publicity which could endanger their funding. The agencies feel duty bound to protect themselves and to ensure their effectiveness; individual officers and personnel feel bound to protect their careers.

The number of whistle blowers within the FBI and CIA has been minimal, although in recent years much publicity has been given to instances of FBI involvement in evidence tampering (both to support prosecution and to cover up department "mistakes").

Congressional investigations have clearly shown the CIA's willingness to act independently of specific Presidential orders and Congressional oversight. Senior officers have demonstrated their capacity to "forget" the details of such actions, even under oath. At the time of this writing, The nation is still attempting to deal with the failure of both the FBI and CIA to share information and proactively investigate incidents related to the attacks of September 11, 2001.[16]

There are still few signs that institutional behaviors of this sort can be eliminated or even significantly corrected.

BOTTOM LINE

The Dallas Police got their man and remain proud of their success. President Johnson charged the FBI with making the case against Lee Oswald and making it quickly. They followed their orders and made sure their own monitoring and use of Lee Oswald as an informant did not become visible.

The CIA protected their "sources and methods" and their personnel at all levels, as well as the secrets of Mongoose, ZR/RIFLE, AM/WORLD, AM/TRUNK and AM/LASH. They also protected their mandate, as they understood it—the President's ability to take all necessary measures for the security of the country, with deniability

Robert Kennedy and the Kennedy family protected the President's secret contacts with Castro representatives and, perhaps more importantly at the time, the AM/WORLD project and efforts to generate an internal coup which would remove Castro and pave the way for a free, provisional government.

Vested interests intrinsically lead to damage control in any venue and the individuals who organized the Dallas conspiracy were professionals with a full understanding of how powerful their chosen patsies would be in affecting the actions of all the agencies which would react to the President's murder. They must also have realized their biggest risk. Their victim's brother was the Attorney General of the United States, fanatically devoted to his brother and a man with absolutely no fear. The use of a Cuba associated patsy was the key to the action against John Kennedy. The Cuba connection could either force a war or expose the secret war and assassination attempts against Fidel Castro by the United States and the Kennedy Administration. The Cuba connection could, and apparently did, initially lead Robert Kennedy to join in the official cover up, going so far as to intervene in Mexico City to help neutralize widespread belief that the Cubans were connected to Lee Oswald and behind the assassination.

But there was another force that could and did aggressively neutralize anyone and everyone, including both Hoover and senior CIA officers who continued to float interest in and indications of conspiracy. That force was the new President of the United States.

There remains little doubt that there was a series executive actions that went beyond the institutional reactions of the FBI and CIA. Given the power and influence of the Oval Office, especially with the reactions to John Kennedy's death, it is foolish to think that we will ever know the full extent to which Johnson exercised his official power or his personal persuasiveness in orchestrating an executive cover-up. It was focused on the primary medical and physical evidence held by the Secret Service and the FBI; it was reactive, piecemeal and just barely good enough to allow the FBI report and Warren Commission reports to carry the day. Executive, Johnson-driven damage control is only briefly described in Chapter 15, but is covered in a much more comprehensive fashion by researchers such as Aguilar, Hunt, Horne, Galanor, Weldon, and, most recently, Waldron—as well as in the autopsy related interviews obtained by William Law.

We now have a taste of Johnson's arguments and persuasiveness in his recruiting conversations with Earl Warren and other members of the Warren Commission. Any orders for the manipulation of the autopsy report, the medical evidence, or physical evidence including the presidential limousine would have been fully protected by National Security, especially as it involved military or government personnel. For that matter, a confidential, Johnson issued National Security Memorandum may still be in effect. The fact that President Johnson personally conducted a campaign against anything other than the official story of a lone gunman is beyond doubt. That Johnson was given explicit information from Mexico City showing one or more individuals impersonating Lee Oswald and creating a KGB–Cuban connection for Lee Oswald is a matter of record. That he and the Director of the FBI dropped the subject and chose not to pursue it is without doubt. That Johnson used rumors of a Communist conspiracy and the threat of world war as leverage to force the official lone gunman story is a matter of record.

President Johnson, on his own personal initiative, killed any government investigation of conspiracy in the Kennedy assassination. The question is simply, why did he do it?

One answer is that the news of the Kostikov incident in Mexico City was the key factor. The indications that the KGB and the Cubans had indeed been behind Oswald and the murder sufficiently convinced

Johnson, and he conducted the cover-up either out of personal fear or out of concern for the fate of the country in the shadow of a third World War. This premise suggests that the Kostikov incident may indeed have been a "fail-safe" device organized by the conspirators. As has been referenced throughout this book, John Newman has developed this view in a powerful presentation at JFK Lancer's 1999 November In Dallas Conference called "Dimming The Switches."[17]

An alternative answer is that LBJ was told something under national security seal in regard to Lee Oswald or something similarly confidential pertaining to Cuban operations which caused him to constrain a true investigation.

The third and most speculative alternative is that Johnson himself was an accessory after the fact and that he based the conduct of the cover-up on his personal awareness of a conspiracy. Of course, Johnson's participation has long been suspected and has been the subject of countless publications. Most notable are Barr McClellan's 2003 volume, *Blood, Money, and Power*, Craig I. Zirbel's 1991 study, *The Texas Connection*, and *MacBird*, a comic send-up of Shakespeare's assassination tragedies by Barbara Garson that appeared as early as 1967.[18] The timing of Johnson's activities combined with disclosures and statements by Johnson associates continue to fuel speculation on this third possibility.

Supporting observations suggesting an executive cover-up conducted by President Johnson

At 1:15 PM on November 22, when the President was known to be dead, Malcolm Kilduff approached Johnson about making a statement. Johnson's response was: "No. Wait. We don't know whether it's a Communist conspiracy or not. Are they prepared to get me out of here?" Johnson's first concern after the shooting appears to be conspiracy. While still at Parkland both S.A. Youngblood and S.A. Roberts approached Johnson with similar concerns and strongly advised him to get out of Dallas and get airborne as quickly as possible:

"We don't know the scope of this thing. We should get away immediately!"
– Youngblood.

"We've got to get in the air!" – Roberts.

Despite his own remark and those of the Secret Service, Johnson appeared reluctant to leave Parkland. When he arrived at Air Force One, his first activities were to watch the national news and to begin making calls regarding taking the oath of office, an oath he had already taken along with John Kennedy.

There is not a single record of Johnson's attempting to contact the National Command Center, the White House Situation Room, the Joint Chiefs, or the Secretary of Defense. Nothing shows him asking about the location of the officer with the missile launch codes. Despite his initial remark, Johnson did not make a single call or contact that would indicate he was worried about a Communist conspiracy or national security.

The Joint Chiefs, on the other hand, had broadcast an alert to all commands at 1:15 PM. Johnson continued to pursue the issue of the oath of office, making a number of calls and holding the aircraft exposed on the ground in Dallas for over an hour and a half, only taking off at 2:47 PM after another oath had been administered. Johnson was sensitive enough to his behavior over the oath that he would later make three different statements (including two of them in his Warren Commission affidavit) putting the responsibility for the delay on Robert Kennedy and Kenny O'Donnell. Johnson's statements were adamantly denied by those individuals.

During the flight back there is also not a single record that indicates that Johnson contacted or attempted to contact anyone within the national security or command structure. There is no indication that he pursued any concerns or actions in response to a conspiracy of any sort, much less a Communist conspiracy suggesting an imminent atomic first strike against the United States. Johnson did not speak to the Secretary of Defense until approximately 6:20 PM EST at the airport in Washington. He had not summoned McNamara; rather McNamara had gone of his own accord. Johnson's first remark to McNamara was, *"Any important matters pending?"*

Before Johnson's departure from Dallas, Lee Oswald had been taken into custody and a frantic background search was underway for information about him as Air Force One was flying back to Washington. We now know that as Hoover was making telephone calls and sending memoranda on Lee Oswald, his own file on Oswald contained detailed information on his recent contacts with the KGB head of assassination and sabotage for the Americas.

None of Hoover's communications on Oswald makes the slightest reference to this connection, and there is no indication that Hoover tried to contact Johnson or anyone in the military or national command structure about this. In fact, it seems that J. Edgar Hoover simply left work at his regularly scheduled time on the evening of November 22. He did not go to the airport to meet the new President as McNamara did; apparently, his first communication was when Johnson himself called Hoover at home at 7:25 PM. The call was described by William Manchester in his book *The Death of a President*. However, the call does not now appear in the official November 22 diary among Johnson's other calls. Of course, if Lee Oswald was working as an informant for the FBI and or CIA, his contact with Kostikov would not have been threatening and Hoover's behavior would make considerably more sense.

The preceding statements are based on anecdotes and quotes from the Manchester book on the assassination. President Johnson was not pleased with Manchester's project and assigned Abe Fortas to monitor Manchester's work. Fortas had been serving as legal council to Bobby Baker in November, but Johnson recruited him to be his "assassination coordinator" by November 26. On that date, Fortas contacted Waggoner Carr, Texas Attorney General in regard to the planned Texas inquiry and introduced himself as the person coordinating all assassination activities for President Johnson. By December 3, Carr announced cancellation of any separate Texas investigation. Abe Fortas was appointed to the Supreme Court by Johnson and in 1969 became the first Justice in history to resign from the Court over the issue of having taken money from a convicted criminal over the individual's appeal.

If we are to believe the official record, neither the CIA nor FBI bothered to tell the new President anything about a direct contact between the KGB assassinations bureau and Lee Oswald during the entire day and night of November 22.

During the evening of November 22, however, there are several people on record who received calls from Johnson's assistant Cliff Carter. On the morning of November 23, the *Dallas Morning News* carried a story quoting Dallas District Attorney Henry Wade that preliminary reports indicated more than one person involved. Regardless of what Wade had thought and told the reporters, the charges filed against Oswald reflected the calls from Washington D.C. the previous evening.

Henry Wade described three calls from Cliff Carter on Friday night. Carter said:

> "any word of a conspiracy—some plot by foreign nations—to kill President Kennedy would shake our nation to its foundation. President Johnson was worried about some conspiracy on the part of the Russians... it would hurt foreign relations if I alleged a conspiracy—whether I could prove it or not... I was to charge Oswald with plain murder."[19]

In addition to Wade, Police Chief Curry and Texas State Attorney General Carr also received similar calls from Cliff Carter, instructing them to avoid any charges or remarks indicating conspiracy.[20]

Officer Frank B. Harrell described a conversation with Will Fritz—Fritz was talking over the days of the assassination with some of his old cronies. Fritz recalled several calls from the President's office between Friday evening and Sunday morning. The calls urged him to cease the investigation because "you have your man." Finally he received a person to person call from the new President who specifically ordered him to cease further investigation. Harrell not only confirmed Fritz's remarks to researchers but also relates that Fritz was ordered to stop the interrogation of Oswald.[21]

Doctor Charles Crenshaw described a telephone call to Parkland Surgical "B" where Lee Oswald was being given emergency medical treatment. Crenshaw had already given surgical clothing to an unknown man with a pistol who had entered the room and was watching the doctors. Doctor Crenshaw related being called out of the room for a call from President Johnson; Johnson instructed Crenshaw that he had a man in the surgery and he was to take Oswald's "death bed" confession. Crenshaw's story has been corroborated by other Parkland personnel including Surgeon Dr. Phillip Williams who was in the operating room with Crenshaw and Parkland chief telephone operator Phyllis Bartlett.

> "There very definitely was a phone call from a man with a loud voice, who identified himself as Lyndon Johnson, and he was connected to the operating room phone during Oswald's surgery." Phyllis Bartlett.[22]

In summary, the new President made no calls and took no action in regard to his originally stated concern about a Communist conspiracy. He displayed no interest in the impersonation of Lee Oswald in Mexico City. However, he and his Texas political aide, Cliff Carter, appear to have made a great many personal calls to ensure that the Texas investigations generated no names other than that of Lee Oswald. Johnson and his new aide, Abe Fortas, also seem to have done a quick job of ensuring that the State of Texas did not conduct its own independent inquiry. At this point there seems little doubt that LBJ personally initiated an "Executive" cover-up in both Washington D.C. and Texas. His motivation remains an open question.[23]

Other commentary on the Johnson speculation

In 1984, a Texas Grand Jury and the Justice Department of the United States were given statements that Lyndon Johnson had indeed been involved in the Kennedy assassination as well as in other murders in Texas. These statements were made by Billy Sol Estes who related that he had been personally told of Johnson's involvement by none other than his long time associate, Cliff Carter. Estes related being told that a convicted murderer named Malcolm Wallace had also been involved.

Estes provided this information to a Texas Grand Jury which apparently declined to pursue it since all the subjects were deceased and not actionable under Texas law.

Estes then approached the United States Justice Department that did respond to him. However, it appears that at the last moment, Estes changed his mind and declined to submit actual concrete evidence in the form of a tape of the Cliff Carter conversation. Carter has named a third party who has heard the tape and this individual has verified Estes' description of the content to researchers.[24]

Estes claims to hold a tape recording of Carter's statements made in 1971 shortly before the deaths of both Cliff Carter and Malcolm Wallace. A friend of Estes, Kyle Brown, is on record as having heard the tape and confirms Estes' conversation with Cliff Carter. Brown's words to Lyle Sardie included the statement: "They prove that Johnson was a cold-blooded killer."

Cliff Carter had replaced Bobby Baker as Secretary of the Democratic National Committee and served as advance man on Johnson's trips even after he took that position. Researchers interested in details on the backgrounds of both Cliff Carter and Malcolm Wallace should become familiar with the material in Glen Sample's *The Men on the Sixth Floor*[25] and the documentation published by Lyle Sardie in support of his film, *LBJ: A Closer Look,* dealing with the Estes information and the Johnson connection.[26]

It may also be worth noting that according to Carter's recorded biography in the Johnson Library collection, Johnson treated Carter as his personal advance man both before and after his ascension to the Presidency. A review of Johnson's daily diary reveals that indeed Carter met with, organized and traveled with Johnson on virtually all his US trips during 1963. The only exception to this appears to be the November trip to Texas, Johnson's home state, where Carter related he had already been relocated and assigned to begin work on the 1964 campaign.

Suggestions for testing and research

1. Johnson's activities in the hours and days after the assassination are a matter of record, although it is possible that pieces of the record have been altered as a matter of national security. Certainly we now know that a large portion of the Air Force One message traffic seems to be missing and the remainder edited. It also seems likely that the rewrite of the log of the National Command Post aircraft approximately one week after the assassination is not a matter of coincidence. A search for the Air Force One record as well as any other source of Executive message traffic on the afternoon of November 22 is vital to the historical record.

2. At this point, it appears highly unlikely that LBJ conceived, organized or led the conspiracy that murdered John Kennedy. However it does appear that he single-handedly drove the major activities that ensured that the conspiracy was not investigated or exposed. Johnson's actions suggest that the Baker-Black connection deserves intense investigation. To date only Mark North has explored this area, in his book *Act of Treason.*[27]

3. Baker was financially and legally associated with Fred Black. Black was one of John Roselli's closest personal friends and next door neighbor to both Baker and Johnson. Black and Baker had met with Johnson in August and Black was intimately aware of the direct association connecting Johnson to the "Serve U Corp" scandal, and could personally have testified to it in court. Black's involvement and his investigation in the "Serve U Corp" scandal must have been well-known to Roselli. Certainly the involvement of Levinson and Sigelbaum made Johnson's exposure known in Las Vegas. Research into the Baker syndicate connections combined with surveillance information on John Roselli and Fred Black could well complete the missing link between the Dallas conspiracy and the executive cover-up of conspiracy.

It is at least within the bounds of possibility that a strategist such as John Roselli could easily have obtained an introduction and extended an offer to Johnson—an offer he could not refuse.

SECTION C

APPENDICES

APPENDIX A: JOHNSON'S DAILY DIARY LOG FOR AUGUST 21, 1963
LBJ MEETS WITH FRED BLACK

#	Time	Activity and Code
1	11:50	To the Capitol, arriving office at 12:15
2	12:15	Meeting w/ Bobby Baker and Mr. Fred Black and Mr. N.A. Storm of North American
3	12:30	Meeting w/ Jim Mathis
4	12:40	Meeting w/ Bob Hilburn
5	12:41	Shook hands w/ Mrs. Morris Jaffe, Jennifer and Judy Jaffee
6	12:50	To Texas Delegation Luncheon, returning to office at S212
7	3:10	Discussion w/ Dale Miller - joined by Walter Jenkins at 3:20 - until 3:45, regarding Melvin Winters' problems w/ Corps of Engineers
8	4:00	Jack Bell
9	4:25 t	Sen. Mansfield - returning his call
10	4:30 t	Joe Stewart
11	4:35	To the White House for dental appointment w/ Dr. Petter
12	5:50	To 4040, arriving at 6:15 pm
13	7:20	To Mayflower Hotel w/ Mrs. Johnson for Dale Miller's reception honoring D.C. Engineer Commissioner, General Clark and Col. Duke
14	8:05	To 4040, arriving at 8:20 pm

Page

SEE VERSO FOR 1...21, ACTIVITY AND CODE

...ould be underscored.

| 411 |

APPENDIX B
CROSSING PATHS IN THE CIA

Names and activities of numerous CIA personnel are presented in Someone Would Have Talked, in fact, so many names and activities that the associations and connections among these individuals may have become confusing. Hopefully the following history will help clarify matters.

IT ALL STARTED WITH **BOB**

Berlin Operating Base was the home base for several of these individuals. Henry Hecksher was stationed there after his service with Army OSS in World War II. He served as acting Chief of Base at the Berlin Station prior to William Harvey's arrival and assumption of that position. Hecksher's 1990 obituary states that he was born in Hamburg, Germany, and became a lawyer and judge there before emigrating to the United States in 1938. He joined the Army during WWII (rising to the rank of captain), participated in the Normandy invasion, and was wounded at Antwerp. He later became an Army intelligence officer and interrogated some of the top Nazis, joining the OSS and going on to head counterintelligence in Berlin after the war.[1] During the 1953 Berlin riots that followed Stalin's death, Hecksher cabled for permission to arm the East Berlin rioters with rifles and stun guns. At that time CD Jackson, Eisenhower's aide, wanted to issue the arms but the request was refused.[2]

In 1946, when Hecksher moved into the OSS, Theodore Shackley was a PFC with Army counter-intelligence in Germany; his Polish language skills were in demand in the new struggle for Eastern Europe. David Morales was serving in the Army in Germany as a corporal (reportedly in Army CIC; counter-intelligence).

When Hecksher moved from OSS into the CIA, he assumed a cover as a State Department employee. David Morales also acquired a State Department cover upon moving from the Army into the CIA. Morales had enlisted in the Army in 1946, and was stationed in Germany after basic training and paratroop training. Exactly when Morales officially moved into the CIA is uncertain, but by 1953 he was enrolled at the University of Maryland and from that point on he operated under his State Department cover.[3]

Shackley had returned to the University of Maryland in 1947 but in 1951, as part of the Army reserve call up during Korea, he returned to Germany as an Army 2nd Lt. He worked in a counter-intelligence unit and was stationed with Lucian Conein who arranged an office and secretary for him. Shackley worked on Polish agent recruiting and penetration.

Chile and the PB/SUCCESS Project

In 1950, David Phillips was in Chile operating a local newspaper. There he was recruited as a CIA contract employee recruiting informants and running intelligence "dangles." Phillips' Latin American experience earned him a place on the CIA's Guatemala project targeting the overthrow of President Arbenz. In his book, *The Night Watch*, Phillips recounted working with E. Howard Hunt on this assignment.

The senior field officer on the project seems to have been Henry Hecksher. While Tracy Barnes was ostensibly in charge of PB/SUCCESS, it appears that he really didn't do much on a day to day basis and matters were largely left in the charge of Haney and his protégé Hecksher. Albert Haney was a CIA officer who had come to the agency from Army counter-intelligence; he was a colonel in the Army CIC. Hecksher went under cover as a coffee buyer and tried to bribe Arbenz's officers, finally recruiting one who reported on an arms buy in Prague. This shipment came in by boat (which Robertson attacked contrary to orders, sinking the wrong ship) and then by train (which Robertson also unsuccessfully attacked). The intelligence on this arms shipment was heavily touted in support of United States' covert action against Arbenz. However, it was eventually found (and not widely reported) that this communist provocation was actually a matter of the Czechs dumping a boatload of junk arms. Frank Holcomb described it as follows: "...once Arbenz's armament officers began to inspect the shipment, they found that everything was virtually useless, a junkyard of cast-off, obsolete antitank guns and artillery, useless in the jungle and the entire array mismatched." This did not prevent Dulles from lobbying over the shipment to force an agreement on proceeding with the coup, presenting Arbenz as having the arms to roll down and seize the Panama Canal.[4]

Hecksher, operating secretly inside Guatemala, personally took David Phillips in country on a fact-finding trip to collect content for his broadcast radio propaganda effort.[5] It seems likely that Hecksher may have been the officer to recommend bringing in David Morales as a paramilitary officer for PB/SUCCESS serving along with his senior, Rip Robertson.

Barnes, Hecksher, Phillips and Morales attained great respect and repute inside the CIA for the success of the Arbenz coup. They were taken to personally debrief President Eisenhower, accompanied by J.C. King and Allen Dulles.

After Guatemala, David Morales moved into an embassy position in Caracas, Venezuela, circa 1955. From there he moved on to Cuba and another State Department cover with the U.S. embassy in 1958. Toward the end of 1958, David Phillips also moved to Havana as an undercover CIA contract employee.

Hecksher moved on from the Guatemala project to become Chief of Station in Laos. He found himself in opposition to the activities of the State Department there and apparently had a good deal of problems with the official U.S. neutrality policies in Laos. He became known for a cable he sent back to CIA headquarters asking "Is HQ still in friendly hands?"[6] His covert opposition to the State Department's activities resulted in a request from Ambassador Horace Smith for his early removal. But Allen Dulles refused to grant the request, allowing Hecksher to serve his full assignment and then moving him down to Thailand to supervise covert trans-border activities in the area of the Golden Triangle.

Following his service in SE Asia, Hecksher went to Japan where he apparently assumed a Station Chief role circa 1959-60. Little is known about his activities there although the Japan assignment is mentioned in his obituary, unlike his later assignment to JM/WAVE in 1963-64.[7]

On to the Cuba Project

By 1960, both Phillips and Morales had returned to the United States from Cuba. They were quickly assigned to the new CIA Cuba project. Morales' files show that he was first reassigned to Washington D.C. and then moved to JM/WAVE HQ in Miami as part of the project JMARC in November, 1960[8].

His assignment in the Cuba Project was counterintelligence; he recruited, assembled and trained the exiles that were to form the new security force for the FRD organization and to establish its anticipated civilian administration in Cuba after Castro was ousted. After the failure at the Bay of Pigs, a number of these individuals would form a covert security/intelligence group operating in Miami, initially under Morales. The Cuban exile in charge of the group was Joaquin Sanjenis. This group has been unofficially tagged as "Operation 40" by some of those in contact with Sanjenis or by individuals writing about its members.

Other names of interest on the initial Cuba Project included David Phillips, who worked out of Washington and Miami. Phillips' stated specialty was propaganda and psychological operations, and when Howard Hunt experienced conflicts in his political action function with the exile leadership, Phillips took over that role as well.

In the area of paramilitary operations, Rip Robertson joined the former PB/SUCCESS alumni. However the officer in charge of paramilitary operations may have been an individual not found in the official (or the CIA histories) of the Cuba project, one Carl Jenkins. According to papers submitted to the ARRB, Jenkins reportedly had served in the Marine Corp in WWII, and in the early 1950's became a CIA paramilitary, survival, evasion and escape trainer for the CIA. From 1955-1958 he served as an instructor for paramilitary tactics and resistance and trained cadre for both the Thai Border Police and the Chinese Nationalist Special Forces. He was also training and operations officer for maritime infiltration and worked in Indonesia, Malaysia, and the Philippines.

Jenkins came into the Cuba project in 1960 and served with it until the Bay of Pigs; he performed selection and training of paramilitary cadre, selected officers, and managed small teams and individual agents in maritime infiltration of Cuba. (More about Jenkins' activities can be found in Appendix J. The material described here and in that Appendix is taken from documents provided to the ARRB pertaining to Jenkins.)

In general terms, it appears that while Morales dealt with the development and deployment of security and intelligence forces in conjunction with the landing, Jenkins selected and prepared paramilitary cadre for small, individual missions in advance and support of the invasion force. There are also documents which connect him to at least one Castro assassination project, involving a small team using rifles. After the Bay of Pigs, Jenkins became Special Warfare Advisor to I Corps in Danang, South Vietnam prior to returning for further service with Cuban exiles in 1963.

William Harvey was selected to run Task Force W, the CIA element of the follow-on Mongoose Project, and he brought along his own special project (ZR/RIFLE, an Executive Action effort approved by Richard Helms which was extended to include the Castro assassination activities of John Roselli). Ted Shackley came to JM/WAVE to serve as Deputy of Operations. When Harvey was dismissed from his position after the Cuban Missile Crisis, Desmond Fitzgerald was brought in to run the CIA effort.

After the Bay of Pigs, David Phillips was assigned to Mexico City, working in a counterintelligence role against the Cuban and Soviet consulates and in general performing intelligence activities for the station. In 1963 Fitzgerald recruited Phillips to become Chief of Cuban Operations and Phillips began a broader coordination of activities and operations with JM/WAVE; this included support for operations being organized by of David Morales.

1963 saw the inauguration of a new and highly confidential project. The CIA cryptonym for its activities in the project was AM/WORLD. In general terms the project involved a new attempt to establish an autonomous Cuban leadership which could assemble the military force and political clout to produce a coup inside Cuba and create the conditions for the United States to come to the aid of a new, non-communist Cuban leadership. Manuel Artime (AM/BIDDY-1) was a key figure in this project and a small task group was organized to support AM/WORLD; it operated out of compartmentalized facilities in the Miami Station (LORKE) and conducted activities in venues ranging from New York to Mexico City to Spain. Henry Hecksher was attached to AM/WORLD as Artime's case officer (among other responsibilities). Carl Jenkins was brought back to oversee paramilitary support and serve as case officer to Artime's second in command, Rolando Quintero (AMJAVA-4).[9]

Jenkins and Hecksher were also involved in the Artime's initial travel to Europe for contact with Rolando Cubela (AM/LASH). These

AM/WORLD activities began in mid-1963 and continued through 1964. Very few CIA station personnel were allowed knowledge of the AM/WORLD project; in Mexico City the only officer authorized for AM/WORLD was David Phillips.[10]

Careers After Cuba

In 1965, David Morales appears to have assumed an AID cover to perform unknown assignments operating out of JM/WAVE. According to Morales' comments to his friend Carbajal, this included the campaign to locate and neutralize Che Guevara in Bolivia. Morales' army cover documents do show him as being assigned to Bolivia from 1965-67, which supports Reuben Carbajal's information. After Bolivia, Morales' next assignment was Laos.

In 1966, Ted Shackley left JM/WAVE to take charge of the CIA's secret war in Laos. He had been highly recommended by Fitzgerald and by 1977 had recruited both Tom Clines and Morales (of his former JM/WAVE staff) into Laos. Morales became base commander at Pakse, a covert operations base focused on paramilitary operations within Laos. Morales' base was known as a key location for launching political action missions and military operations against the Ho Chi Min trail. It was also reputed to be a key drug transfer point for transportation out of Laos, especially in 1966 and 1967 after serious Mekong floods closed off the normal foot trails. Pakse was also a key station for establishing civilian cover for U.S. military operations in Laos.

David Phillips left his Mexico City station assignment to become Chief of Station in the Dominican Republic, a challenging position following United States intervention in that country. And from 1965 to 1966, Carl Jenkins served as Senior Advisor for the Dominican Republic National Police, specializing in counterinsurgency program design and training. After that, Jenkins performed a similar role for the Republic of Nicaragua from 1966-86.

By 1968, Ted Shackley had become Chief of Station in South Vietnam and Morales again followed him the next year, assuming regional responsibilities in the II Corps area, based out of Nha Trang. Although reports associate him with the infamous Phoenix Program, there is nothing in his official records that supports those suggestions.

Jenkins joined the crowd in SE Asia by 1969, going to Laos to serve there until 1973 and becoming Chief of Base for South Laos. He supposedly requested early retirement at the end of hostilities in SE

Asia. However, new documents show that he was still performing some activities for the CIA as late as May 1979. Further details regarding Jenkins are reviewed in Appendix J.

The Latin America Front

Morales and Jenkins had been the first of the JM/WAVE alumni to move to the Latin American fight against Communist expansion. By the early 1970's the list would include Tom Clines at the Chile desk in CIA HQ, while David Phillips had moved to Washington to become Chief of the Cuban Operations Group Western Hemisphere covering all of Latin and South America. He would remain in this position during the CIA's effort to remove Chilean President Allende, eventually being named by the Church Committee as the CIA officer in charge of Track 2 of the Allende project—the track involving CIA efforts to produce a military coup.

Henry Hecksher became Chief of Station in Chile during the CIA's massive effort against the Allende government. He retained his outspoken manner, taking exception to the lack of resources being allocated to the project against Allende and calling for sterner measures. One of his particular targets was a supporter of Allende within the Chilean armed forces, a General Schneider. He also worked separately with the DIA on coup plots against Allende. Reuben Carbajal relates that his friend Dave Morales spoke of having arrived in Chile just in time to support the CIA move against Allende; Morales also spoke of personally killing a Chilean General. Although it may be sheer coincidence, General Schneider was mysteriously killed in the midst of Hecksher's crusade against him.

Following his return from SE Asia, Morales was assigned to Latin America and served as a counterinsurgency advisor to the ultra right-wing military establishments in Argentina, Panama, Paraguay and Uruguay in the period 1971 to 1975. It was during this period that the infamous Condor alliance of right wing governments emerged —involving Paraguay, Uruguay, Argentina, Brazil—and eventually Chile.

Henry Hecksher retired in 1971 after his Chilean service. David Phillips was promoted to Chief of Western Hemisphere (replacing Ted Shackley) but took early retirement in 1975, at the peak of his career.

David Morales also retired in 1975 and died in 1978, shortly before Tony Sforza. Sforza is known to have operated within Cuba and to have conducted JM/WAVE exfiltration missions for Morales. His contact for one such mission involved passing information to David Phillips in Mexico City. Sforza (cryptonym SLOMAN) had been a major CIA covert operative inside Cuba and there is reason to speculate that he used the alias Frank Stevens, known as Enrique inside Cuba, where he operated under the cover of being a professional gambler. If so, he is associated with at least one major CIA Castro assassination attempt and at one point he served as case officer for Morales' AMOT group—an attempt verified in a newly located document and one which was apparently withheld from the Church Committee.[11]

Interestingly enough, another minor name from JM/WAVE would become a media blockbuster a few years later: Edwin Wilson. A number of names mentioned in this appendix would surface again during the Wilson saga, but that's another story. Interested readers might start with *The Death Merchant: The Rise and Fall of Edwin P. Wilson*, by Joseph Goulden. For reference, it appears that Goulden assigns the pseudonym "Brad Rockford" to Carl Jenkins and relates that Quintero went to him for advice when he first became suspicious of Wilson.[12, 13]

APPENDIX C
BARNES, HUNT AND FRIENDS

With the comments provided by readers of the research manuscript of *Someone Would Have Talked*, it became clear that further background information needed to be provided on other career CIA officers involved in Cuban affairs. One of the most senior was Tracy Barnes. He played a key role in CIA's Cuba Project, serving as second to Richard Bissell; next, he took a follow-on assignment to head the CIA's somewhat mysterious Domestic Operations division. It was in this latter position that he recruited E. Howard Hunt to serve as his senior covert operations officer.

Much of the following information is provided courtesy of the intelligence literature research of Pat Speer, especially the available public history of CIA Domestic Operations. The possible link between Domestic Operations and the Domestic Contact Service also raises the possibility of another point of contact with Lee Oswald in1963.

During World War II, Tracy Barnes served in the OSS in Europe, and gained the confidence of Allen Dulles while working with him in an unsuccessful project to obtain an early German surrender. Barnes became one of the first generation of ex-OSS officers who formed the core and leadership of the Central Intelligence Agency when he joined in 1947. With the beginning of the Korean conflict, Barnes joined the CIA as Chief of Political and Psychological Department Staff and devoted much of his energy to CIA operations in that conflict. Years later David Phillips would write that Barnes' first attempt at a report on the successful PB/SUCCESS project in Guatemala had to be entirely reworked (at Dulles' direction) because it had consisted primarily of Barnes' remarks about operations in Korea.[1]

Howard Hunt worked as third in command under Barnes in the Guatemala project; his colleagues in that endeavor included Henry Hecksher, David Phillips, David Morales, and Rip Robertson. Morales' later career shows definite signs of being fast tracked and it may well be that Barnes had something to do with that. It is commonly accepted that Barnes' own fast track within the CIA was heavily influenced by Allen Dulles' sponsorship. At the time he was assigned to the Guatemala project, Barnes was already a CIA supergrade officer (GS18), reporting to Frank Wisner (ADP) who reported to Bissell. Barnes' own next level subordinate report was J.C. King.

There is no doubt that Barnes' career was "made" by the CIA's success in Guatemala and he was personally honored with other PB/SUCCESS personnel in a victory presentation/meeting with President Eisenhower. Rip Robertson seems to have been left out of this celebration; at the time he was on J.C. King's black list for his violation of orders and independent military actions during the project.

After Guatemala, Barnes was assigned as Chief of Station for Germany in Frankfurt and later moved on to become COS in London from 1958 to 1959. He returned to the United States to take the number two position (ADP, Assistant Director of Plans) in the Cuba Project under Bissell. He recruited Hunt, Phillips and Morales into the Cuba project and by the end of 1960 Hunt and Morales were resident in Miami with Phillips, spending much of their time either there or in Washington.

Most sources indicate that Bissell left most of the Cuba Project operational tasks to Barnes (as Hecksher had picked up most of the operational management in Guatemala). It appears that Bissell and Barnes were the individuals who kept abreast of the various Castro assassination projects then in progress. At first glance it seems somewhat strange that Barnes would have this knowledge about such "black" projects, one of which was being run completely separately outside the CIA with John Roselli. Upon closer investigation, it seems that Barnes had a serious history with CIA assassination projects.

Barnes and Helms were the two senior CIA officers who repeatedly dealt with political assassinations, entering into this arena before Richard Helms initiated the relatively limited and conservative ZR/RIFLE project with William Harvey. David Wise, describes Barnes's approval of a plan to disable an Iraqi colonel, a suspected communist sympathizer, with a poison handkerchief.[2] During the tenure of Allen Dulles as CIA Director, such covert projects were proposed to Barnes and Helms who would determine whether they should be brought to the attention of Bissell. It was Bissell's decision whether or not to proceed, and whether or not to inform Dulles (or later McCone) and risk the necessity of informing the President at the cost of "deniability." Based on this approach, many of the Agency's more radical deeds (including assassination projects) seem to have been approved by either Barnes or Helms without specific instructions or approval from above.

This incident with the Iraqi colonel may tell us a good deal about both CIA internal politics and the personalities of Bissell and Barnes as compared to Helms. The Church Report, *Alleged Assassination Attempts On Foreign Leaders*, states quite clearly that Barnes approved the action against the Iraqi colonel on behalf of Bissell.[3] However in Helms' autobiography,[4] he relates that at the time he was acting as Bissell's deputy; Barnes was attached as a deputy in charge of Operation Zapata (the Cuba Project); and that Helms had nothing to do with Zapata. Helms, who had been above Barnes under Wisner, was highly displeased with Barnes' achieving equal status under Bissell. It is apparent from Helms' book that Africa and the Middle East were his own areas of oversight. Elsewhere (and throughout his many hours of congressional committee testimony) Helms expressed his skepticism of assassination as policy. Helms also apparently believed he was bypassed in favor of Bissell because of his reluctance to engage in the more reckless activities favored by Dulles, Bissell and Barnes. This suggests that Helms was reluctant to put his name on an assassination approval even within his own area of responsibility, whereas Barnes was willing to do so. Apparently Barnes was using risky actions to score political points while Helms was standing aside, secretly hoping Barnes would eventually come to grief through his "cowboy" behavior—as he did in the Bay of Pigs.

The Church Committee report documents many incidents where policy was made at the level of the DDP. One of the most infamous incidents occurred on March 31, 1961, where CIA headquarters approved the passage of three carbine guns to dissidents in the Dominican Republic as a token sign of support for their planned assassination of Trujillo. Although the carbines apparently were not fired in the assassination, one was found in the possession of one of the assassins.[5]

What was shocking to the Church Committee was that on April 5 CIA headquarters sent a cable to the Dominican station requesting them to ask the military consul dealing with the dissidents not to communicate with the State Department yet. The military consul testified that he did not tell State because he assumed it already knew. As a result, the State Department was not told until weeks later, when the plan was already far beyond the stopping point. According to an interview with Bissell reported in the book *Spymasters*, the official who approved the transfer of the carbines was Tracy Barnes. When confronted about

Barnes' behavior, Bissell replied, rather disingenuously, "I think almost certainly that the State Department would have been consulted."[6]

It was Bissell, Deputy Director for Plans (and Barnes' boss in the Cuba Project) who originated the idea of contacting "gambling interests" regarding a "sensitive operation against Fidel Castro." Although Bissell denied any knowledge of Castro assassination projects to the CIA's own Inspector General, confirmation of his role is now available from numerous sources including Volume X, State Department memo from May 14, 1962 (used in a briefing for Attorney General Robert Kennedy). This suggests that Bissell and very likely Barnes were at the center of virtually every CIA assassination project of the early 1960's, perhaps explaining Barnes' bland reassurances to Howard Hunt that everything was under control (a response given when Hunt kept proposing that Castro should be assassinated). It may also explain why Barnes was very much aware of *special circumstances* that would have found the Brigade arriving in a leaderless and chaotic Cuba. That would help make a great deal more sense out of the planned invasion. It might also help explain why Bissell apparently ignored predictions of failure from his staff.

On April 9, 1961, Esterline and Hawkins met with Bissell at his home and went over a host of problems, concluding that "*A landing at the Bay of Pigs could not cause Castro's overthrow and would result in the loss of the landing force within a short time after landing.*" Bissell's seemingly inexplicable behavior is covered at length by Don Bohning in the second chapter of his 2005 book, *The Castro Obsession.*[7]

Another indication of Castro assassination projects not revealed to the Church Committee is found in a 1969 memorandum from Miami Chief of Station Anthony Ponchay. It refers to Plan RAPHAEL, related to the assassination of Fidel Castro. Nothing further is known about the date or circumstances of Plan RAPHAEL.[8]

The failure of the Bay of Pigs invasion had a dramatic impact on Barnes' career and reportedly affected him so severely that for a period of several months he became physically ill. This is reminiscent of David Phillips' own physical problems immediately following the failure of the invasion. Although described as normally very even tempered and somewhat detached by Evan Thomas in his CIA history *The Very Best Men,* Thomas reports that Barnes came to speak very strongly against JFK and apparently developed a considerable personal animosity towards him.[9]

Barnes certainly seems not to have dealt with his own apparent failure to properly brief UN Ambassador Stevenson on the invasion. Or for the media disaster that resulted from a Barnes-Phillips plan which landed a purported Cuban Air Force B-26 in Florida (supposedly flown by a member of the Cuban Air Force). The local press quickly discovered this was a CIA disinformation ploy and exposed the US participation in the air attacks on Cuba. In fact, it was the lack of a proper Stevenson briefing and the unveiling of this fake B-26 fraud in the media that forced Stevenson to confront JFK and very likely led to Kennedy's canceling of additional air strikes—the action which Barnes aggressively asserted was the single cause of the failure of the Bay of Pigs invasion.

It well may be that Barnes' uncompromising rhetoric against JFK was at the root of the widespread belief among Cuba Project alumnae that the failure at the Bay of Pigs was solely due to Kennedy's supposed cowardice in not committing air strikes or troops. A relatively recent study published by the CIA itself refers to Barnes' total rejection of the CIA Inspector General's report and his contention that the invasion (JM/MATE) was not "allowed to succeed." The report describes Barnes' denial of the weaknesses in the plan, especially the lack of post landing plans. It refers to Barnes' "delusion" that the invasion failed only due to the lack of ongoing air strikes and would otherwise have succeeded. This analysis specifically identifies Barnes as the single officer who should have had the experience to apply the lessons learned from success in Guatemala to the Cuba Project, and faults him for not doing so. It also speculates that Barnes and possibly Bissell placed too much faith in Castro being eliminated through assassination in conjunction with the invasion.[10]

After the Bay of Pigs failure Barnes apparently was first shunted aside to miscellaneous activities for the remainder of 1961; it is unclear whether his medical problems took him off active duty for any period of time. His assignments are also unclear until he was assigned to head a new Domestic Operations Division in February of 1963, relates that Barnes held a meeting at CIA headquarters in 1961 that floated the idea of using a cigarette factory in Africa as a cover.[11] Harvey's deputy was in attendance at the meeting. This suggests that even before the formation of the Domestic Operations Division, Barnes was assuming responsibility for CIA cover companies. Further corroboration for this is found in Victor Marchetti's book *The CIA and the Cult of Intelligence*.[11]

He also mentions that the Double-Chek Corporation was used to pay the pensions of the dead Alabama National Guard pilots. We know that one of Barnes' duties was payments to the families of the National Guard volunteers killed at the Bay of Pigs; this suggests that Barnes was involved with Double-Chek for some time after the invasion. The *Rockefeller Report* states that "the creation, operation, and liquidation of operating proprietaries is closely controlled by high Agency officials. All such projects must have the approval of the Deputy Director of Operations (formerly Plans) *or his assistant* (Emphasis supplied)."[12] Barnes was undoubtedly involved in the creation of front companies for a variety of purposes, both before and following the Cuba Project.

It also appears that in some cases his association with front companies and with assassination projects overlapped. In *Secret History*, Trento relates a conversation with Robert Crowley, one of his key sources. The incident took place in August, 1961.[13]

Further details of the cigarette factory story show Justin O'Donnell, William Harvey's deputy, was at a high-level meeting where Barnes surveyed current covert operations. When Barnes began discussing the purchase of a cigarette factory in Africa, O'Donnell exclaimed "What in God's name are we gonna do with it?" presumably as a way of giving Barnes grief, since he knew that it was a cover for an assassination project.

According to John Sherwood, another source cited by Trento, O'Donnell was out on the street in three weeks. This strongly suggests that Barnes was every bit the Agency "true believer" and that he wouldn't put up with criticism. It also suggests that Barnes was still operating as Bissell's assistant as late as August, 1961.[14] This "true believer" view of Barnes is also advocated in *Death In Washington* by Donald Freed.[15] Freed presents Barnes as an extremist very much like Hunt, who was recruited by Barnes to work in Domestic Operations in 1963. Later, as part of his Domestic Operations assignment, Barnes also became responsible for the disposition and sales of surplus CIA materiel out of all such proprietary/front companies. The full nature of Barnes' new Domestic Operations Division is undocumented; it seems likely that it included the responsibility for intelligence collection through the previously existing CIA Domestic Contact Service (the Domestic Contact Service made use of both George De Mohrenschildt and Clay Shaw). Clines' book states that the Domestic Contact Service was once called the Foreign Nationalities Branch and conducted debriefings and recruitment of foreign nationals who were living in the United States. By 1992, the recruitment of foreign nationals and National Collections work (targeting U.S. citizens as resources) were both done by the Domestic Resources Division. This merger may well have first occurred with the advent of the Domestic Operations Division under Barnes.

Freed describes the involvement of Barnes Domestic Operations organization with a variety of illegal domestic front companies and projects including the FPCC in New Orleans. This is particularly suggestive as Barnes has also been connected to the QK/ENCHANT domestic CIA project along with Hunt. Clay Shaw was cleared for participation in QK/ENCHANT, and recently available documents show that in late 1960 a CIA background investigation was requested on Guy Bannister and Associates in New Orleans. The request discloses that Bannister's firm was being considered as a cover company, and the related project is listed as QK/ENCHANT. Based on information given to the ARRB, it now appears that QK/ENCHANT may have been a generic cryptonym for both "permission to approach" and "utilization for cleared contact purposes." Clearly it relates to the use of approved individuals and companies as contact covers for intelligence activities.

Given that we now have every reason to believe that Lee Oswald was interviewed and monitored by the CIA upon his return from Russia, it seems that such contacts would likely have been performed by the Domestic Contact Service.

By 1963, Domestic Operations might well have been the starting point for Lee Oswald being considered as an asset in specific CIA intelligence collection projects ("dangles") such as the documented 1963 project targeting the FPCC, first in the United States and then in Latin America. It is certainly possible that Oswald was used in a minor fashion for FPCC intelligence collection, something which grew into a much more aggressive propaganda program in New Orleans and then into an extension of that project in Mexico City. Such an extension would likely have been coordinated by the new Cuban Affairs officer, David Phillips, and monitored by Angleton's CI/SIG internal security group.

Such a scenario would go a long way towards explaining the incident that initiated the well-reported court battle between Howard Hunt and Mark Lane. This case involved a purported internal CIA memorandum reported by Trento. According to Trento, in interviews with Lane and

Russell, the memo came from Angleton and referred to the possibility that CIA would have to explain Howard Hunt's presence in Dallas in November of 1963 (the precise date and location of Hunt's presence were not stated in the memo). Certainly Trento was well connected to CIA sources; he co-authored a book, *Widows: Four American Spies, The Wives They Left Behind and the KGB's Crippling of American Intelligence*, with CIA veteran William Corson.[16] He also had reportedly written *The Secret History of The CIA* with Angleton's blessing. It makes no sense for CIA officers (who denied that they personally had ever heard of such a memo) to continue to associate with Trento (after he'd testified under oath to the memo in the Lane/Marchetti vs. Hunt trial) — unless the rumor had indeed had some element of truth, unless it was being by used Angleton, for purposes known only to himself?

Given our knowledge of a new Domestic Operations division, projects targeting the FPCC both inside the U.S. and beyond, and Howard Hunt's position as "Chief of Covert Operations" for Domestic Operations, Hunt's presence in Dallas in November 1963 might make a good deal of sense. It would not be a great surprise to find Hunt in Dallas, perhaps trying to make contact with a highly visible FPCC advocate who had just returned from trying to obtain a visa to travel to Cuba from Mexico City. It also makes a great deal more sense of the reported observation by Anthony Veciana of David Phillips in the presence of someone resembling Lee Oswald shortly before Oswald's appearance in Mexico City at the Cuban embassy. Intelligence collection at both the Cuban and Soviet consulates was one of Phillips' primary responsibilities. At the time of Oswald's visit there were a number of active intelligence operations going on against Cuban consulate personnel, including recruitment operations in progress against both Veciana's own cousin and Sylvia Duran.

Chapter Forty-Five of *Ultimate Sacrifice* describes an interview conducted with Antonio Veciana. In the interview Veciana relates that "Bishop" had him fly from Miami to Dallas for a meeting which ended up being no longer than ten minutes. The topic of this meeting was killing Castro. Veciana related that when he showed up, Bishop was already talking to a young man whom he later recognized as Lee Oswald. Veciana quotes Oswald as "talking about something we can do to kill Castro."[17] This sounds remarkably like Oswald's remarks as related by Doctor Frank Silva at Eastern Louisiana State Hospital only weeks before. At this distance it is virtually impossible for us to grasp the full relationship that Bishop (Phillips) may have had with Oswald or Oswald's exact assignments and goals in his trip to Mexico City. However, it is certainly clear that his Mexico City trip was not accurately or fully described to the Warren Commission.

Peter Dale Scott relates that David Atlee Phillips was cross-posted as Chief of Cuban Operations in Mexico City, and as Chief of Psychological Operations (i.e. propaganda) in Miami at JM/WAVE. Scott also feels it very possible that Phillips held down three posts in 1963, also serving as a member of Angleton's Special Affairs Counter-intelligence (SAS/CI) staff.[18]

Like Phillips, Hunt is known to have been wearing several hats in 1963. We now know that Hunt was cross-posted to provide support to some of his previously established exile contacts as they were being used in the new autonomous group project being set up off shore by Robert Kennedy's Cuba team. And as further reported by Peter Dale Scott, Hunt seems to have had yet another posting: to assist Allen Dulles in his book and media efforts. "Dulles had resented his being made to take the blame for the Bay of Pigs fiasco: "He thought other people should be resigning before he did, and made it clear that he was thinking of one person in particular, Robert Kennedy".

Peter Dale Scott has written that "Before the assassination, Dulles had fought back in the media, leaking his resentment against the Kennedys to the sympathetic ears of Charles J. V. Murphy of *Fortune* magazine, part of Henry Luce's *Time-Life* empire. Murphy's pro-Dulles apologia, *Cuba: The Record Set Straight,*[19] also served to promote escalated U.S. involvement in Indochina, just before Kennedy's first major Vietnam decision. In this counter-attack, Dulles had Agency support. Dulles asked to have one of his CIA proteges, E. Howard Hunt, go over Murphy's article in detail; and Hunt was accordingly instructed to do so." But Hunt's biographer Ted Szulc says that Hunt was asked to assist Dulles in writing a book, *The Craft of Intelligence,* which Dulles "wrote" following his involuntary retirement in 1961.[20] Just how long it took to complete the book is not clear, but it was published in 1963. Certainly the book would have given Hunt the opportunity to spend many long hours (presumably on company time) with Dulles, his former boss. As Peter Dale Scott states in *The Three Oswald Deceptions,* originally published in: *Deep Politics II: Essays on Oswald, Mexico and Cuba.*

"If Hunt was close to Dulles, he was even closer to his own protégé, David Atlee Phillips. In fact it was probably through Hunt that Phillips became an active player in a small clique within the CIA hierarchy who were almost autonomous in their operational capabilities, an OSS brotherhood of whom Allen Dulles, inside the Agency or out, was the acknowledged leader."[21]

"What merits further investigation is that members of this brotherhood played key roles on both sides of the Oswald phase one- phase two dialectic. The key to Dulles' "agency-within-the-Agency," as Aarons and Loftus have called it, was the power Dulles had conferred on his close friend Jim Angleton. As Counterintelligence Chief Angleton was authorized to spy on the rest of the CIA, and maintain a CI network of assets in other branches. The close connection between Dulles and Angleton endured well beyond Dulles' departure from the Agency."[22]

Barnes was dismissed by Richard Helms in 1966. The reasons for his dismissal don't appear in print. However in Helms' biography, The Man Who Kept The Secrets, Richard Bissell is confronted by Thomas Powers with a story that Barnes told to a friend.[23] The story relates that Bissell had tried to have Helms sent to London right before the Bay of Pigs. The picture painted is that Bissell and Barnes were "cowboys" and that Helms was too conservative for their idea of the DDP (Deputy Director of Plans). When confronted with this story, Bissell told Powers that he thought that Barnes was the one who went to Dulles and tried to have Helms shipped out, suggesting Helms may have had both professional and personal objections to Barnes. It is a matter of record that Helms became Director on June 30, 1966, and Barnes was out of the CIA by July of that same year.

A wilderness of mirrors

In order to understand Lee Oswald in New Orleans, it is important to understand the anti-FPCC joint projects of the FBI and CIA and beyond that the specific role of Barnes and Domestic Operations—not to mention the QK/ENCHANT infrastructure. In order to understand Oswald in Mexico City it is critical to understand Des Fitzgerald's love of false flag and "forward leaning" political psychops projects (such as he allowed Edward Lansdale to conduct in the Philippines).

Combining Fitzgerald's inclinations, Phillips' skills in using "the big lie," and Phillips' intelligence mission against Cuban and Soviet consulate personnel in Mexico City may give us the insight we need to understand what went on in Mexico City in the fall of 1963. In addition, this same context also lends further credibility to certain remarks of Richard Nagell:

1. Nagell's first CIA contacts in the U.S. were with Domestic Intelligence (Domestic Contact Service) in Los Angeles. The CIA-verified names in his notebook provide some interesting definition of that organization.

2. Nagell asked rhetorically if Phillips was a mere accomplice in the "N-matter"; clearly Nagell knew of Phillips, but was unsure of Phillips' real agenda. It may be that none of the individual players was fully aware of the total evolution of Oswald's various roles and uses.

3. Nagell stated that he had done favors for Fitzgerald. This likely occurred in Japan, where Nagell would have crossed paths with Henry Hecksher. Hecksher started his career at Berlin Operating Base and is a very probable candidate for Nagell's mysterious CIA contact in Mexico City, a man he would only designate as "Bob."

These relationships may well explain certain strange remarks and actions of Angleton, including the gossip (per Angleton) that Hunt was used in a very complicated counter intelligence ploy, one involving seemingly crazy and not fully understood exile movements in which nobody could tell who was who and in which everything and everyone seemed to be penetrated by Castro agents (or, according to Martino and Nagell, exiles who were playing everyone against each other). In that context we gain additional insight from Peter Dale Scott:

> "An even more dramatic allegation, also strongly disputed, is that Hunt was in Dallas on November 22, 1963, at the time of the assassination. According to reporter Joseph Trento, a secret CIA memo of 1966, said to have been initialed by Angleton and Helms, emphasized the importance of keeping Hunt's presence there a secret, and suggested a cover story to provide Hunt with an alibi. According to author Dick Russell, Trento later told him that Angleton himself was the source of the story, and arranged for a copy of the internal CIA memo to be delivered to him, as

well as the House Committee."[23]

If this is true, Angleton's role is sinister, and apparently part of a cover-up, whether the memo is real (and Hunt was in Dallas), or whether it was disinformation (and Hunt was elsewhere). Trento told Russell he understood from Angleton that Hunt was in Dallas because "of a serious counterintelligence problem with the [CIA] Cubans," some of whom were known to be "penetrated by Castro's intelligence." Such a remark would be entirely consistent with Angleton's long-term effort to focus conspiracy investigators on Cuban and even Soviet agents–suggesting that Angleton either suspected or had actual evidence of a far more "domestic" conspiracy.

APPENDIX D

THE WAY OF JM/WAVE

Readers will find CIA crypts annotated in this appendix as an aid to reading the related source document exhibits. Without them, the documents (as intended) loose a great deal of meaning.

One of the most significant turning points in the secret war against Cuba was the CIA's decision not to commit to an ongoing operational involvement with some of the most aggressive and experienced exiles and exile groups. This decision may have begun with good intentions early in the Cuba Project, based on concerns for operational security and control. Even so, the expansion of the project up to the Bay of Pigs clearly made security laughable (witness the coverage of the build up and training camps in the Miami papers). Worse, the failure to coordinate the "invasion" with strong local resistance groups led to these groups being totally exposed to the mass arrests which broke the back of the anti-Castro resistance within Cuba in 1961. This led to such significant mistrust of the CIA that eventually the most aggressive exiles rejected any thought of knowing cooperation with the CIA and major amounts of JM/WAVE resources then had to be devoted simply to monitoring these individuals and groups. This lack of access to trained or at least experienced personnel after the Bay of Pigs led to JM/WAVE bringing in Army Special Forces trainers in an effort to train and build operational exile teams; the comments of these teams' trainers and their mission records were far less than encouraging.

However, in the same period, exiles who "blooded" themselves in independent operational missions into Cuba were frequently successful with only minimal supplies and resources. In 1962 and early 1963 the mission records of groups such as the DRE, Alpha 66, and Commandos L were far better than those of the JM/WAVE controlled teams. While this situation has long been a topic of exile complaint, the true scope of this Agency policy failure is only now becoming apparent with increased access to JM/WAVE operational documents and summary reports.

A list of the armed exile military organizations groups potentially most dangerous to Fidel Castro in the early 1960's would likely begin with Unidad Revolucianario/UR, formed within Cuba in 1960 and composed of participants from 27 independent groups including Movimiento Liberation, MRD, MRR, Rescate and 30 November. Apparently Rafael Diaz Hanscomb of the MRR initiated this effort at unification even after being advised against doing so by Antonio Varona, the leader of the "Frente," who would later become the leader of the CIA-sponsored Cuban Revolutionary Council/CRC). Early in 1961 Diaz made a trip from Cuba (cryptonym PB/RUMEM) to the United States (cryptonym PB/PRIME) to obtain external support via contacts at Sinclair Oil. During meetings with U.S. Government officials and the CIA (crypt KU/BARK) the UR was given pledges of supplies, and a plan to establish and staff an office in Miami was developed. At this point the chief leaders of Unidad were Diaz Hascomb (Cuban General Coordinator), Andrews Zayas (Civil Coordinator), and Major Sori Martin (Military Coordinator).

The first materials to be provided from the U.S. arrived in Cuba in late February 1961 and by mid-March the CIA thought Unidad had developed into a significant anti-Castro movement, widely penetrating Cuban police and military forces. Unidad was preparing plans for coordinated uprisings, a rebellion within the Cuban Navy and other operations. But UNIDAD advised the CIA that it was not yet ready to support any actual military action against Castro and that it had so advised its own Cuban network. Unidad was subsequently not advised of the impending Bay of Pigs invasion; as a result, it was not only unable to provide any support but were surprised and extensively damaged by the Castro round-ups. These round-ups occurred as a result of the invasion and Castro's awareness of a planned U.S. backed action against Cuba. A Cuban security forces raid in March of 1961 resulted in the arrest of approximately 38 leading resistance figures; this loss also included the capture and later execution of the UR military coordinator, Sori Martin. The reasons for this disaster (other than a generally heightened Cuban security environment) were unclear, but UR leaders felt that one of the members (Sergio Alonso) of a CIA infiltration team (Jean III) had become an informant to Cuban G-2.[1]

Alberto Fernandez of UNIDAD

Fernandez (CIA crypt AM/DENIM-1) was a graduate of Princeton, attended prep school with John F. Kennedy, and was the Director of the Sugar Stabilization Board of the Cuban Sugar Institute in 1958 and 1959 until his opposition to Castro and his counterrevolutionary activities led to his exile. Initially he had been a strong 26th of July supporter and reportedly raised over $2 million dollars for the movement. An FBI memo dated October 1958 lists companies that he had solicited for payments to Castro and his rebel army. These included United Fruit, Lone Star Cement, Freeport Sulphur, Czarnikow Rionda, Chase Manhattan Bank, King Ranch (Robert Kleberg), Standard Oil, Hilton Hotels, The Texas Company and International Harvester as well as various sugar companies. The FBI report also mentions that Kleberg as well as executives from The Texas Company, Freeport Sulphur, and Lone Star Cement all met with the Assistant Secretary of State over these solicitations from Fidel Castro. In the report Fernandez is mentioned as a contact man for the rebels, demanding tribute for Castro's movement. After the revolution Fernandez vehemently turned against Castro while apparently retaining many of his prior connections to high-level American businessmen.[2]

Clearly, Fernandez enjoyed significant political and financial connections within the United States. He had the confidence of major Cuban businessmen and their commitment of major financing to do whatever needed to be done to oust Castro. Indeed, while the CIA's Cuban Project was still in its infancy, Fernandez was contacting the CIA himself, arranging for intelligence to be brought out of Cuba, and laying the groundwork for a UNIDAD-led counterrevolution.

Much of what we know about Fernandez, his boat the *Tejana III* and related subjects initially came from FBI and CIA contact reports with Michael J. P. "Jack" Malone, Vice President of Czarnikow-Rionda of 106 Wall Street in New York. More recently, the full CIA file on Fernandez and the UNIDAD organization has become available and provides extensive detail in support of Malone's informant data (see Appendix D Exhibits).

Michael "Jack" Malone had worked in Cuba prior to the Castro revolution and had extensive Cuban business and media contacts. Interestingly, one of his activities in Cuba was to prevent the exposure and possible arrest of CIA undercover operative David Phillips. In 1959 Phillips was working a public relations cover inside Cuba under the name Choaden. In August of 1959, several of Malone's Cuban contacts had passed on the information that Choaden was known to be a "KUBARK" operative, and Malone relayed this to the CIA. The Agency performed a risk evaluation and pulled Phillips out of Havana temporarily and then allowed him to return briefly before leaving for good.[3] The memoranda on this incident confirm that "Jack" Malone was personally acquainted with Phillips, and had even written a review mentioning Phillips' performance in a play put on by the Havana Little Theatre and then joined Phillips for drinks at the Hotel Nacional. Following that, one of Malone's Cuban friends advised him that he had better be careful as he had been out with an "American agent" and that could get Malone in real trouble. The editor of the *Times of Havana*, to whom both Malone and Phillips contributed, also warned Malone that it was known that Choaden was KUBARK and told Phillips directly that "he had been pegged as a KUBARK man." After Phillip's return to the United States and his assignment to the Cuban Project, Malone maintained contact with him in regard to the activities of various Cubans involved with the FRENTE and offered to make introductions for Phillips to significant individuals.[4]

Malone (AM/PATRIN) continued to be a frequent and major informant on Cuban affairs for both the FBI and CIA after his return to New York, including the activities of his close personal friend Fernandez. One of Fernandez's first operational moves after his exfiltration to the United States was to use his business connections, including his being known to the Klebergs of King Ranch (Kleberg was not only close to Lyndon Johnson but a diner partner of Alan Dulles). Kleberg helped Fernandez to negotiate and fund the purchase of an ex-Navy sub chaser for penetration and supply missions into Cuba. The ship was located in New Orleans, owned by Texan Robert McCoy, and was purchased jointly with Texas (Kleberg) and Cuban funds, approximately $38,000 each, in November of 1960. Malone was instrumental in the purchase of the *Tejana* and facilitated ongoing contacts between Fernandez and Kleberg. A CIA memorandum records that Malone (AM/PATRIN) recalled being encouraged by CIA (KUBARK) to discuss funding as well as tax write-offs and other compensations for the principals.[5] Though the CIA did not own the boat, it armed and supplied it. Another CIA memo gives an itemized breakdown of the cost estimate for repairs, radar, gun covers, and navigation aids. The *Tejana* was expected to be ready for its first training mission by November, 1960.

Tejana operations, personally led by Fernandez, commenced infiltration missions in March 1961. During its few months of initial operation, the ship made four successful missions into Cuba, infiltrating 27 men and 60 tons of war material and exfiltrating 17 individuals. One of the more familiar names among those infiltrated was Felix Rodriguez, sent in on a one man mission with only a .25 cal. pistol and incendiary devices in March 1961.[6] But on April 7 during its fifth mission into Cuba the *Tejana* broke down en route. At this point the CIA determined that it had better boats available and essentially told Fernandez they wanted nothing further to do with the *Tejana*. The same also contains a complaint about Fernandez. Because Fernandez was connected to very highly placed individuals such as Kleberg, as well as individuals in Washington (his friendship with the Kennedys is mentioned) it was felt to be impossible for CIA officers to maintain their desired level of control over him.[7]

The *Tejana* was captained by Robert Clark Stevens and officered mostly by former Cuban navy officers. George Kappes was its Engineer and Operations officer and Lawrence LaBorde (a CIA DDP contact from February 1961 to April 1962), a former New Orleans port captain, was key to ensuring that its somewhat unique engines remained operational. The *Tejana*'s crew included two men whose names would become legendary in independent exile military operations, Tony Cuesta (AM/DENIM 14) and Eduardo "Eddie Bayo" Perez Gonzalez.[8]

Cuesta and Perez had earlier joined a very special UNIDAD military group called Los Halcones Negros (the Black Falcons) whose chief was former Rebel Army Captain José Lopez (pseudonym "Oswaldo") and which also included Louis Posada Carriles.[9]

After their service on the *Tejana*, neither Cuesta nor Perez were recruited to serve on any other CIA project or operational team. However, they would go on to organize and lead military missions for two of the most aggressive and successful independent activist exile groups, Alpha 66 and Commandos L.

Cuesta and Perez (Bayo) each led missions against targets in Cuba. Cuesta led the first raid against a Russian construction site in September 1962, followed by a mission on October 10 that killed Russians at Isabela de Sangua. After the missile crisis of late 1962, Cuesta returned to the Russians at Isabela de Sangua. On March 18, 1963 he attacked both a Russian freighter and an infantry camp. On March 27, Cuesta led a return mission with a spin off of Alpha 66/SNFE called Commandos L, with photo coverage by *Life* magazine. In this mission the Russian freighter *Baku* was attacked and sunk, precipitating a major diplomatic crisis with the Soviet Union and escalating a crackdown on exile activities by the Kennedy Administration. It was this crackdown that turned the most militant exiles bitterly against President Kennedy. These missions were a huge pain in the side for the Kennedy administration. And although the CIA had orders to penetrate and stop such missions, we can now demonstrate that certain senior officers at JM/WAVE were well aware of these Russian attack missions—in advance—and seemingly did nothing but monitor them and obtain covert debriefings. One of their primary sources for this was Alberto Fernandez.

It is also of interest that the *Baku* raid photos show an unnamed participant in the mission with a strong resemblance to Bernardo de Torres. He had been released only a few months earlier with other Brigade 2506 members after their capture and imprisonment following the Bay of Pigs. Another Commandos L member seen in these photographs was reportedly Ruben Perez, aka. Ruben Victor Ramon (war name "Carlos") who had left Cuba in the fall of 1962. After joining Commandos L, Perez would continue with Menoyo's organization. He was reported as being one of those in a very special Menoyo-affiliated training camp in the Everglades in the summer of 1963, where training was focused on sniper attacks. Diaz Garcia, having arrived in Florida in July of 1963, was also reportedly in the same camp in the summer of 1963.

Fernandez, the *Tejana* and "Jack" Malone

Returning to a more detailed background discussion of Fernandez, we find that he had first become a CIA DDP contact while in Cuba in 1960 and continued in that capacity through 1966. During much of that period he was unpaid and essentially consumed his own personal fortune (he had been a millionaire in Cuba) in anti-Castro activities, going on the CIA payroll only when his own money was virtually gone. He had attended Choate School in Wallingford, Connecticut (when JFK was there as a student) and Princeton University, graduating with a BS in Mechanical Engineering.

Fernandez operated a large ranch and sugar cane plantation from 1944-1959 and became Director of the Sugar Institute in Havana in 1959. After initially supporting the 26th of July movement and actively raising funds for it, he became aware of Castro's communist leanings and began working against him. He left Cuba in December of 1960 while in contact with the CIA and after having come under scrutiny by Castro intelligence due to rumors about his involvement in counterrevolutionary activities. CIA records show that he began reporting to the CIA as an agent in 1960, was granted a provisional operating clearance in January of 1961, and was given a full assignment as an OA (Operational Asset) in April 1963.

In May of 1961, after the Bay of Pigs disaster, Fernandez requested meetings with both the CIA and FBI. In his meeting with the CIA he complained bitterly that his group had not been briefed about the invasion, and that his own warnings that it was not time for something like an invasion had been totally disregarded. He maintained that the exiles and UNIDAD could only succeed if the CIA allowed them contact with senior personnel, independent action, and support from experienced U.S. military advisors. Fernandez also chided the CIA for its trust in Artime and reliance on him.

To the FBI, Fernandez related the story that he and his people had been left totally in the dark about the invasion and that while the *Tejana* was docked at Key West they had watched Navy planes fly in people and supplies to the boat *Santa Ana* which was docked beside them. The *Santa Ana* was crewed by Nino Diaz, with no operational record and nothing like the recent experience of the *Tejana*.

The *Tejana* remained at the dock in Key West. Earlier, in March, UNIDAD's military group in Havana, led by Sori Martin, had been organizing a coup involving Cuban military officers. It would be triggered by using plastic explosives brought in by the *Tejana*. A series of successful attacks (including the gutting of two major Havana department stores) had already been carried out using those devices. The next step was to use them for an attack on Fidel himself. But the pro-Castro militia, alerted by rumors of the pending invasion, chanced upon the leaders of the group and took them captive, seriously wounding Martin in the process. Despite Fernandez's efforts, the UNIDAD group was never able to recover from this loss of its leadership in Cuba.

In April of 1962, Malcolm "Jack" Malone, Vice-President Czarnikow-Rionda Company, arranged a series of meetings with CIA officer Herbert (a direct report to J.C. King) and a second CIA source whose name is still redacted in the released FBI document where Malone informed the FBI on the meetings.

Malone was functioning as an employee of Kleberg in these meetings which followed a March meeting between Kleberg and Lyndon Johnson in which Vice President Johnson had expressed the opinion that JFK would not act against Castro nor commit troops in Cuba. Kleberg apparently dispatched Malone to further investigate this and to lobby for further aggressive action against Castro. Malone was told by Herbert that the opinion expressed to Kleberg by Johnson was out of date and that he should pursue a meeting with Robert Kennedy who was very interested in action against Cuba–obviously good advice considering RFK's role with the Special Group in 62/63. Malone's second, and still redacted source told him that the Cuba project had been separated into it's own operation within the CIA (clearly his informant was aware of the formation of Task Force W and possibly operation Mongoose out of JM/WAVE) and that it had its own counterparts in the DOD and State Department. This informant also seems to have been fully aware of the Special Group led by Robert Kennedy. Malone was also told by Herbert to relay Fernandez assurances that he should be patient as the CIA would certainly be using his abilities and equipment (the *Tejana*) again.[10]

Given Malone's personal connection to David Phillips and Phillip's Texas associates, it is interesting to speculate as to whether Malone was keeping Phillips informed on all these very high level policy matters or whether Phillips was serving as an undocumented backchannel to Malone, Kleberg and other strongly anti-Castro Texans.

It does appear that the assurance passed on to Fernandez was accurate. An FBI memo from Miami to the Director confirms that as of June, 1962, Alberto Fernandez and the Unidad organization were still of operational interest to Ted Shackley, Director of the JM/WAVE CIA station.[11] And Fernandez's records show that he was retained as an operational asset by JM/WAVE and eventually placed on the payroll. He became involved in a variety of somewhat routine operational activities including recruiting of radio operators to be infiltrated into Cuba. However the JM/WAVE monthly operations reports disclose something much more important than that. They relate that Fernandez continued to provide ongoing "spot reports" on developments within the exile community. These included information on the DRE Cuban raids, Alpha 66, and anti-Castro activist Gerry Patrick Hemming.

Most importantly, it seems that Fernandez, due to his association with Cuesta and Bayo, routinely reported on the movements and plans of independent raider groups including Alpha 66 and Commandos L. It is a great surprise to see a statement within a CIA memo that "Both the L-66 raid on the Soviet vessel Baku and the Manuel Quiza raid which aborted on Cayo Blanco were reported pretty accurately in advance by AM/DENMIM/1 (Fernandez) and AM/DENIM/13."

The memo goes on to describe CIA interest in supporting both Alpha 66 and Commandos L with absolute deniability; stating that

> "...current efforts to support them are being made through other channels. The point here is that in order of [sic] obtaining the desired degree of plausibility in our denial of support to them following a raid, which in fact we have supported, it will be necessary for the Commandos (Commandos L) to be unable to trace factually their support to KUBARK in any way. This would be difficult to arrange through AM/DENIM-1."

It would be fascinating to know if this remark might pertain to the Phillips/Bishop dual identity and Phillip's private business community funding sources.[12]

Perhaps even more interesting is another CIA memo which states that Fernandez

> "...has been given no inkling of WAVE's interests in utilizing the Commandos L on an unwitting basis, and would undoubtedly be disappointed to learn that they had acquired a sponsor on their own without his assistance, were this the case."

As for the *Tejana III*, she also eventually did return to service; exactly how is unclear. By that time Fernandez had spent virtually all his personal fortune and had even had to apply for a monthly payment from JM/WAVE, which he did receive up until 1966. The documents make it clear he was trying to divest himself of the *Tejana* and perhaps the CIA assisted him in this. The next time the *Tejana* was reported at sea was in 1963 when it began service as part of Manual Artime's new navy which was building up off Monkey Point in Nicaragua, as part of the rapidly developing Kennedy administration's autonomous group coup project intended to oust Castro. By that time its former engine officer, Larry LaBorde, was long gone, connecting instead with Interpen associates such as Edward Collins, Dennis Harber, Howard Davis, Roy Hargraves and Gerry Patrick Hemming in Miami.

Hargraves and Hemming were reported to have been part of a group which bought a ship, the *Elsie Reichart*, from La Borde in 1962 for clandestine operations into Cuba.[13] La Borde initially worked on coming up with more boats for missions against Cuba. The boats he managed to come up with were nothing like the Tejana and never really seem to have gotten operational, even with some assistance in the boat project from William Seymour, another Interpen associate. In April of 1962 a CIA agent in Key West reported that La Borde was maintaining associations with Tony Cuesta and Collins. He had given up looking for boats and was working with Cuesta on a project to blow up freighters carrying out trade with Cuba. He continued to circulate between Key West, Miami and New Orleans; in that city La Borde was connected to Bartes and Rabel, possibly in support of the projected training camp that Hemming was to set up for the CRC. La Borde himself was reported as having moved back to New Orleans in February of 1963.

It also appears that, in his exit from the *Tejana*, La Borde had become extremely bitter toward the CIA and was viewed as a serious CIA security problem because he was aware of staging areas, warehouses, and arms stores in the Key West area. La Borde and Fernandez would also become significant CIA concerns during the Garrison investigations when La Borde's son informed Garrison of some of his father's New Orleans associations. In listing La Borde and Emilio Santana for investigation, Garrison was definitely naming individuals directly connected with covert CIA operations into Cuba, a real worry for the Agency.

In exposing a link through the *Tejana* to Fernandez, Garrison might also have exposed a whole range of CIA front companies and covert deal makers from Texas to New York City—something which definitely would have been a blow to CIA methods in the secret war against Cuba, and possibly in its domestic operations in general.[14]

Hubris at WAVE

Those who maintain that the Cuban exiles were somehow lacking in military prowess need only to recall individuals such as Fernandez, Cuesta, Perez, Menoyo, Martinez, Williams, Rodriquez and Vidal.

These individuals clearly demonstrated the capacity to be both successful and "dangerous" to Castro. Those who castigate JM/WAVE for not effectively using exile ambition, courage and skills can present a strong case.

The stories of UNIDAD and Alberto Fernandez make the point that CIA planners and officers were simply unable to either comprehend or truly use the power of Cuban rightist patriotism, sacrificing opportunities and a good many anti-Castro Cubans in the name of centralized command and control.

APPENDIX E
STUDENT WARRIOR

Victor Espinosa Hernandez was born in Cuba, the son of a wealthy land owing family which derived most of its income from agriculture and ranching but which was also involved in peripheral business, including an association with a firm which performed industrial inspections of sugar and petroleum refineries. Hernandez related picking up money as a youth by working with inspectors at one petroleum refinery. As a teenager, he attended the University of Havana for one year, becoming heavily involved with radical students and the anti-Batista cause. He would come to be considered one of the "old group" among the student revolutionaries, a close personal friend of Rolando Cubela and Jose Antonio Echeverria. In fact he seems to have devoted virtually all his energy and time while at the University to this political cause, enough so that his father took him out of school in Cuba and sent him to attend Louisiana State University in New Orleans.

Hernandez spent one year at LSU in 1955 and at the age of 18, on the death of his grandfather, he inherited his ranch and returned to Cuba to manage it. For some months he seems to have gotten away from politics and willingly admitted to spending most of his spare time in Havana at the casinos, pursuing gambling and women, rather than the movement against Batista. While making the casino circuit he became acquainted with members of the casino crowd including Mike McClaney, Norman Rothman and their sons.

In 1956, Castro returned to Cuba and called on the student groups to join a revolution. At that time Cubela called on Hernandez to rejoin the movement-but in a much more violent role. Hernandez became one of four assassination teams targeted on leaders of the Batista clique. His team, which included Cubela, became the first to draw blood, killing their target within only days; at that time Hernandez was no more than 20 years old. Afterwards Cubela fled to Miami but Hernandez, due to his youth, stayed in Cuba. Apparently he remained very active with the student revolutionaries and joined the final fighting in Havana, which ousted Batista. Within a short period he became fed up with the Communist trend of the Castro government while his friend Cubela seemingly became trapped within the upper echelon. Hernandez went into exile—first in Miami under the sponsorship of Mike McClaney (living at his home for a time) and then in New York. The HSCA totally failed to explore his associations or activities in New York City but, given the long established Cuban sugar industry and other money connections to New York (as described in Appendix E), it was not surprising to find him in residence there. In side remarks he made during his HSCA interview, it seems clear that his family had significant financial and U.S. government connections. At one point he used a connection to Senator Jacob Javitts' office to gain the attention of the U.S. State Department.

Upon hearing of the recruiting for the CIA Cuba Project, Hernandez returned to Miami and volunteered for the group destined to become the Brigade that would land at the Bay of Pigs. He took military training in Guatemala beginning in June of 1960 and was then transferred to the special training camp at Belle Chase outside of New Orleans. This camp appears to have been associated with paramilitary training and with certain operational activities separate from the Brigade landing at the Bay of Pigs. Hernandez' description of his time there strongly suggests that he was picked as a member of a special paramilitary action group. Given his extensive knowledge of the Castro party cadre, of Havana and in particular, his previous assassination team experience, he would have made a perfect candidate for deniable political operations. His own comments to the HSCA seem to confirm this; he described being moved away from the camp and taken to a series of safe houses from which a team was eventually sent to Cuba, at the same time as (but separately from) the Brigade. He was asked no particular details about the location or activities of his group in this operation and volunteered only that they were told about the landing and then ordered back to Miami. He then describes going on several missions into Cuba after the Bay of Pigs, from a base in the Key West area. He was bitter about these missions because they seemed to accomplish nothing in particular.

He was particularly upset because while on the mission he and others (names mentioned by the HSCA include Miguel Alvarez, Calcie Nundez, and Frank Bernardino) kept opening up ammunition and finding it was not as labeled and did not fit their weapons. Based on that and other glitches, he wondered if someone was trying to arrange for them simply never to come back from Cuba. Hernandez definitely showed no fondness for the CIA and its operations.

Hernandez was very adamant that he directed no personal blame against President Kennedy for the Bay of Pigs. He has all the details of the air raids that didn't happen and the lack of U.S. forces being committed but "nobody bothered blaming Kennedy" about such things. They simply felt that it was all a "CIA screw-up." He also expresses no particular ill will toward the Kennedy administration policy in 1963 that led to the break up of the two attacks against Cuba that he was organizing (and to his own arrest).

The HSCA synopsis notes that it had also located CIA documents which stated that Hernandez was terminated from involvement with the exile military mission in March of 1961 and taken off the payroll at that time. We have noted elsewhere that there was discussion that a group of "malcontents" were removed from the project and returned to Miami during their training. This reference refers to individuals who were trained in Guatemala, given additional training outside New Orleans, and officially separated only weeks before the Cuba invasion. All in all this sounds much more like a cover story created to grant deniability to a small, select group which was intended to perform deniable operations inside Cuba.

Unfortunately, the HSCA made no inquiry into Victor Hernandez' employment or business activities after the period of the Bay of Pigs invasion. We know that he came from a rich family of landowners, completed one year of college, and after apparently abandoning the effort against Castro at the end of 1963, he returned to New York and began making frequent trips overseas, in particular to France. He moved to France in 1967, and then to London - frequently traveling internationally. He seems to have had extensive connections and exile associates in both France and Spain. No inquiry was made into Hernandez' movements or activities between the time he supposedly separated from the CIA (whether in March, 1961 according to the CIA, or August, 1961 according to Hernandez) and the summer of 1963. It was then that he was arrested twice for involvement in separate planned air raids on Cuba.

The CIA itself was interested in what Victor Espinosa Hernandez (alias Victor Papucho Espinosa) was doing during 1962. We have a memorandum from the Deputy Director of Plans to the Director of the FBI, attention Mr. S. J. Papich, requesting all data available to the

Bureau on Mr. Espinosa, residing at that time in New York City, New York.[1] There is as yet no indication of any reply in the available files.

Hernandez willingly discussed his Cuba air attack projects with the HSCA interviewer. He had obtained financial backing from Mike McClaney, logistics support from Sam Benton (previously involved in such schemes with Roy Hargraves), and explosives and other proscribed materials from Richard Lauchli out of Illinois. Among all the experienced exile military leaders that McClaney would have had the ability to fund, we have no explanation of why he would choose to pass his money and support to a 25 year old with no apparent military following. This was yet another question left unexplored in the HSCA questioning, as was the issue of just what other anti-Castro activities Hernandez might have turned to in 1963, or what led him to abandon his activities against Castro.

It is clear that Hernandez had extensive student revolutionary connections, that he was acquainted with Lauchli and Illinois weapons sources, and that he had ties to the Cuban land owner/sugar industry/Julian Lobo money clique. In the summer of 1963 this New York City based clique was also involved with exile initiatives such as that of Paulino Sierra. The financial, political and personal connections of this New York clique are fascinating, ranging from Alberto Fernandez of UNIDAD and the Tejuna CIA naval missions to Kleberg of the King Ranch, to Jack Malone (a major informant on Cuban affairs for both the CIA and FBI), to Malone's long time personal friend from Havana, David Atlee Phillips.

The New York City Cuban exiles (Lobo and his associates) were early supporters of the 1963 Sierra Junta initiative. In the fall of 1963 Sierra was actively buying weapons in the Midwest and that one of his key officers was Juan Francisco Blanco Fernandez of the DRE (student wing of the exile movement). Given the New York and DRE connections, it is at least possible that the "Hernandez" reportedly traveling with Sierra may have been Victor Hernandez Espinosa.

It is fascinating and possibly suggestive that the two major pre-assassination leaks about a plot against JFK came from Homer Echevarria in Chicago (who was shopping for guns with Sierra money) and from Soto Martinez in Miami. Soto Martinez had been sponsored into the United States by Mike McClaney (just as had Victor Espinosa Hernandez) and was living on McClaney's estate in 1963 during the same time frame that McClaney was using Hernandez in the two abortive Cuban raids.

The remainder of the information provided by Hernandez to the HSCA dealt largely with details about his reporting to the FBI, State Department and CIA in regard to information obtained in France and Spain. This information was that his old friend Rolando Cubela was supposedly involved with the CIA in plots against Castro circa 1965. Supposedly some of his Cuban friends in France had learned of this project and were concerned that several of the individuals involved in it were leaking the information. Exactly why they felt so strongly about bringing to the attention of the CIA a project supposedly being organized by the CIA—which was supposedly distrusted by all of the exiles passing on the information—is a bit hard to fathom. It is also difficult to understand why Hernandez made such an effort to bring the information to the attention of the U.S. government. There is no indication of his having had personal contact with Cubela during this period. Hernandez makes it clear that he was not requested to do this by Cubela, and that his effort was only made at the urging of some of his own friends. Their own concerns seem to have been that those involved in the whole affair were not trustworthy, and that sufficient details were leaking among Cubans that the project might already have been compromised.

Victor Espinosa Hernandez was a very interesting young man. He was involved at the very core of the student revolutionary movement against Castro, a member of a political assassination team inside Cuba, and apparently part of special, deniable missions in conjunction with the Cuba Project. We also know that he had connections with well to do exile families in New York City and with the old casino crowd out of Havana—old sugar money, mob funded anti-Castro activities in Miami and New Orleans with McClaney/Benton/Rothman, dealings with Minuteman weapons supplier Richard Lauchli out of Illinois—all this makes for a most interesting set of associates only lightly explored by the HSCA. He was in all the right places to have heard the gossip and all the right places to help spread it. It appears that all sorts of people talked with Victor Hernandez Espinosa; we can only wonder to what extent he might have heard rumors of a plot against JFK, and the possibility that he may have been the source for some of the rumors circulating in Chicago and Miami.

APPENDIX F
ANOTHER RUMOR – SAME SOURCE?

In May of 2004, a set of documents was posted by William Dankbaar, who inquired online as to who among the researchers and historians of the period might be familiar with them.[1] These documents include a written letter (and typed copy) from a former Air Force Security Service member to another individual who had previously served with the writer at Kirknewton, Scotland in 1963. Also included was an internal Air Force Security Police letter relating an investigation of the AFSS letter and its author, and a letter from the senior legal counsel for the NSA to the FBI, bringing this matter to the Bureau's attention. The NSA letter suggested that the FBI might wish to bring the subject to the attention of the congressional committee investigating the assassination of President Kennedy due to the subject of the letter. The NSA letter also confirmed the basic claims made in the original letter in regard to specific intercept targets which were indeed being monitored at the Kirknewton facility in 1963.

The original letter, mailed from a Veterans Hospital in Sheridan, Wyoming, was apparently sent to an active service Air Force Master Sergeant station in Florida. The writer stated that he was in the process of seeking disability payments based both on a physical injury to his leg and mental trauma related to an incident which had occurred at Kirknewton in October, 1963. He requested that the Master Sergeant corroborate the incident in support of the petition to the Air Force. The letter describes the incident as involving the interception of message traffic, which contained remarks about an upcoming attack on President Kennedy. According to the writer, he aggressively attempted to get this intercept filed with NSA but was blocked by his local Air Force superiors. He also made reference to specific channels ("links") and targets that were the source of the intercept (all names and target information have been redacted from his original letter, but the NSA letter to the FBI verifies the described targeting assignments as of 1963). There is a great deal of detail in the letter including a reference to military MOS's; the writer's MOS seems to have been 203 which would have made him a "voice intercept linguist." There is also reference to his getting the Master Sergeant's address from the "outfit in Texas" —which most likely refers to USAFSSCOM at Lackland AFB in San Antonio, Texas. The writer also mentioned at least six other people who would have been familiar with the general incident and at the end gives his own short wave radio handle, YY Prosign. He also described his former wife, Marlene, who was from South Dakota.

It would appear that this letter was turned over to an Air Force supervisor and was in turn referred to the Air Force Security Police, who took the letter seriously, leading to a security investigation. A letter pertaining to this investigation is dated June 2, 1978. It appears the original letter was turned over to OSI because the writer was a civilian at the time, and that OSI did the follow-on investigation. As a result of this investigation, NSA was copied and in turn, due to the subject and based on general corroboration of the individual, the installation, and other details of the letter, NSA counsel Daniel B. Silver brought the incident to the attention of the FBI.[2]

Names mentioned in the correspondence include Silver, James Lear of NSA and Arthur Kerns of FBI Intelligence. All names have been confirmed as legitimate and Silver was contacted by William Dankbaar; he stated that he had no recollection of this particular letter but routinely signed correspondence prepared by his staff.

Based on these posted documents, work by researchers revealed other HSCA documents relating to the Kirknewton incident. In some cases the documents are released and in others they are still classified and we only have access to RIF cover sheets.[3] Further research into the Kirknewton installation shows a historical listing for an individual once stationed there, Mr. Nicholas Stevenson. Calls to Stevenson by Dankbaar eventually elicited the reply from Stevenson's wife that he had been interviewed by the HSCA but that he might not be able to discuss this subject.

A conversation with Stevenson by this author ended with the author being told by Stevenson that he was unable to discuss the subject because of two brain operations which had totally eliminated all of his past memories.

Based on the documents and background available, it seems extremely likely that the incident described by the author of the letter did happen. It was not initially reported to NSA, but NSA was aware that the basic details of the intercept as described in the letter were plausible and worthy of referral to the HSCA. The HSCA apparently was notified by the FBI, conducted its own investigation and prepared reports, all of which still remain classified as of 2006. Which leaves us with good reason to determine if there is anything further we can learn from the details of the letter.

The way it's done

Before describing and evaluating the incident itself, some background on NSA monitoring in Europe circa 1963 is in order. NSA operated a number of intercept/monitoring stations in Europe but for our purposes the two locations of interest were Kirknewton, Scotland and Chicksands, England. The installation at Kirknewton was housed at RAF Station Kirknewton and circa 1963 the unit involved was the 6952 Mobile Radio Squadron of the USAF, operating under control of USAFSS, USAF Security Service. Personnel included Intercept Operators, Voice Specialists and Analysts with responsibilities for collection, processing, analysis and reporting of communications intelligence. Personnel MOS's included 201/Cryptanalyst, 202/Radio Traffic Analyst, 203/Language Specialist and 29X/Morse Intercept and Printer Operations. In general the unit transcribed voice intercepts, screened intercepts for perishable intelligence, and reported to national level "customers"–with overall operations directed by the NSA. Official targets included voice and Morse code traffic with a focus on Soviet military and commercial as well as naval traffic.

At the height of the Cold War, in the early 60s, Soviet air operations and even domestic news services were monitored. Air Force Security Service personnel were said to be an elite group, primarily first and second term non-commissioned officers, all having Top Secret clearance and regarded as dedicated, if generally unmilitary in their day to day dress and address.

Aside from the official history of this NSA monitoring, there is strong indication that other targets in addition to Soviet military and commercial traffic were monitored. Duncan Campbell has done an analysis as part of his article *Inside Echelon*.[4]

It seems that NSA also coordinated the monitoring of targeted traffic involving U.S. allies in Western Europe; both diplomatic and commercial traffic were monitored on international leased carriers (ILC). Such monitoring was referred to as ALLO ("all other countries") and ROW ("rest of world"). While the Chicksands installation focused on Soviet military targets, Kirknewton maintained a Watch List on commercial European traffic. Watch Lists could comprise people by name, companies, or even commodities and were compiled from NSA customers including CIA, FBI, and DIA.

So who was it?

The targeting of the Kirknewton intercept becomes extremely significant as we get to the details of the intercept the author of the letter described. In recalling the "link" that was being monitored, the author mentions that the name of one of the individuals involved was associated with a certain crime branch.

He also mentions that he had recently read information on this branch of crime which indicated that when the intercept was made in 1963, this individual was number four in this organization and that at the time the letter was being written had moved up to a number two position. Because of the redactions in the letter and in the NSA correspondence it is impossible to concretely identify the country, the link, or the name in question. However, based on an insight offered by researcher Larry Haapanen, it is possible to propose at least one specific target which fits this description. A survey of popular literature on crime in the timeframe of the letter reveals that one particular book was drawing widespread national attention–the award winning book had been initially published in 1973, was reissued in paperback in 1974, and went through numerous reprints during the mid-70s. Its title was *The Heroin Trail* and it was researched and prepared by the staff of Newsday.[5] One of the major topics of the book was the Marseilles nexus of the heroin trail and the evolution of the criminal organizations that were moving the drug into the United States.

French connections

As it happens, the Marseilles traffic was under serious investigation in the early 60s and the first significant arrest of one of the founders of the local labs, that of Joseph Cesari, was made in 1964. The book notes a "heavy surveillance and investigation" circa 1963-1964.[6] It also notes that circa 1964 the trade was largely controlled by the Guerini brothers, who were literally at war with another organization headed by Francisci and Dominic Venturi. But by the time of the book's publication in 1974 the Venturis had assumed the top two positions in the Marseilles trade.[7] This transition is not a major theme of the book, but if the author of the letter was monitoring a narcotics Watch List in October 1963 and heard one of these names referenced, it would certainly jump to his attention. *The Heroin Trail* details the fact that in the early 60s Dominic

Venturi and his brother Jean were very busy establishing routes into the U.S. via Canada, specifically Montreal. Venturi was listed by the Federal Bureau of Narcotics as a major importer of narcotics into the United States.[8] It is highly likely that Venturi was indeed on the Drug Agency Watch List as of October, 1963. An associated name of interest would have been that of Paul Mondolini from Montreal, Antoine Guerini's adopted son. Reportedly Trafficante had maintained close ties to Guerini via Mondolini, who had lived in Havana before moving to Montreal. Mondolini may even have been used as an intermediary in the very early Roselli plots against Castro.

Yet another name related to the Marseille drug network and known to assassination researchers very probably was on the Watch List. Victor Michael Mertz, French Resistance hero and an agent for the French SDECE in its war against the Algerian OAS. Mertz was also a major figure in drug smuggling into the U.S. in the early 60s and was a close associate of both Francisci and Venturi Guerini.[9]

Mertz had been smuggling drugs since 1947 and was involved in planning routes, recruiting couriers and workers and in handling finances for the U.S. trade. His system was well developed by 1961 and in March of that year Mertz sailed to New York with a shipment of heroin only to be recalled to penetrate an OAS bomb plot in July of that year. One of the prime movers in that plot was an individual named Jean Rene Souetre who was also traveling into the United States in the early 1960s. To confuse the situation, there are indications suggesting that Mertz may have on occasion used the name "Jean Rene Souetre" as an alias for himself.

After his role in aborting the bomb plot against President de Gaulle, Mertz and his family were relocated by the French SDECE to Montreal where he continued growing his operations through both Montreal and New York. During the period of 1963 and 1964, Mertz began to diversify his network and in 1965 he had a shipment busted which was going through Miami courtesy of the Trafficante crime organization.[10] In addition, there are reports that Mertz was also involved in drug shipments through the Trafficante/Marcello networks that were busted in Loredo, Texas in 1963 and at Fort Benning, Georgia in 1965. Another drug bust on record is that of 22 pounds of heroin being shipped from Paul Mandolini through Joe Stasi in Houston (Stasi was a former co-owner with Trafficante of the Havana San Souci casino.[11] There is little doubt that both Houston and Loredo had become key transit points for the expansion of drugs coming in through France; this fact may also relate to the apparent assassination leaks discussed in Appendix G.

There is also good reason to speculate that Mertz may have continued to operate against OAS moves into the United States. We know that Jean Souetre was actively approaching both agencies and individuals in the U.S. circa 1963. CIA documents show that in May 1963, Souetre presented himself as the OAS coordinator for external affairs and in June he offered the CIA a list of Communist penetrations in the de Gaulle government. OAS contacts have also indicated that Souetre visited General Walker in Dallas in April of 1963 and was in New Orleans in contact with Cuban exiles, though this is unverified. Souetre has also been reported as having done field work for possible assassination attempts in a number of locations and was definitely associated with the ongoing OAS efforts to kill the French President. A history of OAS attempts against President de Gaulle shows two in 1963, five in 1964 and three more in 1965.

A NARA search on CIA and FBI documents pertaining to Souetre reveals a considerable amount of information including a CIA personality file name request on him in March, 1963; a 201 file with no date; a memo on his associates, travel, and finances dated July, 1963; a memo from Angier Biddle Duke on Diplomatic Privileges and Immunities dated June of 1963; and FBI memoranda on him dated in April and May 1963 involving the New York Bureau office. It appears that the FBI was copied on Souetre's contacts with the CIA and there is some indication that an international mail trace may have been placed on Souetre in New York City. An acquaintance of his (Dr. Lawrence Alderson) living in Houston seems to have been identified by the FBI based on a mailing that he sent to Souetre; he was questioned by the FBI after a French inquiry in 1964. There are also several FBI and CIA documents following and related to the 1964 French inquiry to the FBI in regard to Souetre's reported expulsion from Dallas on November 22, 1963. The French inquiry on Souetre's whereabouts may well have been related to the upcoming de Gaulle visit to Mexico in 1964.

As a historical coincidence, James Angleton was very concerned about communist penetration of the French government as a result of information obtained during the Golitsin defection. Angleton recruited the French SDECE chief in Washington D.C. to allow him entrance into the French embassy and personally conducted a black bag job on the embassy, stealing cipher traffic.[12] Reportedly Angleton was meeting with SDECE Col. Gauche at a restaurant in Georgetown on November 22, 1963.[13]

The reason that we have all these records on Souetre in the JFK files is that in April of 1964, the French had contacted the FBI attaché in Paris with a request for information pertaining to the reported expulsion of Souetre from the United States on November 22, 1963. Although both the FBI and CIA investigated this subject for several months in 1964, none of the available documents sheds any specific light on Souetre's travels in the U.S. or his purported expulsion. It is possible that the Souetre "mystery" accounts for the Hoover annotation on a memo about working with the CIA on domestic intelligence which is described in Chapter 15, page 298 of this manuscript: *"OK, but I hope you are not being taken in. I can't forget the CIA withholding the French espionage activities in the U.S.A. nor the false story re. Oswald's trip to Mexico, only to mention two cases of their double dealing!"*

Interestingly, a CIA file summary[14] shows that only three individuals out of several dozen related to the JFK investigation were carried in so called "soft" CIA files. These individuals were Souetre/Mertz, Silvia Duran, and William Seymour. Verbal statements to the HSCA and ARRB suggest that a soft file was maintained on Lee Oswald as well.

It is certainly possible that that the link that was being monitored at Kirknewton in October of 1963 was a commercial channel into France and that the names on the Watch List had come from either DIA, FBI, CIA and possibly from more than one agency. The names involved may have been Venturi, Mertz or even Souetre, but without the redacted information in the related documents or corroboration by the individuals involved this has to remain pure speculation.

Tracing the gossip

If any of the postulated individuals were discussing rumors of an attack on John Kennedy then they had to have a current source as of October, 1963, someone who was at least aware of gossip about JFK being at risk and who was "leaking." As we have traced rumors and leaks in this book, we've come across two very concrete examples in the weeks immediately prior to the assassination. One was in Chicago and referred to someone getting rid of Kennedy; another was in Miami and described someone named Oswald who had the skills to shoot the President between the eyes. In regard to the Chicago gossip, we have seen that the name Hernandez surfaced as being associated with the individuals being the most likely source of the gossip. In Miami, Jorge Soto Martinez was gossiping and the source of his gossip was seen as likely being the circle of Cuban exiles associated with one Michael McClaney—the same McClaney whose brother's property outside New Orleans was used to store bomb making materials in the summer of 1963, with these materials being transported from the Chicago area by one Victor Hernandez. Hernandez had been of interest to U.S. intelligence for some time; as early as November 21, 1962 the DDP of the CIA was asking Director Hoover for "all data available to the Bureau on Victor Espinosa Hernandez... presently residing in New York City".[15] Information collected by the HSCA also revealed that in June of 1963 Victor Hernandez had been under investigation by both the FBI and Customs.

Victor Hernandez has been discussed at some length in this work and it seems extremely interesting that in 1964 Mr. Hernandez left New York City for Paris. In fact for the next couple of years he did considerable international travel with a focus on France and later Australia.

We know about this travel because in 1964, he again came to the attention of both the CIA and FBI in regard to a major leak pertaining to the CIA's AM/LASH and AM/TRUNK projects.

While in Miami, Hernandez had a conversation with an FBI informant in whom he detailed information on an assassination and coup attempt against Fidel Castro being facilitated by Rolando Cubela. At the time, the FBI was "investigating U.S. hoodlum element and Cuban exile plan to assassinate Castro" and they felt that the parties described by Hernandez might be part of that plot.[16] Based on this lead, the FBI interviewed Hernandez in New York in June of 1965 and he related that he had spent the last month in Paris with individuals involved in the plot against Castro. The FBI reported this back to CIA and received a memorandum confirming that "98% of the details" related by Hernandez did confirm to information known to the CIA. Their major concern was over some of the "questionable individuals" who seemed to be associated with Hernandez and to have details on the Cubela project, especially Alberto Blanco aka. "El Loco," and Jorge Robreno.

From AM/LASH documents we also know that this was the time frame in which Cubela was traveling to Spain and France, even receiving bomb-making training at a U.S. facility in France, while under independent observation by French intelligence. Cubela's lawyer, who had also represented Trafficante in Cuba, was also in Spain during this period.

The HSCA eventually located Hernandez in London and he came back to the United States to offer extensive testimony. Unfortunately, as related in Appendix E, his interview was considerably less "investigative" than we might desire. One of Hernandez' old friends from Victor's Bay of Pigs training (and from the McClaney farm incident in New Orleans) told the HSCA that he had heard Hernandez eventually had some problems in France relating to drugs. But the HSCA never asked Hernandez about this remark.

It seems fairly clear that Hernandez was associated with individuals who may have heard rumors about people plotting against President Kennedy. We can speculate that he might even have passed on certain gossip in both Chicago and Miami in the weeks before the assassination. Certainly he was a source for highly accurate information on the ultra-secret Cubela CIA project, and he clearly was in the company of individuals who in turn associated with unsavory characters in locations ranging from Havana to Miami and France. The unanswered question is whether it was the same gossip which not only leaked in Chicago and Miami but was also was picked up in an intercept of someone's call to France.

APPENDIX G

THE WORD IN THE UNDERWORLD

Two days before the assassination Rose Cheramie talked about people who planned to kill President Kennedy in Dallas. That much is perfectly clear. The first and primary witness to her remarks was a veteran police officer of 16 years, Francis Louis Fruge. Officer Fruge presented his information on the Cheramie incident to the House Select Committee on Assassinations in April of 1978. Unless otherwise noted, the material in this appendix is derived from that testimony and from a recently obtained Customs Department report on an investigation of Cheramie's remarks about a drug smuggling activity that she was to be involved with in November 1963.[1] That investigation was based on information provided to U.S. Customs by the Louisiana State Police after its own extended interviews with Cheramie. We have no such follow-up on her Kennedy assassination remarks. Captain Fritz of the Dallas Police was called by the Louisiana Patrol, but he expressed no interest in the Cheramie lead.

Fruge's story begins with a call that he received on November 20, 1963 from the emergency room at Moosa Memorial Hospital. The hospital had treated an accident victim who showed definite signs of being under the influence of some sort of drug. Fruge remarked that the hospital administrator, a Mrs. Guillory, knew he had worked narcotics previously and needed assistance because although the victim (Cheramie) had bruises and abrasions, she had no money and could not be admitted by the hospital. Fruge soon arrived and transported Cheramie to the Eunice jail. He then attended the local Police Department Ball being held that evening. While there, a Eunice police officer came to get him and reported Cheramie had taken off her clothes, was literally climbing the walls, and was obviously going through serious drug withdrawal. At that point Fruge called the assistant coroner who came to the jail and gave Charamie a sedative.

He advised Fruge that she needed to be taken to a hospital and Fruge arranged for an ambulance to transport her to the East Louisiana State Hospital in Lafayette. During the drive to ELSH, Cheramie began a rambling conversation with Fruge, and her remarks centered around two primary subjects.

First, she had been traveling with two men who either were or resembled Italians. The three had stopped at the Silver Slipper Lounge (a house of prostitution well known to Fruge) and had gotten into an argument. Having left that establishment, the men had dumped Cheramie out of their vehicle along with her two cardboard boxes. The second point was that the three had been traveling to Dallas where Rose's baby was, in order to pick up money for a drug purchase and that in Dallas President Kennedy was going to be killed.

Fruge remarked to the HSCA that Cheramie's cardboard boxes contained baby clothes. Later questioning, after the assassination, seems to have primarily dealt with the drug related remarks and revealed that her baby was being held in Dallas to ensure her cooperation. Amazingly, nobody seems to have seriously questioned Cheramie in detail about her Kennedy pre-assassination remarks. Apparently she had heard them from the two men, but that is never clarified nor is there any obvious tie between the drug deal and the attack on the President. Years later, when D.A. Garrison learned about the Cheramie incident and attempted to locate and interview her, he obtained the services of Fruge from the Louisiana Patrol, only to have Fruge discover that Cheramie had recently died. Both Cheramie's mother and sister denied ever having known her and Fruge only managed to develop information on her by having a policewoman pose as a friend to the sister, a friend who had worked along with Cheramie as a prostitute. There is no concrete evidence that either the FBI or anyone else ever investigated her story, although the Customs report previously mentioned makes reference to a letter from the Secret Service which does not accompany the Customs report obtained at NARA. Customs did inform the FBI of the Cheramie drug investigation via the December memo, but it contains no mention of her remarks about the attack on the President. It remains totally unclear how the Secret Service was brought into the matter or what they might have done; there is no indication that they contacted Cheramie, Fruge, or his Colonel. Whether or not they contacted the hospital staff is unknown.

Initially Fruge did not pursue Cheramie's remarks about the drugs or the President Kennedy due to her mental state and the fact that hospital staff felt that it was going to take several days for her to complete withdrawal. However, after the assassination, Fruge contacted the hospital and made arrangements to interview Cheramie the following Monday. At that time he obtained further remarks from her. She had been going to Dallas to pick up her baby and $8,000 for the drug purchase. The drugs were to be purchased in a meeting at a hotel in Houston, and they would be coming into the U.S. with a seaman whose ship would land at Galveston. The seaman was bringing eight kilos of heroin. She was to receive the heroin and then it would be taken to Mexico. Her only remark on the President was that he was "going to be killed," he "had to be killed." At that point Fruge contacted his superior, Colonel Morgan and reported the story to him. Morgan took it to their superior, Colonel Burbank and was told to investigate further. They then contacted Nathan Durham, Chief Customs agent in Port Arthur, Texas.

Cheramie had given considerable detail to Fruge on the drug deal: a boat name, the seaman's name, the location of the hotel in Houston, the alias she was to use in obtaining a room there for the meeting and sale, the name of the man with the money in Dallas, and general information about the "families" involved in the drug deals. This information was provided to Durham and he verified the name of the boat and that the seaman's name was on the manifest. Given that verification Durham told the State Police officers that he definitely wanted to work the case and asked them to bring Cheramie down to be a part of it. A patrol plane was obtained, and Fruge and Morgan picked up Darby and flew to Houston, Texas.

As was noted earlier, Colonel Morgan called Captain Fritz in Dallas on the Kennedy aspect of her remarks but was told that Fritz was simply "not interested."

The HSCA was unable to obtain details of Cheramie's drug information from Fruge; some elements he did not recall by that time, and about others they simply did not ask. It is only with the recent release of the Customs report that we can see the names involved, which will be described in the discussion of the Customs activities which follows. One thing that Fruge did remember was Cheramie's remark made after seeing a newspaper on the plane: that she had worked for Ruby at one time and that Ruby had known Oswald. She mentioned working as a stripper at the Pink Door. Fruge seems to suggest that her employment by Ruby was later verified, but this remains unclear and the author is not aware of any other verification of a connection between Cheramie and Ruby. Similar remarks were reportedly made by her to the doctors at the Charity Hospital during her stay there.

In his HSCA testimony, Fruge related that the Customs agents verified Cheramie's hotel reservation (under her unstated alias) at the Rice Hotel in Houston and confirmed that the man she stated had her baby in Dallas was a suspected drug dealer. He went on to say that the seaman never appeared at the hotel and that he understood that either the Customs tail had lost the man or that he had recognized the tail somewhere on the way and lost it. At that point the Customs people simply put Cheramie back on the street in Houston. The Customs report describes the information which had been relayed to them by the Louisiana State Police including: that she was to be in Houston, Texas on the evening of November 28; to be given $29,000 from Pete Vallone (who supposedly operated the State Door Lounge on Westheimer Road); to register at the Rice Hotel, and be contacted on November 29 by a Puerto Rican seaman called "Luther" (initials L. J.), last name unknown, who was to arrive in Galveston on a ship named the *"Mary Etta"* (phonetic). Cheramie was to accept the drugs, pay the seaman and then deliver the narcotics to Leo Parker in Dallas. Parker appears to be an alias, with the true name on the memo either to be mistyped or typed over – it is something like "Portherillo."

The Customs report states that Agent Harold King of Houston investigated the ships scheduled into Galveston and advised that the SS *Maturata* of British registry was arriving on the 26th and the SS *Mar Negro* of Spanish registry on the 29. Upon Cheramie's arrival in Houston, the Customs agent was given a long and detailed story about her involvement in narcotics smuggling with Vallone and Leo Parker and furnished detailed descriptive data. Captain Morgan confirmed that her story had remained consistent and that the police had not noted any discrepancies in their series of interviews with her. On the afternoon of November 27, the Customs officers decided to proceed to Houston to continue the investigation. While en route and after arrival, Cheramie furnished detailed information regarding members of the Vallone and Tamborello families, their relationship to Pete Vallone, and both their legitimate and criminal reputations. In Houston, local agents Forbey, Harvey and King were able to partially substantiate Cheramie's story.

"Subsequent investigations by those agents… further substantiated more of the informants story" although the agents were to that point unable to locate Cheramie's police record.

> "Police records of the Vallone and Tamborello families revealed that the majority of them had records or reputations for narcotics, white slavery (prostitution) and other criminal activity."

The memorandum confirms Fruge's remarks that the investigation proceeded with Cheramie being registered at the Rice Hotel and plans made for continuance of the investigation.

At this point the discussion of those activities during the next two days simply stops and no mention at all is made of the effort to intercept and tail the seaman; there is no mention of the tail being blown as Fruge described. The next entry (November 29) is a statement that Agent Harvey had located the Houston Police record for Cheramie and determined that her record was extensive under many aliases. She had served time for felonies in multiple State prisons and been in several mental institutions (related to drug use).

For reference, Melba Christine Mercedes also known as Melba Youngblood and Roselle Rene Cheramie had a RAP sheet with 28 offenses including prostitution and drug abuse. At this point it appears that the arrest record currently in evidence contains no felony violations or participation in drug dealing per se. Her arrest sheet shows that she did travel a good deal. There are 1941-1942 arrests in Canyon and Gainesville, Texas and in Shreveport, Louisiana, apparently dealing with an Army Air Force serviceman at Barksdale. This incident seems to indicate that at the time she was married to Robert Rodman and was using the name Melba Christine Youngblood Rodman. The arrest sent her to the State penitentiary at Angola for a two year sentence. In 1947 and 1948 she was in New Orleans and Houston, then back to New Orleans in 1951. From 1951-1957 she was Austin, New Orleans, Galveston, Los Angeles, New Mexico, Arizona and then a patient (drug addiction) at St. Elizabeth's in Washington D.C. In the early 1960's she was arrested in Alabama, Oklahoma and New Orleans using the names Zada Marie Gano, Zada Irene Scars and Zada Lynn Gano. The name Cheramie only shows up on the RAP sheet once, in October 1964 for vagrancy. The official arrest history shows that she was in the East Louisiana State Hospital in Jackson in 1961 as Melba Christine

Mercedes, and there is no reference to the November 1963 incident at all since she was neither arrested nor booked in regard to her injuries on November 20th, 1963.

On October 29, Houston Police had arrested Cheramie for being drunk. At that time she had told of being involved in narcotics traffic although the police report states that is untrue; no details of any actual investigation of the claim are given. It is unclear how the story of a drug deal scheduled for the 29th could have been found to be false before that date, especially when all the preliminary information from Cheramie was checking out positively with Customs? The Customs memo then notes that on November 30, 1963 she failed to appear at a bond hearing and two $1,000 bonds were forfeited. This seems somewhat strange because she was in Customs and Police custody as of the 29th. The report concludes with a statement that the Houston Police Department would not arrest her when approached by the Customs agents. Thus we are left with a Customs memorandum which appears to confirm Fruge's remarks and corroborate Cheramie's claims about the drug deal. A memo which fails to note the real reason for the failure of the investigation and obscures the Cheramie's information with a series of references to Houston Police reports and lack of interest on the part of the Houston police.

Back to Square One

Rose Cheramie heard something from someone that caused her to talk about the President being killed in Dallas. We have a career Louisiana State Police officer as a witness to that fact. For lack of any serious investigation we have no clue whether she had heard the remarks from the men she was traveling with, although Fruge seems to have had that impression, or from gossip she picked up elsewhere. It was one of the things at the top of her mind, along with her baby and the drug deal. And certainly she talked about the same things to staff at the charity hospital while she was coming out of drug withdrawal. It is clear from the Garrison investigation documents that Garrison had received word about the incident via one of these doctors (which one is unclear).

Garrison investigator Detective Frank Meloche sent a memo to Garrison in February of 1967 with a statement by Mr. A.H. Magruder that he had been told by Dr. Weiss during the Christmas season of 1963 about the woman who had talked about the attack on the President before it occurred. One of the doctors (Dr. Victor Weiss) is on record with the HSCA (and in later public interviews) confirming that Cheramie continued to talk about the attack on the President after Fruge transported her and before the assassination occurred. He says that she stated *"the word in the underworld"* was that Kennedy would be hit.[2]

At a minimum we are left with a well-documented case of more "gossip" about an attack on the President, the "noise" that we have seen so much of in the weeks and days before the assassination. The question is whether or not we can infer anything further about its source given the lack of any real structured interrogation of Cheramie in 1963. To date, most conspiracy researchers have focused on the two men Cheramie described, following Fruge's own lead when he resumed the investigation under the Garrison inquiry.

Two Italians from Miami

In his HSCA testimony, Fruge stated that when Rose was first talking to him during the initial transport to the charity hospital, she said that she had been traveling with "two men who she said were Italians, or resembled Italians." The men were going to Dallas where the President was going to be killed, had to be killed. Rose was going to Dallas to pick up some money and her baby. The men were traveling from Florida to Dallas and had stopped at a lounge, the Silver Slipper, for drinks. An argument ensued and the manager of the lounge threw her out, and as she tried to hitchhike she was hit by a car. The Silver Slipper was familiar to Fruge as a house of prostitution and he knew its manager was Mac Manual. Fruge also commented that Rose had in her possession two boxes with clothes and baby clothing.

During his assignment for Garrison and after determining Cheramie was no longer living, Fruge proceeded to the Silver Slipper and interviewed Mac Manual who was still manager there four years later. Manual told Fruge that he remembered the incident and that he knew the two men as pimps who had been to his place before, bringing prostitutes to and from Florida. They had come in with Cheramie. She began acting wild and one of the men slapped her and threw her outside. After this first interview, Fruge obtained a stack of photos from Garrison's office and went back to show them to Manual. But Fruge had no idea who was in the photos, and Manual picked two men from the stack (Fruge does not say how certain Manual was about those identifications or how close the resemblance might have been).

The HSCA photo album contains a photo of Santana that certainly could be taken for an individual of Italian ancestry; unfortunately Fruge did not dig further into the particulars of the two men, the timing of their earlier visits to the Silver Slipper, the identity of the other prostitutes, etc.

This identification has generated a great deal of research, because both individuals named were investigated by Garrison and had associations to various Cuban exile and CIA activities. Garrison did investigate both, however there is no sign that he specifically followed up on the Cheramie incident with either. What we do know about both can be summarized as follows:

In 1967 (during the Garrison investigation) Emilio Santana was married, had six children, lived in Miami, and worked for an auto bumper repair shop. In Cuba he had been a fisherman. After fleeing from Cuba to Miami shortly after Castro's takeover, he was recruited by the CIA, went through training, and became a boat guide for infiltration missions. CIA records are mixed on his dates of service, with one giving a period from 1960 to 1963 and the other 1962-1963. Santana himself told Garrison he had worked for the CIA for two years, having been recruited in Miami, and that his job was smuggling people in and out of Cuba. "His knowledge of the waters surrounding Cuba and its coastline were [sic] very valuable in those operations."

After those two years, he separated from the CIA and moved to New Orleans, spending about three months in the city and then going to work on a fishing boat out of Biloxi. In his February, 1967 interview Santana admitted making inquiries about anti-Castro activities in New Orleans and recalled meeting a Cuban named "Chink" and a man he identified from a photo as Arcacha. Further investigation by Garrison's people identified "Chink" or "Chino" as Jose Llera and also determined that the individual identified as Arcacha was most probably Louis Breto, an Alpha 66 delegate in New Orleans in 1963. Breto closely resembled Sergio Arcacha Smith. Arcacha Smith had left New Orleans sometime before and in 1963 was living and working in Houston, Texas. Another Cuban exile reported that Santana had been trying to associate himself with Alpha 66 at the time.[3]

CIA internal legal memoranda during the Garrison investigation confirm that Santana was a CIA boat guide and that he was involved in operational missions during 1963, until separated from the Agency in October of that year. The CIA was concerned that Santana could identify operational bases and active personnel by location, name and true identities.

Sergio Arcacha Smith attended college in Texas, served as the Cuban consul in India under Batista, and married a woman from Pakistan. He left the diplomatic service to become a hotel manager in Caracas, Venezuela during 1954-1957. He returned to Cuba briefly but went into exile in 1960, traveling to the U.S. via New York, then on to New Orleans and later to Miami where he was appointed by Antonio Verona as the New Orleans delegate of the Frente. During 1961 Arcacha Smith was associated with Guy Bannister, who ran name checks on prospective members and eventually became very close to Frente volunteer David Ferrie. Ferrie and Arcacha Smith were close associates during most of 1961 before and after the Bay of Pigs failure, and late in 1961 Arcacha reportedly introduced Carlos Quiroga to Ferrie. In October 1961 the FRD was absorbed into the new CRC and Smith continued fund raising and recruiting activities for the CRC until January 1962, when he was fired for mismanagement and possible misappropriation of funds. Reportedly some New Orleans exiles suspect him of being a Castro agent; the same suspicions circulated about Quiroga. After his dismissal he went to work for a local PR firm which had served the CRC, but during the summer of 1962 he traveled to Mexico under an assumed name and was fired from that firm.

In October 1962, he left New Orleans for good, moved to Miami, and then settled briefly in Tampa in December. He moved on to Houston Texas in January, taking a job there as an air conditioner salesman in March, 1963. He continued to work in Houston through 1963 and was there on November 22, as verified by his employer Calvin Clausel in a letter to Jim Garrison. Arcacha Smith continued in the air conditioner business until at least 1966, and the files showed that he had applied to travel to Canada in 1964, and to Spain in the following two years.[4]

Cheramie's sources

Due to the lack of any thorough investigation in 1963, we are left with one basic fact: Rose Cheramie *had* heard talk about President Kennedy being killed in Dallas. Given the corroboration of her drug dealing information it also appears likely that she was closely associated with individuals dealing in drugs whether she herself was a courier or not. Where she heard the assassination "talk" and how she may have mixed it in with her drug-related information during the time she was on drugs and going through withdrawal herself is virtually impossible to resolve. It would have been a challenge even in 1963.

The identification of her "Italian" looking pimp companions as Emilo Santana and Arcacha Smith seems questionable; certainly the background of neither man matches someone who would have been seen frequently in the Silver Slipper, transporting prostitutes back and forth between Florida and New Orleans.

Perhaps the most that can be said is that Cheramie's leak can be traced back towards Miami, whence she was apparently traveling, and to "word in the underworld." And perhaps some reader will take the names, dates and information documented in this appendix and develop the Cheramie lead into something more solid than the mystery it remains as of this writing.

One interesting avenue for further research remains the names listed by Cheramie relating to Houston/Galveston drug deals. The only specific major Houston drug bust the author has found mentioned deals with a November 7, 1962 incident involving 22 pounds of heroin. This particular sale was by Paul Mandolini to *Joe Stassi*, the former co-owner along with Santo Trafficante of the San Souci casino in Havana. There also is mention of a drug bust in Loredo in 1963 which appears to have been part of the Trafficante/Marcello/Mertz network – the same network which may have carried the rumors heard in the Kirknewton incident discussed in Appendix F.

APPENDIX H
ODIO REVISITED

The Odio incident illustrates many of the basic flaws in the Warren Commission report. It demonstrates that Lee Oswald was not a lone nut; he was quite definitely involved with others in unexplained activities in the fall of 1963. It illustrates some of the methods that were used to create a false image of Oswald as an unpredictable and possibly dangerous individual. It also associates him with suspicious Cubans who could well be Castro agents. Beyond that, the FBI investigation of the incident demonstrates the lengths to which investigating agencies were forced in order to officially avoid indications of conspiracy – as well as to protect their own intelligence activities and sources.

When pressured by the Warren Commission on the implications of the incident, the FBI produced a reassuring response in the form of a purported Odio visit by Loran Hall, Lawrence Howard and William Seymour. However, at the same time the FBI was communicating that solution to the Warren Commission, we now see that its own internal investigations had already negated such a scenario. On October 2, 1964 a letter from the FBI Miami office related that FBI interviews with Howard and Seymour had determined that Howard had no knowledge of Odio or a visit to her in Dallas, and that Seymour was not in Dallas with Hall and Howard. Seymour's employer had confirmed his presence in Miami in the period from September 5 to October 10, 1963.

In addition, Hall, when visited again by the FBI and shown Odio's photograph, did not recognize her and then stated that he had not visited her in Dallas after all. As Hall would later testify to the HSCA, in the initial FBI visit he had said that he recalled no visit to anyone named Odio. But the FBI had asked if it was at all possible that he could have come in contact with her somehow without recalling her by name. He simply agreed that was always a possibility.

In an additional refutation of the information given to the Warren Commission, the FBI showed photos of all three men independently to both Sylvia and Annie Odio. Both women refused to identify any of the three as their visitors. This negative identification was not reported to the Warren Commission.

The FBI's initial investigation of the three men was apparently so superficial they also totally missed the fact that while all three men were in Dallas in the fall of 1963, they were not there at the same time. Hall and Howard arrived in Dallas on or about October 3, staying a few days. Later, Hall made another trip to Dallas, this time with Seymour, on October 17, a date confirmed by Hall and Seymour's arrest and booking by the Dallas Police.

With all the information now available, we can see that the initial FBI report on Hall was not only incorrect but also lacking in background information held by the FBI itself. It seems that Mr. Hall had been was well known to the FBI long before the autumn of 1964. Hall is found in several FBI reports and was the subject of a prior JFK assassination inquiry.

That investigation involved Hall as a possible suspect in the Kennedy assassination because of his possession of a rifle taken out of pawn in California and possibly taken to Dallas. This investigation began on November 23, 1963 with an FBI interview of Richard Hathcock.[1] Hathcock told the FBI that Hall and Gerry Hemming had been in his office a year earlier and he had lent them money, taking Hemming's 30-06 rifle as security. Ten to fifteen days before the assassination Hall and "a fat Mexican fellow" (almost certainly Lawrence Howard) came in and reclaimed the rifle.

In Hathcock's later remarks to the HSCA, he stated that the FBI came to him the day after the assassination, asking about an employee named Roy Payne and the 30.06 rifle.

> It's my opinion that the reason he [the FBI agent] wanted to see Mr. Payne was because Payne's fingerprints undoubtedly were all over that rifle from his having handled it many times. It's also my opinion that unless that particular rifle had been found [near the scene of the crime] or in some way involved in this whole thing [the assassination], that the FBI would have no interest in it.[2]

Payne was questioned by the FBI and told them that he had seen Hall again on November 18 and asked about Cuban activities but Hall had told him the CIA had stopped his operation in Miami, he didn't have time to talk and had to catch a plane to Dallas. Payne told the HSCA that the FBI secretly searched Hathcock's offices and vehicle and maintained surveillance over them for some time. Payne also claimed he had seen Hall a couple of weeks after the assassination and that Hall had told him he had been in Dallas at the time of the attack, "right in the middle of the lobby of the Hilton, Hotel." Hall himself has repeatedly denied being in Dallas on that date, however, in his HSCA testimony he admitted that on November 22 he telephoned a relative for the purpose of establishing his whereabouts and that he felt the need to establish an alibi for himself.

The FBI's contact with Hall actually began in July of 1959, after his return from Cuba. However, at that time, the FBI determined that the information provided by him time was "considered questionable." The CIA domestic contacts section had also interviewed Hall for two hours in the same 1959 time frame.

Both the CIA and the FBI also had reports on Hall from September, 1963 - related to statements he had made in fund raising appearances in California in regard to his Cuban activities. There is a CIA contact division report relating to Hall with the dates September 12 and 18, 1963 and the subject "Cuban Invasion." At that point in time Hall had also been given a private lie detector test, paid for by the John Birch Society, to verify some of the remarks which he was making in regard to Cuba.

Hall testified to the HSCA about his interrogation by the FBI and CIA after his arrest in Dallas in October 1963. The FBI has denied any such interrogation, however at least one withheld NARA document seems to suggest that Hall may have been telling the truth: "FBI Dallas, October 23, 1963, Interview *of Loran Hall, William Seymour – anti-Castro activities...*"[3] None of this background on Hall shows up in the FBI's Odio incident response to the Warren Commission.

All in all, Loran Hall was a far more interesting subject than the FBI ever indicated to the Warren Commission, even if he was not Sylvia Odio's visitor. Unfortunately, there seems to be no remaining FBI paper trail on the Hall investigation described by Hathcock and Payne. It would be extremely interesting to know what triggered that FBI inquiry on November 23.

Another person of interest seemingly passed over by the FBI (at least as far as official records) was from New Orleans, the self-described point of origin for the Odio visitors.

Carlos Quiroga, prominence in national news coverage immediately following the assassination; he had given extremely inflammatory quotations attributed to Lee Oswald and admitted to having personally met and attempted to infiltrate Oswald's FPCC chapter in New Orleans. Despite this there is no record that the FBI contacted Quiroga after the assassination in regard his admitted contacts with Lee Oswald.

Quiroga would later become an early and key informant to DA Garrison's assassination inquiry. Garrison developed witnesses confirming Quiroga associating with Lee Oswald and introducing him to people associated with retired FBI agent Guy Bannister. At that point the CIA "Garrison Team" was devoting considerable time to damage control in regard to Garrison's investigation. The CIA was worried because some of the names surfaced by Garrison did have real contacts to the Agency and some individuals named by Garrison were claiming to have a CIA relationship. CIA Legal Counsel conducted an extensive survey of all the names being surfaced by Garrison, and even documented the actual CIA association with people such as Santana, LaBorde, Bringuier and Shaw. But the name Bannister is not even mentioned on the internal CIA lists. There was not even an effort to refute CIA contact with him as there was with Novel and Ferrie; he simply was not mentioned.[4]

However a newly available CIA document confirms that as of August 1960, the CIA Cover section was doing a special inquiry on Guy Bannister Associates.[5] That document is followed by another CIA memorandum which calls for an in depth evaluation of Bannister and Associates for possible use as a cover organization in support of the QK/ENCHANT project.[6] It calls for an initial telephonic report by September 11, 1960. While the exact nature of QK/ENCHANT is still unknown, we do know that both Clay Shaw and Howard Hunt were also associated with it.

We have no record as to the outcome of the CIA's Bannister cover inquiry, exactly how Bannister's organization may have been used, or who within the CIA was to be placed under the Bannister cover. These documents do lend additional interest to the witnesses describing Quiroga's introduction of Oswald to Bannister associates–using the name "Leon" Oswald (the name used to introduce him to Sylvia Odio), and to Gordon Novel's description of a CIA propaganda initiative involving Bannister and CIA officer David Phillips.

Carlos Quiroga also appears to figure in some of Lee Oswald's most interesting activities in New Orleans, though not exactly in the fashion that Quiroga himself reported them to the FBI and to DA Garrison.

It appears that Oswald's first action in regard to the FPCC was to simply write a letter (a typical activity for Oswald). In this case it was a letter to the FPCC about a street altercation in which Cuban exile "guasanos" had attacked him, and for which he received a warning from the police. The problem is that Oswald's letter was written on August 4, five days *before* his first actual leafleting in the dock area next to the navy carrier *Wasp* and almost two weeks *before* the exile street confrontation with Carlos Bringuier and other exiles–conducted in front of local news television cameras which had been summoned by Clay Shaw's assistant Jesse Core.[7] The other problem is that is appears that the leaflets used by Oswald, including some of those with the Bannister office street address on them, may have actually been delivered to Oswald by Carlos Quiroga prior to the leafleting. In that regard it may be important to note that the pamphlets distributed with the leaflets were not from the then-current print run (number four) but rather from the very first print run for which a bulk order had come from the CIA.[8]

The contact between Quiroga and Oswald is extremely important, partially because Quiroga and Bringuier apparently misled investigators in stating that Quiroga's visit occurred after the Trade Mart incident and not before. But they also failed to mention that according to Oswald's landlady, Quiroga had arrived with a stack of leaflets five to six inches think, not the one or two leaflets Quiroga described.[9]

Another reason that Quiroga himself is important is that he had been considered a possible Castro intelligence agent by the CIA. Quiroga had also been closely associated with Sergio Arcacha-Smith and the CRC during the period when he himself was strongly pro-Castro–as late as the summer of 1961 after the Bay of Pigs invasion. We know this from the CIA, which had evaluated Quiroga for possible recruitment for return to Cuba as an agent in place but had determined that he was unacceptable. This was due to his having been an "ardent Castro supporter until mid-1961", his supposed homosexual tendencies, and his having made strong anti-U.S. statements.[10] The CIA paid close attention to Quiroga during the Garrison hearings in which he initially served as a major informant for Garrison. It appears that the CIA got much of its information from inside the Garrison investigation by way of Quiroga, relayed from Bringuier to the FBI and on to the CIA.[11]

However, virtually all of Quiroga's leads for Garrison turned out to be apparent misdirections. Garrison began to suspect him and eventually forced him into a polygraph test that showed Quiroga to have guilty knowledge about Oswald and his involvement with other people in some sort of a conspiracy.[12] The polygraph results suggested that Quiroga had been in company with Oswald on several occasions; knew that he was involved in an anti-Castro operation; and was aware of the nature and identity of the heavy set "Mexican" seen in company with Oswald.

Garrison was not the only to grow more suspicious of Quiroga. The CIA further speculated, based on excerpts of a Quiroga interview with Garrison that were supplied to the CIA by the FBI and Bringuier, that Quiroga had been or was still a Castro penetration agent into anti-Castro groups in New Orleans. Among other remarks cited are his statement of loyalty to Cuba and in particular the fact that in 1960 he went to visit his father in Cuba who was "in the Castro revolution".[13]

We know from Quiroga that he represented himself to Oswald as a Castro supporter; what we don't know is how true this may have been and who else Quiroga may have been communicating with other than Bringuier. Quiroga may have passed along the fact that Oswald was playing a role as an informer and provocateur to any number of individuals on both sides of the secret war.

It is also unclear who within the DRE may have heard about Oswald's dual role, either in New Orleans or Miami. A considerable number of CIA DRE reports for the period that should have included reports and commentary on Oswald in New Orleans are either missing or unreleased.

In revisiting the Odio incident, it is critical to view it not in isolation, but in the context of other relevant activities in the August through November time frame. When seen in context, the behavior of her mysterious visitors can be seen as quite consistent with the evolution of Oswald's changing role in the events that led to the afternoon of November 22:

August 4   Oswald writes to FPCC about exiles attacking FPCC demonstration.

August 5   Bringuier has what he will later call his initial contact by an anti-Castro Oswald.

August 7   Oswald seen with suspicious "Mexican/s" in Pena's bar; suspicious Mexicans are reported by Bringuier to FBI as suspected communist agents.

August 9   First Oswald FPCC leafleting near Canal Street docks (no incidents).

Mid August   Quiroga visits Oswald and carries a large quantity of leaflets; represents himself as Castro supporter – which had been only a year earlier.

August 16   Trade Center leafleting and confrontation of Oswald by Bringuier; police arrests.

Late August   Nagell reports to anti-Castro exiles in New Orleans; his first meetings with Oswald, between August 23-27; Nagell takes photo. Cubans represent themselves as Castro agents and recruit Oswald for action in D.C. area in September.

August 29   Oswald begins writing letters to FPCC and CPUSA about a possible move to Baltimore the area.

Early September Oswald reported in the company of Maurice Bishop in Dallas; topic of discussion being elimination of Fidel Castro

September 19 Oswald visits East Louisiana State Louisiana Hospital, inquires about work and is witnessed by Doctor Frank Silva ranting about killing Castro.

September 20 Nagell arrested in El Paso after fleeing from New Orleans.

September 24 Oswald in New Orleans.

September 25 Oswald reported in Austin.

September 24-29 Oswald at Odio's according to Odio; use of the name "Leon"; Oswald at McKeown's last week in September.

Note that Odio's uninvited visitors were men coming from New Orleans in an ostensible effort to get her aid in translating a lettering into English for use in fund raising. The men knew her father's war name but could not give her any associations with JURE. Later her grandfather in New Orleans, a close associate of Tony Verona and Carlos Bringuier (and obviously not a supporter of Ray and JURE) would tell the FBI that Sylvia had mentioned the name "Quiroga" and he might possibly have been one of her visitors – her uncle was unsure of that. Interestingly, her uncle attended the Oswald court hearing in New Orleans although he did not mention to the FBI that he himself had seen Lee Oswald in person.

September 26	Oswald enters Mexico
October 1	John Martino in Dallas, public remarks about Odio daughters in Dallas
October 3	Loran Hall and Larry Howard arrive in Dallas (via El Paso Texas) on their way from California. Hall and Howard come with a U-Haul trailer containing supplies and some arms raised from exiles in California.
October 3	Oswald in Dallas on his return from Mexico, registers at YMCA
October 4	First Oswald "set up" appearance–application as a photographer in the Aldophus Hotel across the street from Ruby's Carousel club.
October 17	Hall back in Dallas from Miami with William Seymour, stopped for traffic violation. Both Hall and Seymour arrested and booked for possession of Dexadrine on that date. Hall reports that he was interviewed by FBI and CIA while under arrest in Dallas; after bail was posted he checked in at the YMCA and saw Seymour's name on the register. The Garrison investigation located copies of the YMCA guest register that suggest the registration name may later have been erased and changed from Seymour to Howard.

October 31   Oswald application for job at Statler Hilton Hotel in downtown Dallas

October 31-   Vidal Santiago in Dallas from Miami, conducting "fund raising."

November 1   Rifle left at Dial Ryder's gun shop to attach scope–in Oswald's name.

November 1   Parrot Jungle incident in Miami, name "Lee Oswald" is used.

November 7   Oswald applies for job at Allright Parking garage on Commerce, where Jack Ruby routinely parks his car.

November 9   Oswald test-drives a car at Downtown Lincoln Mercury

November 11   FBI informant T-1 reported Hall and Seymour had been in Dallas doing fund raising.

November 16   Oswald applies for job at Southland Hotel parking garage and asks about view of downtown Dallas.

November 20-21 Oswald "type" individual hitches ride with Ralph Yates to corner of Elm and Houston, mentions Carousel club and appears to have a rifle in a paper package.

November 21   Vidal back in Dallas from Miami.

Implications

Lee Oswald functioned as a provocateur in New Orleans and was in contact with pro-Castro and anti-Castro Cuban exiles as well as double agents representing themselves as both. By August 20 Oswald had been identified to individuals in Miami as a potential patsy for an anti-Kennedy conspiracy. These individuals contacted Oswald and began to establish him as a patsy after August 27, resulting in his letters about a move to Baltimore.

These individuals included one person known to Oswald as a Castro agent (possibly Quiroga), and one person from Miami representing himself as a Castro agent. The introduction of these imposters was known to Richard Case Nagell—whether some part of the introduction may have actually been made by him remains uncertain. Given Nagell's lack of connections in New Orleans, he may have done the introduction for leverage as he apparently had done with Von Marlowe earlier in Los Angeles. If so, the individual from Miami may have been associated with individuals connected to either Masferrer or McClaney. Masferrer was an object of attention for Nagell in Miami, possibly because of Masferrer's interest in Artime's new activities.

As of the end of August there was no firm plan for an assassination effort in Dallas, Texas. Any specific plans for the DC area were most likely blown due either to (well founded) suspicions of Nagell, to Oswald's failure to obtain a Cuban visa within the three-day period he himself mentioned, or a combination of both elements.

Later the plotters took advantage of Oswald's trip to Mexico City to begin developing a new image of Oswald, not as a political activist but rather as an unpredictable "loose cannon" who could later be associated with a plot by Castro. This approach may even have dovetailed with Oswald's CIA instructions for gaining the interest of Cuban embassy and DGI personnel.

The Dallas plot became firm as of October 1, when it became clear that Oswald would not be getting a Cuban visa and that he would be returning to Dallas to his family. The set up of Oswald in Dallas was done without Oswald's direct knowledge, and in none of his personal actions then or later would Oswald directly implicate himself in that role. This meant that he had to be either managed or impersonated at various points.

At this point the plotters began selecting other patsies to support the story line of Castro agents at work, either double agents or "for hire" players. Individuals selected as possible patsies included Oswald and Jack Ruby, possibly there was some consideration of Loran Hall and Carlos Quiroga as well. All were individuals who could be demonstrated to have had an association with Cuba, to have reportedly associated with Oswald, and to be potential suspects as Castro foils. Following the assassination all these individuals would be reported in contact with Oswald before the assassination and the FBI can be shown to have avoided investigating either Quiroga or Hall (as far as the official record is concerned), possibly frustrating the plotters.

APPENDIX I
ECHOES FROM DALLAS

More than forty years later there are individuals still holding information about the attack in Dallas. They could still set the record straight. Some could verify that a conspiracy was involved, others know the general plan and perhaps even some of the names involved. Some know about the damage control that followed and the real nature of Oswald's use by the intelligence community. Some of the people who know details and names have talked privately, but for them to go public could undermine the decades long Cuban exile crusade against Fidel Castro and Communism in Cuba and that remains an overriding concern. Still, we continue to hear echoes of the conspiracy, remarks about motive, about agendas, and about the type of men who went to Dallas to kill the President of the United States.

Information for the ARRB
In October, 1995, Gene Wheaton faxed a communication to John Tunheim, Chairman of the newly organized Assassinations Records Review Board. Wheaton simply informed Tunheim that he might have some *relevant information* regarding the Board's inquiry. Wheaton included a four page personal biography as background, as well as a letter of commendation from the White House, signed by President Nixon, in recognition of Wheaton's work in the global war against heroin (awarded for his activities while working in Iran).

Wheaton's history is extensive and impressive, representing decades of experience in law enforcement and criminal investigation. It includes Air Force OSI work in criminal investigation and counterintelligence, Army CID training and work, serving as Director of Security for Rockwell's IBEX program in Iran, acting as advisor to U.S. and Iranian agencies on security, police and anti-terrorism, security consulting work with the governments of Egypt, Pakistan and Saudi Arabia as well as for Bechtel Corp in its Saudi Jeddah airport project. It also includes his work as a consulting investigator on the Iran Contra case and the related congressional investigations of the "guns for drugs" aspect of that affair. Wheaton's ARRB correspondence and related documents are provided as exhibits in support of this appendix.

John Tunheim responded to Wheaton's offer of information with a brief letter on October 25, 1995, thanking him for his interest and informing him that a Review Board staff member would be in touch with him. It appears that no further communication was directed to Wheaton until a blanket ARRB notice went out to individuals who had contacted the Board. In response, Wheaton faxed the Board a one page CV he'd prepared for a retired CIA officer whom he described as a "very close friend" in the 1980's. (February 15, 1996)

At that point in time Wheaton was serving as Vice President of National Air Cargo. NAC operated a fleet of 23 twin-engine turboprop cargo planes. Its primary business in the 1985-86 timeframe was support of UPS overnight service. Wheaton stated that he had employed his friend as the company's Washington D.C. liaison officer, overseeing air supply contracts related to Contra support activities. Initially Wheaton did not name his friend and former employee to the ARRB, although he did describe his CIA association and the fact that his friend's wife was also a high level active CIA employee.

Wheaton also described his introduction to a number of Americans and Cuban exiles with whom his friend had worked prior to and after the Bay of Pigs. During his association with the former CIA officer and his Cuban exile friends, Wheaton was privy to their intimate discussions of the Bay of Pigs, covert operations, and the Kennedy assassination. He described his friend as being in charge of infiltrating sabotage and assassination teams into Cuba, beginning in 1960 and continuing after the Bay of Pigs failure. Wheaton also mentioned discussions with the friend and one of his key Cuban agents about coming forward with their knowledge of the Kennedy assassination.

From the CV, we can build a synopsis on Wheaton's CIA officer friend:

- Service in the Marines in the Central Pacific Theatre during WWII, commissioned as 2ndLt of Reserve Rifle Company in 1948 and Paramilitary, Survival, Evasion and Escape instructor for the CIA in 1952-53.

- In the 1950s he trained Thai and National Chinese personnel in paramilitary and resistance tactics as well as prepared maritime infiltration teams in a SE Asian project involving Indonesia, Singapore, Malaysia and the Philippines.

- As a full time CIA officer, he served as Chief of Base in Florida and later Guatemala in 1960-1961. He was responsible for selection and training of cadres for the Exile brigade as well as for selection and management of small teams and agents used in maritime infiltration prior to the Bay of Pigs.

- Following this assignment he served as special warfare advisor to I Corps in Danang, Vietnam prior to returning to become Senior Operations Officer for a still-sensitive Cuban project.

- Recent document releases and research strongly suggests this sensitive duty was the Artime-associated AM/WORLD project, which was heavily compartmentalized within the CIA and which had its own staff independent of JM/WAVE. (Details on this project are provided in Chapter 12.) Based on these new documents, we know that Artime's case officer was Henry Hecksher and that Artime's senior exile military officer was Rafael "Chi Chi" Quintero (a prominent name in Iran-Contra events). Artime and Quintero's senior military advisor was one Carl Jenkins.

For reference, it is worth noting that special military and infiltration training was provided to both Artime and Quintero by David Morales and that the AM/WORLD contact in Mexico City (the only individual authorized to know about AM/WORLD other than the Chief of Station) was David Atlee Phillips. Former officers from JM/WAVE such as Tom Clines and CIA associated exiles such as Felix Rodriquez were also involved in Contra activities.

After service on the special Cuban project, Wheaton's friend was assigned as a senior advisor to the Dominican National Police, then as Senior Advisor on Security and Training in Nicaragua, and eventually as Chief of Base, South Laos in 1971-1973. He requested early retirement from the CIA at the conclusion of hostilities in SE Asia.

After receipt of Wheaton's second communication, Tom Samoluk of the ARRB wrote to Jeremy Gunn in regard to the Wheaton letters. Samoluk pointed out that the Board would need to decide whether or not it should assign an investigator to respond to such correspondence, to evaluate the person's credibility and value in the Board's search for documents. He also noted that he would be available to discuss the correspondence and any larger relevant issues.

Apparently as a result, ARRB staff member Anne Buttimer was assigned to contact Wheaton. There are records of contact with Wheaton in an April telephone call (Buttimer recorded a "outside contact report" for that call) Wheaton informed Buttermer that he had no specific documents that would offer information about the conspiracy but that he could produce documents which would substantiate the nature and general activities of the people through whom he had obtained information about the assassination conspiracy. He cited his sources on the assassination as Cuban exiles who had confirmed that exiles originally trained for attacks on Castro had killed JFK, considering him to have been a traitor. He also stated that *"people above the Cubans wanted JFK killed for other reasons."* Wheaton concluded with the cryptic remark, *"the matter is not complex, but it is convoluted."*

On May 16, 1996, Buttimer followed up the telephone call with a letter to Wheaton in which she offered to meet with Wheaton should he find himself in the Washington D.C. area. We have also a copy of another letter from Buttimer to Wheaton in which she refers to a personal meeting with him in July 1996, at which time Wheaton delivered additional reference material to Buttimer. Unfortunately no contact report has been found for this meeting.

There is no further record of any contact by Buttimer or anyone else from the ARRB with Wheaton. In March, 1998 he again faxed the Board and noted that Buttimer seemed to have departed from the Board. He was never contacted again and only received generic Board news releases. The only response to his effort at follow-up is a very general reply from Eileen Sullivan, Press and Public Affairs Officer. In this "form letter" response, she refers to the Board as having received thousands of leads and suggestions and not being able to link any document releases to information provided by a particular individual.

Apart from this generic "thank you," there is no expression of further interest from the Board. And there was no further record of any comment from Gene Wheaton on the subject until Malcolm Blunt located the Wheaton ARRB files and brought them to the attention of this author, who then pursued the matter with the help of William Law. Law contacted and interviewed Wheaton in 2005, where he confirmed what was in the ARRB records.

A good deal of background research has been done on the Wheaton documents and on the names which Wheaton eventually disclosed to the ARRB in the documents submitted to Buttermer. These include the

CV which Wheaton eventually identified as that of Carl Elmer Jenkins; a copy of Jenkin's passport circa 1983; and business cards for Carl Jenkins (ECM Corporation - International Security Assistance Specialists, New York, Washington DC, California, PO Box in Falls Church Va., Consultants for Human Development, Falls Church Va., identified as a mail drop and National Air, Liaison Officer). The National Air card has a note on it indicating that Jenkins had connected Wheaton to Raphael "Chi Chi" Quintero, Nestor Sanchez, Nestor Pino, Bill Bode, Rob Owen, and Vaughn Forrest.

Carl Jenkins, Paramilitary specialist for the CIA:

Research confirms that beyond a doubt, Carl Jenkins was indeed a senior CIA officer who worked on paramilitary activities in support of the Bay of Pigs project and that by 1963-64 he was indeed directly involved with the AM/WORLD project, with Artime (AM/BIDDY) and Quintero (AM/JAVA-4).

In September, 1963 Jenkins wrote a general memo describing Artime's operational philosophy and concepts. This summarized his views about commando teams, infiltration teams, and guerrilla actions. The memo addresses military operations as Artime conceives them to be organized and conducted under a single organization (AM/WORLD) in which the Cubans can have faith. In a section on Commandos, there is *discussion of the use of abductions and assassinations targeted against Cuban G-2 intelligence informants, agents, officers, and foreign Communists to raise the morale of people inside Cuba.*[1]

In December, 1964, Jenkins prepared a summary report of Quintero's visit to Europe for a dialogue with Rolando Cubela in preparation for further meetings with Artime. The goal of this meeting was to develop contacts with a group inside Cuba which was capable of *"eliminating Fidel Castro and of seizing and holding Havana, at least for an appreciable time that would be sufficient to justify recognition."*[2]

There seems to be no doubt that Jenkins was indeed involved in a very special project in 1963-64 just as the CV Wheaton provided to the ARRB indicates. It should be noted that these AM/WORLD activities were completely segmented from JM/WAVE and communications from Jenkins and Hecksher were not run through JM/WAVE. In fact the AM/WORLD group operated its own facility in Miami (cryptonym "LORK").

Carl Jenkins and the elimination of Fidel Castro:

Perhaps even more surprising is the fact that we now have confirmation of some of Jenkins' activities prior to the Bay of Pigs and corroboration that he was involved with at least one project intended to kill Fidel Castro *prior* to the planned invasion.

This information appears in several memos which were apparently written in conjunction with investigations into assassination projects conducted by the Church Committee; they were located by researcher Malcolm Blunt in 2005 and provided to the author. Whether or not this was ever transmitted to that Committee is unclear; the document was released in 1993 as a part of the CIA historical review program.

The first document is a Memorandum for the Record, dated March 12, 1975 and signed by Edward Cates, Chief, Imagery Exploitation Group, NPIC. It recounts that three NPIC personnel who had formerly worked at JM/WAVE had heard references to assassination plans against Fidel Castro. Eventually eight persons told of plans aimed at Fidel Castro and one relating to Raul Castro.

The incident involving Raul Castro seems to have been an autonomous action by Rip Robertson while engaged in a paramilitary raid on Santiago de Cuba harbor in which the mission personnel took the opportunity to fire on Raul's home as they exited the harbor.

One assassination plan aimed to kill Castro in the Bay of Pigs resort area where he maintained a yacht and was known to vacation. That plan, possibly with the code "Pathfinder" associated with it, evidently did not go into action.

The second project, which apparently did go into operation, was led by Carl Jenkins of the DDP (Directorate of Plans). It called for assassinating Castro at the DuPont Varadero Beach Estate, east of Havana. Castro was known to frequent the estate and the plan was to use a high powered rifle to kill him from a distance. The photo interpretation support involved providing annotated photographs and drawings of the estate. The image personnel had no knowledge of the plan ever being implemented, but other information suggests that up to three attempts were made to insert a shooter for this project.

A second memorandum, of May 1975, from Joseph Seltzer, reflects a search for further information on "Pathfinder" that proved fruitless, turning up only one reference to Pathfinder in a January 20, 1961 FBI memo concerning Frank Sturgis.

Two additional Memoranda for the Record, of June 1975 and August 1975, appear to be part of the CIA's own internal investigation of assassination attempts. The first concerns the claim of a former Cuban agent (then a contract employee) to have made three abortive attempts to land at Varadero Beach for the purpose of assassinating Fidel Castro. The agent claimed that he and another individual made three abortive attempts in February of 1961.

The memo states that a former Miami station case officer said in June of 1975 that he was aware of this mission (though the officer is not named in the memo). According to the Cuban exile, the first mission was aborted when the luxury yacht being used developed engine trouble (they had also forgotten their radio generator). The report continues, but the second page is missing from the file. Cuban names mentioned in this first memo include "Felix" and "Segundo."

The second related memo, of August, refers to the statement of the contract employee (who was being debriefed in preparation for retirement). When asked if he had ever been involved in any activity involving assassinations, he replied that in December, 1960 he had told an Agency officer that the solution to the Cuban problem was to kill Fidel Castro and that he would volunteer for such a mission.

He related that he and two other Cubans made three CIA planned and executed voyages to Cuba for this purpose, but that the craft they sailed in was never met and they never landed. The employee was unable to identify the American he alleged had given them the missions. He said he received no instructions on how to complete the mission nor had he ever fired the scope-equipped rifle provided for said mission. The memo notes that Agency files contain no record of such an assignment.

In *Deadly Secrets*, authors Hinckle and Turner describe an incident related by Felix Rodriguez in his book *Shadow Warrior*.[3] Rodriguez described volunteering to assassinate Castro while in training with the Brigade. He also described being presented with a beautiful German bolt action rifle with telescopic sight. The weapon had been pre-sighted for a location where Castro made frequent appearances. After several abortive attempts to infiltrate Rodriguez into Cuba, the project was abandoned. Felix Rodriguez separated from the CIA in 1976 (as described in *Deadly Secrets*). Though Rodriguez does not name his case officer prior to the Bay of Pigs, when he was infiltrated into Cuba in advance of the Brigade landing, he does acknowledge that Tom Clines became his case officer afterwards.

There seems some reason to at least speculate that both Quintero (who became second in command to Artime) and Rodriguez (who also joined Artime's offshore autonomous effort in 1963) may have been associated with CIA paramilitary officer Carl Jenkins before the Bay of Pigs. It also seems possible that Rodriguez may have been involved with the assassination project described in the NPIC memo and that the project was overseen by Carl Jenkins–this being the operation described by the NPIC personnel.

It appears that Carl Jenkins' paramilitary activities in support of Cuban operations were exactly as described to Gene Wheaton and exactly as summarized in the Jenkins CV submitted to the ARRB. There is also no doubt that Jenkins was very closely associated with Quintero in this period, as described by Wheaton. There are two books in print that also confirm these descriptions of Jenkins.[4]

In *The Death Merchant: The Rise and Fall of Edwin P. Wilson*, author Joseph Goulden presents information from the CIA officer whom Quintero went to when he became suspicious of an assassination assignment being promoted to Quintero and other exiles by Ed Wilson. The officer (given the pseudonym "Brad Rockford") talks about entering the CIA on detached duty from the Marines, being career paramilitary, and running CIA paramilitaries out of JM/WAVE. It seems clear that Rockford was in fact Carl Jenkins.[5]

In his book *Manhunt: The Incredible Pursuit of a CIA Agent Turned Terrorist*, Peter Maas mentions Carl Jenkins by name as the case officer for Quintero prior to the Bay of Pigs. Quintero was part of an advance team sent in before the invasion by Jenkins. After the landing failed, he hid out in Cuba for six weeks before making his way back to Florida. Afterwards Clines would assume a case officer role for Quintero, who would go on make to a number of sabotage and assassination missions into Cuba.[6]

It seems worth pointing out that Jenkins' name has never been mentioned in any of the numerous works on the Bay of Pigs, the Miami station, or the secret war against Castro. Prior to this investigation of Wheaton's ARRB communications, Carl Jenkins had a far lower profile than even David Morales.

Interestingly, Gene Wheaton recommended that William Law read these books in a 2005 interview. Wheaton suggested that they would describe the individuals he had been associating with or had source information on from what has become known as Iran-Contra.

Fellow Travelers?

Additionally, it is of interest that Ted Shackley and Tom Clines (who was to succeed Jenkins as Quintero's case officer) would be familiar names from both JM/WAVE and the Wilson affair. It is also of interest that David Morales's long time friend Ruben independently mentioned that Morales had introduced him to Shackley, Clines and Wilson on a trip to Virginia–and later, to Artime.

Another name mentioned in Wheaton's communication with the ARRB was that of Irving Davidson. Wheaton implies no direct role for Davidson in the conspiracy, however he seems to suggest that Davidson may have unwittingly served as a sort of cut out, bagman, or facilitator. Davidson was a very long time "arranger" in Washington, a registered lobbyist for clients including the Samozas of Nicaragua, the Trujillos of the Dominican Republic, and the Murchisons of Dallas.

In Chapter 16 we examined Davidson's role as the broker of a Murchison deal involving a Haitian meat packing plant in which Bobby Baker had been involved. Baker and VP Johnson had traveled to the Dominican Republic in 1963 and Baker had gone back shortly afterwards, possibly leveraging Johnson's name in regard a casino deal involving his Las Vegas business partners. During the Dominican crisis, tapes record President Johnson and Abe Fortas discussing an intermediary involved in discussions with potential leaders. The name used in the conversation is "Davidson."

Murchison had introduced Davidson to FBI Director Hoover (Anthony Summers relates an interview with Davidson, who lived only a block away from Hoover, in which he describes frequent visits to Hoover and Tolson).[7]

Davidson represented Carlos Marcello in Washington and was running information between Murchison and Marcello in 1963: it was a government sting of a Murchison/Marcello project that resulted in Marcello's arrest. Reportedly Davidson had also been in contact with Marcello after his forced deportation by Robert Kennedy, helping him to covertly return to the United States. In *Interference*, Dan Moldea writes that Murchison had gotten Teamster investments for California land development and that there were many connections between Murchison and Marcello, including their joint use of Davidson. Moldea also describes Robert Kennedy's major 1963 Justice Department initiative against sports gambling and its potential impact on both Marcello and Murchison, both heavily involved with professional sports gambling.[8]

Davidson also had a history as an intermediary in arms transactions, as a collaborator with Cuban exile activities, and as an informant (apparently a protected informant) to both the FBI and CIA. One 1959 FBI memorandum concerns a report by Davidson about a purchase of military weapons. Howard Davis was seeking Davidson's assistance in obtaining quantity of 50 caliber machine guns to be used by Cuban counter revolutionaries. A 1959 CIA report describes Davidson being involved with Cuban exiles interested in forming a government in exile, shows Davidson making introductions for them in Washington.[9] Other memos show Davidson under FBI electronic (ELSUR) surveillance. And in November - December 1963, Davidson was the subject of NSA monitoring, apparently at the request of the FBI. The NSA made reports to the FBI on November 17, 19, and 27, 1963.[10]

Also, as previously noted, Davidson was Jack Anderson's office mate and may have helped focus Anderson's attention on the bombshell lead from John Roselli that JFK had been killed by a team originally formed and trained to kill Castro. Anderson's "scoop" helped undercut Jim Garrison's early focus on CIA officers and anti-Castro exiles as the main actors in the conspiracy.

Real names, real people – real secrets?

Carl Jenkins was a senior CIA officer with exactly the background described by Wheaton to the ARRB. Rafael Quintero was a well respected, covert operations activist associated with anti-Castro and anti-Communist activities over several decades. He was taken seriously at the highest levels of the Kennedy administration. Indeed, DDP Richard Helms himself once commented on an Operational Plan drafted by Quintero to Thomas Parrott, Executive Assistant to the Military Representative of the President in June of 1962.[11]

Quintero had presented the plan to Attorney General Robert Kennedy and General Maxwell Taylor. Beyond that, Quintero was one of only a handful of exiles to be brought into both the AM/WORLD and AM/LASH (Cubela) projects, initiated by Fitzgerald and eventually turned over the Artime autonomous group project. Quintero was well enough respected to be brought into the secret "extra-governmental" Contra effort, and was eventually solicited by Edward Wilson for an assassination project. In both cases Quintero eventually determined that improper activities were going on and informed on them, in the case of Wilson through his old friend Carl Jenkins.

Gene Wheaton claims that he heard discussions of the conspiracy that killed John Kennedy in Dallas during the time when he was in close personal touch with both Jenkins and Quintero. He never raised this issue when he himself attempted to blow the whistle on various aspects of the Contra supply project. He only raised it confidentially to the ARRB–and was quite surprised to find that his correspondence had been released to public view.

However when interviewed in 2005, he continued to stand by his story that he heard from people involved in the "secret war," who knew that Cuban exiles were incited to execute President Kennedy. These individuals had their own agendas. The exile shooters considered themselves above all as patriots. They had been trained to assassinate Fidel Castro, but in the end they turned their guns on John Kennedy.

October 1, 2006

Rafael Quintero died October 1, 2006, in Baltimore at the age of 66. A *New York Times* obituary by Tim Weiner notes that his fellow veteran, Felix Rodriquez, attended the memorial service. The obituary describes Quintero's insertion into Cuba prior to the Bay of Pigs and his escape afterwards. It also states that after his escape from Cuba, Quintero continued working on operations against Fidel Castro, including assassination plots and eventually was paid $4,000 a month to support clandestine arms shipments to the Contras in Nicaragua (despite the Congressional ban on direct U.S. support).

Assessment

Gene Wheaton's name is not unknown to writers and readers of more recent conspiracy material. As Nick Schou related in an *1997 Orange County Weekly* newspaper article, "although he said he was never a CIA employee, Gene Wheaton's experience has brought him into the murky world of agency-connected public-private partnerships."

After a long career with the U.S. Army's Criminal Investigations Division, including several years in Vietnam and Iran, Wheaton went to work for the Anaheim-based autonetics division of Rockwell International in 1976 (the company is now based in Costa Mesa). Three company executives had just been murdered in Tehran, Iran, and Rockwell needed Wheaton to direct its security operations for Project

IBEX, a top-secret airborne electronic-surveillance system the company was building for the CIA in Iran.

At Wheaton's disposal were several other Rockwell officials with either CIA or NSA clearances and an elaborate encoding system provided by the CIA." Schou concluded that whatever else may have been written about Wheaton, his "credentials as a onetime covert operative are impossible to deny."[12]

Wheaton and the Iran-Contra investigation

The reason that Wheaton's name has appeared in print began with his and Carl Jenkins conversations with Paul Hoven in 1985. Hoven worked with a non-profit group devoted to exposing waste in government and the two had some interesting remarks to him about illegal arms shipments and government money being spent for things definitely not approved by Congress. As other leaks eventually began to occur over the North arms deals in the Middle East and Latin America, Hoven introduced Wheaton and Jenkins to Daniel Sheehan. Sheehan was engaged in an attempt to expose a variety of such activities and was happy to receive new sources.[13]

David Corn writes that Wheaton's bottom line for Sheehan was that a "rogue element of the U.S. government was engaged in a host of nefarious activities including assassinations." Corn also describes the names that Wheaton offered to Sheehan. These included: Wilson, Secord, Clines, Hakim, Singlaub, Shackley and Bush.

Sheehan would include Wheaton's (and reportedly Jenkins') information about illegal arms deals and the names of those involved in his crusade and later legal actions.

In 1988 Wheaton offered an affidavit in support of Sheehan's legal action; Jenkins, another source for Sheehan, refused to give a similar affidavit and when questioned asserted that Sheehan must have totally misunderstood any conversations they might have had.

In a 2005 interview with William Law, Wheaton related the following: At some time in 1985/1986 (while he and Jenkins were beginning to talk to parties about illegal arms deals) Wheaton brought up the earlier discussions he had heard in regard to the JFK conspiracy and broached the subject of disclosure of that as well. He states that after a short time the pair declined and told him that if he ever raised the issue they would make him look totally unreliable and ruin his career as a security consultant. It is this author's speculation that once

Wheaton was known to his friends as a "whistle blower", they may immediately have begun providing dis-information which would damage his credibility and undermine any remarks he might make in regard to their earlier conversations about the JFK assassination.

Eventually the Contra portions of Wheaton's assertions seem to have been substantially verified. North's own notebook confirms all the names except Shackley. Shirley Brill, a former CIA official, submitted an affidavit with the same names and claimed she heard Clines, Secord, Quintaro and Shackley plotting to frame Wilson.

Cameron Holmes, a Congressional investigating committee lead investigator, was convinced that Shackley was deeply involved in the Iran-Contra scandal. As he explained when he was interviewed by David Corn: "How could Shackley be the one person in this mob unaware of what was going on? Why was he so insistent he had not picked up a single whiff of the Contra operation or the Iran initiative? There was no crime in knowing. Shackley proclaimed his ignorance too much."[14] Holmes was shocked when special counsel Lawrence Walsh decided not to pursue Shackley. He was not even called as a witness. Walsh did not even take Shackley's deposition until after Congress had finished its hearings on the affair.

However, many of Sheehan's assertions became highly controversial. In particular these seem to relate to a grand elaboration of the "secret team" assertions involving Shackley as the leader of a secret COA "wet ops" unit which had been created as far back as 1976. Sheehan also introduced another crime, the La Penaca, bombing and made it part of his overall case and cause. Clearly Wilson's information and the La Penaca bombing helped raise Sheehan's claims to that of extreme, global conspiracy and had a good deal to do with his losing his legal action. It is also clear that Wheaton's basic information about illegal arms sales, extra-legal "secret teams" and even about sanctioned assassinations dating back to the Cuban secret war have been validated as of 2005.

By virtue of his visibility in Iran-Contra and as virtually the only experienced security person to ever serve as a "whistle blower", Wheaton become sought after for comment in virtually every case to follow where it appeared that the Government might be covering up covert activities. As an example, families from the 1985 Gander crash hired Wheaton to investigate rumors that the government was not telling the full truth about the crash. He concluded the plane was operated by Arrow Airlines which had served as a CIA front company and that the airlines had transported arms from Israel to Iran as part of North's Contra project. Wheaton posited that the bombing of the plane was a form of retaliation by the Iranians for North's arms sale scam.

Eventually mainstream media sources, including *Time* magazine, reached the same general conclusion that the crash was extremely questionable and that Middle Eastern interests of some sort were behind it. Wheaton is even quoted in one *Time* article on Gander.[15]

Wheaton's views, his goal of exposing secret agendas and secret teams plus his willingness to comment result in reporters and writers calls (and citations) whenever anything possibly terrorist associated happens–such as the OKC bombing. For the mainstream press and for some researchers, the fact that Wheaton has become a "lightning rod" for conspiracy commentary and speculation certainly affects his perception as a source. Interestingly there is only one subject he has never addressed in his public remarks, that of the Kennedy assassination. That he saved only for confidential disclosure to the ARRB.

Bottom line

At present, Wheaton's reports of the individuals and conversations he heard discussing the attack on JFK (heard prior to his and Jenkins involvement with people investigating Iran-Contra) appear consistent and credible. However it is reasonable to speculate that virtually anything shared with him following his proposal that Jenkins and Quintaro go on the record about the Kennedy matter may have been "contaminated".

Wheaton himself may have become a target for disinformation at that point, cultivated to ensure that he would be greeted with skepticism if he ever chose to disclose the conversations he had heard.

Research continues….

APPENDIX J

A SMALL CLIQUE IN THE CIA

The day following the President's assassination, Garrett Underhill showed up at the house of friends in New York City. Underhill was a Harvard graduate who had made a career in the field of military weapons. Prior to WWII, from 1938 to 1942, he had worked for David Cort at *Life* magazine, as his assistant on weaponry and military affairs. Cort had lobbied to keep him out of the draft during WWII; Cort described him as the World's No. 1 expert on military weaponry and key to *Life's* accurate coverage of the War. Cort also described him as being key to *Life's* military intelligence and of making a serious contribution in lobbying for rearmament prior to the War.[1]

During the War, Underhill served in Army intelligence (MIS) for two and a half years, serving as a technical and weapons evaluation specialist. He received a war department citation for superior work and was released in May, 1946.[2] Reportedly Underhill's military views had a significant impact on *Life's* coverage of the war and on Luce's views of both WWII and Korea.[3]

Following the war Underhill worked as an analyst and contributor for a number of national publications and information bureaus including *Esquire*, *The Washington Post*, *Colliers* and *Fortune*. He also served as a consultant to an Army Coordinating Group, circa 1956. In the 1950s Underhill became associated with Samual Cummings. Cummings had become the owner of one of the world's largest military and civilian arms trading companies (INTERARMCO); he had worked for the OSI and CSI and in the early 50s, had traveled the world buying foreign weapons with which to supply resistance groups behind the Iron Curtain. Cummings was eventually released as an asset because of being "sharp and difficult to control" but remained a voluntary CIA informant through the 60s.[4]

In 1963, Underhill was working for the Washington D.C. Bureau of *Fortune* magazine in the areas of military, defense and intelligence. He worked under Charles Murphey.[5]

A close friend, Asyer Brynes (*New Republic* contributing editor) reported that one of Underhill's main interests in 1963 was in the Russian missiles that had been placed in Cuba. Underhill felt that the administration story was not the full truth and that there was an outstanding mystery in regard to the missiles. We can only wonder what sources Underhill may have approached in pursuit of his interest in the subject of missiles in Cuba–and wonder if he crossed the path of those who were promoting the Russian defector story discussed in Chapter one, the story that led to the TILT operation.

A Small Clique in the CIA

When Underhill arrived at his friend's, Robert and Charlene Fitzsimmons, home in New York City, it was late and he was excited and scared. The couple was preparing for a trip to Europe and Robert was already asleep. Underhill spoke with Charlene (Charley) Fitzsimmons at length while she continued packing for the trip.

Underhill's concern was that he had become aware of a "clique" within the CIA—a clique dealing with weapons and gun running and making money. These individuals had Far Eastern connections, narcotics was mentioned, supposedly the clique was manipulating political intrigues to serve their own ends. Underhill believed that these individuals had been involved with JFK's murder; he felt that JFK had become aware of their dealings and was about to move against them in some fashion. He also believed that members of the clique knew that Underhill was aware of their dealings and that his own life could well be in jeopardy.[6] Underhill had fled Washington in fear of his life, avoiding his normal haunts at the Harvard Club in D.C. to seek refuge with his friends.

At the time, the Fitzsimmons were totally baffled by Underhill's remarks. His friends were aware that he had separated from his wife a year earlier causing some emotional problems—that was the simplest explanation they could come up with for his behavior at the time. Later, they related Underhill's remarks to certain other close friends and in 1966, when concerns about possible conspiracy began to be elevated due to the Garrison investigation, one of these friends began his own inquiry and re-contacted them. At that point Robert Fitzsimmons remarked that the reason they had really not taken Underhill seriously was that *"we couldn't believe that the CIA could contain a corrupt element every bit as ruthless (and much more efficient) than the Mafia."*[7]

In May of 1964, Underhill was found dead in his apartment. His apartment door was unlocked, he was found in bed dead from a single shot behind his left ear. The weapon used was one of his own pistols. In addition to the wound behind the left ear, the pistol was found under the left side of his body. Brynes felt this to be suspicious as Underhill was right-handed. The police investigation was minimal and the coroner reported the death as a suicide.

Concerns about Underhill's remarks and his death, led to an inquiry by *Ramparts* Magazine eventually published in its June 1967 issue.[8] This article came to the attention of District Attorney Jim Garrison who remarked on Underhill in his famous Playboy magazine interview. In response to those remarks, the CIA (which was tracking all individuals named or contacted by Garrison) prepared a background study on Underhill and his contacts with the Agency. Their study revealed that Underhill had been of interest to them in 1949 and that he was designated for contact on a limited basis, restricted to "Confidential" information. During the 1950s, Underhill had occasional contact with the agency, once reporting an individual who had come to him with photos of Russian weapons while he was working for *Colliers*. In 1957, the CIA Office of Security requested security background checks on Underhill. The CIA study also confirmed that Underhill had been associated with Cummings of INTERARMCO, a significant possible exposure for the agency because of his and the companies services in obtaining and disposing of deniable weapons.[9]

Although not addressed by the FBI investigation nor the Warren Commission report, Underhill's remarks did come to the attention of the HSCA and some attempt was made to determine his possible source of information. Given Underhill's interest in tracking arms shipments, one name strongly considered by HSCA investigators was that of Mitch Werbell, an individual known to be involved with both arms sales and Cuban affairs (Werbell himself frequently touted a long-term relationship with the CIA).[10]

MITCH WERBELL

Although Werbell is certainly an interesting individual, with ties to others such as with Bernardo de Torres (who worked for Werbell in Latin American arms sales in the early 1970's), his potential as an insider source in 1963 remains an open question. CIA documents of the period tell a far different story than the Werbell "legend."

We know this not from the extensive published material on Werbell but rather from actual CIA documents of the period. The story told by these documents is far different than the Werbell "legend" (largely created by Werbell himself) which would evolve in the 1970s–although it does reveal a sudden and significant improvement in Werbell's fortunes towards the later years of the 1960s.

A look at Werbell's WWII OSS associates may also be very worthwhile. Werbell was in the OSS unit that operated in Burma/ China during the War. This unit was commanded by Colonel Paul Helliwell, later Chief of the Far East Division, Strategic Services Unit of the War Department. Other personnel included Howard Hunt, Lucian Conein and John Singlaub. Of course Howard Hunt is well known for his Cuban and Domestic Operations positions. Helliwell is less well known, however his role in assisting with financial covers for CIA's operations deserves considerable discussion, especially in regard to supporting the Cuba Project, JM/WAVE operations and other deniable CIA operations in both Latin America and the Far East. We will return to these names and provide further references at the end of this appendix. Certainly they, along with Ted Shackley and others have been presented as a very special "clique" within the CIA.

Werbell, The Early Years

After service with the OSS in Burma/China, Werbell returned to Atlanta and opened an advertising and Public Relations firm. Reportedly this business effort failed and he moved into Import/Export work in Central America and the Caribbean. Werbell's first contact with the CIA was in July,1959. Apparently using his OSS service and contacts as a reference, he managed to get a call through to General Cabell. He informed Cabell that he was engaged in public relations activities with Cuban exiles and had just returned from the Dominican Republic and a meeting with General Pedroza. They had asked him to assist them in returning to Cuba. Claiming to be seeking CIA advice and having significant intelligence he requested to meet with senior CIA personnel in Washington. General Cabell made no commitment to Werbell but did refer him to the Western Hemisphere staff and they brought Werbell up to D.C. for a meeting.[11]

Details of this interview (at the Statler Hotel) are covered in a lengthy CIA memorandum; the highlights appear to be that Werbell had helped some Cuban exiles (Batista followers) by brokering currency exchange in Miami and this had gained him an introduction to Batista's people in the Dominican Republic. He went down with a Cuban born American citizen who eventually did talk with Batista about doing public relations work (mention is made that Masferrer is doing some fund raising and organization work for Batista in Miami). Werbell also met with General Pedroza and broached PR work, however based on his military experience, Pedroza supposedly asked Werbell to help him set up guerilla operations against Castro. (The CIA memo notes that Werbell talked about his personal military expertise but that his military record shows no actual combat experience). In the end it appeared that Pedroza and Batista were not going to cooperate but Werbell wanted the CIA to back him in para-military operations with Pedroza, requesting to see Cabell or Dulles and asking for equipment and aircraft.

The summary section of the memo refers to Werbell's business difficulties, pictures him as a typical promoter, prone to exaggeration. It suggests he may have some credible sources; among his sources Werbell had mentioned Joe Merola of Miami. Merola was close to Carlos Prio, worked with Batista's brother-in-law (whom he had tried to help get out of Cuba in 1959) and was involved with the syndicate in Havana. Merola was connected to Sam and Gabe Mannarino who had sold the Sans Souci to Trafficante. It has been mentioned previously that Merola was associated with Norman Rothman. Rothman and the Mannarino's had long-time contacts with Pittsburgh Ohio crime figures and both Rothman and Merola had been involved in the 1959 Canton Ohio armory robbery and related attempts to smuggle guns to Castro in Cuba.

The memos' final recommendation is that Werbell may be used as an intelligence source although his motives are questionable and under no circumstances is any commitment to be made to Pedroza. There is concern that Werbell may be difficult to handle.

Based on this meeting Werbell was given provisional operational approval in July, 1959 and activated as a temporary field agent. This status lasted only a little over two months. In October another CIA memorandum recorded a request from Werbell to attend an exile meeting in D.C. and to travel at CIA expense. He had recently requested funding for travel to the Dominican Republic. He stated that he had been invited to attend because of his news agency connections (World Wide International News Service). This generated a CIA evaluation of Werbell and he was terminated as a source in October. His termination was based on the conclusion that he wanted to use the Agency to fund his personal business ventures and that his information was all second or third hand. The Agency felt that only Cuban assets could give them true first hand information. Werbell was advised that he would not be used operationally.[12]

Werbell's next encounter with the CIA was in the fall of 1962. At that point he was working with FINCA, Frutas Intercontinentales in Santo Domingo. This company distributed fruit throughout the region and Werbell claimed to have many important Central American contacts including Miguel Fuentas of Guatemala. He also claimed to be a close personal friend of former General Donovan of the OSS. CIA reports do record an abortive attempt in this time frame by Werbell to sell surplus NATO arms to the Guatemalan army and in Nicaragua. Werbell was also attempting to sell the investigative services of his Worldwide Information Services. Apparently neither effort was successful.[13]

In this same time frame, Werbell was becoming a major concern to the CIA because he was apparently working with (or representing himself to be) Kohly and the United Organization for Liberation of Cuba.

Werbell was making contacts and even extending bribes aimed at gaining recognition for Kohly's organization by the governments of Guatemala and Nicaragua. He had offered a significant bribe to one Nicaraguan government officer. These actions strongly conflicted with U.S. interests. There was a good amount of CIA cable traffic pertaining to CIA concerns and attempts to warn the governments about Werbell and his associates. Werbell and Kohly are both "considered to be wheelers and dealers, peddlers of grandiose schemes and unscrupulous." The cables state Kohly knew the U.S. was opposed to any government in exile and that he was simply promoting himself and private Cuban businessmen.[14, 15]

There are no further released records for Werbell in 1963 but in 1965 and 1966 he was again the object of CIA attention. In 1966 it was serious attention due to his media contacts (including *Time* magazine), in which he was claiming to have a group of 500 men inside Cuba and an assassination team of 26 men preparing to kill Castro. He refused to name his sponsors for this sabotage and assassination program but claimed that he was simply waiting for the CIA "green light." The Agency recorded these claims but expressed extreme skepticism that Werbell was a credible source or that he would have any operational assets inside Cuba. Werbell continued his efforts to sell arms throughout Latin America.

Werbell's Fortune Changes

In 1967, Werbell partnered with Gordon Ingram to distribute the famous, M-11 hand held silent machine gun. At this point in time his profile and apparently his income escalated hugely and he became virtually a legendary figure for weapons sales from SE Asia to Latin America, a friend to right wing dictators and any government concerned about Communist (or leftist) factions. Eventually his Sionics company (better known as The Farm) would become the place for training professional counter-terrorism personnel, from private firms and corporations as well as from governments around the globe. However in 1974, a CIA memorandum still describes Werbell simply as "a gun runner and private eye."

What Underhill Did Know

Garrett Underhill's friends had the impression that he offered no direct knowledge of the conspiracy against John Kennedy. He had not heard any specific "chatter" or "rumors" or names. They felt that his reaction was a response to the initial media coverage of the assassination plus his own special insights into the activities of the "clique" which he described. Their initial skepticism had a good deal to do with their unwillingness to accept that such a clique could really exist within the CIA.

Certainly it would not be unexpected to find an expert in military weaponry, especially one with a long history of experience with foreign military rifles, rejecting the story that the President had been killed with three quick shots from a Carcano. Undoubtedly Underhill would have had many of the same issues with that story that we repeatedly hear from snipers and other expert marksmen.

But, regardless of his emotional state or recent marital problems, Underhill had clearly come across some evidence of the clique that he described. Something that would have led him to believe that they had the will and motive to move against John Kennedy. Something to indicate that they were capable of violent and criminal acts up to assassination.

We have no detailed information on Underhill's own researches in 1963, however we do know that one of his areas of study and expertise was international arms shipments. His friends relate that he was constantly tracking shipments of arms and contraband and clearly he was connected to many of the major sources and agents of such arms shipments, INTERARMCO only being one example. We also know that he was interested in Cuban military issues in 1963, specifically the issue of Russian missiles in Cuba. Where this interest led him and whom he may have contacted we have no idea.

The other clues we do have are that Underhill felt that this clique had Far Eastern connections and that there were some suggestions that drugs may have been involved with some of the gun running. Bringing up that sort of scenario in 1963 would certainly have sounded "wild and preposterous", as preposterous as the fact that such a clique might have been able to manipulate certain political intrigues to their own interests.

Based on the last 40 years of revelations on the American Far Eastern experience and numerous studies of CIA activities, such remarks now suggest that Underhill–rather than being preposterous–had indeed cut the path of a very special CIA clique. A clique that had its beginnings in the Burma/China theatre during WWII, a clique that evolved during the 1960's in the secret war against Castro. A clique that had good reason to object to recent actions of the President. JFK had already moved to transfer CIA "operations" to the American military in Viet Nam. He was focusing covert military operations on Army Special Forces rather than CIA paramilitary.

His 1963 Cuban initiatives were being built around inter-departmental (Army and State) efforts, placing the CIA operations staff (such as JM/WAVE) in a supporting rather than controlling role. None of these moves were well received by the Agency overall, however they were even less well received by the "forward leaning" elements of CIA Plans and paramilitary groups. And there is now solid evidence that he had no intention of American armed forces becoming involved in a long-term ground war in SE Asia.

Discussion of such a clique as Underhill described is far beyond the scope of this appendix or of this book. Readers interested in pursuing the origin and evolution of a possible "Far Eastern" clique are referred to the histories of the operations and personnel of OSS Detachment 101 in Burma/China. Headed by Paul Helliwell and personnel including Howard Hunt, John Singlaub, Lucian Conein, Ray Cline and others. Equally relevant is the history of U.S. support for China (beginning with the creation of the American Volunteer Group before the U.S. entry into WWII), long-term institutional U.S. support for the Republic of China and Chiang Kai–Shek and the creation of CAT (later Air America) through the work of Helliwell, Concoran and Chennault. Of particular interest in studying this history are works by Peter Dale Scott (*The War* Conspiracy), Jonathan Kwitny (*The Crimes of Patriots*[16]) and David McKean (*Peddling Influence*[17]).

The author makes no representation that Garrett Underhill's "clique" actually had any direct connection to the assassination of the President. Underhill only guessed that through his knowledge and speculation on its agendas and capabilities. Underhill's story does not seem to provide a specific clue to the assassination; it may provide an insight into the environment in which the conspiracy may have developed.

NAMES FROM THE WAR AGAINST CASTRO

This book deals with reports, remarks and rumors pertaining to a great number of individuals. In most cases these are in the context of public and secret actions relating to Cuba, actions by the U.S. government, by private citizens, and by the Cuban exiles who sought to remove Fidel Castro and his cadre. To assist the reader, the following list of individuals and groups is provided for reference. Some of the names were well known in media coverage of that period, but many were not. In addition to this brief listing, photographs are provided to assist the reader in viewing individuals as actual people rather than just names.

Further, an effort is made in Chapter 16 to provide additional detail on key individuals and to discuss their activities after the Kennedy assassination.

Alvarado, Gilberto Ugarte:

Gilberto Ugarte Alvarado was a Nicaraguan intelligence informant who went to CIA officials in Mexico City with a detailed story of having observed Lee Oswald inside the Cuban embassy, receiving money for a Cuban sponsored assassination. Alvarado's story was initially strongly endorsed by local CIA officers; David Phillips was initially a leading proponent of Alvarado's information.

Alpha 66:

Alpha 66 was one of the best organized and most militarily effective of the activist Cuban exile organizations. In 1962 and 1963, Alpha 66 was very successful in launching attacks in Cuba, targeting port installations and foreign shipping. Russian ships and assets were among its primary targets. Alpha 66 was also especially effective at private fund raising though exile business connections in New York City and Puerto Rico; the key individual in this effort was one of its principal organizers, Antonio Veciana. The most well known, aggressive and successful Alpha 66 raid leaders were Tony Cuesta and Eduardo (Eddie) Perez (Bayo). Alpha 66 was largely put together by Antonio Veciana and Eloy Menoyo; Veciana had approached the CIA with a proposal to assassinate Castro and his key leaders, in 1961 he helped organized an abortive bazooka attack on Castro before escaping into exile. Eloy Menoyo had been an active Second Front of the Escambray leader during the revolution against Batista. Menoyo was adamant in retaining the "Second Front of the Escambray" name and the consolidated group was often referred to as Second Front Alpha 66.

Many young, activist Cubans also had dual membership in Alpha 66 and in the DRE (Student Revolutionary Directorate). The DRE students had been strongly involved in the Castro revolt against Batista but had been excluded as Castro turned to Communism and Russia; DRE members remained strong anti-Communists and maintained one of the most effective intelligence channels into Cuba under Castro.

AM/LASH:

This CIA cryptonym was associated both with a project and an individual. The individual was *Dr. Rolando Cubela.* Cubela had led DRE forces into Havana to oust Batista but later became associated with Castro and held a variety of minor posts in the Castro regime. These posts did however allow Cubela to travel internationally. After contacts with and recruitment by the CIA, Cubela eventually came to be viewed by the CIA as one option for organizing an internal revolt against Castro. Cubela himself continuously promoted the idea of an assassination attempt against Castro and requested equipment from the CIA for this project.

AM/TRUNK:

The CIA AM/TRUNK project was another effort to identify Cuban military and political leaders who would be willing and able to organize an internal revolt against Fidel Castro. Much of this effort was devoted to a search for military leaders unhappy with the growing Russian military influence and control, which had escalated significantly during 1963. The AM/TRUNK and AM/LASH projects continued for a number of years, even in the face of internal CIA evidence that many of the AM/TRUNK Cuban assets (given AM/WHIP numerical designations) were compromised by Cuban intelligence. There was even CIA security concern that Cubela (AM/LASH) might have been an informant to Castro, who was testing the CIA's willingness to engage in political assassination.

Artime, Manuel:

Manual Artime was one of the early counter-revolutionary leaders (MRR party – Movement for the Recovery of the Revolution) inside Cuba. After fleeing to the U.S he became one of the exile leaders playing a major role in successive U.S. organized exile movements. Artime and other leaders including Tony Varona, Aureliano Arango and Jose Cardona met with Senator John Kennedy as early as the Democratic National Convention in 1960.

In 1963 Artime was sanctioned, along with Harry Ruiz Williams, to be a major leader of a new Kennedy Administration's autonomous group offensive against Fidel Castro. The CIA crypt for the Artime focused project was AM/WORLD. Artime was given far more autonomy than had been previously associated with U.S. backed efforts; in return his charter was to operate totally outside the continental U.S. and to engage in a wide variety of public activities which would make his U.S. sponsorship totally deniable. Newly released CIA documents show that the Artime effort was highly compartmentalized and isolated even from other "secret war" operations within the CIA.

AM/WORLD:

This CIA autonomous group project was part of a larger Kennedy administration multi-agency effort to produce a coup within Cuba which would internally remove Fidel and Raul Castro, allowing their replacement with a new provisional government in which exile leaders would play a key role. The CIA was not in charge of this effort but was limited to supporting Artime's military build-up off shore and other related political actions including helping him establish contacts and infrastructure in a number of Latin American countries. CIA officers playing key roles in this project included Henry Hecksher and Carl Jenkins.

Bayo, Eddie:

Eddie Bayo (Eduardo Perez) initially fought under Raul Castro against Batista. Bayo was a fierce fighter and later turned against the Castro regime. After his rejection of Castro and exile to the U.S., Bayo became a crew member of the Tejana III. The Tejana was a WWII subchaser which had been purchased by persons associated with the King Ranch in Texas and pledged to the CIA's secret efforts against Castro. It was then purchased by Alberto Fernandez Hechaverria, registered under the dummy company name of InterKey Transportation and refitted and "gunned" by the CIA for supply missions into Cuba before the Bay of Pigs in 1961. In 1963 the Tejana was placed under control of Manual Artime and crewed by his MRR commandos as part of the build-up of his forces outside the United States. After leaving the Tejana, Bayo became one of the most aggressive and successful leaders of Alpha 66 boat attack groups, participating in raids against Russian ships and assets in Cuba. In 1963 Bayo helped promote and organize a mission into Cuba known as operation identified by the CIA as operation TILT (and generally known among those involved as the Bayo-Pawley mission). This mission was funded by former U.S. ambassador and millionaire William Pawley who participated personally, as did personnel from Life Magazine and personnel from the CIA's JM/WAVE Cuban "secret war" headquarters in Miami.

Cuesta, Antonio aka "Tony" Cuesta del Valle:

Tony Cuesta had been a businessman in Havana but after going into exile, became one of the most aggressive exile raiders operating first with Alpha 66 and then with Commandos L (Liberty). Cuesta led his first mission into Cuba in September of 1962 shortly before the Cuban Missile Crisis; however, he became a very visible and public figure primarily due to *Life Magazine's* coverage of a raid he led into Cuba in the spring of 1963. Cuesta led a Commandos L team (a spin off group from Alpha 66); the raid resulted in the sinking of the Russian merchant ship Baku and received major media visibility as part of *Life's* photo journalism support for the exiles and their efforts. A *Life* photographer accompanied Cuesta and his crew on the mission.

De Torres, Bernardo:

De Torres was a Bay of Pigs veteran who was held a Castro prisoner with other Brigade 2506 members until December 1962. Upon his release in Florida, he joined his brother Carlos in Miami. Carlos operated a Miami detective agency. Bernardo went on to become the chief of intelligence for the reformed Brigade 2506 and was acquainted with Interpen members including William Seymour and Roy Hargraves. Later De Torres would become involved in the Garrison investigation of the JFK assassination.

DRE (Student Revolutionary Directorate):

Members of the Student Directorate were very active in protesting and opposing the Batista regime and DRE fighters played a major role in the revolution against him. DRE members fought fiercely in Havana and initially took control, later to concede political control to Fidel Castro and his followers when they entered the city. DRE members were later among the first to oppose Castro's eventual turn to communism and the Soviets. The DRE network inside Cuba might be considered one of the best organized and secure during the period of 1962-1963. In the U.S. DRE exiles and members were primarily engaged in fund raising, recruiting and political/media opposition to the Castro regime. DRE and its Miami chapter were one of the few exile organizations actively cultivated and supported by the CIA, both for their intelligence connections and their political value. However DRE members who were more operationally inclined did participate in raids of their own into Cuba and also joined with other operationally focused groups such as Alpha 66/SNFE. During 1962 and 1963, the leader of DRE was Manual Salvat and its military director was Blanco Fernandez. Army intelligence documents note that some members of Alpha 66 were also members of the DRE and we find DRE and Alpha 66 individuals associated in Miami, Puerto Rico and in Dallas during this period. We also find DRE members in New Orleans in contact with Lee Oswald in 1963 and very actively involved in developing propaganda opposing Oswald and the Fair Play for Cuba Committee. DRE members in New Orleans and Miami were also among the very first to seek media attention tying Castro to Oswald and to the Kennedy assassination. Unfortunately, the reports dealing with Oswald which must have gone from the DRE to its CIA case officer have never been made available and as of 2006 are the subject of an ongoing lawsuit against the CIA.

Fernandez,Alberto:

Alberto Fernandez (CIA crypt AM/DENIM-1) was a graduate of Princeton, attended prep school with John F. Kennedy and was the director of the Sugar Stabilization Board of the Cuban Sugar Institute in 1958 and 1959. His eventual opposition to Castro and his counter-evolutionary activities led to his exile. Initially he had been a strong 26th of July supporter and reportedly raised over $2 million dollars for the movement. An FBI memo dated October 1958 lists companies that had been solicited for payments to Fidel Castro and his rebel army. These included United

Fruit, Lone Star Cement, Freeport Sulphur, Czarnikow Rionda, Chase Manhattan Bank, King Ranch (Robert Kleberg), Standard Oil, Hilton Hotels. One of Fernandez's first operational moves after his exfiltration to the United States was to use his business connections, including his being known to the Klebergs of King Ranch, to help negotiate and fund the purchase of an ex Navy sub chaser for penetration and supply missions into Cuba. The ship was located in New Orleans, owned by Texan Robert McCoy, and was purchased jointly with Texas (Kleberg) and Cuban funds (approximately $38,000 each) in November of 1960. This ship would be named the Tejana. Its crew would come to include two men whose names that would also become legendary in independent exile military operations, Tony Cuesta (AM/DENIM 14) and Eddie Bayo .

Harvey, William:

William Harvey was a senior CIA officer who was placed in charge of Task Force W (CIA operations) within the multiple agency, Kennedy Administration anti-Castro project named Mongoose. Mongoose was charged with the overthrow of the Castro regime. Project Mongoose and Task Force W operated out of the same facilities and used the resources of the giant JM/WAVE CIA station on the south campus of the University of Miami. Harvey was ordered by Richard Helms to reactivate the joint CIA-Roselli assassination project in 1962. Helms apparently did this without the knowledge of either the Kennedy administration or the Director of the CIA, John McCone. This effort had originally been organized prior to the Bay of Pigs, using syndicate "fixer" Johnny Roselli and remaining gambling syndicate connections in Cuba which had been part of the Trafficante network. Harvey and Roselli engaged in several efforts to poison or otherwise remove Fidel Castro during 1962 and although the project was officially terminated at the end of that year, the two men continued a close personal association throughout 1963. This association continued even after Harvey was removed from Task Force W and reassigned to Italy. William Harvey had earlier been assigned by Richard Helms to organize and recruit personnel for an overseas CIA Executive Action capability designated ZR/RIFLE. This project was to give the CIA the capability to remove foreign leaders through the use of criminal assets; recent document releases also show this project remained active during 1963 after Harvey's removal from Task Force W / Mongoose and his reassignment.

Hargraves, Roy:

Roy Emory Hargraves was an exceptionally active American supporter of exile anti-Castro activities. Initially he became associated with a group headed by ex-Army Major George Tanner but his longer term association was the INTERPEN group organized by Gerry Patrick Hemming. As part of this group Hargraves was involved with training members of the AAA group headed by Sanchez Arango. AAA was an offshoot of the Authentico party. Arango had been one of the chief leaders along with Varona and Artime during the preparations for the exile invasion of Cuba; however, he had broken from that effort and the CIA entirely at the last minute over concerns that the invasion had been compromised and would be a disaster. Arango's initial funding reportedly came from Rolando Masferrer, a former political power in the Batista regime. FBI documents report that Hargraves received funding from Masferrer to launch a successful raid into Cuba in 1963. Hargraves led in a team of exiles, captured two Cuban fishing boats, engaged in a running fight with Castro forces and successfully extracted his team and the boats to the Bahamas. This ended up causing a minor political crisis with the British when the boats were forcibly recovered by the Cubans (in a raid after Hargraves had returned to Miami). Hargraves was a close friend and associate of independent exile activist Felipe Vidal Santiago. Hargraves continued his anti-Castro and anti-communist activities during the 1960s, becoming involved in a plan to create war with Cuba by simulating an attack on Guantanamo naval base. He eventually moved to Los Angeles where he was involved with bombing attacks on both the SDS (Students for a Democratic Society) and the Black Panthers.

JDGE (Junta del Gobierno de Cuba en el Exilio):

The "Junta" appears to have been largely a paper and media entity, organized to raise funds, buy arms and establish a Cuban government in exile prior to a successful overthrow of Castro. The movement's leader was Paulino Sierra Martinez. Reportedly its designated candidate for the replacement President of Cuba was Carlos Prio Soccares. Soccares was a former Cuban President and had been Fidel Castro's primary sponsor in the movement to overthrow Batista. Sierra actively engaged in major arms purchases as well as in supplying money to several of the more militant operational exile groups. However he had virtually no rank and file and actually hired various INTERPEN associates to transport some of his purchases to Florida and to store them there.

In 1963 Sierra's primary activities were in Chicago and Miami and most of his weapons purchasing efforts were in Chicago and the Midwest. Intelligence reports on the Junta suggest that it had gained major financial pledges from gambling syndicate elements, particularly out of Las Vegas. These pledges were made in return for potential concessions after the overthrow of the Castro regime.

JURE:

JURE, organized and by Manual "Manolo" Ray; it, was socialist-democratic in its politics and generally viewed by other groups and the former Batista associated politicians as being too left wing in its views. Many exiles, especially those from the commercial and landed social classes viewed it virtually as "Castroism without Castro". Ray and JURE were also not trusted by many CIA officers including Howard Hunt, Ted Shackley and David Morales. In one memo out of JM/WAVE, Ray's group is suspected of spying on JM/WAVE/CIA operations. Many of the JURE members were outside the United States and Ray himself spent a good deal of time in Puerto Rico. JURE had been part of the original consolidated exile movement prior to the Bay of Pigs but was not one of the organizations with which the Agency maintained the same sort of ongoing contact as DRE or UNIDAD.

Martino, John:

John Martino was a casino employee in Havana, specializing in electrical installations involved with the gaming. He left Cuba during the Castro take over but continued to make trips back, possibly serving as a courier. During one such trip he and his young son were arrested. The son was returned to the United States; John Martino was imprisoned by the Castro government for several years. After his release in late 1962, he wrote a book (*I Was Castro's Prisoner*) which was published in 1963. The book related the failure of the U.S. State Department to support him while in prison as well as a host of terrible information about the Castro revolution and government. The book mentioned many individuals Martino met in prison and also named David Morales, a U.S. Embassy employee, who had impressed Martino. Martino credited with trying to warn the U.S. government about Castro's communist leanings. In 1963, Martino promoted and personally participated in the Bayo-Pawley mission into Cuba. This mission was staffed with Alpha 66 personnel with military coordination by Rip Robertson who worked for David Morales at JM/WAVE. Robertson had debriefed Martino after his return from Cuba.

McKeown, Robert:

Robert McKeown was a Texan who had participated in transportation of weapons into Cuba. The weapons were purchased by Carlos Prio Soccares for use by Fidel Castro's forces. McKeown organized the transport of these weapons and was active in Texas, Florida and Cuba. Eventually he was arrested for arms smuggling and in 1963 was living outside Houston Texas and on probation. Earlier he had gained media visibility when Fidel Castro visited Houston and asked to meet with his old friend, offering him a position in Cuba. During that same period McKeown was repeatedly contacted by Jack Ruby who wished introductions to elements within Cuba to facilitate his own sales activities and to help gain releases for certain friends from Cuban imprisonment. Those friends had formerly been involved in the casino business there, a business which saw a great deal of reorganization and government control under Castro. In 1963, McKeown was reportedly contacted by Lee Oswald, who was in the company of one of Prio Soccares associates; an individual named Hernandez whom McKeown had worked with earlier in the Castro gun smuggling.

Morales, David:

David Morales was officially an Army NCO and a State Department employee. He had worked out of the U.S. Embassy in Havana (while David Phillips was working as an under cover contract employee for the CIA in Havana), and had earlier participated in the highly successful CIA PB/SUCCESS operation (along with David Phillips) which deposed a leftist leaning Guatemalan leader. After Havana, Morales assumed the responsibility for training and organizing an exile intelligence/security operation in support of the 1962 effort against Castro. Following the Bay of Pigs disaster, he was placed in charge of "secret war" operations run out of the JM/WAVE complex in Miami, reporting to Theodore Shackley. All operational penetration teams were under his supervision and one of his major penetration leaders was Rip Robertson, who had also worked in the Guatemalan coup. David Morales also provided operational support for the Task Force W assassination operations conducted by William Harvey and Johnny Roselli.

MONGOOSE:

The Mongoose project was the follow-on Kennedy administration response to the disaster at the Bay of Pigs. That project had actually originated under President Eisenhower. Mongoose was to be the Kennedy response; it originated in a memorandum from President Kennedy in November of 1961. The memorandum went to multiple agencies and called for all designated parties to follow the lead of Major General Edward Lansdale. Lansdale, designated Mongoose project leader, was to "use our available assets to help Cuba overthrow the Communist regime." These assets were to be largely operated out of the CIA station in Miami known as JM/WAVE and run by station chief Theodore Shackley. Lansdale would run the planning and oversee the grand strategy of Mongoose while William Harvey was assigned to be in charge of the CIA elements known as Task Force W. Lansdale's decisions and planning were to be overseen by a special group of senior administration personnel in Washington, including Robert Kennedy.

Odio, Sylvia:

Sylvia Odio was the daughter of a wealthy Cuban businessman; both her father and mother ended up imprisoned by Fidel Castro for providing aid and comfort to revolutionary activities against Castro. Sylvia and her father were both politically affiliated with Manolo Ray's relatively liberal JURE party. Sylvia and her children eventually moved to Dallas Texas in early 1963 to join other members of her family. While not active with the local JURE organization herself, Sylvia remained in contact with Ray and attempted to locate weapons sources for JURE. Her younger sister, Sarita, a college student in Dallas, was associated with individuals who were active DRE members.

Pena, Orest:

Orest Pena owned the Habana Bar in New Orleans. Although the Habana was frequented by the Cuban and exile community Pena himself was not affiliated with any particular exile party. He had associated with local members of the Cuban Revolutionary Council and later with members of the DRE. His brother was self-described as pro-Batista while Pena himself served as an informant to the FBI, providing information on individuals he suspected might have communist leanings or who might actually be Castro supporters or informants. In the summer of 1963 Pena and his bartender Evaristo Rodriquez observed an individual in their bar whom they later felt was Lee Oswald. This individual was accompanied by a Latin who made a number of remarks about the bar being owned by a "capitalist" or an "imperialist". Pena reported this incident after the assassination and quickly lost his position as a valued FBI informant.

Phillips, David:

David Phillips began his career as a CIA officer as a contract employee and spent virtually his entire career assigned to combat communist influences and oppose Fidel Castro throughout the hemisphere. Phillips worked covertly for the CIA in Havana in 1959. Later he was attached to the Cuba Task Force in support of the Bay of Pigs operation, charged with propaganda and media relations for the Cuban Revolutionary Council. Afterwards he was moved to Mexico City and placed in charge of covert operations and counter-intelligence for the CIA station there. He advanced rapidly in this position, receiving a promotion in the fall of 1963, eventually becoming Chief of Cuban Operations and finally Chief of Western Hemisphere. At that time he held the rank of GS18, the highest position in the CIA not requiring executive appointment. At that rank and before retirement age, David Phillips chose early retirement; shortly thereafter he became involved in founding an association of retired intelligence professionals devoted to opposing media coverage, articles, books and other vehicles which were negative towards the CIA. Eventually Phillips wrote his own autobiography, The Night Watch, as well as other books including one titled The Carlos Contract, dealing with a contract political assassin. One of the major characters in the latter book was clearly patterned on Phillips' long time co-worker and associate, David Morales.

Rip Robertson:

Rob Robertson was a CIA military operations officer; he joined the PB/SUCCESS team in Guatemala, serving as part of the military component with David Morales. Robertson would later become a Brigade 2506 military advisor and was present as an advisor and UDT (underwater demolitions team) leader at the Bay of Pigs. He later become one of the military operations personnel at JM/WAVE, where he continued to demonstrate his personal bravery in Cuban penetration missions. Reportedly Robertson, along with senior boat guide Eugenio Martinez, were part of the unsanctioned group sent into Cuba by William Harvey during the Cuban Missile Crisis. Both men would later be assigned to the CIA supported TILT mission. Robertson had also conducted debriefing and other contacts with John Martino after Martino's return from prison in Cuba. Robertson went on to lead Cuban exile military personnel in Angola (where he used the name "Carlos") and later served in Vietnam.

Roselli, John:

John Roselli spent a lifetime within organized crime, eventually becoming one of the best connected and most respected "fixers", with connections to Chicago, Las Vegas, Los Angeles, New Orleans and Miami. Roselli first obtained success and prominence within the LA movie industry and then went on to become a key "facilitator" for gambling related deals in Las Vegas and later in Havana, Cuba. He was a key organizer of the "skim" from Vegas casinos to syndicate heads in Chicago and the Midwest. When the CIA decided to go to the gambling syndicate to find someone who could use the established syndicate network inside Cuba for the assassination of Fidel Castro, Johnny Roselli was recommended. Roselli was involved in Castro assassination attempts both before the Bay of Pigs and afterwards when the project was reactivated under William Harvey. One of his consistent resources in the Castro efforts was Antonio "Tony" Varona. Varona was a well-respected exile leader but also a man with syndicate connections to the Trafficante organization within Cuba. Santo Trafficante Jr. headed most crime syndicate activities in Florida and Cuba; he was imprisoned by Fidel Castro after Castro began to take major control over the Havana casinos.

UNIDAD:

A list of the armed exile military organizations groups potentially most dangerous to Fidel Castro in the early 1960s would likely begin with Unidad Revolucianario/UR, formed within Cuba in 1960 and composed of participants from 27 independent groups including Movimiento Liberation, MRD, MRR, Rescate and 30 November. Rafael Diaz Hanscomb of the MRR initiated this effort at unification even after being advised against doing so by Antonio Varona, the leader of the

"Frente." Varona would later become the leader of the CIA-sponsored Cuban Revolutionary Council/CRC. Early in 1961 Diaz made a trip from Cuba to the United States to obtain external support via contacts at Sinclair Oil. During meetings with U.S. Government officials and the CIA, the UR was given pledges of supplies and a plan to establish and staff an office in Miami was developed. At this point the chief leaders of Unidad were Diaz Hascomb (Cuban General Coordinator), Andrews Zayas (Civil Coordinator), and Major Sori Martin (Military Coordinator.)

The first materials to be provided from the U.S. arrived in Cuba in late February, 1961 and by mid-March the CIA thought Unidad had developed into a significant anti-Castro movement, having penetrated Cuban police and military forces. Unidad was preparing plans for coordinated uprisings, a rebellion within the Cuban Navy and other operations.

But UNIDAD advised the CIA that it was not yet ready to support any actual military action against Castro. It also advised its own Cuban network of that position.

The CIA did not warn UNIDAD about the impending Bay of Pigs invasion. As a result, it was not only unable to provide any support but its members were surprised and its network extensively damaged by the Castro round-ups.

Varona, Dr. Manual Antonio de Verona y Loredo:

Tony Varona was heavily involved in exile politics and to a large extent became a stand in for former Cuban President Carlos Prio Socarres. Varona became the head of numerous exile parties including the FRD, OA, Rescate and eventually became the acting head of the Cuban Revolutionary Council, supported by the Kennedy administration and the CIA during and after the Bay of Pigs. The CRC worked with various INTERPEN members to set up a training camp outside New Orleans in 1962 (when the administration began cracking down on raids out of Florida) but aborted the effort due to ongoing administration opposition to unauthorized exile military activities. Varona also maintained connections to the powerful gambling syndicate members who had been so influential in pre-Castro Cuba, including the Trafficante organization. It was this connection which resulted in his being used in the Roselli organized poison attempts against Castro; Verona accepted arms, money and supplies in return for his participation. Varona also maintained his connections to key political leaders such as Manual Artime, even after Artime was selected by the Kennedy Administration to move the exile efforts against Castro offshore in 1963.

Veciana, Antonio:

Antonio Veciana had an established and successful accounting business in Cuba, with connections to numerous Cuban professionals and businessmen. However Veciana was firmly opposed to Castro's turn to communism and eventually left Cuba to become one of the chief organizers of Alpha 66. Veciana traveled widely and served as the public spokesman for Alpha 66. He has made it clear that most of the group's strategy and plans were directed by a very secretive American. Veciana went on to work with this American in a variety of efforts, including assassination attempts, directed against Castro. Veciana described one of these attempts (in Chile) as being very similar to the Kennedy assassination.

Vidal, Felipe Vidal Santiago

Felipe Vidal was a Cuban naval officer who went into exile from Castro's communist regime via South America. He was approached by the CIA but no ongoing relationship developed due to mutual distrust. Vidal distrusted CIA's motives and CIA apparently distrusted his associates. Vidal moved into the U.S. via Miami and remained very independent, joining no established exile party but associating with more operationally inclined individuals. He attempted to form his own group for missions into Cuba but could not come up with sufficient funding. During 1962 and 1963 he associated with the INTERPEN group but primarily became a good friend of Roy Hargraves. Vidal was also one of the first people approached by Paulino Sierra when he came to Miami recruiting for the JCGE. Vidal also became a close friend and confidant of John Martino, keeping Martino informed on exile affairs. In the fall of 1963 Vidal made a series of trips to Dallas, Texas.

CRYPTS AND ALIASES

AMBIDDY 1 (Artime)
AMBUD (Cordona)
AMCLATTER (Barker)
AMCONCERT (Verela)
AMDENIM 1 (Fernandez)
AMDENIM 14 (Cuesta)
AMHAWK (Varona)
AMJAVA 4 (Quintero)
AMLASH (Cubela)
AMLILAC (infiltrations)
AMPATRIN (Malone)
AMSCHROLL (Unidad)
AMSHALE (Veciana)
AMSERF (Bartes)
AMSTRUT (on-island asset)
AMTHUG (Castro)
AMTIKI (CRC accountant/payroll)
AMWHIP 1 (Tepedino)
Artime, Manuel (AMBIDDY-1)
Barker, Bernard (AMCLATTER-1)
Berlin Operating Base (BOB)
Choaden (David Phillips)
Cuebela, Rolondo (AMLASH)
Cuesto, Antonio (Tony) (AMDENIM-14)
Fernandez, Alberto (AMDENIM-1)
Fitzgerald, Desmond (Chester Dainold)
Fischetti, Joe (Joe Fish)
Flutter (polygraph)
Hall, Loren (Lorenzo Pascillo)
JMARC (Cuba Project / Brigade)
MONGOOSE (Cuba Project / Lansdale-Harvey)
King, J.C. (Galbond)
Kusoda (interrogator)
KUBARK (CIA)
Los Halcones Negros (Black Falcons)
Malone, Michael (Jack) (AMPATRIN)

Morales, David (Zamka)
NPIC (National Photo Interpretation Center)
National Emergency Command Post Aircraft (Silver Dollar)
ODENVY (FBI)
ODYOKE (United States Government)
Ohare John, Thomas (Colonel Bishop)
PB/PRIME (United States)
PB/RUMEN (Cuba)
PB/SUCCESS (Guatemala Project)
Perez, Ruben (Carlos)
Phillips, David (Chaoden)
RYBAT (Secret classification)
Quintero, Raphael (Chi-Chi) (AMJAVA 4)
Sanjenis, Jose, Joachim, Panderaeo (Sam Jenis)
Sforza, Tony (Sloman)
SGA (Special Group Augmented)
USAFSS (US Air Force Security Service)
Varona, Anthony (Tony) (AMHAWK)
Zamka (David Morales)
ZR/RIFLE (Executive Action project/Harvey)

ENDNOTES

RIFs: The JFK Act of 1992 required agencies that held assassination records to record information about these records on Record Identification Forms (RIFs) for input into a master database. A copy of the RIF is also attached to each document. Those RIFs are used here when possible to guide the reader to assassination records/documents utilized in this book.

Exhibits: References to "Exhibit" in the endnotes refer to the master set of documents available on the *SWHT* website larry-hancock.com and with many previously on *SWHT* CDROM.

CHAPTER ONE: **They're going to kill Kennedy**

1. Martino's wife, Florence, and other members of his family kept John Martino's words of November 22 strictly to themselves for decades, initially denying anything of the sort when questioned by the House Select Committee on Assassinations. The Committee had been given a lead by one of Martino's close friends. However, months before her death, Florence Martino related the truth and details to author Anthony Summers with confirmation from her son.
2. Anthony and Robbyn Summers, "The Ghosts of November" *Vanity Fair*, December 1994. Martino's foreknowledge has also been verified by other researchers, particularly Bill Kelly, in personal communications with surviving members of the Martino family.
3. The FBI reports were largely prepared by Special Agents James O'Conner and were obtained and published by author A. J. Weberman. They include FBI # 64-44838-1, -2, -3, -4 and Summary Report 105-82555-3995.
4. Ibid.
5. Reference HSCA executive session hearing interview with Weiner on May 16, 1979, as well as preparation notes by HSCA staff.
6. Eva Grant, W C, Vol. 14, p. 429 and Vol. 15, p. 321. Also, Lamar Waldron with Thom Hartman, *Ultimate Sacrifice*. New York, (Carroll & Graf) 2005, chapters 24 and 28.
7. Seth Kantor, *The Ruby Cover-Up*, New York (Zebra Books), 1978, pp. 58-63
8. FBI reports in 64-44828 series. See also: Exhibits 1-1, "Cubans Jail Beach Man"; "Cuba Frees Jailed Boy but Daddy Must Remain, Castro Captive

and Only 12"; 1-2, "U.S. Businessman on Trial in Cuba," articles from the *Miami Herald*.

9. Hugh D. Kessler, Protection Officer of American Embassy, advised on September 24, 1959, that "he is aware of Martino's condition; his principal trouble appears to stem from the fact that he is a dope addict." FBI 64-44828-2; Summers, pp. 615-616.

10. HSCA report from Fonzi and Gonzales to Fenton (in Exhibits) as well as the Carswell incident overview in Alan J. Weberman and Michael Canfield, *Coup D'Etat in America*, San Francisco, CA (Quick American Archives), 1992, pp. 156-157. See also Exhibit 1-3, passport office inquiry connecting Martino to Donovan mission.

11. FBI 64-44838-1 Series.

12. Fiorini's remarks are from newspaper interviews primarily; his remarks are also mentioned in the FBI reports on Martino's claims W C documents CD 349 and CD 295 and FBI file #DL 100-10461 and which are covered in detail by Exhibits 1-19 and 1-19A on the website.

13. Exhibit 1-8 White House memorandum, Schlesinger to Goodwin, June 9, 1961, Sam Halpern information on Operation 40 and Sanjenis.

14. Arthur Schlesinger, memorandum for Richard Goodwin (9th June, 1961): "Sam Halpern, who has been the *Times* correspondent in Habana and more recently in Miami, came to see me last week. He has excellent contracts among the Cuban exiles. One of Miro's comments this morning reminded me that I have been meaning to pass on the following story as told me by Halpern. Halpern says that CIA set up something called Operation 40 under the direction of a man named (as he recalled) Captain Luis Sanjenis, who was also chief of intelligence. It was called Operation 40 because originally only 40 men were involved; later the group was enlarged to 70. The ostensible purpose of Operation 40 was to administer liberated territories in Cuba. But the CIA agent in charge, a man known as Felix, trained the members of the group in methods of third degree interrogation, torture and general terrorism. The liberal Cuban exiles believe that the real purpose of Operation 40 was to 'kill Communists' and, after eliminating hard-core Fidelistas, to go on to eliminate first the followers of Ray, then the followers of Varona and finally to set up a right wing dictatorship, presumably under Artime. Varona fired Sanjenis as chief of intelligence after the landings and appointed a man named Despaign in his place. Sanjenis removed 40 files and set up his own office; the exiles believe that he continues to have CIA support."

15. W C document 301, p. 280. See also Exhibit 1-8A FBI report 11/30/63, Marjorie Heimbecker interview.

16. William Hinckle & William Turner, *Deadly Secrets: The CIA-Mafia War Against Castro and the Assassination of J.F.K.* New York. (Thunder's Mouth Press), 1992, pp.188-197.

17. Ibid. p. 189.

18. Exhibit 1-9, *Hear Two Great American Patriots* speaker program, May 8, 1963.

19. Based on 2004 exchanges between researcher John Simkin and Nathaniel Weyl, the following should be noted: Weyl, although strongly anti-Communist, did not consider himself to be right wing. In fact, he had broken association with the John Birch Society and advised Martino against speaking tours sponsored by the John Birch Society. An account of how Weyl became involved with Martino is provided in his autobiography *Encounters with Communism* (Xlibris), 2004. Weyl had also agreed to work with Bill Pawley on a book in 1964 or later, although Weyl did not feel that describing him as a ghost writer was totally accurate. He also pointed out that Bill Pawley was not himself a flyer but that FDR had given Pawley the task of creating the Flying Tiger organization in the months prior to Pearl Harbor. Weyl thought at the time that the Kennedy assassination probably had Cuban or Soviet links but his only information on Oswald's possible Castro associations came from a reporter at the *Sun Sentinel*.

20. It appears that Martino was introduced by Weyl to Julian Sourwine, chief counsel to Eastland's committee, and that Sourwine arranged the briefing meeting with Senator Eastland.

21. Exhibit 1-10, "Pawley Is Named Man of the Year" – 1959; 1-11, "Kennedy Blew Chance in Cuba, says Pawley;" 1-12 "Overthrow Castro – Pawley;" 1-13, "Plan Had Castro Blocked – Pawley." *Miami Herald*.

22. Exhibit 1-14, March 1960 CIA contact memo; William Pawley meeting with J.D. Easterling.

23. Ibid.

24. David Corn, *Blond Ghost; Ted Shackley and the CIA's Crusades.* New York & London (Simon & Schuster), 1994, p. 101.

25. Grayston L. Lynch, *Decision for Disaster; Betrayal at the Bay of Pigs* (Washington & London Brassey's) 1998, pp. 89-96.

26. JM/WAVE support for Operation TILT is described in JM/WAVE report 9342 June 5, 1963; details of the mission are reported and illustrated in "The Bayo-Pawley Affair," Soldier of Fortune Magazine, February 1976.

27. Peter Dale Scott, *The War Conspiracy.* New York (Bobbs-Merrill Company), 1972, p. 112.

28. WAVE-9343 Dispatch; Maritime After Action Report, June 5, 1963, from Chief of Station to Chief Special Affairs Staff. (Leda After Action file)

29. WAVE Dispatch: WAVE-0438; UFGA-9733; WAVE-9712; WAVE-9342 and COS memo UFGA-14348. Exhibit 1-15, Martino CIA 201 cover sheet; Exhibit 1-16, Martino CIA Code Names; Exhibit 1-17 Martino photo with Bayo team on mission; 1-18 Bayo mission photos from *Soldier of Fortune* article including Martino, Bayo, and Martinez.

30. Letter from Carter to Pawley, June 1, 1963

31. Ibid.

32. Billings' New Orleans notes are online at www.jfk-online/com/billings2.html courtesy of David Reitzes.

33. CIA FOIA 18462 to Chief Special Affairs Staff, from COS JM/WAVE.

34. John Martino, *I Was Castro's Prisoner* (The Devin-Adair Company) 1963; CE3108, 11/29/63 – Sylvia Odio FBI interview describes Martino's remarks relayed by her sister to her. Martino reportedly stated that he had been on the Isle of Pines for three years with Amador Odio and that he knew that Odio's daughters were living in Dallas in late 1963: "John Martino spoke, who was an American, who was very clever and brilliant. I am not saying that he is lying at all. When you are excited, you might get all your facts mixed up, and Martino was one of the men who were in Isle of Pines for 3 years. And he mentioned the fact that he knew Mr. Odio, that Mr. Odio's daughters were in Dallas, and she went to that meeting. I did not go, because they kept it quiet from me so I would not get upset about it. I don't know if you know who John Martino is." Page 380. jfkassassination.net/russ/testimony/odio.htm

35. The FBI reports were largely prepared by Special Agents James O'Conner and were obtained and published by author A. J. Weberman. They include FBI # 64-44838-1, -2, -3, -4 and Summary Report 105-82555-3995.

36. FBI report 124-10035-10367. Exhibit 1-19, John Martino, Cuba and the Kennedy Assassination (Human Events), 1964. www.cuban-exile.com/doc_226-250/doc0237.html; Exhibit 1-19A, FBI memorandum, Miami, Florida May 8, 1964. Efforts to locate Cuban Source of John Martino's information regarding Oswald's activities in the Miami area.

37. Sept 24, 60 - Initial meeting is held between CIA Operational Support Chief O 'Connell mobster John Rosselli, and Robert Maheu, a private investigator with CIA ties, at the Plaza Hotel in New York for the purpose of planning assassination of Castro, Church Committee Report, The Assassination Plots. See also, FBI Memo to Attorney General, May 22, 1962, Subject: The Johnny Rosselli Matter, FBI 62-109060-4984

38. JFK authorizes a major new covert action program aimed at overthrowing the Cuban government. The new program, codenamed Operation Mongoose, will be directed by counterinsurgency specialist Edward G. Lansdale under the guidance of Attorney General Robert Kennedy. A high-level inter-agency group, the Special Group Augmented (SGA), is created with the sole purpose of overseeing Mongoose. The Cuba Project, 3/2/62; Alleged Assassination Plots Involving Foreign Leaders, 11/20/75, pp. 139, 144, See also JFK Lancer www.jfklancer.com/cuba/

39. "Executive Action Capability;" i.e., a general standby capability to carry out assassinations when required. Executive Action program came to be known as ZR/RIFLE.

40. Reference RIFs 104-10429-10223 and 104-1048-10216, CIA Segregated Files.

41. Peter Dale Scott, *Deep Politics III, The CIA, The Drug Traffic and Oswald in Mexico* (History Matters) 2000, www.history-matters.com/pds/DP3_Overview.htm.

42. W C Document 59 and 961

43. Waldron, pp. 657-658; 676-677 and index p. 887

44. Exhibit 1-20, HSCA March 1977 memo on Martino and Pawley expedition, Exhibit 1-21, HSCA August memo on initial contact by "Fred" and his detailing of Martino's comments on his involvement in the Kennedy conspiracy, Exhibit 1-22, HSCA October memo on contacts with Martino family.

45. HSCA Martino investigation memos from Fonzi and Gonzales to Cliff Fenton; Record Number 180-10096-10238 and supplemental report.

46. Summer's *Vanity Fair* article and HSCA memo from Lawson to Fenton on John Martino's Cuban Connection, Record # 180-10105-10173.

CHAPTER TWO: ...An Ex-Marine, an Expert Marksman

1. Hinckle and Turner, p.116. Also, Fonzi pp. 109-110.

2. Hinckle and Turner, pp. 52, 53, 366-367; Dick Russell, *The Man Who Knew Too Much: Hired to Kill Oswald and Prevent the Assassination of JFK.* New York (Carroll & Graf Publishers) 1992, Chapter 19; Also, Bernardo de Torres, Bay of Pigs veteran, Brigade 2506 intelligence officer and investigator for DA Garrison stated in his HSCA testimony that he was aware of the existence of Operation 40 although he himself had not been part of the group.

3. WC Volume XI, p. 372; overall Odio testimony on pp. 367 – 389.

4. WC Volume 16, p. 834 and HSCA pp. 138 and 139; best coverage is in Gaeton Fonzi, *The Last Investigation*. New York (Thunder's Mouth Press), 1993, where Fonzi relates his in-depth investigation of the Odio incident for the HSCA.

5. Joan Mellen, *A Farewell To Justice: Jim Garrison, JFK's Assassination, and the Case That Should Have Changed History*. Washington, D. C. (Potomac Books), 2005, pp. 220-221.

6. The Odio incident at the very least destroys the official history of Lee Oswald as a "lone nut." If Sylvia Odio had gone to the authorities with her story on November 22, her story would have supported conspiracy charges against Oswald and also would have implicated the suspicious Latinos – Latinos who had confidential information about her father and who could have easily been Castro agents. Her failure to do so may have been based on fears for her father's safety. Or she may have had the insight to perceive how dangerous (and withal how futile) the filing of such a report would have been. Ruby's murder of Oswald two days later must have made it all too clear that any inside knowledge of the case was dangerous to own.

7. Exhibit 2-1, HSCA memorandum, Gonzalez to Fenton on interview with Amador Odio. See also Noel Twyman, *Bloody Treason: On Solving History's Greatest Murder Mystery: The Assassination of John F. Kennedy* (Laurel Publishing), 1997, p. 321

8. WC 20, p. 690. John Martino definitely knew of Sylvia Odio, although apparently not from her father as he claimed. Martino was not imprisoned on the Isle of Pines.

9. FBI 105-82555-4743.

10. FBI DL 100-10461 10461, 12/19/63.

11. Ibid.

12. Appendix H, Odio Revisited.

13. Summers, *Conspiracy: The Definitive Book on the JFK Assassination, New York (Paragon House) 1989*, p. 415; Russell, p. 777.

14. Fonzi, p. 254.

15. HSCA executive session testimony of Robert McKeown; exhibit 2-3, HSCA executive session testimony of Robert McKeown.

16. Exhibit 2-2, McKeown's passport file, indirectly indicates his supposed communist affiliations; he was forced to deny them for the passport office.

17. Ruby apparently confused McKeown with a man named Davis. Ruby had been involved in gun running with Thomas Eli Davis, and told his first lawyer that Davis' testimony would be potentially the most damaging thing that could happen to his defense case. Given the

McKewon–Oswald encounter, it possible that Ruby's remark to his lawyer was actually in regard to McKeown.

18. HSCA executive session testimony of Robert McKeown; exhibit 2-3, HSCA executive session testimony of Robert McKeown.
19. Russell, p. 432.
20. Ibid.

CHAPTER THREE: They Came From New Orleans

1. *New York Times* interview by Fred Powledge, November 27, 1963.
2. Dick Russell, *The Man Who Knew Too Much*, pp. 400, 770.
3. This exchange is described on pages 59-60 of Mellen's book where she states that Martello lied in saying that he had turned over the original of the note to the Secret Service. Mellen describes a somewhat inaccurate facsimile of the note being handed over while Martello retained the original, now in the possession of his son.
4. The Clay Shaw trial testimony of Regis Kennedy, Criminal District Court Parish Of Orleans, State Of Louisiana January 17, 1969. " Your Honor, I have been directed to say that this is outside of the scope of the authority which I have received from the Attorney General..."
5. John Newman, *Oswald and the CIA*, p. 341 cites CIA Memo of 1967, RIF 199.06.28.15:07:58:030280 – document was misfiled among Fiorini/ Sturgis papers and became available in 1994 release.
6. Paris Flammonde, *The Kennedy Conspiracy: An Uncommissioned Report on Jim Garrison*, (Merideth Press) 1969, pp. 25-26.
7. Ibid.
8. Harold Weisberg, *Oswald in New Orleans: Case of conspiracy with the C.I.A.*, New York (Canyon Books) 1967, pp. 114-115; Andrews interview in WC Volume 11, pp. 325-329.
9. Weisberg, *Oswald in New Orleans*, New York; Harold Weisberg, *Whitewash: The Report on the Warren Report*, (Dell Pub. Co), 1965.
10. For more details on the bar incident, Pena and the reaction of the FBI see HSCA report pp. 193-194 and Mark Lane, *Plausible Denial: Was the CIA Involved in the Assassination of JFK?* (Thunder's Mouth Press) Reprint edition 1992, pp. 55-56 as well as WC Volume 11 pp. 339-346 and 353-363; also Weisberg, *Oswald in New Orleans*, pp. 303-326.
11. WC Volume 11, numerous documents in the 370 and 380 series including 370, 371, 372, 377, 383, 387 and 388. Doyle, April 3, 1967.
12. Weisberg, *Oswald in New Orleans*, pp. 304-308.

13. Richard Billings, *New Orleans Journal*. Available online at: www.jfk-online.com/billings4.html
14.
15. Trial transcript, U.S. vs. Richard Case Nagell, May 4-5, 1964.
16. *Research of Larry Hancock: Richard Case Nagell: Chronology and Documents, John Martino, 112th Intelligence Corp* (JFK Lancer) 2001.
17. Dick Russell, *The Man Who Knew Too Much*, (Carroll & Graf Publishers) Revised edition, 2003, Appendix A: "Nagell and Oswald's ID Card." Russell writes that in 1976, while reviewing Nagell's court files maintained by attorney Bernard Fensterwald, Jr., Russell came across a poor photocopy of a "Uniformed Services Identification and Privileges Card" bearing Lee Harvey Oswald's picture and apparent signature. Neither Fensterwald nor Russell had seen this card among any of the Warren Commission exhibits. The attorney said he had no idea of how the card came into Nagell's possession. Warren Commission historian Mary Ferrell wrote Fensterwald after seeing the card copy, "Where in the world did Nagell get the copy he possessed? Assuming he obtained the original card and xeroxed it adding a different picture and signature, how did he obtain it before it had the postmark (or whatever that stamp is) put on it? I stress the point that this card does not appear in anything else—not the [Warren Commission] Report, not the [commission] volumes, in no other book..."
18. FBI Report, December 20, 1964, "For the record he would like to say that his association with OSWALD (meaning Lee Harvey Oswald) was purely social and that he had met him in Mexico City and in Texas."
19. Nagell letter to Secret Service, January 2, 1964. "I would like to know if this is the accepted procedure of the Secret Service Division when questioning witnesses?"
20. W C Exhibit 1780, Memo from Hosty to Inspector James R. Malley dated November 27, 1963. See also WC Exhibits 1791 and 1793, US Secret Service report of ATSAIC Gopadze accompanying Hosty and Brown to Marina's interview November 27.
21. WC Exhibit 1792, includes interview of Marina Oswald by Leon Gopadze with Paul Gregory, p. 6 specifically asking about Washington and Mexico City; Weisberg, Whitewash II, pp. 20-21.
22. WC Volume 20, pp. 262-264; pp. 266-2667, 270; Volume 19, p. 577. See also Exhibit 3-5, Fair Play for Cuba Committee response letter to Lee Oswald.
23. Robert Gambert to Dick Russell, *The Man Who Knew Too Much*, p. 90; As mentioned earlier, references for this chapter include Russell, as well as *Richard Case Nagell: Chronology and Documents* by this author and

available through JFK Lancer. For specific details on Nagell's letter to Hoover and its retrieval by the FBI, see Russell, *The Man Who Knew Too Much*, second edition, pp. 38-40 and p. 102. The Nagell documents are available primarily through the efforts of Anna Marie Kuhns-Walko. The *Chronology* provides extensive reference documents as well as an analysis of Nagell's route to going public. It also deals with the extent to which his later statements were influenced by his behind-the-scenes battle to recover custody of his children. Additional sources include a section on Nagell in Noel Twyman's *Bloody Treason: On Solving History's Greatest Murder Mystery: The Assassination of John F. Kennedy* (Laurel Pub; 1 edition, 1997) and a series of articles by Lisa Pease in *PROBE* magazine.

Additionally, did Oswald mention he intended to travel to Mexico City, or anywhere else in the near future? The quotes between Ruth and Lee Oswald below are from a 2001 interview conducted by Greg Parker with Mrs. Ruth Peters (married name). (Personal communication between the author and Greg Parker, 2006.)

"He mentioned that he wasn't going with Marina to Dallas because he needed to go to Washington (at least I think that's where he said he was going ... somewhere in northeastern U.S., but then I believe he mentioned several other places as well ... I was only concerned about his lack of interest in being in Dallas with his wife!). In fact, it was his mention of this that triggered my question "but don't you want to be with Marina when she gives birth?" He indicated that he had been present for the birth of their first child so it was no big deal to him; but also that he had "important business" in (I think it was) Washington. When he used that phrase, I remember asking him what business, and his avoiding the question and saying "just business.' I should also mention that we are Quakers, and Quakers do not consider violence an acceptable or appropriate way to solve problems. Thus both my sister Karol and I remember our shock when Karol innocently asked him 'Why did you leave the Soviet Union?' and he answered, "Because they won't let you own a gun there.' One of us persisted with something like 'But why would you need a gun?" And he had said simply, shaking his head nervously, 'you gotta have a gun!' He then went on to tell us that one thing he was going to do in Washington was 'pick up a gun.' This exchange hadn't helped my assessment of his lack of 'normality.' When Karol and I were innocently trying to make conversation with him, he was terribly secretive and evasive about his 'line of work' and about 'his business' in Washington. I wouldn't call him paranoid, exactly; at least he didn't seem to suspect we were part of some plot at the time. But Karol and I couldn't figure out how he was paying his rent and purchasing groceries, and where he was getting the money for all his travel (and guns)!"

Chapter Four: It Begins

1. Don Bohning, *The Castro Obsession: U.S. Covert Operations Against Cuba 1959-1965*. Washington, D.C., (Potomac Books) 2005, p. 125
2. Russell, *The Man Who Knew Too Much*, p. 298.
3. David Corn, p 112.
4. Exhibit 4-1, "Alpha 66 to Take a Bigger Swing at Castro"; 4-2, "Exiles Report Port Attack," 4-3, "Four Targets Struck but Havana Silent."
5. Exhibit 4-4, *Life* coverage of Eddie Bayo on Baku raid; Exhibit 4-5 *Post* coverage "Help Us Fight, Cry the Angry Exiles!"
6. Various U.S. Army memos including those from Lt. Col. Grover King, Commander of AIS; King memo is INSCOM/CSF document 194-10003-10394; *SWHT* Exhibit 4-6, U.S. Army memorandum on Antonio Veciana and Alpha 66 Organization; *SWHT* Exhibit 4-7, U.S. Army reports and memoranda on Veciana and Alpha 66 contacts.
7. Russell, p. 298.
8. *Nassau meeting; Cuban Officials and JFK Historians, December 1997, Transcripts available on Cuban Information Archives at www.cuban – exile. com.*
9. There are violations of correct Spanish name usage in this book. In Spanish names the father's name usually follows immediately after the given name and is in turn followed by the mother's maiden name, such as Diaz (father's name) Garcia (mother's name) the proper short usage is the father's name. For example the short name for Diaz Garcia would be Diaz or Diaz Garcia not Garcia. This could be important in references such as Escalante's where he mentions "Garcia." Standard usage would have him say either Diaz or Diaz Garcia if he meant Diaz Garcia. Although this is true in the critical sense, we know that the FBI and CIA commonly violated standard name convention in their documents; there is also reason to think that some exiles also violated it as a basic misdirection in references to themselves and to each other. It does raise an important issue for the interpretation of Escalante's remark, which cannot be fully resolved without clarifying the question with Escalante himself.
10. Exhibit 4-7A, Memoranda for Deputy Director of Central Intelligence—subject Maheu, Robert A; *SWHT* Exhibit 4-7B, Sheffield Edwards

memorandum for the Record, 14 May, 1962; Exhibit 4-7C, Hoover memorandum to Director CIA, Subject Anti-Castro Activities, and October 1960.

11. Russell, pp. 229-243.
12. FBI Letter of October 2, 1962, Subject: Mr. Richard Case Nagell, Appearance at American Embassy, Mexico City on September 28, 1962. (See Exhibits Ch. 12)
13. Russell, pp.145-147; Also Exhibit 4-8. Lee Oswald, Chronological Record of Medical Care.
14. Russell, pp. 408-411; Exhibits 4-9; 4-10
15. Ibid. Exhibit 4-11.
16. Exhibit 4-9, HSCA document—letter from Garrett Trapnell to Frank Fowlkes; Exhibit 4-10, Certified Statement—Garrett Trapnell to Parole Officer; Exhibit 4-11, FBI Summary Report on Garrett Trapnell; Exhibit 4-12, FBI memorandum on Ingrid Trapnell divorce proceedings with JMWAVE forwarding and CIA tracking sheets.
17. Ibid.
18. Exhibit 4-13, "The Kennedys Greet the Cubans; Dynamite Found at Stadium." Perhaps more importantly, police received reports of an exile sniper in the Bowl itself with a scope equipped rifle in a duffel bag—Cuban male, 25 years old, 5'4," 135-150 pounds and using the name "Chino." See also Richard Mahoney, *Sons & Brothers: The Days of Jack and Bobby Kennedy*, New York (Arcade Publishing) 1999, p. 407 and Miami PD memo Jan 3, 1963, Captain Napier and John Marshall of the Secret Service.

CHAPTER FIVE: Persons of Interest

1. Exhibit 5-1, FPCC reply letter to Lee Oswald's letters of August 28, 1963 and September 1, in regard to Oswald's planned move to Baltimore.
2. HSCA executive session testimony, record 180-10118-10134, Exhibit 5-2.
3. Exhibit 5-3, FBI report on July 31, 1963 Lake Pontchartrain Raid on William McClaney's property.
4. HSCA testimony pp. 72-93.
5. The CRC/Hemming camp is described in exhibit 5-3G, "Adventurer works hard to establish anti-Castro base near Covington," by William Stuckey, *New Orleans States-Item* newspaper, July 1962.
6. This seizure of the U-Haul is sometimes connected to an exile training camp that was on or near McClaney's property, not far from the

farmhouse where the trailer and explosives were seized. This training camp has been connected by other authors to both General Somoza of Nicaragua and to elements of the casino crowd. A series of Garrison investigation documents provide considerably more and different detail on that camp. That camp contained approximately twenty exiles. They were occupied with physical training and expected to move from that location to a larger and much more military-oriented facility in Nicaragua. They had operated for between five and six weeks before the Cubans were hurried back to Miami after the McClaney farm arrests. This camp had indeed been inspired by remarks from Somoza during a visit to Miami. It was set up, and was to have been operated, by the Christian Democratic Movement group–which appears to have been victimized by a con conducted by one Richard Davis. Davis had approached the group with stories of wealthy right-wing Texas and Louisiana supporters, but after collecting a good deal of money for the Christian Democrats and disappearing with most of it, the group determined that his supporters were non-existent. See Alcock-Garrison memoranda of 1967; Details in exhibit 5-3A. The background of the MDC camp is discussed in detail in exhibits 5-3A Alcock to Garrison memo, 5-3B FBI report on Richard Rudolph Davis, Jr., 5-3C FBI report on Guatemalan Lumber and Mineral Corporation, 5-3D CIA Cable on MDC training camp, 5-3E Weisberg memo to Garrison, 5-3F.

7. Exhibit 5-3G DOJ report on INS files, 5-3H HSCA memo on Victor Espinosa, 5-3I HSCA subpoena request for Victor Espinosa Hernandez and Carlos Hernandez and 5-3J HSCA memo on interview with Stuart Cowley.

8. Hinckle and Turner, pp. 216-217. Also, Anthony Summers, *Conspiracy*, 2nd edition [*Not In Your Lifetime*] (Marlowe & Co) 1998, p. 249: The CIA had opened contacts with him in 1961 when he became disenchanted with increasing Soviet interference in Cuban affairs. He spoke of defecting but was asked to stay in Havana as a source. Interviewed in 1978 by Anthony Summers, while serving a life sentence for plotting against Castro, he claimed the proposal to kill Castro came entirely from the American side. According to Summers, the CIA used a leading Cuban exile in its long-running series of contacts with Cubela: Manuel Artime, one of the exiles most favored by RFK. According to interview notes by a congressional investigator: Artime claimed, "...he had direct contact with JFK and RFK personally. They in turn contacted the CIA.

9. Mahoney, p. 286: In an interview conducted in Havana in May 1997, National Assembly president Ricardo Alarcon allowed that Cubella may have been a Castro plant. At the very time the Kennedy administration

was considering normalizing relations with the Castro regime, certain CIA officials were assiduously undermining that possibility. In their incompetence, they allowed themselves to be set up by Castro, a man whom they regarded as a Latin hysteric.

10. Exhibit 5-4, excerpts from "The Dade County Links", *Miami Magazine*, by Dan Christenson, Volume 27, Number 11, September 1976.
11. Ibid.
12. Exhibit 5-4.
13. Exhibit 5-5, HSCA memorandum excerpt with information on Mike McClaney and Martinez, recommending continued investigation into McClaney associates as well as an inquiry into the activities of FBI agents James O'Connor and George Davis.
14. Exhibit 5-6, Justice Department memorandum recommending re-opening of Warren Commission based on reported association of Lee Oswald with known subversives.
15. Sources include Summers' *Vanity Fair* article and HSCA memo from Lawson to Fenton on John Martino's Cuban Connection - Record Number 180-10105-10173.
16. Dallas Police Chief Jesse Curry, *JFK Assassination File*, 1969
17. See Ian Griggs' detailed analysis "The Oswald line-ups and the riddle of Howard Leslie Brennan" in *No Case To Answer: A retired English detective's essays and articles on the JFK assassination, 1993-2005.* (JFK Lancer), 2005, Chapter 10.
18. Ibid.
19. WC v. 24, p. 210.
20. Summers, *Conspiracy*, 2nd edition, p. 76-78.
21. Ibid., p. 42. Arnold Roland interview.
22. Ibid., chapter 4.
23. David Wrone, *The Zapruder Film: Reframing JFK's Assassination,* (University Press of Kansas), 2003, pp. 171-172.
24. FBI Memoranda, Malley to SAC, Dec 11, 1963 and R. Jevons to Mr. Conrad, November 27, 1963; Serial 44-1639-2142 and Serial 62-109060-427.
25. Weisberg v. ERDA and Department of Justice, Civil Action 75-226.
26. Some of the most recent information on the Mexico City Oswald impersonation is online: "Mexico City: A New Analysis", by John Newman. The JFK Lancer web site contains this transcript of an excellent talk given by Newman at the November in Dallas 1999 conference. The text contains links to documents cited.   www.jfklancer.com/backes/newman/newman_1.html. See also, "Tape: Call on JFK Wasn't Oswald" by Deb Reichmann (The Associated Press) with information

from John Newman. www.jfklancer.com/LNE/LHO-Mexi.html. Additionally, Rex Bradford's work on History-Matters website: "We have up here the tape and the photograph of the man who was at the Soviet Embassy, using Oswald's name. The picture and the tape do not correspond to this man's voice, or to his appearance."— FBI Director J. Edgar Hoover, informing President Johnson of an Oswald impersonation. This phone call itself appears to have been erased. www.history-matters.com/frameup.htm

27. Griggs, "An interview with Johnny Calvin Brewer" Chapter 8.
28. FBI Document 105-82555-2704 James O'Conner, March 24, 1964.
29. Further background on Martino's story about Oswald can be found in CD 1020, pp. 691-692; SS report Co234030, and FBI document 105-82555-2704.
30. Exhibit 5-5A.
31. RIF 104-10226-10198; JM/WAVE memo on "Report of Large Scale Operation Against Cuba by Exile Groups", 3/26/63.
32. FBI record 180-10113-10415.
33. Unless otherwise noted, the following material on Vidal and Hargraves is referenced from HSCA 180-10068-10492; "Report on Anti-Castro Activities: Hemming, Gerald Patrick," 79 pages and from exhibit 5-5B, CIA memorandum on Gerald Patrick Hemming and Roy Emory Hargraves, February 10, 1965. This memo contains a resume of the CIA's short-lived relationship with Felipe Carlos Vidal Santiago.
34. Hinckle and Turner, p. 162.
35. FBI 105-86406-28
36. FBI 105-86406-28.
37. Tape 4, *Researchers Bermuda Conference*, Fabian Escalante.
38. This FBI report was located by Anna Marie Kuhns-Walko and presented by Noel Twyman in *Bloody Treason*, pp. 688-9.
39. Ibid.
40. Ibid.
41. Document 0090, Gordon Winslow's Cuban History Web site; Exhibit 5-7, Dunkin Papers, memorandum from Tom Dunkin to Dick Billings. cuban-exile.com/menu1/!menu.html
42. RIF 124-10220-10320.

CHAPTER SIX: "As soon as they take care of Kennedy"

1. He may have said "they" or maybe it was "we," the FBI report equivocates.
2. Reference HSCA pp. 158-9, 302-3; and *Hinckle*, pp. 263 –264.
3. Exhibit 6-1, Secret Service memorandum of Nov. 27, 1963 – Subject Homer Samuel Valdivia Echevarria.
4. RIF 104-10074-10024 and 104-10074-10036.
5. HSCA report p.101.
6. HSCA final report p. 98; also *Hinckle* pp. 203-207.
7. Exhibit 6-2, Bernard Barker personnel folder summary document; miscellaneous papers pertaining to Sierra, JGCE, Blanco, Varona, the "Nevada Group" and Nicaragua.
8. This source is identified only as Dallas File 134-332/DL 282S.
9. Eric Tagg , *Brush With History, A Day in the Life of Deputy E. R. Walthers.* Garland, TX (Shot in the Light Publishing) 1998 pp. 48-61.
10. Exhibit 6-3; FBI HQ report of 12/22/57, record no. 124-10187-10084.

CHAPTER SEVEN: Shadow Wars and Shadow Warriors

1. Treasury Department memo, McBrien to Albrecht, title: "Re-Opening of Warren Commission," exhibit 5-6.
2. W C, Vol. 5 pp. 34-37; Warren Report pp. 441-442; also James Hosty, and Thomas Hosty, *Assignment Oswald.* (Arcade Publishing) 1st edition 1995, pp. 17-19 and 145-146.
3. WC, Vol. 5, pp.34-37; Warren report pp.441-442; Hosty, pp. 17-19 and 145-146.
4. R. Andrew Kiel, *Edgar Hoover: the Father of the Cold War.* Lanham, Maryland (University Press of America) 2000., p.160.
5. HSCA 180-10101-10207; File Number 01263, WC Exhibit 92, Volume 16, pp. 287–336.
6. WC Vol. 16, Exhibit 92, pp. 287–336.
7. WC Vol. 16, pp. 422-3 and analysis in Kiel, pp. 146-147.
8. Exhibit 7-A1, CIA Memorandum on Colby conversations with CBS.
9. Daniel Schorr, CBS television interview with William Colby. Washington, DC, 21 January, 1976.
10. WC Vol. 16, Exhibit 102, pp. 441-442.
11. The best possible sources for understanding the political intricacies

of this period and the opposing agendas of different interest groups are Professor Peter Dale Scott's *Deep Politics III*, along with the CIA Inspector General's Report and the related Schweiker- Hart report on Cuban affairs.

12. Newman, Chapter 14.
13. HSCA 180-10098-10398; file number 011549; Exhibit 7- 4, Secret Service Protective Research Memorandum of December 8, 1962 – Cuban Plot to Assassinate the President, Antonio Rodriguez y Jones and Bernardo Morales; exhibit 7-4A Secret Service report of 11/30/62, Cuban Plot to Assassinate the President, 7-4C Secret Service report of 08/07/63 Cuban Plot to Assassinate the President.
14. Newman, Chapter 14.
15. Scott, *Deep Politics and the Death of JFK*, p. 249.
16. Ray and Mary La Fontaine, *Oswald Talked: The New Evidence in the JFK Assassination*. Louisiana (Pelican Publishing Company) 1996, pp. 168-170 and 231.
17. Fiorini's reports are mentioned frequently in Bernard Barker's personnel overview – Exhibit 7-1, see also Exhibit 7-2, Fiorini 201 file document and 7-3 JM/WAVE memoranda on status change for Fiorini as well as his ongoing reports. Refer to Exhibit 18-1 for these documents.
18. RIF 104-10172-10141; COS JM/WAVE to CIA from Chief of Task Force W.
19. RIF 104-10400-10133, Russell Holmes file plus JM/WAVE correspondence.
20. Scott, *Deep Politics II*, pp. 329-330.
21. Mahoney, p. 270. Mahoney's source is FBI teletype to the Chicago Crime Commission.
22. RIF 104-10506-10040 February 12, 1964.
23. RIF 104-10308-10085
24. Summers, *The Kennedy Conspiracy [Not in Your Lifetime]* Warner Books; Updated ed. with a special postscript edition, 1998.
25. Summers, *Conspiracy*, pp. 514-516.
26. Exhibit 7-5, "The Ever Persistent Miss Howard," by Alan Gill, *TV GUIDE*, Jan 25, 1964 issue.
27. HSCA Executive Session testimony, record 180-10118-10134.
28. This quotation comes from a memo of Deputy Director Helms. All items detailing the Cuban "peace initiative" are from an extended article by Peter Kornbluth, "JFK and Castro – The Secret Quest for Accommodation," *Cigar Aficionado* Magazine, September/October 1999 issue. Another good analysis is provided by Jim DiEugenio,

"Kennedy's Quest for Detente with Castro," *PROBE*, Nov-Dec, 1999.

29. HSCA testimony pp. 72-93.
30. *PROBE* Magazine, May-June, 1999 p. 7.
31. Joseph Califano, *Inside: A Public and Private Life* (PublicAffairs) 2004, pp. 116-122
32. Scott, *Deep Politics II*, Chapter X, pp. 122-124.
33. Newman, *Oswald and the CIA*, Newman's *PROBE* Magazine article of Sept-Oct 1999, and his JFK Lancer presentation available at www.jfklancer.com/backes/newman/newman_1.html.
34. RIF 104-10308-10163, CIA memorandum for the record on AM/SANTA project, 7/10/63.
35. Fonzi, p. 421
36. Fonzi, pp. 307-9.
37. Hougan, *Secret Agenda: Watergate, Deep Throat, and the CIA*, (Random House Inc.T); 1st ed edition, 1984.
38. Hinckle and Turner, pp. 84-89.
39. William Davy, *Let Justice Be Done: New Light on the Jim Garrison Investigation*. Reston, Virginia (Jordan Publishing) 1999, p. 31; CIA memo to the Chief, WH/C 67-336.
40. Exhibit 7-6, Miami Herald 7-30-62, "Anti-Fidel Army is Their Goal."
41. Ibid., pp. 31-3.
42. Ibid., Davy, p. 285; Novel vs. Garrison et al., p. 490; Gus Russo, *Live By The Sword: The Secret War Against Castro and the Death of JFK*, Baltimore, Maryland (Bancroft Press) 1998, p.152.
43. Novel's saga is detailed at length in chapter 5 of Paris Flammonde's *The Kennedy Conspiracy*.
44. Pease, *PROBE* Magazine, July-August 1998 and Sept–Oct 1997.
45. Relevant sections of this transcript are in Davy's *Let Justice Be Done*, pp. 21-24
46. Schweiker–Hart Report, p. 17; Schorr 165; Hersh, *The Dark Side of Camelot*, pp. 278, 377-8.
47. Newman, *PROBE* Magazine, Sept – Oct, 1999.
48. W C Document 1359.
49. Newman at the November in Dallas 1999 conference on Oswald and Mexico City. www.jfklancer.com/backes/newman/newman_1.html. Newman's thesis: "...the plotters killing the president are involved not just in killing him but in neutralizing law enforcement and the intelligence agencies. And in fact these are particularly powerful, and very good intelligence and law enforcement organizations, the FBI, the CIA, the NSA, the Dept. of Defense. So, integral to the plan must have been to neutralize them and make them not do their job. And the story

from Mexico City does that. I use the term, 'planting a virus.' And I like the concept of a virus as opposed to just a false story. Because, it is not all false. Oswald was there. He did go down there, but he didn't make those phone calls. Whoever made them wanted to make damn sure they were in the record, wanted to make damn sure that after 11/22 when the shots ring out everybody goes rushing off to open up their [file] drawers, [that] that's the first thing they see. And so you have a story which is going to be very embarrassing. It is going to be incriminating in some ways, it is going to make lots of people culpable because they had all of this information, Kostikov, Oswald, when they didn't do anything about it.

50. Rex Bradford, "The Framing of Oswald," at: history-matters.com/frameup.htm.

51. JFK's secret move toward rapprochement with Castro provides an obvious motive for Cuban exiles and for a handful of their trusted CIA contacts, all of whom felt betrayed by the Bay of Pigs and the Cuban Missile Crisis. It remains possible, although beyond the scope of this study, that these individuals were influenced by others. That proposition is explored in Ultimate Sacrifice by Waldron and by Matthew Smith in his 2005 book, *Conspiracy – The Plot to Stop the Kennedys*, New York, N.Y. (Citadel Press) 2005.

.

Chapter Eight: "Well we took care of that S.O.B. Didn't We?"

1. The obituary ran in the *Arizona Range News*, May 8, 1978. See also Fonzi, p. 387.
2. Twyman, pp. 437-482
3. Martino, p. 47.
4. FBI 163-34977-2, 1969 and FBI 163-24877-5, 1976.
5. David Atlee Phillips, *The Carlos Contract: A Novel of International Terrorism*, (Macmillan), 1978.
6. From his 201 file, prepared upon his separation –Exhibit 8-1, Record Number 104-10121-10118.
7. Exhibit 8-1, RIF 104-10121-10118.
8. Reference RIF 104-101121-10339; Army Security report to CIA, 1950.
9. See Appendix B for a cross-reference of the assignments and career postings of David Morales, Ted Shackley, and David Phillips.
10. Phillips, *The Night Watch*, pp. 49-50
11. Morales received the Intelligence Medal of Merit for his work on PB/SUCCESS in Guatemala. His recommendation for honors paperwork

describes his work in training a PM (paramilitary) cadre, establishing a training camp in a foreign country, planning actual operations, and inspiring missions. Morales is cited as being the "mainspring" of the paramilitary effort. See RIF 104-10121-10315; Recommendation for Honor Award.

12. David A. Phillips, *The Night Watch: 25 Years of Peculiar Service*, New York (Atheneum), 1st edition, 1977.

13. Joseph Trento, *The Secret History of the CIA*, Prima Publishing, 2001, p. 374.

14. This information is cited from one of the new documents, re: Zamka, in Chapter 8 Exhibits on the SWHT website; see also RIF 104-10121-10300.

15. Lynch, Chapter 15.

16. Chuck Giancana, *Double Cross: The Explosive, Inside Story of the Mobster Who Controlled America*, (Time Warner Books) UK, 1998. Most researchers are aware of this book written by the son of Sam Giancana, a book on his father's life and self-confessed involvement in the JFK assassination. In the book he ties Giancana his associate John Roselli. The majority of the information in this book appears to be nothing more than gossip, rumor and macho mobster talk. However, buried within all of it is an interesting remark that one of the actual Kennedy conspiracy participants was a "Bay of Pigs action officer." As with almost all gossip, this may be the one grain of truth in the Giancana story.

17. Bradley Ayers, p. 27, *The War That Never Was*, The Bobbs-Merrill Company Inc., 1976.

18. David Corn, *Blonde Ghost*, Simon & Schuster, 1994

19. RIF 104-10121-10253.

20. Mahoney, p 396.

21. Comparison of Bissell's CIA Inspector General Bay of Pigs interview statements on assassination with his later statements in 1984; Mahoney, p.107

22. Corn; *Ted Shackley and the CIA's Crusades*, p. 64-74.

23. RIF 104-10241-10064.

24. Interviews with Reuben Carbajal are described and quoted by Fonzi, *The Last Investigation*, pp. 380-390; Twyman, *Bloody Treason*, pp. 447-480.

25. From personal communications between the author and Robert Dorff; material from Dorff's interviews with Ruben.

26. Ayers' affidavit 11-3-89 to Noel Twyman. See *Bloody Treason* for extensive details and corroboration for Ayers' information. Other

references for Morales include Fonzi, pp. 366-390; Bradley Earl Ayers, *The War That Never Was: An insider's account of CIA covert operations against Cuba.* Indianapolis/New York (The Bobbs-Merrill Company Inc.), 1976, Chapters 4, 5, and 6; and Corn, pp. 84-6.

27. RIF 104-10075-10179; JM/WAVE cable concerning Maritime Exfiltration to Director, November 22, 1963.
28. RIF 104-10121-10285; CIA agreement with AID, 1965 and RIF 104-10121-10285, CIA agreement with AID.
29. Joseph Trento, *The Secret History of the CIA*, (Carroll & Graf), Reprint edition 2005, p. 383-386.
30. This is a combination of quotes from both books; the first sentence is from Fonzi, p. 385 and the second is from Twyman, p. 464.
31. Twyman, Chapter 5 contains interviews with Walton and Carbajal.
32. Walton's story and quotation are confirmed by Carbajal; see Fonzi, p. 390.

CHAPTER 9: JOHN ROSELLI, "STRATEGIST"

1. Charles Rappleye & Ed Becker, *All American Mafioso: The Johnny Roselli Story.* New York (Barricade Books, Inc.) 1995, p. 125.
2. Exhibit 9A-1, excerpt from Roselli FBI surveillance records, "Cleveland Group" operations.
3. Rappleye, p. 140.
4. Ibid. p. 16.
5. Ibid. pp.146-163.
6. Ibid. p. 147; David Morales' relationships with gamblers and crime figures as well as his many trips to Las Vegas are described in Rappleye's biography. They are also corroborated by personal remarks from his friend Ruben Carbajal.
7. Exhibit 9-1.
8. Rappleye, p. 178.
9. Ibid. p. 187; also CIA memo to Director FBI, file 105-93264-2.
10. In Richard Bissell's remarks during a CIA internal Inspector General's investigation of the Bay of Pigs operation, he totally denied any knowledge of an assassination project in conjunction with the Bay of Pigs invasion plan giving technically correct but historically misleading information for the official record.
11. Mahoney, pp. 75-6.
12. FBI Airtel, Nov. 3 1960 to Director from SAC Miami, file number 105-93264.

13. From Debra Conway's CIA-Mafia Timeline at www.jfklancer.com: May 22, 1961, FBI Director Hoover sent the Attorney General a memorandum about the Las Vegas wiretap. An attachment to that memorandum quoted Sheffield Edwards as saying that Bissell in "recent briefings" of Taylor and Kennedy "told the Attorney General that some of the associated planning included the use of Giancana and the underworld against Castro." Bissell told the Church Committee that he did not remember any briefing other than for the review of the Bay of Pigs. The Taylor Report. (Bissell, 7/22/75) Taylor told the Church Committee that no mention was made of an assassination effort against Castro.

    The summary of Edwards' conversation with the FBI was accompanied by a cover memorandum from Hoover stating that Edwards had acknowledged the "attempted" use of Maheu and 3 "hoodlum elements" by the CIA in "anti-Castro activities" but that the "purpose for placing the wiretap...has not been determined...." (FBI memo to Attorney General, 5/22/61) The memorandum also explained that Maheu had contacted Giancana in connection with the CIA program and CIA had requested that the information be handled on a "need-to-know" basis.

    RFK writes in the margin of the memo to his aide, Courtney Evans, "I hope this will be followed up vigorously," after being assured the alliance had been discontinued by CIA's Edwards. (Hoover memo to RFK and RFK's notation quoted in Assassination Plots, Interim Report: Alleged Assassination Plots Involving Foreign Leaders, pp127-128)

    Note: Courtney Evans had worked closely with the then Senator John Kennedy and Robert Kennedy on the McClellan Committee which had investigated the relationship between organized labor and organized crime. During the McClellan Investigation Sam Glancana was one of the major crime figures examined. After becoming Attorney General, Robert Kennedy had singled out Giancana as one of the underworld leaders to be most intensely investigated.
14. Photographs provided by researcher James Richards; 1963 print date on back of photos.
15. Exhibit 9-2.
16. Waldren, pp. 111 and 112
17. Twyman, pp. 440-7. Twyman discusses this meeting and the details and implications of the documents located by Anna Marie Kuhns Walko at length.
18. Mahoney, p. 268.

19. Exhibit 9-1A, excerpt from Roselli surveillance file; exhibit 9-1B, Roselli surveillance files for 1961 and 1962; and exhibit 9-1C, FBI telephone surveillance report on Roselli for August - September 1963.
20. "Roselli's run" is described at length in Mahoney, pp. 284 and following, as well as in Twyman's *Bloody Treason*.
21. Rappleye, p. 279
22. Exhibit 9-3, Notes from Chicago Police Department, pp. 9 –10.
23. Jack Anderson shared offices with a very well connected D.C. lobbyist, Irwin Davidson. Davidson represented the Teamsters and others including the Murchison family. He was even reputed to have handled cash payments from Murchison to Baker for some of their very private business dealings. See Twyman, p. 265.
24. Exhibit 9-4, FBI memo Rosen to DeLoach, FBI interview with Morgan; HSCA Request for Immunity Form with notes on Morgan's professed "lack of detail," confirms Morgan's relationship to Roselli and Maheu and 9-4A FBI summary report on Morgan interview and story, March 22, 1967.
25. Rappleye, pp. 274-275
26. Exhibit 9- 5, Memoranda for the Record, Garrison Group Meeting No. 1 and No. 2, September 1967. One of the things that becomes really clear in reviewing the Garrison investigation and Clay Shaw trial is that the CIA was trying to keep from getting pulled in and exposing real operational personnel like La Borde and Santana. On the other hand it was Justice who was working directly with Shaw's lawyers and trying to subvert Garrisons prosecution-there is no doubt that Justice and the FBI were the ones out to do in Garrison. Which of course raises some very interesting questions primarily about what skeletons the FBI had in its closet in regard to Oswald in New Orleans. By far the best detailing of the FBI and Justice's illegal intervention in the Garrison case is in Jim DiEugenio's *The Obstruction of Garrison*, which is pp. 17-50 of *The Assassinations* by DiEugenio and Pease.
27. Hugh McDonald and Robin Moore, *LBJ and the JFK Conspiracy*, Condor Publishing Company Inc., 1978. It appears the book had first been written in 1967 or 1968.
28. FBI report and analysis, Weberman.
29. Rappleye, p. 301
30. Ibid, p. 310
31. Ibid, p. 315. See also Exhibit 9-6, HSCA memorandum from Gary Cornwell to Tiny Hutton, October 25, 1977 – Interview with Roselli's legal counsel during his Senate Intelligence Committee Hearing testimony.

32. Rappleye, pp. 319, 327.
33. Summers, *Conspiracy*, p. 500.
34. Mahoney, pp. 295, 408.

Chapter 10: Standing the "Night Watch"

1. Phillips, *The Night Watch*.
2. Ibid., p. 8.
3. Ibid., pp. 11-25.
4. Ibid., p. 33.
5. Ibid., p. 49.
6. Reference RIF 104-10315-10038, Havana to JM/WAVE, subject "Veciana Report on plot to wipe out Cuban PM and Top Aids."
7. MondOperaio, Rome 2003. The English translation is Kennedy and the left center. Nenni, the missiles and the mystery of Dallas.
8. Ibid.
9. Phillips, *The Night Watch*, page 101.
10. Foreign Relations of the U.S. / Department of State / 1961-1963 Volume X).
11. Exhibit 10-1; Barker personnel file summary memo, page 3 / 11112145; also, exhibit 13-1).
12. John Newman, Oswald and the CIA, pp. 240 –244. Exhibit 10-2, CIA memorandum of February 1, 1961 states that David Atlee Phillips is supervising the operation involving "Court XXX").
13. The shift of domestic spying and infiltration from one agency to another does little to address the unconstitutionality of such activities. That both the Agency and the Bureau conducted surveillance and active infiltration violating First Amendment guarantees became public knowledge during the revelations about Operation CHAOS, conducted against various elements of the peace movement in the late 1960's and 1970's.
14. CIA memorandum for Chief, CI/R&A, "Garrison Investigation; Belle Chasse Training Camp," October 1967, document # WG/C 67-336. The memo is described in William Davy, *Let Justice Be Done*, pp. 30-31 and memo text is excerpted and quoted specifically on p. 31.
15. Ibid., pp. 30-33
16. RIF 104-10113-10082, Memo from Anthony R. Ponchay, C.O.S., WH/ Miami to SAIC, Miami Field Office.
17. Newman, page 290.
18. Davy, pp. 21-4.

19. Fonzi, p. 295.
20. Ibid., p. 297 and, quoting Ron Cross, p. 307.
21. Davy, p. 309.
22. Hinckle and Turner, pp. 90-1.
23. Fonzi, pp. 324-325.
24. Corn, p. 114.
25. Jim Hougan's conversations with Frank Terpil, reported in PROBE, March - April 1966, p. 21.
26. An expanded treatment of the long-term association between Hal Hendrix, the CIA, and David Phillips is detailed by Seth Kantor in *The Ruby Cover-Up*, pp. 376-382. Hendrixs' mis-statements, under oath, are described by Gaeton Fonzi in *The Last Investigation*, pp. 326-7.
27. HSCA Volume X: "Anti-Castro Activists and Organizations, Section IV. Cuban Revolutionary Council: A Concise History", p. 58. After the October 1962 missile crisis, the policy of the United States toward the Castro regime changed drastically. In his book *The Losers*, Paul Bethel, former press attaché at the Havana Embassy noted, "There is no doubt that President Kennedy and his brother, the Attorney General, consciously set about the business of stopping all efforts to unhorse Fidel Castro-from outside exile attack." Paul Bethel, "*Te Losers*, New Rochelle, N.Y., (Arlington House) 1969, p. 398.
28. Personal correspondence between Shawn Phillips (James' son) and researcher Gary Buell. Phillips, *Nightwatch*.
29. Phillips, *The Night Watch*, pp. 114-122.
30. HSCA Lopez Report
31. HSCA Lopez Report, pp 13-30; footnote 363 on p. A-25, as quoted in *Deep Politics II; Essays on Oswald, Mexico, and Cuba*, p. 9.
32. RIF 124-10003-10052; FBI memo from Legate, Mexico City to Director, FBI, February 2, 2004.
33. Ibid.
34. Exhibit 10-3, "Rebel Raids to Continue"; "Exiles Say Soviets Killed in Raids," HSCA interview of Antonio Veciana.
35. Exhibit 10-3A, HSCA Veciana notes, Liebengood and Routh December 1976 and Tom Moore, January 1977.
36. Fonzi, p. 142.
37. Ibid., pp.137-139, 272.
38. Ibid, p. 272.
39. Exhibit 10-5; HSCA memorandum from Gonzales to Fenton, Aug 25, 1977.
40. This last comment followed a personal introduction. David Phillips (propaganda chief for the Cuban Project, Chief of Cuban Operations,

and Chief Cuban Operations Western Hemisphere) stated and later testified that he had never heard of Antonio Veciana, head of Alpha 66, the most visible and successful independent anti-Castro exile group during the period of Phillips' service.

41. Fonzi, p. 396
42. Ibid., p. 313-315
43. Ibid., p. 309
44. Lisa Pease, *PROBE*, March-April, 1996.
45. Exhibit 10-4, Jul 14, 1963 "Backstage With Bobby" by Hal Hendrix, *Miami News* Latin American Editor. Detailing RFK's role as the architect of the "Nicaragua-based front against Castro." Also FBI memo Re: Anti-Fidel Castro Activities Internal Security, 105-1742, 19 July, 1963, HSCA, AA. Additional information found by Debra Conway in the National Security Files: This newspaper story was discussed in the Jul 16, '63 meeting of the "Standing Group": Report by Mr. FitzGerald. "There was a discussion of the wide-spread press reports that the U.S. was backing Cuban exiles who are planning raids against Cuba from Central American States. One news article shown the Attorney General was headed "Backstage with Bobby" and referred to his conversations with persons involved in planning the Cuban raids. In the discussion as to how to deal with the press reports, the Attorney General suggested that we could float other rumors so that in the welter of press reports no one would know the true facts. Mr. McCone agreed that it would be possible to confuse the situation in this manner." [5 lines of source text not declassified] Kennedy Library, National Security Files, Meetings and Memoranda Series, Standing Group Meeting, 7/16/63.
46. Summers, *Conspiracy*, p. 518.
47. This exchange between James Phillips' son, Shawn Phillips, and researcher Gary Buell was posted electronically and confirmed in personal email with the author. In addition, Shawn Phillips confirmed the events in personal communication with author Dick Russell. A recently available document indicates that as far as JM/WAVE was concerned, David Phillips was to be in Mexico City on November 23. The document describes arrangements for the maritime exfiltration of a CIA Headquarters asset. An individual traveling out of Cuba was to be carrying a priority message via "pouch" and was expected to arrive in Mexico on November 22. "Sloman" was to contact Phillips in regard to this information. Sloman is reported to be Tony Sforza, an individual known to be associated with the CIA and a close associated of both David Morales and David Phillips (Fonzi, *The Last Investigation*, p. 384). The CIA document states that "Sloman will contact Choaden

(Phillips CIA crypt) by phone either at the station or at home 23 Nov to arrange pick up." Reference JM/WAVE Cable concerning Maritime Exfiltration, 11/22/63; RIF 104-10075-10179.
48. Quote from copy of Phillips' manuscript provided by researcher Malcolm Blunt to the author.

CHAPTER 11: "CUBA, THE GUNS, NEW ORLEANS, EVERYTHING"

1. Kantor, See also Chapter 4.
2. Louis McWillie's FBI record, number 4404064, shows that he used the aliases of Martin, Chapman and Olney.
3. Schiem; Exhibit 11-3A, "The Secret Life of Jack Ruby" *New Times*, 1/23/78 p. 48.
4. RIF 124-90100-10308; FBI Memorandum 11/12/59. Also FBI Memorandum RIF 104-10182-10273 discusses Mitch Werbell and his connection to Joe Merola. In Cuba, Merola had been an aide to Mannarnio, the man who sold the San Souci to Trafficante.
5. Material summarized from *Miami Herald* articles by Al Finklestein, Gene Miller and Arthur Johnsey, 1960 and 1961.
6. JFK Document 007235, April 6, 1978, p. 56.
7. Exhibit 11-1, "Miami Gun-Runners Go To Prison"; exhibit 11-2, "Gun Running Plot Links Miamian with Appalachian"; exhibit 11-3 State Department Passport summary report on international travel, by Norman Rothman.
8. Scott, *Deep Politics*, p. 200.
9. CD 84, p. 215; HSCA report p. 152, p. 167; Blakey and Billings, *The Plot to Kill the President*, pp. 293-4.
10. Hubert/Griffin memo to Lee Rankin, May 14, 1964 p. 4; HSCA Volume 5, pp. 197-198; HSCA Vol. 5, pp. 204-205. See also Lisa Pease's travel analysis of Ruby for this period, excerpted from her article "Gunrunner Ruby and the CIA," *PROBE* 1995, Volume 2, No. 5.
11. W C Exhibit 1689.
12. Exhibit 11-3A, "The Secret Life of Jack Ruby" *New Times*, 1/23/78, contains numerous revelations about Jack Ruby left unanswered by all the official investigations.
13. HSCA Volume 5, pp. 355-367.
14. *The Dealey Plaza Echo*, Volume 10, Number 1, March 2006, Ian Griggs "An Interview with Andrew Armstrong, Jr," pp. 26-30.
15. Memo series from 112th Intelligence Corps Group, San Antonio–Cuban Exile Training in Nicaragua and Cuban Officer Training Program;

author's research work on the 112th MIG available from JFK Lancer. www.jfklancer.com/

16. Exhibit 11-4, Garrison investigation Outside Contact Report and related memoranda–Girnus interviews, photo and flight plan.

17. Ibid.

18. Ibid.

19. Ibid.

20. Details on the Kimble flight are taken from Garrison, p. 136-139, *On the Trail of the Assassins* and from Kimble's statements to Garrison provided by researcher David Boylan.

21. Exhibit 11-5, David Ferrie's Long Distance Telephone Call List, November calls missing from record, courtesy of researcher Larry Haappenen.

22.. HSCA record number 180-10108-10170, memo from Moriarty to Fenton, 3/25/77 and exhibit 11-6, HSCA memorandum Moriarty to Fenton on Robert Price.

23. 1963-64, rare book collection, microfilm, Washington D.C., Microcard Editions, 1967

24. Exhibit 11-7, "Suspect Nabbed on 5th Green; Partner Held in Armed Robbery."

CHAPTER 12: THE "ANTI-CASTRO PEOPLE"

1. All quotations and references are from a series of memoranda on the Cuban Officer Training Program prepared by Region 1, 112th Intelligence Corp Group, San Antonio, Texas, dated November 1, 1963; exhibit 12-2.

2. Exhibit 12-A1, CIA Memorandum of 9 August 1963, Desmond Fitzgerald to McGeorge Bundy.

3. Summary from Hinckle and Turner, pp. 152-167; pp. 207-213 and 217-221.

4. Exhibit 12-1,"Anti-Castro Sea Raiders Fire Imagination of Exiles," March 13, 1963.

5. Exhibit 7-1

6. Exhibit 6-2; Barker personnel summary report.

7. Barker's file also records his communication with Carlos Hernandez in February of 1963. This is further confirmation of Hernandez's remarks in his HSCA deposition, when Carlos was one of the McClaney raid informants also in contact with the CIA.

8. As outsiders they had to find their own money. They had to look for their own men and their own arms. Their natural inclination was to seek these from individuals and power structures who shared their own politics and their visceral reactions to anything "pink." These groups ranged from the ultra right militias and the arms dealers who supplied them, to the political action groups and wealthy conservative individuals who might be expected to contribute.

9. Tagg, pp. 46-57, Details of Walthers and the house on Harlandale. As this book was going to press, researcher Steve Thomas brought attention to a series of Dallas FBI memos by SA Haitman (Heitman served in a counter intelligence role in the Dallas office, one of his areas of focus was Cuban exiles and exile groups). WC Document 1085 incorporates information from Heitman and relates that certain Cuban exiles had been under surveillance at least as early as November 27, 1963 (perhaps earlier, the search is on for earlier related documents for 1963). Mail for these individuals was being tracked and recorded; they received mail from Mexico City on November 27 and from Cuba in December. The two individuals in question were Juan Francisco Quintana Maya and Raul Castro Baile. These individuals were Cubans who had come into the U.S. from Mexico and married to sisters; they were in residence in Garland Texas. Lee Oswald was reported in attendance at a DRE meeting in Garland prior to the assassination but this sighting could not be positively confirmed (Commission Document 205 - FBI Report of 23 Dec 1963). It would appear from the FBI memos that these individuals were Alpha 66/SNFE members, had attended meetings at the Harlandale house and were associates of Rolando Orccarberro. Informants also told the FBI that a Rambler station wagon was first observed at their Garland residence six to eight weeks before the assassination and that the Rambler had a bumper sticker with the message "Kan the Kennedys" but at some point in time someone had freehanded the message to read "Kill the Kennedys". After the assassination an attempt was made to remove the sticker. Further research on the exiles in question reveals two interesting points. First, the background FBI documents on both individuals (9 and 10 pages respectively) are still postponed in full as of 2006. Second, there are FBI reports on both individuals, generated out of the Dallas office which *associate each of them with John Martino* (RIF 124-9033-10125 and RIF 124-90033-10126). Research on these associations continues.

10. Secret Service Report on Manual Rodriquez (Orcarberro), 4/24/1964 RIF 180-10095-10401.

11. Exhibit 6-3; FBI HQ report of 12/22/57, RIF 124-10187-10084.

12. Frank Ellsworth to Dick Russell, *The Man Who Knew Too Much*, p. 543.
13. Exhibit 12-3, FBI Memo SAC San Antonio to Director and SAC Dallas, October 24, 1963, Subject: John Masen.
14. Exhibit 12-4, series of FBI reports on Nonte's contacts with Masen.
15. Sworn Testimony of Frank Leslie Ellsworth II, July 25, 1978, Select Committee on Assassinations of the House of Representatives. RIF 180-10091-10125.
16. Exhibit 12-4, series of FBI reports on Nonte's contacts with Masen as well as the FBI's own independent investigation of Masen and the named exiles, October 25- November 8.
17. Exhibit 12, Report of Military Police Investigation; Texas National Guard, Terrell, Texas – subjects Whittier and Miller.
18. Ibid.
19. Ibid.
20. Exhibit, 11-5, HSCA memorandum from Allen to Wizelman on "Gun-Running activity and Jack Ruby, Donnell Darius Whittier, James Miller, Lawrence Miller and James Elrod.
21. Exhibit, 12-7, *PROBE*, July-August, 1996, article illustrated with November 22 Masen arrest fingerprint card. See also Exhibit 12-8.
22. References for the Ellsworth, Masen and Elrod incidents include the relevant portions of the LaFontaine's *Oswald Talked*; Twyman's *Bloody Treason*; a monograph by Carol Hewett ("Masen Talked" in *PROBE*, July – August, 1966, *Brush with History* by Eric Tagg, and a series of documents on the Terrell robbery which are provided as exhibits.
23. Ibid.
24. Ibid.
25. William Scott Malone quotations excerpted from Tagg, p. 85. Malone did stories on crime figures, Rothman, Roselli and Trafficante. Exhibit 11-3A, "The Secret Life of Jack Ruby" *New Times*, 1/23/78 Exhibit 12-9, series of Secret Service and FBI memos pertaining to the Echevarria investigation in Chicago.
26. Exhibit 12-9, series of Secret Service and FBI memos pertaining to the Echevarria investigation in Chicago.
27. The source for the Schaumberg incident is an FBI report obtained and in the possession of researcher John Armstrong.

Chapter 13: Patsies

1. Exhibit 13-1, FBI reports and memoranda on Dallas Downtown Lincoln-Mercury Oswald incident, September 1964.

2. Excerpt from document CIA 104-10300-10078; exhibit 13-2.
3. FBI Memo, November 27, 1963, FBI Report DL 44 1639 SA Ben S. Harrison.
4. Exhibit 13-3, FBI report of 11/27/63; interview with Ralph Yates and his uncle, Mr. J. O. Smith.
5. The Jones interview was conducted by SA Arthur Carter; Dallas File DL 44-1639.
6. George O'Toole, *The Assassination Tapes*, New York (Penthouse Press Ltd.), 1975, Chapters 9-11 and Dale Meyers, *With Malice: Lee Harvey Oswald and the Murder of Officer J.D. Tippit*, (Oak Cliff Press) 1998, pp. 287–304 (demonstrating the possible finding of an Oswald wallet at the Tippit murder scene).
7. Earl Goltz, *Dallas Morning News* article 1976; Kantor, page 392-393 and Marrs, *Conspiracy*, pp. 410-411; Exhibit 14-3.
8. Exhibit 13-5, September 16, 1967 memorandum. A September 18, 1967 letter to Jim Garrison from Matt Herron (described as a *Life* magazine informant) reported details on telephone calls made by Jack Ruby to Lee Oswald at Oswald's 1026 N. Beckley address. Ruby to Oswald calls were also supposedly reported to Dallas Police by telephone company Ray Acker (whom was said to have been promoted and moved out of Dallas not long after the assassination). The Herron letter also identified a local Dallas telephone operator, Faye Massey, who reported that an insistent and abusive man called on November 22, 1963, at 12:45 PM, wanting the number of Lee Harvey Oswald at 1026 N. Beckley. Since Oswald's connection to Kennedy's death was unknown at 12:45 PM, this urgent request appears suspicious. Researcher Robert Howard has verified that the Dallas 1963 residential telephone directory does list Faye Massey and he has also verified from *Dallas Morning News* archives that Ray Acker did indeed receive a promotion and moved out of Dallas in 1964. Author's personal communication with Robert Howard.
9. Blakey and Billings, pp. 360-361.
10. The visitor's log is shown on Tagg's page 93.
11. Exhibit 13-6, Department of Justice Memo, April 6, 1977, Assassination of President John Fitzgerald Kennedy, November 22, 1963, Dallas, Texas.
12. Exhibit 14-6; photo of Jack Ruby and Oswald press conference.
13. Russell, p. 704.
14. Lynch, p. 155.
15. Ibid. 168.

16. Rolando Otero's testimony to the HSCA was classified, although researcher Dick Russell obtained a copy. Russell, p. 538. See also Chapter 18.
17. *Nassau meeting; Cuban Officials and JFK Historians, December 1997.* Transcripts available on Cuban Information Archives at *www.cuban–exile.com.* Also, article by Dick Russell, "JFK and the Cuban Connection."
18. Peter Kornbluh "JFK and Castro, the Secret Quest for Accommodation", *Cigar Aficionado,* September-October 1999.
19. In September 1963, Associated Press' American journalist, Daniel Harker, interviewed Castro at a gathering inside Havana's Brazilian Embassy. Harker's article quoted Castro saying: "United States leaders should think that if they assist in terrorist plans to eliminate Cuban leaders, they themselves will not be safe."
20. *Researchers Bermuda Conference;* Also, article by Dick Russell, "JFK and the Cuban Connection."Interestingly enough, John Roselli (not an avid fan of international political coverage) referenced and commented at length on this same purported Castro statement. In his HSCA testimony, Roselli stated that he felt Castro's attitude towards efforts to eliminate him might have led to a Castro sponsored conspiracy to kill President Kennedy. See Fonzi, p. 321 and letter from David Belin to CIA, April 1975; September 7 1963, Castro interview by Daniel Harker; exhibit 14-7, HSCA analysis of Harker interview.
21. Interestingly enough, John Roselli (not an avid fan of international political coverage) referenced and commented at length on this same purported Castro statement. In his HSCA testimony, Roselli stated that he felt Castro's attitude towards efforts to eliminate him might have led to a Castro sponsored conspiracy to kill President Kennedy. See Fonzi, p. 321 and Letter from David Belin to CIA, April 1975; September 7 1963, Castro interview by Daniel Harker; exhibit 14-7, HSCA analysis of Harker interview.
22. FBI RIF: 124-10290-10075, Subject: SUBJECTS : CC, INTV, JAMES, DANIEL, ASST and FBI RIF: 124-10063-10383, SUBJECTS: JFK, OPINION, DANIELS, JAMES D.
23. References to this and the following include RIF #180-10083-10419 and 154-10002-10419 as well as Palamara analysis and Secret Service trip reports/timeline found in Palamara, *Survivors Guilt,* 2005 edition, pp. 21-24.

CHAPTER 14: "ALL SORTS OF RUMORS"

1. Palamara, JFK Web Pages and *Survivors Guilt.*
2. *Assassinations Records Review Board Final Report*, Chapter 8, Secret Service section pp. 135-6
3. Exhibit 11-3A, Malone, "The Secret Life of Jack Ruby" *New Times*, 1/23/78
4. Robert Maheu, and Richard Hack, *Next To Hughes*, New York (Harper Paperbacks) 1993.
5. Dan Christensen, *Miami Magazine*, September 1976 and Summers, *Conspiracy*, p. 447.
6. Secret Service Agent James Griffiths to HSCA interviewer Harold Rose, February 2, 1978.
7. Raw data regarding JFK's cancelled trip to Chicago, Illinois, 11/2/63, Palamara, JFK Web Pages and *Survivors Guilt.*
8. References include court documents, a letter from Abraham Bolden to Senator Edward Long in April of 1965 and the HSCA interview with Abraham Bolden in 1978, Record Number 180-10070-10273; exhibits 14-1, Bolden letter to Senator Edward Long.
9. Exhibit 14-2, exhibit 14-2, HSCA interview memorandum of Abraham Bolden; exhibit 14-3, HSCA memorandum on Bolden, 1/19/78.
10. Hosty, p. 50.
11. Tagg, Chapter 1, p. 28. Tagg interviewed Walthers friends and family extensively about Walthers experiences on Nov. 22 and the following weekend and wrote a book on Walther's activities in conjunction with the assassination. In reference to the metal boxes, it was the Sheriff's Department that had to get the search warrant for the Paine search since the residence was outside of Dallas city limits. Walthers actually obtained the warrant and was a main figure in the search on Friday afternoon although DPD officers met him at the location and did much of the actual search and evidence recovery. Tagg describes the search in some detail and notes major items Walthers talked about later including the fact that they "found the six or seven metal filing cabinets full of letters, maps, records and index cards with names of pro-Castro sympathizers." Apparently Walthers himself transported those small metal file boxes back to the Sheriff's office in the trunk of his car. The boxes were seen by the DPD officers and reportedly there was local talk about their possible implications. Sheriff Decker mentions seven metal boxes including literature and pamphlets in his official follow-on report, which was provided to the Warren Commission; Volume XIX; Decker Exhibit 5323 - Dallas County. Apparently there

was sufficient talk about the boxes, their contents and implications to cause the Warren Commission to address the matter. However, they did so simply by stating that no such items were listed or inventories on the official report provided by the Dallas Police and FBI. *Report of the President's Commission on the Assassination of President Kennedy*, Appendix 12: Speculation and Rumors. Walthers Deputy Report filed on 11/22/63. This is towards the end of his report:

"Upon searching this house we found stacks of hand bills concerning "Cuba for Freedom" advertising, seeking publicity and support for Cuba. Also found was a set of metal file cabinets containing records that appeared to be names and activities of Cuban sympathizers. All of this evidence was confiscated and turned over to Captain Fritz of the Dallas Police Department and Secret Service Officers at the City Hall." jfkassassination.net/russ/testimony/walther1.htm

However, during his WC testimony taken on 7/23/64, he told Wesley Liebeler:

"...and then we found some little metal file cabinets. I don't know what kind you would call them, they would carry an 8 by 10 folder, all right, but with a single handle on top of it and the handle moves.

Mr. LIEBELER. About how many of them would you think there were?

Mr. WALTHERS. There were six or seven, I believe, and I put them all in the trunk of my car and we also found a box of pictures, a bunch of pictures that we taken. We didn't go to the trouble of looking at any of this stuff much---just more or less confiscated it at the time, and we looked at it there just like that, and then we took all this stuff and put it in the car..."
-
Mr. LIEBELER. I have been advised that some story has developed that at some point that when you went out there you found seven file cabinets full of cards that had the names on them of pro-Castro sympathizers or something of that kind, but you don't remember seeing any of them?

Mr. WALTHERS. Well, that could have been one, but I didn't see it.

Mr. LIEBELER. There certainly weren't any seven file cabinets with the stuff you got out there or anything like that?

Mr. WALTHERS. I picked up all of these file cabinets and what all of them contained, I don't know myself to this day.

www.jfkassassination.net/russ/testimony/walthers.htm. For further reading, John Armstrong addresses this issue on p. 879-880 of his book, *Harvey and Lee*, (John Armstrong) 2003, and the reader is also referred to Armstrong's JFK Lancer presentation and his articles on discrepancies in the evidence as listed in Dallas vs. the FBI's listings for the Warren Commission.

12. In Hearings of the U.S. Senate Select Committee to Study Governmental Operations With Respect to Intelligence Activities, vol. 5 (Oct. 21, 22, 1975). The hearings focused on an illegal CIA mail intercept program, in operation at the main post office in New York City from 1953 until 1973, under which the first class mail, sometimes even the registered mail, of Americans was, in violation of criminal laws, opened, examined, and sometimes photographed. Under this program, code-named HTLINGUAL, over 215,000 letters were unlawfully opened and photographed.

"Just a few days prior to the assassination, a letter [from Oswald] to the Soviet Embassy in Washington was intercepted. Purportedly written by Oswald, this letter referred to '*my meetings with comrade Kostin*" and noted that *"had I been able to reach the Soviet Embassy in Havana as planned, the embassy there would have had time to complete our business.'* Mysteries surround both the phone calls and the letter—there are indications that both may have been part of a frame-up of Oswald." Rex Bradford, Valeriy Kostikov and Comrade Kostin, www.maryferrell.org/wiki/index.php/Valeriy_Kostikov_and_Comrade_Kostin.

13. The Revill memo: November 22, 1963, Captain W. P. Gannaway Special Service Bureau, Subject: Lee Harvey Oswald 605 Elsbeth Street.

Sir: On November 22, 1963, at approximately 2:50 PM, the undersigned officer met Special Agent James Hosty of the Federal Bureau of Investigation in the basement of the City Hall. At that time Special Agent Hosty related to this officer that the Subject was a member of the Communist Party, and that he was residing in Dallas. The Subject was arrested for the murder of Officer J. D. Tippit and is a prime suspect in the assassination of President Kennedy. The information regarding the Subject's affiliation with the Communist Party is the first information this officer has received from the Federal Bureau of Investigation regarding same. Agent Hosty further stated that the Federal Bureau of Investigation was aware of the Subject and that they had information that this Subject was capable of committing the assassination of President Kennedy.

Respectfully submitted, Jack Revill, Lieutenant Criminal Intelligence Section.

Regarding the last sentence of this memo, on April 27, 1964, William A. Murphy, a retired FBI agent who had been the Dallas SAC, wrote to Shanklin stating Murphy was shown the original memo by Curry and that sentence was not included. Hosty, *Assignment Oswald*.

14. Harold Feldman, *The Nation*, January 27, 1964, exhibit 12-5, article excerpt.
15. Note that John Roselli would later go to jail for participating in a card swindle in Los Angeles.
16. 17 H 566 in the Warren Commission volumes, located by Vincent Palamara.
17. FBI reports 44-24016-288, 44-24016-121, 92-3267-260.
18. RIF 198-10004-10011
19. Exhibit 12-5, 70 pages of sworn testimony by William Walter delivered to the HSCA on March 23, 1978.
20. Exhibit 14-6, recreation of teletype prepared as sample by Walter.
21. Exhibit, 14-7, FBI Memorandum of 10/23/75–cover memo (letters missing) for series of internal FBI letters pertaining to Walter's allegation.
22. LaFontaines, pp. 209-306.
23. *Dallas Morning News*, June 10, 1979.
24. Message from Sixth Floor Museum Curator Gary Mack to alt. conspiracy.jfk newsgroup June 9, 1998. Mack had been shown a copy of the application; the signature was *Lee H. Oswald*.
25. DPD report, Detective Bob Carroll to Captain Gannaway, Dallas Police Archives Box 1, Folder #11, Item #9.
26. Dallas Police Archives Box 18, Folder 18 & 7, item #34.
27. The details of Roselli's ruse are elaborated in Mahoney, pp. 284-285.
28. HSCA document 180-10074-10394.
29. HSCA document 180-10038-10419.

30. Matthew Smith, *Vendetta, The Kennedys*. Edinburgh and London (Mainstream Publishing), 1993

31. September 19, 1963, RIF 104-10241-10034

32. Joe G. Biles, *In History's Shadow: Lee Harvey Oswald, Kerry W. Thornley & the Garrison Investigation*, 2002 pp. 146-147.

33. HSCA Vol. IX, pp. 1090, 1093 and WC Vol. XXV, p. 254.

CHAPTER 15: "IF I TOLD YOU"

Many documents and their explanations referred to in this chapter can be found online in *Mexico City, A New Analysis* by John Newman at JFK Lancer's "November in Dallas Conference", November 19, 1999, transcribed by Joe Backes and Debra Conway. www.jfklancer.com/backes/newman/newman_1.html

1. Exhibit, 15-1 text of Martino article "Cuba and the Kennedy Assassination" from January 1964; exhibit 15-2, *On Target*, July 1966– featured speaker list for Patriotic Party organizational meetings as published in Minutemen monthly newsletter.

2. Exhibit 15-1, series of letters to Lee Oswald, Robert Kennedy, President Johnson as well as the Voice of America.

3. Scott, *Deep Politics* p. 103. Scott references several primary sources including Mexi CIA documents of November 27 and 29; numbers 174-616 and 260-670, Phillips own book *The Night Watch* p. 182 and Managua CIA cable of November 26, 262237Z.

4. Reference RIF 104-10404-10386, "Info Developed By CIA On The Activity Of Lee Harvey Oswald In Mexico City" 28 Sept-3 Oct 1963, Russ Holmes Work File.

5. The best reference for this incident is *Deep Politics II* by Peter Dale Scott. The key sources for the information are described on page 103 and include HSCA 11 AH 162, 3 AH 595, WR 307-8, WCD 1000A and Mexico cables 7104 and 7156. See online, *CIA Files and the Pre-Assassination Framing of Lee Harvey Oswald* by Peter Dale Scott. This piece was originally published in *Deep Politics II: Essays on Oswald, Mexico and Cuba*, 1994. www.assassinationweb.com/scottc.htm

6. WC CD 897 and 916.

7. William Manchester, *The Death of a President*, New York, Evanston and London (Harper & Row Publishers) 1967.

8. Max Holland, *The Kennedy Assassination Tapes* (Knopf) 2004, pp. 148-149. Further, on the afternoon of November 29, Johnson had a

previously scheduled meeting with Dr. Glenn Seaborg, chairman of the AEC. Johnson uses details from Seaborg on American casualties from a Soviet first strike as key ammunition in his meeting with Warren. It is improbable that Johnson had such a scheduled meeting with Seaborg from before November 22. If not, that implies that Johnson was either a) seriously anticipating a Soviet first strike should Oswald not be found to be a lone nut, and we are missing all the history behind that concern or b) Johnson was really stacking the deck for his recruitment of Commissioners. The motivation for the meeting with Seaborg would be telling if we had some way of finding when and how the meeting was scheduled.

9. Anthony Summers, *The Secret Life of J. Edgar Hoover*, p. 383, interview with Billy Byars, Jr.
10. FBI Legat Memo/Mexico City 2/24/64 RIF 124-10003-10052
11. Newman, p. 404. See also Jefferson Morley, "What Jane Roman Said, A Retired CIA Officer Speaks Candidly About Lee Harvey Oswald." www.history-matters.com/essays/frameup/WhatJaneRomanSaid/WhatJaneRomanSaid_1.htm
12. Scott, *Deep Politics II*, pp. 98 and 99.
13. Personal communications between the Author and James Hosty, 2004. However, basically the same information is in Hosty's book *Assignment Oswald* on page 215, he was just not as specific in his book that it was DeGuire that was his source for the surveillance remarks.
14. Exhibit 15-6.
15. RIF 104-10438-10078, Exhibit 15-9, also John Newman's NID 1999 presentation. www.jfklancer.com/backes/newman/newman_5a.html
16. Scott, p. 14 (quoting Col. Nechiporenko and General Leonov).
17. Exhibit 15-6.
18. Exhibit 15-3, CIA document on surveillance of Kostikov in November of 1963.
19. Exhibit 15-4.
20. Exhibit 15-5.
21. Exhibit 15-8.
22. Exhibit 15-9.
23. Exhibit 15-10.
24. Exhibit 15-11.
25. Exhibit 15-12.
26. Exhibit 15-13.
27. Doug Horne, ARRB report on AF1 Records. Available at JFK Lancer.

28. Rex Bradford, "The Fourteen-Minute Gap," *Kennedy Assassination Chronicles*, Volume 6, Issue 1, spring 2000. See: history-matters.com/essays/frameup/FourteenMinuteGap/FourteenMinuteGap.htm

29. RIF 80-10110-10484. www.jfklancer.com/backes/newman/documents/goodpasture/goodpasture.htm. Selected pages from HSCA Testimony of Anne Goodpasture, 04/13/78, contained in the "Lopez" Report, *Report on Lee Harvey Oswald's Trip to Mexico City.*

30. Tarasoff interview in Scott's *Deep Politics II*, p. 99 gives the full quote there p. 85. He also cites Newman, p. 371 and gives a primary reference to the Lopez Report, p. 85.

31. RIF 104-10015-10116.

32. RIFs104-10015-10082 Arrest of Silvia Duran, 104-10015-10114 CIA Cable Requesting Lienvoy Tapes and Transcripts, 104-10015-10290. Online at www.jfklancer.com/backes/newman/documents/10082/10082.htm, www.jfklancer.com/backes/newman/documents/10114/10114.htm, www.jfklancer.com/backes/newman/documents/10290/10290_1.htm.

33. See www.jfklancer.com/backes/newman/newman_2.html

34. Memo is a record of a phone call from "Scelso" to Helms, then as noted, Helms called Angleton "the warning", December 11, 1963, Exhibit 15-11. See also Hosty, *Assignment Oswald* pp. 294-5 for the unredacted version.

35. Richard B. Trask, *That Day In Dallas*, pp. 85--91 which presents several of Jim Murray's photos. Page 85 has a full page blow up which clearly shows the two men coming down the knoll beyond the pergola and although small certainly one individual clearly resembles Oswald. Researcher Anna Marie Kuhns-Walko first presented this finding at JFK Lancer's November In Dallas Conference in 1998 and has been continued by photo researcher James Richard.

36. Marvin Robinson CD 5, p. 70 and HSCA volume 12 p.18 and Roy Cooper of Euless, Texas.

37. Manchester, p. 287.

38. Edward Osford, "Destiny in Dallas", *American History Illustrated*, November 1988. W C, Vol 5, p. 259.

39. RIF 179-30003-10203, transcript of call, "Mr. J Edgar Hoover Said As Follows".

40. *PROBE*, Volume 4, No. 3 March-April 1997.

41. Russell Jack Smith, *The Unknown CIA; My Three Decades with the Agency*, (Potomac Books) 1989, p. 163; reference courtesy of Larry Haapanen.

42. From the transcript:
    LBJ: Have you established any more about the visit to the Soviet embassy in Mexico in September?

Hoover: No, that's one angle that's very confusing, for this reason—
we have up here the tape and the photograph of the man who was at
the Soviet embassy, using Oswald's name. That picture and the tape
do not correspond to this man's voice, nor to his appearance. In other
words, it appears that there is a second person who was at the Soviet
embassy down there.
November 23 10:01 AM LBJ-Hoover call. The transcript is available
from the LBJ Library. Also excerpted in *Taking Charge*, Michael R.
Beschloss ed., (Simon & Schuster) 1997, p. 23. The transcript is also
excerpted in the Lopez Report, Addendum to Footnote #614 (RIF #180-
10110-10484).

43. In "Gerald Ford and the Agency," (Counterpunch.org, October 18,
2001), Jamey Hecht wrote: President Johnson overcame their resistance
with the threat of nuclear war: he brandished some secret evidence–its
source was J. Edgar Hoover, and it has long since been discredited–
indicating that Oswald was working with the Soviets as an assassin,
and if that were to get out, Johnson warned, "there could be war,
nuclear war...40 million Americans could die." So: conscience and
duty demanded that these chosen men destroy their old conscience
and their old duty (loyal to President Kennedy, concerned with the
question of what really happened), and put on the new (loyal to
Johnson, and concerned with the future). To men like Earl Warren, this
entailed a kind of moral suicide, the source of those legendary tears he
shed on agreeing to serve on the Commission that will bear his name
forever.

44. Chapter 17 demonstrates the Texas Court of Inquiry was initiated
solely by Johnson himself.

45. Exhibit 15-14; The President's Daily Diary, logs and entries for Nov 22-
24.

46. Primary references: Donald Gibson, "The First 72 Hours," *PROBE*,
November–December 1999 and Peter Dale Scott, *Deep Politics II*,
selected CIA documents as provided in exhibit 15 – NNN.

47. RIF 144-10001-10203; NSA internal memo copied to FBI's Sullivan

48. Jesse E. Curry, *JFK Assassination File: Retired Dallas Police Chief Jesse
Curry*, 1969.

49. Hinckle and Turner, pp. 349–350.

50. Recall, however, that John Newman has argued that the plotters
deliberately assembled an easily falsifiable Oswald impersonation for
Mexico City, making the Kostikov connection fully flexible: it could
be used to coerce participation in a cover-up (as Johnson used it), but

then neutralized to prevent U.S.-Soviet war if necessary. See Newman, www.jfklancer.com/backes/newman/newman_1.html

51. See Bibliography for details.

52. Thomas P. "Tip" O'Neill, with author William Novak, *Man of the House: The Life and Political Memoirs of Speaker Tip O'Neill* (Random House) 1987, pp 271-272.

53. Doug Horne, ARRB interview 07/15/97.

54. Graduate student James Gouchenaur filed a report with the House Select Committee in June of 1977 (HSCA File #180-101109). Gouchenaur described an extended conversation with former Secret Service Agent Elmer Moore who had been sent to Dallas after the assassination. Moore expressed his remorse for badgering Doctor Perry into changing his testimony about the entrance wound in the throat. Moore stated that his assignment was to manage the Dallas doctors' testimony. However, the remarks that most startled and frightened Gouchenaur were made in a rant by Moore on the subject of John Kennedy. Moore stated that Kennedy was a traitor and had been giving things away to the Russians. He even remarked that it was a shame people had to die, but maybe it was a good thing. If we knew the source of Mr. Moore's perspective on John Kennedy, it might help us understand more about the cover-up and what people conducting the most sensitive elements of it might have been told. James H. Fetzer, PH.D., *Murder in Dealey Plaza: What We Know Now that We Didn't Know Then.* Chicago (Catfeet Press), 2000, pp. 115, 165, 256.

55. Robert Groden, *The Killing of a President: The Complete Photographic Record of the Assassination and the Conspiracy.* (Studio) Reprint edition *1994*, pp.86-8.

56. *Murder in Dealey Plaza*, pp. 175–218

57. "The Converging Medical Case for Conspiracy," *Murder in Dealey Plaza*, p. 213. Other mandatory reading for fully appreciating the manner in which the autopsy was hijacked after the fact includes: Dr. David Mantik, "Paradoxes of the JFK Assassination: The Medical Evidence Decoded," *Murder In Dealey Plaza*, pp. 219-298 and Douglas Horne's accompanying article, "Evidence of a Government Cover-Up: Two Different Brain Specimens", on the evidence for a brain substitution and two separate brain examinations, pp. 299-310.

58. *Murder In Dealey Plaza*, p. 29.

59. Boswell HSCA interview, Aug. 16, 1977, also Harrison Edward Livingston, *Killing Kennedy: Deceit and Deception in the JFK Case,* New York (Carroll & Graff Publishers Inc.), 1995, p 188.

60. James Folliard "Blaming the Victims", *The Fourth Decade*, Vol. 2, No. 4, 1995.

61. "Discrepancies in the Evidence - Phone Transcript Between Acting AG Ramsey Clark and LBJ", Audio provided by Gregory Burnham and transcribed by Debra Conway, *Kennedy Assassination Chronicles*, pp. 18-19, Vol. 5, Issue 3, Fall 1999. Available online at jfklancer.com.

62. Manchester, page 405, and November 22-24 diary entries from "The President's Daily Dairy"; Lyndon Baines Johnson Library and Museum.

63. Jim Marrs, *Crossfire: Crossfire: The Plot That Killed Kennedy* (Carroll and Graf) 1989, p. 356 and Mark Oakes' video interview with Wade.

64. "Achilles in the White House," a discussion with Harry McPherson and Jack Valenti, available online at www.questia.com.

65. John Newman, "Oswald, the CIA and Mexico City: Fingerprints of Conspiracy," *PROBE*, September-October, 1999, p 29.

66. "Poison pill is a term referring to any strategy, generally in business or politics, which attempts to avoid a negative outcome by increasing the costs of that outcome to those who seek it." (Wikipedia.org). The October 1963 impersonation of Oswald linking him to Kostikov was a poison pill to the FBI and CIA themselves, in that Oswald's abundant connections to them would be embarrassing to their entire membership, not just to the plotters among them.

67. It is now known that Dr. Humes destroyed both his notes and his first version of the autopsy report; his assistant, Dr. Boswell, reportedly "lost" his notes the night of the autopsy (David Lifton, 1999 JFK Lancer presentation). Dr. Humes' credibility has been severely challenged in forums ranging from the ARRB medical records work to the lawsuit filed and won by Dr. Crenshaw (of the Parkland Hospital staff in 1963). It is perhaps worth noting that when giving his extremely reluctant interviews to the ARRB, Dr. Humes wore and proudly remarked on the cuff links that had been given to him personally by President Johnson. See Doug Horne's 1998 JFK Lancer presentation.

68. Charles A. Crenshaw, M.D., *Trauma Room One: The JFK Medical Coverup Exposed*. New York (Paraview Press), 2001, pp. 131-4.

69. David E. Scheim, *Contract on America: The Mafia Murder of President John F. Kennedy* (S.P.I. Books) Reprint edition 1992, p. 250; conversation between Johnson and John McCormick reported by lobbyist Robert Winter Barger in *The Washington Payoff: An Insider's View of Corruption in Government* (Dell) 1972.

70. Joachim Joesten, *The Dark Side of Lyndon Baines Johnson*, London (Pater Dawney), 1968.

71. G. R. Schreiber, *The Bobby Baker Affair*, Chicago (Henry Regnery Company), 1964, p. 23.
72. Johnson Daily Diary, Appendix A.
73. Mark North, *Act of Treason*. New York (Carroll & Graff Publishers Inc.) 1991, p. 63
74. Schreiber, p.138.
75. North, p. 282.
76. Schreiber, pp. 23-31.
77. Black–Baker references are from *North*, pp. 63, 121, 132, 248, 309, 472 and 502; Scott, *Deep Politics*, p. 235; Rappleye and Becker, passim.

CHAPTER 16: WHEELING AND DEALING WITH BOBBY

1. Robert "Bobby" Gene Baker, with Larry L. King, *Wheeling and Dealing: Confessions of a Capitol Hill Operator*. New York (W.W. Norton & Company) 1978, p.78.
2. Exhibit A16-1, "Playgirl Threat to Security" and A1-2, "The Elusive Ellen Does a Fade Away."
3. Mahoney, pp. 278. Special Investigation Division, FBI Memorandum of 4 November 1963.
4. Judith Campbell incident and Roselli association, reference Rappleye and Becker, pp. 209, 215.
5. Baker, p. 168.
6. Ibid, p. 211
7. Ibid.
8. Schreiber, pp. 117 – 129.
9. Baker, p. 170.
10. Beschloss, p. 321.
11. Robert Lacy, *Little Man Meyer Lansky and the Gangster Life*, New York (Little, Brown and Company) 1992, p. 364.
12. A minor investor in Levinson's Stardust casino was one Milton Jaffee, whose phone number appeared in Jack Ruby's address book. See WC CE 1322; Vol. 22 p. 504.
13. "Licensed Casino Owners and Percentages as of April 1, 1962," Ed Reid and Ovits Demaris, *The Green Felt Jungle*, New York (Trident Press) 1963, Appendix.
14. *The National*, "Little Man," pp. 291-292, 379.
15. Ibid, page 390; Reid and Demaris, pp. 99-106.
16. Ibid, Chapter 8.

17. Belli became Ruby's lawyer.
18. Hinckle and Turner, p. 222.

CHAPTER 17: "WE CAN'T CHECK EVERY SHOOTING SCRAPE"

1. Manchester, p. 405. "At 7:25 he telephoned J. Edgar Hoover. The Director was at home…[LBJ] wanted a complete FBI report on the assassination. Depressing the receiver, Hoover called his office, ordering a special assistant and thirty agents to Dallas."
2. Carter calls to Texas, November 22.
3. Russell Jack Smith, *The Unknown CIA*, p. 163.
4. Holland, p. 66.
5. Waldron, p. 212.
6. Holland, p. 98; Alsop, Joseph 1910–89, American political journalist. As examples of his political reach, here are two quotes: "Together with Robert E. Kintner from 1937 until the war, with his brother Stewart from 1946 to 1958, and alone thereafter until 1974, Alsop wrote a highly literate column that relied, in equal parts, on his erudition, his ideological fixation, his dinner party guest lists, and his considerable legwork. He was obsessed with what he saw as the nation's need to prove its collective manhood and was forever wondering whether this or that president was "man enough" to stop the Reds at some critical juncture. From a review by Eric Alterman of *I've Seen The Best Of It* by Joseph W. Alsop with Adam Platt, W. W. Norton & Co in the *Columbia Journalism Review*, May/June 1992. "[Joseph and Stewart] were columnists with a huge reach. They were in 200 newspapers with a combined circulation of 25 million, and they wrote insistently for the *Saturday Evening Post*, which was a major magazine at the time with six million subscribers and twenty million readers. So they had an immense reach in a country that had 170 million people, maybe 180 million people." Robert Merry, executive editor of the *Congressional Quarterly*, author of *Taking on the World: Joseph and Stewart Alsop, Guardians of the American Century*.
7. Waggoner Carr & Byron Varner, *Texas Politics In My Rearview Mirror*. Texas (Rep. of Texas Press), 1993.
8. Manchester, p. 568.
9. Holland, p. 96-103.
10. A memo by the FBI's Courtney Evans on November 26, 1963 indicates that Hoover himself drafted the Katzenbach memo. See also John H.

Davis, *Mafia Kingfish: Carlos Marcello and the Assassination of John F. Kennedy*, (Mcgraw-Hill) 1988, pp. 250-251.
11. North, pp. 430, 436.
12. Beschloss, p. 53.
13. Ibid.
14. North, pp. 460-470; also FBI memorandum from De Loach.

CHAPTER 18: AFTERWARDS

1. Hinckle and Turner, p. 44, interview with William Pawley.
2. See *Life*, April 12, 1963, "Aboard A Defiant Cuban Raider" and *Post*, June 8, 1963, "Help us fight, cry the angry exiles."
3. Evan Thomas, *The Very Best Men: Four Who Dared: The Early Years of the CIA*, p. 291. "Desmond Fitzgerald now officially became head of the successor to Task Force W, the newly designated Special Affairs Staff, on January 25, 1963."
4. Ibid. p. 194 "'Fitzgerald was given to sayings, two of which he repeated like mantras. 'We are not here to monitor communism, we are here to destroy it,'" he would instruct his operative.
5. Ibid., p. 298.
6. Twyman, p. 731.
7. RIF 157-10005-10186.
8. RIF 124-10291-10330.
9. Hinckle and Turner, pp. 268-269.
10. Twyman, p. 632.
11. Ibid, p. 672.
12. Ibid, p. 715.
13. Ibid, p. 716.
14. Major Thomas Odom, *Dragon Operations; Hostage Rescues in the Congo, 1964-1965*, (Combat Studies Institute) *Leavenworth Papers*, 1988, p. 116.
15. Corn, p. 113.
16. Ibid., pp. 107-108.
17. Jonathan Kwitny, *The Crimes of Patriots: A True Tale of Dope, Dirty Money and the CIA* (W.W. Norton and Company) 1987.
18. Alfred McCoy, Cathleen Reed, Leonard Adams II, *The Politics of Heroin in SE Asia*, 1972.
19. Thomas, p. 324.
20. Corn, pp. 306-308.
21. Association of Former Intelligence Officers (AFIO). www.afio.com.
22. Twyman, pp.745, 624.

23. FBI unnumbered report, Miami, April 1963.
24. Twyman, p.637.
25. Russell, p. 587.
26. Ibid, p. 601.
27. Ibid, p. 600.
28. Hinckle and Turner, p.136.
29. Exhibit 18-2, photograph of Herminio Diaz Garcia.
30. Hinckle and Turner, p. 78
31. Exhibit 18-3, newspaper article on Trafficante's expulsion from Cuba.
32. Tanenbaum memo to Purdy, March 14, 1977, exhibit 18-4.
33. Rappleye and Becker, p. 309.
34. Summers, *Conspiracy*, p. 500.
35. Rappleye and Becker, p. 315.
36. Executive Session, March 16, 1978, p. 58.
37. W C; CD 23.4.
38. W C; CD 1085; WC CD 853.
39. Exhibit 18-5, selection of newspaper reports on Quesada activities and remarks.
40. Hinckle and Turner, p. 183.
41. Schweiker-Hart Report, p. 78, and IG Report, p.103.
42. IG Report, pp. 101-104.
43. Fonzi Memoranda to Tannenbaum, June 15, 1977, Re: Adames & Otero interview. "Although we get a partial corroboration of what Otero had told us Adames had told him about De Torres having some connection with the Kennedy assassination, from Adames we don't get the information that De Torres was involved or that he was on the scene on November 22, 1963. That's specifically why I went back to Otero. From him I again got the very detailed contention that Adames told him, when both were in the Broward County Jail, that De Torres was involved in the Kennedy assassination and that he personally knew Lee Harvey Oswald. Otero said he would be willing to testify under oath to that. Corroborating to some extent Otero's story is what Otero's girlfriend Kathy told Otero's lawyer, Bob Rosenblatt, a few weeks ago. She said that during the brief period that Adames was out on bond, he came to see her regarding possibly helping Otero. However, without being asked about it, Kathy volunteered that Adames seemed interested in what Otero might have told her about this fellow De Torres."
44. Exhibit 16-6, memorandum from Louis Ivon to Jim Garrison regarding Bernardo De Torres; exhibit 18-6A Miami, Florida Police Memo, Suspect in Presidential Assassination, exhibit 18-7, Garrison expense payments to De Torres.

45. Exhibit 18-8, selection of Miami and New Orleans newspaper articles in reference to the involvement of De Torres in the Garrison investigation.
46. Exhibit 18-18
47. Ibid.
48. For a fuller appreciation for De Torres' connections and potential importance see Fonzi; also see exhibit 18-9, a collection of HSCA memoranda, observations and reports on De Torres.
49. Richard Saunders, *Dallas Morning News* ad salesman, WC Vol. 15, pp. 577-85.
50. WC Volume 15, pp. 71-96; Vol. 20, pp. 428-429.
51. WC Volume 15, pp. 392-394.
52. Kantor, pp. 88-89, 114-115.
53. WC Volume 25, pp. 143, 245; Vol. 5, p. 186; Vol. 20, p. 49.
54. Kantor, p.62.
55. Ibid., p.104.
56. WC Volume 25, pp. 154, 476-7; also <u>John Kaplan</u> and <u>Jon R. Waltz</u>, *The Trial of Jack Ruby: A Classic Study of Courtroom Strategies*. (Macmillan) 1966, pp. 130-131.
57. WC Volume 15, pp. 615-7.
58. WC Volume 21, pp. 309-11.
59. WC Volume 25, p. 229.
60. Kantor, p.130, and Bill Sloan, *Breaking The Silence*. Texas (Taylor Publishing Company) 1993, p. 69.
61. Rheinstein, WC Volume 15, p. 356 and Phillippe Labro, WC Volume 25, pp. 200-1 Labro met Ruby on the third floor that afternoon and received a Carousel advertising card and invitation to come to the club for a drink.
62. Kantor, p. 112.
63. Mellen, pp. 28, 29 128, 183, and 307.
64. Ibid. pp. 59-60.
65. Davy, p. 201, document 1272 – 1028, 1992 release.
66. Exhibit 18-10, Justice Department memorandum from Vinson and Yeagley (Assistant Attorneys General) to Ramsey Clark, U.S Attorney General meeting with Shaw attorneys; exhibit 18-11, CIA Garrison Team Meeting notes for Team Meeting 1 and 2.
67. Memo from CI/R&A to Sara Hall, Security, February 11, 1969.
68. Memo from Angleton to Hoover and Papich, February 28, 1969.
69. CIA Memo March 18, 1969, David Phillips to Director.
70. Weisberg letter to Jim Garrison. Davy, pp. 39-41.
71. Davy, pp. 39-41.

72. Fensterwald interview; *PROBE*, May-June 1997.
73. Bannister's heavy drinking has been verified by comparison of bar bills from November 22 with those of other tabs at the same bar, the Katz and Jammer; Davy, p. 279.
74. Garrison, p. 3.
75. Davy, pp. 178-9.
76. DiEugenio, pp. 198-202.
77. FBI document 62-109060-4720.
78. Davy, pp. 48 -52; HSCA FBI Investigation files on Lee Harvey Oswald, Box 2, Section 8.

CHAPTER 19: End Game

Some sections of this chapter are reflections and summaries from the previous chapters and not all sources are noted again.

1. *Researchers Bermuda Conference* Proceedings between Cuban Officials and JFK Researchers, Nassau Beach Hotel, December 1995, available at JFK Lancer.
2. RIF 104-10400-10133; Russell Holmes work file documents plus WAVE correspondence. In addition, JMWAVE internal memoranda seriously express the view that JURE (coming into an influential position with the advent of the AM/TRUNK project) began in March, 1963 to infiltrate a number of U.S. agencies including KUBARK. JURE is described as positioning informants within JM/WAVE and building lists of KUBARK agents and tasks. JURE was also described as beginning a program of propaganda against the U.S. Government and CIA prior to Ray's personal meeting with RFK in June of 1963. Ray left that meeting highly impressed with RFK and the new AM/TRUNK initiative which has been adopted after the idea had been floated by Tad Szulc, based on input from Jorge Volsky aka Chico. Volsky himself was considered a security risk and likely JURE informant, being especially dangerous due to his high level leverage with the Kennedy Administration and his direct working relationship for most of 1963 with COS JMWAVE (Shackley aka Tad Brickham) and Operations Chief Stanley Zamka (David Morales). This information is derived from a 14 page CIA memo on Volski which is presented as a new document on the *Someone Would Have Talked* web site, www.larry-hancock.com.
3. See Chapter 7.
4. Palamara, pp. 17-24.

5. RIF 104-10308-10092; CIA memoranda from Henry Hecksher, subject: Dr La Saga.

6. This deduction was made by FBI agent DeBrueys in New Orleans and is reported by James Hosty, *Oswald Talked*, p. 76.

7. Exhibit 19-1, *Dallas Morning News*, June 10, 1978, "Cubans' friend believes Oswald contacted exile leader," by Earl Goltz; from Volume 3, Issue 12 of Penn Jones, *The Continuing Inquiry* newsletter.

8. HSCA 180-10147-10205.

9. Details of this group's activities are elaborated throughout *Deadly Secrets*, by Hinckle and Turner.

10. Exhibit 19-4, *Biographical Summary of Russell Douglas Matthews*, excerpted from Volume 5, issue 12 of Penn Jones' *The Continuing Inquiry* newsletter.

11. Smith, *The Second Plot*, pp. 268-74.

12. Aubrey Rike, ambulance driver, speech at JFK Lancer's November in Dallas conference, 2002; Also personal conversation between Rike and the author.

13. Jim Marrs gives the most extensive details on the incident in *Crossfire*, pp. 246-248.

14. Ulric Shannon, *The Third Decade*, Vol. 9, January 1993.

15. Richard B. Trask, *That Day In Dallas*, (Yeoman Press) 2000, pp. 85--91 presents several of Jim Murray's photos. Page 85 has a full-page blow up that shows Craig watching as the two men come down the knoll beyond the pergola and one individual clearly resembles Oswald. This individual was first noticed by researcher Anna-Marie Kuhns-Walko. She presented her findings at JFK Lancer's 1998 November In Dallas Conference. Photo researcher James Richards continued studying the Murray photos and put together an entire series that shows what is described by Craig and are available on the SWHT photo pages on the website. www.larry-hancock.com.

16. See for example "Failure and Crime Are Not the Same: 9/11's Limited Hangouts," by Jamey Hecht, November 22, 2003, *From the Wilderness*: www.fromthewilderness.com/free/ww3/112203_failure_crime.html.

17. See www.jfklancer.com/backes/newman/newman_1.html.

18. See Bibliography.

19. Twyman, pp. 792-793. Also *American History Illustrated*, "Destiny in Dallas," by Edward Osford, November 1988.

20. W C, Vol 5, p. 259.

21. Twyman, pp. 793-795.

22. Crenshaw, pp. 132-134. Additionally, Mrs. Bartlett stated when interviewed by researcher Debra Conway that she surely recognized

LBJ's voice and that another operator overheard the voice also. She told Conway she didn't note the call in her written report of the weekend due to her decision not to record anything she felt was official or top secret, such as calls to and from the White House by Secret Service men or others. She only later spoke out to support Dr. Crenshaw when his story of the LBJ call was questioned.

23. In speculation on Johnson's motivation it may be helpful to have an insight into his own thoughts about the cause of the assignation. These are reflected in private remarks that have emerged over the years:

The day after John Kennedy's funeral, Johnson pointed at a portrait of Diem and told Hubert Humphrey that, "We had a hand in killing him; now it's happening here." Johnson later told Pierre Salinger a story about "divine retribution" and implied that perhaps that also applied to Kennedy's death.

A few days after Kennedy's funeral, Kennedy aide Ralph Dungan was working late in his office in the West Wing when he heard a noise at the door. Dungan looked up and there was President Johnson, in nothing but a T-Shirt and boxer shorts. He told Dungan he wanted to talk to him and motioned him to the Oval Office where he forced him to sit on the sofa and in a low voice said, "I want to tell you why Kennedy died." A stunned Dungan sat while Johnson pointed his finger and said "Divine retribution...he murdered Diem and then he got it himself." (Mahoney, pp. 302-303, from Mahoney interview with Dungan .)

Shesol also relates that, Johnson told Jack Valenti that his inner political instinct was that Castro was behind the killing. Johnson expanded on that thought to Joseph Califono - President Kennedy tried to get Castro, but Castro got Kennedy first. Apparently Johnson made a similar remark to Richard Helms of the CIA. When was by a Congressional Committee if he had ever heard the theory that Castro might have been behind the assassination of President Kennedy, Helms replied that the very first time I heard such a theory (that Oswald might have shot the President on Castro's behalf) was in a very peculiar way from President Johnson. Later, Johnson would relate to Acting Attorney General Ramsey Clark that, then he (Castro) called Oswald and a group in ...and said go set it up and get the job done (killing Kennedy). (Jeff Shesol, *Mutual Contempt: Lyndon Johnson, Robert Kennedy, and the Feud That Defined a Decade*, (Norton and Company), New York, 1997, pp. 131-134.)

Johnson's best known biographer, Robert Caro remarked, that Johnson could believe whatever he wanted to believe...could believe it with all his heart....he could convince himself of anything, even something that wasn't true. (Robert A Caro, *Means of Ascent: The Years of Lyndon Johnson, Volume 2*, (Knopf) New York, 1982, Chapter 2.) Had, in the end, Lyndon Johnson convinced himself that an agent of Fidel Castro had killed John Kennedy–a sort of divine retribution" for Kennedy's program to kill Castro?

24. Exhibits 19-5, "Billy Sol Links LBJ to Murder," *Dallas Morning News*, March 23, 1983; 19-6 Letter from Stephen S. Trott, Assistant Attorney General to Douglas Caddy, Attorney at Law re. Billy Sol Estes, May 29, 1984; 19-7, response letter to Mr. Trott from Mr. Caddy re Billy Sol Estes–with details on Carter information, August 9, 1984.
25. Sample, Glen and Mark Collom, *The Men on the Sixth Floor* (Sample Graphics) 1997.
26. Lyle Sardie, *LBJ: A Closer Look* (Timeless Multimedia), 1998.
27. North.

APPENDICES

Appendix B: CROSSING PATHS IN THE CIA

1. *Hecksher Obituary;* 1990, Princeton NJ, byline Alfonso A. Narvaez
2. Thomas, Powers, *The Man Who Kept The Secrets: Richard Helms & the CIA* (Knopt) 1979.
3. RIF 104-10121-10133 and 104-1021-10246.
4. Burton, Hersh, *The Old Boys: The American Elite and the Origins of the CIA* (Tree Farm Books) 2001, pp. 344-6.
5. Powers, p. 98.
6. Ibid.
7. RIF 104-10308-10091, "Memo on Washington Meeting with AM/BIDDY-1," 7/10/63.
8. RIF 104-10121-10264.
9. RIF 105-10241-10-20, Hecksher memo "Improvement of AM/BIDDY-1 Image," 10/03/63 and RIF 104-10308-10094, Jenkins memo "AM/BIDDY-1's Operational Philosophy and Concepts."
10. RIF 104-1038-10096; Jenkins memo on AM/JAVA-4 visit to Europe; meeting with Cuebela, December 1964.
11. RIF 104-10113010082.
12. Goulden, Joseph, with Alexander W. Raffio, *The Death Merchant: The Rise and Fall of Edwin P. Wilson* (Bantam Books) 1985.

13. Michael Ruppert, "Ed Wilson's Revenge: The Biggest CIA Scandal in History Has Its Feet in the Starting Blocks in a Houston Court House" *From The Wilderness*, January 2000. www.fromthewilderness.com/free/ciadrugs/Ed_Wilson_1.html.

Appendix C: BARNES, HUNT AND FRIENDS

1. Phillips, *The Night Watch*, p. 49.
2. David Wise, *The American Police State: The Government Against the People* (Random House) 1978, p. 222.
3. The Church Committee Report, *Alleged Assassination Attempts On Foreign Leaders*. p. 181.
4. Richard Helms, with William Hood, *A Look over My Shoulder: A Life in the Central Intelligence Agency* (Random House) 2003.
5. The Church Committee Report, p. 200.
6. Ralph E. Weber, Editor, *Spymasters: Ten CIA Officers in Their Own Words*, Wilmington, DE., (Scholarly Resources, Inc.) 1999, p. 88.
7. Bohning, *The Castro Obsession*.
8. RIF 104-10113-10082
9. Evan Thomas, *The Very Best Men: Four Who Dared: The Early Years of the CIA* (Simon & Schuster) 1996.
10. This report, titled "The CIA's Internal Probe of the Bay of Pigs Affair" by Michael Warner, is viewable at: www.cia.gov/studies/winter98.
11. Marchetti, Victor, and John Marks, *CIA and the Cult of Intelligence*, New York, (Dell Publishing) 1974, 1989, p.125
12. Ibid. p. 219
13. Trento, *The Secret History of the CIA*, p. 211.
14. Ibid.
15. Donald Freed, *Death In Washington: The Murder of Orlando Letelier*. (Lawrence Hill) 1980, p. 46.
16. Joseph Trento, with Susan B. Trento and William Corson, *Widows: Four American Spies, The Wives They Left Behind and the KGB's Crippling of American Intelligence*. New York (Crown Publishers, Inc.) 1989.
17. Waldron, p. 530.
18. As noted in Peter Dale Scott's "The Three Oswald Deceptions: The Operation, The Cover-Up And The Conspiracy":
19. Charles J. V. Murphy, "Cuba: The Record Set Straight." *Fortune*, September 1961.

20. Allen W. Dulles, *The Craft of Intelligence: America's Legendary Spy Master on the Fundamentals of Intelligence Gathering for a Free World* (Greenwood Pub Group) July 1977.
21. For further reference on Scott's remarks and sources please see *The Three Oswald Deceptions*, originally published in: *Deep Politics II: Essays on Oswald, Mexico and Cuba*, and available at www.assassinationweb.com/scottd.htm.
22. John Loftus, and Mark Aarons, *The Secret War Against the Jews: How Western Espionage Betrayed the Jewish People* (St. Martin's Griffin) 1997.
23. Thomas Powers, *The Man Who Kept The Secrets: Richard Helms & the CIA* (Knopt) 1979, p. 123.

Appendix D: THE WAY OF JM/WAVE

1. RIF 104-10226-10285, memorandum from Acting CIA Chief of Station, Havana, 12/28/60; RIF 104-10166-10226, CIA internal study report on Unidad Revolucionaria, 4/6/63.
2. See FBI New York office Case letter on Alberto Fernandez Echavarria aka Alberto Fernandez, Albert Casas; Registration Act Investigation, 12/22/58; and Department of State Memoranda on Activities of Cuban Rebels, dated October 25 and November 6, 1958.
3. RIF 104-10128-10330, cable from Director to Havana on Security Review of Phillips.
4. RIF 104-10240-10222; CIA document, letter from Malone to Phillips, February, 1961.
5. RIF 104-10172-10088 and 104-10173-10197, CIA Memoranda on AM/PARTIN and AM/DENIM.
6. RIF 104-10172-10438; JM/WAVE memo *"Tejana* Returned Key West," 3/31/61.
7. RIF 104-10172-10150; CIA memo from Martha Thorpe on Fernandez, 6/27/62.
8. RIF 104-10172-10067; JM/WAVE memo requesting crypts for *Tejana* crew, 2/22/61.
9. RIF 104-10226-10162; COB JM/WAVE to Chief WHD, subject AM/CHEER-1, 1/1/61.
10. RIF 105-35253-991; FBI memo from NY to HQ on Anti Castro activities, March, 1962 also FBI memorandum of April 5, 1962 from SAC New York to Director on Anti Fidel Castro Activities.
11. RIF 124-10200-10182, FBI memo SAC Miami to Director, 6/6/62.

12. These remarks are from the Chief of Special Affairs Staff at JM/WAVE (David Morales) to Chief of Station at JM/WAVE (Shackley) JM/WAVE operational memos September 1962 - 1963 including RIF 104-10172-10141 and RIF 104-10172-10129.
13. RIF 104-10106-10468, CIA memo on contacts of Robert Brown in Garrison case, 9/16/68.
14. RIF 104-10137-10114; CIA memo on LaBorde, Fernandez, Harber, March, 1962; also CIA Garrison team notes/personality diagrams.

Appendix E: STUDENT WARRIOR

Unless otherwise noted, information in this appendix is derived from RIF 180-10075-10071, HSCA summary of Deposition taken June 7, 1978 and 180-10075-10072, Deposition of Victor Espinosa.
1. RIF 157-1007-10315; 11/21/62.

Appendix F: ANOTHER RUMOR

1. The documents were made available on his website: www.jfkmurdersolved.com/NSA.htm.
2. NSA letter dated September 7, 1978.
3. These documents include a seven page communication to the HSCA pertaining to RIF 180-10130-10010 (which may be "Overseas communication of the assassination," the same material posted by William Dankbaar); an Air Force Security Service letter to NSA on "Proposed action concerning former security service member" RIF 180-10130-10009; an HSCA Outside Contact report of three pages referencing the name "Stevenson, Nicholas" RIF 180-10130-10006; and an HSCA transcript pertaining to Nicholas Stevenson with the subject "Kennedy, John, Assassination, Leads and Information" RIF 180-10130-10011.
4. Duncan Campbell, *Inside Echelon*: www.100megsfree4.com/farshores/s_ech03.htm. Article originally published in Telopolis, Hannover - July 25, 2000.
5. *Newsday* Editors, *The Heroin trail: The first journalistic investigation to trace heroin traffic from Turkey to France to its ultimate customer, the young American addict* (Signet) 1974.
6. Ibid. p. 76.
7. Ibid. p. 95.

8. Ibid. pp. 95, 146.
9. Ibid. pp. 109-114.
10. Ibid. pp. 110-114.
11. Douglas Valentine, *Strength of the Wolf*, London and New York (Verso) 2004.
12. Russell, *The Man Who Knew Too Much*, p. 558.
13. Valentine, p. 317
14. RIF 104-10428-10001.
15. RIF 104-10400-10200.
16. RIF 104-10419-10021; SAC Miami to Director, 8/7/64.

Appendix G: WORD FROM THE UNDERWORLD

1. RIF 180-10105-10003; memorandum of 12/10/63.
2. Chris Mills, "Rambling Rose," a study published in *Dateline Dallas*, July 1994, Volume 1, Issue 3.
3. Alcock memo to Garrison on the interview of Emilio Santana, February 15, 1967.
4. Garrison File memo from Sgt. Fenner Sedgebeer, February 11, 1967.

Appendix H: ODIO REVISITED

1. Allied International Detectives, Hollywood Boulevard, Los Angeles California.
2. HSCA 180-10107-10443.
3. RIF 180-10097-10177.
4. RIF 104-10400-10151 and 104-10404-10441.
5. RIF 104-10109-10374.
6. RIF 104-10109-10376.
7. "guasanos" = worms on Cuba.
8. Summers, *Conspiracy*, p. 303.
9. DiEugenio, pp 218-219.
10. La Fontaine, p. 162.
11. RIF 104-10404-10445.
12. RIF 104-10428-10178.
13. RIF 104-10535-10033 and DiEugenio, p. 287.
14. RIF 104-10435-10333.

Appendix I: ECHOES FROM DALLAS

1. RIF 104-10308-10094, AM/BIDDY-1's Operational Philosophy and Concepts, from Jenkins to CIA.
2. RIF 104-10308-10096, Report on AM/JAVA-4 Visit to Europe, Jenkins to CIA.
3. Hinckle and Turner, p. 410; Rodriguez, Felix I. and John Weisman, *Shadow Warrior: the CIA Hero of a Hundred Unknown Battles* (Simon & Schuster) 1989.
4. These books were recommended in a 2005 interview with Gene Wheaton conducted by William Law. Wheaton suggested that they would describe the individuals he had been associating with or had source information on from what has become known as Iran-Contra.
5. Joseph Goulden, with Alexander W. Raffio, *The Death Merchant: The Rise and Fall of Edwin P. Wilson* (Bantam Books) 1985, p. 65.
6. Peter Maas, *Manhunt: The Incredible Pursuit of a CIA Agent Turned Terrorist.* (I Books) 2002, p. 65.
7. Summers, *Official and Confidential: The Secret Life of J Edgar Hoover, p. 268.*
8. Dan Moldea, *Interference: How Organized Crime Influences Professional Football* (William Morrow & Co) 1995.
9. RIF 124-10294-10046 and RIF 124-10294-10066.
10. RIF 124-10299-10041.
11. "Operational Plan Submitted To CIA By Quintero" is available for viewing on the book web site: Appendix I, RIF 145-10001-10121 and 145-10001-10122.
12. *Orange County Weekly*, November 5, 1997.
13. Daniel Sheehan served as Chief Counsel on The Iran/Contra Civil Case against the Reagan-Bush Administration (forcing the appointment of Iran/Contra Special Counsel Lawrence Walsh, but failing to obtain any civil judgment against the Iran/Contra conspirators when George Bush, Sr. granted Presidential Pardons to the main conspirators and this case was dismissed by Miami's Chief Federal Judge). Full bio at www.be-in.com/12/bio_sheehan.html
14. Corn, p. 390
15. *Time Europe*, April 27, 1992

Appendix J: A SMALL CLIQUE IN THE CIA

1. Cort, David, *The Sin of Henry Luce; An Anatomy of Journalism* (Lyle Stuart) 1984.
2. This information on Underhill is taken from a CIA memorandum RIF 104-10170-10145; Ramparts, John Garrett Underhill Jr., Samuel George Cummings and INERARMCO), and from remarks in a 1966 letter from Asher Brynes, long time friend of Underhill.
3. CIA memorandum; RIF 104-10170-10145.
4. There is a copy of a letter from Murphy to Lansdale, found in Col. Burris files; Burris was V.P. Johnson's military and international affairs advisor. In the letter, Murphy remarked that he was loyal to Dulles, not JFK.
5. Remark contained in May, 1966 letter from Asher Brynes, long time friend of Underhill.
6. These concerns are described in May and June 1966 correspondence from Charlene and Robert Fitzsimmons.
7. Jim Garrison's Playboy Interview, vol. 14 no. 10 - October 1967 available online: www.jfklancer.com/Garrison2.html.
8. CIA memoranda, RIF 104-10170-10145 and 104-1019-10401.
9. The author's personal communication with Gaeton Fonzi.
10. CIA memorandum to Chief, Western Hemisphere, RIF 104-10182-10135.
11. CIA memorandum of October 13, 1959; RIF 104-10182-10119.
12. CIA memorandum from Chief of Station, Santo Domingo, to Chief WHD; RIF 104-10182-10093.
13. CIA memoranda, Guatemala to Director, August, 1962 and February, 1963; RIF's 104-10182-10109 and 104-1082-10098.
14. CIA memorandum, RIF 104-10182-10090.
15. Jonathan Kwitney, *The Crimes of Patriots: A True Tale of Dope, Dirty Money and the CIA* (W.W. Norton and Company) 1987, also (Bookthrift Co.) 1990; David McKean, *Peddling Influence: Thomas "Tommy the Cork" Corcoran and the Birth of Modern Lobbying.* New York. (Steerforth Press) 2004.

NO POSTAGE
NECESSARY
IF MAILED
IN THE
UNITED STATES

BUSINESS REPLY MAIL
FIRST-CLASS MAIL   PERMIT NO. 25   FLAGLER BEACH FL

POSTAGE WILL BE PAID BY ADDRESSEE

CRUISING
WORLD

PO BOX 420375
PALM COAST FL   32142-7196

BIBLIOGRAPHY

Government Reports and Documents

President's Commission on the Assassination of President Kennedy 26 Volumes of Hearings and Exhibits, referred as the "Warren Commission", after its chairman Chief Justice Earl Warren.

Investigation by New Orleans District Attorney Jim Garrison into the assassination of President Kennedy, including Clay Shaw Trial Transcripts and Orleans Parish Grand Jury Transcripts.

Senate Select Committee to Study Governmental Operations with Respect to Intelligence Activities, known as the "Church Committee" after its chairman Frank Church.

House of Representatives Select Committee on Assassinations Investigation of John F. Kennedy and Martin Luther King, Jr., referred to as "HSCA". 95th Congress, 2nd Session. Includes the report from staff members Dan Hardaway and Edwin Lopez Oswald, the CIA, and Mexico City referred to as the "Lopez Report". 1976

President's Commission on CIA Activities Within the United States, was formed by President Gerald Ford. Headed by Vice-President Nelson Rockefeller, known as the "Rockefeller Commission." 1975

CIA Inspector General, "Inspector General's Survey of the Cuban Operation," October 1961, CIA History Staff files, HS/CSG-2640.

LBJ Library in Austin, Texas

Government Documents held at the National Archives and Records Service, College Park, Maryland:

- Assassination Records Review Board
- Central Intelligence Agency, John F. Kennedy Files
- Federal Bureau of Investigation, John F. Kennedy Files
- President's Commission on the Assassination of President Kennedy

BOOKS

Ayers, Bradley Earl, *The War That Never Was: An insider's account of CIA covert operations against Cuba*. Indianapolis/New York (The Bobbs-Merrill Company Inc.) 1976.

Baker, Robert "Bobby" Gene, with Larry L. King, *Wheeling and Dealing: Confessions of a Capitol Hill Operator*. New York (W.W. Norton & Company) 1978.

Beschloss, Michael R., *Taking Charge; The Johnson White House Tapes, 1963-1964*. New York (Simon & Schuster) 1997.

Bethel, Paul D., *The Losers: The Definitive Account By an eyewitness, of the Communist Conquest of Cuba and the Soviet Penetration in Latin America*. New Rochelle, N.Y., (Arlington House) 1969.

Biles, Joe G., *In History's Shadow: Lee Harvey Oswald, Kerry W. Thornley & the Garrison Investigation* 2002.

Blakey, G. Robert *The Plot to Kill the President*, (Time Books) 1981.
— and Richard N. Billings, *Fatal Hour: The Assassination of President Kennedy by Organized Crime* (Berkley Publishing Group) Reissue edition 1993.

Bissell, Richard, with Jonathan E. Lewis and Frances T. Pudlo, *Reflections of a Cold Warrior: From Yalta to the Bay of Pigs*. New Haven, CT (Yale University Press) 1996.

Bohning, Don, *The Castro Obsession: U.S. Covert Operations Against Cuba 1959-1965*. Washington, D.C., (Potomac Books) 2005.

Califano, Joseph A., *Inside: A Public and Private Life* (PublicAffairs) 2004.

Robert A Caro, *Means of Ascent: The Years of Lyndon Johnson, Volume 2*, (Knopf) New York, 1982

Carr, Waggoner and Byron Varner, *Texas Politics In My Rearview Mirror*. Texas (Rep. of Texas Press), 1993.

Corn, David, *Blond Ghost; Ted Shackley and the CIA's Crusades*. New York & London (Simon & Schuster) 1994.

Cort, David, *The Sin of Henry Luce; An Anatomy of Journalism* (Lyle Stuart) 1984.

Crenshaw, Charles A., M.D., *Trauma Room One: The JFK Medical Coverup Exposed*. New York (Paraview Press) 2001.

Curry, Jesse E., *JFK Assassination File: Retired Dallas Police Chief Jesse Curry*. Dallas 1969.

Davis, John H., *Mafia Kingfish: Carlos Marcello and the Assassination of John F. Kennedy*, (Mcgraw-Hill) 1988

Davy, William, *Let Justice Be Done: New Light on the Jim Garrison Investigation*. Reston, Virginia (Jordan Publishing) 1999.

DiEugenio, James, *Destiny Betrayed: J.F.K., Cuba, and the Garrison Case*. New York (Sheridan Square Press) 1992.

Dulles, W. Allen, *The Craft of Intelligence: America's Legendary Spy Master on the Fundamentals of Intelligence Gathering for a Free World* (Greenwood Pub Group) July 1977.

Fetzer, James H., PH.D., (Editor) *Murder in Dealey Plaza: What We Know Now that We Didn't Know Then* (Open Court) 2000.

Flammonde, Paris, *The Kennedy Conspiracy: An Uncommissioned Report on Jim Garrison*, (Merideth Press) 1969.

Fonzi, Gaeton, *The Last Investigation*. New York (Thunder's Mouth Press) 1993.

Freed, Donald, *Death in Washington: The Murder of Orlando Letelier*. (Lawrence Hill) 1980.

Galanor, Stewart, *Cover-Up*. New York (Kestrel Books) 1998.

Garson, Barbara, *MacBird* (Random House Trade Paperbacks) 1967.

Garrison, Jim, *On the Trail of the Assassins: My Investigation and Prosecution of the Murder of President Kennedy* (Sheridan Square Press) 1998.

Giancana, Chuck, *Double Cross: The Explosive, Inside Story of the Mobster Who Controlled America*, UK (Time Warner Books) 1998.

Goulden, Joseph, with Alexander W. Raffio, *The Death Merchant: The Rise and Fall of Edwin P. Wilson* (Bantam Books) 1985.

Groden, Robert, *The Killing of a President: The Complete Photographic Record of the Assassination and the Conspiracy*, (Studio) Reprint edition 1994.

Griggs, Ian, *No Case To Answer: A retired English detective's essays and articles on the JFK assassination, 1993-2005*. Southlake, Texas (JFK Lancer Productions and Publications) 2005.

Hancock, Larry, *Research of Larry Hancock: Richard Case Nagell documents, John Martino, 112th Intelligence Corp. Texas* (JFK Lancer Productions & Publications) 2001.

Helms, Richard, with William Hood, *A Look over My Shoulder: A Life in the Central Intelligence Agency* (Random House) 2003.

Hersh, Burton, *The Old Boys: The American Elite and the Origins of the CIA* (Tree Farm Books) 2001.

Hersh, Seymore, *The Dark Side of Camelot*, (Little, Brown) 1997.

Hinckle, William and William Turner, *Deadly Secrets: The CIA-Mafia War Against Castro and the Assassination of J.F.K.*. New York (Thunder's Mouth Press) 1992.

Holland, Max, *The Kennedy Assassination Tapes* (Knopf) 2004.

Hougan, Jim, *Secret Agenda: Watergate, Deep Throat, and the CIA.* (Random House Inc.) 1984.

Hosty, James and Thomas Hosty, *Assignment Oswald.* (Arcade Publishing) 1st edition 1995.

Joesten, Joachim, *The Dark Side of Lyndon Baines Johnson.* London (Pater Dawney) 1968.

Kaplan, John and Jon R. Waltz, *The Trial of Jack Ruby: A Classic Study of Courtroom Strategies.* (Macmillan) Second printing edition 1966.

Kantor, Seth, *The Ruby Cover-Up.* New York (Zebra Books), 1978.

Kiel, R. Andrew, *J. Edgar Hoover: the Father of the Cold War.* Lanham, Maryland (University Press of America) 2000.

Kwitney, Jonathan, *The Crimes of Patriots: A True Tale of Dope, Dirty Money and the CIA* (W.W. Norton and Company) 1987.

Lacy, Robert, *Little Man Meyer Lansky and the Gangster Life.* New York (Little, Brown and Company) 1992.

La Fontaine, Ray and Mary, *Oswald Talked: The New Evidence in the JFK Assassination.* Louisiana (Pelican Publishing Company) 1996.

Lane, Mark, *Plausible Denial: Was the CIA Involved in the Assassination of JFK?* (Thunder's Mouth Press) Reprint edition 1992.

Law, William, with Alan Eaglesham, *In The Eye Of History: Disclosures in the JFK Assassination Medical Evidence.* Southlake, Texas (JFK Lancer Productions and Publications), 2005.

Livingstone, Harrison Edward, *Killing Kennedy: Deceit and Deception in the JFK Case.* New York (Carroll & Graff Publishers Inc.) 1995.

Loftus, John, and Mark Aarons, *The Secret War Against the Jews: How Western Espionage Betrayed the Jewish People* (St. Martin's Griffin) 1997.

Lynch, Grayston L., *Decision for Disaster; Betrayal at the Bay of Pigs.* (Washington & London Brassey's) 1998.

Maas, Peter, *Manhunt: The Incredible Pursuit of a CIA Agent Turned Terrorist.* (I Books) 2002.

Marrs, Jim, *Crossfire: The Plot That Killed Kennedy.* New York (Carroll & Graf Publishers Inc) 1989.

Martino, John, *I Was A Prisoner in Castro's Cuba,* New York (Devin-Adair) 1963.

McDonald, Hugh and Robin Moore, *L.B.J. and the J.F.K. Conspiracy,* Westport
Connecticut (Condor Publishing) 1978.

Mahue, Robert, and Richard Hack, *Next To Hughes,* New York (Harper Paperbacks) 1993.

Mahoney, Richard D., *Sons & Brothers: The Days of Jack and Bobby Kennedy.* New York (Arcade Publishing) 1999.

Manchester, William, *The Death of a President.* New York, Evanston and London (Harper & Row Publishers) 1967.

Martino, John, *I Was Castro's Prisoner* (The Devin-Adair Company) 1963.
—*Cuba and the Kennedy Assassination* (Human Events) 1964.

Marchetti, Victor, and John Marks, *CIA and the Cult of Intelligence,* New York, (Dell Publishing) 1974, 1989.

McClelland, Barr, *Blood, Money, and Power: How L.B.J. Killed J.F.K.* (Hannover House), 2004.

McKean, David, *Peddling Influence: Thomas "Tommy the Cork" Corcoran and the Birth of Modern Lobbying.* New York. (Steerforth Press) 2004.

McCoy, Alfred, Cathleen Reed, Leonard Adams II, *The Politics of Heroin in SE Asia* (Harper & Row) 1972.

Mellen, Joan, *A Farewell To Justice: Jim Garrison, JFK's Assassination, and the Case That Should Have Changed History*. Washington, D. C. (Potomac Books) 2005.

Meyers, Dale, *With Malice: Lee Harvey Oswald and the Murder of Officer J.D. Tippit* (Oak Cliff Press) 1998.

Moldea, Dan, *Interference: How Organized Crime Influences Professional Football* (William Morrow & Co) 1995.

Murphy, Charles V., *Cuba: The Record Set Straight*.

Newman, John, *Oswald and the CIA*, New York (Carroll & Graff Publishers Inc.) 1995.

Newsday Editors, *The Heroin Trail: The first journalistic investigation to trace heroin traffic from Turkey to France to its ultimate customer, the young American addict* (Signet) 1974.

North, Mark, *Act of Treason: The Role of J. Edgar Hoover in the Assassination of President Kennedy*. New York (Carroll & Graff Publishers Inc.) 1991.

Odom, Major Thomas, *Dragon Operations; Hostage Rescues in the Congo 1964-1965*, (Combat Studies Institute) *Leavenworth Papers* 1988.

O'Neill, Thomas P. "Tip", with author William Novak, *Man of the House: The Life and Political Memoirs of Speaker Tip O'Neill* (Random House) 1987.

O'Toole, George, *The Assassination Tapes: An electronic probe into the murder of John F. Kennedy and the Dallas coverup*. New York (Penthouse Press Ltd.) 1975.

Palamara, Vincent, *Survivors Guilt: The Secret Service and the Failure to Protect the President*. (Self) 2005.

Phillips, David Atlee, *The Night Watch:* 25 Years of Peculiar Service. New York (Atheneum) 1977.
—*The Carlos contract: A Novel of International Terrorism*, (Macmillan) 1978.

Powers, Thomas, *The Man Who Kept The Secrets: Richard Helms & the CIA* (Knopt) 1979.

Ragano, Frank and Selwyn Raab, *Mob Lawyer: Including the Inside Account of Who Killed Jimmy Hoffa and JFK*. New York (McMillan Publishing Co.) 1994.

Rappleye, Charles & Ed Becker, *All American Mafioso; The Johnny Roselli Story*. New York (Barricade Books, Inc.) 1995.

Ratcliffe, David, *Understanding Special Operations*. Santa Cruz California (rat haus reality press) 1999.

Reid, Ed & Ovid Demaris, *The Green Felt Jungle*. New York (Trident Press) 1963.

Rodriguez, Felix I. and John Weisman, *Shadow Warrior/the CIA Hero of a Hundred Unknown Battles* (Simon & Schuster) 1989.

Russell, Dick, *The Man Who Knew Too Much: Hired to Kill Oswald and Prevent the Assassination of JFK*. New York (Carroll & Graf Publishers) 1992.

Russo, Gus, *Live By The Sword: The Secret War Against Castro and the Death of JFK*, Baltimore, Maryland (Bancroft Press) 1998.

Sample, Glen and Mark Collom, *The Men on the Sixth Floor* (Sample Graphics) Second edition 1997.

Scheim, David E., *Contract on America: The Mafia Murder of President John F. Kennedy* (S.P.I. Books) Reprint edition 1992.

Schreiber, G. R., *The Bobby Baker Affair*. Chicago (Henry Regnery Company) 1964.

Scott, Peter Dale, *Deep Politics and the Death of JFK*. Berkeley, Los Angeles and London (University of California Press) 1993.
—*Deep Politics and the Death of JFK II*, Grand Prairie, Texas (JFK Lancer Productions & Publications) 1996
—*The Three Oswald Deceptions*, originally published in *Deep Politics and the Death of JFK II*, www.assassinationweb.com/scottd.htm.
—*Deep Politics III, The CIA, The Drug Traffic and Oswald in Mexico* (History Matters) 2000, www.history-matters.com/pds/DP3_Overview.htm
—*The War Conspiracy*. New York (Bobbs-Merrill Company) 1972.

Jeff Shesol, *Mutual Contempt: Lyndon Johnson, Robert Kennedy, and the Feud That Defined a Decade* , Norton and Company, New York, 1997.

Sloan, Bill, *Breaking The Silence*, Texas (Taylor Publishing Company) 1993.

Smith, Matthew, *Conspiracy-The Plot to Stop the Kennedys*. New York, N.Y. (Citadel Press) 2005.
—*JFK; The Second Plot*. Edinburgh (Mainstream Publishing Company) 1992.
—*Vendetta, The Kennedys*. Edinburgh and London (Mainstream Publishing) 1993.

Smith, Russell Jack, *The Unknown CIA; My Three Decades with the Agency*, (Potomac Books) 1989.

Summers, Anthony, *Conspiracy: The Definitive Book on the JFK Assassination*. New York (Paragon House), 1989.
—*Official and Confidential; The Secret Life of J. Edgar Hoover*. New York (Simon & Schuster, Pocket Star Books) 1994.
—*The Kennedy Conspiracy [Not in Your Lifetime]* Warner Books; Updated ed. with a special postscript edition 1998.

Tagg, Eric, *Brush With History, A Day in the Life of Deputy E. R. Walthers*. Garland, Texas (Shot in the Light Publishing) 1998.

Thomas, Evan, *The Very Best Men: Four Who Dared: The Early Years of the CIA* (Simon & Schuster) 1996.

Thompson, Josiah, *Six Seconds In Dallas; A Micro-Study of the Kennedy Assassination* (Random House) 1968.

Trask, Richard B., *That Day In Dallas* (Yeoman Press) 2000.

Trento, Joseph, *The Secret History of the CIA* (Carroll & Graf) Reprint edition 2005.
—With Susan B. Trento and William Corson, *Widows : Four American Spies, The Wives They Left Behind and the KGB's Crippling of American Intelligence.* New York (Crown Publishers, Inc.) 1989.

Twyman, Noel, *Bloody Treason: On Solving History's Greatest Murder Mystery: The Assassination of John F. Kennedy.* Rancho Santa Fe, California (Laurel Publishing) 1997.

Valentine, Douglas, *The Strength Of The Wolf.* London and New York (Verso) 2004.

Waldron, Lamar with Thom Hartman, *Ultimate Sacrifice: John and Robert Kennedy, the Plan for a Coup in Cuba, and the Murder of JFK.* New York, (Carroll & Graf) 2005.

Weber, Ralph E., Editor, *Spymasters: Ten CIA Officers in Their Own Words*, Wilmington, DE., (Scholarly Resources, Inc.) 1999

Weberman, Alan J. and Michael Canfield, *Coup D'Etat in America.* San Francisco, CA. (Quick American Archives) 1992.

Weisberg, Harold, *Whitewash: The Report on the Warren Report*, *(Dell Pub. Co)*, 1965.
—*Whitewash II; The FBI–Secret Service Cover-up.* Hyattstown, Md. (Harold Weisberg) 1966.
—*Oswald in New Orleans: Case of conspiracy with the C.I.A* , New York (Canyon Books) 1967.

Weyl, Nathaniel *Encounters With Communism* (Xlibris) 2004.

Winter-Berger, Robert N., *The Washington Payoff: An Insider's View of Corruption in Government* (Dell) 1972.

Wise, David, *The American Police State: The Government Against the People* (Random House) 1978.

Wrone, David, *The Zapruder Film: Reframing JFK's Assassination* (University Press of Kansas) 2003.

Zirbel, Craig I., *Texas Connection: The Assassination of President John F. Kennedy*, self published 1991 and 1992.

JOURNALS

Electronic Assassinations Newsletter

The Continuing Inquiry, Editor Penn Jones

From the Wilderness, Editor Mike Ruppert

The Kennedy Assassination Chronicles, Editors George Michael Evica, Robert Chapman, Larry Haapanen, and Alan Rogers

The Third/Fourth Decade, Editor Jerry Rose

PROBE, Editors Jim DiEugenio and Lisa Pease

The Dealey Plaza Echo, Editor Mark Bridger

INDEX

Note: For detailed page listings of individuals with name crypts, please refer to the person's alphabetical name listings in the index. Some crypts are provided for document reference and do not appear in the book itself.

A

AAA (Athentico Party)   78, 372, 511

Air Force One   283, 301, 307, 402, 406

Alba, Adrian   109, 113

Alderson, Lawrence   456

Aldophus Hotel   498

Aleman, Jose   187, 344

Alexander, William   211, 288, 307

Allende, Salvadore   135, 179, 419

Allright Parking   273, 499

Alpha 66   6, 10, 46-47, 50-52, 55-56, 59, 62, 67, 77, 79, 85, 87-88, 97, 99-101, 103-108, 113, 123, 147, 162, 173, 177-178, 181, 192, 199-200, 204-206, 212-213, 215, 335, 337, 344-346, 357, 370, 372, 375-376, 380-381, 433, 437, 440-441, 468, 505-506, 508-509, 513, 518, 528, 543, 546,

Alsop, Stuart   327, 329, 561

Alvarado, Gilberto   220-201, 238, 273-274, 287, 293, 328-331, 505

AMBIDDY 1 (Artime),   133

AMBUD (Cardona) - for document reference only

AMCHEER   387, 570

AMCLATTER (Barker)   77

AMCONCERT   (Verela)   -   for document reference only

AMDENIM 1 (Fernandez)   103, 123, 570

AMDENIM 14 (Cuesta)   437, 510,

Ameritas   6

AMFAST   387, 367

AMHAWK (Varona)   - see Varona for detailed listing

AMJAVA 4   (Quintaro)   417, 437, 485, 568, 572

AMLASH (Cubela)   118, 167, 199, 205, 347, 378, 399

AMOT   86, 131

AMPATRIN (Malone)   436, 570

AMSANTA   113, 135

AMSTRUT   (on-island asset) - for document reference only

AMTHUG (Castro)   - for document reference only

AMTIKI (CRC accountant/payroll) - for document reference only

AMTRUNK   103, 104, 106, 111, 118, 148, 199, 200, 399, 459, 506

AMWHIP   506

AMWORLD   86, 99, 111, 128, 129, 132, 133, 148, 199, 200, 203, 205, 257, 271, 366, 374, 399, 417, 418, 483, 490, 485, 507

Anderson, Jack   146, 151, 152, 154, 490, 540

Andrews, Dean 36, 37, 47, 109, 349, 355, 361, 370

Angleton, James   234, 283, 286, 356, 357, 428-432, 456, 556, 564

Arango, Sachez   78, 511

Arbenz, Jocobo   98, 414, 415

Armstrong Andrew 544
Arnold, Carolyn 71, 72, 393
ARRB (Assassination Records Review Board) 94, 240, 255, 258, 283, 303, 306, 358, 416, 427, 457, 481-485, 488-491, 494, 555
Artime, Manuel (See also, AMBIDDY-1) 23, 111, 133, 148, 192, 200-205, 216, 249, 257, 366, 417, 483, 485, 488, 489, 507
Attorney General Robert Kennedy 142, 202, 292, 314, 326, 327, 399, 522, 525, 539, 542, 543
Ayers, Bradley 124, 132, 134, 146, 537, 538

B
Baker, Bobby 154, 308-310, 313-322, 403, 489
Baker, Samuel 211
Baku 101, 103, 438, 441, 508, 528
Bannister, Guy 35, 117, 168, 358, 359, 474
Barbara J 9
Barker, Bernard (AMCLATTER-1) 5, 6, 9, 77, 165, 169, 204, 205, 207, 344, 533, 534
Barnes, Tracy 143, 161, 415, 421-427, 429-431
Bay of Pigs 20, 21, 49, 50, 98-100, 114-116, 130, 165-167, 202-204, 231-233, 416, 417, 423-426, 446, 447, 482, 483, 485-488, 512-517, 536-539
Bayo, Eddie (see also Eduardo Perez Gonzalez) 6-8, 11, 16, 50, 61, 76, 77, 108, 336, 437, 440, 505, 507, 508, 522
Belle Chase, LA 115, 166, 167, 446, 541
Belli, Melvin 156, 318, 384, 561

Belmont, Alan 282-284, 292, 293
Bennett, Glen 236, 237
Benton, Sam 449
Berlin Operating Base (BOB) 128, 413, 431
Bertrand, Clay 193, 356, 359, 360
Bethel, Paul 163, 171, 173, 274
Bethesda Medical Center 295, 299-302, 307
Billings, Richard (Dick) 9, 11, 81, 522, 544, 548
Binion, Benjamin (Benny) 317
Bishop 97, 114, 171, 176-181, 183, 233, 428, 429, 441
Bishop, Maurice 97, 113-114, 117, 162, 171, 176, 178-179, 181-182, 297, 477
Bissell, Richard 422-425, 430, 539
Black Falcons (Los Halcones Negros) 437
Black, Fred 154-155, 309, 311, 313, 316, 322, 345, 407, 411
Blanco, Alberto (El Loco) 458
Blanco, Cesar 106, 374
Blanco, Juan Francisco 85, 106, 374, 533
Blunt, Malcolm 111
Bohning, Don 49, 424, 528, 569
Bolden, Abraham 243-245, 252, 550
Boswell, J. Thornton 301-303, 558, 559
Bowers, Lee 388, 394
Boylan, David 211
Boyles, Bob 54
Bradford, Rex 119, 532, 536, 552, 556
Branigan, Bill 290
Brennan, Howard 70, 224, 282
Bringuier, Carlos 13, 33-34, 37-38, 47 65, 109-110, 474-478

Browder, Donald 87, 213, 214
Browder, William 85, 87, 213, 214
Brown, Kyle 43, 560
Brynes, Asher 497
Bucaro, Richard 361
Bucknell, David 55
Bundy, McGeorge 234, 286, 306, 324, 325, 328-331
Burkley, George 295, 301-303
Butler, Ed 168
Buttimer, Anne 484
Byars, Billy 276, 555

C

Cain, Richard 13, 105, 142, 143
Califano, Marshall 111, 249
Campbell, Don 357-358
Campbell, Judith 314, 315, 560
Campesi, Joe 3, 228
Carbajal, Rueben 127, 130, 133, 135-137, 538
Carr, Waggoner 325-329, 331, 332
Carrilles, Louis Posada 437
Carswell, Daniel 4, 5, 520
Carter, Clifford (Cliff) 275, 289, 295, 305, 306, 324, 403, 404
Carter, Marshall 8, 10, 336
Cash, Ben 226, 227, 396
Cellar, The 386, 389
Charles, Pedro 13, 273, 294
Chase Manhattan Bank 435, 510
Cheramie, Rose 461-470
Chicksands 453
Childs, Jack 118
Choaden (David Phillips) 436
Christ, David 4, 5
Church Committee 142, 155, 178, 179, 339, 341, 345, 362, 379, 419, 420, 423, 424, 486, 539
Civello, Joe 228
Claasen, Fred 15

Clark, Ramsey 152, 398, 564
Cline, William 370, 371
Clines, Tom 133, 418, 419, 483, 488, 489
Cohen, Mickey 318
Colby, William 533
Coll, Thomas 242
Collins, Edward 442
Commandos 85, 99, 101, 103, 105, 108, 192, 337, 372, 375, 433, 437, 438, 441, 485, 508
Condor 126, 136
Corcoran, Tommy (the Cork) 574
Corn, David 492, 537, 538, 542, 562
Craford, Laverne 352
Craig, Roger 288, 337, 393-395, 401, 566
CRC 63, 165, 167, 178, 204, 343, 346, 434, 442, 469, 475, 517, 529
Crenshaw, Charles 404
Cross, Ron 114, 180, 541
Cruz, Miguel 38
Cuban Revolutionary Council 20, 130, 164-166, 514, 515, 517, 542
Cuebela, Rolondo (AMLASH) 65, 118, 339, 340, 347, 378, 445, 449, 458, 490, 506, 530
Cuesta 52, 337, 362, 437, 440, 442, 508
Cummings 5, 15, 16, 375, 376, 495, 497
Cuneo, Ernest 173, 236
Curington, John 343
Curry, Jesse 249, 288, 289, 355, 553, 557
Czarnikow Rionda 435, 510

D

Daelitz, Moe 86, 140, 141, 317, 318, 373, 375
Dankbaar, William 451, 452, 571

Davidson Irving   153-154, 489, 490, 540
Davis, Ricardo 349, 350
Day, Carl 296
de Brueys, Warren 34, 356, 565
de Freese, Lubert 254
de Joseph, Larry 63
de Torres, Bernardo 347, 348, 438, 498, 508, 523, 533, 563
Dealey Plaza   194, 213, 298, 350, 361, 558
Deauville, Hotel and Casino 2-4, 15, 66, 381
Desert Inn Country Club 140, 317, 318, 375, 376, 383
Diaz, Nino 116, 166
DiEugenio, Jim 554, 560
Domestic Operations 306, 421, 425-428, 430, 442, 498
Domestic Resources Division 427
Donovan, James 100, 234, 292, 520
Dorff, Robert 537
Double-Chek Corporation 426
DRE 10, 33, 34, 62, 65, 79, 84, 85, 87, 97, 108, 169, 193, 199-201, 204, 208, 509
Dulles, Allen   164, 292, 415, 421, 422, 429, 430
Duran, Sylvia 297, 299, 448
Durham, Nathan 463

E
East Louisiana State Hospital 21, 462, 465, 477
Eastland, James 7, 8, 521
Echevarria, Homer 83-85, 87-89
Edward Lansdale 336, 430
Egerter, Ann 278
Einspruch, Burton 24
El Indio 124–128, 162, 170
Ellison, Seymour 318

Ellsworth, Frank 207-212, 547
Elrod, John 210-212
Escalante, Fabian 52, 233, 528
Escapade Lounge 195
Estes, Billy Sol 405, 406
Eunice, LA 461
Exner, Judith Campbell 314, 560

F
FAL (rifles) 146, 147
Fernandez, Alberto (AMDENIM-1) 478
Fernandez, Blanco 105, 107, 529
Ferrie, David 35, 63, 115, 116, 189, 194, 195, 257, 356, 358, 359, 545
Ferror, Kiki 484
Finck, Pierre 302
Fischetti, Joe (Joe Fish) 134
Fitzgerald, Desmond (Chester Dainold) 111, 203, 336, 339-341, 361, 378, 417, 418, 431, 490, 562
Fitzsimmons, Charlene 496
Fitzsimmons, Robert 496
Flammonde, Paris 507, 525
Fontainbleau Hotel 86
Ford, Gerald 318, 577
Forini, Frank (See Sturgis, Frank)
Fort Benning   201, 221, 249, 269, 475
Fort Hood 208-209
Fortas, Abe   45, 319, 321, 324, 326, 330, 332, 403, 405, 489
FPCC 33, 47, 59, 95, 97, 98, 110, 112-114, 117, 118, 165, 166, 168, 178, 183, 369, 427, 428, 474-477
FRENTE   130-131, 204, 434, 436, 469, 517
Fritz, Will   225, 227, 343, 350, 355, 404, 463
Fruge, Francis 461-468

G

Garcia, Hermonio Diaz   52, 141, 156, 337, 362, 367, 376, 438, 528

Garrison, Jim   34, 35, 115, 116, 151-154, 168, 169, 343, 348-350, 357, 359, 442, 466-469, 474, 476, 496, 497, 540, 545

Giancana, Santo   105, 142, 144, 145, 150, 155, 156, 197, 314, 365, 366, 537, 539

Girnus, Edward   193, 194, 196

Gonzalez, Eduardo   20, 252, 253, 350, 524

Gonzalez, Pedro 23, 252, 381, 383

Gruber, Alex 352, 382-384, 395, 586

H

Habana Bar   57, 534

Habighorst, Aloysius   379

Hall, Loren (Lorenzo Pascillo)   24, 471,473,478,480

Halpern, Sam   540

Hanscomb, Rafael Diaz   434, 516

Hathcock, Richard   472, 473

Harber, Dennis   441, 570

Hargraves, Roy   78-81,342,362,441, 442,448,598,511, 518, 532

Hargraves, Roy   98-101, 362, 462, 531, 552

Harker, Daniel   255-256, 569

Harlandale   107, 108, 232, 233, 365, 392, 400-402, 566

Harlandale Street   87,88,212,313,34 5,372,380,382,546

Harvey, William   12, 100, 104, 105, 132, 133, 139, 145-148, 156, 149, 204, 417, 464, 510, 514, 516, 552

Hathcock, Richard   492, 493

Hecksher   99, 128, 129, 135, 337, 413-415, 417, 422, 431, 485

Helliwell, Paul   498,505

Helms, Richard 8, 13,77,118,128,14 6,330,229,234,283,285,286,287,34 0,347,377, 417,422,423,430,431,4 90,510,534,550,567

Hemming, Gerry 5, 63, 337, 338, 341, 342, 346, 440, 472

Hendrix, Hal   7, 114, 170-173, 181, 542, 543

Hecksher, Henry   39, 111, 128, 133, 135, 413, 414, 417, 419, 431, 483, 566

Hernandez, Victor Espinosa 26, 29, 52, 62-65, 85, 87, 141, 167, 193, 213-216, 346, 371, 376, 445-449, 458, 459

Holland, Sam   561

Hoover, J. Edgar   13, 14, 24, 44, 144, 275, 276, 284-289, 291-294, 305, 306, 314, 315, 318, 319, 323-327, 330, 331, 402, 403, 489, 561

Horne, Doug   420

Hosty, James   43, 44, 68, 69, 91, 92, 101, 245, 246, 278, 280, 282, 289, 290, 338, 369, 382, 383, 526, 533, 555, 556

Hotel Luma   74

Houma, LA   55, 136, 137, 188

Howard, Lisa 107, 109, 117, 118, 235

Humes, James 303, 559

Hunt, Howard 6, 114, 144, 164, 169, 180, 204, 343, 344, 414, 416, 421, 424, 427-429, 474, 498

I

INCA   86

Ingram, Gordon   501

INTERARMCO   116, 208, 497, 502, 586

INTERPEN   7, 25, 78, 81, 86, 346, 347, 441, 442, 509, 511, 512, 517, 518

J

James, Daniel   173, 182, 186, 236, 532, 542, 549, 558

January, Wayne 71, 225, 383

JDGE (Sierra Junta) 63, 84, 89, 104-106, 199, 204, 346, 373-376, 448, 511, 512

Jenkins, Carl 132, 416-418, 420, 483, 485, 486, 488, 490, 492, 507

JFK Lancer   16, 276, 421, 543, 546, 547, 551, 555, 565, 574-576, 579, 585, 586

JGCE 84, 373, 375, 533

JM/WAVE vi, 8-16, 30, 50, 58, 67, 74, 77, 84-86, 97, 103-114, 121-204, 233, 273, 336, 339, 361-380, 393, 415-420, 429, Appendix D

Johnson, Lyndon (LBJ) 45, 153, 303, 307-310, 312, 313, 315-316, 319, 327, 330, 404-405, 436, 440, 556-567, 567, 568

Jones, Clifford 310, 315

Jones, Dempsey 223

JURE   20-23, 338, 478, 512, 514, 565

K

Karamissines, Thomas 278

Karnei, Dr. 302, 303

Katzenbach 327,328,331, 561

Kennedy, Regis 34,308,525

Kennnedy, Robert (see also RFK) 85, 105, 110, 111, 139, 140, 144-146, 200, 202, 203, 256, 293, 339, 399, 429, 440, 489, 490, 539

Kirknewton 451, 453, 457

Kirkwood, Pat (The Cellar) 386

Kleberg, Robert (Bob) 85, 373, 435, 436, 437, 440, 448, 510

Kostikov, Valery 119,120, 277-287, 294, 311, 324, 329, 340, 378, 400, 403, 552, 556, 555-557, 559

KUBARK 77, 436, 441, 565

Kuhns-Walko, Anna Marie 15, 547, 550, 552

L

La Borde, Larry 442, 540

Lafayette, LA 482

LaFontaine, Mary   251, 376, 547, 553

Lake Charles, LA 151

Lamaru, Rene 77

Lansky, Meyer   106, 140, 141, 142, 156, 186, 190, 310, 317, 318, 319, 374, 310, 317, 318, 318, 374, 560, 579

Law, William 400, 484, 488, 492, 573

LBJ, 303, 309, , 401, 405, 406, 540, , 559, 561, 568

Lechner, John   126, 394

LeChuga, Carlos 235

LEDA 9, 200, 522

Levinson, Edward   309, 310, 316-318, 322, 407

Lobo, Julio 77, 162, 448

Lopez, Gilberto 14, 15

Lopez, Jose (Oswaldo) 34, 35

Los Halcones Negros (Black Falcons) 437

Luce, Claire Booth 163, 172, 178

Luisa, Maria 273

Luma Hotel 54

Lynch, Grayston 130, 232, 521

Lyndon Johnson 303, 305, 307-310, 312, 313, 315, 320, 323, 326, 330, 404, 405, 436, 440, 567, 568

M

Mabra, W.W. 388, 390, 586

Maheu, Robert   142, 144, 151, 539, 540

Mahoney, Richard 149, 530, 534, 537-541, 553, 560, 567
Malone, William Scott 241, 435, 436, 438-440, 448, 547, 550, 570
Mann, Thomas 293, 294
Marcello, Carlos 140, 141, 156, 366, 470, 489, 490
Marlowe, Vaughn 56, 59, 95, 95, 107, 112, 120, 480
Martin, Jack 239, 358, 359, 544
Martinez, Eugenio 9, 10, 21, 108, 123, 376, 516,
Martinez, Jorge 9, 10, 65-67, 87, 208, 209, 442, 522, 531
Martinez, Jorge Soto 65, 66, 241, 448, 458
Martino, Florence 1, 2, 61, 519
Martino, John 1-4, 11-13, 15-19, 29-31, 48, 49, 60, 61, 66, 67, 74-76, 86, 91, 92, 107, 108, 121, 123-126, 221, 239, 240, 367, 368, 374-376, 522-524
Masen, John Thomas 207-213, 547
Masferrer, Kiki 25
Masgerrer, Rolondo 25, 65
May, Robert 196
McDonald, Hugh 173, 560
Mertz, Michael Victor 455-457, 470
Mondolini, Paul 455
Morales, David 76, 104, 123-139, 141, 143, 145, 169, 170, 232, 234, 372, 374, 414-416, 418-422, 513, 536-538
Murchison, Clint

N

Nagell, Richard Case 39-47, 53-56, 59, 60, 96, 98-100, 104, 107, 110, 128, 129, 232, 371, 431, 477, 480, 526, 527
Neal, Sam 26-28, 154

Nevada Group 89, 156, 216, 373, 375, 533
Newman, John 112, 278, 279, 306, 401, 525, 531, 532, 541, 554, 555, 557, 559
Nonte, George 207, 208, 209, 219, 546, 547
Norman, Harold 71
North American Aviation 309, 310, 311, 316
Norton, Howard 237, 560-562, 567, 574
Novell, Gordon 35, 115, 116, 168, 358, 475
NPIC (National Photo Interpretation Center) 486, 488
NSA 295, 451-453, 490, 535, 557, 571

O

Odio, Annie 492
Odio, Sarita 40
Odio, Sylvia 40-46, 50, 53, 56, 57, 67, 85, 121, 233, 239, 260, 358, 391, 394, 493, 494, 544
Operation 40 5 6, 21, 131, 167, 372, 374, 378, 436, 520, 523
Oswaldo 437
Otero, Rolondo 233, 347, 348, 349, 364, 548, 563

P

Palamara, Vincent 236, 237, 239, 549, 550, 565
Parrot Jungle 65, 66, 87, 241, 479
Patterson, William 70, 92, 280, 245, 246, 369
Pawley, William (Bill) 6-11, 50, 61, 67, 77, 104, 147, 171, 172, 206, 335-336, 338, 343, 361, 377, 508, 513, 521-523, 562

Payne 472, 473
Pearson 151, 163, 164, 173
Pena, Orest 37, 38, 47, 109, 167, 370, 477, 515, 515, 525
Perrel, George 208
Phillips, Shawn 182, 542,543,586
Ponchay, Anthony 424, 541
Powell, John 92
Prewitt, Virginia 178, 236
Price, J.C. 388

Q

Quesada 85, 86, 104, 105, 346, 375, 563
Quigley, John 250, 256
Quintero 49, 111, 132, 133, 417, 420, 483-491
Quiroga, Carlos 34-36, 469, 474-480

R

Racoosin, Theodore 7, 79
Ralston, John 148
Ralston, John 168
Ramon, Ruben, Victor 438
RAPHAEL (Plan) 424
Ray, Manolo 20, 22, 23, 104, 512, 414
Red Bird Airport 255, 256, 383, 394, 395
Reitzes, Dave 522
Revill, Jack 92, 246, 247, 552
REX 9, 200
Reynolds, Don 253
RFK 14, 63, 105, 118, 139, 146, 147, 188, 249, 288, 294, 365, 440, 530, 539, 565
Rheinstein, Frederic 354, 564
Rice Hotel 464
Robertson, Rip 8-10, 67, 76, 77, 108, 123, 126, 130, 147, 232, 338, 339, 374, 414-422, 486, 513, 514, 516
Roca, Roy 152, 356, 357
Rockford, Brad (see Carl Jenkins) 420, 488
Rodriquez, Everisto 37
Rodriquez, Felix 133, 378, 437, 483, 487, 572, 582
Roland, Arnold 71, 72
Roman, Jane 278, 555
Rometsch, Ellen 314, 315
Roselli, John 5, 32, 106, 124, 125, 159-161, 165-169, 171, 173-175, 333, 334, 363, 364, 384-386, 393-396, 401, 402, 427, 569
Rosen, David 142
Roth, Alan 2, 15
Rothermel, Paul 342
Rothman, Norman 187, 188, 192, 213, 214, 337, 344, 346, 445, 449, 499, 544, 547
Ruby, Earl 3, 317, 319
Ruby, Jack xvii, 3, 3, 13, 27-35, 66, 86, 149, 151, 156, Chapter 11, Chapter 12, Chapter 13, 241, 248-257, 272, 317, 318, 332, 350-362, 380-389, 395, 397, 479, 480, 513, 544
Ruiz-Williams, Harry 23, 63, 105, 110, 204, 249, 442, 507
Russell, Dick xvii, 28, 29, 40-46, 50-56, 232, 343, 431, 523
Russell, Richard 276, 291, 298, 307, 329

S

Saez, Miguel, Casas 294
Salvat, Manual 208, 509
Sam Jenis 5
Samoluk, Tom 483
San Souci 27, 52, 99, 141, 188, 455, 470, 492, 544

Sanchez, Goicoecha, Fermin 208
Sanchez, Nestor 485
Sanjenis, Jose, Joachim, Panderaeo (Sam Jenis) 5, 21, 167, 378, 416, 520
Santana, Emilio 442, 468, 469, 470, 474, 540, 572
Santiago, Vidal 5, 76, 78-80, 89, 234, 341, 342, 382, 383, 442, 479, 518, 532
Schneider, Rene 135
Schorr, Daniel 94, 95, 535
Scott, Peter, Dale 101, 112, 119, 278, 280, 429, 431, 503, 521, 523, 554, 557, 569
Scott, Win 132, 273, 276, 294
Seltzer, Joseph 486
Serifin, Aldo Vera 106, 108, 375
Seymour, William 24, 25, 442, 457, 471, 472, 479, 508
Sforza, Tony (Sloman) 134, 419, 420, 543, 586
Shackley, Theodore 8, 10, 104, 121, 124, 128, 130, 132, 133, 135, 145, 146, 171, 234, 290, 335, 337-341, 361, 377, 378, Appendix B, 440, 489, 492, 493, 498, 512-514, 421, 536
Shanklin, Gordon 284, 287, 288, 533
Shannon, Ulric 390
Shaw, Clay 35, 152, 153, 168, 193-195, 308, 356, 361, 398, 426,427, 474, 475, 525, 540, 564, 575
Shelley, Bill 71
Sierra, Paulino Martinez 84, 85, 104, 108, 192, 204, 215, 374, 376, 448, 518
Sikes, Richard 243
Silva, Art 80, 81
Silva, Frank 21, 22, 183, 219, 369,

428
Silver Slipper Lounge 462, 467, 468, 470
Singlaub, John 492, 498, 503
Singlebaum, Benjamin (Benny) 315, 316
Sionics 501
Sloman 134, 420, 543
Smith, Joe, Marshall 388
Smith, Matthew 255, 256, 536
Smith, Orville 388
Smith, Russell Jack 290
Smith, Sergio, Arcacha 115-117, 166-168, 468-475
SNFE 56, 85, 99, 192, 204, 345, 346, 372, 375, 376, 437, 509
Snipes, Vaughn 46, 56, 59 95, 107, 112
Soccares, Prio 4, 26-31, 65, 77, 78, 84, 86, 104, 105, 141, 142, 144, 187, 190, 199, 202-205, 213, 216, 254, 337, 366, 499, 511, 513, 517
Soutre, Jean Rene 455, 456
Spagnoli, Joseph 243
Speer, Pat 421
Special Group Augmented (SGA) 8, 145, 523
Spengler, Lillian 65, 241
Sprague, Richard 301
Springer, Eva 360
Stardust 317, 375, 376, 560
Stassi, Joe 470
Storm, N.A. 310
Stublefield, Robert
Sturgis, Frank 5, 6, 9, 13, 27, 63, 76, 77, 103, 169, 177, 187, 188, 192, 204, 213, 214, 274, 341
Suarez, Christina 6
Suarez, Miguel 6
Summers Anthony 17, 126, 134, 183, 196, 509, 550, 575

Szulc, Tad 147, 148, 429

T

Tagg, Eric 229, 546, 547, 550
Tanner, George 78
Tarasof 378
Task Force W 120, 124, 152, 153, 163, 165, 166, 224, 356, 437, 460, 530, 531, 534, 554, 582
Tejana (Tejana III) Tejana 26, 393, 455-462, 527, 528, 530, 590
Terpil, Frank 229-232, 567
Terrell Armory 229-232, 567
TexAir Terminal 415
Texas Court of Inquiry 326-329
Texas Theatre 36, 89, 95, 102, 245, 292, 411
Thompson, Josiah 604
Thomas, Steve 197
Thorneberry, Homer 54, 326
Thunderbird Casino 24, 160, 230, 231, 330, 335
TILT 6, 8, 11, 61, 67, 108, 147, 336, 508, 516, 521
Tolson, Clyde 304, 314, 509
Trafficante, Santo 3, 22, 52, 53, 59, 106, 143, 145, 155-156, 156, 187, 188, 190-191, 197, 198, 254, 362, 470, 366, 367, 372, 373, 455, 516, 517
Trapnell, Garrett 57, 58, 529
Tropicana 47, 161, 206, 208, 269
Trull, William 85, 86
TSBD (Texas School Book Depository) 69-72, 225, 252, 355, 371, 382, 383, 385, 387, 392
Tumbleweed 279, 282, 286
Twyman, Noel 358, 536-540, 562, 563, 566

U

Underhill, Garrett 494-497
Underwood, Marty 239, 240
UNIDAD 97, 182, 454, 455, 459, 463, 532, 536, 537

V

Valencia, Pedro 175
Valenti, Jack 306, 558, 559, 567
Vallone 464, 465
Varona, Anthony (Tony) (AMHAWK) 22, 23, 65, 86, 144, 145, 202, 205, 216, 343, 344, 366, 367, 374, 381, 511, 516, 517, 520, 533
Veciana 51, 56, 97, 113-115, 162, 176-180, 183, 204, 233, 297, 385, 428, 505, 518, 528
Venturi brothers 454, 455, 457
Vera, Aldo 106, 108, 375
Vidal, Felipe Santiago 5, 76-80, 86, 89, 123, 234, 341, 342, 362, 364, 375, 382, 383, 370, 442, 479, 511, 518, 532

W

Wade, Henry 227, 305, 353-355, 393, 403, 404, 559
Wallace, Malcolm 405
Walter, William 250-252, 553
Walthers 72, 87, 88, 206, 533, 546, 550-552
Warren 151, 153, 228, 291, 307, 331, 533, 555
Weberman, A. J. 367, 519, 540, 542, 584
Weisberg, Harold 73, 525, 526, 531
Weiss, Victor 467
Werbell, Mitch 347, 497-501
Weyl, Nathaniel 12, 221, 521
Wheaton, Gene 481-485, 488-494,

573
Whittier, Donnell Darius   547
Williams, Harry   204, 249, 404, 442,
    507
Wilson, Edwin   133, 420, 488, 489,
    491-493, 568, 569, 573
Witt, Steven   387, 390
Wood, Court   97, 117, 165
Wray, Gill   195

Y
Yaras, Dave   197
Yates   197, 222-226, 238, 383, 392

Z
Zamka   129, 133, 537
ZR/CLIFF   257
ZR/RIFLE   13, 104, 128, 132, 133,
    143, 145, 146, 148, 149, 154, 257,
    374, 378, 399, 417, 523

Printed in the United States
144593LV00002B/1/A